ANTHROPOLOGY
FOR
CHRISTIAN WITNESS

ANTHROPOLOGY FOR CHRISTIAN WITNESS

CHARLES H. KRAFT

ORBIS BOOKS

Maryknoll, New York 10545

Library of Congress Cataloging in Publication Data

Kraft, Charles H.
    Anthropology for Christian Witness / Charles H. Kraft.
      p. cm.
    Includes bibliographical references and indexes.
    ISBN 1-57075-085-8 (alk. paper)
    1. Mission—Theory.   2. Ethnology—Religious aspects—
Christianity.   3. Christianity and culture.   4. Evangelistic work—
Philosophy.   I. Title.
BV2063.K756   1996
226'.001—dc20   96-38716
                                        CIP

CONTENTS

v

PART II
CULTURE

PART III
RELATING TO THE NONHUMAN UNIVERSE

PART V
CULTURAL AND WORLDVIEW CHANGE

PART VI
RESEARCH AND STUDY

INTRODUCTION

This volume is the product of twenty-six years of teaching anthropology to missionaries and international church leaders at the School of World Mission, Fuller Theological Seminary. It is the fruit of my attempt to integrate my Christian faith with my commitment to the importance of anthropological insight to effective cross-cultural Christian witness.

Back in the early 1950s when my wife and I were training to go to Nigeria as missionaries, not much of this kind of training was available. God blessed us, however, with the opportunity of attending a Christian college (Wheaton) where one could major in anthropology. He also led us to a mission board (The Missionary Board of the Brethren Church) that supported us while we obtained graduate level anthropological, linguistic and theological training before we went to the field. Though this background put us at odds with much of what our mission was doing in the field, it contributed greatly to the effectiveness of our work there.

THE IMPORTANCE OF ANTHROPOLOGY TO CHRISTIAN WITNESS

This background has contributed significantly to the present volume in several ways. In the first place, my experience in Nigeria strongly confirmed for me the importance of approaching cross-cultural Christian witness from a perspective that integrates anthropological insights with those that come from church involvement and theological training. As cartoonist Walt Kelly (*Pogo*) points out, *the enemy is often us*. Though Christian experience and theological input enable us to better understand the messages God wants us to communicate, an anthropological perspective makes it possible for us to avoid being crippled by the enemy within us—our own ethnocentrism.

A second lesson I learned is, however, just as important as the first: it is possible to go too far to the relativistic extreme advocated by most secular anthropologists. We are committed to Jesus Christ and to the extension of His Kingdom. Nothing we do, no perspective we learn, should detract from that commitment. There is a "capital R" REALITY God (*see* chapter 2) above the "small r" reality cultural world in which humans live. Our commitment to that God and His purposes requires that we go beyond simply accepting culture-bound human behavior. Anthropologists have taught us a great deal about the need to take everyone's culture seriously. As committed Christians, we need to combine this insight with something we could not learn from anthropologists: the fact that God desires to use human cultures to interact with His creatures, to change their allegiances, their perspectives, and their behavior in the direction of His ideals. Our commitment to Christ requires that we see culture as context and instrument rather than as an end in itself.

A third important insight that came to me was that my understandings concerning God and His works, including how I understood the Bible, needed to be culturally adapted if they were to speak to the people God had called me to. It came as a bit of a shock that most of what I had learned in Christian college and seminary, in the forms in which I learned it, was inappropriate or irrelevant to the Nigerians I worked with. The content was indeed important, but my western ways of interpreting and understanding needed to be replaced by Nigerian ways of understanding, if God's messages were to be perceived as genuinely relevant to the real life of rural, traditional Nigerians. It came as a pleasant surprise to me, however, to discover that traditional Nigerians often understood biblical events and teachings more clearly than I did, due to the fact that their culture is more similar to those of most of the Bible than is mine.

In short, my anthropological training opened my eyes to an incredible amount of understanding in three important areas: 1) of myself and my people as culturally formed and constrained, 2) of the people to whom I was called within their cultural context and 3) of the Bible as a cross-cultural book. That training, however, also gave me tools with which to get beyond at least some of my cultural conditioning. These tools enabled me to serve God and the people He called me to with a deep awareness of the need to free the people to understand and respond to God in terms of their way of life, rather than to seek to convert them to my way of life to be acceptable to God. I believe in anthropology as a tool, a perspective in terms of which to better understand and present the life-changing message of Jesus Christ to peoples living in cultural and subcultural contexts other than our own.

Since returning from Nigeria I have become very aware of the need for an anthropological perspective on Christian understanding and witness, even within my own society. Cultural differences are at base the differences between people conditioned in different ways within different families. On the one hand, even within our own society, we are in daily contact with people from families whose perspectives and behavior have their roots in cultural worlds other than ours. On the other hand, even when those different families speak the same language and live in the same neighborhoods, there frequently are differences of understanding, perspective, and behavior that are best understood from an anthropological perspective.

So, I believe in anthropology for everyone—but only as a means, never an end. Respect for people of other cultural worlds is a Christian principle. But the absolutization of tolerance that often underlies rhetoric about "multiculturalism" is in no way Christian. The Gospel, not simply tolerance, is to be communicated into everyone's world (Mk 16:15). Though the material learned about the Gospel in Christian college and seminary may not have been useful in Nigeria in the form in which I learned it, the Christian message, even though presented in those irrelevant forms, was and is worth dying for. It is for the sake of that content that we go to the ends of the earth as missionaries, and it is for the sake of making that content maximally intelligible to people of different cultural worlds that we use anthropological and communication tools in the cause of Christ.

So we use anthropology. It is a tool, not an end in and of itself. We apply its perspectives to a task that far transcends the anthropologist's goals of accumulating insight concerning other peoples and, in the process, learning to respect them. Our mandate is still the Great Commission. God has allowed humans to learn, through anthropologists, quite a number of things that enable us to respect and work with people as He respects and works with them, so we study anthropology and seek to integrate our Christian perspective into the way it is presented here.

NOT FOR SCHOLARS BUT FOR PRACTITIONERS

In this presentation, I am not trying to be theoretically sophisticated or even up-to-date. Nor do I seek to break new ground for the sake of scholarship. Those are valid reasons for other treatments, but not the aim here. I am not writing for other scholars but for practitioners who may neither know nor care what professional anthropologists spend their time debating. I have made no attempt to present the latest theoretical approaches to the issues I deal with or even to deal with all of the issues that are currently in vogue within the discipline. I intend this to be an introduction of anthropological insights to an audience that has had very little contact with our discipline but needs very much to incorporate some of the most basic of our perspectives into its ministry.

I have chosen a selection of theoretical concepts (many of which have been around for a long time) that I believe to be useful and important to Christian communicators and attempted to combine them with tried-and-true approaches that will be helpful to that audience. I make no apology for the fact that many of my sources are old. Though our discipline may in many ways have moved away from the theoretical perspectives of the Lintons, Redfields, Goodmans, Fosters, Nidas, and Luzbetaks, the audience I am concerned with may never have even heard of the concepts these scholars pioneered. My audience is looking for the ABCs approached from a Christian perspective and their applicability to the problems of cross-cultural Christian witness.

Basic insights concerning issues such as the distinction between forms and meanings (Linton 1936), worldview (Redfield 1953, Kearney 1984), the individual and culture (Goodman 1967), status and role (Linton again), education (Beals and Spindler 1973), communication (Nida 1954, 1990), issues of culture change (Foster 1973, Barnett 1953, Luzbetak 1963) and the like are, I believe, timeless and crucially important for cross-cultural Christian workers to consider, whether or not they are currently of interest to professional anthropologists. My aim is utilitarian, whether or not scholars are impressed. My desire is to be helpful to those who, like Jesus, seek to communicate messages from God to people whose cultural ways of life differ from theirs.

Not that there is nothing up-to-date or distinctive here. I (and others) would contend that my treatment of worldview has some pioneering dimensions to it. I believe also that the distinction I have attempted to consistently make between culture as structure and society as people is an important contribution, though it is hardly new. My attempt (following Nida) to incorporate communication theory into an anthropological perspective is, I believe, a major contribution. Further, I believe there is at least some newness in the way I have treated religion, family, the distinction between REALITY and reality, and several other areas. As one professional who reviewed the manuscript put it, "Your sources are largely old, but I feel you are on the verge of some kind of a breakthrough." Breakthrough or no, I pray that those who use this volume will be helped to be more effective for God than they would have been had this not been made available to them.

This text has been developed over about two decades. That means that there are quite a large number of people who have helped along the way, many of whom I do not remember as I write. I want to thank them all, however, even though they remain nameless in print. I express gratitude to each of the secretaries who worked on the various stages of the manuscript. Among the most recent ones, I thank Nancy Thomas and Betty Ann Klebe. I am also very grateful to Anne White and others in the Fuller word processing office for their fine work, both in the preliminary stages and in putting the text into final shape.

I thank Chuck Lindquist and Scott Grandi, former students at the Fuller School of World Mission, and Beth Meres, a present student, for helping me with the writing. I am grateful, too, to doctors Douglas Hayward of Biola University and R. Daniel Shaw, my colleague at Fuller, for going over the manuscript and making helpful comments on it. Thanks also goes to my longtime graduate assistant, Alex Haarbrink, for numerous kinds of help, to my daughter Karen for editorial assistance, and to my wife Marguerite, for her patience and encouragement.

Finally, I am very grateful to Dr. William Burrows and the staff at Orbis Books for their encouragement, patience, and willingness to publish such a large book.

May God richly bless all who use this volume and enable it to serve whatever purposes He has in mind for it.

PART I

THE PERSPECTIVE

CHAPTER 1

WHY ANTHROPOLOGY FOR CROSS-CULTURAL WITNESSES?

INTEGRATIONAL THOUGHT

A key question for Christians who study anthropology is, What is God's view of culture? I believe we have our answer in 1 Corinthians 9:19–22, where Paul articulates his (and God's) approach to cultural diversity:

> I am a free man, nobody's slave; but I make myself everybody's slave in order to win as many people as possible. While working with the Jews, I live like a Jew in order to win them; and even though I myself am not subject to the Law of Moses, I live as though I were when working with those who are, in order to win them. In the same way, when working with Gentiles, I live like a Gentile, outside the Jewish Law, in order to win Gentiles. This does not mean that I don't obey God's law; I am really under Christ's law. Among the weak in faith I become weak like one of them, in order to win them. So I become all things to all men, that I may save some of them by whatever means are possible.

From the very beginning of Scripture, God has shown Himself willing to work with people *within* their cultural frames of reference. He has always worked in terms of Jewish culture to reach Jews. Through Paul, He states what is illustrated

1

in the Book of Acts—that He wants to accept Gentiles within their cultures also, without the necessity of their changing cultures in order to do things in a way that is acceptable to Him.

If we are to take a scriptural approach, we are to adapt ourselves and our presentation of God's message to the culture of the receiving people. If we demand that they become like us in order to be acceptable to God, we, like most of the early Jewish Christians (*see* Acts 15:1), have misrepresented God. We, the witnesses, are to make the cultural adjustments, not they, the potential respondents.

As we begin this study of anthropology for Christian witness, we are seeking to learn how to be as open to cultural differences as God is. As we see from 1 Corinthians, the desire of God is that we adapt to cultural differences. The early believers, however, were Jewish. They, therefore, naturally believed that the cultural context in which they received the Gospel was to be normative for all others. That is, if one is to come to Jesus, he or she must also convert to Jewish culture.

The Apostle Paul, though Jewish himself, learned otherwise. As pointed out in the above text, he chose to live like a Gentile when working with Gentiles, lest they get the impression that God's message was simply about culture change. And in Acts 15:2ff we find him arguing fiercely against the majority position of the early Church for the right of Gentiles to follow Jesus within their own sociocultural contexts. God Himself had shown first Peter (Acts 10), then Paul and Barnabas, that this was the right way by giving the Holy Spirit to Gentiles who had not converted to Jewish culture (Acts 13–14).

But the Church has continually forgotten the lesson of Acts 15. We have continually reverted to the assumption that becoming Christian means becoming like us culturally. A major component of the Protestant Reformation was the discovery that God would accept people who spoke German and worshiped in German ways. They did not all have to convert to Roman language and customs. The discovery that God was pleased to use English language and custom was a part of the Anglican break with Rome, and when Wesley moved away from Anglicanism, it was to a great extent in recognition of the fact that God accepted the common people of England as they were culturally.

One of our major aims in this approach to the study of anthropology is to learn to protect the people of other societies from our own inclination to make them like us. It is a sad fact that, though Paul learned from the Holy Spirit to be a Jew to Jews and a Gentile to Gentiles, many of today's cross-cultural witnesses have not learned that approach. We pray that the Holy Spirit will use anthropological insight in our day to show us how we are to go about adapting ourselves and our presentation of the message of God to those immersed in other cultures.

INTRODUCTION

For many Christians, the term *anthropology* is either an unknown term or one that they associate with those who attack Christianity. It is often seen by them as a discipline that advocates evolution and ethical relativism and is often regarded as anti-Christian. In fact, I often have people ask me, "How can you be both an anthropologist and a Christian?"

Anthropology has not ordinarily been a part of Bible school or seminary curricula, either in Euroamerica or in the Two-Thirds World. For many Christians, it has an anti-Christian reputation. Why, then, require it for contemporary missionaries, national church workers, and others whose primary concern is to communicate the Gospel and lead God's people in the Two-Thirds World?

I once asked this question myself. In my first year at a Christian college, I began to inquire of upperclassmen concerning what I should specialize in. I wanted a subject that would prepare me for missionary work. After receiving a number of suggestions, I came upon a student who was planning to become a missionary himself. In response to my question, he replied simply, "There's only one subject for a prospective missionary to specialize in." I said, "What's that?" "Anthropology," he answered. And I said again, "What's that?" I had never heard of anthropology before. His answer, though, showed me that he had thought this thing out and really knew what he was talking about.

He pointed out that our western college curricula are pretty out of balance. Though things have improved a bit now, at that time (early 1950s) every subject except one dealt almost exclusively with the western world. If we studied history, we studied European and American history, as if the rest of the world had no history. If we studied philosophy or literature or languages, we studied Euroamerican philosophy or literature or languages. Even specializing in Bible meant we were specializing in the interpretation of the Bible from a Euroamerican point of view. Only one subject, my friend said, aims at dealing with the other thousands of cultures of the world: anthropology. That, he said, is the only subject that will give a prospective missionary the help needed in preparation for going "into all the world."

I regard this as some of the most important advice I have ever received, and I'd like to pass it on to you in the form of the following ten reasons why anthropology is a crucial area of study for cross-cultural witnesses like yourselves.

Before I do, though, let me say a word to those of you who are not Europeans or Americans. You may assume that since you are already from the Two-Thirds World, you don't need a subject like this. After all, you are working in your own language and culture and so don't need to learn about other cultures. Or perhaps you have already learned and worked in several languages and cultures. So you wonder what a subject like this could possibly contribute to your ministry.

You will discover a number of things on your own, but let me just mention two benefits that past generations of international students have shared with me.

1. Even though you come from non-European languages and cultures, you have been rather thoroughly westernized through the schooling you have received. Usually this schooling (plus the tremendous impression western societies make in the area of technology) leaves internationals with some sort of inferiority complex. This study will help you to overcome many of the harmful effects of that inferiority complex and realize that your own culture is not inferior to western culture. One Chinese student said to me recently, "You're making me proud to be Chinese!" I pray that this book has the same effect on you.

2. Though you may be communicating the Gospel to "your own people" in "your own language," one result of your western schooling has been to separate you culturally from the traditional people around you. The way this works in many parts of the world is that there develops a westernized segment of the population that is in most ways quite distinct from the traditional segment of the population. They all speak the same language but live on opposite sides of a very definite cultural boundary. You may wonder why you have such a difficult time really communicating with the traditional people in your society. In fact, you may find yourself look-

ing down on them and expecting them to become like you before they can really experience Christianity. This is, of course, the way the early Jewish Christians felt about the Gentiles. They didn't realize that they were imposing cultural, not spiritual, requirements on the Gentiles in the name of Jesus.

In this book we are just as much concerned with such cross-cultural (or cross-subcultural) problems between members of the same language group as we are with the problems faced by those of us from the West who call ourselves missionaries. Both westernized internationals and we from the West are faced with the problems of cross-cultural witness. This book is, therefore, directed to all of us.

Let's, then, begin answering our question, Why anthropology for cross-cultural witnesses?

1. ANTHROPOLOGY ATTEMPTS TO DEAL WITH WHAT PEOPLE ACTUALLY DO AND THINK

Anthropology is a *behavioral science*. This means that anthropologists attempt to study what human beings do, how they behave. We try to avoid (not always successfully) simply philosophizing about what people *ought* to do. Anthropologists try to discover and describe what is there before they start theorizing about what ought to be there. Other sciences classified as behavioral sciences are sociology, psychology, linguistics, and communication science.

Anthropologists are interested in people's total behavior, not just how people think. Many academic disciplines spend almost all their time dealing with how people think. Anthropologists are interested in how people think but also in what people do in their everyday activities. This includes their work, their rituals, their child rearing, their play, their music and art, their religion, their philosophizing, their education, their politics, their food getting, their family organization. In short, we are interested in everything people do and think in their ordinary lives. There is nothing that people are involved in that anthropologists aren't interested in.

This kind of realism is very important to cross-cultural witnesses. We are (or ought to be) concerned with people *as they are*. We want, then, to communicate Christian messages (messages from God) to them in those terms.

Unfortunately, many of us have gone out to work with peoples of other societies with rather unrealistic (often negative) views of what people in these societies do and think. Without trying to understand the reasons behind their customs, we often simply say, "People shouldn't practice such a custom." We take a negative attitude toward that custom, condemn it, and act as if we know God's will in the matter. This is done without even attempting to understand or to show the kind of love and acceptance that God has showed us in spite of some of the things we practice.

God wants us to treat others as we would want to be treated if we were in their position (Lk 6:31). We need, therefore, to find out where people actually are, try to understand them, and accept them as God has accepted us. Anthropological study is a human tool that enables us to start where God wants us to start. We thus gain freedom from our own cultural biases to be the kind of cross-cultural witnesses God desires.

Such study can enable us to learn about the people we seek to reach before we make too many mistakes. It can help us find out their point of view, their understandings of life, and to approach them with the Gospel in terms of what their perception of reality is, rather than in terms of our understandings. Anthropology can be a great help in this area since it is a behavioral, not a philosophical, science.

As a footnote to this discussion, let me note that anthropologists are not always successful in their attempts to observe and record correctly what people actually do and think. Anthropologists make many mistakes in their work. We, like all other people, are often misled by our presuppositions. Many of you from the Two-Thirds World have read anthropological descriptions of your cultures that are quite inaccurate at many points. It must, however, be said that usually descriptions of nonwestern cultures done by non-anthropologists (travelers, government officials, and even missionaries) are even less accurate than those done by anthropologists. Anthropologists are not always right, but their insights can often be very helpful to us as cross-cultural communicators of the Gospel.

2. ANTHROPOLOGY HISTORICALLY HAS DEALT PRIMARILY WITH NONWESTERN PEOPLES

As my college friend pointed out to me, the division of labor in western academics is a very strange one for our present world. In western universities we have a wide variety of academic specialties. Among them are philosophy, religion, literature, history, sociology, psychology. These all deal largely with one small group of societies, often referred to as if they practiced one culture called "western culture." Judging from the number of distinct languages that have been counted in the world (approximately 6,000), we can estimate that there are at least 6,000 separate cultures in the world, and I suspect this estimate is quite low.

But western academic interest developed before westerners were much concerned with studying the rest of the world, so each of these disciplines was developed within the very limited perspectives of this handful of western societies, with little or no concern for the rest of the world except as westerners bumped into its peoples (in conquest, trade, or missionary work) or as those peoples bumped into the West (as when some nonwestern group would attack a western group).

Such a very limited perspective on the world has been particularly damaging in two respects:

1. It has tended to perpetuate the ignorance of westerners who have sought to relate to people in other societies. We fall into all kinds of misunderstanding of other people's customs and the myth of the presumed superiority of our customs to those of other peoples.

2. When exported as has been widely done through western schools, such western perspectives have led many nonwesterners to look up to western societies and to look down on their own. Indeed, nonwesterners studying in western schools have often learned more about the history, literature, technology, music, language, economics, education of the colonial power than they have of these aspects of their own society.

As westerners came into more frequent contact with peoples of other societies, whether through colonialism, trade, travel or missionary endeavor, some began to develop a new academic discipline called anthropology. The purpose of this new discipline was to study the remainder of the 6,000 sociocultural entities not dealt with by the other disciplines. The division of labor is a strange one in our day. We have many academic disciplines dealing with one small group of closely related societies, while only one academic discipline deals with all the rest. Anthropology is, therefore, particularly important to those of us who work in any of these other societies or languages, since anthropology has been the only academic discipline focusing specially on them.

Having said that, I should note that there has been a change fairly recently. You'll find, for example, that in good-sized universities nowadays history departments that once only dealt with western history sometimes have specialists in the history of the Orient, the Middle East, or other nonwestern areas. Sometimes they will have someone who specializes in "ethnohistory." This is history from a perspective that is influenced by anthropology. Likewise with music. Sometimes you will find an "ethnomusicologist," one who studies the music of nonwestern societies. Occasionally you will even find people specializing in ethnobotany, ethnomedicine, ethnoart, ethnopsychology, oral literature, and the like. Such scholars have usually been influenced by anthropology.

Anthropology is important to cross-cultural witnesses because it deals primarily with these other thousands of societies in the world.

3. ANTHROPOLOGY HAS DEVELOPED THE CULTURE CONCEPT

As Louis Luzbetak has said, "The concept of culture is . . . the anthropologist's most significant contribution to the missionary endeavor" (1963:59). All down through history there have been very important discussions about whether people are more influenced by their biological heritage or by their environment. When anthropology came along, we began to discover that we must take biological heritage seriously. Then there is the environment around us. That also has to be taken seriously.

But there is something in between the physical and the environmental, something intangible but very real and very influential in human life. This is the thing we call "culture." It consists of all the things that we learn after we are born into the world that enable us to function effectively as biological beings in the environment. We are each carefully indoctrinated from before birth into the patterns of behavior that the adults around us feel to be appropriate. By the time we become aware of what's going on, we have already been pressed into a cultural mold. Though anthropology is not the only discipline that deals with culture, anthropologists have contributed most to our understandings of the concept. In fact, one definition of anthropology is that anthropology is the discipline that studies human culture.

As we learn our culture, we organize ourselves biologically and environmentally according to it. Human biology requires that we eat. Each environment provides a certain range of edibles and imposes limitations (no bananas in the Arctic) that tend to keep us from obtaining other edibles. But it is in terms of our cultural patterns that we choose to eat certain things (e.g., beef) provided in our environment and refuse to eat other things (e.g., cat meat). We ordinarily follow cultural guidelines concerning what to eat, where, how often, at what times, and with what implements (fingers, forks, chopsticks, tortillas).

Human biology requires that we sleep. Our environment provides various possibilities and limitations (darkness, different types of material on which to sleep). But we follow cultural structuring, not biology or environment, in deciding when, where, and on what (if anything) we sleep, as well as who (if anybody) we sleep with and in what positions. Environment often dictates that we protect our bodies (e.g., from weather). But it is cultural patterning that we follow in deciding what (if any) clothing and housing we use and when and how we use it. Furthermore, with respect to any given aspect of environment or biology, it is the values of our culture that we follow when deciding either to submit to such forces or to try to master and rearrange them.

As we will learn later, anthropologists regard cultures as essentially equal to one another. They find no evidence of any given cultural structuring that is superior to any other in every respect. It looks, rather, as though one structuring can be rated superior to another in certain aspects but will fall below that other structuring in other aspects. Anthropologists don't believe it is right to line cultures up in a sequence from supposedly "inferior" to supposedly "superior" as westerners have tended to do.

Popularly, however, westerners have looked at the cultures and the peoples of the Two-Thirds World and often called them "primitive" or "underdeveloped" because they don't do things the same way we do. We have often then lined up the cultures of the world so that those that look technologically most like ours are considered "superior," while those that look technologically least like ours are at the bottom end of the scale. This is our ethnocentric way of looking at things. Anthropologists, of course, cannot agree.

Well-functioning societies appear to be reasonably adequate for meeting the needs the people within the culture consider to be important. Even healthy societies, however, do not ever seem perfect or without flaws. Nor do they provide for meeting every conceivable need. There always seem to be loose ends, areas where people are left dissatisfied, even when the cultural structures are working well. Increasingly, though, the intense culture contact of modern days is resulting in widespread inadequacies in the patterns of life (cultures) people have been taught. People are left, then, with customs that don't work in modern situations and develop social and psychological problems that defy the best efforts of scientists and governments to solve.

Whether the people we deal with live with adequate or inadequate cultural structuring, cross-cultural witnesses for Christ need to know all they can about culture and its relationships to people. Most of the rest of this book will be devoted to this subject.

4. ANTHROPOLOGY TAKES A HOLISTIC VIEW OF PEOPLE

To deal adequately with culture, anthropologists must be concerned with the people who live according to cultural patterns. Most other academic disciplines, of course, deal with people. But anthropology treats people in what we call a "holistic" manner. That is, we try to deal with the whole range of human behavior within one discipline. Rather than segmenting humans into various compartments such as psychology, religion, philosophy, history, language, science, and so forth, anthropologists try to look at the whole spectrum together. What we try to do is to discover and integrate all that can be known about the relationships between human beings and the cultural patterning in which they live. We try to be holistic and integrative with respect to human behavior, rather than specializing in a single aspect of it.

In many ways, anthropology may be called interdisciplinary or multidisciplinary in comparison to the more traditional "monodisciplinary" approaches to

studying human beings. We who have been through western schooling have traditionally studied specific topics related to human life in the West. Our scholars
have led us to specialize in subjects such as the philosophy of western people, the
religion of western people, the literature of western people, and so on. In the West,
we are fond of dividing even human beings into such compartments.

Anthropology, however, tries to reverse this trend to a certain extent and to
deal with human beings in a holistic sense. This is partly because anthropology is
more focused on human beings as its subject, whereas the other disciplines are
focused primarily on their topics. It is, however, also because anthropology has
taken a cross-cultural approach to the whole curriculum (see next point). Whatever has to do with human beings, especially cross-culturally, is a part of anthropology. This makes anthropology perhaps the most holistic and comprehensive discipline there is.

One part of anthropology even deals with the biological and physical aspects of
human beings: "physical anthropology." We will only deal with a part of this sub-
discipline (in chapter 7). Another part of anthropology, "anthropological linguistics," deals with the languages of people. Other subsegments of anthropology deal
with archeology (the cultures of people in the past), ethnology (or cultural anthropology), and applied anthropology. We will be primarily concerned with the last
two of these subdisciplines.

People are like fish swimming in cultural water. Whether it is us or God dealing with people, the cultures in which people exist must be taken into account.
People must, furthermore, be treated holistically. The holism of anthropology is,
therefore, another crucial dimension for cross-cultural witnesses.

5. ANTHROPOLOGY IS A PERSPECTIVE, NOT SIMPLY A SUBJECT

It follows from what we have been saying that anthropology is consciously different from other academic disciplines in a number of ways. I would say, though,
that the most important of these differences (at least for our purposes) is the difference in perspective. By dealing holistically with people in terms of their
involvements in culture, and by being informed in this quest primarily by the
experience of studying people in nonwestern societies, anthropologists come to
look at people from a different perspective, a different point of view. This we call a
cross-cultural perspective.

So, the fifth thing we want to say is that anthropology is valuable to cross-cultural witnesses because it seeks to generalize about human behavior from the
vantage point of this cross-cultural perspective. That is, it seeks to generate
insights into how human beings behave based on experience with people in many
cultures. *A cross-cultural perspective is a point of view that attempts to understand
and make generalizations about what people are like based on what we have discovered about the interactions of the thousands of peoples of the world with the
thousands of distinct cultural structurings in which they live their lives.*

This perspective contrasts with what we call a *monocultural perspective*, in
which the point of view is based on the limitations imposed by one's own culture,
with little or no attempt to get beyond those limitations. We will deal more with
this contrast in chapter 5.

As indicated above, most western academic disciplines work from a monocultural perspective. Those specializing in these areas have typically had no experi-

ence in another culture, so they generalize on the basis of the experience they have had within western culture(s). One example of this is the generalization that has often been made (both by scholars and nonscholars) that teenagers just naturally rebel against their parents. By this they mean that such behavior is a biological given for all teenagers of all societies. There is, of course, a good bit of evidence to prove that teenagers do rebel against their parents within western societies. A monocultural perspective, having no understanding of data from nonwestern societies, generalizes that this is a basic human characteristic.

Anthropologists, however, have found that such rebellion, though very real in western (and westernizing) societies, is not a biological phenomenon but a cultural one. They collected data on this topic from a wide variety of different societies, assuming that if teenage rebellion is a part of inherent human nature (biologically produced), it would be found in each of these ways of life. If, however, teenage rebellion is a cultural thing, it will only be found in those societies that in some way produce it.

They found that in many of the traditional societies they studied, the transition to adulthood was a fairly smooth one. Indeed, the teenagers in those societies wanted so much to be like their parents that, far from rebelling against them, they were actively and happily imitating them. Since they wanted to be like them, rather than unlike them (as is true with many western young people), the transition was very smooth.

The conclusion, then, is that western teenagers *learn* to rebel against adults. Somehow, in the process of growing up, they are taught patterns of behavior that lead them to challenge their parents and, often, others of their parents' generation. This ideally results in constructive self-determination on the part of the adolescents. It causes no end of consternation for the parents, however.

Learning to look from a cross-cultural perspective at how we train our youth (as we will do in chapter 17) would at least alert people to some of the major causes for this situation. Hopefully such an approach will suggest possible solutions, as well. We will be employing this cross-cultural perspective to attempt to analyze and point to solutions for quite a number of the problems of cross-cultural witness and cultural life in general as we proceed through this book.

Overall, we can expect major benefits from a cross-cultural perspective in at least four areas:

1. Understanding and interpreting ourselves in our own sociocultural matrix.

2. Understanding and interpreting those to whom we go in their sociocultural matrix.

3. Understanding and interpreting the Bible, couched as it is in the cultural patterns of other times and places. Since all that is reported there happened in societies other than our own, interpreting the Bible is a cross-cultural problem.

4. Understanding how best to communicate a message given to us in cultural forms other than ours to people who live by customs and assumptions other than ours.

Since everything we do with people and with the Bible faces us with cultural issues, we all can profit much from taking a cross-cultural perspective. Westerners and the westernized can especially be helped, since most of the cultures of the world (including those of the Bible) are more like each other than any is to western cultures. There is, however, much in contemporary cultures that helps us to better understand the events recorded in the Scriptures. Anthropology, then, becomes a very important tool in arriving at helpful interpretations both of life in general and of the Bible itself.

6. ANTHROPOLOGY FOCUSES ON COMMUNICATION

A sixth important contribution of anthropology to cross-cultural ministry is its focus on the elements of human behavior that relate to communication. Anthropology tries to understand people in relationships, and a major part of human relationships is communication. In fact, the quality of the relationships is tied closely to the quality of the communication. Communicational topics such as perception, felt needs, acceptance and appreciation of people of other societies and the like are, therefore, important focuses in the study of anthropology.

As cross-cultural workers, our aim is first to understand the people to whom we go. When we come to understand the people in their culture, then we are in a better position to communicate the Gospel in such a way that they will not misunderstand it. We hope that understanding will bring acceptance of the Gospel, but this does not necessarily happen. Indeed, understanding may result in them rejecting the message. As with the man called the Rich Young Ruler (Lk 18:18–22), they may reject the message not because they misunderstand but precisely because they understand and are not willing to pay the price.

Unfortunately, as we look at Christianity around the world, we find there have been many people who have responded positively on the basis of misunderstanding. There are also many who have rejected Christianity because they misunderstood it. It is our desire to apply the insights of anthropology in such a way that people will understand the message. Whether they accept or reject, it will be on the basis of understanding, not misunderstanding.

Anthropology can help us go even farther: it can help us communicate the Gospel in a way that our hearers will feel meets their felt needs. Anthropological study of a people can expose to our view needs that the receptors already feel and alert us to ways in which the good news from God can be applied to the meeting of these needs. It can enable us to communicate the Gospel to them in such a way that they will say, "Here is the answer to a need that I am already feeling."

7. ANTHROPOLOGY DISTINGUISHES
BETWEEN FORMS AND MEANINGS

A seventh important contribution is that anthropology deals with the relationship between cultural forms and their meanings. There has been a considerable amount of confusion among Christians (and others) concerning the nature of the cultural forms (e.g., rituals and ceremonies) that we use regularly. Many assume that forms such as baptism, the Lord's Supper, and even preaching and other church customs are sacred in and of themselves. But an anthropological perspective helps us realize that the form or ritual is important not because the form itself is sacred, but because the meanings that may flow through that form are sacred. It is idolatry to exalt the form to a position where our focus is on it rather than on what God seeks to communicate through that form. An anthropological perspective can, therefore, provide protection against idolatry.

As an example, let us take the cultural form called monologue preaching. Many have gone to a people and sought to communicate to them through monologue preaching, assuming that that cultural form—standing up and monologu-ing—is a Christian thing. They do not realize that lecturing like that is simply a cultural form that may be used for Christian purposes or may be used for non-Christian purposes. There is nothing sacred about the cultural form we call "preaching." Likewise with the cultural forms we call "baptism," "The Lord's Sup-per," and "sacred music." Any sacredness lies only in the meanings that can flow through these forms when they are properly used. Though the proper forms must be chosen if the meanings are to be right, that choice needs to be based on how the receptors interpret the form in their context. Forms that properly convey given meanings in one cultural context often convey different meanings in another cul-ture. We will deal with this matter in considerable detail as we go along (especially in chapters 2 and 9).

8. ANTHROPOLOGY HAS DEVELOPED THE CONCEPT OF WORLDVIEW

Culture consists of two levels: the surface behavior level and the deep worldview level. At the core of culture and, therefore, at the very heart of all human life, lies the structuring of the basic assumptions, values, and allegiances in terms of which people interpret and behave. These assumptions, values, and allegiances we call *worldview.*

With regard to *assumptions*: When we from the West assume that the only per-sonal beings in a given room are the ones we can see, we are following a worldview assumption taught us as we learned our culture. Or, when those from the Two-Thirds World assume that in a given room there are many very active personal beings that we cannot see (spiritual beings), they are following a different world-view assumption—one taught them as they learned their cultures.

With regard to *values*: When we from the West value individual rights and freedoms, capitalistic economics, democratic government based on 51 percent votes, high mobility, interpersonal competitiveness, and so on, we are following our worldview values. When members of other societies value family loyalty above individual privilege, government by consensus requiring 100 percent votes by cer-tain leaders, bartering that places a high premium on the developing of a personal relationship between the barterers, the suppressing of competitiveness, and so forth, they are following the worldview values of their own cultures.

With regard to *allegiances*: When we in the West commit our loyalty primarily to ourselves, secondly to our jobs, thirdly to friends, fourthly to country or some organization, fifthly to family, and only sixthly (if at all) to God, we are following our worldview prioritizing of allegiances. For members of other societies, alle-giance to family often comes first, with allegiance to job or nation far down on the list.

Whether in the area of the assumptions from which behavior springs, or in the area of what is positively or negatively valued, or in the area of allegiances, world-view provides the structuring in terms of which people govern their behavior. As such, it is of primary concern to anthropologists.

Christian anthropologists are especially concerned about worldview, since it is a person or group's worldview that is at stake whenever an appeal for conversion (whether to Christianity or any other ideology) is made. When people become Christians, they make certain changes in their deep-level worldview assumptions, values, and allegiances. The importance for cross-cultural witnesses to understand such a concept and approach people in terms of such an understanding cannot be overestimated. We will devote chapter 4 and several of the later chapters to various aspects of worldview and worldview change.

9. ANTHROPOLOGY HAS DEVELOPED THE RESEARCH METHOD MOST HELPFUL TO CHRISTIAN WORKERS

A ninth area where anthropology can be of great help to us is in discovering insight into human behavior on the field, for anthropology uses the field method that is of greatest usefulness to cross-cultural workers: *participant observation*. It has been traditional for scholars to do their research either in libraries or, in the case of the laboratory sciences, in laboratories, but anthropologists find it very difficult to study people that way. You can't put people into test tubes or into books. Long ago, anthropologists discovered that there aren't books written on most of the peoples they sought to study, so they had to develop a way of learning about people by studying people themselves in field situations.

Anthropology has said that in order to study people, we have to observe people by living with them and participating with them in their everyday life. We must live with them, learn their language, and do as much as we can to learn to look at the world from their point of view. We need to discover what their assumptions are concerning reality and ask ourselves questions such as, "If I assumed reality to be what they assume it to be, how would the world look to me? And if it looked that way to me, how would I behave?" On the basis of the understandings gained through seeking answers to such questions, applied anthropologists (including missionaries) have often been able to help people discover answers to problems they previously could not solve.

This field method is particularly appropriate for Christian cross-cultural workers. We want to find out what the world is like from their point of view. We also want to discover what they feel to be needs not now solved by the cultural practices they have been taught. We then want to communicate the Gospel to them in ways that will be meaningful to them from within that point of view and in relation to those needs. We will deal further with this anthropological field method in chapter 28.

10. ANTHROPOLOGY DEALS WITH CULTURE CHANGE

The final thing that I want to mention is that anthropology has come to a good bit of understanding of the processes of culture change. It used to be thought that traditional peoples do not change their cultures much, if at all. Even now we occasionally read in the newspapers about some society that has supposedly remained unchanged for thousands of years. But such reports are not written by anthropologists. Anthropologists know that no people has left its culture unchanged for even one year, much less for a thousand years.

There are, of course, societies that change their customs more rapidly (like western and westernizing societies) and those that change less rapidly (like societies that are more or less isolated from contact with other peoples). But there is no such thing as a culture that has not been changed over a given length of time. All peoples are changing their cultures at all times. The only things to be investigated, then, are the hows and whys of change.

As Christian witnesses, we are eager to see certain changes take place among the peoples with whom we work. It is important, however, that such changes take place in ways that will be less disruptive rather than more disruptive to the people. The wrong kinds of change or too rapid change can often be seriously disruptive even if brought by well-meaning people. A study of anthropology should enable us to understand the processes of culture change so that we can work for the kinds of change that Christianity asks for in ways that are less disruptive rather than in ways that are more disruptive. By learning what anthropology has to offer in this area, we can learn to work constructively and often in terms of the change processes already going on, rather than destructively and counter to those processes. In this way, Christianity can be built on the foundation already provided by the society rather than in opposition to what the people are already familiar with. Chapters 22–26 deal with issues of cultural and worldview change.

These are ten reasons why it is important for all who seek to witness wisely in cross-cultural contexts to study anthropology. You will discover many more reasons as we go along. Many of us who train people for cross-cultural ministries feel that anthropology is both the most important and, usually, the most neglected of the areas that should be required. Since everything we do and think, plus everything done and thought by those to whom we go, plus everything recorded in the Scriptures, is totally affected by culture, we can at least contend that no one should attempt to work cross-culturally for Christ without a pretty solid understanding of culture. And that is what anthropology is about.

So we seek in this text to develop from a Christian perspective certain crucially important anthropological insights into three areas:

1. The people to whom we go in their cultures,
2. Ourselves within our culture, and
3. The biblical message presented within the biblical cultures.

CHAPTER 2

REALITY, PERCEPTION,
AND MENTAL MAPPING

INTEGRATIONAL THOUGHT

Toward the end of the "Love Chapter," Paul makes an interesting statement: "What we see now is like a dim image in a mirror; then we shall see face to face. What I know now is only partial; then it will be complete—as complete as God's knowledge of me" (1 Cor 13:12).

Paul says we only see dimly. Our view is fuzzy. Not only that, but our knowledge is merely partial. We cannot see clearly and know completely, as God sees and knows. Though someday we get to see and know clearly and completely, that day has not yet come, so we either have to be content with our limitations or kick against them.

When Satan tempted Eve and Adam, his promise was that they would know as God knows. Since then, many have been trying to attain such knowledge, and the amount of knowledge amassed over the years is truly impressive. But no matter how much we learn, we cannot transcend the limitations of our human condition; we cannot see and know as God sees and knows.

Do these limitations apply even to our understanding of the Scriptures inspired by God and illumined by the Holy Spirit? What about anthropology, or physics, or medicine? Whatever the area, and no matter how impressive our knowledge, we never approach either total clarity or total completeness. Indeed, the more expert we get in any area, the more obvious it becomes that we see dimly and know only partially.

Is there then no certainty? I believe there is, and we are to witness to that. We will deal further with this question below. We must be careful, however, lest our certainty lead to dogmatism, for knowledge and understanding are to be held in humility and love. That's why the above verse occurs in the love chapter.

We cannot know as God knows. Therefore, love. Accept those with differing opinions and practices as likely to be at least partly right. Be humble about one's own opinions and practices, since they are at least partly wrong. Love each other, whether or not we agree, for "to love is to obey the whole Law" (Rom 13:10).

INTRODUCTION

The terms *reality*, *perception*, and *mental mapping* may sound overly philosophical or technical for an introductory approach to anthropology. This chapter is, however, intended to lay a foundation for the approach presented in the pages that follow. Dealing with philosophical issues is not unknown in anthropological writing and should be considered legitimate, given the all-inclusive nature of anthropology. Indeed, much of what I'm saying is based on some things that my former colleague Paul Hiebert has written in the first chapter of his excellent text, *Cultural Anthropology* (second edition, 1983). To pursue these ideas further, *see* Barbour (1974) and Kraft (1979a).

THE BASIC PROBLEM: HOW DO WE KNOW?

The basic problem of analysis, whether in science or in life outside of science, is, How do we know what we know? Or to put it more tentatively, How do we know what we think we know? The technical (philosophical) term for this kind of investigation is *epistemology*. Those who specialize in epistemology ask (largely from western cultural points of view), What is the nature of knowing? How do we know, and what do we do about it once we find out?

Another way of approaching this problem is to ask, Is what we see exactly what is there? When I look at you, is what I see exactly what is there? When I ask this question, I often think of the glasses I wear. They are bifocals and give me at least two views of reality. They are made so that part of them helps me to see close up, another part to see things at a distance. When I look at close things through the top of the lenses, everything is blurred. Likewise, far things are blurred if I look at them through the bottom of the lenses, because that part of the lenses is meant for something about eighteen inches in front of my eyes.

The question is, Is what I'm looking at really like what I'm seeing? Or do my glasses alter or distort what is there? In our normal life experiences, is what we see what is there? Or are we seeing something else? If we see what is actually there, how come others see things differently?

Have you ever heard a report of the same event from two different people? Why are the reports different? Even sincere, honest, trustworthy people regularly describe similar experiences quite differently. Have you ever heard two or three people describe an automobile accident? In the Scriptures, we have four different gospels. Why are four inspired accounts not the same?

The fact of human variation in reporting and interpreting is such, however, that if Matthew, Mark, Luke, and John had all written exactly the same thing, we would doubt the reliability of the Gospels. We would assume that somebody must have indoctrinated them into a single story so they all came out with the same account of their experiences with our Lord. But we know that when two or three or four people look at the same event, they come out with slightly different emphases, different focuses. Different things are important to different people. Some people see one set of things and don't see another set of things. Other people see that second set of things and miss the first set of things. That's the way human beings are.

THE TRADITIONAL APPROACH TO THIS PROBLEM

The traditional western approach to this problem, both in popular and in academic life, assumes a real world that can be accurately observed and accurately described. Observations of physical reality seem to support these assumptions. If one sees a mountain, westerners assume the mountain is real. If there appears to be a mountain, to us it really exists. It is not just something in the observer's imagination. If the mountain exists, we assume a careful observer can be objective and describe that mountain as it really is. It is assumed that any hypothesis or theory of the observer can be proven to be true either by experiment or by logic. These theories, once proven, are accepted as unchanging "laws" of nature, like the law of gravity or the laws of mathematics. They are believed to be unchanging and immutable.

This approach has resulted in scientific theories and philosophical propositions with the following characteristics:

1. Such generalizations are seen as parts of closed systems. All the parts of each system are seen to be tightly knit into a whole. No part of the system can be challenged without threatening the total structure. Whether it is a philosophical or a scientific system, such systems of analysis are set up as if they were eternal, consisting of unchanging laws, propositions, and basic truths.

When a group (whether a cultural group or a group of scientists) starts with an unconscious presupposition—such as the base 10 assumption in mathematics—and builds its system on that assumption and others (equally unquestioned) derived from it, the resulting system tends to be fairly consistent internally but closed to other assumptions. The reason a system is closed is because the absoluteness of its validity is threatened if the validity of other presuppositions is admitted. This is why both cultural and scientific or philosophical or theological systems tend to be closed off by their adherents from other points of view.

Many of us have been brought up to understand Christian doctrine as a closed system and are carefully warned (often unconsciously) against doubting or even examining certain symbolic parts of the system. In my experience, the impression was given that my orthodoxy (and even, perhaps, my salvation) was in jeopardy if I ever questioned certain doctrines. Among them were the literalness of the early chapters of Genesis, conservative views of the authorship of various books of the Bible, the verbal plenary theory of inspiration, inerrancy, or any of a number of other doctrines. We were taught that these conservative beliefs were so tightly tied together that questioning any of them would inevitably result in our becoming liberal and, therefore, lost to the cause of Christ.

2. Those who hold such views, whether in mathematics or in theology, tend to become dogmatic. Because the basic assumptions underlying our knowledge are not examined, we assume that our knowledge is absolute, or nearly so. The old approach to mathematics that didn't examine the base 10 assumption was dogmatic. We were certain because we didn't even imagine another system. We claimed to operate under immutable and universal laws of mathematics. Any deviations from the system were considered wrong or heretical. That's what everyone, including our teachers, always told us. In Christian doctrine, only one way could be right—our way—for there are laws of doctrine, as well, and we are the ones who know them.

3. Under this old approach, the system (whether cultural, mathematical, theological, or some other) was regarded as an unchanging final statement of fact. Philosophers, theologians, behavioral scientists, and all others who considered themselves scientists gave themselves to the pursuit of "laws" of their disciplines that would parallel in absoluteness the laws of the physical sciences or mathematics. When they discovered what they felt to be such immutable laws, they tended to become quite dogmatic about them.

ALTERNATIVE UNDERSTANDINGS OF REALITY

But what happens when there are alternative ways of looking at the same thing? What do we do about different understandings of reality?

Perhaps the old story about the blind men and the elephant can illustrate the point. You'll remember, there were four blind men trying to understand an elephant. The first blind man touched the elephant's tail and said, "The elephant is like a rope." Another man got his arms around the leg of the elephant and said, "The elephant is like a tree." Somebody else pushed against the side of the elephant and said, "The elephant is like a wall." Somebody else got hold of the trunk of the elephant and said, "The elephant is like a hose." Each examined the same reality (or, rather, a part of the same reality) but came to a different conclusion. Which of them was wrong? All were responding to something real (the elephant), and all were understanding some part of that reality. None was really wrong in his analysis, but none understood the whole elephant.

This is the problem. No matter how sincere and trustworthy we are, as human beings, we never see the whole picture as God sees it. We always see "in part" and dimly (1 Cor 13:12). Yet we often ignore this limitation and lock ourselves into certain understandings of reality, dogmatically asserting them as if we knew the mind of God. Then we come across somebody who sees it differently, and we find we can't deny the possible validity of that person's perspective. What approach do we take? There are at least three possibilities.

1. One of those blind men could argue that all the others were wrong, because only he perceived it correctly. He knew that the elephant is like a rope. Why? Because he felt it, touched it, and he knew. So he could say that all the others were liars or stupid. And if he had prestige or power over those others, he might be able to "convince" them, even against their will, that he was right.

This approach is what Barbour (1974) and others label *naive realism*. I prefer to call it *direct* or *unmediated realism*. This is the approach that says, "My view is the only valid one. I see things as they really are." This approach denies that others are understanding a matter accurately unless they agree with me.

2. But some are beginning to understand that our points of view are not always right, while those of others are not always wrong. They also see that often one cannot make a clear choice between two points of view. That is, each point of view often seems to be just as valid as another. So they postulate a different understanding.

Some of them tend to absolutize a relativistic view toward reality. They at least profess to believe that any view of reality is valid, as long as it is held sincerely. (Whether they are completely consistent in such a belief is another story—many are not.) Such an approach attempts to regard reality as totally the product of people's minds. Such views have been labeled *mentalistic, idealistic*, or *intuitive*.

The *idealism* or *intuitionism* of India fits in here. This perspective is now coming into the West in a big way through the New Age movement. The contention is that reality is totally what we make it. We think we see those mountains out there, but they're not really like we think they are. Whatever reality the mountains have exists because we have created it—not because (as we in the West have traditionally assumed) they exist in and of themselves. If someone thinks an elephant is a kind of tree, it is a kind of tree for that person. If someone else thinks it's a rope, it is a rope for that person. To him it's a tree, to you it's a wall, because the only reality is what's in our minds.

Most westerners would not ordinarily go that far in dealing with physical reality, but, especially in philosophical, religious, or similar areas considered intangible by westerners, we might say that we create our own reality.

3. Still others adopt a position that we may label *mediated* or *critical realism* (Barbour 1974). This is the position I am recommending. It holds that there are two realities. There is a REALITY "out there"—the world outside ourselves does exist, it is REAL. But there is also a reality inside our minds. That, too, is REAL. This position believes that *there is both an objective REALITY and a subjective reality*. We look at external REALITY and take a photograph of that REALITY with our minds. Then we operate on the basis of the pictures of reality in our minds. Thus the REALITY "out there" is mediated to our minds through a mental picture that we ourselves construct.

We can summarize these positions as follows, with big R standing for objective REALITY and little r standing for perceived reality:

Position 1: (Unmediated, Direct or Naive Realism): Only R exists. My perceptual r = objective R because I see R directly and clearly.

Position 2: (Idealism, Intuitionalism, or Absolute Relativism): Only perceptual r exists. The only reality that counts is that in my (or someone else's) mind.

Position 3: (Mediated, Indirect, or Critical Realism): Both absolute R and perceptual r exist and are to be taken seriously. I only understand R through my picture of it (r). I need to constantly compare my r with other understandings of R and adjust it to more adequately approximate R.

CRITICAL/MEDIATED REALISM

The mediated realism view would explain the differences between the blind men's understandings as based on the different mental pictures each of them developed. These mental pictures were constructed independently by each man on the basis of such things as present and past experience, psychological makeup, and cultural training, but none of their perceptions altered what the elephant actually was—the REALITY.

One great advantage of this position is the potential for lessening dogmatism. Another advantage is the freedom that this position allows to learn from others. If, for example, your picture of REALITY differs from mine, we can sit down and discuss the differences and learn from each other. Yours may be more accurate than mine in some details. Mine may be more accurate than yours in some details. We can both learn by discussing and comparing, thereby possibly bringing both of our understandings into closer correspondence with REALITY as it actually is.

It really thrills me to reflect back on what I have learned about the Scriptures (not to mention about life in general) from discussing, sharing, and comparing African perspectives with my western perspectives. My experience leads me to believe what Dr. Jacob Loewen said several years ago, when he suggested that God has buried so much treasure in the Scriptures that we will never find it all until the interpretive perspectives of each of the languages and societies of the world have been applied to them. As we work with different languages and peoples, we find that each perspective asks different questions of the scriptural data. When we can see the questions that African and Asian and Latin American peoples ask of the Scriptures and see the tremendous comprehensiveness of the revelation, then we can enter into a grander understanding of God than we ever could when we simply asked the questions of that data that our one cultural perspective brought to our attention.

The puzzling question is, How do we know whether the picture in our minds of some aspect of reality is even close to the way things actually are? The answer is, We never can know *absolutely* (as God does). Indeed, one of the problems with the direct or naive realism approach (position 1) is the arrogance that we easily fall into when we claim to see and know reality as God sees and knows it. We believe, however, that we can know *adequately.* As humans, we seem to be able to understand reality well enough to know what we have to do to survive biologically and socially. In the Scriptures (and probably in other ways, as well) God reveals what we need to know to survive spiritually. But this aspect of REALITY (Scripture) is also subject to our human interpretation and, therefore (like all else), can only be understood adequately, never absolutely.

For example, even with respect to the God we serve, we have to distinguish between the REALITY of God (God as He is) and how we perceive Him. Even with the biblical revelation available to us, we develop different perceptions or understandings of God. Indeed, within the biblical revelation we see God allowing different perceptions of Himself. This position keeps us from absolutizing our own understandings of God. We can only contend that God is—there is who He is— whether or not we see and interpret Him correctly. In our interpretations of Scripture and Christian things, we have to say that our understandings are not absolute, although they can be adequate. They can be adequate for God's purposes even though we never see the absolute God absolutely.

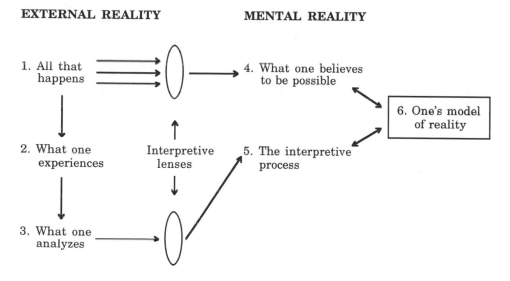

EXTERNAL REALITY   **MENTAL REALITY**

1. All that happens
2. What one experiences
3. What one analyzes

Interpretive lenses

4. What one believes to be possible
5. The interpretive process
6. One's model of reality

Figure 2.1 Constructing a model of reality

In some areas of life it is more difficult, and in other areas less difficult to prove the adequacy of our understandings. In spiritual and psychological areas, it is more difficult to check up on our perceptions. In material and physical matters, however, it is often quite a bit less difficult. Checking out the law of gravity, for example, or the rule that states that two material objects cannot occupy the same space at the same time, is fairly easily done.

The medical realm illustrates both the possibility of fairly accurate understanding of reality and the great difficulty of measuring accuracy. If, for example, somebody comes to a medical doctor with a seriously diseased part of her or his body and the doctor treats some other part of the body, while the patient dies from the original problem, that's a pretty good indication that the doctor did not accurately understand the situation. Suppose, though, a patient has a ruptured appendix and the doctor diagnoses a ruptured appendix. He or she operates, removes the appendix, and the person gets well. We then say the doctor's view of reality was close enough to REALITY that what she or he did to take care of it was adequate.

In most areas of medical diagnosis ranging from common aches and pains to diagnosing some forms of cancer, even a doctor's ability to see REALITY clearly may not be very great. He or she has to take educated guesses. Due to experience and training, those educated guesses are likely to be closer to the REALITY of the situation than the uneducated guesses of a nonspecialist.

What goes on in our minds when we perceive and construct our models of reality is apparently quite complex. In an attempt to be helpful, but at the risk of greatly oversimplifying, we may picture some of this material as charted above.

Note that there are at least three dimensions to external reality (1, 2, 3) plus two aspects of mental reality (4 and 5). From these latter, which we learn as children and modify (often only slightly) as we mature, we construct our model of reality (6). We employ at least two lenses for interpreting external reality, one for interpreting what happens and the other for interpreting what we analyze of our experiences. All that happens (1) seems always to be larger than either what we believe to be possible (4) or what we actually experience (2). What we experience, furthermore, always seems to be greater than that portion of our experience that we interpret (3) and from which our model of reality is constructed. Nevertheless, there seems to always be some interaction between one's model of reality (6), the materials in boxes 3 and 4, and the process in 5 above.

In this process, the assumptions we are taught become the primary influences on the conclusions we arrive at. Here are four illustrations of the close relationship between assumptions and conclusions:

1. If we assume that God does not exist, we conclude that miracles cannot happen.

2. If we assume that God exists, but that He is distant and unconcerned about us, we conclude that though miracles could happen, they don't. God doesn't care enough to interfere.

3. If we assume that God exists but perceive of Him rather philosophically and relegate Him to corners of life carefully designated as "religious," we may conclude that miracles used to seem to happen. Now, however, we explain such things differently ("scientifically"), and we marvel at how naive people used to be.

4. If, though, we assume that God is very active in human affairs, we conclude that miracles happen around us all the time. We assume that He's very active, so we interpret many things as manifestations of His activity.

SUMMARY AND AMPLIFICATION

There are four basic assumptions to note that underlie critical/mediated realism:

1. Critical/mediated realism, like direct realism but unlike Indian mysticism, assumes a REAL, structured world that can be experienced in part by people.

2. Critical/mediated realism says, however, that we have to distinguish between that REALITY and the human perception of it.

3. Critical/mediated realism assumes that REALITY is much bigger and more complex than we can grasp all at once. With the blind men, the elephant was too big for them to grasp all at once. This led to their differing theories as to what the elephant was like.

4. Critical/mediated realism sees the observer as both very important and very limited in the observational process. Indeed, as you read, your differing perspectives may result in quite a variety of understandings of what is written here. And you (not I) will have the final word. Your part, then, becomes at least as important as mine in determining the reality of what I intend.

Observers, however, are subject to certain limitations:

1. First of all, we're limited by our senses. There are many things happening outside our experience—some of them, indeed, are probably outside of any human's experience. But we can only experience what our senses give us.

2. Secondly, we limit ourselves by being highly selective in choosing the data we consider. We tend to screen out (unconsciously or consciously) data that we've been taught not to notice or that we aren't interested in or don't understand. In this presentation, you, the reader, are already involved in this selection process. You are accepting and understanding certain things and probably ignoring those things you don't understand. Some of the things I consider important will be the things you don't understand and either ignore or, worse yet, misunderstand.

3. In addition to the limitation of such personal selectivity, there is the screening or filtering of REALITY produced by our society in accord with our cultural patterns. This is a broad-gauged type of limitation in which we learn as members of a society to notice certain things and describe them in certain ways while ignoring other things. Many nonwestern peoples, for example, divide the color spectrum into three or five categories, or assume that the universe is full of very active malevolent spirits, or tend to regularly ignore the passage of time (including other commitments) if something meaningful is in process, or consider every decision still negotiable, even if a vote has been taken and a rule or law passed. Such practices result in culturally inculcated differences between the members of such societies and the members of western societies in what aspects of REALITY are noticed and how they are perceived.

In dealing with color, we in the West tend to make more distinctions than many peoples. But when it comes to spiritual beings, we tend to ignore or even deny their existence. When it comes to distinguishing heat and cold, I found that my western upbringing did not provide me with all of the categories I needed to be able to speak the Hausa language of northern Nigeria. As I found out by trial and error, they are taught to divide heat and cold into four categories, each with a specific word to label it: dry heat, damp heat, dry cold, damp cold.

4. In the fourth place, we are influenced in our perceptions by the limitations and distortions imposed by human sinfulness. Secular scientists, of course, usually ignore this factor. It is not a part of REALITY that their subculture focuses on, though some seem to notice (e.g., Goldschmidt 1966; Menninger 1973).

Sinfulness undoubtedly affects perception at both individual and cultural levels in a multitude of ways. Among them would presumably be the many times when the selfish interests of persons or groups intrude into the way REALITY is understood. Whenever, for example, we perceive REALITY as endorsing our good at the expense of the good of others, we can assume that it is sin that is distorting our vision. Indeed, every perception of REALITY is tainted in some way by the sin factor.

The critical realist position starts from the observation that, though we do observe REALITY, we do not see it directly. It goes on to point out that we strive to make sense of what we see by organizing our perceptions into a mental ordering that may be labeled by such terms as *mental map*, *model*, *picture of reality*, or *perspective*. This mental ordering consists of a more or less integrated understanding of REALITY built largely from the system or systems we have been taught before we knew of any alternative perspectives. The perspective taught to us, mainly in unconscious ways, by the adults in our lives while we were growing up has a big head start on any other perspective that we may seek to adopt later on.

CHANGE

We have been carefully and effectively taught what to perceive, yet we always seem to modify our perspectives. Though we will deal more fully with this topic later in this volume, when we deal with culture and worldview change, it will be helpful here to note at least three reasons for this.

1. We always seem to learn imperfectly. Though each generation tends overall to adopt the perspective of the previous generation rather fully, there always seems to be some slippage from generation to generation. This is most likely due to imperfect understanding or lack of complete acceptance on the part of the learners. Often parents, due to their own life experience, become less convinced of a given understanding than their parents were and, therefore, will pass it on to their children in such a tentative way that their children will alter or reject it.

2. A second reason for change in our mental maps is the fact that as we experience life, we seem to constantly test our models in relation to that experience. Since the perspectives we were taught were developed to fit the experiences of previous generations, there is likely to be some lack of fit, at least in certain areas, with our own experience. This fact faces us with the choice of ignoring the lack of fit, altering the perspective, or denying any interpretation of our experience that does not conform to the perspective. People seem to choose each of these options fairly frequently. When, however, we choose to alter our mental map, change takes place, at least in the way we use the patterns of our own culture.

3. A third pressure for change in our mental grid occurs when we are faced with a conflicting model of, or approach to, some aspect of reality. In traditional societies (at least in the past) and in more isolated segments of western societies, exposure to other options tends to be minimized. But in the mainstreams of both western and nonwestern societies today, people are being faced in an unprece-

dented way with models of reality that often conflict in whole or in part with what they have been taught. There are at least two frequent results of such pressure.

a. Frequently a person or group will be so convinced of the greater validity of the new understanding of REALITY that they make what has been called a *paradigm shift*, a conversion to a new perspective (*see* Kuhn 1970; Barbour 1974; Kraft 1979a, 1989). Such a shift happens whenever nonwesterners convert from a spirit-centered view of REALITY to a materialistic "scientific" perspective, or when non-Christians convert to Christianity, or when westerners brought up in a Christian "paradigm" (perspective) convert to a secularistic perspective or (in a more restricted context) when scientists who have learned to understand their science (or some part of it) in one way abandon that picture of REALITY for a different understanding (e.g., flat earth to round earth or earth-centered universe to sun-centered universe).

b. When people convert from one perspective to another, they usually retain a major portion of the old view, often compartmentalizing it in case they need to use it again later. They may switch back and forth between the two, as when people of nonwestern societies who have been taught secularism in western schools employ that secularistic perspective when involved in activities associated with western culture (business, school, politics, church) but switch to a spirit-centered perspective learned within their home society when faced with life experiences not adequately handled by the western paradigm (illness, breakdown of interpersonal relationships, oppression by spirits, personal or group misfortune).

WHERE ARE WE?

Models, perspectives, grids, mental maps, paradigms, and perceptions such as we are discussing here are, therefore, to be understood as ways of seeing things rather than as absolute declarations about the essential nature of things. They are interpretations of the REALITY (or parts of it) seen imperfectly and partially by human beings through lenses affected by culture, personality, experience, sin, and probably a myriad of other limiting and distorting factors. Only God sees REALITY and TRUTH fully. We see as partially as the blind men examining the elephant. The best we can claim, therefore, is glimpses of REALITY and TRUTH—glimpses that prove to be adequate in the living of life and are revealed to be adequate in our preparation for eternity.

These are tentative ways of perceiving REALITY and should be subject to constant reevaluation, change, refinement, and replacement. Models of REALITY are intended to be improved on. Meanwhile, they are important to us in at least two ways:

1. They help us understand and relate to REALITY, whether that of the world around us or that of the realm that lies beyond human time and space.

2. In addition, such models provide us maps for action, enabling us to chart our course in relation to both this world and the next.

The perspective (critical/mediated realism) being presented here may already have become your point of view, or it may require a paradigm shift for you to accept it. In any event, you may notice that even in presenting this view, I have at times tended to present it as TRUTH rather than (as the theory requires) simply a tentative perception of truth.

This is easily done, and I need to apologize for it. But let me also take this opportunity to give two reasons why I think this has happened.

1. I suspect that I, like most others who advocate the critical realism paradigm, am actually in the category of those described above who actually hold within them two mutually incompatible perspectives. I'm afraid that I regularly switch back and forth between critical/mediated realism and naive/direct realism. If so, you may detect in this chapter and elsewhere in the book touches of the dogmatism of the direct realism that I seek to avoid. Sorry. But look out for the same tendency in yourself.

2. Secondly, there seems to be something about an attempt to be persuasive that requires a high degree of certainty in the words and phrases used. Such certainty in vocabulary should be accepted as I intend it—as designed to present my ideas as persuasively as possible. It should not be interpreted as an unconscious repudiation of the position I am arguing for.

UNDERSTANDING PERCEPTION

In the following figure, each r stands for the perception of reality understood by a given person. Each number stands for a person. If we imagine each person to be from a different culture and imagine the REALITY she or he is looking at to be Christianity, the stage will be well set for the following discussion.

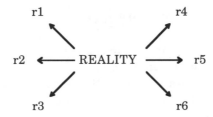

Figure 2.2 Multiple perceptions of REALITY

As humans, we apparently always interpret. Furthermore, we always interpret in relation to ourselves. We seem to be incurably subjective. When we interpret, then, we interpret holistically. Everything observed (words, gestures, posture, setting, context, timing, and so on) plus quite a number of factors internal to us (past experience, present disposition, cultural and psychological conditioning, and so forth) become parts of the message. In response to all of this, we construct the meanings that make up our interpretations (*see* Kraft 1991a for a more detailed treatment of communication theory).

The upshot of all of this is that every communication results in three realities:

1. The first reality is that of the communicator. As I write, I have an idea of what I want to communicate to you. That's my reality.

2. The second reality, or set of realities is that of the receptor. In response to what I say, each of the readers of this volume generates a picture of reality based only partly on what I say. This perception, filtered as it is through my words, the medium of print, and the variety of factors specific to you, the reader, can end up

quite distant from my intent (especially if your overall attitude toward me and this material should be negative).

3. Then there is objective REALITY. This is REALITY as God alone sees it.

Though we can't hope to attain 100 percent accuracy in our grasp of God's REALITY, it is all-important to understand and seek to overcome any discrepancies between the other two realities. Following are a series of documented misperceptions stemming from such discrepancies.

ILLUSTRATIONS OF MISPERCEPTIONS

Here are a few illustrations of misperceptions or misinterpretations stemming from differing views of reality.

1. A Nigerian once asked me, "What was wrong with Jesus?" I said, "What do you mean, what was wrong with Him? There was nothing wrong with Jesus." He said, "He was a shepherd, wasn't He?" "Yes, the Bible talks about Jesus as the Good Shepherd." "Then what was wrong with Him? He was grown up, wasn't He? Wasn't He an adult?" "Yes, He was an adult." "Then what was wrong with Him?"

This man from northeastern Nigeria (this is not true for all of Nigeria) had something in his perception that led him to the conclusion that there must have been something wrong with Jesus. Assuming that there must be some valid concern behind his question, I asked myself, Who in this part of Nigeria tends sheep? That question, then, led me to the answer: there are two kinds of people herding sheep—young boys and mentally deficient adult men.

To present Jesus as the Good Shepherd communicates well to Hebrews, since it lines up well with their perception of REALITY. But these people in northeastern Nigeria were getting the message that Jesus must have been mentally deficient. What is a marvelous analogy for one people misleads another.

2. I was talking to our Kamwe leaders one time, and asked, "If you men were to present this message of Christianity to the village council down under the tree where they meet, how would you do it?" They said, "We would stand up and pick out the oldest, most respected man in the group and ask him a question. We might say, 'Father, what did our people believe about God before the missionaries came?' He would start speaking and answer at length. Some of the other old men would chime in, and it might take them ten, fifteen, twenty minutes to give the answer. Then we'd ask him another question, and he'd give the answer. And so on, until eventually we would be doing more of the talking than the older men."

I said to them, "Apparently this is your indigenous way of preaching." They said, "Yes, it sounds like it." I said, "Why don't you use this method in church?" "Oh, we haven't been taught to do that in church. In church the preacher stands up and does all the talking."

I asked, "Could this be why no old men come to church?" They said, "Of course. We've alienated all the old men, because they have not been given their due respect." In such a society, you have to give proper respect to the old leaders of the group by letting them speak first. Once you have given that respect, you have won the way to present your message, in essentially a monologue fashion. Until you have shown that respect, though, you have not done things properly. The perception that these old men were getting was that Christianity is not for old men.

3. In a very instructive article by Pike and Cowan (1959) we are made aware of a unique misperception of Christianity occurring among the Mazateco people of southern Mexico. These people believe that Jesus speaks to them via hallucinations induced by eating certain mushrooms. The mushrooms, they believe, are the result of the blood of Jesus dropping to the ground as He flew over it at the time of His crucifixion. Because of some confusion of their indigenous ideas with the message as it came to them, they blended their pagan meanings with the foreign Christian meanings so that the overall understanding was quite different. Though the result seems weird, we must take it seriously if we are ever to get any other view across.

4. "Would God forget a man who has given Him his first wife?" asked a Cameroonian chief rhetorically in a discussion with William Reyburn (1958). The discussion centered around what this chief and his elders were doing about their desire to be recognized (accepted) by God in spite of the fact that the church rejected them because they each had several wives.

What they had done was each ordered his first wife to join the church. "God would not turn away a man who gave Him his first wife," they reasoned. This very clever strategy stemmed, of course, from their misperception of the Christian God and His system. Western missionaries, seeing these wives in church regularly, would assume the wives were properly motivated (in spite of their marital situation). It is unlikely that they would have learned the real reason for these wives' regular attendance. For them and their husbands, however, this was a creative and culturally appropriate response to a very different perception of the Christian message.

5. The story is told by Don Richardson (1974) of a time when he related to the Sawi people of Irian Jaya the story of Jesus' betrayal and crucifixion. "How can we be like that?" his hearers asked. In response, Richardson began to tell them how to be like Jesus. Interrupting him, the Sawi said, "No, not Jesus. We want to be like Judas!" Sawi society puts a high value on being clever in treachery, so they were anxious to hear more of the story of Judas and his clever betrayal of Jesus, so they could learn to be even more adept at betrayal.

6. One of the most disturbing cases of misperception is presented in an article by John Messenger (1959) on forgiveness among the Anang Ibibio. The Anang people believed in a god of rules and regulations, one who punished harshly if a person overstepped the bounds. Their understanding sounds very much like some of the Old Testament portrayals of Yahweh.

Then came Christian missionaries presenting a loving, accepting, and forgiving God. This God was apparently perceived as different from their traditional god but attractive to them. Over the course of a generation or so of intensive missionary effort, centering in schools and hospitals as well as in churches, more than 50 percent of the Anang people have come to profess Christianity. Women, boys, and young men have been especially receptive.

Though traditional Anang moral standards were quite similar to those of Christianity, young people especially have come to widely disregard them. According to Messenger, the reason lies not in a questioning of those standards but in a belief that the Christian God will not punish "if belief is maintained" (the Protestant approach) or "if sins are confessed and absolved" (the Catholic approach). Wearing crosses and praying and sacrificing to the Holy Spirit are believed to be especially effective in assuring "God's forgiveness for an immoral deed." Thus a misperception of the nature and requirements of God has given rise to a belief in the compatibility of Christian allegiance with gross immorality.

It apparently did not occur to the missionaries that the indigenous Anang god might be the same as the Christian God and that it would have been wise to present the Christian message as essentially continuous with traditional belief and practice, rather than in competition with it.

I had this kind of expression from a member of the neighboring Igbo tribe. A group of us were invited to visit at his home in Michigan. He was a student whom I had enlisted to help me orient three missionary recruits who were preparing to go to Nigeria. This man prayed before the meal, "Oh, Lord, help these young men to realize that it is You who are taking them to Nigeria, not they who are taking You." As soon as he said the "amen," I asked, "What in the world did you mean by that prayer? Please explain."

> When the first missionaries came out, they came with what they saw as a new religion and a new God. And many of us accepted this new religion and the new God. We took them at their word that they were presenting to us a new God.
>
> You know, it took us about two generations to realize that this wasn't a new God that they were bringing. This was the same God that we have always known, though very imperfectly. It was our God, not a different one, who had brought them to instruct us more perfectly about Him and how to get into a better relationship with Him. But they didn't seem to know this. Nor did we, until recently. I don't want these young men to make that same mistake.

OTHER POSSIBLE PERCEPTIONS

Perceptions of Christianity that don't square with ours are not, however, always negative.

1. Jacob Loewen tells of a time when he wanted to demonstrate differences of perception between Africans and western missionaries. He asked a group made up of missionaries and Africans to write down what they believed to be the main message of the story of Joseph in the Old Testament. The Europeans' responses added up to, "Joseph was a man who, no matter what happened to him, always remained faithful." The African responses, however, showed quite a different focus. Their interpretation was, "Joseph was a man who, no matter how far he traveled, never forgot his family."

Neither perception is, of course, really wrong. Western individualism is evident in the one interpretation, while the family orientation of African societies leads to quite a different focus.

2. In working with Nigerian leaders, I once started with my understanding of God's greatest demonstration of power in the Scriptures—the resurrection of Jesus. I found, to my dismay, that pointing to Jesus' resurrection carried less impact than I had expected. In probing the reason for this, I found that these people regularly referred to a person who had been knocked out and come to as having risen from the dead. Since being revived after having been knocked out was a reasonably common occurrence, whereas rising from the dead was virtually unimagined, the interpretation these people would normally give to talk of Jesus' resurrection would mislead them.

"Since the impact of the account of the resurrection is thus seriously diminished among your people," I asked the leaders, "what approach should we take?"

The discussion was not very productive until I asked, "What is the biggest problem that your people feel?" Their ready answer was, "Evil spirits." I then asked how impactful would be a presentation of Christianity that focused on God's power over the spirits. "That would be genuine good news," they answered.

Without denying the truth of the resurrection, we chose to focus first on another part of the biblical message—a part that they perceived as an answer to a problem they couldn't solve themselves. By proclaiming the God who could and would free them from the tyranny of the spirits, we gained an immediate hearing. The importance of Jesus' resurrection and the fact that He was really dead, not just knocked out, could be dealt with more slowly.

3. At one point, I suggested to my Nigerian colleagues that I thought I saw important similarities between their system of sacrifices and that in the Old Testament. As we discussed the matter, however, it became clear that the similarities were only on the surface, since the basic motivation was quite different. The Kamwe people, like many of the peoples of the world, are more concerned with the ability of evil spirits to harm them than with their relationship to God. As the Kamwe reasoned, God will be good to us; it's the evil spirits we have to watch out for. We sacrifice to the spirits to appease them and keep them from hurting us.

Similarly, Beekman (1959) reports that the Gospel has been presented to the Chol Indians of southern Mexico in relation to their perception that the devil is "the owner of the world and the ruler of the spirits in the realm of nature . . . [he] is the one who causes the hardships of life and who must be satisfied with sacrifices." God is perceived as being benevolent toward humans and can, therefore, be ignored.

The Christian witnesses among the Chol studied and took these perceptions seriously. They then presented the Gospel as a message about a Holy Spirit more powerful than either the devil or the spirits controlled by the witch doctor. In this way "the very core of their pagan belief was dealt with in a manner that each one could understand, and was replaced with the heart of the Gospel." We found the same to be true among the Kamwe.

4. Missionary annals are full of accounts of people who, for one reason or another, were expecting the first Gospel witnesses when they arrived. Several of these stories are documented by Richardson (1981). Another is told by Barney (1957). Note the importance of the receptors' perception in the following account concerning the coming of the Gospel to the Meo of Laos in 1950.

The missionary had left his station for a few weeks and put a young Christian from a neighboring tribe in charge of the station while he was to be away.

> Nai Kheng went about town telling of his Christian faith. One who listened intently was Po Si, an old Meo shaman who lived close to town. He stated that a female shaman had prophesied two years before that in two years someone would come to tell them about the true God, Fua-Tai. Po Si was convinced that Nai Kheng was telling him about the same God and became a professing Christian. He took Nai Kheng to his own village, where the chief led his entire group in expressing faith in Fua-Tai-Yesu, as Jesus came to be called in Meo (Barney 1957:34).

The account goes on to tell of the presenting of the message to the female shaman who had made the original prophecy. She was convinced that Fua-Tai-Yesu was the God about whom she had prophesied and "led her village in placing faith in" Him. Hearing this, other villages sent for Nai Kheng and, in turn, responded in faith to the extent that when the missionary returned, he "was amazed to find nearly 1,000 Meo tribespeople who had announced their faith in Christ" (p. 34). The missionary, Nai Kheng, and Po Si then went from village to village and, with permission, destroyed the people's fetishes. The Christians' primary joy was in their freedom from the powerful evil spirits that they could not control but which Jesus could. This is a refreshing example of an approach to Christian witness that succeeded because it worked with the receptors' perceptions.

WE ARE MESSENGERS FROM GOD

Our concern for perception leads us to a concern for how we, as cross-cultural witnesses, are perceived, for, as communication studies show us (*see* Kraft 1991a), the person communicating is the major component of the message he or she tries to get across. How we are perceived strongly influences this perception of God and His message.

This thought hit me one time in a way I've never gotten over. I was standing near our home in Nigeria, looking up and down the valley in which we lived, pondering the fact that I was the only missionary within fifteen to twenty miles, when crowding into my mind came the realization that to these people I was Jesus Christ. The thought scared me then, and it scares me now. Whatever they would know of Jesus Christ in that pioneer situation would come from their perception of me. This was the first contact most of them had had with the Christian message and Christian messengers. Most of them probably thought that Jesus was a brother or close friend of mine. Many had no understanding of the historical facts. I symbolized this new approach to God, and what I did and said and how they interpreted me became major components of the message we were presenting.

I regretted very much that the likes of me would be so important in the communication process. But God seems to have set things up in this way. Paul refers to us as letters from God in flesh and blood (2 Cor 3:1–3). God writes His letters in flesh and blood, not simply in words on paper. God sends us as His messages to others.

What does reality look like from the point of view of those to whom we go? Does God's love really come through to them? What is their perception of the Gospel, and does our influence enhance the message and its accuracy so that the objective reality of God shines through? Or do we disturb that message, distort it, and turn it in a different direction? How should this kind of realization affect our approach to ministry? With reference to this book, how should these kinds of questions affect our understanding?

It is my contention that much of the material in this book should help us understand the point of view of the people to whom we go and enable us to produce the kind of behavior that will bring about a bridge between us and them over which properly Christian messages will pass. Our goal is that the meanings in their heads be accurate perceptions of the message that God has entrusted to us. To that end I dedicate the chapters that follow.

CHAPTER 3

A PERSPECTIVE ON CULTURE

INTEGRATIONAL THOUGHT

We live our lives largely according to the rules and patterns we have been taught by those of the previous generation who brought us up. These rules and patterns, our culture, have been produced and modified by generation after generation of our forebears and represent the accumulated knowledge of our predecessors. We are taught to trust it (and our predecessors who produced it) as an adequate set of guidelines in terms of which to live our lives.

Most people consider their customs and the assumptions that underlie them to be correct, sacred, and often even absolute. This was the view the Hebrews took toward their customs. They saw their culture as given to them by Yahweh (even though it can be proven historically that most of it was in place before God made His covenants with Abraham). They thus considered it obligatory to obey these sacred customs to express their commitment to God.

The normal Hebrew word for their culture is usually translated "Law." This term signifies Hebrew tradition or culture. In the excellent play (and movie) about Jewish life, titled *Fiddler on the Roof*, the lead character, Tevye, exults over these traditions. Tradition is what tells us who we are and what God expects, he says at one point. Then he sings and dances his joy over these traditions. Similarly, the Psalmist writes a whole psalm (Ps 119) of rejoicing over his involvement with these commands and customs, at one point exclaiming, "How I love your law!" (v. 97).

People today may not sing and dance in exultation over their customs, but they may be just as attached to their customs as the Hebrews were to theirs. This fact must be recognized at both ends of the communication process. We may be so attached to our ways that we cannot imagine other peoples not wanting to do it our way. And they may be so attached to their customs that they may be quite resistant to changing them.

The Apostle Paul tackles the problem of extreme reverence for custom in the Letter to the Galatians. He is appealing for freedom from the tyranny of a legalistic commitment to a particular set of customs. The Galatians had apparently started where Abraham started—with a covenant relationship with God (Gal 3:6–9). Having started well they then turned back to their commitment to Hebrew custom. In condemning this behavior, Paul says,

> Tell me this one thing: did you receive God's Spirit by doing what the Law [= Hebrew custom] requires or by hearing the gospel and believing it? How can you be so foolish! You began by God's Spirit; do you now want to finish by your own power? . . . Does God give you the Spirit and work miracles among you because you do what the Law requires or because you hear the gospel and believe it? (Gal 3:2–5).

Relationship precedes custom in God's ordering of things. We and the people we minister to are to be free from legalism, and this is true whether our legalism be cultural or denominational. We all need customs, but not somebody else's customs. We all need a certain amount of ritual, but not somebody else's ritual. Our customs, no matter how valuable to us, are not to be imposed on others. And their customs, no matter how sacred they may be to them, are not sacred to God.

Cultural structuring is important. We all need it, both in church and in all of life. But when it gets in the way of the freedom we have in Christ to develop customs that spring out of our relationship with Him, cultural structuring becomes an obstruction.

INTRODUCTION

The term *culture* is the label anthropologists give to the complex structuring of customs and the assumptions that underlie them in terms of which people govern their lives. Every society has its own cultural way of life. Apparently, human beings cannot live without such structuring. At least, no group of people has yet been discovered without culture.

A culture may be likened to a river, with a surface level and a deep level. The surface is visible. Most of the river, however, lies beneath the surface and is largely invisible. In a river, what happens on the surface is both a reaction to external phenomena and a manifestation of the deep-level characteristics of the river. For example, if something is thrown into a river, there will be a splash as the surface of the water is affected by the external phenomenon. That item, however, will in turn be affected by subsurface phenomena such as the current, the cleanness or dirtiness of the river, the presence of other objects in the river, and the like.

So it is with culture. What we see on the surface of a culture is the patterning of human behavior. This patterning or structuring of behavior, though impressive, is the lesser part of the culture. In the depths are the assumptions we call worldview (*see* chapter 4), in terms of which the surface level behavior is governed. When something affects the surface of a culture, it may result in a change at that level. The nature and extent of that change will, however, be influenced by the deep-level structuring (worldview) of the culture.

With humans, unlike with rivers, there is a still deeper level. We will call this the level of person. Culture (including worldview) is a matter of structure or patterns. Culture does not *do* anything. Culture is like a road. It provides a surface with boundaries on which people may walk or drive. People may choose to walk or drive off the road. They may creatively forge a new path, develop a new custom that may or may not be followed by others. If that new custom is followed by others, it becomes a part of their culture, as well. If not, it remains idiosyncratic and dies with the person who invented it.

Ordinarily people govern themselves by habit. Though people are creative and some very creative in devising new strategies, most of what we do and think is more habitual than creative. It is our regular habit to follow the cultural guidelines (roads) taught to us as we were growing up. *The apparent power of a culture to govern a person's behavior lies in the human propensity to live by habit. Culture has no power in and of itself.* The interaction between people and cultural structuring will be explored further below and becomes an important part of the undergirding of our whole treatment.

I am frequently asked, Where did culture come from? And how did there get to be so many cultures? My assumption is that God both created into humans a culture-creating (and modifying) capacity and gave Adam some kind of culture to start with. Since we know of no language without a culture, the fact that Adam spoke a language would seem to indicate that he also had culture.

As for the vast number of cultures in the world (probably more than the 6,000 languages that have been counted), my theory is that the primary reason for such diversity is *human creativity* (a part of the image of God in humans). In spite of our propensity to behave habitually, humans are just too creative to continue to do things, think things, feel things, say things in the same way(s) all the time. People innovate, and enough innovation and isolation (geographical or social) over a long enough period of time results in cultural and linguistic divergence and splitting.

CULTURES ARE TO BE RESPECTED

We cannot live without culture. It is that matrix within which we "live and move and exist" (Acts 17:28), the nonbiological, nonenvironmental part of our lives that we learn from our elders, that we share with our community, and in which we are totally submerged from one end of life to the other.

Cultural structuring is both outside of us and inside of us. We relate to it in many ways as a fish relates to water (though it is more influential in our lives than even water is to fish). But we are usually as unconscious of it as fish must be of the water in which they exist or as we usually are of the air we breathe. Indeed, many of us only notice culture when we go into another cultural territory and observe customs different from our own. Then we often feel sorry for those people and, if we are able, seek ways to rescue them from their customs.

Historically, many have reacted to other people's customs by trying to rescue the people from them. They responded to other people's ways like the monkey in the Southeast Asian story of the monkey and the fish. It seems Monkey and Fish got caught in a flood. As the waters rose higher and higher, Monkey found a tree and climbed to safety. As he got above the water level, he looked down and saw his friend Fish still in the water. So, out of concern for his friend, he reached down, rescued Fish, and held him tight to his chest as he climbed higher in the tree. This, of course, was the end of friend Fish, since he cannot live outside of water.

Human beings, like fish, can live inside a culture but not outside of one. Thus, any persons "rescued" from one culture can only survive if they are quickly immersed in another. Some from the Two-Thirds World are studying or living in America, feeling they've been "rescued" from the culture into which they were born, since they no longer fit there. When they're in their home country, they don't any longer feel at home. They have been pulled out of their home culture. The sad thing is that, having been pulled out of one culture, they have usually not been made to feel completely at home in the other. They feel, as one of my Nigerian friends put it, like the bat—they don't get along either with birds or with animals.

The way of Jesus is, however, to honor a people's culture, not to wrest them from it. Just as He entered the cultural life of first-century Palestine in order to communicate with people, so we are to enter the cultural matrix of the people we seek to win. If we are to witness effectively to human beings, we have to take account of the culture in which these human beings live. If we fish for fish, we have to know whether the fish are swimming in deep water or shallow water, in water that is running rapidly or is stagnant, in water that is clean or dirty, cold or warm. We have to know these things if we're going to fish for fish. This text is designed to help us learn about the cultural water in which people live and move and have their being and without which we are not human beings.

We who are missionary anthropologists believe that we really can't do what we seek to do very effectively if we live in ignorance of the cultural dimensions of human beings. Much good Christian witness has resulted from the activities of perceptive people who, though working cross-culturally, have dealt with people sympathetically and understandingly in terms of the kinds of principles we are talking about. As Eugene Nida states, "Good missionaries have always been good 'anthropologists'" (1954:xi). What he means is that good missionaries didn't need a basic anthropology course to alert them to these things. They did the right things naturally. Unfortunately, too many of us, like those who have sought to rescue people from their cultures, don't do the right things naturally. We need books like this to inform us concerning the relationships between people and their cultures, to enable us to be the kind of cross-cultural witnesses we intend to be.

A POSITIVE OR A NEGATIVE VIEW OF CULTURE?

An important basic concern of Christians who take anthropology seriously is whether we should take a positive or a negative attitude toward culture. As I have suggested above, I believe God takes culture seriously and, as I will discuss further in chapter 6, is pleased to work through it to reach and interact with humans. Culture is seen here as usable by God and us to fulfill God's purposes on earth.

But is culture good, bad, or neutral? Some have felt that when John refers to the "world" as something we should hate in 1 John 2:15–17, he is condemning culture. Recently, Sherwood Lingenfelter of Biola University has published a view of culture that takes this position and challenges the view I stated in *Christianity in Culture* (1979a):

> I see cultural structuring . . . as basically a vehicle or milieu, neutral in essence, though warped by the pervasive influence of human sinfulness. Culture is not in and of itself either an enemy or a friend to God or humans. It is, rather, something that is there to be used by personal beings such as humans, God, and Satan. . . .
>
> Culture is seen as a kind of road map made up of various forms designed to get people where they need to go. These forms and the functions they are intended to serve are seen, with few exceptions, as neutral with respect to the interaction between God and man. Cultural patterning, organizing, and structuring of life, the functions they are intended to serve, and the processes cultures make available to human beings are not seen as inherently evil or good in themselves (113).

Lingenfelter says, however, "I reject the notion that culture or worldview is neutral," adding, in at least partial contradiction of a view he once participated in,

> Analogies such as Kraft's "map" or "a tool for communication and interaction" (Lingenfelter and Mayers 1986:122) are inadequate to capture the pervasive presence of sin in the lives and thought of human beings. Using the tool analogy, culture is more like a "slot machine" found in Las Vegas' gambling casinos than a wrench or screw driver. Culture, like a slot machine, is programmed to be sure that those who hold power "win" and the common players "lose" . . . The structures and organizations of cultures are not neutral; people define and structure their relationships with others to protect their personal or group interests, and to sustain or gain advantage over others with whom they compete (1992:18).

A page before this statement, Lingenfelter had said,

> [T]hese social systems and worldviews become prisons of disobedience, entangling those who hold them in a life of conformity to social images that at their roots are in conflict with God's purpose for humanity as expressed in Jesus Christ. Paul suggests that human beings are in a prison, a cell of disobedience: "God has imprisoned all human beings in their own disobedience only to show mercy to them all" (Rom 11:30-32 *NJB*). He repeats the same theme in Galatians 3:22, paraphrasing Psalm 14:1-3. He observes that "the whole world is a prisoner of sin." God has penned up all people in their self-created cells of culture, including Jew and Gentile, pagan and missionary (1992:17-18).

Lingenfelter contends that "the gospel contradicts society and worldview" and that Jesus' "'good news' brought conflict and change," challenging the system operated by the power brokers of His day, inducing them to react in defense of that system in such a way that the Christians experienced "great distress" (1992:19). In response to my position that God wants to transform people by enabling them first to live up to their own ideals, then to transcend them to approach scriptural ideals (1979a:245), Lingenfelter holds that "the Scriptures will inevitably *contradict the ideals of a culture* (1992:20, italics his). He concludes that while I and Mayers hold "a 'high' and neutral view of culture," his "is a 'low' view," a view that sees culture as "inextricably infected by sin" (1992:20).

I have attempted to present Lingenfelter's argument in some detail because it deserves to be taken seriously. There are problems inherent in taking a positive view of culture. Sin is a fact. The constant misuse of power is a fact, as is the ease with which those in power are able to manipulate cultural structures to serve their ends. The selfishness of those in power is a fact. *But it is also a fact that cultural structures are usable by people, both Christians and non-Christians, for good purposes*. People are *not* determined by cultural structuring (*see* chapter 10). That is, in spite of the boundaries and rules of culture within which we operate, there is room for choices. As Christians, however, we find ourselves living our lives within structures that seem to make it easier to do the wrong thing than to do the right thing. We play, as it were, on an "uneven playing field." It is as if we are playing soccer or football on a field that is definitely slanted and we are obliged to defend the downhill goal. For our enemies to score, they move the ball downhill. For us to score, however, we have to move it uphill. So the playing field is uneven, the slot machine is rigged. But our experience is that not every game is won by the evil side.

I think, therefore, that picturing cultures as "prisons/cells of disobedience" is misleading. A prison is something a person cannot get out of. A person is locked up in a prison, totally unable to use most aspects of his or her environment for positive purposes. Such is not the case with culture. Though culture may not be as neutral as I once thought it was, it is not the structures of culture that lock people in prisons but, rather, the sinful choices of *people* who are continually affected by the uneven playing field of the structures but are not totally determined by them. Within those structures other people put pressure on us or attempt to entice us to use our cultural structures sinfully. We may or may not go along with them. *But it is people-pressure and people-choices that determine whether the structures will be used as instruments of Satan or of God, not the slantedness of the structures themselves.*

True, it may be easier for a person to play to the downhill side of an uneven field. It is a part of our human condition that it is easier to sin than to do what is right. But this fact is a comment on the nature of persons, not the nature of the structures within which we function. These cultural structures, though slanted, may either be allowed to become a prison of disobedience for those who are disobedient to God or be used by Christians, utilizing the power of the Holy Spirit to play effectively uphill, as structures in terms of which they use options allowed within the cultural structures to express obedience to God. Though cultural structures are infected, they are not beyond usefulness.

In summary, I can agree with most of what Lingenfelter says with respect to the evilness, conflict, and misuse of power that surrounds us. But I contend that *these are people things, not structure things.* The structures are infected, to be sure, but the real problem lies in the people, not the structures. When, in 1 John 2:15-17, John warns us about "the world," he is talking about *people* (what I call "society" below), those within whom there is a sin nature, not about *culture*, the structures within which people operate and which they often manipulate to their advantage. People behave in prideful, manipulative ways that are displeasing to God, and we are not to love these sinful behaviors of society if we are to properly relate to God.

Though Lingenfelter and I may disagree as to whether to be negative or positive toward the structures of culture, the way he finds to escape from the morass of determinism he has fallen into is by reaching out for the kind of separation between people and culture described below. In his final chapter, he points to what he calls "the duality of culture" (1992:204) as the way out. This is very similar to the separation I made (1979a) between what I called "cultural patterning" and "cultural performance," a concept that is more fully developed below by making use of the distinction between culture as structure and society as people. Lingenfelter refers to a book by Anthony Giddens (1979), who proposes

> that structure and interaction must be addressed as separate levels for analysis. The structural dimension focuses on the systemic factors that define the enduring cultural components of relationship, the features that are reproduced over time and provide meaning for the participants. Interaction, on the other hand, focuses on the actors engaged in communication within the institutional framework yet with the freedom of individual choice characteristic of social behavior. Actors in every social situation formulate an interpretive scheme, a modality of the structural and interaction systems available to actors (Lingenfelter 1992:204).

Lingenfelter then refers to a book by Margaret Archer, who makes a similar distinction, calling the categories "the cultural system" (cultural structure) and "the sociocultural level" (people) (1988:134). Critiquing, then, theories of worldview such as Hiebert's (1985) that "have combined or conflated these two distinctive levels into one unified system" (Lingenfelter 1992:205), Lingenfelter agrees with Archer that this "myth of cultural integration" deludes us into ignoring "the recurring inconsistencies within every cultural system . . . and the volatility and unpredictability of human behavior" (Lingenfelter 1992:205). Recognizing the distinctness of the cultural structure level from the personal/social level "allows us to examine much more carefully the interplay of these two and the transforming processes that occur when the gospel brings contradiction into the life of the individual and into the systems of cultural and social relationships" (1992:205).

I agree. Though Lingenfelter chooses to be more negative than I concerning the influence of cultural structures on human behavior, I believe we are not that far apart with respect to strategy. In any event, I offer the approach to culture and worldview presented in this book as a start in the direction both of us are calling for. In spite of our differences, I am largely in agreement with the thrust of the following paragraph, with which he concludes his book:

> The key to the power of the gospel for transforming culture is an unwavering commitment to the Word of God. Missionary and national alike are frequently blinded by the relationships and values of their own social environment. While they are committed to a common Christ and a common gospel, they have integrated that gospel into a cultural system that reflects in large part a transformation of their preconversion knowledge and worldview. The pressures of the old cultural system and the old social order continually work against the liberating power of the gospel and the call to discipleship in Christ. By searching the Scriptures for those kingdom principles that call believers to antistructural relationships, such as freedom from property, giving and receiving at risk, loving family relationships, and servant leadership, missionary and national discover the "trigger mechanisms" that set them free from the bondage of their cultural systems and their sociocultural environments (Lingenfelter 1992:212).

PEOPLE AND CULTURE

As mentioned above, we need to distinguish carefully between people and the cultural structures in which they operate. It has been too common with both non-specialists and specialists to confuse the two. For example, it is common to hear statements such as "Their culture *makes* them do such and such," or "A people's culture *presses* them into its mold," or "A people's worldview *determines* their view of reality, enabling them to see certain things clearly but blinding them to other aspects of reality," or "Their culture *doesn't allow* them to . . ." Note that the italicized verbs in these statements convey an assumption of personal initiative and power on the part of culture.

Such statements represent what has been labeled a *superorganic* view of culture or "cultural superorganicism." People who subscribe to such a view picture culture as if it were an enormously powerful being that molds and pushes people around, determining or at least strongly influencing their beliefs and behavior, sometimes helpfully, sometimes harmfully. A culture, from this point of view, is a living organism, existing independently of those who practice it, with great power to influence their lives.

Those who hold to a superorganic view of culture are attempting to deal honestly with a big problem. The question they seek to answer may be stated as follows: How do we explain the fact that people within any given society behave in incredibly similar ways? All anthropologists have to answer that question. Some choose to see the source of such conformity in culture. Some choose to see it in the people themselves. I choose the latter.

For this reason I attempt to make a clear distinction between culture as structures and patterns and people as the active agents either in maintaining those structures and patterns or in changing them. This position has great theoretical significance both for our approach to anthropology and for our approach to Christian witness.

As I have written elsewhere in a treatment of worldview,

> Culture is not a person. It does not "do" anything. Only people do things. The fact that people ordinarily do what they do by following the cultural "tracks" laid down for them

should not lead us to treat culture itself as something possessing a life of its own. Culture is like the script an actor uses. He follows it most of the time. But occasionally, either because he has forgotten his lines or because he thinks he has a better way of reaching the goal, he departs from the script and does something else.

The "power" that keeps people following the script of their culture is the power of habit, not any power that culture possesses in itself. People ordinarily follow the patterns of their culture, but not always.

Cultural (including worldview) patterns, then, do not force people to follow them. *It is force of habit that keeps us following custom.* But even a habit can be changed with some effort. If the change is considered serious, however, others in the society will exert great pressure on the one who is deviating to get him or her to conform. If the deviation is not considered serious, little or no pressure may be exerted to get the person back in line (1989:56–57).

The distinction we are making is embodied in the contrast between the words *culture* and *society*. Culture refers to the structured customs of a people. Society refers to the people themselves. Note in the final paragraph of the above quote that it is the pressure of people (social pressure) that is brought to bear to keep people obeying certain customs, while the lack of such pressure leaves them free to make changes. There is no power in culture to press for conformity.

	PERSONAL BEHAVING	CULTURAL STRUCTURING
S U R F A C E	**BEHAVING**	**PATTERNS OF BEHAVIOR**

	Habitual Behaving
	  Overt (Doing, Speaking, Emoting)
	  Covert (Thinking, Feeling)
		Overt Customs that Pattern Doing, Speaking, Emoting, etc.

	Creative Behaving
	  Overt (Doing, Speaking, Emoting)
	  Covert (Thinking, Feeling)
		Covert Customs that Pattern Thinking, Feeling, etc.

D E E P	**ASSUMING** **(Usually Habitual, Often Creative)**	**PATTERNS OF WV ASSUMPTIONS**

	Primary-Level Assuming
	  Willing (Choosing)
	  Emoting
	  Reasoning
	  Assuming Motivations
	  Assuming Predispositions
		Patterns Underlying Primary Behavior
		  Willing (Choosing)
		  Emoting
		  Reasoning
		  Deciding Motivation
		  Being Predisposed

	Assigning Meaning
	  Interpreting
	  Evaluating
		Patterns of Meaning Assignment
		  Ways of Interpreting
		  Ways of Evaluating/Validating

	Responding to Assigned Meanings
	  Explaining
	  Committing/Pledging Allegiance
	  Relating
	  Adapting
	  Regulating
	  Seeking Psychological Reinforcement
	  Striving toward Integration/Consistency
		Patterns of Response to Meaning
		  Ways of Explaining
		  Ways of Committing/Pledging Allegiance
		  Ways of Relating
		  Ways of Adapting
		  Ways of Regulating
		  Ways of Getting Psychological Reinforcement
		  Ways of Integrating/Attaining Consistency

Figure 3.1 Surface and deep, personal and cultural

The chart above summarizes the distinction I am making between the behavior of persons and the cultural structuring of that behavior. Note that on the left (personal) side of the chart, we describe the activities by using verbs. People behave and assign meaning. On the right (culture) side of the chart we use nouns to indicate the static nature of the patterns people learn, by means of which they guide their behavior. Note the distinctions made between habitual and creative behavior and between overt behavior (doing and speaking) and covert behavior (thinking).

I have included the deep structure (worldview) part of the chart to give the whole picture even though we will not deal with the specifics of worldview until the next chapter.

We may liken the interaction between people and their cultures to that between actors and their scripts. In preparation for performing a play, an actor memorizes his script. During the performance he speaks his lines as creatively as possible within the limits set for him by the script and the physical setting on the stage. There are, however, conditions under which the actor will depart from the script. For one, he may forget some lines or make a mistake and have to improvise. For another, one of the other players may miss a cue or do something the first actor hadn't counted on, requiring him to improvise. Or some external circumstance (a prop misplaced or falling over) might motivate him to say or do something other than what he has memorized. Or he may simply create something new right on the spot to spice things up.

Though cultural lines are carefully memorized and most of the cultural performance proceeds according to habit, there is also room for creativity. When people follow the patterns, whether by habit (ritual) or by conscious choice, they are, in a sense, "performing their culture." They are following the cues. When they make mistakes or innovate, they are also performing, but in a more creative way. This kind of performance relates to the cultural script but does not follow the guidelines exactly.

In the drama of cultural performance, it sometimes seems good to change the script. This is done by agreement between the parties concerned: director, actors and actresses, stage manager, and so on. Cultural patterns (scripts) are both maintained and altered by the people who use them. The performance of people as they use their cultural patterns results in the continuance of most of the patterns, though always with some changes.

CULTURE DEFINED

Culture may be defined as the "total life way of a people, the social legacy the individual acquires from his group," a people's "design for living" (Kluckhohn 1949a:17). Or, to be more specific, we may see a culture as a society's complex, integrated coping mechanism, consisting of learned, patterned concepts and behavior, plus their underlying perspectives (worldview) and resulting artifacts (material culture). Diagrammatically, this definition is shown in figure 3.2 below.

Let's look more closely at our definition.

1. First, culture is seen as *a coping mechanism*. Another term that might be used is *a strategy for survival*. Culture is the mechanism by means of which every human group and individual copes with human biological makeup and the surrounding geographical and social environment. We experience three basic givens: our person (including biological, mental, psychological, and spiritual components), the environment in which we live (including both physical and social components), and the culture, in terms of which we relate to the other two. The latter provides us with the plans (strategies) and patterns that we employ in dealing with the givens of our psychobiological makeup and those of our geographical and social envi-

ronments. We will come to understand more of this coping mechanism as we go along.

A complex, integrated coping mechanism	Belonging to and operated by a society (social group)	Consisting of: 1. Concepts and behavior that are patterned and learned 2. Underlying perspectives (worldview) 3. Resulting products, both nonmaterial (customs, rituals) and material (artifacts)

Figure 3.2 A definition of culture

2. Secondly, we have labeled a culture as *belonging to and operated by a social group* (*society*). A culture is owned by the people who are trained in it and live according to it. As pointed out above, it is a "social legacy," an inheritance from a people's ancestors. It is very precious to a people and, under ideal conditions, is operated happily and confidently by those for whom it is the only "life way" or "design for living" that makes sense to them. A people perceives their culture as having been created by concerned and revered forebears to enable them to deal effectively with the concerns of life.

3. Such a cultural system *expresses ideas or concepts*. These ideas are where things start. There is no lever to enable us to move large rocks without an underlying concept, no wheel, no wedding ceremony, no eating custom, no pottery or basketry, no naming or puberty rite. Underlying every custom, every cultural strategy and probably historically prior to each, is one or more concepts in the head of the originator and of each one who practices the custom or employs the strategy.

4. These concepts underlie *cultural behavior*. Behavior is simply what we do with body or mind, alone or in groups. It is the most visible type of cultural activity. Some examples are listed in the above paragraph.

5. The concepts and behavior of a culture are *patterned*. In the past, certain westerners (often missionaries or travelers) went to other parts of the world, observed the behavior of the people there, and made statements such as, "These people don't have any organization to their life. They just do what they feel like, without rhyme or reason to their customs."

As anthropologists and others began to really study other people's cultures, however, they discovered that that is not an accurate point of view. Every group of people has rules and regulations according to which they live. There is always structuring, always regularity, always system, and a very high degree of predictability, since most cultural behavior (thinking as well as doing) is quite habitual. People act habitually and unconsciously according to the patterns they have been taught.

Due to these patterned regularities and the habitual behavior that stems from them, cultural behavior is interpretable by insiders—the other members of the cultural group. If cultural behavior were random, there would be no way for other members of a society to understand what that behavior means. Suppose, for example, a given person greeted others sometimes by waving, sometimes by punching them in the nose, and sometimes by disrobing in front of them. Unless everyone in the society agreed that each of these methods was appropriate greeting behavior, this person would be greatly misunderstood. *Understanding requires agreement*.

Agreement requires predictability, which, in turn, requires patterning. Cultural behavior is (and must be) patterned.

6. Culture is *learned*. We get it from our parents and others from whom we learn. It is not transmitted biologically. Nor does it come from the environment. It is a human thing, passed from generation to generation very effectively via familiar processes of imitation and teaching. Most of these processes take place quite unconsciously, leading us often to underestimate the difficulty of culture learning and the complexity of what we have learned.

Sometimes I'm asked, "How come you westerners with all your education and intelligence can shoot rockets to the moon, but you can't even learn our culture and language, the simplest in the world?" I tell them we had the wrong mothers! If we had their mothers, we would have learned their culture and language. But we didn't. Our mothers didn't know their culture and language and so didn't teach it to us. But there's a fair chance that these people won't understand what I'm saying unless they try to learn another culture and language themselves.

7. Culture also consists of the *underlying perspectives* (*worldview*) on the basis of which the cultural concepts and behavior we have been discussing are generated. As pointed out already, this constitutes the very important deep structure of culture.

8. Lastly, we point to the *products* produced by people as they follow cultural rules and patterns. These products may be nonmaterial or material. The majority of the products are nonmaterial. These include the concepts and behavior patterns practiced by a people. All the customs and rituals practiced by a people are nonmaterial cultural products. So are the ideas that underlie the material artifacts produced by a people. Those artifacts are the material cultural products of a people. These include the tools, containers, utensils, houses, vehicles, clothing, and so on that people use in their cultural behavior. Some anthropologists (e.g., Spradley and McCurdy 1975) would exclude material products from a definition of culture, contending that culture is totally a matter of knowledge and ideas. It has, however, been traditional to include them, and I follow that tradition.

LEVELS AND TYPES OF CULTURE AND SOCIETY

The terms *culture* and *society* can be used at several levels. Though these two terms are often carelessly used interchangeably, we need to be careful to use *culture* when referring to the structuring of life and *society* when referring to the people who live by that structuring.

Since each person is immersed in a culture, it is possible to speak of the most specific level of cultural structuring as a personal culture. At the other end of the spectrum we may lump together large groupings of cultures that manifest similar characteristics. Such terms as western culture(s), African culture(s), Latin American culture(s) are used to label such groupings. Equally appropriate as designations of the peoples who live by these cultures would be western society(ies), African society(ies), Latin American society(ies).

A sequence of terms to designate cultural structuring may be charted as follows:

    1. Personal Culture
      2. Family Culture (or Subculture)
        3. Community Culture (or Subculture)
          4. Regional Culture (or Subculture)
            5. National Culture (e.g., American Culture)
              6. Multinational Culture (e.g., Western Culture)

Another way of grouping cultures and societies is on the basis of one or more shared characteristics. Such labels as traditional cultures/societies, peasant cultures/societies, and industrial cultures/societies are often employed to distinguish cultural structures and peoples on the basis of one set of economic features. Shaw (1988), starting from Dye's (1980) economics-based, three-culture-type classification, has helpfully worked out a more detailed typology. In it, Shaw presents several typically contrasting characteristics in four cultural "subsystems" (*see* chapter 8): the economic, the religious, the social and the political. Shaw's chart on pages 42–43 illustrates this type of classification.

Another set of economic features is in focus when anthropologists designate a people as participating in an agricultural or settled farming culture or a herding or cattle-herding culture. The people may be called an agricultural society or a herding society. Sometimes social characteristics are used as the basis for grouping as when reference is made to polygamous or monogamous cultures/societies or when peoples are grouped according to family characteristics such as extended family cultures/societies or nuclear family cultures/societies. Religious designations are frequently used to lump cultures and peoples, e.g., Muslim cultures/societies, Buddhist cultures/societies, Roman Catholic cultures/societies, Hindu cultures/societies.

The above designations are appropriate for labeling differing levels of a type of culture and society that might be called "natural." A natural culture is one that is owned by a given society, usually speaking a single language, and that is passed on through that language to those born into the society. But the term *culture* may also be legitimately applied in a kind of "horizontal" way to common patterns exhibited by certain categories of people in many societies. For example, it has been observed that poor people of many societies structure their lives in very similar ways and develop similar strategies for coping with their poverty even within quite different cultures. This led to the coining of the term *culture of poverty* by Oscar Lewis (1959). Similarly, we can observe cultures of drug addicts, deaf people, urban gangs, athletes, factory workers, and any number of other life situations that impose conditions similar enough to require the development of similar coping strategies.

CULTURES AND SUBCULTURES

A society may be made up of a smaller or a larger number of people. In general, the larger the number of people, the more complex will be the cultural structures they produce and live by. For example, a large population will typically develop more specialization than is necessary in a smaller population. Whereas in smaller societies any given head of a family may serve as a leader in political, economic, religious, and social matters, in larger societies, there are likely to be specialists in each of these areas.

Larger societies will also develop more subgroupings. These subgroupings are usually referred to as *subcultures*. Since this term is usually employed to refer to the people in the subgroupings rather than to the structuring of such groups, it would be more precise to call them *subsocieties*.

A large population such as that of Anglo-American society, for example, will contain such subcultures/subsocieties as those of youth, blue-collar workers, white-collar workers, farmers, even computer specialists, taxi drivers, clergy, and any number of others.

BASIC CONTRASTS:	KINSHIP SOCIETIES
1. Government	Monocultural-cultural independent groups
2. Dominant institution	Clan, kin group
3. Economic base	Gardening, hunting
4. Occupations	Generalists
1. ECONOMY:	SUBSISTENCE
1. Land	Group owned, shared
2. Land value	Valuable for corporate use, available
3. Source of energy	Human, animal, simple tools
4. Food produced	Used by "family"
5. Goods produced	Few goods, generalists, for personal use
6. Hard times	Dependent on nature and family cohesiveness
7. Dominant economic relationships	Egalitarian
8. Education	Informal
9. Goal of education	Control supernatural
10. Ideal life style	Village people
11. Time orientation	Timeless
12. Leisure	Varies, often considerable
2. RELIGION:	ANIMISM
1. Importance of religion	Permeates all life, no sacred/secular distinction
2. Ancestors	Ghosts nurtured, placated
3. Function for society	Unity
4. Function for individuals	Control environment, establish individual's place
5. Religious buildings	None, or not elaborate
6. Religious specialists	Part time
7. Importance of mythology	Sacred tales which validate the belief system
3. SOCIAL RELATIONSHIPS:	FAMILIAL
1. Kinship	Everything
2. Type of family	Extended family
3. Marriage function	Build kinship ties, trade ties, labor force, etc.
4. Polygamy	Functional
5. Dominant dyads	Brother-brother, father-son
6. Old, sick, jobless	Cared for in home
4. POLITICAL ORGANIZATION:	COMMUNITY
1. Structure	Small independent units
2. Internal control (law)	Negative sanctions; shame/restitution
3. External control (government)	Non-kin relations, warfare between locally defined groups
4. Participation by common people	Alliance/defiance, community in control, full rights
5. Leadership	Local leaders, achieved
6. Power of rulers	Weak

Figure 3.3 Contrastive features of three different culture types

Peasant Societies	Industrial Societies
States, regional interdependence	Interdependent nations
Lord-Servant	Corporation
Farming, crafts	Industrial (agro-business)
Specialized occupations	Multiplied roles
Market	**Commercial**
Individually owned by elite	Individual, less important
Valuable to elite for use by peasants, scarce	Monetary value
Human, animal	Fuel powered machinery
Sell part, eat part	Raise for sale, buy food
Many goods, artisans for trade	Vast number of goods, laborers, for money
Dependent on nature and elite	Locally independent, internationally dependent
Competitive, unequal	Commercial
Apprenticeship, special schools for elite	Extensive, formal, specialized
Maintain social structure	Technological knowledge
Idealized behavior of elite	Upper middle class
Busy, but not time oriented	Focal value on time
For elite only	Regulated and organized
Animism and National Religion	**Many Religions**
Important, sacred/ secular sometimes distinguished	Unimportant, sacred/secular sharply separated
Respected	Forgotten
Acceptance of roles in society	Obedience to law
Comfort, reaffirm personal worth	Sense of belonging, identification
Extensive temples sponsored by elite	Equal to other buildings
Full time, important	Full time, less important
Tales which relate to the past, thereby revealing a heritage	Fairy tales with no relevance to present (Science provides functional substitute)
Hierarchical	**Impersonal**
Extra means of coping	Unimportant
Varies widely	Nuclear (old, sick, excluded)
Economically helpful	Meet personal needs, basic unit of society
Recreational	Dysfunctional
Parent-child, patron-worker	Husband-wife, friend-friend
Old respected, all cared for	Institutionalized
Kingdom	**Republic**
National, regional autonomy	National and international
Shame, gossip, civil law	Civil/criminal law
Regional inter-dependent, warfare within region, interest groups, etc. religious sanctions	International politics, warfare between nations
Alien control, limited rights	Politics at all levels, citizens' control
Hereditary roles from elite	Politicians
Very great (Lords)	Power divided among many specialists

(slightly modified with permission from Shaw 1988:36–9)

In addition, it is common for national and multinational sociocultural entities to contain other societies (called "included societies"), each with its own cultural structuring. In a country such as Nigeria, for example, there are hundreds of distinct societies, each with its own language and culture, all functioning as parts of a larger national society and culture. Likewise, in the United States, there are included societies speaking Spanish, Korean, various Chinese languages, Japanese, Tagalog, Cambodian, various American Indian languages, and any number of other languages. In addition, there are communities of Blacks, American Indians, and the second and third generations of many of the above language groups who speak English but retain a good bit of their non-Anglo sociocultural identity. These sometimes class as included societies, sometimes as subcultures/subsocieties within the larger society, depending on the degree of integration into the mainstream of American society.

MORE ABOUT CULTURE

With this background, let us turn to a series of additional characteristics of culture. Though each of these characteristics applies primarily to fully formed "natural" cultures, they also apply, to a greater or lesser extent, to the more limited types of culture discussed above.

1. Culture is *complex*. All cultures are complex (though some are more complex than others). Anthropologists have never yet discovered a simple culture. Some groups have a simple technology. Their material culture might even be called "primitive," though this is a poor word to use for their culture as a whole. No matter how simple their technology and material culture might be, their ways of living, their customs, their perceptions of and responses to the reality around them are patterned in a complex way that often defies the attempts of outsiders to learn or even understand them.

2. We also know that culture tends to show *more or less tight integration* around its worldview. The basic worldview assumptions provide the "glue" in terms of which people tie each of the various subsystems (see below) of culture to the worldview and also to each other. Thus, in addition to their relationship with worldview itself, within a cultural system, politics is closely related to economics, and both of these subsystems are closely related to religion and social structure (family, social control), while all are tightly tied to language, artistic expression, and so on. Tighter integration of these internal parts of a culture tends to result in a more satisfied people. A breakdown of integration usually increases a people's dissatisfaction and psychological stress (often leading to breakdown).

3. The culture of a people provides for them *a total design for living*. It is comprehensive, dealing with every aspect of life. A culture provides a given people with the means of answering the vast majority of the questions they feel are important regarding the human problems they face. Such questions are usually so well taken care of that the people may not be able to even articulate questions or answers. They simply accept both answers and questions as their way of life.

Cultural answers are designed to cover all facets of life, whether routine things such as eating or dressing or less tangible things such as how to decide when to plant or how to think about relational, judicial, philosophical, or spiritual issues. One implication of this totality of cultural coverage is the fact that when we bring something like Christianity to a people, we should not be misled into thinking we can simply add it to their culture as if there were a void that their culture wasn't filling. Rather, we are appealing to them to replace something that is already there. We're not coming to people who are not committed to anything. We're asking people to commit themselves to Christ in place of whatever other primary commitment they are taught to have. Their society has already shown them what their supreme commitment is expected to be.

4. Culture is an *adaptive system* or, as mentioned above, a *mechanism for coping*. It provides people with patterns and strategies by means of which they can adapt to the physical and social conditions around them. Cultural patterns show great adaptation to the geographical environment. That's why cultures in the tropics differ from those in snowy countries. If you're in a tropical area where you can grow food all year round, the cultural patterns show adaptation to that particular circumstance. If you're in a cold area where you can grow only during a very limited growing season that requires you to store food for the rest of the year, the cultural patterning is adapted to that.

Cultural patterns also show adaptation to social circumstances. If you're in a situation where you have been conquered by another people, your cultural perspectives are adapted to that circumstance. If you're in a situation where you're free from that oppression, your patterns are adapted to that circumstance. There is also cultural adaptation to biological givens. People of short stature will develop at least some cultural patterns that differ from those of taller peoples. People whose stomachs cannot digest sweet (nonsour) milk will adapt culturally to that fact.

5. *No culture seems to be perfectly adequate* either to the realities of biology and environment or to the answering of all of the questions of a people. There are always areas of life that are not handled perfectly. Another way of saying this is that while a cultural system is designed to answer all of people's questions, it's apparently true that all peoples, of whatever culture, always have some questions left over that are not very well answered.

One of the important things to recognize about Christianity is that there are lots of ways of approaching people with our message. One of the best ways is to find the questions people are asking for which their culture is not providing answers. Perhaps the Christian perspective can provide answers for some of those questions. If they can see that the new approach answers some questions they have never before been able to answer, they may be attracted to it initially as a supplement to what they already understand. The local chief in our area of northeastern Nigeria once asked me if Christianity could provide the answer to a major question his people were asking. This question was based on the belief of his people that God had gone far away due to a bad mistake they had made in the past. So he asked me if I knew where God had gone and how they could get back in contact with Him. We were able to make use of the felt need for an answer to this question to enhance the entrance of the Gospel into that society.

6. Culture is *learned as if it were absolute and perfect*. Before we (or any other people) knew or even suspected the existence of alternative ways of life, we as children were indoctrinated into ours. We learned our customs unconsciously, before we had any ability to compare and evaluate them, so we often consider them the only possible approaches, the best and only right way. We thus developed an attitude called ethnocentrism, the belief that our customs are the best. Ethnocentrism is one of our worst enemies, since it leads us to impose our ways on others. It is,

however, a disease both we and the people we go to suffer from, unless we or they have been intimidated by another people into believing our customs to be wrong. We will treat this problem in detail in chapter 5.

7. Culture *makes sense to those within it*. When we look from our own cultural perspective at other people's ways of doing things, many times they don't make sense to us. "Why do they do it that way?" we may ask. "We would discipline our children if they did that." From our point of view, based on our worldview assumptions, their custom may seem illogical or at least ill-advised. Yet the more we learn about other cultures, the clearer it becomes that what people do tends to be consistent with the assumptions they start with. Just as we aim at consistency, so do they. But since their assumptions, their starting points, differ from ours, naturally what they end up with will differ. Cultural behavior itself (whether theirs or ours) only really makes sense when you understand the underlying assumptions.

I often wonder how many of the things I did and said looked strange to the Nigerians of the area in which we worked. If their customs seemed strange from our point of view, ours must have looked doubly strange from theirs. I imagine them getting a lot of entertainment from their contacts with me. They didn't have television to entertain them, but they didn't need television as long as they had a white man around! I'll bet they just laughed and laughed at all the crazy things I did (just as we missionaries laughed at the things they did).

One serious mistake I made was to carry my small children on my shoulders. It made sense to me to carry them that way, especially if we were walking any great distance and wanted to go faster than their little legs would carry them. That custom didn't make sense to the Nigerians, however, since in their world only corpses were carried on a person's shoulder!

I'm very thankful to my Nigerian colleagues for being bold enough to tell me about this mistake. I wonder, though, about the thousands of other times they didn't tell me what they thought and probably got the wrong impression, not about me only, but about Christianity. How are they going to know what Christ is like except by looking at me? And when they draw their conclusions from looking at me, how are they to know that they shouldn't trust their conclusions? Do they know and will they make allowances for the fact that my behavior is based on different assumptions than theirs? Any given set of customs makes sense to those who practice them, but not necessarily to people of another culture, whose behavior is based on other assumptions. Yet we all evaluate what we see others doing on the basis of our own cultural assumptions. Watch out!

8. Cultural practices are *based on group or "multipersonal" agreements*. A social group is made up of many persons (i.e., it is multipersonal) who unconsciously agree to govern themselves according to the group's cultural patterns. Influenced by the social pressure toward conformity to these patterns they ordinarily behave similarly and make decisions according to those patterns. Homer Barnett (1953) called such group behavior "multi-individual." I prefer to call it *multipersonal*.

Everything underlying culture depends on people's agreements to do things one way or another. The things people agree are right are considered right. Things they agree are wrong are considered wrong. Culture is based on those agreements. This fact has particular relevance to those who seek to initiate change in a culture, for a change of custom or belief is itself the result of an agreement to change. Such an agreement to change, for its part, is usually the result of individual agreements on the part of the members of the group to follow the lead of one or more prestigious members (opinion leaders) who have decided to change. That is, prestigious persons ordinarily suggest changes. Others follow, usually after a period of time devoted to consideration and discussion, so that what appears eventually on the surface to be a group change has very definitely a multipersonal basis. Those (like Christians) who seek to encourage culture change need to study this process. We will devote several chapters to this subject later in the book.

9. Culture is *a legacy from the past*. The customs we practice were developed by past generations as they saw fit to deal with the problems of life. They therefore represent the learning our ancestors arrived at and saw fit to pass on to us. This fact provides cultural continuity from generation to generation. It also provides the present generation with wisdom from the past.

Often we can be proud of the cultural wisdom of our ancestors. Their ways of dealing with the multiplicity of life problems we face serve us quite nicely most of the time. Many of the techniques they developed have enabled us to thrive and even become great in certain areas of life. All we do is strongly influenced by and usually built on foundations developed and passed on to us by our forebears.

Some of what is passed on, however, seems to be either unnecessary or counterproductive. Many things that seem to be no longer useful are preserved in the transmission of a culture from one generation. The buttons on the sleeves of men's coats would be one illustration of this fact in American culture. The English spelling system is another. We will further discuss this factor in chapter 22.

In another area, however, the legacy of the past may present those of the present generation with even greater problems, especially in rapidly changing societies, for what is passed on to us by our parents is the culture adapted to the problems of previous generations. Thus, many of the answers we are taught are answers to questions that people were asking in the last generation or the generation before, and frequently we find certain portions of the last generation's patterns not fitting the current generation very well. This is what's happening in many rapidly changing situations. Here in America, for example, we have to learn how to conserve resources such as trees and water. Previous generations learned to exploit these things and simply use them in their manufacturing. They didn't worry about the pollution or depletion of such resources; the possibility of a problem never occurred to them. The answers of the last generation in this area have become problems for us in our generation, and we must change our cultural habits.

10. Culture provides people with *a way to regulate their lives*. It provides people with patterns as to how to do things: when and how to eat, sleep, go to the toilet, laugh, cry, work, play. Our whole lives are regulated by what we are taught is appropriate in such areas and in nearly all else, as well. We are provided, for example, with customs regulating our behavior when we meet someone, when we marry, when there's a death, when we worship. Usually quite unconsciously, we obey certain rules when we stand, walk, or sit, when we communicate, even when we think. Whether we are with others or by ourselves, we regulate our behavior by the cultural patterns we have been taught.

11. *A culture may be pictured as a maze of roads, and a description of the culture as a map of those roads.* As mentioned above, people ordinarily follow the roads (practice the customs) but may, whenever they choose, create new ways to arrive at the same destinations. When people create new roads, others in the soci-

ety may object and apply social pressure to attempt to get them back on the established path. Or, especially if the one who innovates is an opinion leader, others may like the new path better and imitate it themselves. In the latter case, a new cultural road is created that then becomes a part of the legacy passed on to the next generation. *See* chapter 24 for more on this subject.

A description of a culture is, like a map, an abstract representation of the reality of that culture. Knowing the information concerning the cultural patterns enables one to get around in a society, just as a road map enables one to get around when traveling. Insiders in the society, of course, learn the map while growing up and conduct their lives' journey according to those patterns. Maps concerning when and how to eat, sleep, toilet, cry, work, play, think, reason, love, hate are all imprinted in their minds. If the cultural map is presented to outsiders (in, for example, an ethnographic description of the cultural patterns), they can learn to negotiate the maze of cultural pathways according to that map.

12. There is *conscious (or explicit) culture and unconscious (or implicit) culture*. Conscious culture includes the ways of behaving and thinking that people are aware of and usually can see and explain. Unconscious culture, on the other hand, consists of those patterns of behaving and thinking that lie below the level of a people's consciousness. This distinction is not the same as that between surface culture and deep culture (worldview), though a greater percentage of the latter will be in the unconscious category, for much surface-level behavior is unconscious, and a fair number of the deep-level assumptions can be consciously articulated by a people.

If outsiders ask about those parts of a culture the people are conscious of, an insider can usually describe and explain the customs. These include cultural patterns that parents (and other elders) openly explain to children. Many customs, rituals, and even assumptions fall into this category. More difficult to get at, both for insiders and for outsiders, is unconscious culture. This consists of unconscious habits, attitudes, assumptions, values, and the like that people learn largely by imitation and inference and seldom, if ever, discuss.

Not infrequently, insiders are so unaware of such customs that it takes a perceptive outsider to call them to their attention. Sometimes when an unconscious custom is called to an insider's attention, the person will either deny that such a custom exists or give an inaccurate explanation of the reason for it. If, for example, someone asks a typical American why we are so competitive, we may answer (wrongly) that we are not competitive or we may explain that we are competitive in order to "get ahead." Though there is some truth in the latter explanation, it masks the fact that we follow an unconscious underlying assumption that it is right for people to get ahead, even though it involves (carefully) overriding the interests of others. The real reason for our competitiveness, as for most of the rest of our customs, is that we have been taught to be this way. Rational (conscious) reasons for why a people eat, sleep, dress, speak, and live in particular ways are almost always less accurate than the simple explanation, "We do . . . this way because our parents/elders taught us to do it this way."

13. There is *ideal culture and actual culture*. Every people has its ideals. In American society, for example, we believe that all people are created equal. But an outside observer may notice that certain people in our society are regularly granted more privileges than others. The reason is, we don't live up to our ideal in this matter (as in many other areas of life). Instead, we live at another level called

the "actual" (or "real") level. This level may fall slightly or greatly below the ideal level.

People regularly idealize their behavior when they attempt to describe it. Often the ideals they describe are seldom, if ever, practiced. It is probably a part of the effects of sin that we regularly live below our ideals while claiming to live according to them.

The need to distinguish between ideal and actual relates to this text and our attitude toward other people's cultures in an interesting way. If we are to respect other people's ways of life, it is important to try to understand the intent (the ideal) of the customs being discussed. For example, in dealing with the custom called polygamy (marriage of one man to more than one wife), we need to understand that it can be defended at an ideal level just as rationally as we would defend monogamy (*see* chapter 18 for the arguments). Occasionally it is practiced in a relatively ideal way. Usually, like monogamy, plural marriage is practiced at a subideal level. In comparison ideal polygamy and ideal monogamy each (from a human point of view) can be quite satisfactory, while actual (subideal) monogamy or polygamy can be very destructive.

In an attempt to get us to respect other people's cultures, I will frequently direct our attention to ideal expressions of their customs. In attempting to combat the tendency both of westerners and of westernized nonwesterners to idealize western customs I will frequently criticize the actual (subideal) expressions of western customs. Though I take these positions to make important points, we need always, in considering any given way of life, to pay attention both to the ideals and to the actual expressions of its customs. This is especially important when we compare one set of customs with another. It is unfair to compare the ideals of one society (e.g., ideal monogamy) with the actuals (e.g., subideal polygamy) of another.

THE SUBSYSTEMS OF CULTURE

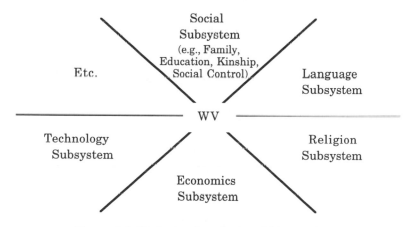

Figure 3.4 Typical subsystems within a culture

To conclude, I want to briefly present a diagram picturing what I am calling the subsystems of culture. These subsystems are seen as divisions of surface-level culture and, as such, provide various behavioral expressions of worldview assumptions. Each of these subsystems will be dealt with in the following chapters, as will worldview.

I will leave a detailed discussion of this diagram until chapter 8. It is presented here simply to complete our overview of culture.

I trust that this chapter has alerted the reader to such things as the nature, extent, and importance of culture, the various ways in which the term *culture* is used, and the relationships between culture and people. Culture is an extremely important factor in human life and, therefore, in any attempt to carry Christian witness to humans. I hope this chapter helps us see how crucial it is that cross-cultural witnesses take culture seriously.

If we are to reach people, we will have to reach them within their culture. We will do this either wisely or unwisely. It is hoped that by understanding more of what cultures are all about we can deal with them more wisely than might otherwise have been the case.

CHAPTER 4

A PERSPECTIVE ON WORLDVIEW

INTEGRATIONAL THOUGHT

In Acts 14:8–18 we have the account of an interesting encounter involving misunderstanding due to differences in worldview. Paul and Barnabas had begun their ministry at Lystra. They apparently ministered in Greek and did not understand the language of the people of Lystra. Nor did they understand how a healing in the name of Jesus Christ would be perceived.

As Paul spoke, a man who had been lame from birth listened, and "Paul saw that he believed and could be healed" (v. 9). So Paul commanded him to stand, and he "jumped up and started walking around" (v. 10). The apostles had used a form of communication much used by Jesus to convey the message of God's love and concern for human beings in physical or spiritual bondage.

What the Lystrans understood, however, was "The gods have become like men and have come down to us" (v. 11). Since they shouted this in their own language, Paul and Barnabas had no idea they were being misinterpreted until the priest of Zeus began to bring out bulls and flowers to make a sacrifice to them (v. 13). At that time, Paul and Barnabas sent another message by tearing "their clothes and [running] into the middle of the crowd, shouting, 'Why are you doing this? We ourselves are only human beings like you!'" (vv. 14, 15). We do not know if the Lystrans understood the Jewish habit of showing distress through the tearing off of clothing. What we do know is that "Even with these words the apostles could hardly keep the crowd from offering a sacrifice to them" (v. 18).

The communication problem was based on an underlying difference in basic assumptions (worldview). The apostles assumed the miracle was performed by God as an act of love. The people assumed it was performed by the gods Zeus and Hermes (v. 12), who had decided to take on human form and to visit them. Such worldview differences frequently result in misunderstandings of the messages brought by people from other societies. We can expect misunderstandings, but we must do our best to minimize both the number and the importance of such occurrences by learning whatever we can about differences in basic assumptions and what to do when they cause us difficulties.

INTRODUCTION

In chapter 2 we came to the recognition that a model or map of reality provides for us a patterning in terms of which we can chart our life's course. Such patternings are not, however, simply operative at the individual level. A whole group (society) may chart its course according to a single map of reality. That is, within a range of allowed variation, large numbers of people employ (largely in response to

51

their training) a single perception of the REALITY around them. We call such a perception shared by a social group a worldview, and we see that worldview as the core of a culture, functioning, on the one hand, as the grid in terms of which reality is perceived and, on the other, as that which provides the guidelines for a people's behavioral response to that perception of reality.

WORLDVIEW DEFINED

As is probably obvious by now, I define worldview as the culturally structured assumptions, values, and commitments/allegiances underlying a people's perception of reality and their responses to those perceptions (Kraft 1989:20). Worldview is not separate from culture. It is included in culture as the structuring of the deepest-level presuppositions on the basis of which people live their lives.

Like every other aspect of culture, worldview does not *do* anything. Any supposed power of worldview lies in the *habits* of people. People are the ones who do things. But worldview provides the cultural bases and part of the structuring for people's actions.

1. A worldview is *culturally structured*. That is, as a part of culture, it participates in the structuring of that culture and is not independent of it. Like culture, a worldview is a human product, resulting from the fact that humans are culture-producing creatures. The material within a worldview is organized and structured according to principles that are themselves based on worldview assumptions.

2. A worldview *consists of assumptions (including images)*. Since many, perhaps most, of our underlying assumptions seem to be stored in our brains as pictures or images, it is important to note that images are a kind of assumption. We dare not let ourselves believe, therefore, that our basic assumptions are easily described verbally. In addition, though I often list values and allegiances/commitments as if they were parallel to assumptions, the term *assumptions* covers values and allegiances as well. That is, it is the assumptions underlying values and commitments that are in view, as well as all other more general assumptions. In terms of such assumptions, we assign meaning and respond to the meanings we assign. In doing so, we follow the worldview patterns taught us as we do such things as interpreting, evaluating, explaining, committing ourselves, relating, and adapting. We will deal more specifically with these facets of worldview below.

3. These assumptions *underlie a people's perception of reality and their responses to it*. Worldview assumptions provide the structuring of perceived reality. We respond not to God's REALITY (*see* chapter 2) but to the reality we perceive, our interpretation of REALITY.

As with culture, we may speak of an individual worldview, a family worldview, a community worldview, subcultural, national, and multinational worldviews. As with cultures, there will be increasing variety within the worldviews at each level in accord with the increasing number of people involved. Furthermore, it is possible to refer to the worldview assumptions of such transcultural groups as poor people, factory workers, agriculturalists, women, youth, the deaf, and so forth.

WORLDVIEW AND SOCIOCULTURAL SPECIALIZATION

The concept of worldview is important to our understanding of culture. It is, however, only relatively recently that anthropologists have begun to use the term.

Not long ago, certain anthropologists began to focus, not so much on the vast assortment of different customs (as had been their primary concern) as on the assumptions underlying these customs that seemed to relate them coherently to each other. For a high percentage of the peoples that anthropologists have studied, a preponderance of these assumptions related to supernatural beings and powers. From a western point of view "religion" seemed to be at the core of most nonwestern cultures.

Thus came about a tendency, still apparent in the writings of many anthropologists and nonspecialists alike, to confuse the core of a culture (worldview) with a people's religion. Increasingly, though, it is being recognized that even in "supernaturalistically oriented" societies there appear to be deep-level, core assumptions that are not easily labeled "religious." Furthermore, as greater attention is being given to cultures whose core assumptions are largely non- (even anti-) supernaturalistic (e.g., western), it is becoming obvious that the term *religion* as the designation for the core of culture is misleading.

It seems better to use the term *worldview*, introduced by Redfield (1953), to label the central assumptions, concepts, premises, and values to which the people of a sociocultural group commit themselves, whether or not those are supernaturalistic.

This approach leaves us with one major problem: how to explain the fact that many societies seem to be dominated by religious concepts and practices. As I will explain more fully in chapter 8, this fact is paralleled by the fact that many other societies (e.g., many western peoples) seem to be dominated as much by economic concepts and practices as others seem to be by religion. Others (e.g., traditional Chinese) seem to be dominated more by family concerns than by either religion or economics.

I explain each of these situations as *sociocultural specialization*. In any given society, as with any given individual, greater attention is given to certain things than to others. Just as individuals specialize so do groups of individuals (societies). Certain peoples give more attention to religious matters, other peoples to economic matters, others to family. The surface-level behavior that a people specializes in will have a greater influence on the core assumptions, values, and allegiances (worldview) than the behavior that they do not emphasize as much.

In terms of a subsystems diagram like that introduced at the end of the previous chapter, we may picture this fact as shown in figure 4.1 below.

The differential emphases of a *supernaturalistically oriented society* might be pictured as in figure 4.1 (with the amount of space in each "piece of the pie" representing the amount of emphasis).

The differential emphases of a society (e.g., western) *focused primarily on economics and material culture* might be pictured as in figure 4.2 below.

As illustrated, the primary concerns of a people dominate the surface level of their culture. These same areas will influence the worldview more than will the other subsystems. In supernaturalistic cultures, we say that the religious subsystem influences the worldview more than, say, the economics or the concern for the material world or some other aspect of the culture as a whole. In western societies, though, we would say that subsystems dealing with economics and the control of the material world influence the worldview more than the religious subsystem. Such differences in focus suggest that we may characterize different societies as centered around a supernaturalistically oriented worldview or a materialistically oriented worldview or a social relationship oriented worldview, or a worldview that emphasizes some other orientation.

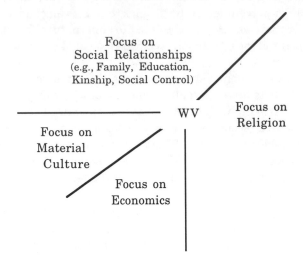

Figure 4.1 Differential emphases in a supernaturalistically oriented society

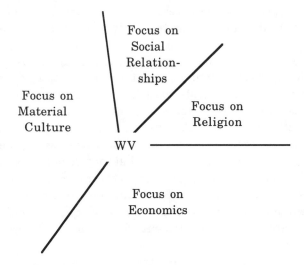

Figure 4.2 Differential emphases in a naturalistically oriented society

Worldview assumptions, values, and allegiances (commitments) vary little from member to member and from subgroup to subgroup of smaller, more tightly knit societies. There is, however, considerable variation from member to member and from subgroup to subgroup of larger, less tightly knit societies, such as that of America. Though there is, apparently, always some allowed range of variation at the worldview level, that range tends to be wider in proportion to the size of a society and the intensity of contact with other societies. Again, smaller societies with little contact with other groups tend to exhibit a smaller range of allowed variation, while larger societies with greater contact with outside groups will show a wider range of variation.

Indeed, in large, diverse societies with strong outside influences, the tendency is for their people to experience a good bit of conflict at the worldview level among competing assumptions, allegiances, and values. Such competition results in many people in such societies assimilating at least an important portion of one or more worldviews in addition to the one they learned as children. These whole or parts of worldviews are often only partially reconciled with each other, leading to a situation where a person or group applies worldview perspective in one set of circumstances and another, at least partially contradictory, set of assumptions in other circumstances. Western Christians commonly experience such "worldview split personality" at any point where they need to decide whether to interpret an event from a naturalistic perspective or in terms of Christian supernaturalistic values.

To illustrate, picture an American Christian driving along a highway and narrowly avoiding an accident. How does she or he react? The naturalistic American worldview into which we have been trained will push us to respond with some such statement as, "Boy, was I lucky!" Our Christian perspective, which we have probably only partly assimilated, brings to our attention the fact that God is involved in every such event to protect us from harm (Rom 8:28). An appropriate reflexive response stemming from that assumption would be something like, "Thank you, God."

Such differences in our automatic (habitual) response to such a situation come from competing worldview assumptions within us. Some of us will have so integrated our lives around our Christian assumptions that we will automatically say, "Thank you, God. You saved me from that accident. You protected me," rather than "Boy, was I lucky!" But many of us will show less integration of our Christian values and sometimes go one way and sometimes the other. Such experiences bring to our attention the conflict between worldview assumptions going on within us.

Some internationals may even have parts of three or more sets of worldview assumptions competing within them—those they were brought up with, western assumptions taught them in western schools, and Christian assumptions (possibly infected by a western perspective). The situation can get quite complicated.

CHARACTERISTICS OF WORLDVIEWS

1. Worldview assumptions or premises are *not reasoned out, but assumed to be true without prior proof.* By definition, assumptions are simply accepted without the requirement that someone prove them. They are deeply imbedded in the structure of culture. The surface-level customs serve as the behavioral acting out of these unconsciously accepted and agreed upon presuppositions. These assumptions are taught to each new generation so persuasively that they seem absolute and are seldom questioned. People then interpret their life experiences in terms of these assumptions and feel that they are proven.

To illustrate, let's look at a people's definition of life. Philosophically, we may ask, When does life begin? The answer for most of the peoples of the world is assumed rather than proved. People in one society grow up with the assumption that life begins at conception. Those in another society may assume another starting point before birth, or at birth, or at some point after birth. The Kamwe, like many peoples, make a distinction between the start of biological life and the start of human life, with the latter starting about a year and a half to two years after birth. For many peoples (including the Hebrews), life as a full-fledged human, as opposed to simple biological existence, starts at the naming of the child.

Assumptions concerning disease provide another example. Americans assume that disease is caused by germs. Recently when I "caught" a cold (or did the cold "catch" me?), I assumed what my American elders had taught me—that I came in contact with some germs that got into my system and caused the cold.

When I got to Nigeria, though, I came into contact with people whose parents taught them differently. These people learned that it is spirits, not germs, that cause disease. When we would discuss our differing points of view, they would contend that their theory handles the situation better because it explains that you got sick because a personal spirit chose to attack you and to leave me alone. The germ theory attempts to explain that aspect of disease in terms of the chance that the right (wrong?) germ came along at a time when the person's resistance was low. This doesn't make a very convincing explanation to a traditional Nigerian.

They, like I, had been taught theory as fact. We could argue with them that our theory is more "scientific" than theirs. But is it? What we often don't take into account is the fact that our science is based on the assumption that if there is any reality beyond the physical world, it is irrelevant when dealing with causation. This, however, is a very challengeable assumption, especially from a Christian perspective.

Any argument between those who espouse these different theories of disease is complicated by the fact that, in terms of a broader view of reality, it is probable that neither theory is wrong, except when it is advanced as the whole truth, for it is entirely possible that a given disease may be caused ultimately by a spirit but that the spirit uses a germ to bring it about.

A third theory believed by many is that disease is caused by loss of or damage to a person's soul. When a person is ill, they say that somebody has stolen the person's soul or that she or he has fallen and jarred the soul loose. To us westerners this seems like a very strange theory. But, like each of the other theories, it is taught convincingly, believed implicitly, and accepted as truth in each instance of illness (and of healing). They, like us, interpret whatever happens as proving their assumption. All worldviews are like this.

2. A people's worldview *provides them with a lens, model, or map in terms of which REALITY is perceived and interpreted*. We talked in chapter 2 about lenses through which people look out at what goes on around them. Those lenses have a variety of components. It may be argued that the cultural (worldview) component is the most pervasive, since it assures that most of the people in a society will understand and interpret most things in essentially the same way.

The vast majority of the assumptions we live with are not idiosyncratic. They are given to us by those who taught us our culture. Others of that generation taught others of our generation the same model of reality. We and all others of our generation in our society learned to follow that map, to view through that lens habitually. And to the end of our days we follow most of the pathways of interpretation we were taught.

3. In terms of its worldview, *a people organizes its life and experiences into an explanatory whole that it seldom (if ever) questions unless some of its assumptions are challeng*ed by experiences that the people cannot interpret from within that framework.

When people become aware of such a challenge in areas considered very important, the result can often be widespread demoralization. Take, for example, the many peoples of the world (Anglo-Americans, many American Indian groups, the ancient Hebrews) who live(d) with the worldview assumption that they could not be defeated in war. When the unbelievable happened, they were forced either to change their assumption or to reinterpret the event in such a way that the defeat was not allowed to challenge the assumption. Many Americans have taken the latter course in interpreting the Vietnam war (which we did not win) as a "police action." Many American Indian groups, however, found themselves unable (or unwilling) either to change their assumption or to reinterpret. They became demoralized (due to this and other factors) and died out. The ancient Hebrews assumed they were "the People of God" (meaning to them that God would always protect them, regardless of how they related to Him). They were able to survive by developing a broader understanding of the close relationship between their faithfulness to Him and His assistance in war.

A second type of situation in which a people may question some portion of its worldview occurs when it becomes aware of alternative explanations or assumptions that both seem to work and cannot be explained away. Such a situation may occur either with or without outside pressure. This type of situation is widespread in nonwestern societies, enhanced by the pressure of western schools. Under such conditions, assumptions concerning agriculture, disease, God, the spirit world, and a myriad of other theories are being altered, replaced, or otherwise accommodated.

4. Of all the problems that occur when people of different societies come into contact with each other, *those arising from differences in worldview are the most difficult to deal with*. Since worldview is a matter of assumptions, it seldom occurs to the members of a social group that there may be people of other groups who do not share their assumptions.

This is a major reason why culture shock (better, "culture stress") is such a problem. If we are in another society, not only are they behaving on the basis of different assumptions than ours, they may not even understand why we are having a problem. We may be off balance because our assumptions aren't working, and we get no help because it never occurs to the people of the other society that we are having a problem.

In addition to culture stress problems, worldview differences underlie most of the problems we face as we attempt to communicate Christianity cross-culturally. The Gospel is intended to influence and change people at the deepest possible level—the worldview level. The changes brought about by Christianity should be basically changes in the worldview, changes in the basic assumptions. Worldview provides the guidelines in terms of which people assign meanings. It's these meanings that are to be influenced by Christianity.

Often the process goes afoul, however, since we tend to tangle up Christian assumptions with those of our own society, often quite unconsciously. In our attempts to discover and remedy such a problem, we need to become conscious of which of our assumptions stem from our Christian commitment and which from our culture. It is one of the aims of this volume to assist us in this process. Another aim is to provide tools that will better enable us to learn and to work productively in terms of the worldview of those to whom we are called.

5. As should be obvious by now, though we need to treat people and cultural/ worldview structuring as separable entities, *in real life, people and worldview function together*. We do not have people in one place and worldview in another. People cannot say or do or think anything without behaving on the basis of their worldview assumptions. Those analyses of worldview that do not clearly make the person-structure distinction tend to attribute to worldview certain personal characteristics.

Such is the perspective of Paul Hiebert, who holds that worldview (not simply people) consists of cognitive, affective, and evaluative dimensions (1985:30–49). I hold that it is not worldview—the structures—that has these dimensions, but the people who carry out their activities according to worldview patterns who think, feel, and evaluate. The dimensions Hiebert points to are indeed there in real life as people conduct their lives. But the dimensions he points to are people things, not culture/worldview things. The problem, as I see it, is that Hiebert is looking at worldview as a combination of structure and people and using "people terminology" to label the structures. I feel that this approach is confusing.

We can, however, reconcile our two approaches by seeing my analysis in which people and cultural/worldview structures are kept distinct as our starting point, with Hiebert's approach as a second step. We can then say that *"people*, following worldview guidelines, function cognitively, affectively, and evaluatively." Step one: people and structures analyzed separately (as in figure 4.3 below). Step two: people function in terms of their structures to think, feel, and evaluate.

FUNCTIONS OF WORLDVIEW

In our attempt to understand worldview and the part it plays in the cultural life of a people, let's focus on the way people use worldview assumptions. Though it is people using worldview, not worldview doing something by itself, we will label these *the functions of worldview*. To deal with these functions, let us return to the chart of personal behavior and cultural structuring presented in the last chapter (*see* figure 4.3). Focusing on the lower (deep level) portion of the chart, we will examine the categories portrayed there one by one, keeping in mind that it is always people who are the doers, with the worldview patterns used as guidelines for their habitual behavior.

1. The first set of patterns provided by a worldview is that for the *structuring of deep, underlying personal characteristics*. We may call these "primary-level characteristics." Among them are willing, emoting, reasoning, motivation, and predisposition.

a. *Patterning the way we use our wills*. We are taught the socially approved ways of choosing and deciding. Individualistic societies teach children to assert their wills individualistically. Group-oriented societies teach their children to use their willpower to conform to the group. "It is the one who wanders away from the group that gets in trouble," they are told.

b. *Patterning the use of emotions*. All societies structure the use of emotion. In few, if any, is it considered proper to express any emotion at any time. Though some allow great latitude in emotional expression, some are very repressive.

c. *Patterning logic and reason*. People in different societies reason differently. Westerners are known for what is called linear logic. We tend to reason in a straight line. If such and such is true, then it follows that such and such is also true. We then tend to make rather sweeping generalizations on the basis either of logic or of a few experiences that we feel point in the direction of the generalization.

	PERSONAL BEHAVING	CULTURAL STRUCTURING
S U R F A C E	**BEHAVING** *Habitual Behaving* 　　Overt (Doing, Speaking, Emoting) 　　Covert (Thinking, Feeling) *Creative Behaving* 　　Overt (Doing, Speaking, Emoting) 　　Covert (Thinking, Feeling)	**PATTERNS OF BEHAVIOR** Overt Customs that Pattern Doing, Speaking, Emoting, etc. Covert Customs that Pattern Thinking, Feeling, etc.
D E E P	**ASSUMING** **(Usually Habitual, Often Creative)** **Primary-Level Assuming** 　　Willing (Choosing) 　　Emoting 　　Reasoning 　　Assuming Motivations 　　Assuming Predispositions **Assigning Meaning** 　　Interpreting 　　Evaluating **Responding to Assigned Meanings** 　　Explaining 　　Committing/Pledging Allegiance 　　Relating 　　Adapting 　　Regulating 　　Seeking Psychological Reinforcement 　　Striving toward Integration/Consistency	**PATTERNS OF WV ASSUMPTIONS** **Patterns Underlying Primary Behavior** 　　Willing (Choosing) 　　Emoting 　　Reasoning 　　Deciding Motivation 　　Being Predisposed **Patterns of Meaning Assignment** 　　Ways of Interpreting 　　Ways of Evaluating/Validating **Patterns of Response to Meaning** 　　Ways of Explaining 　　Ways of Committing/Pledging Allegiance 　　Ways of Relating 　　Ways of Adapting 　　Ways of Regulating 　　Ways of Getting Psychological Reinforcement 　　Ways of Integrating/Attaining Consistency

Figure 4.3 Surface and deep, personal and cultural

Many of the peoples of the world, however, reason contextually. They see each event encased in a context that is different from any other context. The uniqueness of each context makes each event unique and difficult to generalize from. In building a case for something, they will tell story after story, in great detail, rather than making what we would consider logical point after logical point. The writer of Hebrews used a kind of contextual reasoning to make his points.

d. Worldview assumptions also *affect and pattern motivation*. What motivates people to behave in certain ways differs from society to society according to differential patterning at the worldview level. Though there are certain basic biologically based motivators (the need for food, water, sleep, sex, exercise), there are also socially inculcated wants (desire for prestige, wealth, comfort, freedom from trouble) that motivate people in powerful ways. Worldview assumptions govern both the motivators and the expected responses to them.

e. Even *predispositions are patterned by worldview*. Such attitudes as optimism versus pessimism are based on worldview assumptions and expressed differently from society to society. Though each of these attitudes will be found in every society, certain societies will teach their children in such a way that the vast majority of them will look on the positive side of things most of the time. Other societies teach their children to focus on the negative side.

2. The next two worldview functions (the patterning of interpreting and evaluating) relate to *the patterning of the assignment of meaning*. Assigning meaning is perhaps the most frequent activity human beings engage in. It is important to recognize, as I detail in chapter 9 and in Kraft 1991a, that meaning is assigned by people. Meaning is not inherent in the vehicles we use to convey it.

a. *Interpreting*. We have been taught how to interpret. For example, in the West, it is common for us to interpret landscapes and flowers as beautiful. We interpret them that way in accord with the way we have been taught. In many societies, however, beautiful is not a word the people would use for landscapes and flowers. They have not been taught to assume such things are beautiful. With regard to beauty, Americans recognize that "beauty is in the eye of the beholder." That is, beauty is a matter of interpretation. The same is true for everything else in life.

The assignment of meaning is a matter of personal interpretation based on social agreements concerning how to interpret cultural forms. These people agreements are, for the most part, quite predictable, since they are based on the worldview structuring of assumptions that people have been taught. There's a sense in which all that we say and illustrate concerning worldview applies to this interpretation function. This being true, we will not further elaborate on this function here, allowing the following discussion to fill in additional details concerning it.

b. *Evaluating*. As we interpret, we also evaluate. Indeed, the evaluating, the "feeling" of the meaning, is an extremely important part of the assignment of meaning. We are taught to feel differently about different words and other cultural items. When I say the word *dog*, for example, not only do hearers think of a canine animal, they react positively, negatively, or neutrally to that thought. People either like dogs (or a dog), dislike them, or are neutral toward them. Whatever the evaluation, it becomes a part of the meaning they assign to the concept.

Evaluational assumptions provide the bases for judgments concerning what is good and what is not good. Typical areas in which these assumptions are applied are esthetics (e.g., judgments as to what is visually or aurally pleasing), ethics (e.g., judgments as to what is moral and what immoral), economics (e.g., judgments as to what ought to be more or less expensive), human character (e.g., judgments concerning proper versus improper or admirable versus criticizable conduct or character traits), and the like.

Most cross-cultural problems stem from differences in meaning assignment. Indeed, the examples of cross-cultural differences in understanding we have already given in this and the preceding chapters all relate to this area of worldview. When we go into another society, we are accountable for their assumptions, not ours. To the extent that we can assign meaning according to their assumptions, rather than ours, we can understand and function properly within their world. Learning their language and culture, however, means learning their assumptions.

3. The next seven worldview functions relate to *the patterns of how people respond to the meanings they assign*. These patterns include ways of explaining, pledging allegiance, relating, and adapting.

a. *Patterns of explaining*. Explanatory assumptions concern the way things are or are supposed to be. They include basic assumptions concerning God (e.g., God exists or God does not exist), concerning the universe (e.g., the universe is like a machine; the universe is like a person; the universe is predictable; the universe is capricious and unpredictable; the universe is controllable by humans; the universe is to be submitted to by humans; the universe is centered around the world; the universe is centered around the sun), concerning the nature of human beings (e.g., human nature is sinless, sinful, or neutral), and the like. The various explanations concerning disease that we have discussed also fit in here.

In addition to explanations concerning the origin and nature of the universe, we look to worldview assumptions for explanations concerning such things as how people, animals, plants, and geographical phenomena got here and what we should expect of them. Areas covered by science, history, myth, legend, and the like fit in here. Whether such explanations can be proven or not is irrelevant. If they are assumed by a people, they are a part of their worldview.

b. *Patterns of pledging allegiance.* A worldview provides a map in terms of which people develop and prioritize allegiances. It thus enables us to sort out, arrange, and make differential commitments to the things we assume, value, and do. That is, we don't simply assume, believe, value, or relate to everything in the same way. We assume, believe, and relate with some degree of intensity, committing ourselves quite strongly to certain of our beliefs, values, and behaviors, but quite weakly to others. We are likely, for example, to be less strongly committed to the brand of toothpaste we use (even though we may use it because we believe it to be the best on the market) than we are to our parents (even though we may see faults in them).

How we have prioritized our allegiances becomes most obvious when we are forced to choose between them. Americans frequently have to prioritize allegiances in choosing between job and family, between self-interest and the best interests of loved ones (e.g., spouse, parents, children, friends), between self and community, and for Christians between God and any of these. For nonwesterners, the need to choose between allegiance to God and that to community is often excruciatingly difficult. Our real commitments are often most obvious when such choices are made unconsciously—as when during wartime most Christian citizens of a nation unconsciously agree to put allegiance to nation or tribe above an allegiance to their Christian brothers who are on the other side. The test of which are the highest allegiances is the question, Which of these commitments would one die for?

In general, the more intense the commitment of groups or individuals to an assumption, value, or practice, the less likely they are to change it. If, on the other hand, they become dissatisfied with the custom or discover an attractive alternative, the strength of their allegiance is likely to lessen and they will become more open to the possibility of change.

c. *Patterns of relating.* A worldview provides assumptions concerning how people are to relate to one another. Perhaps most peoples (following their worldview) assume that it is good for people and groups within the society to relate cooperatively with each other. Working together would be seen as good, and competing with each other as bad. People are taught according to worldview patterns how men should relate to women, how youth should relate to their elders, how people of low prestige should relate to those of higher prestige, how one occupational group should relate to another, how followers should relate to leaders, and the like.

Relating to outsiders is a different matter for most peoples. A worldview structures assumptions concerning who is in our "in-group" and therefore to be treated as one of us, and who is in our "out-group" and to be treated differently. Various out-groups are to be ignored, treated with reserve, or treated as enemies.

Even our relationships with animals, plants, and other parts of the material universe are patterned by worldview assumptions. Are we to dominate the world around us or submit to it? Relationships to any invisible beings and powers a people believes in are also patterned. Likewise with relationships to ideas, moral values, and rules and regulations. Since we believe such and such, how should we behave? And if we don't behave as we are taught to, what will be the penalty? A society is in difficulty when the relationships between the various potentially competing groups within the society are not well-managed.

d. *Patterns of adapting.* We are not always able to handle everything that comes our way by following the guidelines of our worldview, so there are worldview assumptions concerning what to do when we perceive that things are not as we believe they ought to be. When this happens, we usually attempt to handle it without altering our assumptions. We try to interpret what we see in such a way that it is either conformed to our worldview or dismissed as unreal.

On occasion, however, either because of personal or group openness or because of the persistence of an uncongenial perception that we find ourselves unable to deny, we may choose to make a change in some aspect of our worldview. For example, nonwesterners under constant pressure from the teaching of western naturalistic interpretations of reality may choose to replace part or all of their supernaturalistic assumptions with naturalistic ones. Or, under these kinds of pressure, persons and groups may attempt to retain two sets of mutually contradictory assumptions and thus live their lives with the kind of worldview "split personality" spoken of at the beginning of this chapter.

In this regard, our values and allegiances come strongly into play. We are committed so strongly to certain things that we would rather "fight than switch" if they are called into question. We may close our eyes to any other evidence to protect such assumptions. On the other hand, there are behaviors and assumptions that are not that important to us. So, if faced with evidence that change would be a good idea, we change.

If the challenges are too great or for some other reason the worldview assumptions are unable to handle the pressures for change, a people can lose confidence in its worldview. When this happens, and it is happening more and more in our day, there is breakdown at the worldview level commonly issuing in demoralization. Such demoralization is manifested in symptoms such as psychological, social, and moral breakdown and, unless it is checked and reversed, in cultural disintegration. See chapter 26 for more on people's reactions to such pressures.

e. *Patterns for regulating.* As we will see in chapter 21, societies provide guidelines for steering behavior in directions considered appropriate and for stopping behavior considered inappropriate. These guidelines are grounded in worldview assumptions, especially in evaluative assumptions. As westerners we assume that it is proper to wear clothes. We assume therefore that public nakedness is to be punished. On the basis of certain assumptions concerning appropriateness we regulate what kind of clothing is to be worn in what situations.

We have, in addition, a plethora of assumptions concerning the regulation of interpersonal behavior, including ownership of property, politeness, appropriate treatment of each other, patterns of interpersonal behavior, patterns of childrearing, and the like. We add to these regulatory assumptions a large number of assumptions concerning appropriate sanctions or punishments for those who overstep the boundaries we assume to be proper.

f. *Patterns for getting psychological reinforcement*. When things seem to be in order at the worldview level, people can relax psychologically. Because of our worldview assumptions, we know what to do in life when faced with normal and most abnormal situations. We usually have learned worldview assumptions that enable us to know what to do in transitions and crises, as well as in everyday life situations.

When we're trying to make a decision, for example, we work on the basis of the underlying assumptions we have been taught concerning how to go about decision making. A baby is about to be born. Someone is to get married. Someone is ill. Someone has died. We have been taught to assume that it is proper to do thus and so. We do it and are psychologically at ease because we have done the proper thing.

Often what is expected is a ritual. The ritual may be religious or secular, elaborate or simple. It may involve many people or only a single individual. Passage rituals such as those that commonly are prescribed at times such as birth, naming, puberty, marriage, retirement, and death are one kind. Crisis rituals such as those surrounding illness, accident, failure, and decision making may be similar to or dissimilar from passage rituals. All of these and more are prescribed by a society and embedded in its worldview assumptions, and people feel satisfied when they conform to such assumptions.

g. *Patterns for integrating and attaining consistency in life and the way it is structured*. The fact that groups of people assume an incredibly large number of the same things provides a kind of glue holding a society together. People with a common worldview tend to apply the same principles and values in all areas of life. If, for example, their worldview value in one area of life is (like Americans) individualism, they are likely to be individualistic in virtually all areas of life. Their life and culture are integrated around such a principle. If, on the other hand (like many nonwestern peoples), their worldview principle is communalism in one area of life, they are likely to practice communalism in virtually all areas of life. Likewise with other core values such as freedom, hierarchy, male/female dominance, materialism, supernaturalism/naturalism, past/present/future time orientation, competitiveness, conformity, and the like.

Though such common assumptions push sociocultural life and structures toward integration, it is doubtful that any culture is or ever was perfectly integrated. But most seem to be integrated well enough that anything that is changed in the worldview automatically produces ramifications throughout the rest of the culture. This is because the whole of the culture is centered in the same worldview assumptions. The worldview, then, functions within culture much like a radio transmitter. Anything fed into it, whether normal operations or changed procedures, gets broadcast throughout the rest of the culture.

UNIVERSALS OF WORLDVIEW

We may (largely following Kearney 1984) speak of six worldview universals. These are the areas of life with which every known worldview deals. We will simply outline these universals here. See Kraft 1989 for a more detailed presentation.

1. The first of these is *classification*. All peoples classify the reality they perceive around them according to the categories laid down for them in their world-

views. Whether it's plants or animals, people or things, material objects or social categories, natural or supernatural entities, the visible or the invisible—all are labeled and put into categories together with other items and entities believed to be similar to them. These categories are paralleled by other categories made up of other items and entities believed to be dissimilar from those in other categories.

2. A second area that all worldviews treat is that of *person/group*. The nature of the human universe and both its internal and external relationships needs to be understood in the same way by all the members of a society. A worldview provides this understanding. We are taught whether to see people primarily as individuals (as in America) or primarily as groups (as in many other societies). We are taught whether people are expected to dominate the physical environment (as in western societies) or to submit to it (as in many nonwestern societies).

We are taught who is in-group and who out-group, and how to treat each. We are taught the characteristics of good people and bad, of rich and poor, of leaders and followers, of wise and unwise, of respectable and not respectable. We are taught what is appropriate for men and what for women, what for adults and what for children, what for youth, what for parents, what for grandparents, what for various statuses and occupations. In short, whatever a society deems necessary for its members to know concerning people, their nature, and behavior is codified in a society's worldview.

3. A third area addressed by every worldview is the matter of *causality*. The questions being answered under this label are questions of power or cause. What forces are at work in the universe? And what results do they bring about? Are the forces personal, impersonal, or both? The answers provided have names like God, gods, spirits, demons, luck, fate, mana, chance, cause and effect, political and economic structures, the power of persons, and so on.

All questions of supernatural, natural, or human causation fall into this category. As we have seen, many peoples focus greatly on supernatural causation. Other peoples virtually ignore the possibility of supernatural cause and focus almost entirely on human and natural causation.

4. *Time* is another worldview universal. All worldviews codify their society's concept of time. Daily, weekly, monthly, yearly, seasonal, and other cyclical entities are conceptualized. The passage of time is also noted, whether or not it is quantified into seconds, minutes, and hours, as in the West. Something is done about remembered events (e.g., myth, history), present events, and anticipated events (the future). But the systems may be quite different from each other.

Many peoples, for example, are more event oriented than time oriented. That is, they are more concerned with what happens than with how long it goes on. In the West, we set rather strict time limits on most of our activities. Whether or not the activity (e.g., church) is satisfying we cut it off when the time is up. One wonders if God is pleased with the way we limit our time with Him on Sunday mornings.

5. All worldviews likewise provide people with assumptions concerning *space*. Whether it's a matter of how to arrange buildings, structure the space within buildings, structure interpersonal standing space, sleeping space, eating space, or how to conceive of and relate to geographical features or the universe as a whole, a people's worldview provides the rules.

Questions concerning the material universe, how it got here, and how to arrange ourselves in relation to it are the subject of worldview assumptions of all peoples. But, as we would expect, the assumptions of each group will differ. Should we dominate nature or submit to it? Should we live in one place, or should we move around? Should we sleep all in one room, or should we sleep in separate rooms? These and millions of other questions regarding space and the material universe around us are answered in terms of worldview assumptions.

6. People find it necessary to define the *relationships* between the various components of worldview and culture. Whether it is a matter of enabling people to relate time to space, or classification to causality, or space to persons and other relationships between categories, or a matter of relating one kind of time to another (e.g., seasonal time to calendar time), or individuals to groups, or one cause to another (e.g., God to spirits) within the various categories, a worldview provides the guidelines.

CONTRASTING WORLDVIEWS

Though one needs to oversimplify to do so, it is helpful to present a chart like figure 4.4 to point out in summary fashion some of the more distinct contrasts between American worldview assumptions and the assumptions of other peoples. In column two are several typical assumptions held by other peoples that contrast with American assumptions. Each letter (a, b, c) labels an assumption coming from a different worldview. The assumptions do not represent a single worldview.

WORLDVIEW AND CULTURAL CHANGE

Solid culture change is a matter of changes in the worldview of a culture. Just as anything that affects the roots of a tree influences the fruit of the tree, so anything that affects a culture's worldview will affect the whole culture and, of course, the people that operate in terms of that culture. Jesus knew this. When He wanted to get across important points, He aimed at the worldview level. Someone asked, "Who is my neighbor?" So He told them a story and then asked who was being neighborly. He was leading them to reconsider and, hopefully, change a basic value down deep in their system. Paul and Philemon discussed a runaway slave. Paul said to Philemon, "Accept your slave back, but recognize that now he is a Christian." Poor Philemon had to figure out on what basis he could accept a slave who was now a Christian. Onesimus was both a slave and a Christian brother. Paul was pressuring Philemon in the direction of a worldview change.

Jesus said, "You have heard that it was said, 'Love your friends, hate your enemies.' But now I tell you: love your enemies and pray for those who persecute you. . . . If anyone slaps you on the right cheek, let him slap your left cheek too" (Matt 5:43, 44, 39 GNB).

Again the seeds were being planted for change at the deep worldview level.

When things are changed at a deep level, however, it frequently throws things off balance, and any disequilibrium or unbalance at the center of a culture tends to cause difficulty through the rest of the culture. We have spoken above of the demoralizing effect of defeat on a society that believes it cannot be defeated in war. Such a defeat causes disequilibrium at the deepest level.

Something even more bothersome to us, though, is the fact that the introduction of Christianity has sometimes resulted in unforeseen negative consequences because it has threatened people at the deepest worldview level. The account by

American Worldview (Middle Class)	Other Worldviews
Basic Assumptions	
1. Orderly universe	a. Capricious universe b. Different rules for different groups
2. Life analyzable in neat categories	a. Everything fuses into everything else
3. Natural and supernatural dichotomized	a. No distinction b. Dichotomized but psychological phenomena in the supernatural category
4. Linear time divided into neat segments	a. Cyclical (circular) time b. Spiraling time c. Time flows and can't be quantified
5. Can validly generalize about others from one's experience	a. Can't generalize. Experience always unique
6. Humans can understand truth	a. Humans can't understand truth
7. Human-centered universe	a. God- or spirit-centered universe b. Tribe- or family-centered c. Uncentered
8. Money/material the measure of value	a. Family relationships the measure b. Personal/family prestige the measure c. Spiritual power the measure
9. Unlimited good (i.e., wealth, power, prestige) available	a. Limited good available b. Amount of good getting less
10. Future orientation	a. Past orientation b. Present orientation
Etc.	
Values	
1. Competition good (need to "get ahead")	a. Competition evil b. Cooperation good (want everyone at same level)
2. Change good (= "progress")	a. Change bad (= destruction of traditions) b. Change neither bad nor good
3. Individual good valued	a. Group good valued b. Individualism destructive
4. "51%" democracy	a. Consensus (100%) democracy b. Certain people "born to rule"
Allegiances	
1. Most frequent for men and career women 1) self, 2) job, 3) family 2. Frequent for mothers 1) family, 2) self 3. Christian varieties 1) God, 2) self, 3) job, 4) family 1) God, 2) family, 3) self, 4) job	a. 1) Family/clan, 2) job, 3) self b. 1) God/gods, 2) clan/family c. 1) Ancestors/family, 2) self
Etc.	

Figure 4.4 Contrasting worldview emphases

John Messenger (1959) referred to in chapter 2, plus several of the other examples given there, illustrate how well-meaning people can introduce apparently good changes that turn out to be culturally as well as spiritually damaging. Add to this the enormous damage (again both cultural and spiritual) that has been done through the influence of western schools introduced and run by missions, and you can understand that there are at least a few valid reasons (among the invalid ones) for certain anthropologists to be critical of missionary work.

In addition to the changes that flow from worldview throughout the culture, there are changes that flow the other way, as well. Changes made (often in response to coercion) in peripheral customs lead people automatically to change the worldview assumption(s) that relate to that area of life. The requirement that Nigerian Christians reject polygamy and become monogamous led even Christians to certain undesirable worldview assumptions concerning the Christian God. Among these were: God is against the real leaders of Nigerian society; God is not in favor of women having help and companionship around the home; God wants men to be enslaved to a single wife (like whites seem to be); God favors divorce, social irresponsibility, and even prostitution. None of these conclusions is irrational or farfetched from their point of view. Undirected worldview change of this kind frequently results from a mandated change such as this one in a peripheral custom.

Similarly, people who, in the name of Christianity, change from indigenous medicine to western medicine often come to assume that God condemns their medicine and endorses western medicine. If they get deeply enough into secularized medicine they may even conclude (as do most western medical personnel, including many Christians) that God is irrelevant to the healing process. People who in Christianizing change from task-centered work (i.e., one works to accomplish a task, then stops working) to time-intensive work (i.e., one works every day simply for the sake of working) often come to assume that God does not value their family and communal interactions and rituals, since these can no longer be maintained in the face of a daily work schedule. They will often assume that God wants them to be more oriented to money than to personal (family/clan) relationships. Changing from traditional types of religious rituals to western rituals often leads to worldview assumptions that regard western rituals as more powerful in a magical way than their own.

We will deal with worldview change in greater detail in chapters 22–26. Suffice it to say here that cross-cultural witnesses would do well to learn as much as possible about this whole area.

IS THERE A SINGLE CHRISTIAN WORLDVIEW?

In concluding this chapter, I will briefly state my position with regard to whether or not there is a single Christian worldview. We have indicated in several ways that the coming of Christianity is intended to bring about change at the deepest level of a people's cultural assumptions. Helping people to develop those assumptions and the habitual behavior appropriate to them is a major concern of Christian growth.

In spite of this fact, I do not believe there is a single Christian worldview. If there were, Christians would need to have a single approach both to things like moral values and to things like time, space and categorization. There are those who speak of a Christian worldview (e.g., Sire 1976; Schaeffer 1976). They are not understanding, however, the all-encompassing nature of worldview in the anthropological sense. They are speaking of the influx of Christian assumptions, values, and allegiances into a worldview as if that input constituted the whole worldview. It does not.

Christian Africans, Christian Asians, Christian Europeans, and the multitude of committed Christians from the other societies of the world simply do not see most things the same way, in spite of their commitment to Christ. The question is, should they? My answer is no. There will be certain very important similarities. But most of the differences in worldview, as in surface-level cultural behavior, remain—unless, of course, in the process of becoming Christian, these people also change their culture. This latter is not, however, a Christian requirement.

Jesus had a worldview (*see* Kraft 1989, chapt. 9). It consisted of His "Kingdom perspectives" integrated into His first-century Hebrew worldview. Our task is to follow His example by integrating those same perspectives into our cultural worldview. We are to assume Christian assumptions and live habitually by them, each within his or her own cultural context, just as Jesus did within His context.

CHAPTER 5

A CROSS-CULTURAL PERSPECTIVE

INTEGRATIONAL THOUGHT

The Apostle Peter seemed to have a more difficult time than Paul did in developing the ability to accept people of other societies into Christianity. In Acts 10, God resorted to a rather spectacular vision (vv. 9–16) to prepare Peter for the request from Cornelius to come present the Gospel message to him. Though Peter did not obey God in the vision by eating the "unclean" animals, he did get the message God was trying to communicate. He stated, "God has shown me that I must not consider any person ritually unclean or defiled" (v. 28). And he went with the messengers to the Roman centurion's home.

There, of course, he articulated the general principle he had learned: "I now realize that it is true that God treats everyone on the same basis. Whoever fears him and does what is right is acceptable to him, no matter what race [i.e., culture] he belongs to" (vv. 34, 35).

But in Galatians 2:11–14 we see Peter wavering in his acceptance of Gentiles who remain Gentiles. He identified with them as long as there were no Jewish Christians around, but when those who believed Gentiles had to convert to Jewish culture arrived, "he drew back and would not eat with the Gentiles, because he was afraid of those who were in favor of circumcising them" (v. 12). So Paul "opposed him in public, because he was clearly wrong" (v. 11).

God endorses what we call *sociocultural adequacy*. The perspective we want to develop accepts people and meets them where they are, within their familiar sociocultural contexts, in the same way God and Paul did. We should be careful not to imitate Peter's Galatians 2 behavior. What we need is a cross-cultural perspective.

INTRODUCTION

Since one of the aims of this book is to help the reader develop a cross-cultural perspective, it is time to clarify and discuss just what is meant by this term. To do this, we will first discuss several varieties and characteristics of its opposite—a monocultural perspective. With this in mind we will attempt to define and discuss a cross-cultural perspective and the "doctrine" of sociocultural validity that provides the basis for it. Finally, we will discuss what I have termed *biblical sociocultural adequacy* in order to highlight the convergence of anthropological and biblical truth in this area.

MONOCULTURALISM

A naive monocultural perspective looks at reality (including other people's) from one point of view only, the cultural (worldview) point of view of the monocultural person. Sometimes we refer to such a perspective as monocultural myopia. *Myopia* is a technical word for nearsightedness. Myopic people can only see things close to them. Monocultural people typically only take their own worldview perspective into account. That is, they simply interpret and evaluate the way they have been brought up, for we are all taught to be monocultural.

1. Monoculturalism is naively *ethnocentric*. People who are monocultural judge all other customs and perspectives from the point of view of their own cultural (worldview) values only. Ethnocentrism is at the cultural level what egocentrism is at the individual level. It prevents a person or group from appreciating or often even understanding points of view different from their own. Monocultural people are captured by the point of view of their own society. It's almost like looking through a tube: you see nothing on either side of the tube.

The Hausa picture a person with extremely limited understanding as a fish in a well, which fits the monocultural person. The fish looks up, and all he can see is what's in the well and a little bit of daylight at the top of the well. His experience is restricted to what he sees in the well.

2. A monocultural point of view is *absolutistic*. Monocultural people regard as absolute the points of view of their own society. Though nearly all peoples are taught to be monocultural, such an attitude is particularly dangerous when held by people in power. Monocultural westerners who believe their perspectives are the only right ones and wield power over other people have caused incredible damage throughout the world. Unfortunately, many who have held such views considering any other approach to life as wrong have been advocates of Christianity. This has hurt the cause of Christ immeasurably.

Often we extend our monoculturalism to subcultural allegiances such as denominations, social classes or castes, a particular theological perspective, or the like. We may believe that our theological perspective is the only right one. Some are committed in a monocultural way to Reformed Theology, some to Wesleyan or Charismatic theologies. Such people feel that God Himself endorses only their understandings. No allowance is made for the possible rightness or validity of another point of view. Any other perceptions of reality are automatically wrong because they are different.

3. A monocultural perspective *buys into naive realism*. Monocultural people equate their perceptions of REALITY with REALITY itself and make no allowance for the possible rightness or validity of other perceptions. They see only their view of REALITY as true and claim God's endorsement of this point of view.

4. Monocultural people seem to *assume that their views have been arrived at because they are superior*. You get the impression they think their ancestors looked at all the possible ways of doing things, rejected all other ways as inferior, and chose their way as the best way. Indeed, many seem to assume God gave their ancestors these customs. Unfortunately, many Christians have felt this way and considered other societies' homes, clothing, tools, music, strange-sounding language, and other supposedly inferior customs to be the result of sin, or at least a lack of intelligence. They will often point to their customs as superior and the result of the closeness of their society to God.

5. A monocultural perspective *has no respect for other people's ways*. It is proud of its own way of life, looks down on other people's languages, perspectives, and behavior, and blames these people for choosing such "ridiculous" customs; it doesn't want to try to understand them. It simply condemns them.

6. Such condemnation stems from the monocultural habit of *always evaluating other people's customs and perspectives in terms of one's own culturally learned assumptions and values (worldview)*. Monocultural people tend to evaluate other people's customs as if they were inferior (or defective) parts of their system (the only correct system), rather than well-functioning parts of a completely different system. From this point of view, there is no need to try to understand another people's customs from their perspective, since there is no validity to that system anyway.

Recognizing that we western Christians have often been guilty of such an attitude, we need first to repent, then to learn from our mistakes. As missionaries we have often been guilty of first condemning a people's customs, then teaching against them, and then letting them make "their own choice." Very often this was the reason for western schools—to teach them how to think straight. But are people really uneducated, unintelligent, or inferior simply because they have not been to school and learned to read?

7. People with a monocultural perspective readily *use pejorative terms to contrast their ways with those of others*. Look at the terms we often use. We say, "their customs are *primitive*, ours are *advanced*." What does it mean to be advanced culturally? The use of such terms is merely a way of taking the things we are best at and grading other people down because they are not as good at them as we are.

I did a similar thing at a personal level while in college. As an athlete, I was part of a group that thought that people who weren't good at athletics were inferior to us. People on the other side of campus did things like playing violins, pianos, and trumpets. In our estimation, what they were good at was not nearly as important or valuable as what we were good at. We could do things like throwing a football or hitting a baseball or making baskets with a basketball. Because they were not good at the things we were good at, we considered them inferior. But I found out later that some of them were looking at us and doing the same thing! Whether at a personal or cultural level, we readily take the things we are good at and condemn other people because they are not skilled in the same fields. We should, rather, cheer on others in the use and development of their abilities.

Another of our favorite terms is *uncivilized*. Our western tendency is to call other people uncivilized and ourselves civilized. But are western societies civilized? Just in the United States alone, we kill approximately 50,000 people a year on the highways. Is that civilized? No society in all of history has been able to kill more people in warfare than western societies. Is that civilized? If we compare our ways with those of any number of smaller, more traditional societies, with all of their faults, they often appear more civilized than we.

We call ourselves *superior* and them *inferior*, ourselves *developed* and them *underdeveloped*, but these are ethnocentric terms designed to show approval of our way of life and disapproval of theirs. Just what does *underdeveloped* mean? It means they are not as good as we are at the things we choose to be good at. I'm afraid, though, that the real problems in this world are not with the underdeveloped peoples but with the "overdeveloped" peoples. I had a college roommate who was a wrestler. He had developed certain of his muscles to enable him to wrestle well, but he found that developing his muscles for one purpose kept him from using them for other purposes. For example, though his shoulder muscles were very helpful when he was wrestling, they kept him from raising his arms above his head, so he had great difficulty reaching for things over his head.

Our western "developed" societies have done the same thing. In order to become good at using the material environment to our advantage, we have developed ourselves to an incredible extent in this area. In the process of becoming expert in that area, we have neglected other areas, so we now live in a polluted environment. One area we have failed to develop is the art of getting along with each other. Failure in this area has led us to overdevelop our ability to conduct war. So now we live in fear of annihilation. Perhaps instead of calling ourselves developed and other people underdeveloped, we should call them developed and ourselves overdeveloped!

We often refer to others as *pagan* or *heathen* and to ourselves as *Christian*. Many internationals have a rude awakening when they find out how unchristian this country is.

We often call other people *superstitious* but ourselves *religious*. In using such labels we ignore the fact that there is much superstition in our religion and that what we may see as superstition in other societies is usually a part of a religious system fully as complex and functional as ours. They have superstition, but so do we. We have religion, but so do they.

Often we refer to the approach of traditional societies to the past as *myth*, while we call ours *history*. When we look more closely, however, we find that a lot of our history is really myth in the worst sense. We also find that a lot of nonwestern oral tradition has a lot more truth value than we previously suspected.

Sometimes westerners refer to other peoples' customs as *quaint* or *childlike*. Of course, we see ourselves as *mature*. "Look how little it takes to make these people happy," we say. "Why, they dance and play just like children. They even eat with their fingers!" Though often such comments are intended to be positive rather than critical, they are ethnocentric and betray an assumption that when these people learn a bit more, they will "grow up" to be like us.

Another term that is used pejoratively is the designation *"dialect"* for what is really a full-fledged language. In India and several other countries, for example, it is common to refer to certain "major" languages as languages and to those designated "minor" as dialects. Such a use of these terms betrays the fact that they have been taken in by a western kind of ethnocentrism that says, "Those varieties we respect we call languages; those we don't respect we call dialects." In reality, all mutually unintelligible varieties of speech, whether westerners respect them or not, are distinct languages. Technically a dialect is a variety within a language that differs slightly from another variety of that same language but is understandable to those speaking that other variety. Any two varieties of speech that are not mutually intelligible are separate languages.

Though I have been illustrating largely from western ethnocentrism, there is a tendency for most people to use one set of terms to designate their customs as superior and another set of terms to designate the customs of others as inferior. *Ethnocentrism is not limited to westerners*. It just may be more visible in western society because westerners tend to be more visible and vocal. The fact that we westerners are not the only ones who are ethnocentric came to me quite forcefully a few years ago when talking to a student from Vietnam. About halfway through the anthropology course, he said to me, "Now I realize that we Vietnamese are not supposed to make those mountain people into Vietnamese." I chuckled, because behind his statement lay the fact that the American missionaries working in his area had tried to make him into an American. He had rejected that, saying he wanted to be a Christian Vietnamese, but when he went as a missionary to the mountain people within Vietnam, he started trying to convert them to his Vietnamese culture!

This Vietnamese missionary, like so many Euroamerican missionaries (and the early Christians—*see* Acts 15), had gone out to serve the Lord with the monocultural ethnocentric belief that the culture within which God dealt with him was to be normative for others as well. Such an attitude is particularly troublesome when those who hold it have high prestige with or power over those to whom they go. Under such circumstances, the people often gladly convert to the culture of the witness with the understanding that this is required by God.

THREE OTHER MONOCULTURAL POSITIONS

Though the above-described naive monocultural perspective is the most typical position in this category, it is possible to describe at least three other positions that may also be called monocultural.

1. The *Eclectic Monocultural Position*. This position is but slightly different from the above and ends up just as arrogant. It simply believes that the selection process by means of which a culture gets to have all of the best customs is still going on. This, by the way, is quite American. We believe that other peoples do on occasion come up with better ways of doing things. So we feel obligated to observe and evaluate other peoples' ways with a view toward adopting those customs that we view as superior to ours and rejecting (and criticizing) those we don't like. A fairly high percentage of customs (especially technological customs) in American culture originated in some other culture.

There is a very clever write-up by an anthropologist named Ralph Linton (1936:326–7), who entitles his article "100% American." He points out how we borrowed one thing from the Chinese, another from Europeans, still another from the Middle East, and something else from the American Indians. He shows a typical American using all these things and then sitting back to read a newspaper printed on paper developed in China by a print process developed in Germany, and thanking a Hebrew God in an Indo-European language that he is 100 percent American. This is the eclectic monocultural position: we take things from other peoples, combine them with what is already there, and, forgetting where any given custom came from, take pride in the superiority of our way of life, as if we had invented it.

This eclectic position is particularly troublesome in mission situations when one who holds it tries to evaluate someone (missionary or national) who recommends leniency toward a custom such as polygamy or common-law marriage. People who are eclectic monoculturalists often can only conceive of three reasons why someone might advocate acceptance of those who have come to faith but still practice such customs. They would conclude that the one willing to accept such persons either 1) believes the custom to be a superior custom and is, therefore, condoning it, 2) has impure motives (e.g., may be oversexed), or 3) is lowering the standards for Christians.

2. *Reactionary Monocultural Position*. Then there is the kind of attitude that people fall into either because they have become culturally demoralized or because they overglamorize some other culture or type of culture. They conclude that their own culture is inferior or bad and seek to escape from it into that other culture or type of culture. Many people in western societies have moved in this direction.

Some writers have suggested that the people who are the happiest are those who are closest to nature, so they go to some so-called primitive society to become like them because they believe they are happy. They believe that the complexity of western societies is the reason for our unhappiness. The problem with this position is that once you begin to know people, you discover that though they may not have the same troubles as westerners, they do have others, and they are not necessarily as happy as they look to us.

Many nonwestern people have been intimidated by westernization into believing that western culture is good and the customs of their fathers and grandfathers inferior and bad. Such people are often reaching out to become more and more western with very little respect for their traditional cultures or for the traditional people within their cultures who have not westernized. They have been taught in western schools that everything good comes from the West and that little, if anything, from their traditional cultures is worth preserving.

A lot of problems come along with such an attitude, including psychological problems for those who can no longer feel at home within their own societies yet, in spite of their best efforts, never quite become totally accepted as westerners, either. Christians in the Two-Thirds World have often been led into this kind of mentality to an even greater extent than others in their societies since they have often been in closer, more intense contact with western influences.

3. *One-World-Culture Monocultural Position.* A final monocultural position springs from the idea that the world is all moving in one direction and it is just a matter of time before everyone will be westernized, speaking English, and thinking in western ways. Many of us as westerners (and not a few nonwesterners) assume that this process is inevitable, that it is based on the relatively free evaluation by nonwesterners of the superiority of western cultures, that people are westernizing because they choose to, and that the best policy for us westerners to follow is to do whatever we can to assist people to move in this direction. I have frequently heard missionaries justify an all-out commitment to a school-centered approach to mission work on the basis of the belief that such an approach is helping people to better cope with the world of the future.

In the short run, they may be right. At the present time, the world is moving rapidly in a westernizing direction. But the assumption that this is to be a permanent thing betrays a shortsighted view of history, and the assumption that such a movement is a good thing betrays (in my opinion) a naive view of culture. When we look back at history, we find that at one time everybody thought the world would become Greek. All the differences between societies would be stamped out. But after a while, the Romans came along, and for a time everybody was going to become Roman. Now it's the turn of those of us who speak English, but this too is only a passing phenomenon. It's probably only a matter of time before China or some other nation takes over. Then everyone will have to learn whatever language the new rulers speak.

A CROSS-CULTURAL PERSPECTIVE

To avoid the deficiencies of a monocultural perspective, we recommend what we call a *cross-cultural perspective*. As we will see below, this is a different thing from "multiculturalism," a politically correct term to signify total tolerance for every kind of perspective and practice except the traditional values historically associated with Judeo-Christian morality. Though multiculturalism advocates respecting and taking seriously every group's approach to life, it ignores and even denies "big R" absolutes to which every human is accountable.

Assuming that there is a God and a REALITY beyond our reality to which we are held accountable by Him, our cross-cultural perspective is built on three principles.

1. The first of these is the observation that *there is right and wrong in every society and its culture*. No culture seems to be perfect, not even our own. All seem (like individual persons) to have both strengths and weaknesses and, again like individuals, to be deeply affected by sin. In spite of the impressive way that a people's culture provides adequate guidelines for most of life, no culture seems to provide satisfactory answers for all of life's problems. There always seem to be flaws.

Cultures, furthermore, seem always to get off balance. The culture of a people becomes specialized (warped) around those approaches to life most highly valued by its people, at the expense of other values that may ultimately be just as important as (or even more important than) the values in primary focus. Western cultures, for example, tend to be warped in the direction of technological accomplishments at the expense of interpersonal, family, and broader social relationships.

Nevertheless, it would be unfair to take a reactionary monocultural position and suggest that any culture (western or nonwestern) does not also possess impressive strengths. Western cultures are, of course, very impressive in technological areas and are rightly admired by peoples of other societies for these strengths. Many nonwestern societies, however, though not nearly as accomplished in technological areas as we are, have developed truly admirable patterns of interpersonal, family, and group interaction and relationship. While we in the West have poured our energies into the area of our interest and specialization (technology), these peoples have devoted themselves to constructing social monuments.

2. The second principle is to recognize that *there are many equally effective approaches to the solving of most of life's problems*. It is just as effective, for example, to get food to one's mouth by fingers or chopsticks as by fork. It works just as well for people to sleep on mats as on mattresses (as long as they're used to it) or to squat as to sit when going to the toilet, or to speak one language as to speak another, or to be governed in one way as to be governed in another, or to buy and sell in one way as to buy and sell in another, or even to organize their marriages and families in one way as to organize them in another.

I wonder if God really has a preference as to how we eat or sleep or what kind of family, economic, or political organization we have? Many Americans would say that God favors democratic government and is opposed to all other kinds of government. But the Bible shows that God didn't set up a democracy when He had the chance. God can work in and through any kind of government.

Does God really have a preference concerning what language is spoken? Some people say God endorsed Hebrew, Greek, or Latin, but linguists can point to many languages that are at least as pictorial as Hebrew and as precise as Greek. There is no way of designating one language as better or more effective than another overall, though each has strengths in the areas related to the special interests of the people who use the language. The fact is that all languages are effective and usable for all types of human communication, and God uses whatever language is available. He used Hebrew because that was the language of the people He was dealing with, in spite of the fact that when He started using Hebrew, only one Hebrew family was following Him—the rest were "pagans." When His message was taken to people who understood Greek, He used Greek, in spite of the fact that the formation and use of that language was in a "pagan" crucible. He can even use English for His purposes!

3. Following from these principles is the principle I will call *sociocultural adequacy* (often referred to as "cultural relativism" or "cultural relativity"). What this principle asserts is that though no cultural way of life is perfect, each is adequate and to be respected. I believe this recognition of sociocultural adequacy enables us to practice the Golden Rule at the cultural level. The Golden Rule says, "Do to others what you would like them to do to you." If you want them to respect you, you respect them.

Recognizing the adequacy of each sociocultural system enables us to advocate respect for other peoples and their ways of life. This is the way to be loving and concerned. These people were born into their society and taught their culture, just as we were born into our society and taught our culture. We cannot legitimately condemn one culture as if it were totally bad or elevate another culture as if it were totally good. We must, rather, see each in terms of its capacity to enable people to handle most of their life needs and wants. In providing for this, each culture is relatively adequate. If it weren't, its people would not survive.

By advocating the doctrine of sociocultural adequacy we are not going to the extreme position that some anthropologists (and others) sometimes claim to advocate—that of absolute relativism. That position would claim that there are no absolute standards existing outside of culture. Any kind of culturally approved behavior is, therefore, just as good as any other kind for anybody at any place and time.

Sociocultural adequacy does not claim that every way is right, only that every way that survives has met enough of the required criteria to be respected. It is in this sense that we use the word *adequate*. We could alternatively speak (as I sometimes do) of cultures as "valid," if by valid we mean to indicate that each way of life does reasonably well at carrying out its intended functions and is, therefore, worthy of respect. To me the most helpful analogy is to suggest that most cultures are like most people—never perfect, yet adequate enough to survive and valid enough to be respected.

EVALUATING CULTURES

As mentioned above, if we took the position of absolute relativism, we could not evaluate or criticize a culture, especially one other than one's own. To the advocates of that position (if there are any), what is, is right. Sociocultural adequacy, however, allows evaluation under certain conditions.

1. The first condition is *that any evaluation be done on the basis of an understanding of the culture from the inside*. Technically, this insider's view is known as *an emic perspective*. Kenneth Pike, a linguist for many years associated with Wycliffe Bible Translators, developed this term to highlight the contrast between a cultural insider's view and that of an informed outsider. The latter he called *an etic perspective* (Pike 1967). These terms are now widely used by anthropologists.

Cultural insiders have rights and privileges that outsiders do not have when handling their culture (*see* point 2 below). They have been conditioned to see things from the perspective being evaluated and therefore have an understanding that outsiders rarely attain, though insiders can often be quite naive in their understandings and evaluations. Outsiders, however, if they learn to understand and appreciate the insider's point of view (learn an emic perspective), can often be very helpful in the process of cultural evaluation, for informed outsiders can often see certain things more clearly than the insiders themselves.

The crucial requirement for outsiders to attain such understanding is the ability to see beneath the level of surface forms to the deep-meaning level. For outsiders, learning to understand another people's culture at the deep-meaning level is ordinarily a long and difficult process, requiring of them much more involvement than simply learning the language. And while one is learning to understand, it is necessary to attempt to suspend one's tendency to make judgments. This is very difficult but very important, especially if one seeks to communicate Christian love and acceptance.

Some western Christians feel that a procedure where one suspends judgment and does not speak out against apparent evils in another society is unchristian compromise. Nothing could be further from the truth (or more indicative of our enslavement to monocultural ethnocentrism). As will be seen below, God Himself has shown us that the way of patience and love is His way in such matters. What frequently leads us to make such a mistake is our misunderstanding of who has the right to be a prophet. A prophet is a cultural insider, not an outsider. As long as we are outsiders, we are obligated by our Christian principles to take the posture of patience and love as we strive toward understanding (and even after we understand), since we are outsiders and guests in someone else's cultural home.

2. When evaluating cultural phenomena, *there is a crucial difference between the rights and privileges of a cultural insider and those of an outsider*. I believe that insiders have a responsibility to critique and try to change those aspects of their cultures that they find to be in some way deficient. Outsiders, however, should take quite a different attitude. They must recognize their position as guests of another people and be very careful what they say and how they say it. When people are allowed to enter someone else's home, they have no right to criticize the arrangement of the furniture, no matter how disagreeable they find it—unless, of course, the owner of the home asks their opinion. This kind of courtesy is especially important for Christians to observe. Love allows no other option.

The reader will note that I am quite critical of American culture at many points. See the section on my attitude toward American culture below.

3. A third condition for evaluating is that *whatever judgments are made be made concerning parts or aspects of the culture, not the culture as a whole*. We have already contended that no culture is totally good or totally bad. Since no culture is perfect, however, there will always be aspects of the culture that can be criticized. These may be evaluated and, if necessary, critiqued, especially by insiders, as if they were defective parts of a machine that still works, even with the defective parts. That is, the whole structure should not be condemned, even if some parts of it may rightly be evaluated as flawed. Furthermore, any attempt to evaluate the flawed aspects of a culture should be balanced by a positive assessment of those aspects that seem to be measuring up well to the criteria (*see* below) in terms of which the judgments are made.

4. A fourth condition is that *the one who evaluates (whether negatively or positively) cultural behavior do so according to transcultural principles*. As indicated above, any evaluation based simply on a monocultural assumption of rightness

and wrongness as taught by the evaluator's society is selfish, inconsiderate, and totally inappropriate to a cross-cultural perspective. It is certainly out of bounds for Christians to evaluate other ways of life on such a basis. Christians, of all people, need to have a transcultural basis for our evaluations. I would contend further that cultural insiders also need to evaluate their cultures on the basis of transcultural principles.

What, then, are these principles? How can we know that they are not simply derived from our own culture? To take the second, more difficult question first, we cannot be totally sure, since we can never see or understand without interference from our cultural grid. I believe we can, however, at least tentatively approach the developing of transculturally valid principles from two angles. I will label the first of these "the human well-being criterion" and the second "the God's-intent criterion."

The extensive study of the cultures of humankind has led anthropologists to the conclusion that the first and most important function of a culture is to provide its society with effective strategies for dealing with the challenges of life. These strategies need to be characterized by such things as organization, order, meaning, continuity with the past, guidelines for the present, and the like. When these are well provided, people function well. When they are not well provided, people break down. A well-functioning culture provides its people with a high degree of physical, psychological, and spiritual security. Such security results in what I call human well-being. Just how much of such security needs to be provided by a culture for the people to be in a state of well-being is not known. Perhaps it differs from people to people. Nor do we know for sure how much of that security can be sacrificed before people begin to break down and their lives fall apart. Perhaps this, too, differs from people to people.

What does seem clear is that a point has been reached in many societies where large numbers of people cease to obey many of the rules of the culture, where psychological illness and breakdown increase dramatically, where people lose hope and become demoralized, where individual selfishness and crime increase, where people dramatically decrease their rate of reproduction. When such symptoms are evident, the security and well-being of the people seems minimal and the demise of the society with its culture appears imminent. Even before that point arrives, however, we may find it possible to raise questions concerning the adequacy of certain of the structures of a given culture to provide for the well-being of those governed by them.

We might, for example, raise such questions about contemporary American society. Though enabling most Americans to survive biologically, the extent of family breakdown, business and political abuse, and moral infection through the media within the society currently is exacting a high psychological and social price. Increasing numbers of our people are in deep difficulty. Society would seem to be failing to meet the well-being criterion.

Interestingly enough, it looks as though the "God's-intent criterion" would lead to a questioning of all of the same things raised by the application of the human well-being criterion. This fact follows from our Christian assumption that God is positively disposed toward people and wants the very best for us. This criterion would, for example, employ the Ten Commandments as one of its basic statements. Six of those apply to horizontal human relationships and, if followed, lead to human and social well-being in the areas dealt with.

I would see the God's-intent criterion as also supporting the broader well formedness of cultural structures, without which things fall apart for human beings. I assume that it is God who put within humans both the capacity to create and change culture and the necessity to live within it, so I judge it to be God's intent that culture-bound life provide a maximum of human well-being.

The ultimate revelation of God's intent is, I believe, found in statements such as that recorded in Matthew 22:37–40 (also Mk 12:30, 31; Lk 10:27; Lv 19:18; Dt 6:5) concerning loving God supremely and neighbor as self. The more specific rendering of the Ten Commandments (Ex 20:3–17) and Jesus' reinterpretations of the murder (Mt 5:21, 22) and adultery (Mt 5:27, 28) commandments are other examples. Cultural structures may, I believe, be judged according to how well they permit and encourage such ideals.

We also see in Scripture, however, another very important aspect of God's intent with regard to cultural life—His patience with subideal customs. He shows great patience with Hebrew henotheism, for example, where for generations after the Hebrews committed themselves to the true God, they continued to believe that many other gods existed. God did not force them to abandon these gods. He only said, "make Me your chief God." See Exodus 20:3, "Worship no god but me," which allows the continued belief in (though not primary allegiance to) the other gods. Eventually, of course, the Hebrews came to contend that these other gods did not exist at all (2 Kgs 19:17–19; Jer 2:11, 5:7, 16:20), but it took them a while to come to that conclusion. Likewise with polygamy—God accepted the custom, even though He had not ordained it. By New Testament times, however, the custom was virtually dead (though still allowed) in Hebrew society. It did not occur in Greek.

God seems to respect people's involvement in their cultures, even though this involvement entails practices that He does not endorse in any ultimate way. God's principles in this regard seem to be those articulated by Paul in 1 Corinthians 14:40 and 1 Corinthians 9:19–22. In the former text, the standard for Christian behavior is that things be done in a culturally "proper and orderly way." I believe such propriety and orderliness, however defined by any specific society, is both highly valued by God and highly important for the psychological well-being of the participants in a society. The principle in 1 Corinthians 9:19–22 is that of the viability of any culture as a way of life and the usability of any culture for God's purposes.

BIBLICAL SOCIOCULTURAL ADEQUACY

Though conservative Protestant Christianity has ordinarily shied away from acceptance of anything labeled "cultural relativism," it has done so in ignorance. The Bible seems quite clear on this point when looked at from a cross-cultural perspective (which, since the Bible is a cross-cultural book, is the only appropriate way to interpret it). But when a monocultural perspective is combined with a lack of understanding of what is meant by cultural relativism and a confusion between cultural relativism and ethical relativism, such a mistake is predictable.

We have not yet dealt with the confusion between cultural and ethical relativism. Ethical relativism is the irresponsible position taken by those within a given society who, because they know that a given custom is practiced in some other society, insist that it is allowable for them to practice it. This is directly contrary to the doctrine of sociocultural adequacy (relativism), which requires that the mandates of each culture, whether one's own or another, be taken seriously. Ethical relativism is disallowed by the doctrine of sociocultural adequacy, which sees customs as valid only within their own systems (*see* Kraft 1979a:124–8 and Mayers 1974 for more on this subject).

Here we contend, following Nida (1954:48–52), that God endorses a "biblical cultural relativity" principle. This is, however, a relative (not an absolute) relativism. Only God Himself is absolute. All else, including cultures, is relative in the sense that it derives from and relates to Him as the absolute.

God treats people in their cultural contexts in terms of this relativism. That is, He does not absolutize one way of life and require everyone to convert to it. Rather, He respects and works within each of the several varieties of culture represented in the Bible. He is not, of course, uncritical of people's cultural behavior. But judgment is according to what people claim (Mt 7:1–5), rather than in terms of their closeness to or distance from some particular cultural patterning. As Nida states, God recognizes "that different cultures have different standards and that these differences . . . [have] different values" (1954:50).

Continuing Nida's discussion, we see that God relates to people in terms of a threefold relativism:

1. First, God takes into account *a relativity in the endowment and opportunities of people*. The parable of the talents (Mt 25:14–30) and of the pounds (Lk 19:12–27) seem to indicate this. Much was expected of the person who had a lot. The one who had only a little was expected to produce a small amount. The expectation related to the kind of endowment and opportunity that they had, not to the absolute amount that they had. According to these passages rewards and judgments are relative to people's endowments. The summary in Luke 12:48 says, "For to whoever much is given, of him shall much be required."

2. Secondly, God takes into account *a relativity in the extent of revelation*. Not all peoples have available to them the same amount of information concerning God. Romans 2:14 says, "When Gentiles who have not the law do by nature the things contained in the law, they, though not having the law, are a law to themselves." People have standards within their cultures that correspond with God's standards. These standards, however imperfectly perceived, will be used by God in His judgments. The Jews, of course, were provided with a clearer vision and will be judged by that standard. Jesus raised even those standards, pointing frequently to distinctions between the former revelation and His own (*see* Mt 5:38–44).

3. Thirdly, He takes into account *a relativity in cultural patterns*. In the Old Testament, the enslaving of Gentiles is accepted (Lv 25:39–46), but this is neither endorsed nor even mentioned in the New Testament. In Numbers 5:11–31, God endorses trial by ordeal for jealousy. This, too, doesn't come up in the New Testament. Polygamy is sanctioned in 2 Samuel 12, but not mentioned in the New Testament. Divorce is simply regulated in the Old Testament (*see* Dt 24:1–4) rather than condemned, even though, as Jesus pointed out (Mk 10:2–12), God never intended that there be any divorce at all.

Paul's approach to different cultures (and subcultures) is God's approach. Paul sought to be all things to all people (1 Cor 9:20–21). He sought to take seriously the customs of whatever people he was among, in order to use those customs as vehicles for communicating the Gospel. In Galatians 2:11–16, Paul even rebukes Peter for not following this sociocultural adequacy principle. Peter was working properly with Gentiles by adapting to Gentile customs. When some Jews came along, however, Peter switched and started acting like a Jew. Paul reprimands him for his inconsistency.

But after speaking so intensely against such accommodation to Hebrew culture, in Jerusalem (Acts 21:17–26) Paul thoroughly identified with Hebrew culture again. He took a vow, shaved his head, and went through the whole purification ritual. He probably made sacrifices as well, accommodating to Jewish expectations. At another time he advised Timothy to get circumcised (Acts 16:3) so he would have a hearing among Jews.

Such biblical relativism may appear to be inconsistency, but it is not. It is simply a realistic "recognition of the different cultural factors which influence standards and actions" (Nida 1954:52). Nida goes on to contrast this biblical position with that of Islam (which, by the way, is very similar to that of most monocultural Protestant conservatives).

> While the Koran attempts to fix for all time the behavior of Muslims, the Bible clearly establishes the principle of relative relativism which permits growth, adaptation, and freedom under the lordship of Jesus Christ. The Bible presents realistically the facts of culture and the plan of God by which He continues to work in the hearts of men, "Till we all come in the unity of the faith and of the knowledge of the Son of God unto a perfect man unto the measure of the stature of the fullness of Christ." *The Christian position is not one of static conformance to dead rules but of dynamic obedience to a living God* (1954:52, emphasis mine).

Those are powerful words. The Christian position does not endorse one culture, one set of rules. In Acts 15 it was decided that Gentile Christians did not have to become Jews in order to be Christians. But as different groups have come to power within Christianity, the typical attitude of the group in power has been to require converts to convert both spiritually and culturally. So it was when Roman Catholicism dominated Europe. People had to convert to the Roman Catholic perpetuation of certain aspects of Latin culture until Luther and the other reformers fought the same battle against the domination of Christianity by the Romanizers as Paul had fought against the domination of the Judaizers. Likewise when the Wesleys and others broke from the domination of Anglicanism in England. Likewise with nearly every denominational split.

There can only be one absolute—God. All else is relative to Him, since it is created, finite, and limited. Therefore, "Biblical relativism is an obligatory feature of our incarnational religion, for without it we would either absolutize human institutions or relativize God" (Nida 1954:282). The tendency of a monocultural position is to absolutize the customs of one culture (or subculture). The tendency of non-Christian anthropologists is to relativize God. We certainly do not want to go to the non-Christian extreme of relativizing God. But we also do not want to go to the extreme of those who in God's name absolutize their own culture or subculture. We want a cross-cultural perspective that sees the value of every people's culture to themselves and the usefulness of that culture in the communication of the Gospel.

MY ATTITUDE TOWARD AMERICAN CULTURE

One important area that needs to be brought to the surface when we talk about a cross-cultural perspective is how all of this applies to our view of our own society and culture. The reader has noticed that I often make disparaging remarks about American culture. I have a right to be critical, because this is my culture.

Indeed, I consider it my responsibility under God to use my expertise in cultural matters to evaluate and critique my own way of life. Perhaps thereby I can have some influence on the bettering of some of our customs, or at least make a contribution toward a more knowledgeable use of our customs by other Americans. I can also, perhaps, help outsiders who might be in danger of regarding some of our customs too highly to see some of the problems with these customs.

Note, however, that I take a much more tentative and charitable attitude toward other people's customs. It is the right and responsibility of those who own those customs to critique them. As an outsider, I have no such right (though I may have questions and opinions) unless invited by insiders to express myself. It is important that missionaries and other cross-cultural witnesses recognize that though they have the right and responsibility to speak as prophets when in their home culture, they have no such right when they serve as witnesses (Acts 1:8) and ambassadors (2 Cor 5:20) in someone else's culture.

In what follows I seek to state my reasons for being tough on American culture. There are at least five.

1. First, *I believe all of us should take a different attitude toward the society and culture of which we are a part than we take toward those of other people*. With respect to other cultures, we must do all in our power to understand them. Then, whether or not we like what we understand of them, we should be very charitable (loving) toward both the people and their customs. Their culture is their way of life, not ours, and they have rights with respect to it that we simply do not have. We are guests when we enter their frame of reference and should never forget it.

On the other hand, the culture of which we are a part is ours. Though the guests we invite in need to be respectful and charitable toward our way of life, we need to be constantly evaluating it, to see if it is meeting the needs it is supposed to meet. Our culture belongs to us, on the one hand, and strongly influences us, on the other. If those influences are not for the best we need to rework our possession (our culture) to see if it cannot serve us better. We are insiders in our own culture and (as we will see in chapter 24) it is only insiders who can make changes in a culture. If there are things wrong with a culture, it is the responsibility of the insiders to do something about it. If they don't, no one will.

You non-Americans, however, do not have the same right that I have to criticize American society and culture. Though I want you to understand some of the problem areas in my society, I don't want you to make the mistake many of us have made of becoming overcritical of someone else's way of life. What I'd like you to learn from my approach is not that you should critique my society and culture, but that you should take a similarly critical attitude toward your own. Yours is the culture you must take responsibility for.

2. A second thing is perhaps not so much a criticism as it seems, though it often comes up when I am critiquing American or western culture. *Western cultures, especially the American variety, show the greatest quantity and quality of differences from the majority of the other cultures of the world*. When we compare societies, we find that if any group differs markedly from what would be considered normal for most of the rest of them, it is those societies called "western." In fact, western societies (and especially American) often seem to be far out on a limb, taking positions and advocating customs that are very, very different from those of the majority of the other peoples of the world.

One interesting (and frequently disturbing) aspect of this fact is that, since our way of life is so different, we who have been conditioned by western ways usually have a very difficult time learning to identify with the more "normal" ways of life of other peoples. This makes for real problems since, due to our financial and other resources, we have been the most able of all the peoples of the world to send out missionaries. It means that, although we can get them out there, they usually have a much more difficult time adjusting and ministering than would the members of societies more similar to the receiving ones.

3. Third, *I fully believe American society to be sick.* I believe this fact is directly responsible for the tremendous amount of psychological illness in this country. I believe culture is the creation of God. It is His will that there be culture. But a people's culture is supposed to do certain things for that people, such as providing security, support, and all the other underpinnings that people need in order to function properly. When the culture no longer provides the kind of security, support, and guidance that its people need to function properly, it may legitimately be referred to as sick. I believe we have gotten off balance in many areas, due at least in part to certain wrong choices that have been made. Whether we will recover or not is anyone's guess. The least we can do, though, is to warn others not to imitate us.

People are amazingly resilient. It may be that the American people, who have been so creative technologically, will straighten themselves out socioculturally. It's possible that even though we have moved some distance toward destruction, we may be able to bounce back, reformulate our values, and survive (as Wallace 1956 has demonstrated for other societies). At the moment, though, I am not optimistic about that. I fully expect our future to parallel the history of great societies in the past. That is, I expect the process of internal self-destruction we see taking place in America to continue for awhile longer and to be followed by conquest from outside.

4. Fourthly, *American and other western societies are highly visible, very wealthy and very powerful.* If indeed we are sick, the peoples of other societies need to understand that any time they get near us, they risk contracting our illness. One of the last things that should be done is to imitate a sick approach to life. This is why I am anxious that some of these things be made explicit. Furthermore, we as Americans need to understand what our society and culture look like in comparison to those of the rest of the peoples of the world. We need to understand this in order to give us a fair chance of fighting our own ethnocentrism. We who have been brought up in this society are often ignorant of other approaches to life and are likely to simply assume that our way is not only the right way culturally, but God's way as well.

I had missionary colleagues who were trying to introduce the Christian form of funeral, the Christian form of wedding. What they sought to impose on the Nigerians as the Christian wedding ceremony or the Christian form of funeral, however, looked strangely American. I believe these cross-cultural witnesses were captured by their culture because they didn't know God's ways very well. My hope is that the next generation of western witnesses will be more knowledgeable.

Nonwesterners need to understand our western cultures and learn to protect themselves better from their enticements. Nonwestern Christians also need to come to understand the involvement of us Americans in this culture. Very often the high respect in which we are held leads nonwesterners to assume that we are more in control of such things than we really are.

Very often when internationals begin to see the difference between western customs and Christianity, they remark, "That's why you Americans do such and such! It's because of your culture. We thought that was Christian!" A Christian American acts according to American culture, and many of us do the very best we can to be Christian in this kind of culture. But that does not mean that nonwestern Christians need to act the same way. There may be better patterns, more constructive patterns, patterns that more effectively express and exhibit Christianity in your culture than our patterns.

5. A fifth thing in my mind as I critique American culture is *the desire to combat the high prestige of western ways of life*, especially in the minds of nonwesterners. I would like us all to recognize that we in the West are in a prominent position in the world not because of cultural superiority but because of gunpowder. It is our technology, primarily our implements of war, that have given us prominence. If there ever was an anti-Christian reason for being in power, we have developed it and exploited it. Daily in the papers we find reports that we in the so-called "Christian West" are supplying the whole world with arms. Our businesspeople are so much more interested in money than in doing good that they are willing to sell arms to anybody willing to pay the price. Sometimes our government restricts these things and sometimes it doesn't. We not only make war ourselves, we encourage others in their war making, and often their reasons for making war are even worse than ours.

Is this a society worthy of the high prestige we are granted? I would like us to recognize that this high prestige proves little or nothing concerning our supposed cultural superiority. We do have superior technology, but we have often used that very badly. Those of us who are insiders need to beware, lest we naively assume that we are a superior society. I would like us to know that there is a difference between the power we have and the quality of our culture. Internationals especially are often misled into assuming that there is a direct relationship between the quality of western society and the power it wields in the world. I would like all of us to be warned against assuming any necessary connection between the prestige of our culture and its quality.

With specific regard to biblical Christianity, western perspectives have crippled us when it comes to understanding and dealing with the spirit world. While our theologians and biblical scholars have devoted incredible energy and talent to the study of biblical and Christian things, due to worldview blindness, they have largely missed this facet that is so prominent in Scripture. While we can be very thankful for what western biblical scholarship has achieved, we need to be warned against considering western views of Scripture as complete.

These are five reasons for my criticisms. There may be other valid reasons as well. Perhaps these will suffice to help you understand why I come down so hard on western societies and their cultural structures.

CHAPTER 6

GOD, CULTURE, AND HUMAN BEINGS

INTEGRATIONAL THOUGHT

In Genesis 1:26, 27 we read: "Then God said, 'And now we will make human beings; they will be like us and resemble us. They will have power over the fish, the birds, and all animals, domestic and wild, large and small.' So God created human beings, making them to be like himself."

Just what it means to be "like" or in the "image" of God has been discussed endlessly by students of the Bible, and I doubt that I can solve all problems here. One subject that keeps coming up in such discussions, however, is the possibility that human creativity is a manifestation of the image of God in us. I tend to agree.

In fact, I believe God likes creativity and diversity. I also believe it is human creativity that is ultimately responsible for the vast number and diversity of human cultures and languages in the world today. People are so constituted that they will not go very long before they create a new way of doing things. The creation and practice of increasing numbers of new ways by one subgrouping of people given enough time, leads inevitably to their breaking away from the rest and forming a new society of their own. As long as such breaking away is not done angrily, it can have God's blessing, as was the case when Abraham and Lot separated (Gn 13:1–13).

Such a high percentage of human behavior seems to be governed by habit and to follow cultural patterning that many seem to ignore the much more interesting creative behavior that results in new cultural patterns. If 95 percent of human behavior is habitual and only 5 percent creative (consider this a wild estimate!), it is still the 5 percent that is most interesting and, perhaps, most godlike.

Perhaps this is why Jesus and Paul speak out so forcefully in favor of freedom and against bondage. When Jesus announces the theme of His ministry in Luke 4:18, 19, He uses the phrases "proclaim liberty to the captives" and "set free the oppressed." He then speaks in John 8 of the freedom that springs from obedience to the Father (vv. 31, 32), of the power of the Son to set us free, and of the quality of that freedom (v. 36). Paul speaks of freedom from such things as sin (Rom 6:18, 22), cultural constraints (1 Cor 9:19–22), and the Law. He furthermore exhorts us to not "let the world around you squeeze you into its own mold" (Rom 12:2 *JBP*), lest the freedom (and creativity?) we have in a proper relationship to God be squelched. James exhorts us to use our wills to keep free from Satan (4:7).

Though we are pressured by society to conform in various ways, we are not compelled to submit and thus lose our godlikeness. We are creative and intended to live free of such artificial compulsions, both by virtue of creation and because of redemption, the latter providing us with the power to resist even Satan, self, and the "world."

INTRODUCTION

We have already begun to deal with the question of how God relates to culture, and it is appropriate that we have not been able to completely wait to treat such a topic until now. One of the aims of this book is to develop an integrated perspective on these matters. If we are to do this we have to start working on it at the very beginning. It will be helpful here to review and elaborate on the understandings underlying our approach.

The question in focus is, What is the relationship between God, culture, and human beings?

HISTORICAL OVERVIEW

Historically, westerners (like nearly all people) have tended to treat culture the way we treat the air we breathe: we simply assume its existence and ignore it. Those who have taught and written on our relationship with God have usually made little or no overt reference to the cultural waters in which humans exist. Theologians and biblical expositors have rightly described the attributes of God and those of humans and discussed the relationships between the perfect God and sinful humans. This was done, as we would expect, in terms of the cultural and disciplinary perspectives of the scholars who gave themselves to such pursuits.

In the western scholarly world, philosophy was the major academic discipline for hundreds of years. To this day, our doctorates are called "Doctor of Philosophy." Under the umbrella of philosophy, other disciplines developed and split off which are now, with philosophy, referred to as the humanities (theology, history, literature, language). Eventually a larger split took place and the physical sciences (biology, botany, zoology, physics, chemistry, etc.) came into being as separate entities. The physical sciences, with their empirical approach to research became the model for the development of the "people" or behavioral sciences (sociology, psychology, anthropology).

In this process, at least in part as a reaction against theology, scholars turned more and more to the study of the creation and away from the study of the Creator. The concern of the physical sciences was (and is), of course, the material universe. The humanities from a philosophical perspective, and the behavioral sciences, from an empirical perspective, have made human behavior their focus.

Though the medieval attempt of theologians and philosophers to focus on God and His activities may not have been balanced by a corresponding interest in coming to understand the human end of things, the contemporary interest in the latter goes to the opposite extreme. Though God is left out, one can discover a fair number of common interests between the most recent of the disciplines (the behavioral sciences) and the oldest (philosophy and theology). As we attempt to work out a balance between the insights of these two sets of disciplines, we need to start by recognizing their common interests. Note both the common interests and the differences in the answers given to the list of problems in figure 6.1 below.

With respect to ultimate authority, theology (at least conservative theology) looks for it in God, while the behavioral sciences know no authority beyond that of human beings. Ultimate truth has been primarily a matter of revelation for conservative theology, while the behavioral sciences look for truth in empirical discovery. "Empirical" simply means looking at the universe around us and conducting experiments, largely with the things we can see, touch, or observe.

	Theology	Behavioral Sciences
1. Ultimate Authority	Rests in God	Rests in Humans
2. Final Truth Comes	Via Revelation	Via Empirical Discovery
3. We Are Circumscribed	By God	By Nature, Psychology, Culture
4. Interest	Absolutes in the Universe	Relativities in Human Life
5. Evil Is	In Human Beings	Inherent in Human Systems

Figure 6.1 Common interests and differences between the behavioral sciences and theology

Both sets of disciplines are concerned about limitations, asking, What is the limiting factor? Theologians have seen human beings as limited by God, the all-encompassing REALITY. The physical sciences see the limitations of human being-ness as in nature. Psychology sees human beings as limited by their psychological being. Anthropology talks about culture as the limiter.

Then there's the concern for what in life is absolute and what relative. Theology tends to focus on absolutes, while the behavioral sciences focus on the relativities in human existence.

Regarding evil, the orthodox theological position has always been that evil lies in human beings; we are sinful. Since human beings operate structures, then those structures are seen as sinful as well. The behavioral sciences, however, have ordinarily opted for seeing the evil as in the structures. If we could only straighten up those structures, they say, we would find that human beings are basically good.

WESTERN THEOLOGY—STRENGTHS AND WEAKNESSES

In seeking to develop a perspective that balances the insights of theology with those of the behavioral sciences, we will turn first to theology with a focus on evangelical theology. A person, culture, or academic discipline develops strength in its area of specialization. Conservative theology's specialty is in dealing with the biblical revelation, and it has developed definite strengths in dealing with the Scriptures. Very often, however, the discipline of theology ranges more widely than the biblical revelation, into the experience of people. In that area the results are mixed. We can, however, look to western theology for help in at least two important areas.

1. The first is theology's *focus on God and His works*. Theology is strong when it comes to dealing with such topics as the nature of God. Theological interests include who He is and what He is like, God's creating and sustaining activity, the way God interacts with human beings, how He has revealed Himself, and the like.

2. The second area in which western conservative theology is strong is in its *focus on such things as human beings in relation to God*, on human sinfulness, on human response to God (conversion and faith response), on moral issues, and on other concerns related to the things that human beings have in common, as opposed to the things that differentiate between one group of human beings and

another. The focus has been on how people, no matter who they are or where they are, are similar.

There are undoubtedly other strengths that could be added here, but I want to point to these two as representative.

There are, however, *certain weaknesses* in the approach that theology has taken to the world. One group of weaknesses is what gave rise to the development of the other sciences. Scholars felt that this perspective was too narrow, so they split off into other disciplines that developed other specialties. But these battles have been resolved and need not concern us here.

1. What should concern us is the fact that theological study as we know it is *largely captive to western cultural ways of thinking*. Theology, being western, asks and seeks to answer questions generated within western societies and ignores those not asked by westerners.

2. Worse yet, theology tends to be *quite academic*, so the questions asked and answered tend to be those of a very narrow segment of the members of western societies. This discipline (like all other academic disciplines) involves specialists talking to other specialists about subjects of interest to specialists. Even when these subjects might be of interest to nonspecialists, the language used is often too technical to be readily understood.

3. A third weakness is the tendency for theologians (who are usually academics) to be *more concerned with concepts than with practice*. A major difficulty stemming from this weakness is that pastors trained by such academics tend to teach, whether explicitly or implicitly, that what God requires is proper doctrine. Many in the churches have come to believe that if they believe correctly (that is, have correct theory), God will accept them, even if their behavior does not correspond with their belief.

You don't find that approach in the Scriptures. There was probably no group in Jesus' day that had more correct doctrine than the Pharisees, and yet there was no group that Jesus condemned more forcefully than the Pharisees—not on the basis of their doctrine but because of their behavior. He said to them, "You know this, but you act in a different way." Much of what we do in theologizing is in danger of falling under that same criticism. Not that correct doctrine is wrong—even the doctrine of the Pharisees was mostly right—but that the focus on correct belief needs to be balanced with a strong focus on correct behavior. But behavior is not taught well in classrooms—doctrine is. Because of the classroom orientation of the way we train pastors, we specialize in only part of what needs to be done—those concepts that are easily bought and sold in the classroom. This is a serious weakness.

4. Another weakness is that when dealing with human life, western theology *tends to settle for philosophizing about how life ought to be at the expense of "hands on" study of how life actually is*. The discipline operates in the heady atmosphere of people's ideals, rather than in terms of the realities of everyday living. Without denying the value of this kind of focus on ideals, it is often accurate to accuse theologians of being impractical and not very relevant to real life and its problems as perceived by ordinary people.

5. A fifth weakness is theology's *book orientation*. Along with most academic disciplines (especially the humanities), theology tends to depend almost totally on written accounts and analyses, even when dealing with highly person-oriented problems (e.g., moral behavior, sex roles). Though there is some improvement

lately, the use of the more person-oriented methods of research developed by the behavioral sciences has gone largely unnoticed by most theologians, even when they deal with topics that would be greatly helped by such research methods.

THE BEHAVIORAL SCIENCES—STRENGTHS AND WEAKNESSES

On the behavioral sciences side, there are also strengths and major weaknesses. There are at least four areas in which the behavioral sciences (especially anthropology) are strong that are relevant to us as we seek to develop a balance between theological and anthropological insight.

1. The first of these is the anthropological *focus on what people actually do and think*. Anthropology attempts to focus on the empirical—what is, rather than what ought to be. Such an emphasis can be used to complement the focus of theology and philosophy on what ought to be. This focus on what is leads, among other things, to a concern for ways in which human beings differ, both from each other and from the kinds of generalizations made about humans by westerners. Such a concern (though it may easily be carried too far) can provide a valuable complement and corrective of the concern of theologians for the more general and ideal in human life.

2. A second strength is the development of *the culture concept*. The perspective abroad in the churches (under the influence of theological thinking) focuses on God and human beings as if there were nothing in between. Anthropology provides informed understanding of the cultural "water" in which divine-human interaction takes place. Though anthropologists (like the philosophers, historians, etc. on whom theologians have traditionally depended) tend not to take God seriously, we can use their insights concerning human beings in culture to fill gaps not well handled by scholars who do take God seriously.

The culture concept helps us learn about human beings at the level of human perception. Though theologians have been very concerned with how things look from God's perspective, they have often showed less concern for and less preciseness in dealing with how things look at the level of human perception. The behavioral sciences, however, work almost totally at this level. This is a strength of the behavioral sciences that can be used in the development of a more inclusive perspective.

3. A third strength is that anthropology, especially (and the other behavioral sciences to a lesser extent), *seeks to deal with people as people*, not simply as relatively impersonal subjects for philosophical generalization, historical description, or statistical calculation. For an anthropologist, participant observation, personal interview, and oral biographical narrative are at least as valid research tools as library study of the analyses of other scholars (often dealing with people and problems in contexts quite different from those of the present).

4. The fourth strength is the *development of the cross-cultural perspective*, in which generalizations concerning human beings are made on the basis of experience in many societies, rather than on that of just a few western societies. It is not possible to overestimate the importance of a cross-cultural perspective either in the area of communication or with respect to the understanding and interpretation of the Scriptures. The Scriptures are cross-cultural documents and only yield part of their treasures to those who approach them from a monocultural perspective.

But anthropology and the other behavioral sciences also have weaknesses, and some of them are severe.

1. First of all, the behavioral sciences *tend to be naturalistic, as if there were no God*, or, if God exists, He is not considered very important. For these scholars, a belief in God is irrelevant at best and harmful at worst. Some very snidely turn the Scripture around and say, "Human beings create God in their own image," as if God is a matter of our imagination.

2. The *extreme relativism* that anthropology and the other behavioral sciences often get into is another weakness. When you cut yourselves off from your moorings, your ties to an absolute God, what do you have left? You're into a sea of relativity. Though there are few, if any, who embrace absolute relativism, without God they have nothing solid to stand on when they choose to evaluate. Evaluating cultural behavior is, therefore, something they tend to shy away from, even when they believe it is possible.

3. A third problem is the *emphasis on human diversity*. Often the incorrect impression is given that people of different societies are so different from each other that they really have very little in common. People are often seen as so influenced by their involvement in culture that they are virtually helpless even to understand, much less adapt to, people of other societies. This is, of course, not true (and is often not an impression intended by anthropologists). Anthropological literature is full of evidence that, as Goldschmidt has said, "people are more alike than cultures" (1966:134; *see also* Donald Brown 1991; Kraft 1979a:81–89).

POSSIBILITY OF COMBINING STRENGTHS

Is it possible to combine the strengths of the theological disciplines with the strengths of the behavioral sciences? Many would say no. They feel that the discipline of anthropology is so infected with an anti-God attitude that it is not redeemable. We who are Christian anthropologists, of course, deny this. We don't deny that most anthropologists deny God, but so do most historians in the western context, as do most geographers, linguists, and other western academics. We don't refuse to use their insights, so why should we refrain from using the insights of non-Christians who operate the behavioral sciences?

We must, however, be very careful with and critical of their insights, especially of their underlying assumptions, lest we follow them into assumptions that are counter to our basic principles and commitment to God. With such care, however, I believe we can use these strengths and combine them for our purposes.

This is, however, an enterprise that requires care and humility. For example, though we believe that God is working in and through human cultural structures, we may not mention Him very much. In fact, we may spend so much time focusing on the structures themselves that we actually do forget to discuss the place of the Holy Spirit in it all. We don't mean to do this. We simply assume all of us know that the Holy Spirit is constantly at work. We often do not know how culture works, so we try to fill in our understandings in this area.

Though I may not mention the activity of the Holy Spirit as often as some would like, I really do believe He is operating in everything, whether or not we even notice what He's doing. Our experience has been, however, that the real problem areas lie in what we are doing, not in what He is doing. So we tend to focus more on these areas. Furthermore, it looks as though when we do our job better (in dependence on Him), He is able to do His job better.

For example, in dealing with intercultural communication, we find that when we learn to communicate better, the Holy Spirit is able to work more effectively through us. Though it seems to be true that the Holy Spirit often makes up for our mistakes, it is also true that often He does not. Very often when we make a mistake, the Holy Spirit seems to do nothing about it. We can't always be sure that our sincerity and our prayers will overcome our ignorance.

Since the Holy Spirit is, from our point of view, very unpredictable, we can't simply take the attitude that if we make a mistake, the Holy Spirit will automatically correct it. That doesn't seem to be true in missionary work and Christian work in general. Many of us have made mistakes that the Holy Spirit did not correct. Was it because we weren't spiritual enough? Could be. Or maybe there are some other principles operative here. What are those principles? I hope this doesn't sound sacrilegious, but hopefully by learning more about culture and communication, we can make the Holy Spirit's job easier, so that He has less of our mistakes to correct. This is our real desire. We have no desire either to do away with or to ignore God's part in the ministries to which He calls us.

Trying to avoid that pitfall let us try to combine the strengths of both perspectives to look both at God and at human beings from as informed a point of view as possible. We want to look at God and human beings on the basis both of revelation and of empirical study. In doing this we will seek to take advantage of the strengths of each approach to compensate for the weaknesses of each. Thus, while we seek to utilize the strength that theology provides us in our attempt to understand God, we seek to compensate for its weakness by adopting a cross-cultural perspective in our approach to interpreting the Bible and formulating (or reversing) theological insights. Likewise, while we look to anthropology for insight into humans in culture and the whole area of human perception, we seek to compensate for a weakness of anthropology by assuming the existence, importance, and pervasive activity of God.

Our aim is an informed approach to God, human beings, and the culture within which they interact. We reject either a God-and-human-beings-minus-culture approach or a human-beings-and-culture-minus-God approach. We advocate, rather, a comprehensive approach involving the study of God, culture, and human beings as necessary for any adequate understanding of any of these three elements and their relationships.

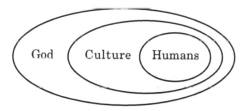

Figure 6.2 God in relation to culture and humans within culture

Read: God, who exists apart from culture, relates to and interacts with human beings in and in terms of the cultural waters within which humans are immersed.

AN INTEGRATED APPROACH

Though we will not go into great detail here concerning the implications of this perspective, the following three examples should help increase our understanding of the kind of approach we are recommending. A more detailed presentation of the approach will be found in my *Christianity in Culture* (1979a).

Example 1: God's Attitude toward Culture

Many have debated this topic. The Christian sociologist H. Richard Niebuhr (1951) has discussed the largely unconscious positions of quite a number of theologians. His was a long step in the direction in which we are heading. We will, therefore, largely incorporate (with modification) his presentation into the broader framework toward which we are moving.

Five basic positions on this issue can be distinguished.

a. Many secularists see God as *the product of culture*. They do not regard God as anything more than the product of human imagination. They observe that the peoples of each society have a different perception of God (or gods) and conclude that the only God/gods there are, are the ones people create. Though this is the position of many anthropologists, we cannot accept it as our own, since it denies a basic tenet of our Christian position. We must, however, accept the very valuable truth that this position points out (though it carries that truth too far)—the recognition that the people of each society see even the true God in slightly different ways.

People do, of course, both create false gods and bow down to evil spirits. The Bible makes this abundantly clear. But the helpful thing is to recognize both the importance of cultural differences at the perceptual level and the fact that recognizing such differences is no threat to our belief in a single God. The true God exists as He is, outside of culture, whether or not He is accurately perceived by those within culture. Accepting this cultural conditioning of perception enables us to explain both the differences in perceptions of God described in Scripture and God's patience with these differences.

b. Many Christians have assumed that God is *against culture*. They point to verses such as 1 John 2:15, "Love not the world, neither the things that are in the world. If any man love the world, the love of the Father is not in him," and assume that what God means by "world" is what we mean by "culture." But that point of view can be challenged, since the same term for world (*kosmos*) is in John 3:16, "God so loved the world." The term is used in two ways—one to designate the people for whom God gave Himself in love, the other apparently to designate a system governed by Satan.

But the opposition to the latter, as well as the communication of the message of God's love, takes place within human culture and language. For this reason, plus the fact that we see in the Bible both God and His people actively using human cultures for His purposes, I assume that whatever world means in passages such as 1 John 2:15, 16, it is something that occurs within culture. It is not all of culture itself. That is, God is opposed to Satan, not to the cultural structures that both God and Satan use to interact with human beings.

The truth of this God against culture position is, of course, in the fact that there is much within culture that Christians need to oppose. But it ignores the fact that there is also much cultural behavior that is approvable by Christians. It is, therefore, a form of overkill to oppose all of culture. Nor is it possible to oppose it all, since culture exists inside as well as outside of us. We must, therefore, use cultural means to do whatever we do—even if this is to oppose part or all of culture. Thus those who have taken this posture and attempted to escape from their cultures (e.g., into monasteries or other forms of Christian segregation) have unwittingly taken their cultures with them and only been able to modify, never to escape from, them.

c. Still others have seen God as *endorsing a culture or subculture*. This has been the position of many missionaries, including the colleague of mine mentioned above who was always looking for the "Christian" way to do things. At one time he was quite exercised to discover "the Christian form of funeral." He believed there is only one Christian way to bury or marry or do any such thing, but whenever he found such a custom, it was always some adaptation of the western way. He believed what we were looking for is a single set of Christian cultural forms that every Christian would be expected to adopt. He didn't believe that American culture is always Christian but seemed to feel that we are pretty close and simply need a bit of shaping up to finish the job.

Many Christians fall into that kind of mentality (especially when we have power over others). They tend to idealize our culture, as if it were a special Christian culture and, often, our nation as if it were a Christian nation. This is the mistake the Hebrews made. They felt that since God was willing to use their culture, He must be endorsing it as the proper way for everyone. Paul, of course, fights such an idea in Acts 15, Galatians, and elsewhere in the New Testament, maintaining that God is willing to use Gentile cultures to reach Gentiles (1 Cor 9:19–22). On that basis, I would claim that God endorses no culture but willingly uses any culture. I would contend (as indicated in chapter 4) that there is no such thing as a "Christian culture," even though Christians are to strive to change their cultural structures in ways that will facilitate rather than hinder the work of God.

d. A fourth position is to see God as *above culture and unconcerned*. Those who take this stance typically assert that God created the universe, got it going, and then virtually left it. Many tribal groups (e.g., many African peoples) believe in God but largely ignore Him, because they feel He is too far away to be concerned about them and their problems.

Likewise, those within western societies called *Deists* sometimes speak of the universe as similar to a clock that God created and wound up. They see it as operating according to natural laws, with no interference by God until such a time as the "clock" runs down and the whole thing is destroyed. Such groups see God's transcendence but not His immanence. Many of the founders of the United States (e.g., Jefferson, Franklin) held to this belief.

e. The view presented here sees God as *above culture and working through it*. We see *culture as a vehicle* usable by God, Satan, or human beings. We see no dichotomy between so-called Christian forms and cultural forms. The forms God uses are cultural forms; none are sacred in and of themselves. What we want is to be able to use cultural forms with Christian meanings. We see God wanting to reach each people group today in terms of their own culture, just as He sought in biblical times to reach Hebrews via Hebrew culture and Greeks via Greek culture. These are the cultures that were available to God in biblical times, so He used them. Each of them could have been called pagan when God first started using them.

If God could use pagan Hebrew or pagan Greek cultures, He can use even pagan American culture or pagan African or Latin American cultures. Was there ever a society more pagan than Greek society? Yet God was able to use even the cultural structures of that society for His purposes. I think the message here is that there is no culture that is unusable. Therefore, conversion happens within culture. The Church happens within culture. Whatever changes happen as a result of Christianity are transformation of the culture from within, especially at the worldview level.

Example 2: Distinguishing between Data and Perspective

The direct (naive) realism perspective that until quite recently underlay most academic study (including theology and, though perhaps to a lesser extent, anthropology) was not very aware of the large part played by the observer's perspective in scientific investigation. In Church circles, it has usually been assumed that the greatest necessities for accuracy in biblical interpretation were sincerity, spirituality, and expertise in such things as the original languages and the history of interpretation. With enough expertise and spirituality it was felt that the original authors' intended meanings could be discovered with a minimum of difficulty. Such interpretation, however, was often skewed by the unconscious influence of cultural assumptions quite different from those of the original authors.

Such expert interpretations were expected to yield a single, authoritative interpretation. Differences in interpretation meant that someone was in error, leading those committed to each position to argue among themselves to support their position as the correct one while contending that all the others are wrong. Though there is truth in this approach, it often did not occur to scholars that, due to cultural differences, all interpretations might be wide of the mark. Interpreters needed to be much more humble about their ability to understand accurately what was written from the perspective of another set of cultural assumptions—assumptions often quite different from ours.

A mediated (critical) realism perspective, however, attempts to take a less dogmatic approach. It sees the probability that at this distance in time and culture, it is quite unlikely that anyone can claim for sure that he or she has discerned the precise intent of the author of a portion of Scripture or of God who inspired it. It also recognizes that equally honest and godly people may arrive at equally plausible though quite different interpretations, especially if they come from different backgrounds.

This view makes a distinction between the reality observed (the data) and the viewpoint from which that data is observed (the perspective). With regard to traditional theology, therefore, we ask such questions as,

- What is the perspective from which this interpretation springs?
- How does that perspective differ from other possible perspectives?
- Might approaching the Scriptures from another perspective be both valid and helpful?

Once we recognize a difference between the data as it is (i.e., as seen by God) and the perspective in terms of which the data is interpreted, such questions become obligatory. This helps us understand that the wide variety of interpretive perspectives yields a wide variety of theologies. See for example figure 6.3 below.

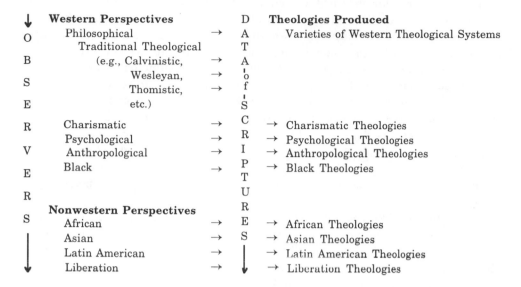

Figure 6.3 Differing perspectives yield differing theologies

There are at least two points to make here. First, the perspective one takes when approaching the data has a great influence on the kind of system one comes out with. Secondly, there is a large number of possible theologies, each with its own strengths and weaknesses. Since they all have to deal with the same data, there will be a great number of similarities between them. In those areas in which the scriptural meaning is most clear, there will be the greatest amount of agreement between the theologies. Theologies will differ most in areas where Scripture is less clear and in areas where the special focus of one perspective differs from that of another perspective.

Example 3: Theologizing from a Cross-Cultural Perspective

In 1973 and in a more detailed way in 1979a, I have proposed that the data of Scripture may be interpreted and systematized just as validly from an anthropological as from a philosophical perspective. All theologizing is done for someone as well as by someone. That is, all theology is contextualized. I have contended, therefore, that a shift from a western academic philosophic mode (i.e., by western academics for western academics) to a cross-culturally perceptive mode for analyzing scriptural data would greatly benefit all who seek to deal with the Christian message in nonwestern cultures. Such a shift would also be of great value to monocultural western theologians sincerely interested in pressing beyond the limitations of western cultural perspectives in their attempts to understand a book written entirely in nonwestern thought forms and language.

I have named this approach to theologizing *Christian ethnotheology*. I see it as a discipline that springs naturally from the kind of integration of anthropological insight with Christian belief and commitment that this book is aimed at initiating. The subject matter of Christian ethnotheology is the same as that of traditional theology, but it is approached from a broader, cross-cultural perspective. Thus my *Christianity in Culture* (1979a) deals with topics such as God, human beings, hermeneutics, revelation, the Bible, inspiration, sin, salvation, Church, conversion, theologizing, God's working within culture, Christian witness, and the like.

Here I would like to outline a few of the basic assumptions that underlie that presentation, in order to make our approach more explicit before we turn in the following chapters to more traditionally anthropological subject matter.

a. Assumption 1: *The God of the Bible exists outside of culture* (He is supracultural). He is omnipotent, omniscient, omnipresent, perfect, etc., and the only absolute in the universe (all else is created by and dependent on Him). God is absolute (in contrast to angels, demons, and humans, all of whom are nonabsolute). He and the angels and demons are, however, all supracultural (in contrast to humans, who are cultural). We may, therefore, label God as absolute and supracultural; angels and demons as nonabsolute and supracultural; and humans as nonabsolute and cultural.

b. Assumption 2: *Human beings, though created by God in His image and without sin, now are sinful as well as limited* (by space, time, genetic factors, culture, experience). Though humans do not (presumably cannot) exist outside of culture, they are too creative to leave their cultures unmodified. Humans are thus always creatively interacting with and modifying the cultural structures in which they exist.

c. Assumption 3: *God communicates to humans via human communicational vehicles* such as speaking, dreams and visions, writing (especially the Bible), interpersonal interaction, and the like within human cultural contexts. Though human perception of God Himself and of His communications is always limited and faulty, it is adequate for enabling acceptable understanding of and response to God.

d. Assumption 4: *God seems to ordinarily use cultural structures*, such as language, other vehicles of communication (e.g., interpersonal and mass structurings), rules of groupness (e.g., patterns of Church), rules of economics, rules of politics, religions (and other) ritual in culturally normal ways and without perfecting them. In this way, however, He provides supernatural (not simply natural) and trustworthy leading, including inspiration (e.g., of the Bible) and revelation.

e. Assumption 5: *Since none of the writings of Scripture record events from a western cultural perspective, it is extremely helpful for westerners who seek to probe the intent of the original authors to experience life in contemporary societies similar to those of biblical peoples and the writers of the biblical texts.* Though there is enough "on the surface" of the Bible to enable even uninstructed hearers/readers to understand the rudiments of God's messages, rich treasures lie at a deeper level available only to those with a cross-cultural perspective. These insights are particularly important to those who are called to communicate scriptural messages to those of other societies, since they often elucidate how God works as well as what He seeks to get across.

With this extremely brief sampling of some of our basic assumptions, let's turn to a survey of several areas with which anthropologists have traditionally concerned themselves.

CHAPTER 7

HUMAN BEINGS AND RACE

INTEGRATIONAL THOUGHT

"In the beginning God . . ." (Gn 1:1). This is where it all started. Once this has been said, though, we must quickly admit that what we see concerning how He started things is unclear and even what we think we know about our beginnings is only partial (1 Cor 13:12). We cannot be dogmatic about our understandings. We confidently assert, however, that whatever was done was done by God, for there is no better theory.

This world didn't get here by chance. Some try to tell us it did, but they don't try to explain the presence of automobiles, buildings, and millions of other material objects by contending they got here that way. A university student once took this position as we talked. So I asked her if I could convince her that a bowl on the table we were sitting at got there by chance. She said, "No way!" I replied, "But you're asking me to believe this body got here by chance? I'm afraid I just don't have that much faith in chance. I only have enough faith to believe that if something like that bowl or this body exist, someone made them." She said, "I get your point."

So logic, as well as faith, assures us that someone made what exists. A scientist would not deny that a personal cause lies behind physical objects in any other area of life. Our Christian position that God is the Someone who created the universe is, therefore, at least as logical a theory as any that science has come up with.

But we, like scientists, cannot explain all the details, and we need to admit this. The problem of many Christians dealing with this topic is that they often claim to know too much, but we, as well as the scientists, see indistinctly (1 Cor 13:12). The author of Proverbs warns us, "Never rely on what you think you know" (Prv 3:5 *GNB*). This is a good warning to heed in this area.

I will confidently assert, therefore, that God did whatever was done. I will also seek to look at some of the theories concerning how He did what He did. But I will assert further that we do not know for certain how to resolve many of the issues raised in this chapter. At this point, God alone knows, and He's not explaining.

So let's not claim to know as God knows. It is no credit to Him in this area or in any other for His people to claim to know too much. In fact, I believe we are a considerable embarrassment to Him when we claim to see as He alone sees and to know as He alone knows. Such claims may even border on idolatry. They are certainly a poor testimony to those around us.

So we assert, "In the beginning God . . . ," and recognize that the rest of our discussion is theorizing. Hopefully, our speculations will be helpful as we attempt to understand what God has not revealed to us, but let's not attribute too much authority to human speculations, even those done by Christians. By all means, let's refuse to break fellowship with other sincere Christians who prefer a theory other than the one we prefer, for we are called above all else to love each other, whether or not we agree (1 Cor 13).

INTRODUCTION

Though our primary focus is to be on cultural anthropology, there are a certain number of questions related to physical anthropology and prehistory that cross-cultural witnesses should be able to deal with. The two most obvious of these concern the fossil record and race. Though as evangelical Christians we have no doubt that humans are here because God created us, we need to deal with the fossil record, especially since it is so often used to suggest that creationism is untrue.

The subject of racial differences is another area treated by anthropologists in which it is better for cross-cultural witnesses to be informed than to be ignorant. We are often asked whether people of different races differ in intelligence. Any differences would have important implications for what is to be expected of those peoples with lesser intelligence.

The area called "prehistory" deals with questions concerning cultural evolution. Have the societies of today evolved from more "primitive" societies? Are some of today's societies the "ossification" of more primitive forms of societies like our own? The anthropological subfield of archaeology is particularly concerned with discovering answers to such questions.

BELIEVING IS SEEING

In matters of ultimate faith, what one believes is crucial. As we have seen, the worldview of a society serves an explanatory function. Thus, when dealing with understandings of events long lost in history, such as the beginnings of the human race, people tend to simply trust their worldview assumptions. Such trust or belief provides the basis for explanations concerning beginnings.

As biblical Christians, we point to the accounts of creation in the Scriptures as the foundation for our faith that the universe and its inhabitants got here through Divine activity. But interpretations of Scripture differ, even among those thoroughly committed to Jesus Christ.

Scientists, too, have their faiths (called theories). Those committed to biblical Christianity usually share with Christian nonscientists the faith that it was God who brought the universe and its contents into being. Those who are not committed to biblical Christianity often share with a large number of non-Christians a kind of agnosticism concerning the ultimate origin of things. That is, they have given up on attempting to understand how things began and concentrate on the scientific concern to explain what has happened and continues to happen now that the universe and its contents are in existence.

In any discussion of these issues, it is important to keep clearly in mind just what is being discussed. Many such discussions have generated more heat than light, simply because the participants were not really on the same topic.

1. One topic frequently in focus is that of *ultimate origins*. If this is the topic, we need to be aware that creationists (by faith) have committed themselves to the belief that God created the universe and at least its original contents. Scientists have not necessarily committed themselves one way or another on that issue,

since it is generally conceded that science cannot prove or disprove how things originally got here.

Scientists do, however, often have their own faith statement (theory) to make concerning ultimate origins. This faith statement is often that there is no God. When they make such a statement, it needs to be recognized that what they have said is a statement of faith, not of scientifically provable fact. It is parallel to the faith statement that we Christians make concerning the existence of God. So, if the discussion is to be on the same level, it needs to be about the comparative merits of opposing beliefs concerning the existence of God, not (as the discussants may desire) on the comparative merits of creation versus evolution.

2. If *creation versus evolution* is to be discussed, it needs to be noted that there are two topics at issue: (a) How did things get started? and (b) What has happened since things got started? A simple statement that God created the universe should not bother evolutionists if they are only interested in what their scientific investigations have uncovered, since their investigations deal only with the second of the above questions. Nor should statements concerning the fossil record upset creationists, unless they are extending their faith concerning creation into areas not specifically dealt with in the Bible.

Unfortunately, many members of both camps regularly trespass on the territory of the other, often without realizing it. That is, scientists who believe in evolution often make statements that imply that things started totally by chance. Such statements fall outside of what their sciences can legitimately be expected to provide, since science is only a tool for examining what is, not for explaining how things got to be here in the beginning. Such statements are a part of worldview belief. They are an interpretation based not on science but on faith.

Creationists often make poorly informed statements concerning what has happened since the creation. They often have very little knowledge of what science has come up with, and often react more to the faith statements of scientists than to their discoveries. Such reactions, unfortunately, often become the basis on which scientists ridicule creationism.

In all such discussions, it is important that we compare faith (theory) with faith (theory) and data with data. For example, all statements concerning the origination of the world and its contents are faith statements. On the other hand, there are quite a number of fossils and other geological data. Though these can be interpreted differently (that is, on the basis of different faiths), creationists cannot deny their existence and the need to interpret them.

THE PERSPECTIVE

Our perspective starts with the recognition that we have two theories of origins: 1) creation by God and 2) chance. From that point on, we have data. This data comes largely from science, though there are occasional references in Scripture that are pointed to by some as data. The primary thing we get from Scripture is, however, our perspective on whatever data is presented. As to origins, it is clear that we opt for the creation by God theory rather than the coming into existence by chance theory—especially since it takes less faith to believe in God as creator than to believe that chance brought about the existence of this universe.

How the data of science is to be interpreted, however, is another matter, and Christians are often deeply divided on the issue. Some seem to believe that since most of those digging out the data are not Christians, we should not accept their findings. But we do not reject the findings of non-Christian historians, medical researchers, physicists, engineers, and the like on this basis. Instead, we take what they discover as from God and to be used for God. We simply don't ask whether or not it was a Christian who discovered this medicine or developed the principles that enable this airplane to fly or came across this historical or physical fact or principle. In keeping with that approach, many of us find it exciting that God has given scientists the tools to discover at least some insight into how He has guided things since the creation.

We start, therefore, with the faith that whatever happened is the result of God's working, and attempt to interpret all of the data from that perspective. Whatever the biases of those who ferret out the data we insist on interpreting it from a perspective that sees God at the very beginning as creator and now as sustainer and director.

We assert, furthermore, that human beings carry the "image of God." We are not certain we know all that this means or how badly this image was damaged by the Fall, but we suspect that scientific discoveries concerning humans are likely to teach us something about this image.

We know that all data is interpreted. Both biblical and scientific data are capable of being accurately or inaccurately interpreted, with no assurance often of which is which. Thus, whatever conclusions the following presentation may lead us to must be considered quite tentative. We know, furthermore, that sincere, dedicated Christians do not always see eye to eye on many of these issues. Our ability to maintain our commitments to each other as brothers and sisters in Christ should not be hindered by differences in understanding or opinion in this area. Two excellent recent books presenting an informed Christian perspective are Phillip E. Johnson, *Darwin on Trial* (1993) and Buell and Hearn, *Darwinism: Science or Philosophy?* (1994).

THE FOSSIL RECORD

An impressive amount of data has been gathered concerning prehistoric humans. We will not attempt to go into that data in detail. Some of the books in the bibliography can be referred to by those who wish to go into the matter further (e.g., Campbell 1974, Jolley and Plog 1976). Suffice it to quote a summary of current thinking from a 1984 publication of the American Anthropological Association. Note the mixture of data with interpretation. Though we are not compelled to agree with the interpretations, we must recognize the existence of the data.

We have seen that humans are members of the Order Primates, along with apes, monkeys, and prosimians. Our last common ancestor with chimpanzee and gorilla lived about 8–10 million years ago. Between 4 and 2 million, early humans known as *Australopithecus* lived in Africa, walked upright on two legs, had brains larger than those of apes of equal body size and ate mainly plant food. The first members of our own biological genus *Homo* appeared in Africa before two million years ago, differing from *Australopithecus* in having a larger brain and more modern walking ability, as well as by making stone tools that allowed them to prepare vegetable foods and cut up mainly scavenged meat. These *H. habilis* people were succeeded by *H. erectus*, who lived between 1.75 and 0.25 million years ago, had still larger brains, tamed fire, hunted large game animals, and spread throughout much of tropical and temperate Africa and

Eurasia. By half a million years ago, the earliest member of our own species, *H. sapiens*, appeared and spread outward from Europe and Africa, replacing the last *H. erectus*. In Europe and western Asia, these early *H. sapiens* people evolved into the Neanderthals, while an African variety may have evolved into the earliest fully modern people like ourselves. By 90,000 years ago, early Africans were living in the southern part of the continent, and moderns appeared in Eurasia somewhat later, finally replacing (and probably mixing with) Neanderthals. Asian peoples continued to spread outward as populations increased, reaching both Australia and the Americas. In the geologically short time since then, *Homo sapiens* has taken advantage of cultural rather than biological means to conquer all the climatic regions of the world and begin the exploration of the universe (Delson 1984).

Though this brief presentation of informed opinion does not detail the data on which these opinions are based, it is important that we recognize that we have to take seriously at least the following facts:

1. There are *a large number of fossils*, many of which are clearly human, some of which are clearly simian (apes), and some of which appear to be intermediate. Though scientists who are committed to an evolutionary perspective have themselves disproven the validity of some of these fossils (e.g., Piltdown Man), the vast majority of them will not go away.

2. There is *quite a range of variation in these fossils*. As mentioned in the above quote, those considered closer to the present show larger brain capacity and more upright posture. How much this range of variation proves concerning evolutionary development is not always clear, however, since at least the more recent fossils often differ no more from each other than contemporary peoples.

3. The sophisticated dating methods used for determining the age of these fossils indicate both the *great antiquity of the earth and the great antiquity of humans on the earth*. The dating estimates are, however, based on the assumption that decay in the past took place at the same speed as it does today. This assumption could well be wrong. That is, decay could have proceeded faster or slower in the past than it does today. If so, the dates given could be greatly or slightly off. Even if they are inaccurate, though, it seems quite unlikely that they would be so far off that any of the "young earth" theories advanced by certain creationists would be supported.

4. *The physical structuring of human beings is remarkably close to that of the "higher" mammals*. Indeed, "All the methods show that the African apes and human beings are far closer genetically than anyone had imagined. Human and ape differ no more than many animals that have always been regarded as very similar—horse and zebra, for example" (Washburn, n.d.).

Since physical "evolutionary" changes have certainly taken place in such mammals, it is to be expected that similar changes may have taken place in humans. For example, the horse was once about eighteen inches tall, with five toes and teeth appropriate for tearing, but has changed a lot over the years. It could be expected that as much change may have taken place in humans (*see* Beals and Hoijer 1977:141–2).

5. *In spite of such changes, there seem to be certain limits*. The major limit is that change within species ("micro-evolution") is much easier to prove than change between species ("macro-evolution"). As Beals and Hoijer put it:

Speaking of biological inheritance, it is a commonsense observation that like produces like. Cats give birth to cats, and birds produce birds.... Each living organism is unique.... Cats resemble other cats more closely than they resemble any other living thing.... This fact of variation within limits is inherent in the basic processes of sexual reproduction.... The important point here is the fact of continuous variability within species (1977:138).

6. A major difference between animals and humans lies in the area of a specialized versus a generalized adaptation to the environment. "Generalized species are more capable of surviving environmental changes than are specialized species, but specialized species are usually more capable of surviving in unchanging environments" (Beals and Hoijer 1977:139). Though many animals tend to be quite specialized, humans are more generalized physically, depending on culture (which is not characteristic of animals) to enable them to adapt to the wide variety of environments they occupy. An interesting comment by Beals and Hoijer on this difference in relation to evolutionary theory lends support to our Christian contention that the differences between humans and other primates are more significant than the similarities:

> The primate brain, most particularly the human brain, is large and complex but it tends to be used for generalized rather than specialized adaptations. The fossil record suggests that the general trend of evolution has been from very simple and generalized forms in the oldest geological periods towards more complex and specialized forms in recent times.... Human beings are presumably an exception to this tendency, for although they are complex, they are generalized (Beals and Hoijer 1977:140).

7. One further fact that needs to be reckoned with is that the early chapters of Genesis are written in a highly creative, often poetic, "largely symbolic, pictorial" (LaSor, et al. 1982:74) literary style. This does not mean that what is recorded there cannot be taken as literal fact. Factual events can very easily be recorded in poetic or dramatic style. Job and Jonah are two other biblical examples of writings cast in dramatic style. In spite of the kind of literature employed, most evangelicals would contend that the events recorded in Job and Jonah actually happened.

The fact that these early chapters of Genesis are written in such a style gives legitimacy to a variety of interpretations. Whether or not one interprets them as an account of literal fact should not be made a test of orthodoxy. It is one's assumptions concerning how God administered those early events that result in either a literal or a nonliteral interpretation. The simple fact that needs to be stated is that these materials are not, like those from Genesis 12 on, written in a straightforward historical style. Allowance must be made for those who interpret them as presenting truth without attempting to be totally factual.

IMPLICATIONS

What are we to make of the fossil data? Can we simply dismiss what scientists have found? Or can we develop some combination of their understandings with our own? If we believe in God, we must hold that whatever happened was superintended by God. But must we believe that He brought everything into existence immediately? If so, is the whole fossil record simply put there by God to fool us? Or does Satan have the power to put the fossils there?

Some Christians try to ignore the fossil record or consider it a plot by non-Christians against Christians. But the number and variety of fossils are too great for us to simply write the whole matter off as a plot by non-Christians to discredit creationism. Indeed, many non-Christian scientists share the view articulated by one of the "leading authorities on the evolution of humanity," S. L. Washburn, chosen by the American Anthropological Association to articulate their view of the subject.

> Everyone accepts the end products of the process of evolution, that is all the forms of life as they exist today. Traditionally viewed as the results of creation, it would have been irreligious to deny their existence. But creation was not limited to the external forms; the processes of life were also created. The processes are as real as their products, and it is an odd twist of human thought to believe that it is religious to accept the products of evolution but not the process that created them. The processes are far more remarkable and complex than anything our ancestors could have conceived.
>
> The study of evolution is only one small part of the attempt to understand the nature of the universe. Each decade brings new understandings of the size and wonder of what was created (n.d.).

If we can combine our belief in God's creatorship as asserted in Genesis with an understanding that the process that scientists seem to have uncovered is God's process, we can, I think, live quite well with the implications of the fossil finds. Whether or not we feel these positions can be combined, we can choose one or another position (or a combination of them) such as the following:

1. A kind of agnosticism on the issue that simply contends that God did whatever has been done but we're not sure how

2. That God did all of the creating by immediate fiat, whether or not in twenty-four-hour days, putting the whole fossil record into the creation at the same time

3. That God created everything in literal twenty-four-hour days, but that there were long periods of time between the days during which evolutionary developments took place

4. That God created then destroyed through the flood after perhaps 2,000 years and the flood was responsible for the fossils

5. That God brought all of the creation except humans into existence through some sort of evolutionary process but stepped in at a certain time to do something special when He brought humans into existence

6. That God stepped in at many points along the way to bring new forms of life into existence; those holding this theory often suggest that each new category represents a new creation of God

7. That God brought all into existence through evolution, including human bodies, but that at a certain time He breathed His image into humans

8. That God produced a good creation, probably with prehistoric animals roaming the earth, as recorded in Genesis 1:1; between Genesis 1:1 and 1:2, however, there was a catastrophe (perhaps occasioned by the fall of Satan) that rendered "the earth formless and desolate" (Gn 1:2) so that the account that follows is that of a new creation of what had been destroyed

9. That though God took a long time to create, He revealed the creation story to Moses in seven twenty-four-hour days.

My own preference is for positions six or eight. If position six is correct, Adam and Eve may well have looked like one of the earlier forms of humanity identified by the physical anthropologists. I am, however, open on this issue (as on many others), since I believe it possible that these earlier forms preceded Adam and Eve. If so, theory number seven might be more accurate.

I am also open with regard to whether the early chapters of Genesis are to be taken literally or not. For cultural reasons, the original hearers and writer(s) would not have held our western expectations concerning how the facts are to relate to the account. We should not, therefore, simply apply our scientific expectations to those texts unless there is some evidence from the sociocultural context in which they were produced that such standards are valid. Western societies differ from most of the peoples of the world in assuming that to be true, something must be scientifically factual.

It is characteristic of poetic literature that truth is presented figuratively or by analogy in such a way that the broad outline, though perhaps not each specific detail, is factually accurate. Speakers and writers of poetry, even in our society, carefully protect the truth of the crucial points in the account but feel free to elaborate on (or contextualize) the details. What we do not fully know about the early Genesis accounts is which of the truths are presented factually and which (if any) may be presented figuratively.

As westerners, we have been carefully taught to identify truth with fact and to regard nonfact as nontruth. Yet even we have no difficulty with statements such as "The Lord is my Shepherd" (Ps 23:1). This statement presents an important truth—that the Lord cares for us as a good shepherd cares for his sheep. But it is stated as if it were a literal fact that the Lord is a sheepherder and I am one of His sheep. We understand, however, that Psalm 23 is in poetic form, so we don't get upset over the nonfactual statement of a truth.

Nor do we get upset when Jesus presents important truths in His parables, though it is shocking to realize that the Good Samaritan and the Prodigal Son were probably not real people (though they could have been). We understand that parables are an effective way to teach truth. The first eleven chapters of Genesis are in poetic, parabolic form.

For example, the Hebrew term *Adam* means "of the ground." And *Eve* means "life giver." Are these terms intended to be the names of actual persons, or are they intended as symbols? That is, is the account simply presenting the truth that God started things with a single pair of humans, or is the account to be taken as literal fact? The original hearers probably would have taken it as truth (perhaps as a parable) but not necessarily as fact. It may, however, well be fact (in the scientific sense) as well. A problem such as this should not simply be swept under the rug and ignored. But since the answer is no more clear than this, we should not deny committed Christians the right to come up with differing opinions.

Again, is the story of Cain and Abel to be taken as literal fact or as parable? Anthropologically, it would seem unlikely that two members of the same biological family would practice such divergent economies—agriculture and herding. It is possible that at the start of the world, God would set things up that way, but ordinarily, any given family (and the larger society to which it belongs) is committed to one or the other of these economies. Anthropological insight would tend to bias even Christians in the direction of regarding the account as more symbolic than factual. Suspicion that the story is not to be regarded as factual is further engendered when we note that the Hebrews who wrote and passed on the story were herders who would automatically be biased toward the herder in the story, Abel, rather than toward the agriculturalist, Cain. Neither of these considerations force us to deny the factuality of the Cain and Abel story, but they do raise questions that have to be considered.

Questions can also be raised concerning the necessity of interpreting literally many of the other stories in those first eleven chapters of Genesis. I find helpful the position articulated by LaSor, et al.(1982:74, 75):

> Recognizing the literary technique and form and noting the literary background of chs. 1–11 does not constitute a challenge to the reality, the "eventness," of the facts portrayed. One need not regard this account as myth; however, *it is not "history" in the modern sense of eyewitness, objective reporting.* Rather, it conveys theological truths about events, *portrayed in a largely symbolic, pictorial literary genre.* This is not to say that Gen. 1–11 conveys historical falsehood. That conclusion would follow only if it purported to contain objective descriptions. The clear evidence . . . shows that such was not the intent. *On the other hand, the view that the truths taught in these chapters have no objective basis is mistaken.* They affirm fundamental truths: creation of all things by God; special divine intervention in the production of the first man and woman; unity of the human race; pristine goodness of the created world, including humanity; entrance of sin through the disobedience of the first pair; depravity and rampant sin after the Fall. All these truths are facts, and their certainty implies the reality of the facts. . . .
>
> How then, finally, is the unique literary genre of Gen. 1–11 to be understood? One may suppose that the inspired author, informed by God's revelation to Israel of the nature of the world and humanity and the fact of sin which resulted in mankind's alienation from God and one another, was led to true understanding about the nature of beginnings and stated them in contemporary language. Even more, the author marshalled current literary traditions to teach the true theological facts of humanity's primeval history. The author of Gen. 1–11 was not interested in satisfying biological and geological curiosity. Rather, he wanted to tell who and what human beings are by virtue of where they came from: they are of divine origin, made in the image of the Creator, yet marred materially by the sin that so soon disfigured God's good work. (emphasis mine)

Personally, I both accept Genesis 1–11 as true and choose to believe the events actually happened essentially as they are presented (in spite of the literary style). Whether or not they happened exactly as they are presented, it is clear that they were recorded in a way appropriate to the culture and expectations of the original hearers. The Bible is trustworthy because here, as always, its truths are presented appropriately for those to whom it was originally written. Those who demand that God present things in ways appropriate to our requirements (i.e., with scientific accuracy), rather than according to the expectations of the original audience, misunderstand how God does things.

I don't intend to raise doubts about the inspiration or trustworthiness of the first eleven chapters of Genesis (or of any other portion of Scripture). I believe this portion and all the rest is inspired by God and trustworthy, whether or not the events actually happened as they are presented. Our views of inspiration should fit what Scripture is, not set up a mold that Scripture must fit into. So we should have no fear about recognizing these facts about how this portion of Scripture was recorded. It is our cultural conditioning that may mislead us into expecting something else. Because of this, we should hold our own interpretation humbly and have patience with those who interpret the facts we have been presenting differently than we do.

My hope is that this discussion will enable us 1) to look honestly and squarely both at the findings of science and at the literary facts concerning Genesis 1–11 and still hold to the inspiration of the Word of God and 2) to not break fellowship with brothers and sisters in Christ who happen to sift the evidence and come to different conclusions than we do. Our fellowship with and commitment to each other as members of the body of Christ are too valuable to allow them to be broken over nonessentials such as those we are discussing here. We have a real Devil to fight. Let's stop fighting each other.

One organization that does a good job of attempting to integrate evangelical faith with the findings of science in this and many other areas is the American Scientific Affiliation. Their journal, the *Journal of the American Scientific Affiliation*, frequently carries informed and perceptive articles on these topics written by committed Christians who are also experts in one or another of the scientific disciplines on which the scientific community depends for data.

HUMAN PREHISTORY

For the sake of tying our consideration of the fossil record to what we experience with contemporary cultures, the following brief overview of an *anthropological understanding of human prehistory* is offered. This may not seem as relevant as other portions of this book to the tasks of cross-cultural witness, yet there may be some value in recognizing that present-day culture change is not completely without precedent. Indeed, it becomes obvious that many parallels exist between the kinds of culture change that apparently took place in prehistory and those taking place today.

To look at human prehistory, we will have to take seriously the fact that there seems to have been a development in culture. This development is often referred to as the "evolution of culture." Cultural evolution is, however, quite a different thing from biological evolution. For one thing, it is much easier to prove. For another, it is no threat to a Christian view of origins. As will be seen in the chapters on technology, there is much truth in at least certain of the contentions of cultural evolutionism. Note that here, as in the preceding section, the data often can be interpreted in more than one way, and the dating may or may not be accurate.

In the following we will lean heavily on Haviland 1979 and 1982 and Beals and Hoijer 1977. There are many excellent treatments of this subject, but these will suffice to provide the broad outline.

The *beginnings of human culture* are traced back to a period of time called the "Pleistocene" (thought to extend roughly from 3 million to 10,000 years ago). During the early part of this period (before 850,000 years ago) *Homo habilis* developed a crude "all-purpose generalized chopping tool" that enabled them to add "meat to the diet on a regular basis because people could now butcher meat, skin any animal, and split bones for marrow." This "may mark one of the first known times that an animal species made a cultural rather than a physical adaptation to its environment. It appears that . . . [they] lived in very small groups that moved from place to place" (Haviland 1979:150). Hunting required more complicated forms of coordination than the simple gathering of food that is thought to have preceded it. This type of challenge, plus the change in diet, is thought to have stimulated further development of the brain.

Homo erectus fossils dating between 1.5 million and 400,000 years ago show evidence that fire was used "for protection, warmth, and cooking; tool making was well developed; and apparently cannibalism was practiced" (Haviland 1982:146).

With *H. erectus* we find a greater interaction among cultural, physical, and environmental factors than ever before. Social organization and advanced technology developed along with an increase in brain size. The result was that *H. erectus* became a more efficient hunter. With their new ability to modify their environment in advantageous ways, these early hominids expanded into new geographic areas and their populations increased. At various sites in Europe and Africa, a number of fossils have been found which date between about 200,000 and 300,000 years ago, and which show a mixture of traits characteristic of both *H. erectus* and *H. sapiens* (Haviland 1982:146).

Homo sapiens, including Neanderthal Man, who lived from about 100,000 to 35,000 years ago, is the species presently inhabiting the world. Only fossils tell us of the earlier species. According to Haviland,

> The brains of Neanderthals and their contemporaries had reached modern size, although their skulls retained some primitive characteristics. With a larger brain, they were able to utilize culture as a means of environmental adaptation to a far greater extent than any of their predecessors; they were capable of an advanced technology and sophisticated conceptual thought (1982:146).

Much has been made in popular circles of the supposed primitivity of the Neanderthals. The above quote, however, does not support the assumption that they were greatly inferior to today's peoples. Indeed, according to Haviland, they even looked similar enough to contemporaries that "they could probably pass almost unnoticed among living human populations" (1982:138). They continued, like their predecessors, to be basically hunters and gatherers. They did, however, develop a new tradition of tool making involving the "pressure flaking" of certain types of rock.

Modern humans are dated from the emergence of people called "Cro-Magnon" around 35,000 years ago. Crucial to the more recent development of modern cultural characteristics has been the receding of the glaciers.

> By 10,000 B.C., glacial conditions in the world were moderating, causing changes in human habitats. Throughout the world, sea levels were on the rise, ultimately flooding many areas that had been above sea level during periods of glaciation, such as the Bering Straits, parts of the North Sea, and an extensive area that had joined Indonesia to southeast Asia. In northern regions, milder climates brought about marked changes as tundras were replaced by hardwood forests. In the process, the herd animals upon which northern . . . peoples had depended for food, clothing, and shelter disappeared from many areas. Some, like the reindeer, moved to colder climates; others, like the mammoths, died out completely. Thus, the northerners particularly were forced to adapt to new conditions. In the new forests, animals were not as easy to hunt as they had been, and large, cooperative hunts were no longer very productive. However, plant food was more abundant than before, and there were new and abundant sources of fish and other food around lake shores, bays, and rivers. Hence, human populations developed new and ingenious ways to catch and kill animals, while at the same time they devoted more energy to fishing and the collection of wild plant foods (Haviland 1978:195).

The world as we know it was coming into existence. Outside of Europe at this time, the recession of the glaciers allowed "specialized seed gathering leading to incipient agriculture" (Beals and Hoijer 1977:215). These authors continue,

> With the development of agriculture, the distribution of cultures took the basic form that it still has today with expanding regions dedicated to intensive agriculture surrounded by zones occupied by incipient or marginal agriculturalists and by surviving

specialized hunters and collectors or unspecialized hunters and gatherers, nearly all of whom have been influenced by agricultural peoples. Little is known of the details of the transition from seed collecting or other forms of collecting to incipient agriculture or from incipient agriculture to intensive agriculture and animal domestication. In several parts of the Old World a village farming way of life, perhaps independently invented, had developed perhaps as early as 8000 B.C. . . .

In favored spots, such as the lowlands of Mesopotamia, use of the plow and of irrigation led to increasing populations and to the eventual transition from a village way of life to a town and city way of life. This urban revolution was accompanied by the development of the complex economic, political, and religious institutions required for the perpetuation of cities, states, and empires. The urban revolution was accompanied by the development of the wheel, of metallurgy, and ultimately of writing. With the discovery of iron smelting in about 1500 B.C., the urban revolution was essentially complete, and the dominant historical picture became one of the rise and fall of empires. Radical change in a world dominated by peasant farmers and the empires they supported depended upon the discovery of a new source of energy, fossil fuels, and the beginnings of the industrial revolution only a few centuries ago (Beals and Hoijer 1977:215).

In the New World, the process was essentially the same. American Indians seem to have first specialized in hunting, with some of them developing agricultural economies at about the same time this change was going on in Europe. Somewhat later (c. 2500 B.C.) we find settled farming villages in Mexico and Peru, with towns appearing in the same places by around 1000 B.C. By the time of Christ we find cities, especially in Mexico. Due to the lack of domesticated animals in the New World, neither the plow nor the wheel were developed. Nor was steel developed, though other forms of metallurgy were widely employed (Beals and Hoijer 1977:215–16).

According to Haviland (1978:276), the development of cities necessitated at least four basic changes in culture. The first was in agriculture. New farming methods had to be developed, including the possibility—through such techniques as irrigation—of increasing crop yields.

Secondly, it was necessary to develop new specializations to serve the needs of the larger populations.

With specialization came the development of new technologies, leading to the beginnings of extensive trade systems. An outgrowth of technological innovation and increased contact with foreign people through trade was new knowledge; within the early civilizations sciences such as geometry and astronomy were first developed (ibid.).

Thirdly, centralized government became necessary "with authority to deal with the complex problems associated with cities." With the development of writing, ancient law codes, temple records, royal histories, records of governmental transactions, and the like could be kept and passed on. Important kingdoms such as those of the Near East (e.g., Babylon, Assyria) and of the New World (e.g., the Inca, the Maya) emerged.

The fourth concomitant of urbanization was social stratification with resulting differentiation of social classes. Status and privilege appeared, "and individuals were ranked according to the work roles they filled or the position of their families."

Along with these changes came some less desirable things, however. Then, as now, cities required highly organized ways to look after sanitation. In the absence of such, infectious diseases were common. In addition, stress was common due to such things as the density of the populations, the often despotic nature of the governments, the rigid structuring of the class systems, and the constant threat of hostilities from other urban centers. Armies had to be created and maintained and the cities fortified. Thus so-called civilization was born.

RACE

Much has been said, written, and felt on the subject of race, most of it based not on scientifically attested facts concerning biological differences between peoples, but on culturally inculcated evaluations of those differences. One of the primary purposes, then, of a discussion such as the following is to help us realize that there is a good bit less to race than meets the eye. As we will see, any belief in deep-seated racial differences in intelligence or ability has no scientific foundation.

By way of definition, "a race may be defined as a population of a species that differs in the frequency of some gene or genes from other populations of the same species" (Haviland 1982:154). Early anthropologists attempted to subclassify the human species on the basis of geography and physical features such as skin color, hair texture, head shape, nose shape, body type, and the like. At a later date, rigorous classification was attempted on the basis of blood types. The problem was that all such attempts kept coming up with "individuals who did not fit the categories, such as light-skinned Africans or dark-skinned 'Caucasoids'" (Haviland 1982:153). At first, these were regarded as hybrids, mixtures, or even mutants. But before long it became obvious that such explanations would not do. For

> no examples of "pure" racial types could be found. These categories turned out to be neither definitive nor particularly helpful. The visible traits were found to occur not in abrupt shifts from population to population, but in a continuum that changed gradually, with few sharp breaks, from Africa to Norway. There were many variations within each group; the in-group variation was often greater than the variations between groups (ibid.).

To start our discussion, let us relate the subject of race to the subject of culture history dealt with above. *If one race were superior to another, we could expect a consistent correlation between cultural and racial superiority.* What we see, though, indicates that "all races are equally capable of cultural development and that culture operates independently of racial heredity" (Hoebel 1972:240). Hoebel suggests that three underlying principles combine to lead us to this conclusion.

> (1) Although all cultures are fundamentally similar in their nuclear cores, the range of cultural variability as manifested by human societies is truly remarkable. Limits to the range of culture are imposed by the physical nature of man. These limits are so basic and so generalized, however, that they are common to all races of man. The forms of variation are the result of the processes of culture growth, not of racial predisposition. (2) The behavior and cultural ingenuity of different peoples within any given race are so variable that obviously the racial factor can be of little importance. (3) The same people may exhibit astounding cultural energy at one period of their history and be almost wholly devoid of it at another. Peoples who have been culturally quiescent for centuries suddenly burst into a veritable fury of cultural development without any determinable change in racial composition. The Japanese are the most spectacular example in modern times (1972:240–41).

Though Euroamericans often claim racial superiority, we have come to our present position quite recently (only in the last 500 years) and seem unlikely to last much longer. Hoebel points to three American Indian societies belonging to the same race and speaking related languages whose histories turned out quite differently for cultural reasons. Seven hundred years ago the Aztecs, Comanches, and Shoshones all lived in the western deserts of North America "as lowly hunters and gatherers at the bottom of the cultural scale" (1972:241). The Aztecs wandered south, and by 1500 "were overlords of the land: maize growers, road builders, astronomers, artists, and possessors of a city with public buildings of cut stone so magnificent that Cortez cried out that in all Andalusia there was nothing to compare with the glory of this city" (ibid.).

The Comanches at a later date obtained horses and guns from the Spanish and became feared robbers and fighters in the southwestern plains of the United States. The Shoshones, however, remained essentially as they were and were chased into the desert by the Blackfeet. "They developed a strong inferiority complex, and . . . welcomed the coming of the whites" (ibid.).

Racial differences are, like other genetic variations, the result of prolonged inbreeding. Such inbreeding is typically the result of geographical or social isolation. The key factor is reproductive isolation, for "when interbreeding takes place between adjacent breeding populations, the resulting transfer of genetic materials between the two populations will tend to reduce the extent of the biological differences between them" (Beals and Hoijer 1977:97).

There is ample evidence to suggest that isolated breeding populations also adapt to their environment. This causes further differentiation between those populations and any they may have split off from. Furthermore, mutations or genetic changes may occur which, if they are adaptive, will become characteristic of the split off group, increasing their distinctness from the other group. Since a human generation is so long (20–30 years), and since there has not been all that much isolation between reproductive populations, not enough of such changes have occurred to result in the development of separate species (ibid.). Enough surface changes have occurred, however, to attract a good bit of attention.

There are several rather important limitations to the concept of race.

First, race is an arbitrary category, making agreement on any particular classification difficult; second, humans are so complex genetically that often the genetic basis on which racial studies are based is itself poorly understood; and finally, "race" exists as a cultural as well as a biological category. Many anthropologists view the race concept as useless . . . (Haviland 1979:229).

A statement on race formulated by a panel of physical anthropologists and geneticists convened in 1950 by UNESCO is worth including here by way of summary:

We have thought it worth while to set out in a formal manner what is at present scientifically established concerning individual and group differences.

(a) In matters of race, the only characteristics which anthropologists have so far been able to use effectively as a basis for classification are physical (anatomical and physiological).

(b) Available scientific knowledge provides no basis for believing that the groups of mankind differ in their innate capacity for intellectual and emotional development.

(c) Some biological differences between human beings within a single race may be as great as or greater than the same biological differences between races.

(d) Vast social changes have occurred that have not been connected in any way with changes in racial type. Historical and sociological studies thus support the view that genetic differences are of little significance in determining the social and cultural differences between different groups of men.

(e) There is no evidence that race mixture produces disadvantageous results from a biological point of view. The social results of race mixture, whether for good or ill, can generally be traced to social factors (Shapiro 1952, quoted in Hoebel 1972:242).

It is probably best, then, to join the growing number of scientists who consider race to be an unscientific concept.

RACISM

Racism is *a cultural interpretation of racial differences* in which a people with one set of racial traits attributes their supposed superiority to their possession of those traits and the supposed inferiority of another group to their racial characteristics. Racism is, therefore, a type of ethnocentrism that, like other types, has no scientific validity. This fact does not, however, cause it to go away. As Nida says,

> Everywhere in the world people recognize the in-group.... and the out-group.... The establishing of an in-group consciousness is part of the psychological drive for a sense of belonging. The hostility which is so frequently a part of the out-group consciousness is in a measure a fortification of the in-group solidarity by sentiments of superiority; but in more instances than not, it is simply the poultry-yard complex, that is to say, each chicken knows what other chicken can be pecked at with reasonable guarantee of getting by with it. In other words, the out-group is a kind of scapegoat for one's hate satisfaction (1954:55).

Though such prejudice is universal, it is not always attached to racial differences. Indeed, according to Nida, the present "type of rationalization has been primarily the development of the last two hundred years," principally among Anglo-Saxons (ibid.). This attitude has produced negative social stereotypes of people who possess certain physical ("racial") features that set them apart from those who see themselves as "superior." Such attitudes are passed quite unconsciously from generation to generation as if they were established facts and get played out in habitual behavior. As a result, members of the group in power react to differences in behavior on the part of the "lower" group by considering both the behavior and those who acted that way to be inferior.

Nida helpfully traces the origin of white racism as follows:

> By the beginning of the nineteenth century colonialism, imperialism, and slavery were in dire need of some social and moral justification. The fact that missionaries were being sent out to raise the moral level of the "benighted peoples" scarcely sufficed to warrant the unabashed exploitation of so many millions of people. Some persons were ready to employ the supposed Biblical doctrine of damnation to the Negroes by citing Genesis 9:25 in which Canaan as a son of Ham was cursed. However, even this was not the kind of "scientific" basis which seemed necessary for the nineteenth century. Such a basis was found, however, in the ethnocentric appeal of the evolutionary hypothesis. The theory of biological evolution provided the basis for ideas about social evolution. These related concepts were popularly accepted, and Western Europe soon had a "scientific" basis for its superiority, founded so largely on gun powder (which was invented in China), on navigation (which was improved, but not invented, by Europeans), and on a desire for wealth (scarcely a unique cultural contribution).
>
> On the basis of the evolutionary hypothesis, social scientists of the day rated the Negroes as the least evolved and, of course, the white race (especially the people of Western Europe) as the most evolved. Races such as the Chinese and the American Indians were some place in between. ... Matters of social organization, economic life, and religious concepts were all scaled from the "lowest" to the "highest." Invariably the

victims of colonial exploitation were in the lowest categories and the imperialists' culture rated the highest. Perhaps never in the history of the world have those who claimed to speak in the name of science been so infected with the plague of racial egotism.

It is to the credit of present-day scientists that they have thoroughly discredited such ideas of racial superiority; but for the average man there lingers the idea that his contempt for other people is scientifically justified. It will take a long time to erase such cherished prejudices (1954:56–7).

Such prejudices lead people to the widespread assumption that there are behavioral differences between the members of different races. These people then look for such differences and attribute them to biology rather than, as they should, to culture. The fact that American blacks tend to score lower than whites on so-called intelligence tests is often pointed to in this regard, sometimes even by learned people (e.g., Jensen 1981). The preponderance of research in this area, however, points not to biological difference but to cultural bias on the part of the examinations. The examinations "are designed by whites for whites from similar backgrounds. It is not realistic to expect individuals who are not familiar with white middle-class values to be able to respond to items based on knowledge of these values" (Haviland 1979:229).

Though it is possible that some sort of relationships between genetic makeup and types of intelligence will someday be demonstrated, it is not presently possible "to separate the inherited components of intelligence from those that are culturally acquired" (ibid.). The same is true of other racial characteristics as well.

MISSIOLOGICAL APPLICATIONS

Many have seen the material dealt with in the early sections of this chapter as quite threatening to their faith. If God did not do things as we have been taught, they say, how do we know what to believe? Could non-Christian anthropologists have a clearer view of the truth than dedicated biblical scholars and theologians?

Though it may be disconcerting to accept, there is ample evidence coming from numerous fields of study that those who specialize in these areas, though they may not be Christians, are indeed the ones to look to for expertise. We would not, for example, trust a lay Christian over a specialized non-Christian in areas such as medicine or aeronautics when our life is at stake. We would demand the most expert person possible! So it should be (and usually is, for the informed) in areas of thought such as history, economics, politics, and anthropology. Not that experts are always right and (Christian) laypersons always wrong in their analyses, but the percentages lie with the experts.

People expert in one area are not, however, equally expert in all areas. One who is expert in theology, for example, is not necessarily expert in paleontology (the study of fossils). Nor do we necessarily trust a paleontologist in the area of history, philosophy, or theology. There are, furthermore, the crusaders for a particular interpretation of Scripture who seem to have closed their minds, like the Pharisees of old, to the possibility that the God of all the universe may have done things differently than their theories allow for.

Though I would not contend that non-Christians are always more right than Christians or that experts are never wrong or even that crusaders are always wrong, I would strongly recommend in these issues that we take seriously the views of the experts and look for ways to correlate their views with our commitment to God and the Scriptures. There is a lot of "world" out there that God has not yet made known to us, a lot yet to learn—and absolutely nothing to be gained by fighting with fellow Christians over how to interpret fossils. However God did it should be good enough for us, both in creation and in the inspiration of the Scriptures.

If, for example, we decide to change our previous view and accept that God (probably) used certain evolutionary processes to bring about much of what we observe in the world, perhaps we will also have to alter our view of how He guided the writing of at least parts of the Scriptures. If so, what have we lost? We have simply recognized that since we are not ourselves omniscient, we are still learning how God did things (both creation and inspiration). We can still hold firmly to what the Bible asserts (i.e., that it is inspired) without arrogantly contending that we know as much as God does about these matters, for it is not the Bible that requires us to interpret the early chapters of Genesis as literal history. It is certain Christian leaders and groups who require this (though, interestingly enough, this group includes very few real experts on the cultural and linguistic backgrounds of Genesis). We should therefore feel a certain freedom in this area to explore the fossil data and, without giving up our conviction that the Scriptures are inspired, to adjust our view as to how God led the author(s) to record the report.

The race issue may be just as difficult, but in a different way. For most of us, the problem in this area is not the intellectual acceptance of the invalidity of the concept of race and especially of racism. It is the difficulty of eradicating from our behavior the habits of thought and action that we have been unconsciously following. Those of us who are white Euroamericans have usually been deeply infected with racism, whether we admit it (or even see it in ourselves) or not. Once we see it in ourselves, it is likely to be a lifelong battle to try to overcome it.

Though people may start at different points in this battle, it is likely that all of us will have to follow some such process as the following:

1. Work it out intellectually. The discussion here plus that in Nida (1954:54–72) are good places to start. The big hurdle is our habit of stereotyping people of other races. Though we will ultimately need to get rid of the problem at a deeper emotional level, we need first to work at extricating that stereotype from our minds by admitting people of other races into our "person" (i.e., human being) category. Humans seem regularly to divide others into the "us" (in-group) and the "them" (out-group). The "us" are persons (human beings) we consider to possess ordinary "person" characteristics; the "them" are thought of in terms of stereotypes such as "blacks," "Hispanics," "Africans," "New Guineans," etc. Though thinking our way toward victory over the stereotype problem is the first step, it is unlikely that we will have completely overcome the problem with any given individual until we no longer reflexively think of the person in terms of his or her racial category. I had a happy experience with this matter once when someone asked me if my friend Ernie was black and I couldn't remember.

2. That kind of reflexive response is not, however, likely to happen in the abstract unless we have taken steps to develop a close personal relationship with one or more persons of the other race. By close, I mean the kind of relationship that involves deep mutual sharing, including the confession to that person of whatever we have seen of our racism and the request that that person help us to deal with it. As Nida says, "It is not enough that we should understand others (this can be a subtle form of patronizing); they must also understand us" (1954:72). We

will probably find it very difficult to retain a racist view (at least toward that person) if we really get close to him or her.

Basically, the antidote to racism is a close personal relationship. This will include confession of sins (such as racism) that are the result of our conditioning (worldview) rather than of our wills. This then issues in reconciliation and mutual trust. This may be difficult to do, but since the success or failure of our ministries may depend upon it, it should be a top priority item. God has called us to relate person to person, not stereotype to stereotype. If these chapters can get only that thought across, they will serve their purpose.

PART II

CULTURE

CHAPTER 8

A MODEL OF CULTURE

INTEGRATIONAL THOUGHT

Perhaps at this point in our presentation it would be good to deal with risk. For many, this subject matter raises feelings of tension and fear. They may fear that some of the solidness of their Christian convictions is being eroded as they expose themselves to this material. But Jesus seems to have had a rather positive view of risk, especially the kind of risk people took when they left all and followed Him. He says to the disciples, "Anyone who leaves home or brothers or sisters or mother or father or children or fields for me and for the gospel, will receive . . . a hundred times more . . . and in the age to come he will receive eternal life" (Mk 10:29, 30).

Would He not have said the same thing about those who leave "home base" with regard to their thinking? Would He not counsel us to risk our paradigms as well as our possessions and relationships? In the Parable of the Talents (Mt 25:14–30), He illustrates His attitude toward those who are conservative in their use of what God has given them. Does this not apply as well to those who are conservative (e.g., the Pharisees) in their thinking?

In the parable, the servants were given according to their ability. Those with the greater amounts risked what they had received and gained more. The one who received one talent, however, refused to risk it. He preserved it and presented to the master just what he had received. There was neither loss nor gain, because he didn't even try, and the master calls him "bad and lazy" (v. 26).

Many of us get the point of that story with respect to economics. "Nothing ventured, nothing gained," we say when it comes to money matters. Jesus would perhaps add, "Use it or lose it." But this is a rule in much of the rest of life as well. Use our muscles or lose the ability to use them, no solid growth without exercise, use our talents or they, too, atrophy. Likewise in the intellectual area. Our previous perspectives may have served us well in the past, but unless we risk them in obedience to the Master we seek to serve, we are not likely to learn the next thing He seeks to teach us.

Many of us who call ourselves "conservatives" have, I believe, put ourselves intellectually in the position of the man who buried his talent. We have come to comfortable positions on most issues and are content to preserve those positions without reexamining them. We stop growing. We also cease being faithful to our Master, who led us to those positions at one time in our lives in order that we might "invest" them in the process of growing into better positions at a later time.

I'm not talking about giving up basic convictions such as the centrality of Jesus Christ in God's redemptive plan or about the need for a commitment to Him as the basis of our salvation. We must hold to certain cardinal doctrines of the Christian faith or what we believe ceases to be Christian. But we need to grow as our experience grows in our understanding of even these tenets of our faith. Then there are many less-crucial things (e.g., ways of understanding God's relation to mankind, methods of doing His work) where we must change from the understandings of our early days as Christians in the direction of more mature understandings. If we don't grow in these areas, we will dry up and die in our spiritual lives.

This is scary because it involves risk, but risk under the direction of God is but another name for faith. As John Wimber says, "Faith is spelled R-I-S-K." So let's listen fearlessly to whatever God may be saying. Then let's invest the good perspectives He has given us in the past, seeking to discover and follow, under His direction, whatever new perspectives He would like to lead us into in the present and future.

INTRODUCTION

In the preceding chapters we have attempted to draw up a perspective from which to view cultural and human phenomena. Unlike traditional approaches to anthropology, we have sought to lay a foundation that sees God as present and active in human experience. With this as our basis and with a commitment to use cultural phenomena to serve God's purposes we turn to the more traditional material of anthropology. First, we look more closely at culture (part II), then at how humans relate to the nonhuman universe (part III) and the human universe (part IV), and conclude with parts on change (V) and research (VI).

In chapter 2 we talked about models in general, then about worldview as providing us with a model or mental mapping of reality which, when followed, results in cultural behavior. We have also indicated that there are hundreds of at least slightly differing understandings of culture. Now, as we turn more specifically to the treatment of culture, we want to make explicit the understanding or model of culture that underlies this presentation. First, let's look at the relationship between human commonality and cultural diversity.

BASIC HUMAN COMMONALITY AND CULTURAL DIVERSITY

The discussion of what stems from "nature" and what is the result of "nurture" in human behavior has been a long one (*see* D. Brown 1991 for a detailed treatment of this topic). From the very beginning of disciplined anthropological investigation, this has been a major concern, though, as Brown emphasizes, much anthropological investigation has assumed rather than proven that the major influences on human life are in the nurture area. In fact, Brown scores anthropologists for this bias, saying,

> Although [anthropologists] were sent into the field with the charge of getting the whole picture, so that they could come back relieved of parochial views and thus tell the world what people are really like, anthropologists have failed to give a true report of their findings. They have dwelt on the differences between peoples while saying too little about the similarities (similarities that they rely upon at every turn in order to do their work). At the same time, anthropologists have exaggerated the importance of social and cultural conditioning, and have, in effect, projected an image of humanity marked by little more than empty but programmable minds. These are distortions that not only affect the way we look at and treat the rest of the world's peoples but also profoundly affect our thoughts about ourselves and the conduct of our own affairs. These distortions pervade the "whole secular social ideology" . . . of our era (1991:154).

A major problem, as Brown sees it (and I agree), is that while we as anthropologists have claimed to have special expertise in this area, we have allowed ourselves to become both victims and perhaps the major perpetrators of the nurture/relativism ideology of the age. This ideology was and is so concerned to discover and proclaim the differences between human groups that an incredible body of similarity was ignored. To prove his point, Brown fills his book with general and specific illustrations of similarities between peoples that are rooted in human nature and support Goldschmidt's contention that "people are more alike than cultures" (1966:134). When we give the impression that everything cultural is relative, variable, arbitrary, and radically different from society to society, we are simply wrong. Both for the sake of truth and in order to conduct anthropological comparisons, we must recognize a substantial basic substratum of characteristics common to all humans, even though we dedicate ourselves to the study of that which varies from group to group—culture.

Customs A	Customs B	Customs C	Customs D	Customs E
Worldview A	Worldview B	Worldview C	Worldview D	Worldview E
Similar Basic Principles such as, take care of biological and social needs in socially approved ways (e.g., don't murder, steal, commit adultery, etc. within the in-group), support the society, its culture and its leaders, reproduce to keep the society in existence, etc.				
Common Basic Needs and Problems such as biological, psychological, sociocultural, and spiritual needs				

Figure 8.1 A general overview of human commonality and culture

Figure 8.1 above is an attempt to picture an anthropologically orthodox view of the relationship between what is common to humans and what is culturally different.

Note that this diagram has three levels to it. The top level is the cultural level. The middle level suggests that underlying culture are certain basic principles of human life that spring from a still deeper level of basic human needs and problems. The greatest diversity between peoples lies in their customs, with less diversity at the worldview level and commonality below the worldview level.

Note especially the middle box, where it is pointed out that every group has the need to take care of biological and social needs in socially approved ways. Here's where several of the Ten Commandments—don't murder, don't steal, don't commit adultery, don't bear false witness, and so on—exist in some form in every society. These are social regulations, present in all societies, without which social life could not continue.

Figure 8.2 below shows the same kind of progression in more detail.

As I have indicated, we can speak of cultural diversity only on the assumption that there are a great number of basic human commonalities of the kinds noted in these diagrams. On these foundations we observe that the diverse cultures of the world's peoples constitute just so many different answers to essentially the same sets of questions posed by human situations (*see* D. Brown 1991; Kluckhohn 1953; Luzbetak 1963:321).

I have divided universal human needs into four categories—biological, psychological, sociocultural, and spiritual. Under each category I have tried to present a sampling of the basic needs every society has to provide for and of the functions that need to be performed to provide for those needs. Though each society provides for these needs in ways that may differ from those of other societies, each must be provided for, and this is done in culturally structured ways.

The boxes at the top of the chart are designed to briefly, and in a generalized way, portray three types of cultural systems that are well-known in the world. Each has to deal with the same set of basic problems, but each does so in at least partially different ways. People are too creative to all agree on a single way to deal with their needs and problems. Note the similarities between cultures A and B and the wide differences between them and culture C (western). We westerners tend to be the most different from other societies in the world.

Various lists of elements found in all societies have been developed. Perhaps the most famous of these is that by George Peter Murdock. This is not a complete list, but about seventy-three categories of human ways (listed alphabetically) are mentioned. Here is the list:

> age-grading, athletic sports, bodily adornment, calendar, cleanliness training, community organization, cooking, cooperative labor, cosmology, courtship, dancing, decorative art, divination, division of labor, dream interpretation, education, eschatology, ethics, ethnobotany, etiquette, faith healing, family, feasting, fire making, folklore, food taboos, funeral rites, games, gestures, gift giving, government, greetings, hair styles, hospitality, housing, hygiene, incest taboos, inheritance rules, joking, kin-groups, kinship nomenclature, language, law, luck superstitions, magic, marriage, meal times, medicine, modesty concerning natural functions, mourning, music, mythology, numerals, obstetrics, penal sanctions, personal names, population policy, postnatal care, pregnancy usages, property rights, propitiation of supernatural beings, puberty customs, religious ritual, residence rules, sexual restrictions, soul concepts, status differentiation, surgery, tool making, trade, visiting, weaning, and weather control (1945:124; *see also* Luzbetak 1963:317).

	Culture A	*Culture B*	*Culture C*
	Hunt for food Live in caves and lean-tos	Cattle-herding or Settled agriculture Build round huts of mud	Settled agriculture Elaborate rectan- gular housing of wood or stone
	Personal security and meaning in kinship relation- ships and depen- dence on super- naturals Group oriented	Personal security and meaning in kinship relation- ships and depen- dence on super- naturals Group oriented	Meaning more in freedom than in security Individualistic Competitive Achievement orientation
	Extended families Informal education Kinship-based social control	Polygamous extended families Education informal and formal Social control through family and chief	Nuclear families Elaborate formal education system Specialists main- tain political sys- tem and enforce social control
	Supernaturals close and active Elaborate mythology	Supernaturals close and active Elaborate mythology Ancestor reverence	Naturalistic man and technology- centered belief system and myth called "science"

	Biological	*Psychological*	*Sociocultural*	*Spiritual*
F U N C T I O N S	Obtaining and maintaining bio- logical necessi- ties—Food, Air, Shelter, Sex, Excretion	Obtaining and maintaining psy- chological neces- sities—Meaning in life, Personal security, A mea- sure of freedom	Obtaining and maintaining sociocultural necessities— Language, Fam- ily Education, Social control	Obtaining and maintaining spir- itual necessi- ties—Beliefs, Rituals, Mythology
N E E D S	Food, Air, Health, Shelter, Sex, Excretion, etc.	Meaning, Maintenance of individual psyche, etc.	Communication Provide for transmission of culture, Maintenance of social system, etc.	Understanding of and relating to supracultural beings and factors, etc.

Figure 8.2 Universal needs and functions and diverse cultures

Humans have so much in common that such a list could be extended considerably (*see* D. Brown 1991). Note, though, that not everything on this list is at the
same level. Some things are quite specific, some quite general. Some even seem
trivial. The number of things that all human beings have in common is, however,
very impressive. As we focus on diversity and the differences between people, we
should never lose sight of this.

If we didn't have a lot in common, the quest to communicate cross-culturally would be worthless. If each culture were so distinct that everything was totally different, there would be no way of communicating from one society to another. The fact that people are able to understand each other, even across very large cultural gaps, gives us the clear indication that we have much in common. Though we dare not minimize the difficulties, it is very important to recognize that we have something at the base that enables us to get together.

This being true, anthropologists are far from agreeing on how much of any given area of life is properly attributed to human nature and what to culture. One area concerning which there has been a considerable amount of discussion down through the years is whether human commonality extends to logic and reasoning. Some have maintained that at least certain nonwestern peoples have a kind of "prelogical mentality." This position was advocated in print by the French anthropologist Levy-Bruhl (1923), though he renounced the position before he died. Certain American racists seem to have developed a similar belief (e.g., Jensen 1981).

Just what we are to conclude from this depends somewhat on 1) how we define terms and 2) what our presuppositions are. If, for example, we assume that nonwestern peoples reason differently, there is plenty of evidence that can be interpreted to support that contention. If, however, we assume that people reason in essentially similar ways, we can easily conclude (with Nida, Luzbetak, and many secular anthropologists) that "human psychology is the same the world over" (Luzbetak 1963:158).

This is the position I favor. Within each society, I expect that research will discover (as has been shown in western societies) people who reason according to a variety of "cognitive styles," one or more of which is favored by the society. Such linear "devices" as literacy favor a certain style of thinking, and people who learn to read are pressed into it. This fact probably explains the kinds of variation that have been pointed to as indications of differences in reasoning between western and certain nonwestern peoples. As Cole et al. (1971) discovered, West African children who learned to read reasoned more like Europeans than like their nonliterate relatives. Other differences are probably the result of cultural pressure in the direction of acceptance of the preferred cognitive style.

The major reason for differences in the way people think seems, however, not to lie in the thought processes themselves so much as in the fact that when people (creatively) start with different assumptions, they are almost certain to come out with different conclusions. Differences in worldview assure that there will be many differences between peoples at the level of their presuppositions, even if the way they get from their assumptions to their conclusions is the same.

However impressive the array of common needs may be, we observe that since most of the problems we face are capable of different answers, different societies have radically different approaches to dealing with these needs and problems. Human beings are too creative to simply go about solving the same problems in the same ways. We develop different answers to the same problems and, over time, groups who prefer one set of approaches split off from groups that prefer another set of approaches. Then, in isolation from each other, they move even more rapidly in different directions.

Some would theorize that differences in human culture are the result of our sinfulness. If we weren't so sinful, they say, we would all come to the same answers to our problems. Though sin does play a part in everything we do, say, and think, I believe the differences between cultures are more a function of our similarity to God than of our rebellion against Him. Because we are in the image of God, we are able to develop creative approaches to problems, and God seems to like creativity and diversity.

This understanding of culture sees differences between cultures as the result of different approaches to answering essentially the same array of problems. To illustrate what I mean, let's look at a series of examples.

1. All peoples ask the question, Who is in charge here? One group says God. Other groups theorize that there are many gods, or that human beings are in charge, or that the universe is eternal and runs itself, or that a force such as fate controls things. There are still other theories. Some of these answers are wrong. Some are partly right, partly wrong. Human creativity, combined with human limitations and sinfulness, does lead to wrong and partial answers quite often. The underlying creativity and ability to come up with different approaches to the same problem is, however, not to be denied.

2. Another nearly universal problem is, What do we do about uncongenial weather? If it's cold, we may assume that there is only one answer—warm clothes and sturdy housing with a fire inside. However, some groups don't bother with the warm clothing or the sturdy housing. The Tierra del Fuegans who used to live in a very cold climate off the southern tip of Latin America were known to go practically naked. But even when they paddled in their canoes out in the cold water, they had a little fire in the middle of the canoe in order to keep warm. That was their creative way of handling the problem.

3. The need to obtain enough food to live on is another universal problem. Though the physical environment places certain limitations on people, there is great variety and creativity in the way food is obtained, which foods are eaten, and how the foods are prepared. With regard to getting food, some gather, some hunt, some herd, some plant and grow. There is great creativity in the ways people carry out each of these activities. With regard to planting, for example, some people scatter seed (as in the Parable of the Sower), some dig a hole and carefully place one or a few seeds in it. Some people plant only one kind of crop (e.g., rice, yams, guinea corn), others may plant several. Some cultivate fertile plains near rivers, others construct and plant in terraces on steep hillsides.

4. With regard to housing, most societies aren't much concerned about comfort in housing. This comes as strange news to some of us in the western world, but it seems to be true. Their main concern seems to be simple protection from the environment, so many people are content to live in what looks to us like very simple kinds of housing. But they creatively build their homes out of whatever material is available—mud, dung, grass, sticks, trees, ice, stone. They may make their homes round, square, or oblong, simple or ornate, but they create in ways that often leave us westerners amazed at their abilities.

5. Many societies provide personal security and meaning largely via kinship relationships. Family and relatives are the big things to them. Those with family are wealthy (whether or not they have any money). Those without family are poor (even if they have money). Other societies see personal security and meaning in terms of kinship plus relationships to supernatural beings, and elaborate that to some extent. Western societies tend to see meaning mainly in terms of freedom and associational kinds of relationships outside the family, rather than in terms of kinship relationships.

6. People are often most creative in the area of language. A society will create abundant vocabulary, idioms, and even grammatical structures to facilitate communication in areas its people value highly. When new items and concepts are introduced into the society, the people create or borrow the necessary words to enable them to deal with the new things and ideas.

A MODEL OF AN INDIVIDUAL CULTURE AND ITS SUBSYSTEMS

Figure 8.3 below pictures the internal organization of culture from this point of view. It is similar to one of the diagrams presented in chapter 3, where we focused on the centrality of worldview in culture. Here we will focus on the part of culture external to worldview, the surface level of culture made up of the "cultural subsystems."

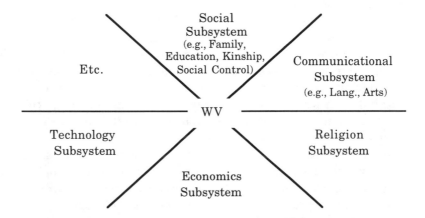

Figure 8.3 Cultural subsystems in relation to each other and WV

These subsystems are interdependent yet readily identifiable substructures that we label by such terms as *social structure, political structure, economic structure, religious structure, linguistic structure*, and so forth. Notice that one segment on the chart is labeled "etc." to indicate that there are several additional subsystems that could be listed.

Each subsystem consists of at least three components: assumptions, habitual (ritual) behavior, and creative behavior. This aspect of subsystem structuring is pictured in figure 8.4 below.

1. To start at the bottom of the diagram, each subsystem contains *subsystem-specific assumptions*. These are assumptions that relate only to the subsystem in which they are found. They differ in this respect from worldview assumptions, since the latter apply to and underlie all of surface-level culture.

One set of specifically economic assumptions relates to the proper way to go about buying and selling. In the West, we assume that all we need to do is pick out what we want to buy and present it impersonally with our money to a nameless person behind the cash register. In many other societies, the assumption is that there will be a time of personal dickering prior to coming to agreement on the price to be paid. These assumptions are not worldview assumptions, since they apply only within the economic subsystem.

ECONOMICS SUBSYSTEM	FAMILY SUBSYSTEM	RELIGION SUBSYSTEM
Creative Behavior	Creative Behavior	Creative Behavior
Habitual Behavior (Ritual)	Habitual Behavior (Ritual)	Habitual Behavior (Ritual)
Subsystem-Specific Assumptions	Subsystem-Specific Assumptions	Subsystem-Specific Assumptions

Figure 8.4 Internal structuring of the subsystems

In the family subsystem, in certain societies, it is considered proper for family members to show a lot of overt affection. In other societies, it is assumed that little or no such overt expression will occur. In the religion subsystem specific assumptions might relate to times and places of worship, appropriate religious leaders and how they are to behave, beliefs and doctrines that only relate to the religious subsystem (as opposed to any generally supernaturalistic worldview understandings that apply to the whole culture).

2. *Habitual or ritual behavior* makes up the majority of the subsystem behavior. The behavior for buying and selling, for example, is largely habitual. Whether the underlying assumptions are those of the West or those that prescribe dickering, the way we go about purchasing something is ritualized. The habitual practice of choosing an item, going to the cashier, presenting enough money to cover the amount specified, and walking away with the item and change is every bit as much a ritual as anything we may do in the religion sphere. Likewise, with respect to most of what we do within our families. Among such family rituals are the greetings we exchange when we first meet a family member in the morning, the way we gather for meals, and the ways in which the various members treat each other. Even the ways we think of and respond to each other are largely habitual.

Habitual behavior and ritual in the religion subsystem includes how and when we worship, where we go to perform religious acts and what we believe in this sphere. Religious traditions are often well worked out and so ritualized that the correct performance of them is considered magical and incorrect performance is considered very serious.

3. Beyond such ritual and interspersed with it at every point will be *creative behavior*. This is by far the most interesting kind of behavior, and the most difficult to predict. It occurs in such activities as the choices made between alternatives and the innovations that are made as people think and behave. In dickering to buy something in Nigeria, for example, I have frequently found it helpful to treat the progress toward agreeing on a price as if it were a trip. Once when the seller's price seemed to me to be too high, I suggested that he was at a city somewhat distant from the city we were bargaining in. He warmed up to the analogy and suggested that he was at a closer city. We creatively played out this game within the dickering ritual until we came to agree that the price put us in the same city. At that point, the deal was made.

Within the family, we may create, for better or worse, different relationships than those prescribed by the society. Such creativity may incur serious sanctions if the new relationship is incestuous. If, however, what is created is a new pseudo parent-child relationship to substitute for the failure of a parent to do his or her job properly, the results can be very constructive. The creation of blood brother-

hood, which admits an outsider into the family, may or may not be regarded negatively. Jonathan's admitting David into his family in this way incurred King Saul's
wrath. Often, though, such creative behavior meets with the approval of all.

Creativity in religious behavior is often more the prerogative of the leaders
than of the laypeople. It may be more acceptable, for example, for a leader to vary
a ceremony or advance a new doctrine than for a layperson to attempt the same
thing. Creativity is, however, often encouraged and greatly honored in religious
artistry such as music, drama, and carving.

Creativity often happens inadvertently through people making mistakes. It
also happens deliberately through invention and borrowing, often because people
face some new problem they have no answer for. Some people are more creative
than others. When their creativity is respected, others imitate them, and new traditions come into existence. We will come back to the subject of creativity when we
deal with culture and worldview change in later chapters of this book.

STRUCTURAL INTEGRATION OF CULTURE

Culture, according to our model, is an integrated thing, with each aspect of culture interdependent on each other aspect. Some have thought of culture as if it
were like a bag full of blocks. They picture a religious block, an economic block, a
political block, a social structure block, and so on, as if a culture exists as a collec-
tion of customs and institutions unconnected to each other. Where this theory has
appeared in missiology is the suggestion that our job as cross-cultural witnesses is
to go to another people, to "operate" on their culture by "surgically" cutting out
their religion and replacing it with ours. This approach is quite naive, because it
fails to recognize the intricate interconnection of the various parts of a culture.

The fact is we are talking about something that is very much like an organism—like a human body—with everything connected to and dependent on everything else. While recognizing such interdependence, however, doctors find that
they can deal with the parts of the body separately. They can talk about the heart
separately from the rest of the human body, but know that they also have to talk
about its relationships with everything else. When dealing with its functions they
cannot treat it as separable from the other parts. When, however, something is
wrong with the heart, they can deal with it alone to repair it so that it functions
properly in its relationships.

Even though we reject the "bag of blocks" analysis, a chart such as the above
one could give the impression that the various subsystems are separate, self-con-
tained entities. We are, however, simply doing what medical people do, focusing on
parts as well as the whole. So, for analytical purposes, we will from time to time
lift out the various parts of culture for special individual treatment. Here, however, our focus will be on cultural integration.

The integration of culture, like that of a human body, makes it difficult to discuss one part without reference to other parts. We cannot, for example, properly
describe the religious aspect of a culture without dealing with the extensive network of interrelationships between religion and politics, religion and economics,
religion and social structure, and every other aspect of the culture. Nor can we
deal with the social structure without referring to the interrelationships between
social structure and religion, social structure and politics, and so forth. This
means that any change brought in by Christian witnesses will have ramifications

throughout the rest of the culture. There will be influences on the economic structure, the political structure, the worldview, etc., whether we plan it that way or not. In order to do our job properly, it is important that we understand cultural integration.

A culture is integrated, but this integration never seems to be perfect or totally satisfying. Ideally, each culture is designed to meet all the needs of its people, but no culture ever really does a complete job because cultures, like everything else human, are flawed. Whether we study the economic subsystem, the religious, or the social, we will find each only *relatively* adequate. There will always be places where there seem to be loose ends, where the people recognize that their culture is not providing all the answers they seek. At this point they may be open to suggestions from outsiders, if they are approached correctly.

As cross-cultural witnesses, we need to look for people's felt needs. Some of the needs they feel will be met reasonably well by the sociocultural patterns and processes in which they participate. Others, however, will not be taken care of, leaving the people with questions for which they have no satisfactory answers. As we work with the people, we need to find out what kinds of questions they are asking for which they are unable to find answers within their culture.

In spiritual matters, they probably have many questions that are not being satisfactorily answered. I remember the old Nigerian chief who told me what his people believed about God before we came. He painted a picture of a god who had once been near and had since gone far away and left them. They felt hopeless and helpless. Then he looked at me and said, "White man, can you tell me where God has gone?" Here was an indication from within. I wasn't coming to him with answers before I learned his questions. This gave us opportunity to speak from his text—a god who is distant, and this distance bothers them. So we talked about a God who, though distant, has built a bridge through Jesus Christ. We could talk about the bridge that he didn't know anything about.

One way of highlighting the integration of culture is to focus on what happens when change occurs. When a new custom is introduced into any part of the culture, it often puts into greater imbalance the already imperfect cultural integration that did exist. Even if the custom was introduced or developed to solve a problem, there will usually be some disruption. New customs, like medicine, usually have side effects that are often not anticipated. When a new custom is introduced, then, the people have to work to integrate it into their system and make whatever adjustments are necessary in other parts of the culture.

What is happening in a large number of the world's societies is that changes are occurring more rapidly than they can be assimilated. The upset produced by such rapid change puts many people in a kind of culture shock within their own context. No longer are changes coming one or two at a time; people are forced to deal with large numbers of major changes all at once. Before they have a chance to assimilate one group of changes, another group comes. Like the rapid current of a flooded river, they never stop coming, and people find themselves continually off balance. It was to describe such a situation in American society that Alvin Toffler wrote the book *Future Shock* (1970). Many societies crumble and move into danger of extinction under this kind of pressure.

Even under pressure, however, there seems to be a large measure of integration in cultural structures and resiliency in people. Furthermore, there seems to be a human drive to push cultural structures toward consistency and integration.

These facts probably explain both why societies are often able to survive even under great pressure and why, even when there is considerable disintegration, influences on one area of culture ramify throughout the culture.

It is a sad fact that even the introduction of positive, helpful changes such as those brought by Christian witnesses can result in sociocultural breakdown if they come too fast or in the wrong way. Often the ways we went about seeking to bring people into God's family have produced cultural breakdown. A society's system of social control is often damaged so that the authority of the elders is no longer effective in keeping the people in line. We say, "We didn't say or do anything to cause that. Christianity doesn't disrupt the authority of the elders." Yet the way we have brought Christianity in has constituted a threat to the elders because women and young people have been attracted and chose to obey the foreign system at many points where its requirements conflicted with those of the elders.

Perhaps the most famous example of such disruption is described by Lauriston Sharp (1952) among an Australian aboriginal society known as Yir Yoront, into which missionaries brought steel axes. By giving axes to women and young men who would traditionally not have easy access to such implements, the missionaries unwittingly challenged a major part of their authority structuring. Previously young men and women, when they needed an ax, would have to go to an authority figure (a chief or older person who possessed a stone ax) and borrow it from that person. In doing so, they had to obey certain well-defined social patterns. Women and young men who acquired axes because they were liked by the missionaries and other westerners, however, no longer had to keep on good terms with the older men. In addition, they had a superior implement with which to do their work.

As a result, authority patterns began to break down internally and trading relationships externally, so that the society faced extinction. When the article was written in 1952, it looked as though the whole society would fall apart, and indeed it was in deep trouble. Human resiliency is such, however, that the society has been able to regroup, make its peace with the ideas coming in from the outside, and survive (J. Taylor 1988), probably at least in part because it has been able to remain relatively isolated.

Though the risk of disruption is great when change is introduced, the drive within people to discover better answers to unresolved problems seems even greater. People will not remain as they are, even if they are warned against the dangers of accepting too much too fast. There is a great feeling of need for change abroad in the world today. This gives Christian witnesses great opportunity. It is incumbent upon us, as we seek to introduce change, to recognize the implications of cultural integration, even as we seek to identify and appeal to a people's felt needs. See chapters 22–26 for more on culture change.

PATTERNING AND PERFORMANCE

As pointed out in chapter 3, our discussion involves us in dealing with two phenomena: culture and people. Culture provides the patterning, people do the performing. Culture provides the roads that people drive on or the script that people follow as they live their lives, but it is people who drive the roads or follow the script.

We have focused on the patterning of culture and will deal with culture change in more detail toward the end of this volume. But it will be useful here to point out four ways in which cultural performance leads to changes in cultural patterning:

1. A major reason for cultural improvisation is the fact that *the cultural script is never completely or perfectly passed on to the next generation.* As the cultural patterns are taught to the next generation by their elders, parts are not covered by the adults or are missed by the children. In addition, the adults pass on mistakes they have made in their own performance. Since people didn't learn the script perfectly or completely, they frequently find it necessary to improvise at various points in their journey. Though many of the things missed or learned incorrectly are eventually corrected, there are always many that remain, especially in a society such as American, which tends to isolate the younger generation from their parents at an early age, putting them on their own to develop many of their own patterns in reaction against those of their parents.

2. Another circumstance that requires creativity in cultural performance is the fact that *cultural patterns passed on by a previous generation are always to a certain extent "regressive."* That is, the patterns provide answers to the questions asked by the members of the previous generation, whether or not those answers are appropriate to the problems of the new generation. In most contemporary societies, however, things are changing so rapidly that yesterday's answers don't satisfy. They may (or may not) have worked for the last generation, but when this generation's problems are approached with the last or even prior generation's answers, things don't work, and today's people have to improvise. Thus each generation needs to change the script in order to perform well in the present.

3. Just as an actor may make a mistake in a drama, so *cultural performances frequently contain mistakes.* People may have been taught the correct pattern but make a mistake in carrying it out. Many such mistakes are made by children while they are in the process of learning the script. Some of them result in creative nicknames such as "Dampa" for Grandpa, or "Tewin" for Karen. Though these and other mistakes made by children are seldom adopted by others, they are creative responses to the need to perform culturally. The difference between imperfect learning and mistakes is that mistakes were not intended that way. They are, however, a common occurrence in cultural performance.

4. Then, of course, there are those who perform their culture creatively by *deliberately seeking to invent, discover, or borrow new things.* Such inventions and discoveries happen quite often, especially in societies in which innovation is encouraged. New words are invented to label new items or ideas that come into the life of a people, new techniques are discovered or developed for doing old tasks more efficiently, old ideas or techniques are put together in new ways to create something not previously known. When such new ways of performing are adopted by whole groups, they become new cultural patterns. These new patterns and recommendations concerning performance may be passed on to the next generation.

Change in patterns is thus initiated by change in performance. As I have said before, though, it is people who are the doers, the performers. The script (culture) doesn't do anything. Most of it is followed, parts of it changed, parts perhaps even ignored as people conduct their lives either according to the script or in departure from it.

DISSECTING CULTURE

At this point, we will attempt to dissect cultural structuring like a medical student dissects a cadaver. When we see sociocultural events happening, the drama being played out, the patterning may be less obvious than the players. Everything seems to be moving. Likewise with a living person. She or he is always moving, and whether we try to analyze that person biologically, emotionally, or mentally, it's difficult to get him or her to sit still. Whether with a person or with sociocultural phenomena, however, it helps sometimes to take a still photograph and then to try to dissect it. The picture is presented in figure 8.5 below.

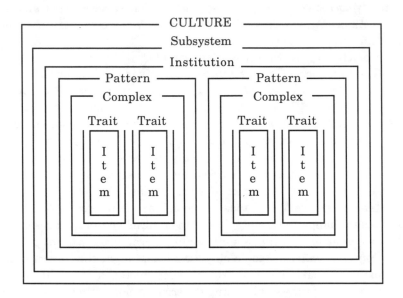

Figure 8.5 The internal structuring of culture

Starting with the smallest entity, we can say that each of the items (the smallest things in the culture) is organized into traits. That is, each trait has a number of identifiable items that pattern to form that trait. Each of the traits is patterned to form complexes. Each of the complexes is patterned with other complexes to form patterns, and each pattern forms, with other patterns, an institution. Each of the institutions is patterned with other institutions to form the subsystems that, in turn, make up a subculture that with other subcultures makes up the culture as a whole. This is, of course, an oversimplification for the purpose of trying to raise to our consciousness a bit of what's going on within this particular body that we call culture.

Ralph Linton (1936) illustrates this analysis by applying it to the Comanche, an American Indian culture, as shown in figure 8.6 below.

Within Comanche culture are the economic subsystem, political subsystem, religious subsystem, and so on. On the chart, we choose to focus on the economic subsystem. We then choose the hunting institution, within which are patterns such as those developed for hunting on horseback, hunting on foot, hunting in various seasons, and hunting various animals. We choose the hunting on horseback pattern, within which are complexes such as the bow and arrow, the horse, the tracking or hunting complex. Our choice is to focus on the bow and arrow complex, within which are certain traits such as the bow, the arrow, the quiver, the method of shooting, and so on. We choose the bow trait, within which are items such as the wood, the polish, the length, the string tightness, and so on.

Cultures	Comanche Navaho Anglo-American	← We Choose Comanche Culture
Subsystems	Economic Political Religious	← We Choose Economic Subsystem
Institutions	Hunting Gathering House building Trade	← We Choose Hunting Institution
Patterns	Hunting on Horseback Hunting on Foot Hunting in Winter Hunting Rabbits	← We Choose Hunting on Horseback Pattern
Complexes	Bow and Arrow Complex Horse Complex Tracking Complex	← We Choose Bow and Arrow Complex
Traits	Bow Arrow Quiver Method of Shooting	← We Choose Bow Trait
Items	Wood Polish Length of Bow String	

Figure 8.6 Comanche cultural patterning

MISSIOLOGICAL APPLICATIONS

These terms and categories are very useful to help us analyze the component parts of a whole culture. They can also be used to dissect for analysis a cultural structure such as a church. I have written on this in *Readings in Dynamic Indigeneity* (Kraft and Wisley 1979). To see how this would work, let's look at figure 8.7 below for a selection of patterns, complexes, traits, and items within the cultural institution called church, which is part of the religion subsystem of a given culture.

In the chapter in Kraft and Wisley referred to above, I have used this type of analysis as a basis on which to develop a scheme for measuring the indigeneity (contextualization) of a church. Indigeneity or contextualization involves the use of largely indigenous cultural forms for Christian purposes.

We can analyze what goes on in the worship of a given church in terms of the complexes, traits, items, and so on. If we look at worship in culture X, let's choose to focus on corporate worship and under that on the singing. We can ask, What kind of music is being used—indigenous or foreign music? If it is foreign music, that makes a particular impact on the worship. What about the preaching? Is the way the communication is done an indigenous way or a foreign way? If it's a foreign way, then that has a particular impact on people and signals to them that this particular worship is of a particular kind.

What about the prayer? Is the prayer in the kind of language that everybody uses everyday, or is it in an archaic language or some kind of constructed language

PATTERNS	COMPLEXES	TRAITS	ITEMS

WORSHIP	Corporate Worship
	
	Private Worship
		Corporate:
		  Singing
		  Preaching
		  Prayer
		  Order of Worship
		  Scripture Reading
		Private:
		  Bible Reading
		  Prayer
		  Meditation
			Singing:
			  Voice
			  Words
			  Music
			Preaching:
			  Language
			  Text
			  Illustrations
			  Tone of Voice

ORGANIZATION	Government
	
	Leadership
		Government:
		  Regulations
		  Procedures
		  Decision Making
		Leadership:
		  Qualifications
		  Performance
		  Interaction
			Regulations:
			  Meeting Times
			  Ruling Body
			  Membership
			  Chairman

BELIEF	Doctrine
	
	Values
		Doctrine:
		  Salvation
		  God
		  Sin
		  Eschatology
		Values:
		  Worldview
		  Morals
		  Ethics
			God:
			  Omnipotent
			  Omniscient
			  Loving
			  Righteous

WITNESS	Individual Witness
	
	Corporate Witness
		Individual Witness:
		  Verbal
		  Life
		  Personnel
		Corporate Witness:
		  Personnel
		  Organizations
		  Own Society
		  Elsewhere
			Corp. Person:
			  Missionaries
			  Street Witnessing
			  Mission Committee
			  Chairman
			  Street Witness Chair

EDUCATION	Formal Education
	
	Informal Education
		Formal:
		  Instruction
		  Initiation
		  Times
		  Techniques
		  Personnel
		Informal:
		  Places
		  Times
		  Personnel
		  Techniques
			Formal Initiation:
			  Baptism
			  Mode of Baptism
			  Times
			  Place
			  Audience

CEREMONIAL	Small Group Ceremony
	
	Large Group Ceremony
		Small Group:
		  Nature
		  Types
		  Frequency
		  Participants
		  Leadership
		Large Group:
		  Nature
		  Types
		  Frequency
		  Participants
		  Leadership
			Large Group Types:
			  Christmas Pageant
			  Easter Pageant
			  Choir Cantata
			  Children's Programs

Figure 8.7 Analysis of cultural structure applied to the church

or foreign language? If it's in a foreign or archaic language, that has a particular impact on the people concerning how they regard these worship services. If it's in the indigenous language, that has another kind of impact. Is the order of worship a normal kind of thing that might be used in other situations in this same society, or is it a pretty foreign thing?

If most of the people in a church are not literate or only minimally literate, what kind of impact is created if hymnbooks and Bibles are required to follow what goes on? And what kind of impact is there if the Bible is read in a language that is not that of the hearers?

This kind of analysis can be very profitable in helping us discover just how indigenous and effective the church we are working with is. If we discover that some of these items and traits on the right side of the chart are giving the wrong kind of signals, creating the wrong kind of impact, then we should ask the question, How can we move this church toward greater indigeneity, so that the message that is communicated is more in line with what is intended to be taught?

Let's take another of these patterns, the organizational pattern of a given church, and analyze it the same way. We can, first of all, split organization into at least two components—government and leadership. Under government, among the traits are regulations, procedures, decision-making processes, etc. Under leadership are qualifications, performance, the interaction between the leader and his followers and between the leader and other leaders, etc.

The Kamwe leaders were puzzled over the way our mission organized and taught them to lead their churches. One of the leaders once asked me, "Which is more inspired—the Bible or *Robert's Rules of Order*?" I said, "Which do you think?" He replied, "You people don't follow the Bible like you follow *Robert's Rules of Order*." He had been getting an impression at the trait and item end of the chart that it was more important to govern that church according to *Robert's Rules of Order* than by the Bible. We need to take such impressions seriously and to find out what was giving that impression. We would, of course, *say* that the Bible is inspired and that *Robert's Rules of Order* isn't. The first step toward rectifying the situation would be to discover what is coming through to give the impression that we are bound by *Robert's Rules of Order* more than we are bound by the Bible.

We can do the same thing with the belief patterns. We can divide belief into at least two categories: doctrine and values. Under doctrine are such things as salvation, God, sin, eschatology, etc. Under values are worldview, morals, ethics, and the like. By describing the actual situation, rather than talking about what we hope and pray will happen, we can get a better grip on what is actually going on in this particular church at this time. What kinds of values do they see endorsed by Christianity? What kinds of values do they see that are contradicted by or forbidden by Christianity? This will give a better understanding of any hindrances to indigeneity and what to do about them.

Likewise with each of the other aspects of church life.

CONCLUSION

We started our discussion of a model of culture with a consideration of basic human commonality. We then looked at cultural subsystems and cultural integration on our way toward bringing into focus several levels of structuring. We also dealt with the relationships between cultural structuring and the personal performances that transform it into something exciting to watch and to participate in. We now turn to another crucial dimension of the relationships between human beings and their cultures: the distinction between form and meaning.

CHAPTER 9

FORMS AND MEANINGS

INTEGRATIONAL THOUGHT

The Scriptures provide a good bit of insight concerning one of the major subjects of this chapter, what a Christian needs to know concerning cultural forms and the meanings people assign to them. One important passage dealing with this issue is Romans 14:13–23. With respect to the meaning of food considered to be unclean, Paul says, "no food is of itself ritually unclean; but if a person believes that some food is unclean, then it becomes unclean for him" (v. 14).

The cultural form is the eating of the food. Eating food is a cultural form regularly engaged in by all people (or else!). A problem arises, however, with the fact that not everyone attaches the same meaning to certain foods. In American society, for example, it is considered improper to eat horse, dog, or cat meat. That is, the meaning attached by most Americans to the very normal cultural act of eating, when applied to those kinds of meat, would be "improper, wrong." Americans do not feel the same way toward either beef or pork. For people of Hindu or Muslim backgrounds, though, the meaning of eating beef (Hindus) or pork (Muslims) is even more negative than the eating of domestic animals is for Americans.

In the New Testament at least two kinds of food problems are raised. The one concerns food considered ritually unclean (e.g., this passage, Acts 10). The other concerns food that has been offered to idols (e.g., 1 Cor 8). Both types of occasion raise the form-meaning problem. They also raise two other types of problems dealt with in the next chapter.

As we will learn later in this chapter, the forms of culture are the external, often observable part. The meanings are the personal part, based on how persons interpret the significance of the cultural form. People always interpret cultural behavior and attach meaning to it. When food is eaten, both eater and observer(s) will attach meaning to the activity. The question for Christian witnesses is, Will the meanings attached be helpful or harmful for either the eater or the observer?

In Romans 14:22, 23, Paul deals with the meaning attached by the person doing the eating and concludes, "Happy is the person who does not feel guilty when he does something he judges is right!" Apparently in situations such as this involving simply a ritual, rather than a moral precept, the freedom we have in Christ allows us to not attach the meaning "guilt" to our behavior.

In the rest of the passage, Paul gives instructions to the potential eater concerning how he or she should behave if an observer is likely to take offense. That teaching is summed up in the statement, "Do not let the food that you eat ruin the person for whom Christ died" (v. 15), since that person is attaching to your behavior meanings that both misconstrue your intention and mislead her or him.

Because of this problem, "you should decide never to do anything that would make your brother stumble or fall into sin" (v. 13).

INTRODUCTION

In 1936, Ralph Linton analyzed culture as consisting of four aspects: forms, functions, meanings, and usage. Along with many anthropologists of his day, he lumped the cultural with the personal into a single entity. Thus he saw the personal part of the culture-person interaction—the functions, meanings, and usage—as part of culture itself. Though some anthropologists continue to treat culture as if it has a life of its own, that is not the perspective taken here.

Rather, we see culture as the forms, structures, and patterns that humans use in the process of living. As has been mentioned, culture is the script; people are the actors. Culture is a system of roads; people are the ones who either use those roads or construct new ones.

It is possible to speak of the *function* of a road or a script, but only if we understand that the road or script does nothing by itself. The function of a road is to make it possible for a person to drive conveniently from one place to another. It is a mistake, though, to picture that road as itself moving. Rather, the road has been constructed by one group of people and is used mostly by other people as they carry out their activity of getting from one place to another. The function of the road is dependent on the use made of it by people.

We can say that there is a *use* dimension to culture only if we understand that it is people who use, not something that culture does itself. We can say that the potential for use is built into a culture by the people who produced it and that the interaction between people and culture is characterized by the use people make of cultural structures, but use is a characteristic of people, not of culture.

As for *meaning*, this too is a person thing, not a structure thing. Cultural phenomena do not have meaning in and of themselves. They are assigned meaning by people, usually on the basis of group agreements taught to the people as they learned the cultural forms.

What we have, then, are two very distinct components—people and culture—that work together so effectively and unconsciously most of the time that they seem to be a single entity. People are fond of saying things like, His culture made him do such and such, rather than He did such and such because he was following the cultural script he had been taught (by people) as a youngster.

It is not culture that has forms, functions, meanings, and usage, as Linton and others have taught. Culture has only forms. People *use* cultural forms to perform certain *functions* and attach *meaning* to them, ordinarily according to habits that come from inside, often in response to people pressure from outside, rather than according to some inherent power in the cultural structures themselves. This is an extreme position, but seems to me to avoid the pitfalls of cultural determinism and to enable us to understand how and why cultures get changed.

FORMS, SURFACE AND DEEP

We have already seen that there are surface and deep dimensions to culture. On the surface, we see human behavior usually following the guidelines of cultural patterning. At the deep level, we see human worldview assumptions following cultural guidelines as well. We call all of these guidelines, whether surface or deep, plus all of the other structured and structuring components of culture, the *forms* of culture.

What we mean by *cultural forms* is all of that complex of items, patterns, and structures—visible and invisible, surface and deep—that people use in particular ways (functions), usually according to habit and in terms of which they guide their lives. All of the structural levels discussed in the preceding chapter are levels of form. Lest, however, the term *form* not seem adequate to cover the items of culture plus all of these structural levels, I will frequently refer to forms, patterns, and structures as the components of culture.

Any cultural element, whether a material object or an idea or a ceremony, is a cultural form. Most cultural forms are nonmaterial, such as marriage customs, family structure, educational procedures, ceremonies of all types, linguistic structures, and the like. Material objects such as automobiles, machines, buildings, tools, and so on are also cultural forms. Each custom, pattern, or structure is a cultural form. From a cultural point of view, a church service is a cultural form. So are the clothing we wear, hairstyles, gestures, words, foods, eating patterns, furniture, sleeping habits, and so on.

Cultural forms are complex. As we saw in the previous chapter, cultural forms such as institutions are made up of cultural forms called patterns which, in turn, are made up of forms called complexes, then traits and items. That whole analysis was of the forms of culture. The form called "church service" is made up of a whole lot of other forms, some of which are called "singing," "prayer," "announcements," "offering." Each of these is divisible into smaller forms.

C U L T U R	SURFACE LEVEL	ITEMS (e.g., material objects, ideas, words) PATTERNS (e.g., building plans, rituals, grammatical patterns) STRUCTURES (e.g., buildings, institutions, language structure)
A L F O R M S	DEEP LEVEL (WORLDVIEW: ASSUMPTIONS AND IMAGES)	ITEMS (e.g., assumptions, values, allegiances) PATTERNS (e.g., paradigms) STRUCTURES (e.g., themes)

Figure 9.1 Cultural forms, surface and deep

The forms of a culture are static. Forms don't "wiggle" in and of themselves. They are, however, used by persons to serve various functions and convey various meanings. To illustrate how forms are used to serve functions and convey meanings, let us take a cultural form like the bow and arrows mentioned in the previous chapter. Quite a number of the peoples of the world still use bows and arrows as implements of food getting and warfare. A few years ago, when I went to Papua New Guinea, I saw the people carrying such implements. These material artifacts are cultural forms that I as an American was quite attracted to, so I arranged to buy some arrows. I thought they might look good hanging on the wall of our living room back home. I'm not sure what the man I bought them from was thinking. Perhaps he thought that I would use the arrows to kill some animals, the way he uses arrows. Or perhaps he simply thought that selling them to a white man was an easy way to make some extra money. I don't know, but I bought them, and if you come to my home today, you'll see several arrows from Papua New Guinea hanging on my wall.

These are cultural forms that I have carried far from their place of origin. I use them quite differently than the man I bought them from, and because I use them as decorations rather than as hunting implements, I assign them quite a different meaning than he assigned them. The forms are the same, whether in New Guinea or in the United States, but the personal elements are different.

What I have just said about cultural forms, surface and deep, is charted in figure 9.1 above.

USAGE, FUNCTION, AND MEANING

As indicated, usage, function, and meaning stem from persons. Persons may, however, operate individually or in groups. With respect to ordinary habitual cultural functioning, people usually function in accord with their group. With respect to the creative dimension of cultural usage, they tend to function more individualistically.

Meaning is the label we give to the interpretation, including all the impressions, associations, values, attitudes, and the like, that a person or group assigns to any given cultural form. All forms are given meanings, and meanings are conveyed from person/group to person/group through forms. The meanings attached to the forms are, however, usually socially agreed upon. That is, whether the form be a word or a ritual, an item or a pattern, the people of a society have been taught to interpret it in essentially the same way—unless the form is new to them. Even when new things are introduced into a society, however, there is usually a high level of consistency in the way the various members of the society interpret it. If there is not such agreement, it usually only takes a short time for the group to come to agreement concerning how to interpret the new thing.

Once a form is a part of a people's cultural inventory, however, the assignment of meaning is as habitual (and therefore as predictable) as any other cultural behavior. The reason for this is that humans learn well what the society teaches them. Though often we despair over the weaknesses in our formal educational system, the informal system through which our children learn cultural patterns and social habits is very effective. Children have an incredible drive to learn, coupled with an equally incredible ability to learn quite unconsciously. One of the major things they learn is to apply meaning to the cultural forms with which they interact.

A form is a structural thing, made up of items and patterns. Meaning, though usually attached quite habitually, is a personal thing. Though there is some individual creativity in the way meanings are attached, as mentioned, group agreements are usually followed. Thus when a given cultural event occurs, whole groups of people in the same society will attach the same or greatly similar meanings to that event. There will be some individual variation, but the meanings attached will be highly similar. In fact, the whole process of communication depends on people agreeing on the meanings of the forms they use. If we did not agree as a group concerning the meanings of the words and other grammatical

structures we use, we couldn't communicate. Words are among the most prominent kinds of cultural forms.

This assignment of meaning is performed by people according to their learned
worldview patterns. Thus it is ordinarily done in accord with the deep level (i.e.,
worldview) cultural forms taught us. Meaning assignment, though personal and
different from cultural forms, is performed in terms of and in dependence on
forms. This is one reason why many people confuse the personal and the cultural.

The way we plan to *use* the cultural forms we deal with has a direct bearing on
the meaning we attach to them. To return to the arrows I bought from the Papua
New Guinean, they meant quite a different thing to me than they did to him,
because I planned to use them quite differently than he did. Indeed, I didn't even
buy a bow (without which the arrows would be useless from his point of view),
since I felt it would be too large to carry home with me on the airplane.

All of this was in accord with what most of my fellow Americans would have
planned. I (or my fellow Americans) did not need the arrows for food or protection.
Americans, however, value implements like these prominently displayed in our
houses to remind ourselves and indicate to our visitors that we have been to exotic
places. I planned to use the arrows quite differently than the seller did—as decorations rather than as a means of food getting. Therefore, they have quite a different meaning for me.

We see that the meaning of a cultural form is closely associated with its use,
and we have illustrated how the intended use may give rise to a difference in
meaning. But the converse is also true—the meaning intended can give rise to a
difference in usage. Recently I needed to reach something stored in a high cabinet
in our kitchen. To do so, I needed a cultural form that would mean "something to
climb onto to reach something high." I knew we had a small ladder made especially for that purpose, but instead of finding that ladder, I chose to use a chair, a
form with the normal meaning of, "something to sit on." By assigning that chair
the meaning ordinarily assigned to a ladder, I was able to conceive of a usage different from its normal use and then to use it in that way.

By imagining other possible meanings for cultural forms, we may regularly
use a nail file as a screwdriver, use secular anthropologists' ideas to aid Christian
witnesses, use classes we aren't interested in to achieve degrees we are interested
in, use plates to cover saucepans, and so on. What is happening when we do such
things is that we are discovering and assigning new uses and, therefore, new
meanings for known cultural forms and using them accordingly.

Cultural *function* is the way the use and meaning of a form relate to the people
who use and interpret them. We can say that a function of bows and arrows in
many Papua New Guinean societies is to enable these people to get food or conduct
war. Another function might be as means to earn money (by selling them to
whites). It is likely that at least some of the deep need for security felt by such peoples is satisfied by the knowledge that they have such weapons and people who
can use them, so we can say that as weapons, bows and arrows also function for
them as symbols of security.

To take another example, we can say that among the functions of a wedding
ceremony in many societies are the following: 1) to legitimize a decision for a couple to live together, 2) to bring about close interaction between nonrelated families
(those of the bride and the groom), 3) to provide an opportunity for members of the
same families to interact closely with each other, 4) often to bring about close

interaction between people and their religious leaders, 5) to provide a celebration for all involved, 6) to lead both participants and observers to think deeply about marriage, and 7) to initiate the participants into a new stage of life.

Though function and meaning (as well as usage) overlap greatly, and though each may vary from person to person even within the same event, there are distinctions to be made between them. The primary distinction is that function tends to be a broader thing, relating primarily to the system, while meaning tends to be more individual and personal. With regard to the wedding illustration used above, we can say that a wedding functions within the cultural system to legitimize the fact that from this point on a given man and woman will be living together and producing and raising a family. This change in behavior and the children produced because of it are made legal because the society agrees that that event serves a legitimizing function with respect to that behavior. The fact that the wedding ceremony symbolizes that function contributes to both the social and the individual meanings of the event.

The fact that meaning, function, and usage are so tightly intertwined leads us to frequently use only one of the terms to refer to all three. Thus many will speak of the "form-meaning" distinction or the "form-function" or "form-usage" distinction, with the intention that the latter term be interpreted to mean "function, meaning, and usage." My preference is to use the term *meaning* as the cover term. I will therefore frequently speak of the dichotomy between form and meaning in the pages that follow.

FORMS HAVE MULTIPLE MEANINGS, FUNCTIONS, AND USAGES

To make certain that we properly understand both the distinctions and the close relationships between these aspects of culture and person, let us look at a series of further examples.

1. Let's look at the *form of a traditional hymn in a worship service*. When we go to a worship service and sing a hymn, we do so with certain underlying felt needs and motivations that influence how we *use* the cultural form. We may, for example, consciously or unconsciously use a hymn for any or all of the following purposes: worship, showing off a good voice, participating with others, following a ritual, relaxing, remembering an individual or group experience, relating to history. In addition, the pastor or other leader may have other usages in mind. He or she may desire (consciously or unconsciously) to get people warmed up, to relax people, or to start or finish a service.

Very often hymns are used as transition devices. When the leader wants to move the people from the introduction of the service to another part—say, the offering—he or she announces a hymn. Or at the end of the service a hymn is scheduled to provide a transition between the service and whatever is to happen next. I hear music directors sometimes complaining that the pastor of the church sees the music only as a vehicle for making transitions between parts of the service. Music directors often feel that such an attitude demeans both their product and their position. They have quite a different attitude toward how music should be used in church.

All of these usages are, of course, closely tied to the (conscious or unconscious) interpretations of the participants. If, for example, we interpret this act as an act of worship and our intention is to worship, the *meaning* we are expressing is "worship." We are singing our praise and worship to God. Perhaps at the same time or at other times, however, we are expressing through singing a connection with the past. Most of the hymns in our church were written by people at least a century or two ago and provide a connection with the past. We sing "A Mighty Fortress Is Our God" and tend to think of our connection with Martin Luther and the Reformation. Quite often there are meanings of fellowship—we are singing these hymns along with other people whom we love in the Lord.

Sometimes we feel that the hymns are beautiful, so the meaning "beautiful music" fills our minds. We may pride ourselves on our good voice, so we sing loudly to show it off. Often, though, the meaning that our leaders intend will not correspond with the meaning in our minds. Suppose they intend worship or beauty or connection with a valued tradition but we sing with a meaning in our minds that this is a worthless tradition or an irrelevant or archaic song. There are certain hymns that we may not like to sing because we consider the words objectionable. Some hymns we may be able to sing only if we don't think about the words. Such discrepancies between the intended meanings of leaders and followers are, unfortunately, quite common in all cultural behavior, so a single form—a hymn—used in a worship service may have quite a variety of meanings.

It may also serve a variety of conscious and unconscious *functions*. Sometimes a hymn serves a given function (such as providing a transition or relaxing people or putting them in a worshipful mood) because it is designed or expected to serve that function. At other times hymns serve a function that nobody planned; it just happened. Hymns usually function to tie worship services together and provide transitions, whether or not the leaders intend it that way. They sometimes function to cut down boredom, or increase boredom at other times. Sometimes it seems as though their main function is participation in what otherwise is a nonparticipatory occasion.

From a social (as opposed to an individual) point of view, a hymn functions to identify a particular type of music and the allegiance of those who use it. If that type of music and that allegiance happen to be respected by the society at large, this fact will be a part of the perception of the people as they sing (though they will probably be quite unconscious of it). If, on the other hand, such music and allegiance is looked down on by the society, that fact will be in people's unconscious thinking as they use hymns.

2. As a further example, let's take the word *dog*. Any word is a cultural form. The animal is not a cultural form; the animal is a physical form, but the label of that animal is a cultural form. What meanings do we attach to that word? If you like dogs, you get a warm feeling when you hear the word. If you dislike dogs or are neutral toward them, you attach a negative or neutral meaning when you hear the word. If you come from a society that eats dog meat, you will attach still a different meaning to that word form. (Some from such societies have misinterpreted the American term *hot dog* as indicating that Americans, too, eat dogs!)

Note that interpreting may involve emotion. We find from our studies of communication that meaning is more felt than reasoned (*see* Kraft 1991a). With respect to a dog, the people within a society will largely agree on whether a given animal is a dog or not, although in some societies the category will not correspond exactly to that of English. That part of the meaning that simply identifies the animal as a part of the worldview category labeled "dog" is not likely to be argued about within the society. Nor will a people ordinarily argue about any culturally prescribed emotional reaction, such as the culturally prescribed intense negative reaction to dogs of Arabic (and many other) peoples. But in many societies the cultural guidelines allow people to develop either positive, negative, or neutral attitudes toward dogs.

In American society, a variety of attitudes toward dogs are allowed. For example, my wife and I have quite different attitudes toward one particular breed of dog called a St. Bernard. My family had one while I was growing up, and he was my best friend, so in my mind the nicest kind of dog is this very large, slobbering, lovable animal. But when my wife was a little girl, she was knocked over by a St. Bernard! The name St. Bernard is one word form, symbolizing one kind of animal, but the meaning I attach to it is very positive, while my wife's meaning is little short of terror!

3. We have illustrated the form-meaning dichotomy by pointing to differences in the meanings of a church service and a word form like the word *dog*. Now let's look at the cultural form *American wedding ceremony*. Though the ceremony may be a single event, let's ask, What does that event mean to the different participants? As we focus on the couple about to be married, we ask, What thoughts are going through their minds? What does this event mean to them? Presumably this is something they want, so they are positive toward it, but they may have quite a bit of apprehension as well. They may wonder how they will ever make it together, or they may be concerned about their parents' attitude.

What about the parents? The mother of the bride may be thinking, "Oh, my, am I glad this is happening! I thought she would never attract a man." Or maybe she's saying, "I wish she had waited. She's settling for someone who is really not worthy of her." The poor father of the bride, who has to pay for the wedding according to middle-class American custom, may be saying, "Oh, why didn't she go out and elope? It would have been so much less expensive."

What is the meaning of this ceremony to the guests? Some of them are close friends of either bride or groom and are very happy to share their joy. Others may be there more out of duty than because they chose to come. They will attach quite a different meaning to the ceremony than will the close friends. What meanings are in the minds of the musicians? The organist may be a poor struggling college or seminary student who doesn't know the participants but can make $50 by playing for weddings. The wedding means something quite different to her or him than to the family or the couple. What does such an event mean to the preacher? He or she feels good about some of the couples he or she marries. Others he or she would rather not marry. Lastly, what does the wedding mean to the janitor? He may attach still a different meaning to the event. If it is a Saturday wedding, it may mean that he has to work well into the night to get the church all cleaned up for Sunday. Even if it is not a Saturday wedding, it still will probably be a lot of work for him. Again, we have one cultural form but many different meanings (and functions) channeled through it by those who are using (participating in) the form.

4. Next let's look at an item of material culture such as an *automobile*. What does that mean? For most people, it means the possibility of traveling from one place to another quite rapidly. For some it is a symbol of prestige or status. For a young American just getting a license to drive, it means "At last I can get away from home. I don't have to ask Mom or Dad to drive me places." He or she has a

new sense of freedom and power, a new way to show off. At least on occasion, a car means trouble. But when a car means trouble to its owner, what does it mean to a mechanic? My mechanic likes to see me drive in, since my trouble is his livelihood! Again, the same thing means different things to different people.

5. A ritual such as *baptism* is also a cultural form. We should ask the same kinds of questions about its meaning that we ask about other cultural forms. We hope that people will interpret the ritual positively as a channel for showing one's commitment to Christ and His Church, but what about people who join an immersionist church but are afraid of the water? We had many people like this in northeastern Nigeria. They were terribly frightened by the thought of someone pushing their heads under water. Is that a Christian meaning? Are people getting the proper message through that form when they are expected to go through something that frightens them to death? It may be that they are getting the proper meaning, because they feel that if they survive that, they have literally been raised from the dead! I'm afraid that many simply see baptism as a silly ceremony. When we use this ritual to bring people into Christianity, we must take account of the meanings in people's minds.

God's message is a message of meaning, not a message of form. The forms are extremely important, for they are the vehicles through which meanings are communicated. As such, the forms used by Christians either serve God's meanings or counter God's meanings. For this reason, we have to give careful attention to the cultural forms we employ if we are going to convey the proper meaning.

FIVE PRINCIPLES

There are at least five principles concerning the relationships between cultural forms and their meanings that those who serve God cross-culturally need to understand.

1. The first of these has already been mentioned. It is that *meanings are transmitted from human being to human being only through cultural forms.* As we have said above, meanings are arrived at through the process of interpretation. Though humans interpret physical (e.g., geographical features, animals) phenomena and perhaps other noncultural phenomena, as well as cultural phenomena, the latter are always cultural forms. Anything produced by humans automatically results in cultural forms. The interpretation by humans of the cultural forms produced by other humans is the way meanings are transmitted, so if we want to communicate Christian meanings, we have to use cultural forms like words, customs, ceremonies, rituals, and beliefs.

When we think of communicating to people of another society, however, we have to ask what forms should be used. Do we import our forms and require them to learn them before they can understand what we are saying and doing? This has, of course, frequently been done by Christian witnesses from earliest times. The early Jewish Christians imposed circumcision and several other distinctively Hebrew customs on Gentile Christians; the Roman Catholic Church has down through the years imposed Latin language, ritual, and other customs on Roman Catholics of many societies; and Protestants of various denominations have regularly imposed their denominational distinctives on their converts.

Do we seek to adopt and adapt the cultural forms of the receiving culture for Christian purposes? This also has frequently been done. The early Church used Greek, the language of commerce, rather than Aramaic, the language of Jesus, when they took the Gospel outside of Palestine, and both Roman Catholic and Protestant churches regularly adopt many of the practices of the peoples to whom they take the Gospel.

Whichever approach is taken, though, cultural forms must be used, since only thus can meanings be gotten across. Yet the forms of any culture, whether that of the receivers or that of the Christian witnesses, already have their own meanings in their home context. At least some of the forms of the receptor culture may very well regularly convey meanings that seem incompatible with Christian meanings. Should we use those forms for the communication of Christianity? Or do we reject them and introduce forms from another culture, recognizing that these will be interpreted by the receivers in accord with their relationship to the people from whose culture the forms are taken?

One of our worst enemies in our attempts to help people feel "at home" in Christianity is the presence of cultural forms within their Christianity that feel foreign to them. Such foreign forms are often adopted, even when the missionaries may be against such a procedure because the receiving people think God intends things that way. One of our aims in this text is to seek a way out of such a dilemma.

We will not seek to answer such weighty questions at this point, however. Let them simply serve to underscore the great importance for us as Christian witnesses to seek to find the right fit between the forms we use and the meanings we seek to convey.

2. A second principle that is important for us to recognize is the fact that *the same form in different societies will have at least some different meanings*. Several years ago, on my first visit to Korea, I became very aware of the fact that I was likely to make some serious mistakes. So I asked one of our former students to watch me and tell me when I did something that might be misinterpreted so I could correct my mistake. The first thing he pointed out had to do with how I sat when we prayed. He noted that I had been sitting on the platform in clear view of everybody with my legs crossed during a prayer. I asked him what was proper in Korea, and he said, "We would put our feet flat on the floor and take a more dignified posture for prayer. Having your legs crossed during prayer is showing disrespect to God." Having crossed legs during prayer in my society, of course, would not usually be interpreted as showing disrespect to God, but that same form in Korean society had a different meaning.

This principle is operative also in the language area. Literal Bible translations, for example, often carry over concepts that were perfectly acceptable in Greek or Hebrew, but are not in English. The use of the word *bowels* (*see* Phil 1:8, 2:1; Col 3:12; Phlm 7, 20; 1 Jn 3:17 *KJV*) is a case in point, since the bowels were considered the seat of pity or compassion in New Testament Greek. Such an expression is, however, crude at best and obscene at worst in English. Similarly, the symbol *fox* (*see* Lk 13:32) means slyness in English but treacherousness in New Testament Greek. Portraying God or Jesus as a shepherd was fine for Hebrews, but sheep and shepherds have little meaning for ordinary (unchurched) Americans. In certain parts of Nigeria, however, to see Jesus as a shepherd is to see Him as insane (*see* chapter 2).

As pointed out above, a dog can be regarded very positively in the United States. But in the Middle East, parts of Africa, and in many other areas, the same form, dog, usually carries very negative connotations. The intensity of such feeling came home to me one day when my northern Nigerian teaching assistant came into the office absolutely distraught. I asked what was the matter and he blurted out, "Don't you Americans have anything better to do with your money than to spend it on dogs?" In northern Nigeria, dogs are to be tolerated at best and kicked whenever they get too close. He had heard of somebody who had spent $40 at the veterinarian to get a dog well. He just couldn't conceive of that and made some pointed remarks about how wasteful Americans are with their money. Here, as often, we have one form but two (or more) meanings for people of different societies.

3. This being so, what happens when a cultural form from one society is taken to another? One thing that happens is that *any form borrowed by one society from another will have at least some different meanings in the receiving society*. Forms are, of course, regularly borrowed by one society from another, and there is no reason for us to be against this, even within Christianity, but we must recognize what happens.

To illustrate, I'll tell a story that has happened numerous times in a number of rural parts of the nonwestern world. For me, it happened a generation ago in rural northern Nigeria. I saw a man wearing a heavy army overcoat in the middle of the day, when the sun was shining brightly. It was hot, and the man was sweating profusely. I wanted to go up to him and ask, "Why in the world are you wearing an overcoat in the hot tropical sun?" But I knew exactly what would happen (because I have friends who have tried it). He would look at me as if to say, "Why would anybody ask that question? I wear an overcoat because I own an overcoat!" The point is, how would anyone know that this man is wealthy enough to own an overcoat if he doesn't wear it? The fact that the sun is hot is not the point; showing the world that you own an overcoat is. There is some self-protection here too, because there, as in many other parts of the world, if you own an overcoat and don't wear it but leave it at home, your brother will wear it. It gets worn-out just as fast anyway, so you might as well wear it to keep him from wearing it.

This is a case where an item of clothing has been borrowed from another society but the meaning has been changed (at least for this man—not all Nigerians would reason this way). You ask us whites what an overcoat means and we'll talk about keeping warm in cold weather. This Nigerian might find that a very strange meaning, since to him the same cultural form connotes prestige. The same item in Culture 1 has meaning 1, but in Culture 2 it will have meaning 2.

A similar illustration would be the difference in meaning that shoes have in many societies from the ordinary European meaning. For many peoples who regularly go barefoot, shoes are only worn for decoration, not for protection. Indeed, often their feet are so callused that putting shoes on them is very uncomfortable. Nevertheless, when in a town, many will wear shoes to make themselves appear more like city folks who wear shoes than like country folks who go barefoot.

A missionary who had worked in Iran told me that when he lived there, it was to be expected that one would use his automobile bumpers for bumping! Whenever he would go out in his car, he said, he could expect to accumulate several more dents on it before he got back home. If there was any kind of space between cars, somebody would try to get through that small space by bumping other vehicles out of the way. It was like a continual game of bumper cars, he said.

Much more serious is the example of the use of the word *Dios* for God in Latin America. The Spanish missionaries assumed that there was only one adequate word for God—the Spanish word. They knew that the local peoples had their pagan gods and words to designate those gods and assumed (as many other missionaries have) that the indigenous concepts were not adequate as labels for the Christian God. They therefore imported their word for God into the Indian societies, thinking that by so doing they were assuring a correct concept of God.

What happened, of course, was that the Indians gave the borrowed form, *Dios,* a new meaning. They asked themselves, "What do these people mean when they use this word?" and concluded that the Spanish word was simply a new label for one of their traditional gods. After they became Christians, they had two words for God. They gave to the new word form the meanings they had already attached to their word for God. To this day, many Latin Americans use the Spanish word forms to label God and saints, but the meanings they attach to those words are often closer to those of their pre-Christian ancestors than to those of orthodox Christianity. This is the kind of system that is often called Christo-paganism. It looks like Christianity on the surface, but at the deep level are indigenous meanings.

This example raises the issue of just what to do concerning the labeling of concepts newly introduced into a society. We might legitimately ask, What should the Spanish missionaries have done? Wouldn't it have been just as risky for them to have used the indigenous word forms? The answer is yes, that approach is also very risky. Yet the experience of Bible translators is that, in general, it is less risky to use indigenous forms than to import foreign labels for concepts that already exist in the language. It is apparently easier to keep track of what is going on at the deep level of a society when the surface-level forms continually remind everyone of the need for deep-level transformation of meaning than it is if those surface-level forms seem to signal a deep-level meaning that needs no transformation.

What happens is something like the following: When outsiders introduce foreign forms (such as a foreign word for God), and the people start using those forms, it is very easy for the outsiders to assume that the people are meaning the same thing by those forms that the outsiders mean when they use them. So the outsiders (and their converts) soon stop applying pressure on those within the society to redefine the concept thus labeled. Meanwhile, the people—in their own minds, without telling the outsiders—are retaining the indigenous meaning. If, however, the indigenous word is being used, everybody (outsiders and insiders) is kept constantly aware that the terms used have to go through a process of transformation, so the Christians keep the pressure on for as long as they are growing in the faith. If, of course, they stop being serious about Christianity, things revert naturally to the pagan meanings.

In such a case, it is clear that the terms chosen cannot be considered adequate when they are first used. They will probably be no more adequate than the terms used throughout the Bible for theological concepts were when they were first used. The vast majority of the biblical terms for crucial concepts such as God, sin, conversion, justification, church, love, repentance, salvation, plus the majority of the rituals used both in Judaism and in the early Church (e.g., circumcision, baptism, the Hebrew festivals, speaking in tongues, church) were concepts and customs with pagan meanings when first adopted by God's people. Adoption by God's peo-

ple, however, started these concepts and rituals on the road to transformation in
the direction of becoming more adequate vehicles for the transmission of God's
meanings. *See* Kraft (1979a:345–81) for a more detailed discussion of this issue.

When the concept in question does not exist at all in the society, the situation
is a bit more difficult. Sometimes there seems to be no better choice than to borrow
a term or custom from another culture. When this is done, however, the Christian
witness needs first to recognize the truth of the principle we are discussing and
then note that it is less disruptive for a people if the borrowing is done from a culturally similar people than from a culturally dissimilar people. The ideal is for a
people to borrow from a culture from which they regularly borrow—often a neighboring culture or one that is highly regarded in their area. Borrowing from such a
source tends to reduce the radicalness of the reinterpretation that takes place in
the borrowing process.

By way of illustration, let me point to what I believe to have been a poor choice
that was made in the Hausa language of northern Nigeria. The early Christians
needed a term for *church*. There are, of course, several terms in the language that
signify gatherings or groupings of various sorts that probably could have been
used, but for some reason the early church leaders seemed to feel that none of
them was adequate to designate the entity they had in mind. Nor did they turn to
Arabic, a language from which Hausa people have been borrowing for hundreds of
years, or even to English, from which Hausas had started to borrow quite heavily.
Instead they decided to borrow a term from Greek! They settled on the term *ekklesia*. Hausa, however, has no tradition at all of borrowing from Greek, especially
from ancient Greek (though English does have such a tradition for certain scientific purposes). So we end up with a technical term for church that is bound to confuse anybody and everybody from the outside and most people from the inside. I
suppose we could imagine a worse choice, but it would be very difficult.

In summary, whether we are talking about fairly trivial things such as the different meanings attached to coats or automobiles, or about crucial concepts such
as God and salvation, there is ample evidence that when terms and customs move
from one society to another, they are reinterpreted by the receiving people and
given at least some different meanings.

4. A corollary to these last two principles is the fact that *what is essentially the
same meaning is often represented in two cultures by quite different forms*. For
example, Bible translators are frequently puzzled over just how to represent an
idea when it appears that the people have no clear word for the concept. One
group of translators was looking in a particular language for a word for forgiveness. They kept asking, "What is the word for forgiveness?" There were a few candidates suggested, but none of them seemed to be quite right. Then one of them
decided to approach the matter by describing a situation. So he asked, "If two people were enemies and they decided to make up, what would they do to symbolize
that they had forgiven each other?" The people replied, "They would spit on the
ground in front of each other. They would hand each other a bit of guinea corn and
each would chew it and then they would spit on the ground in front of each other."
It became clear what to do in that Bible translation. The form that would get
across the meaning of forgiveness is to say, "God spits on the ground in front of us."

5. All of these principles being so, *we must, in moving from society to society,
choose and use the appropriate cultural forms, or the meanings will be wrong.*

Though the forms used may be changed as we move from society to society, it is extremely important that the forms chosen be the ones most likely to be interpreted by the receptors as conveying the intended meanings. Cultural forms are extremely important, but priority has to be given to the meaning conveyed over the preserving of the original forms if communication is to be effective. There must be an appropriate fit between the meaning and the form, or the meaning gets changed.

Suppose we (like Paul) wanted to say that God doesn't want non-Christians to be able to criticize Christians because they act improperly. What forms would we use? In 1 Corinthians 14:34, 35, Paul showed the women one thing they could do to communicate this meaning (i.e., to not speak in public) and in 1 Corinthians 11 he showed them another thing they could do (i.e., to cover their heads). In 1 Timothy 3:2, 12, he showed church leaders (men) one thing they needed to do to communicate this message (i.e., not remarry if his wife dies or leaves him). In American society, none of these forms will convey the meaning Paul intended. Instead, we would have to warn women about such things as clothing styles and men about such things as boasting, drunkenness, and immorality.

If, for example, we in America keep women from speaking (appropriately, of course) in public, the meaning that gets across is likely to be something like, "the Christian God (or His representatives) are against women." In African and other contexts, the importation of western hymns has led to meanings such as, "the Christian God only approves of western music and African music is evil." In English, the continued use of Bible translations in archaic or stilted language (e.g., *KJV, ASV*) leads to meanings such as, "God is very out-of-date."

POSTSCRIPT

I regard the form-meaning distinction as crucial, and a large number of cross-cultural witnesses who have gone through my classes have testified that this concept is the most important thing they learned from my course. There are, however, those anthropologists who dispute the value of this distinction. Some have even gone so far as to state that in given situations (especially with regard to rituals), "the form *is* the meaning." Hiebert (1989), for example, following Mary Douglas (1973) and the perspective within anthropology called "symbolic anthropology," makes such a claim. That perspective, however, confuses message with meaning and ignores the need to focus on person/group interpretation as the operative element in assigning meaning. Though the bonding between form and meaning can be very tight in many situations, the attempt to equate form with meaning reveals a fundamental misunderstanding of the distinction being made.

1. First of all, the form-meaning distinction is an analytical distinction. In real life, they occur together. That is, in real life it is impossible to point to one thing as being a form and another a meaning, except conceptually. In cultural experience, meanings require forms and forms will be assigned meanings by the people who observe and use them. It is of the nature of culture that it be made up of forms (as I have defined them here). And it is of the nature of human beings that they interpret (assign meaning to) the various cultural items, patterns, and structures they observe and participate in.

2. The fact that different people (especially those from different societies) can assign different meanings to the same cultural form indicates that form and

meaning can be separated conceptually. As we have seen, if we want to understand what happens to meanings when cultural phenomena are taken from society to society, we need some such conceptual tool.

3. The fact that different persons can observe any given cultural form and assign it different meanings proves that a form cannot *contain* its meaning. Even within the same society, not all people interpret their cultural forms, even rituals, the same.

4. Though the sources of meaning have been discussed endlessly, the arguments for meaning being external to human beings all founder on the fact of variability in interpretation. If meaning was inherent in forms, both individual and cross-cultural differences in interpretation of cultural phenomena would be virtually, if not totally, nonexistent. Since there is great variability in interpretation of the same phenomena, the source of that variability must lie within the human interpreters, not within the phenomena themselves. For further discussion of the source of meaning in people, *see* Kraft (1991a).

From my point of view, there is no better option than the form-meaning conceptual distinction for enabling us to deal with cultural data and the transfer of cultural phenomena from one society to another. Are there difficulties in the theory? Yes, some.

For example, not infrequently the form of poetry in one society is radically different from that in another. This is the case between Hebrew and English. When, therefore, translators attempt to render the Psalms in English, they have to choose whether to focus on form or on meaning. If the translator renders the Psalms in Hebrew parallelistic fashion, the English reader may well decide that the extreme repetitiveness indicates some deficiency in the authors. The English reader may not know that such repetitiveness was required by Hebrew poetic structuring. If, however, the translator makes the choice to bring the meaning over as clearly as possible to English readers (as most contemporary translators choose to do), the translation will seldom come out looking like poetry to the receptors.

The problem arises when some part of the meaning is dependent on the form of the cultural phenomenon. In the case of poetry, the translator has to consider that part of the meaning to the original hearers lay in the fact that a poetic form was employed. In the case of Hebrew hearers, poetry was very much respected, especially when used to convey messages from or about God.

With ritual, it is undoubtedly true that meaning is assigned both to the way the ritual is performed and to whatever messages it is intended to convey. But this does not demonstrate that the form *is* the meaning. It simply illustrates the well-demonstrated communicational principle that all that surrounds the message is interpreted and becomes part of the message. For example, when a speaker tries to get across a message, in addition to interpreting what he or she says, the receptors interpret clothing, tone of voice, posture, the setting in which the interaction takes place, the time of day, and whatever is going on inside of them. The meanings assigned to all of these elements become a part of the message communicated. That is, a multiplicity of forms are assigned meaning when a communication is interpreted. The same is true of ritual, poetry, and every other cultural event.

Nevertheless, Hiebert has a point when he sets up a scale to try to calculate the tightness or looseness of the bonding between given forms and their meanings. He says, "In many symbols the links between form and meaning are arbitrary. In others, however, the links vary along a continuum ranging from loose ties based on similarities and analogies, to more direct ties based on direct connections, and to symbols in which form and meaning are one" (1989:111).

This continuum of linkages is charted as follows:

Type of Linkage	Examples
1. Arbitrary Linkage	Names, ordinary words chosen arbitrarily to label things
2. Loose Linkage	Words for common human experiences; color terms; association of blood with life, of land and women with fertility, of males with violence and warfare
3. Tight Linkage	Eating together as expressing close relationship; bowing or prostrating to show subservience; dance and music to express emotion; precise rituals and chants conveying magical power
4. Forms Equated with Meanings	"Specific historical facts tied to specific times and places" (e.g., the Incarnation); legal statements such as "guilty," or "I pronounce you man and wife," the saying of which transforms a person's social status; boundary symbols such as fences, walls, lines marking lanes on roads or boundaries on athletic fields

Figure 9.2 Hiebert's scheme for linkages between form and meaning

Though I believe the equation of form and meaning in the latter part of the above quote and the chart to be erroneous, the recognition of difference in the tightness of the relationship is valuable. When, for example, people interpret words or rituals as tightly associated (in their minds) with certain meanings, it will be very difficult for an advocate of change to lead them to reinterpret them, at least in the first generation. When meanings are more loosely associated with their referents, however, it is usually because they are considered less crucial to their lives, and are more easily changed. Note, though, that it is *people*, not the forms themselves, that tie the forms to their meanings. *The meanings are assigned to the forms by people, whether the connection is a tight one or a loose one. They are never inherent in the forms themselves.*

Are those who interpret and assign meaning aware of a difference between cultural forms and their meanings? Usually not. Most of life for most people in every society (including western societies) goes on quite well without awareness of this distinction. The analytic value of the form-meaning dichotomy, however, in no way depends on people being conscious of the difference.

CHAPTER 10

THE INDIVIDUAL AND CULTURE

INTEGRATIONAL THOUGHT

There are two additional considerations in the discussion concerning form and meaning. The first is raised in both the Romans 14 and the 1 Corinthians 8 passages: the issue of *intent or motivation*. It is not clear to me whether to consider this a meaning or to see it as something deeper. My inclination is to associate it with one's will and to consider it to be at a deeper level than even meaning. It would still be at the personal, rather than the cultural level, but deeper.

In any event, it needs to be considered strongly as we think of the significance/meaning that people attach to our behavior. I believe, what we intend when we do something in relation to others is of great significance to God, and should be to us. If we mislead them, is it by intent or by accident?

Jesus was hard on the Pharisees for willfully using their positions to oppress people. He calls them hypocrites, those who do things intended to lead others to think more highly of them than they deserve. In Matthew 23, for example, He critiques their motives in harsh terms, saying,

- They do everything so that people will see them (v. 5).
- They love to be greeted with respect (v. 7).
- They lock the door to the Kingdom of heaven in people's faces (v. 13).
- They sail the seas and cross whole countries to win one convert; and when they succeed, they make him twice as deserving of going to hell as they themselves are (v. 15).
- They give to God one tenth . . . but neglect to obey the really important teachings of the Law, such as justice and mercy and honesty (v. 23).

Jesus called people like this "whitewashed tombs," saying further, "on the outside you appear good to everybody, but inside you are full of hypocrisy and sins" (vv. 27, 28). They used forms of behavior they hoped would be interpreted in such a way as to bring them honor and respect as religious leaders, but their motivation was to use the prestige they received for their own devious purposes.

Cultural forms can and regularly are used by people to mislead receptors into the impression that the motivations of the users are better than they really are. That's why Paul is strong on the fact that the Christian's motivation in whatever we do must be love. We are to consider the meaning our brother or sister may derive from our actions and, in love and concern, even go to the extent that we "will never eat meat again, so as not to make my brother fall into sin" (1 Cor 8:13). If the Pharisees had only behaved in love, much of their behavior would have been exemplary, but beneath the forms they used and the meanings they sought to convey lay the wrong motivations.

There is still another matter that relates to cultural forms and meanings: *empowerment*. Most of what we (and others) do falls simply into the human realm. That is, it is normal human behavior—cultural forms used for ordinary human purposes and empowered by no one else than the humans who perform those acts. There are, however, other empowerers in the universe: God and Satan.

The food spoken of in Romans 14 and 1 Corinthians 8 does not seem to have been dedicated to (and thereby empowered by) Satan or evil spirits, though the biblical authors are usually very much against eating food that has been offered to idols (*see* Ex 34:15; Ez 22:9; 1 Cor 10:21; Rv 2:14, 20). But often in cross-cultural situations we come across food, amulets, items used in worship, idols, and the like that have been empowered by satanic power and cannot be regarded as merely neutral cultural forms. These must be destroyed or freed from the empowerment they carry if the work of God is to go on unhindered in that area. "For," as Paul says, "we are not fighting against human beings but against the wicked spiritual forces in the heavenly world, the rulers, authorities, and cosmic powers of this dark age" (Eph 6:12).

God can, however, also empower cultural forms. We call this "blessing." When we bless our food in Jesus' name, God empowers it to fulfill the purpose it was blessed for. Likewise when we bless the elements in the communion service, the words we preach, or the oil we use to anoint the sick. We can even bless water, salt, letters we write, or other physical objects, empowering them to convey blessing to those who use them. God empowers our hands and words as we lay our hands on people and pray for their healing.

Most western Protestants have shied away from this area due to cultural conditioning in part based on a reaction to the excesses of Medieval Roman Catholicism. But in the Scriptures we read of the empowerment by God of Paul's handkerchiefs and aprons (Acts 19:12), Jesus' garment (Mt 9:20), even Peter's shadow (Acts 5:15). Paul, speaking of the communion elements, points to the empowerment conveyed in the blessing when he asks, "The cup of blessing which we bless, is it not the communion of the blood of Christ?" (1 Cor 10:16 *NKJV*).

Then, in the same passage, Paul warns concerning empowerment when he says, "You cannot drink from the Lord's cup and also from the cup of demons; you cannot eat at the Lord's table and also at the table of demons" (v. 21).

So learn to distinguish between forms and their meanings, but also be aware of the deeper levels of motivation and empowerment. These areas are crucial to Christian ministry.

INTRODUCTION

Anthropologists are often critical of other academic disciplines for being so individualistically oriented. Psychologists deal with much of the material that anthropologists consider important, but they focus so completely at the individual level that they (from our point of view) tend to miss quite a bit of the significant material that affects individuals. Having said that, we must admit that anthropologists (perhaps in reaction against this individualistic emphasis) often go to the other extreme and deal so much with groups that you can go through a whole anthropology course and say, "What about the individual? Aren't individuals important? Aren't human beings as single persons important at all?"

To partly rectify that lack, I want to treat a topic that is very legitimately part of any anthropological survey. This is the matter of the individual and culture, focusing on the relationship between people as individuals and the cultural matrix in which we find ourselves. In what follows, I am greatly indebted to Luzbetak (1963) and Goodman (1967).

RELATING THE INDIVIDUAL TO CULTURE

We are conceived without culture, but immediately embark on a process that anthropologists call enculturation, socialization, or education (in the anthropological sense of the term—*see* chapter 17). In this process we learn a particular set of habits—habitual patterns of perceiving reality, behaving, thinking, and so forth. By being trained into these habits we are automatically trained out of other habits. Because of this, we find it very difficult to understand the habitual behavior and habitual perception of people of other societies.

The perspectives and behaviors we have learned become automatic—so natural that we take our patterns as normal, as natural for all humans. We often cannot even conceive of the fact that the reactions we have within our society are not natural for everybody, for our cultural behavior, though relative, "is learned as if it were absolute, as if it had a value as universal as mankind" (Luzbetak 1963:76). This process is so pervasive, so thorough, and so subtle that even our emotions and muscular coordination reflect our cultural conditioning. The introduction of sit-down toilets, for example, has led to constipation among "squatters" in many parts of the world (Foster 1973:103). This is cultural conditioning at a fairly deep physical level!

 Our enculturation is so effective that we are 100 percent culturally conditioned. Note that we said "conditioned," not "determined." Many people take the phrase "culturally conditioned" to mean culturally determined. This is not what we mean. Culturally conditioned means that 100 percent of our behavior is *affected* by our cultural conditioning in every aspect. This includes the ways we think and the things we think about, as well as the things we do and how we do them. Our psychology and mental processes are thoroughly conditioned.

Sometimes Christians (and others) feel threatened when we talk about the pervasive influence of culture on us. We seem to have learned as we grew up (at least in American society) that we are basically free, with only a few things that restrict us—such as other people's freedom. But along come the psychologists to tell us that we are strongly influenced by the way we have been taught and that such influences frequently push us to do things that we would not otherwise do. As Christians, we have learned that sin affects everything we do, but we tend not to see sin and evil as seriously limiting our individual freedom. Now we're learning that culture affects everything we do, so we may well wonder, How many things are there in life that can restrict our freedom?

Case against Cultural Determinism

As a first step toward the perspective we are developing here, let us recognize that, whatever else we say about human freedom or lack of freedom, we are ultimately limited by God. He has set the outer limits of our freedom. There never has been any possibility that humans could be absolutely free; we have always had to live within a sphere defined for us by our Creator. We are, furthermore, limited by such things as space, time, biological makeup, genetic capacities, the idiosyncrasies of our own life histories, and many other similar factors that characterize our human beingness. Some of these will be charted below.

In spite of all of this, however, it is a part of the worldview of many (most?) westerners to believe that we are more free than it now appears we are. We may illustrate this fact by suggesting that many have seen human freedom as covering the whole range between the following lines in figure 10.1.

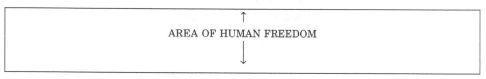

Figure 10.1 Many see humans as having a wide area of freedom

There are, however, those who would completely deny such a belief. B. F. Skinner is probably the most prominent of those within psychology who have made such an assertion. He says that before we got as far as we have in scientific investigation, we thought that human beings had some free will. But in his book *Beyond Freedom and Dignity* (1971), he suggests that until we learn that there is no freedom and that we have no such thing as dignity in so-called freedom, we are not being scientific. We should recognize that we are *totally determined*. Now, in our present state of knowledge, we still see a little bit of what we call free will, but it's only a matter of time until scientists (he would probably say behaviorist psychologists) will prove that free will is only an illusion. In terms of figure 10.1, he is saying that the lines we once thought were fairly wide apart actually converge—there is no free will at all!

I'm not quite sure how an intelligent man like Skinner could say such a thing, since it seems as though he must have used some measure of what we call free will to think it up and put it in print. Perhaps what he means is that everybody is determined except himself! It sounds to many of us as if he's using something that we have learned to call freedom (whether it's a lot of freedom or a little freedom) to state that everybody is determined.

Within anthropology, the most prominent recent determinist is Leslie White. In his writings we find the contention that when something becomes culturally possible, it becomes inevitable (1949)! Again here is a very intelligent man making what I would consider an obviously unintelligent statement. I was amused to find that my former colleague Alan R. Tippett had written in the margin of his copy of White's book, "Do you mean that as soon as it becomes culturally possible for someone to become a Christian, it becomes inevitable?" Since many people for whom it is possible to become Christian have chosen not to be Christian, White's statement would seem to be wide of the mark.

It seems clear, rather, that human beings are not simply hapless victims of either psychology or culture. True, we are not as free as westerners once believed, but in recognizing this fact, it does not seem that we must go all the way to the other extreme, as Skinner and White have. There are other options short of concluding that we are totally determined. We could draw our lines as in figure 10.2.

The reasonable position would seem to be that we are pressed into a psychocultural mold, but that there is within that mold some leeway, some space within which we have a degree of freedom of choice, what I like to call some room to wiggle. We are pressed into a mold, but it's a mold that has some room in it. I think of a person with a broken leg who has to wear a cast. The cast is there to guide the process of healing and protect the damaged leg. But it cannot be too tight and it cannot totally restrict all movement (at least not for a long period of time) or the leg will become useless, even if the break heals. There must be some room to wiggle, some space, no matter how small it may be, within which the person can flex the muscles and move the leg. Within certain sectors of a culture, there is a lot of freedom, a lot of room to wiggle. In other parts of the culture, there may be only a little room to wiggle. But there is always some room. We are not totally determined.

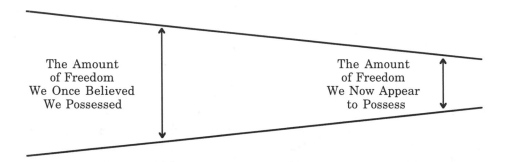

Figure 10.2 The amount of perceived freedom is now less

The valid point the determinists like Skinner and White make is that once we felt that we had freedom over a fairly wide range. Human beings were seen as very free to create and to make choices. Then, as the process of scientific investigation (specifically behavioral science investigation) went on, it was discovered that the range within which we have freedom is not nearly as wide as we once thought. It's much narrower. We see ourselves as more determined now than we saw ourselves 200 or 100 years ago. With this in mind, Skinner and other determinists take a leap of faith and say it's only a matter of time until we discover that these borders between which we think we have freedom really converge and we are totally determined.

Though it is common practice for people to plead in court that they were forced by circumstances beyond their control to commit whatever crime they committed, I don't think the anthropological evidence can support such a claim. The data suggest it is quite possible that certain people are conditioned in such a way that criminal behavior is highly likely. But this is not the same as saying that people are conditioned in such a way that criminal behavior is *determined*. For every example of a person who is conditioned to become a criminal, you could find many examples of people conditioned in the same way, or worse, who somehow have kept from becoming criminals. At some point there is an area of choice where some people use whatever freedom they have to become criminals, while others in the same circumstances choose to transcend these pressures.

I reason the same way with regard to Lingenfelter's view of culture as a "prison of disobedience" (*see* chapter 3). Though it may be culturally easier for humans to do wrong than to do right, we are not imprisoned (determined). It may be more difficult, but we can, even within the same cultural structures, obey God. We are not imprisoned by the structures. We can *use* those structures for good or for evil.

As I see it, the evidence suggests that in all cases there is some element of choice as to what we do with our cultural conditioning. The cards may be stacked against us. There may be a lot of pressure for us to become victimized and to go into some kind of antisocial or criminal activity. But there is, I believe (and this has to be a statement of faith rather than actual knowledge), always some room to wiggle. There is always some way to do something else with those particular defects.

From a Christian perspective, we believe there is enough free choice for us to be held responsible and accountable for our actions before God. If we look at the Parable of the Talents, we see one man with five, another with two, another with one. They all started with different abilities, capabilities, and obstacles. The man with one obviously did not have the resources to do what the man with five had. But they were accountable before God for what they did with what they had, not for measuring up to some other people's standard.

Personality

When it comes to personality, each of us starts with something biologically distinctive: our genetic makeup. This is something that anthropologists often don't know what to do with. In spite of the limitations and lack of interest of certain anthropologists, *there seems to be something distinctive at the individual level to which culture must be adapted* (*see* Goldschmidt 1966:135).

Why do two children in the same home, presumably having the same cultural conditioning and the same family conditioning, turn out so differently? One accepts whatever the parents suggest, the other rejects the parents' way. There seems to be something essential to individual personality, probably rooted in genetic characteristics, that predisposes one child to accept whatever is taught and the other to reject whatever is taught. Notice I said "predisposes" rather than "determines."

Personality seems to be created as a response to the interactions between what people are given genetically and the cultural patterning into which they are introduced by parents and others from whom they learn. This is an interactive process in which there is pressure toward conformity to the cultural patterns exerted by the society. It results in 1) a fair amount of diversity stemming from genetic differences and personal choices and 2) a large amount of psychological similarity among the people of any given society. Some anthropologists have labeled such similarities in group personality characteristics "modal personality" or "national character," but such social pressure is not totally determinative, since within each society the number of variations seems to be endless.

Boundaries, Patterns, Press, and Pull

As we have pointed out in chapter 8, the patterns within which human beings work are embodied in their culture. Within most patterns, however, we are allowed a range of options from which we may select according to our own individuality. Given customs provide the channels within which we choose the specific form of the custom that we employ in any given act. Our behavior may be according to this alternative or that, depending on which we choose. But once we have chosen one alternative, other choices may be more limited than before we made the first choice.

Each custom provides us with boundaries within which we conduct our lives.

> But boundaries are not directives. Within the life space defined by his boundaries our
> man is at liberty. It is within this space that he exercises those faculties . . . to which
> self-determination can be attributed. Moreover, the boundaries are potentially alter-
> able. Fortuitous circumstances (e.g., to spend his savings on travel) may significantly
> expand his life space. Man's potential for mastery of his conditions is, of course, limited,
> yet it is the less limited the more he becomes aware, thoughtful, and confident of his
> own powers (Goodman 1967:57).

Within those boundaries human beings act out what Goodman calls a "drama of individual thrust" that is met by social "press" (1967:3). This drama takes place as we feel either pressured or pulled (enticed) to behave in certain ways by those with whom we interact. Such press and pull are exerted by people as they follow the cultural patterning they have been taught. As humans, we seem to know intu- itively that if the structures are to be preserved, they must be obeyed. People therefore attempt, with varying degrees of success, to press or pull each other into conformity to those structures.

In many areas, group pressure seems to allow little room for individual free- dom—we are simply pressed, pushed, or coerced in given directions. Societies develop laws with severe penalties attached, and authorized persons (e.g., police) or structures (e.g., feuding) enforce them. Even without such laws, however, cer- tain behaviors are so strongly enforced by means of public opinion that they also fit into this "press" category. In terms of our individuality, then, we may either (with most people) choose to submit to that pressure, or we may try to "thrust" against it, even at the risk of being regarded as deviants. If enough others join us in resisting rules and laws that we don't like, we may be successful in getting the rules changed and thereby widening the range of allowed behavior. In areas of cul- ture where there are more allowed alternatives, the pressure is more subtle. This makes us feel that we have a fair amount of freedom to respond positively or nega- tively to the attractions and enticements held out before us without suffering severe penalties. This is the "pull" factor. In such areas, the society seems to say, "You can do whatever you want in this area, but if you want to be respected by peo- ple, do this." That's an enticement. The person can choose either to do as the soci- ety recommends and be respected by people or to do something else and pay the social consequences.

We have an analogy that fits here about a horse pulling a wagon. The horse doesn't want to move, so the person driving the horse holds out over its head a stick from which a carrot is hung. The horse sees the carrot and goes after it. Of course, as the horse moves, the carrot moves ahead of him, since it is held by the driver who is sitting in the wagon. The horse never catches up with the carrot, but is too dumb to realize he's never going to get it, so he keeps on trying and, in the process, pulls the wagon that he didn't want to pull. Social life is something like this. The society holds certain standards out before us and says, "You will get cer- tain goodies. You will feel good about yourself. Other people will look up to you, if you achieve this particular goal." So we, like the horse, work hard to achieve such goals, whether or not they are really important or fulfilling, simply because they are the goals valued by our society.

For example, who are more important to western societies, professors or gar- bage collectors? If the professors stop working, who cares? Only a handful of students and their families, plus the employees of the institutions in which they teach, are really inconvenienced. With only a few adjustments, our society could get along reasonably well without professors. But if the garbage collectors go on strike, we're in big trouble! Yet western societies say it's more prestigious to be a professor than a garbage collector. There's the pull, the enticement. Professors don't ordinarily make a lot of money; garbage collectors often make more money than professors. It often happens that the necessary occupation is without very high prestige, while the unnecessary luxury occupation is held as very desirable. Who would be a professor if it didn't involve prestige? That's the pull of society.

Sometimes even harmful things are presented by society as attractive and prestigious. This is the case in western society with drinking and smoking. We are enticed into believing that to be really "in" with the attractive people of our society we have to be able to drink the right drinks and smoke the right cigarettes. If you smoke a certain cigarette, they say, you will be truly happier than if you smoke another brand or don't smoke at all. Or if you drink such and such a beverage, you will have great pleasure and be truly "in" with the people who count. Within this "life space," we have our room to wiggle. The press of society is in effect when we hear, Don't you dare do that or "they'll get you." If you steal, the policeman will get you. If you speed, watch out for the red lights behind you. The pull of a society is expressed in the enticement offered to lead people to do certain things rather than other things. Nobody will put you in jail if you don't become a professor. But you know that if you do become a professor, people will look up to you. The society uses enticement, not pressure, to get people to become professors. These processes are important to recognize whenever we consider the relationships between individuals and their cultures.

At many points in sociocultural life, several choices are possible, none of which is inevitable. In some cases, we may be conditioned so that the chance of our choosing a given alternative is about 90 percent. But there is one chance in ten that we will choose another alternative, and there are always those who choose one of the other alternatives.

As Goodman points out, there are at least three categories of cultural behavior to choose from:

1. *Modalities*—those things that most people do or believe they should do because they believe them to be prescribed and proper. These are usually done habitually.

2. *Alternatives*—behavior allowed with no penalty. These are chosen rather than habitual behaviors.

3. *Deviances*—alternative behavior considered outside the range of that allowed without penalty. These, too, are the result of choices (1967:5).

In even the best regulated and most orderly of societies, as in families, there will be less than perfect conformity. It may be merely a matter of imperfect reproduction of patterned roles. It may be deviance of sorts explicitly or implicitly invited by the very nature of the patterned values. But always individuality will find expression somehow, whether it is rewarded or punished. The press of society is uneven and never wholly adequate to suppress or sublimate the thrust of individuals (Goodman 1967:5).

Social pressure is toward conformity to prescribed or modal behavior for most of the participants. We are pushed or pressed in certain directions both by the people we relate to and by the habits we have developed as we learned our culture.

Such pressure evokes in a certain number of people a rebellious response. These people become known as rebels and are often ostracized and may even leave their society if the opportunity presents itself. Many who move from rural homes to the city do so in an attempt to escape such social pressure. Likewise with many who emigrate to another country.

At least certain people in a society are, however, pulled or enticed to select alternatives not open or recommended to the majority. These are the specialists and those expected to be creative and innovative. Allowance is made for people such as Dr. Albert Einstein and other pioneers who seem so absorbed in their special concerns that they don't dress or talk or behave like other people in the society. Indeed, for these, the society's prescribed or modal behavior is different. But children will be warned not to "go off the deep end" by imitating them.

In addition to what has already been said concerning social pressure and individual choices, we may list the following principles:

1. Small-scale traditional and peasant societies, where homogeneity is high and conformity both highly valued and highly enforceable, tend to exert more pressure on individuals to bring about modal behavior.

2. The larger the scale, the more diversity and complexity in a society, the more enticements there are to choose alternative behavior rather than that recommended by the society.

3. Societies with a high degree of urbanization tend to provide and allow more alternatives than societies that are primarily rural.

4. Greater contact with peoples of other societies tends to encourage more diversity in behavior than does isolation from other ways of life.

5. Societies that highly value individualism tend to allow more alternative behavior than societies that are highly group oriented.

As Christians, we must believe that there are choices available within cultural structuring if we are going to appeal to people to respond to Jesus Christ. If we are to appeal to them to respond to our message, there must be some possibility for them to do something that perhaps the rest of the people in their society are not doing. The determinists would have us believe that once society has molded us, we have no choice. Any change in us, they say, is the result of a change in the culture. The widespread choosing of alternatives as opposed to modal behavior, however, proves the determinists wrong.

In areas where the Christian message has not been effectively communicated, we are anxious to introduce the possibility of becoming Christian as an alternative. We would like to see this alternative selected by so many people so often that it becomes a modality, the norm. The first thing we're aiming at, though, is that such a choice be accepted as an allowable alternative. Unfortunately, in many situations, Christianity is first perceived as a deviance. Those who turn to Christ often see their conversion as a way of joining another group's culture to escape from the pressure of their society to conform. We're not anxious to see Christianity permanently regarded as a deviance in any society.

ELEMENTS INVOLVED IN RELATING
THE INDIVIDUAL AND CULTURE

Goodman (1967:26–27) presents three helpful propositions concerning the ways in which individuals relate to culture.

1. *The individual is endowed with will and creativity*, as well as with intelligence and awareness. (It's good to hear an anthropologist talk about will and creativity; not many of them do.) The individual is therefore creator and manipulator of culture, as well as receiver and reactor. Culture is what individuals receive and react or respond to. Individuality is that characteristic of humans that interacts creatively with culture.

2. *Within any given society, there is great variability between individuals*. We find active and passive individuals within every society. We find those who worry a lot and those who never seem to worry. In spite of the social pressure to conform, it appears that the range of variation between individuals is approximately the same for every society—though, due to the social pressures, the percentage of people of each type probably differs from society to society (*see* Goldschmidt 1966). That is, if a society pressures people to be "uptight" as, for example, Japanese society seems to, we can expect a higher percentage of uptight people in such a society. But we would also expect to find a certain (probably low) percentage of people in the culture who do not seem to be as uptight as the majority.

It is very important for us to recognize that there is great individual variability within each society. It is very easy for an outsider to come to a people and, on the basis of a cursory look at them, to assume that they are all the same. We may look for someone to help us with the language and culture and assume that if we learn from one person, we have learned all that is necessary. Such a view is simplistic.

Rather, there are people in all societies who have learned their culture or language imperfectly or do things idiosyncratically. There are those who, often through no fault of their own, will lead us into a nonprestigious or idiosyncratic form of their language and culture that will hurt our relationships with those we seek to reach.

There are also generational variations within most societies. If we learn the culture and the language from an old person, the young people will say, "You speak our language like an old person." If we learn the language from a younger person, we may receive a similar criticism from the elders. Each group, of course, practices a valid variety of the culture, but not the only variety. The point is that there are variations within every culture. When we learn the language and culture, we should learn one variety of it, but with our eyes open to the fact that we are learning that particular variety—we are not learning the "whole" culture. In fact, when we choose who we're going to learn from, we should make sure that the persons are practicing a form of the culture and language that is not looked down upon by those we seek to win. We need to be aware that there are variations and to study them to discover which variations carry prestige and which do not. Sometimes we will want to choose a variation that is not highly prestigious. This is what Jesus did, of course. He did not choose the most prestigious place in Palestine to live, nor did He choose the most prestigious social class. He chose the one that suited His strategy on the basis of His knowledge of the variety of possibilities available. Interestingly enough, He chose to fill a respected position within the segment of the society with which He identified. A carpenter was a respected person in Galilee. So were fishermen.

3. The third proposition is that *the forces of society and culture acting on the individual may be either helpful or unhelpful* in terms of personal well-being, That is, people's psycho-social health and well-being may be either strengthened or weakened (or both) through their interaction with their cultural norms and guide-

lines. Sociocultural influences are seldom as bad as Freudian psychology suggests. Freud seemed to have the idea that all influences from outside are bad, and we are psychologically incapacitated because of them.

On the other hand, the data doesn't allow us to regard sociocultural influences as thoroughly benign or good, as another psychologist named Maslow seems to suppose. These influences lie somewhere in between. On the one hand are pressures and enticements toward growth, maturation, and health, while on the other are those that at best challenge psychological health and growth, and at worst can press and pull strongly toward psychological illness and dysfunction.

A chart that can help us visualize this great complexity of factors in the relationships between culture and the individual is found in Goodman 1967:57 (based on Kluckhohn and Mowrer 1944) and reproduced in figure 10.3 below.

Levels of Individuality	Antecedents and Influences			
	Biological[A]	Physical Environmental[B]	Social[C]	Cultural[D]
Universal[4]	4A Birth, death, hunger, thirst, elimination, etc.	4B Gravity, temperature, time, etc.	4C Infant care, group life, etc.	4D Symbolism, taboo on incest and in-group murder, etc.
Communal[3]	3A "Racial" traits, nutrition level, endemic diseases, etc.	3B Climate, topography, natural resources, etc.	3C Size, density, and distribution of population, etc.	3D Traditions, rules of conduct and manners, skills, knowledge, etc.
Role[2]	2A Age and sex differences, caste, etc.	2B Differential access to material goods, etc.	2C Cliques, "marginal" men, etc.	2D Culturally differentiated roles
Idiosyncratic[1]	1A Peculiarities of stature, physiognomy, glandular makeup, etc.	1B Unique events and "accidents" such as being hit by lightning, etc.	1C Social "accidents" such as death of a parent, being adopted, meeting particular people, etc.	1D Folklore about accidents and "fate," etc.

Figure 10.3 The individual and culture (from Goodman 1967:57)

Goodman provides a good summary of the chart as follows:

a. The individual, though he has much in common with his fellow tribesmen or nationals (role and communal levels), and much in common with humanity at large (universal level), is also and everywhere unique (idiosyncratic level).

b. The sources of his uniqueness are not entirely accounted for when we have catalogued what are certainly the principal antecedents and influences by which his development and his actions are affected. What these factors of heredity and environment represent are more accurately described as boundary conditions than as determinants.

c. Certain boundary conditions are of course unyielding. No man can defy the genetic forces through which he is endowed with feet, not fins. The pull of gravity, the need for nurture in infancy, his restless mind—these are forces to which he is subject.

He reacts to these forces. He reacts to the drives inherent in his biologically given nature and to those learned so early that he feels them as equally, or almost equally, inherent.

d. There is an immutable condition of life to which much of idiosyncrasy is traceable, that is, the impossibility of truly exact replications of behavior either by or between individuals . . .

e. Diverse though they are, the individuals of a given society tend to cluster and to be classed. Social differentiation is inevitable because of individual diversity, and social differentiation is conducive to ranking and to social stratification. Once it has developed, a system of stratification becomes an antecedent-influence factor affecting new generations (1967:62).

Notice the labeling of the chart. Along the left-hand side are what the authors call levels of individuality—universal, communal, role, and idiosyncratic. The categories indicated along the top are the antecedents and influences, the inevitable contexts—the biological, physical environmental, social and cultural—within which this individuality will be played out. Each compartment on the chart gives examples of the kinds of things that occur in the life of every individual at that particular intersection of the individual and the contextual. Note the kinds of things specified under each category. For example, all human beings, whatever their culture, experience birth, death, hunger, thirst, etc. Likewise with regard to the physical environment, all experience the force of gravity, temperature, time, space limitations, etc. In the social area, all experience infant care, group life, and other social concomitants of our humanness. Likewise all experience within the cultural realm things such as symbolism, taboos against incest and in-group murder, etc. These are universal things.

At the communal level, such factors as one's racial group, the climate of the area in which one lives, demographic realities, and cultural traditions come into play. One is born into a community already possessed of certain characteristics. One chooses none of the things that are labeled communal here. Yet all of them regularly impinge on one's cultural experience, making it unique in many ways yet similar in many ways to that of any others who share the same communal characteristics.

As to role, it makes a difference in any society whether you are male or female (box 2A). Every society has differing roles for males and females. This is a response to a biological pressure that inclines people to produce cultural structures that require men and women to relate differently to members of the opposite sex than they do to members of their own sex. It is a cultural fact that these and other roles with a nonbiological basis (e.g., leadership, occupation, education, wealth, etc.) are assigned or achieved (box 2D). Physical environment, however, may play an important part in this by either facilitating or inhibiting access to the goods and services necessary for such desirables as wealth and schooling (box 2B). One's particular role in a social group (box 2C) is also important to one's cultural experience. Being a leader, for example, provides one with quite a different experience than that of a "marginal" person.

Perhaps the most interesting part of the reality charted here is the bottom row, labeled idiosyncratic. At the idiosyncratic level biologically, each of us has our own peculiarities of stature. We are five feet tall or six feet tall or somewhere in between. That's a given of our individual biological makeup. Externally, we have particular facial characteristics, particular bodily characteristics. Internally, we have a particular metabolism, a particular energy level. Within every society there are people with high energy levels and people with low energy levels.

Under physical environment, everyone experiences certain unique events and accidents. A person hit by lightning who lives through it is never the same afterward. Anyone who has experienced a broken leg is immediately on common ground with any other person who has had that same experience, even if that person happens to be from another society. The same is true of those who have given birth to a child. In this respect, all women who have borne children have more in common with each other cross-culturally than with any man, even one of their own society.

Then (box 1C) there are social accidents. For one whose parent has died or who has been adopted, the cultural experience may be quite different than for someone whose experience is more normal. Since such events happen fairly often, humans develop explanations concerning why such things happen and why they happened to certain people and not to others. These are the idiosyncratic part of the individual's experience (box 1D).

THE INDIVIDUAL AND CULTURE CHANGE

All this interplay between individuals and their cultures is highly relevant to the subject of culture change. Though we will be dealing with this subject in several later chapters, it will be helpful to point out here the importance of individuals in the process. As Barnett (1953:1–16) says, the place where a cultural change is initiated is always in the mind of an individual (*see also* Luzbetak 1963:196–97). This is especially true if the individual in question is an opinion leader in a group. If such a person makes a change, others are likely to follow, and the change is likely to become a part of the group's behavior. In this way it becomes a cultural thing rather than simply an individual thing.

The process goes something like this: a given woman decides to make a change in her cultural behavior by cooking something in a slightly different way. She cooks it, and her family likes it, and so she or they tell a friend. The friend responds by trying the recipe, liking it, and from that point on always using that recipe in place of her former one. She has adopted the change and made it a part of her habitual behavior. Another lady visits the friend, hears of the recipe, copies it, takes it home, and tries it on her husband, who likes it and tells his friend, who tells his wife. Soon we have a group change, rather than simply an individual change. In this way, new recipes and even new foods may be introduced into a society by a given individual who both adopts the change and becomes an opinion leader for others who imitate her.

Whether it is new items such as foods or mechanical things or new techniques, this is the way innovation happens. There is always a given individual, usually with fairly high prestige, to initiate the change. It is unusual for an individual with low prestige to do something different and have other people imitate him or her. When individuals of low prestige innovate, people tend to evaluate the ideas as strange or even dumb. Ordinarily they will reject the innovation, not because it's not a good idea, but because of the person introducing it. Indeed, not infrequently when an idea comes from a high prestige person, it is at least tried, even if it is not a good idea. The prestige of the innovator is often more important to the acceptance of the innovation than the quality of the idea. We may ask how an individual gains high prestige in a given society. As we will discuss in chapter 19, prestige is either assigned by the society on the basis of such things as birth or inheritance, or it is earned by achievement. In many societies, the primary means of becoming prestigious is by being born into certain families. Maintaining that prestige is ordinarily a matter of simply responding positively to those presses and pulls of the society that are designed to keep prestigious people prestigious. In many other societies, the major ways of becoming prestigious are by attainment. Such attainment involves even more attention to responding properly to those presses and pulls of the society that will assure the desired prestige. A person learns how to work the mechanics of the sociocultural context so as to become someone who people will listen to.

One fact of present-day situations is that the process of westernization has often introduced new techniques for getting prestige. In most of today's societies, there is a traditional segment within which people aim to attain according to more or less traditional rules. In the westernizing segment, however, the rules are some modification of western rules. Often these techniques result in people having a fair amount of prestige, but often not much influence, especially within the traditional segment of the society. Such people may find that they have been trained to operate in another society, like that of America or Europe, and trained out of knowing how to relate to the guidelines of the society in which they have to live (even though those guidelines may have been modified to some extent in a western direction).

There are quite a number of nonwestern people who have gone to a high level of western schooling, only to find that there are no or not enough positions for them in their homeland. We often see international students trained in Europe or America who don't go home when they finish their schooling. Frequently the problem is that they have been trained to do something that is valid only in Euroamerica. There's no use for their training in their home country. Or if there is some use for it, people don't value it highly enough to provide the expected salary. One type of individual response to such cultural factors is for the person to not go home.

When we look at change, then, we must look at the individual. It doesn't seem to matter what the ideas are; whether agricultural innovation or innovation of Christianity, the processes seem to be the same. As Luzbetak points out, "there is no essential difference between a culture change affecting tractors and farm techniques . . . [and that] affecting culture elements of a more abstract nature . . . say, philosophy, art, or religion, for psychologically all ideas are the same" (1963:196–97).

Insiders of high prestige (as long as they also have influence) make changes that are imitated by their friends, until there is a group of people making the change.

The fact that at least certain individuals are so important in the process of culture change has important ramifications for the way we present Christianity. We want people to change their minds concerning their relationship to God and the supernatural and to pledge their primary allegiance to God through Jesus Christ. In order to do this effectively, especially in group-oriented societies, we want to appeal to those people who will both make decisions for themselves and, as opinion leaders, influence others to make the same decision.

We want to see Christianity introduced as a viable alternative within the society, an alternative that is attractive to all, not simply to those who are "marginals." Often those who have responded most enthusiastically to the Christian message have been individuals who, either because they are young or for some other reason, have not been allowed to fully participate in the society. Many such people have been attracted to the new message at least partly because it offers them a way to gain stature in the society more quickly or more surely than if they sought to attain their status by following the traditional guidelines. Such people are classified as marginals or even deviants in the society, and any movement (such as Christianity) that they follow is automatically classified by the rest of the society as a deviant way of dealing with life rather than as a valid alternative.

This is not to say that we should not witness to marginals. But we need to be aware of the ramifications of any approach that does not take account of the differences of influence between individuals in the society. The importance of individuals in the decision-making process, plus this "reputation factor" should provide us with great incentive to strategize the Christian witness so that those with proper authority and status in the society are the ones to whom the primary appeal is made. It also means we can't simply dump our message (as is often done in preaching) on a whole group or attempt to appeal to groups in general. As Luzbetak says, we are not postmen who simply come to a house, dump the mail, and leave (1963:205). We are called to interact with people in such a way that the communication is seen as desirable, and appealing to the proper people, those with prestige and influence, is ordinarily understood to be the proper way of going about the communication of anything important. The response, then, can be on the basis of the fact that respected people in the society, people whose opinions are respected, have evaluated the message and found it attractive.

One thing that is widely misunderstood by westerners is the way in which decision making takes place in group-oriented societies. It has been commonplace for westerners to speak of "group decisions," as if the group had a mind of its own that it imposes in some mysterious way on all of its members. This is certainly not true. Nor is it always the case that in such societies there are strong leaders who make decisions and impose them upon their subjects forcefully. Though we know of many such cases, both in history and in contemporary situations, the process that has been and still is more typical in traditional societies is one labeled by Barnett and Tippett "multi-individual, mutually-interdependent" decision making (McGavran and Wagner 1990:227–229).

In this process, important ideas are thoroughly discussed by higher-level leaders (e.g., tribe, clan) with family leaders who, in turn, discuss them with family members in such a way that all those designated by the society as participants in the decision-making process come to agreement on the decision. When such agreement is achieved, the primary leader of the group simply announces the decision that has, in effect, already been made. Outsiders looking on are often misled into thinking that the primary leader has made the decision independently of his people. On the contrary, his function in this process, as in much of the rest of his responsibility, is not that of an imposer but an announcer.

SUMMARY

In summary, though in anthropology we are basically talking about groups, we need to recognize the great importance of individuals, at least certain individuals, in sociocultural dynamics. Social life involves constant interplay between individual and group, on the one hand, and between individual in-group and the cultural structures within which they operate, on the other. Pressures and enticements coming both from within and from outside of the society crowd in on people and require response in terms of whatever freedom they possess.

Within the society, people have their "significant others." These are the people, usually within the immediate subgroup of the persons in question, to whom a person looks for guidance and confirmation. When people think of possibly making a change, they ask, "What would my family or friends think of me if I made this change?" Often the change is rejected out of concern for what the group might think.

This kind of situation is a typical case of interaction between individual and group. Sometimes in such a case, an individual decides that the group is not important and makes the change, even though it costs membership in the group. That, too, is an example of individual-group interaction. Such interaction, and the possibility for individuals to make different decisions in such cases, argue against a deterministic view of the relationship between culture and the individual.

In conclusion, Luzbetak (1963:83) provides us with three very important guidelines for dealing with the individual-culture relationships that we encounter.

1. In the first place, in this area as in all others, we need to study the situation in as thorough and systematic a way as possible, to get as good a picture as we can of the intensity and effectiveness of the social pressures on individuals (*see* chapter 28). We need to assess the amount of leeway allowed people in the areas of life in which we seek to help them change.

2. Secondly, we need to develop a proper appreciation for the deep influence of a people's enculturation. They have been carefully trained and have come to practice their habits just as automatically as we have come to practice our own— often with no clearer logic than ours. Such a recognition should help us appreciate more God's patience with us and enable us to be more patient with them as we wait for them to understand and change.

3. Thirdly, we need to recognize that the struggle for change is usually with the habits of people as they have been trained, rather than with ill will or indifference. It is often not so much that people are against the message as that they realize that to accept this message might involve so much change in their basic habits and behavior or so much antagonism from their "significant others" that they regard the cost to be too high.

PART III

RELATING TO THE NONHUMAN UNIVERSE

CHAPTER 11

MATERIAL CULTURE AND TECHNOLOGY

INTEGRATIONAL THOUGHT

Materialism is a very obvious feature of the world today. There are so many "things," so many gadgets, so many "laborsaving devices," so much prestige to be gained by accumulating houses and lands and vehicles and gadgets. In many ways, the world seems to be gripped in the clutches of a desire to accumulate the visible. We even have a bumper sticker that says, "The one who dies with the most toys wins!"

Don't we know? Haven't we heard? We can't take it with us. Generation after generation of materialists have proven, that happiness does not consist in the amount of things we possess. Material goods and money are very hard taskmasters. Serving them is a real "drag."

This is true whether the interpretation of material possessions is like that of the West, where we brag "we earned all these things ourselves," or like that of much of the rest of the world, who believe (as did the ancient Hebrews), "these possessions mean that God is blessing us." Either attitude can lead to our serving the things rather than the things serving us.

Jesus knew this and warned us against allowing ourselves to be enslaved to material things. As Christians, we especially need to keep our allegiances straight, for "No one can be a slave of two masters. . . . You cannot serve both God and money" (Matt 6:24).

So stop worrying, Jesus says, even about food, drink, clothing, and the other necessities of life (not to mention the non-necessities). God takes care of birds and flowers and decks them out gloriously. Will He not then look after our needs, even though our faith is small?

Let's get our priorities straight. The Provider is infinitely more important than His provision. It is He we are to pledge allegiance to, not the material goods we think we need to have a happy life. If we cannot serve two masters, let's be sure we choose the right one.

It is His Kingdom and obedience to Him alone that can satisfy our longings for security, happiness, freedom from worry, and all the other good things we seek. It is that commitment alone, that relationship with our gracious Provider, that we can take with us into eternity. Only that will last.

> So do not start worrying: "Where will my food come from? or my drink? or my clothes?" (These are the things the pagans are always concerned about.) Your Father in heaven knows that you need all these things. Instead, be concerned above everything else with the Kingdom of God and with what he requires of you, and he will provide you with all these other things. So do not worry about tomorrow; it will have enough worries of its own. There is no need to add to the troubles each day brings (Mt 6:31–34).

INTRODUCTION

As we look at each aspect of human culture, we find ourselves entering the whole of culture, for no subsystem of culture sits off by itself in a corner. Rather, each may be seen as a kind of layering that covers the whole territory of culture and interacts with every other aspect.

In this chapter and the next, we will treat the subsystems of culture that deal with the material universe. These subsystems are often labeled "technology" and "economics." Just as Hall (1959) says, "culture is communication," so it is possible to say "culture is technology." What such a statement would mean is that culture is a mechanism that provides for people the techniques (technology) they need for living. Societies differ, of course, in the extent to which they develop various kinds of technology, but no sociocultural group has been discovered without a well-developed system of technology.

DEFINITION

Robert B. Taylor defines technology as *"All of the social customs by which people manipulate material entities and substances of all kinds"* (1973:137). Manipulating or working with material entities and substances involves techniques and tools by means of which we extend our human capacities.

Notice that we are talking about *social customs*, not simply material items. The thing most visible may very well be a material item such as a tool or some product produced through the use of tools, but what cultural anthropology is concerned with is the custom or technique that either results in that item or makes use of it.

These social customs involve a vast number of skills, a wide variety of implements, and a large number of substances serving a multiplicity of purposes. Among the implements, we think of tools and machines. Substances include such things as wood, stone, plastic, clay, cloth, leather, metal, and the like. The purposes served include shelter, clothing, transportation, food getting, food preparation, art, recreation, and so forth. There is no part of any society that is not deeply influenced by material technology.

> Technology is the aspect of culture that is responsible for [human] adaptability. Technology is the stored knowledge of how to do things. It includes the practical knowledge for wresting a livelihood from the jungle, the desert, or the soil. It includes the knowledge of how to prepare and preserve the food man gets. It includes the fabrication of clothes and the building of houses to give him protection against the inclemency of the weather. It includes the manufacture of weapons of the chase and warfare for protection and aggression. It includes also the tools with which he makes all these other things, and many, many more (Goldschmidt 1957, I:76).

Human arms are not strong enough to move the heavy loads people want to move, so we develop techniques such as levers and machines to push, pry, lift, or carry. In these ways we can move loads that far surpass what we could handle with only our normal human capacities. Our bodies do not protect us from the elements (heat, cold, rain, hardness, etc.) to the extent that we are always comfortable, so we extend our bodily abilities by adding such techniques as clothing, housing, bedding (to protect us from hardness when we sleep), etc. Clothing provides us with another set of skin, as it were, to enhance our protection from the elements. We get carried away with the process, of course, and sometimes use more or less clothing than required for protection due to the fact that we also have other values (beyond the need for protection) that we seek to serve through a technique such as clothing.

People find it uncomfortable, sometimes life threatening, and not very private to sleep and perform certain other family activities out of doors. So we add housing, different styles for different societies, built of different materials of greater or lesser permanence and greater or lesser comfort. Within the housing, most of us like to lie down when we sleep, although that's not necessarily a universal posture for sleeping. There are people who sleep regularly in a sitting position. We may try to enhance the comfort of sleeping by producing mats to spread on the ground, floor, or platforms (beds) and mattresses to keep us above the ground or floor. Though not every people is as concerned for comfort as we in the West seem to be, many peoples seek to increase comfort, as well as protection, via technology.

Our feet don't carry us as fast as we would like to go sometimes. Some of us can run faster than others, but still we cannot cover 3,000 miles in four or five hours, so we develop machines to enable us to travel that far, that fast. Early technological advances in transportation used animals such as horses to speed travel time. Then came other modes of travel, such as bicycles, cars, trucks, airplanes, rockets. Food getting also has gone through an evolutionary process in many societies, from the use of such skills as hunting and gathering to the kinds of skills, implements, and processes that allow a comparatively small number of farmers to produce enough food for very large populations.

Our voices don't carry as far as we would like them to be carried, so we develop voice-extending devices such as loudspeakers, records, radio, television, cassette tapes, and the like. We can't see as far as we would like to see, so we develop glasses, binoculars, telescopes, microscopes, and the like. We can't remember as well as we would like to or preserve records or transfer them from group to group very efficiently with only our unaided human capacities. So we develop writing, printing, and publishing. In these and many other ways, we seek to extend our normal human capacities through technology.

As we all realize, western societies have so emphasized this aspect of culture that it causes us great problems. We, like other societies, have developed technology to serve us, but it looks very much as though in many ways we have become enslaved by the technology we created, so that now we often seem to serve it rather than it serving us.

For example, it is usually crucial to be *efficient* when employing technology. When working with people, however, efficiency is often destructive, rather than constructive. We westerners have become so captured by the technological value of efficiency that we regularly organize and relate to people according to this value (e.g., scheduling fifteen-minute appointments or one-hour church services), even when it is destructive to do so.

Another example of our enslavement to technology becomes apparent when we consider the efforts to get Americans to cut down on our use of automobiles in order to reduce smog. These efforts don't seem to be working. Apparently we are so attached to our automobiles that we would rather choke on smog than give up our ability to move quickly (efficiently) from here to there. Many of us go into great psychological stress if our automobile breaks down. Add to this our extreme dependence on a multiplicity of other laborsaving (efficient) devices such as running water, electricity, washing machines, telephones, writing, and it becomes apparent that to talk of enslavement to such devices may not be an overstatement.

Many of us westerners have taken such techniques and gadgets with us to other parts of the world and shown so much attachment to them that the people there easily identify these as the things we really value. Often, for example, we could not refrain from using our cars, even if we came to realize that communication is done better when we are walking with people than when we are driving past (or even with) them in an automobile. Though we often assert that our main aim is the communication of the Gospel, we unwittingly allow attachments to techniques such as cars to get in the way. We often unconsciously assume that we need to get from here to there as quickly (efficiently) as possible, without considering what this does to our relationships with the people we are (or should be) with.

TECHNOLOGY: FORM, FUNCTION, MEANING, USAGE

A technique is a way of doing something. As such, it is a cultural form. A tool is an implement that a human being may use to do something. It, too, is a cultural form. Techniques and tools can be used to serve a wide variety of functions. The meanings attached to techniques and tools are also widely varied.

Take housing *forms* as an example. There are a wide variety of forms used by the various peoples of the world. In many parts of the world, housing techniques involve the use of wood. In many areas, the primary substance is mud. Cement, grass, metal, and many other substances are also used. Both the substances and the techniques are cultural forms.

We have mentioned that housing *functions* to provide protection from the elements. This is but one of the functions provided by housing forms. Among the others are such functions as signifying status, providing a central meeting place for family units, providing a place for eating, sleeping, privacy, sex, childbirth and rearing, entertaining, and the like. Often within housing are spaces—sometimes open, sometimes partitioned into rooms or huts—assigned to various persons and functioning to provide various functions such as privacy, personal identity, relative status, and room for storage of valuables.

Housing is *used* according to cultural conventions for the above-mentioned functions. When so used, the *meanings* attached by those who use the housing in these ways will be appropriate to the given functions. When used in other ways, as, for example, when a given home is used as a museum, the meanings attached will differ accordingly.

BASIC ASSUMPTIONS

Throughout our discussion of the various aspects of culture, we are constantly confronted with the human propensity for evaluating. It is apparently characteristic of humans that we constantly make value judgments concerning what we observe. We have spoken of ethnocentrism, the tendency to evaluate one's own cultural practices as superior to those of others. We have also spoken of the tendency of westerners to be strongly biased toward evaluating many aspects of life in terms of criteria that are specifically appropriate to technology but not as appropriate to other aspects of life. We specifically mentioned *efficiency* as the primary criterion in terms of which we tend to evaluate many things. There are, however, two other values that intersect with the efficiency criterion when we evaluate technological matters: *degree of control* and *complexity*.

We believe that technological devices (and many other aspects of life) are "better" if they are *efficient, complex, and able to control* more rather than less of whatever they operate on. We apply these criteria to our own technological products and to those of other societies. Since technological products are so visible and we Euroamericans are so focused on this aspect of culture, we tend to fall into the habit of evaluating whole societies in terms of how similar to or different from our own technology theirs is, especially with regard to these values. Unfortunately, we are likely to do this quite unconsciously.

It would be good for us to recognize what we are doing and to ask about the reasons for and the consequences of such behavior. Among the reasons are, of course, our own preoccupation with technological things and our great cultural expertise in this area. One important consequence is that we end up with very little respect for most of the world's societies for at least two reasons:

1. They are often not very good at what we are best at, and
2. By evaluating them by what we are best at, we miss the many other aspects of life that they often handle much more competently than we do.

For example, in contrast to our preferred criteria, another society may attempt to organize its life around such values as "the greatest security (personal and group) for the greatest number of people" or "patience with and acceptance of people on their own terms" or "make no decision on an important matter until every household head agrees" and the like. Each of these would involve a measure of inefficiency and lack of control (from our point of view) that would seriously decrease a westerner's ability to tolerate social behavior based on such a principle.

We do, of course, have a sizable tension within western societies between our technologically oriented criterion of efficiency and our attempts to be democratic governmentally. In America, this tension tends to be resolved by settling for a facade of democracy on the surface of our organizations, with the real running of them being done in the background by administrative personnel working less visibly but much more efficiently than true democracy would allow. The myth that our structures are democratic, however, satisfies us that they are indeed superior to other people's structurings.

Apart from such inconsistencies, our American tendency is simply to say (or assume), "such and such is better than such and such," without realizing what the underlying criteria for such a judgment are. For example, we assert that airplanes are better transportation than horses. We can assert this, however, only as we assume that the inconveniences of air travel are worth putting up with in order to receive the benefits. Our underlying evaluational criteria lead us to believe that it is so "good" for us to be able to move quickly over great distances that we are willing to put up with such inconveniences as the fact that the carrier belongs to someone else, is quite expensive, can only land at designated (often quite inconvenient) places, usually involves quite a bit of discomfort due to crowding, and so forth.

When talking about warfare, we say that guns and bombs are better weapons than arrows and stones. That is, they can kill more efficiently and control more effectively than arrows and stones. It is also satisfying to know that our preferred weapons are more complex. If these are our basic criteria, guns and bombs are indeed better than arrows and rocks. If, however, we had other criteria, such as ease of obtaining/manufacture or portability, our judgment would be different. Note, however, that things that are more efficient, complex, and controlling (whether guns or airplanes) often tend to depersonalize. War can be waged person to person or impersonally. Formerly all wars were waged person to person. People fought one-on-one or small group against small group. They often could see and shout to each other (see some of the Old Testament descriptions of battles for examples). But in the West, our values lead us to want to kill more efficiently, so we have developed techniques that enable us to kill people without even knowing them, without even seeing them. We prefer depersonalized warfare, waged efficiently.

We can say mass production is better than handcrafting, since we value producing things in large quantities at low prices. Perhaps we couldn't dispute such a statement as long as our criteria are efficiency and control, but we shouldn't make the mistake of saying that mass production is better than handcrafting in every respect. Apart from the quality of the product, when you start considering the interaction between this custom and the psyche of the people who participate in the system, we find that mass production does something negative to the worker's feeling of accomplishment. Among other things, this technique tends to depersonalize and reduce any meaningfulness of the work to a bare minimum, and industrialists have to deal with workers who break down under the strain of such depersonalization and meaninglessness.

Handcrafting enables workers to feel they have done something worthwhile. People engaged in mass production often feel they have not done anything worthwhile since they often never see the product through from start to finish and therefore don't feel they have had a really important part in constructing it. In terms of efficiency, control, and complexity, mass production may be better than handcrafting, but in terms of other criteria, it has severe deficiencies.

Whenever an evaluation is made of a technique, it is important that the criteria on which that evaluation rests be made clear, especially if there is any thought of introducing that technique into another society. It is also important, whenever the possible introduction of technique into a culture is considered, that its "fit" with the rest of the culture be considered. Unfortunately, there are by now thousands of illustrations of techniques that fit quite well in the donor society but proved to be unsuited at best, and disruptive at worst, in the receiving context, often because the meanings attached to them by the receiving people were quite different from those assumed by the donors (*see* Rogers 1983; Foster 1973).

The influence of techniques and tools on other aspects of culture is clear. But when a custom is borrowed by another society, will the influence be for good? This is much harder to assess. Would societies that don't seem particularly interested in technological development be improved if they had more freedom from food getting? Take a society where each family grows its own food. If they could have more freedom from workaday activities, would they use that leisure to develop their culture constructively? Unfortunately, the picture is not encouraging.

The story of the introduction of steel axes into Yir Yoront society is a classic example of the problems that may arise (Sharp 1952). Clearly the intention of those who introduced the axes was that such an introduction would be for good, but it turned out to be destructive. One assumption made by the outsiders was that if these people just had a more efficient tool, one that gave them a better opportunity to control their environment, they would have more time and energy to put into more productive activities. In addition to the assumptions concerning efficiency and control was the western assumption that work is burdensome and ought to be simplified, if possible. What happened (in addition to some large-scale social breakdown) was that the people became lazier. As they began to use the steel axes, they found they had more time on their hands, so they slept and became lazy. You can't always predict the influence of a new technological development. Introducing something new needs to be considered carefully, lest something that was intended to be helpful ends up being a disaster.

It looks as though it is easy for people to neglect other important aspects of their culture if they focus their attention simply on a single aspect such as technological achievement. It looks very much as though technological development is addictive, even for us in western societies. Even though we have benefited greatly through the simplification of our work through technological achievements, instead of using the extra energy and time available to build better social relationships, we use this time and energy to develop more technology. It's like a person who takes one drink not being satisfied until he gets another drink. We get in the habit of developing more technology rather than using the leisure that a better technology has given us for more constructive purposes.

EARLY ANTHROPOLOGY

The early anthropologists were people of their times and therefore infected with the western propensity for evaluating societies on the basis of their technology. In keeping with the evolutionary view of human history then (and, by and large, still) in vogue within western societies, the first anthropologists were cultural evolutionists. When they gathered their data on the cultures of the world, they rather unconsciously (and ethnocentrically) made judgments concerning that data and lined up the cultures from simple to complex on the basis of their technology. This approach both corresponded with and contributed to the popular tendency we are critiquing. It supported the use of words such as primitive and civilized or advanced. It frequently got into missionary writings. Indeed, the early anthropologists made wide use of materials gathered by missionaries.

The most important of the early American anthropologists, Louis Henry Morgan, is a case in point. Combining missionary (and other) data with evolutionary assumptions, he wrote a book entitled *Ancient Society* (1877), in which he proposed a classification of the stages through which the world's cultures have developed or are developing. He saw these stages both as the ones through which "civilized" cultures (like ours) have passed and as the positions in terms of which it is possible to classify all contemporary cultures that have not yet progressed to the "civilization" stage.

For us, his scheme is simply of historical interest. Probably no western anthropologists follow Morgan's approach in detail, though there are many who espouse a much more carefully worked out and, from my point of view, reasonable evolutionary approach to anthropological data. Interestingly enough, his approach is considered anthropological orthodoxy in the Communist world. Unless things have changed recently, Morgan's evolutionary analysis is the only anthropological theory allowed in China, the former USSR, and their satellite nations.

According to Morgan, human culture evolved through the stages shown in figure 11.1. Each stage was marked by the invention or discovery of an important technological development (Hiebert 1983:69).

Period of Savagery

Older Period: From the first humans to the domestication of fire and subsistence on fish.
Middle Period: From fishing to the invention of the bow and arrow.
Later Period: From the bow and arrow to the invention of pottery.

Period of Barbarism

Older Period: From pottery to the domestication of plants and animals.
Middle Period: From the domestication of plants and animals to the invention of iron smelting.
Later Period: From iron to the invention of the alphabet.

Period of Civilization

From the alphabet to the present.

Figure 11.1 Morgan's scheme of cultural evolutionary stages

In spite of the fact that terms such as savagery and barbarism strike us as terribly demeaning and inappropriate (their connotations weren't quite as bad in the nineteenth century), this organization of anthropological data was regarded as quite a breakthrough in its day. First of all, Morgan had collected and organized an impressive amount of data. Secondly, he had provided a rational explanation for the similarities and differences among the various societies of the world. He had developed a "big picture" into which others could fit additional data.

There were, however, serious flaws in the scheme—flaws that only became apparent once anthropologists began to examine the assumptions on which the scheme was built. One flaw that we now see is the fact that *the focus was almost exclusively on material cultural products*. The classification was almost solely based on the observation by outsiders of material artifacts and techniques. Considerations of meaning and the influences of different cultural contexts on the meanings were virtually ignored.

A second problem, related to the first, is the fact that *the analysis was done entirely by outsiders and from the perspective of the outsiders' cultural interests and assumptions*. This allowed anthropologists to remain largely unaware of their evolutionary assumptions (which they had inherited from their western worldviews). In keeping with these assumptions, they arranged their data in a single line from simple to complex (technologically) and felt that they had solved a great mystery concerning the relationships between cultures. What they really sought (again in keeping with western worldviews) was an explanation of how western societies got to be so magnificent (Langness 1987). Their interest was more in the way they felt nonwestern societies portrayed previous stages of western culture than in the characteristics of those cultures in and of themselves.

This fact accounts for a third major mistake. What Morgan and most of the other anthropologists of that day did was *to take all of the societies they knew of that displayed a certain set of characteristics and lump them into a single category*. Those that displayed the characteristics of the next "higher" level of development went into that category, on the assumption that the latter had developed from the former. The problem is that often the majority of the cultures in one geographical area fell into the same stage of development, while those in the next stage were geographically quite distant from them. This fact makes it unreasonable to expect that the higher cultures developed from the others, since they had never inhabited the same places. The possibility that the cultures in a higher category could have developed from those in a lower category without any contact is virtually unimaginable.

There seems to be a good bit of truth both to the general direction of cultural "development" pointed to by Morgan and to the fact that many societies do go through many of the stages he outlined. However, a great deal of refinement of the theory was necessary before it could be properly disentangled from the ethnocentric assumptions concerning the presumed evolutionary development of western societies. These assumptions are still very much with us among western peoples and need to be fought against if we are to be as free as we desire to serve God cross-culturally.

MEASURING CULTURE CHANGE TECHNOLOGICALLY

We often unconsciously measure the rate at which a society is westernizing (changing) by looking at the number of things in that society that we recognize as coming from the West. When people borrow western gadgets, we often assume that they are adopting western culture as a whole. This is not, however, true, as the Japanese (among others) have clearly proven. They have adopted much of western technology but accepted very little else from western societies. The problem is that technological and material things are the easiest things to borrow and are among the most visible parts of a culture once they have been borrowed.

Outsiders tend to notice people adopting western dress, radios, tape recorders, bicycles, cars, television sets, and a myriad of other material items, and assume that their culture is changing just as rapidly in every area as it is in technology. What happens is that people borrow those things that most obviously help them with surface-level problems. These are technological and material things, borrowed for their utilitarian value. Outsiders, however, frequently miss the fact that these familiar items are usually invested with meanings other than those attached to them in the donor culture.

Some speak of a "global village" (McLuhan 1964), but that is a very misleading label for a situation where only the surface is similar from society to society. When it comes to meanings, the differences between peoples with similar technologies (e.g., Japan and America) may be vast. There are, of course, influences that trickle down from the surface to affect other aspects of a culture, but the change in basic worldview assumptions, religious customs, political customs, and economic customs tends to be much slower.

In addition, the interaction between western and nonwestern societies produces a certain number of customs that are neither western nor traditional, but somewhere between. Some of these are quite puzzling to westerners who think they know how a given item should be used. I remember my consternation at seeing Nigerians using handsaws in a different way than I was used to. Americans use a saw with the teeth facing them, one-handed, and cutting toward them. The Nigerians were using the same kind of saw, but turned it around so that the teeth faced away from them. They then sawed with both hands, cutting away from them. It startled me to see them using "our" implement in a way that I thought it shouldn't be used!

In some parts of the world, they have a very interesting (and disturbing) custom that is neither traditional nor western, but a new custom resulting from combining certain aspects of each. Girls go to school and get schooled out of contact with their society and its customs. This means their families have a difficult time arranging a marriage for them, so many of them simply don't get married. Instead they take a job in the city as a clerk or a teacher and live as singles (like many westerners do). But they often don't give up becoming mothers. They work in the city until they get pregnant, then go back home to deliver the child. After a while, they turn the child over to the parents and return to the city to start the process again. I understand that some of these girls' families are beginning to like this arrangement, since in a patrilineal society, if the girl got married, her children would become a part of her husband's family. If she doesn't get married, though (as in this custom), the children become a part of her parents' family. This is a mix of the traditional values and the new possibilities that have arisen through the process of westernization.

Another different usage of a western borrowing is the widespread belief that western schooling exempts a person from manual labor. Though such an assumption is not unknown in some parts of Euroamerica, it is especially surprising for many of us who worked our way through college to hear it articulated by people in societies where we'd expect people to recognize the need for combining schooling with manual skills. I was once startled to hear a Nigerian say, "If you see me bending over (in the typical hoeing posture), I am not hoeing, I am throwing up!" What he meant was that, since he had been to school, the only reason for him to assume that posture would be for throwing up. He never planned to hoe again.

In spite of the apparent rapidity of such surface-level changes, the point is that we cannot assume an equal amount of change at the deeper levels of culture. Though there is change in worldview—some of it quite significant—the fact of such change needs to be established quite independently from the changes occurring in the technological area. Usually change at deeper levels is much slower.

COMPARING WHOLE CULTURES

We should not, like the uninformed of today or the anthropologists of yester-day, naively rate cultures on the basis of their approximation to western cultures in areas such as technology in which we excel. *If we want to evaluate on the basis of technology, we should limit ourselves to evaluating technology alone.* It is valid to speak of a culture as *technologically* fairly simple (or even primitive) in compari-son to the technology of another society, but it is wrong to evaluate the whole cul-ture as simple or primitive on the basis of one subsystem. We westerners would not like it if we were considered simple or primitive because some powerful people evaluated our whole culture on the basis of our primitive family and kinship system.

Cultures are more complex than simplistic attempts to evaluate them allow. If we are to compare whole cultures, we need to recognize that complexity and dis-cover some better basis for evaluation. One possibility would be to use some such criterion as a culture's overall ability to provide a satisfactory life for its people. If this were our basis, we would find many diverse cultures in the "adequate" cate-gory and many other diverse cultures in the "inadequate" category. Each category would include both technologically primitive and technologically complex societies. There would be no single line from simple to complex based on sophistication in a single area of culture. Furthermore, the evaluation would be more people ori-ented—based on the assumption that the primary purpose of a culture is to serve the people within it.

One approach to evaluating how well a culture serves its people might be to devise some way of rating societies in terms of their overall healthiness. One of the underlying assumptions in this approach to evaluation would be that a healthy society exhibits an appropriate, "well-fitting" culture. A healthy society would practice a culture that is well-integrated structurally and provides a maximum of meaningfulness for its people. Its people agree on and obey its rules. They get along reasonably well with each other and experience relatively low levels of psy-chological disorder. A sick society would score low in such areas. Crime, delin-quency, and other forms of disobeying the rules would be common. So would psy-chological dysfunction, high levels of meaninglessness, unbridled competitiveness between individuals, generations, and other social groupings, self-centeredness, and constant complaining about the inadequacy of the cultural structures.

In a healthy state, a society possesses the ability to satisfy at least the press-ing needs of its people most of the time, though it appears that no sociocultural structuring is ever totally satisfactory for its people. Indeed, one area in which many societies have allowed people to develop unsatisfied needs is in the area of control over their environment. This provides a powerful drive on the part of many peoples for new gadgets. The wholesale borrowing from the West that that drive tends to engender, however, is leading more and more societies into what looks like social illness.

Today's peoples seem to be on a binge to gobble up as much technology as pos-sible and, like those who overeat or overdrink, seem to be throwing their systems off balance. In a sense, what they are doing is satisfying a felt need that was not previously adequately satisfied. In another sense, though, they are becoming addicted in such a way that only the strongest or most resilient may be able to sur-vive the unbalance and cultural breakdown that is occurring. For those who do survive, what may develop is a surface level where most cultures look reasonably similar to each other, with deeper levels that differ to a greater or lesser extent.

TECHNOLOGY AND CULTURAL COMPLEXITY

As pointed out above, the purpose of technology is to enhance human abilities to manipulate the environment. Note the three-way interaction pictured in figure 11.2 below between biology (the biological makeup of human beings), the physical environment, and culture.

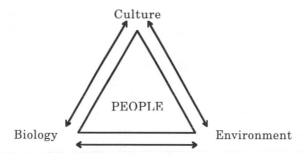

Figure 11.2 Interaction between culture, biology, and environment

In each of the relationships in the diagram, the interaction goes in both directions. People interact with their cultures. From within and in terms of our cultures, we interact with our biological makeup and our physical environment. In a sense, we can talk of person- and culture-mediated interactions between biology and environment. We can point to at least four culturally significant factors in these interactions:

1. The first is *worldview*. Our worldview provides us with guidelines concerning what attitude and approach to take toward our biology and our environment. Peoples of certain societies believe that our bodies are to be enhanced and our environments to be controlled as much as possible. Western worldviews provide little or no restriction on human attempts to enhance and control. Other peoples believe we should keep bodily enhancement and any attempts to control the environment to a minimum. To them, propriety demands total submission to what is. Most societies fit somewhere between these extremes.

2. Generated by such worldview values are *strategies* for implementing these attitudes and approaches. To the extent that a people believes in enhancing and controlling, they develop strategies that involve various kinds of technology.

3. That *technology* increases our biological capacities and consequently our ability to control our environment.

4. These techniques, in turn, require *strategies* for their use.

Implicit in such considerations is the fact that those peoples who believe in doing as much as possible to enhance their physical capabilities and control their environments will develop more and more technology. If, in addition to the drive to develop such techniques, there is the worldview belief that such knowledge should be widely shared, plus the ability (largely through literacy and other mass media) to effectively pass it on both from person/group to person/group and from one generation to the next, the kind of situation develops that we see today in the West (and increasingly throughout the rest of the world).

One important facet of this situation is the fact that *technological development in and of itself increases the complexity of a culture*. It also enables a people to spend less time and energy looking after the essentials of life, thus providing the potential for them to do other things with their time and energy. This doesn't always result in a people using their energies for constructive purposes (e.g., the steel ax example above), but it does allow for development of facets of a culture that might have been neglected before. There is, therefore, a strong correlation between technological development and overall cultural complexity.

People who have to spend 90 percent of their time and energy making sure they have enough food and protection from their environment only have 10 percent of their time and energy for all other activities. On the other hand, people who only have to spend 10 percent of their time dealing with food and protection have 90 percent of their time for other pursuits. By enabling people to extend the abilities of their bodies to control their environment more efficiently, technology makes other things possible. This is the point that modern cultural evolutionists make, and it would seem that there is indeed a strong relationship between the development of technology and the development of other parts of the culture, especially in the complexity of the rest of the culture.

Leslie White, who took this position to a deterministic extreme, held that societies are able to grow both in size and in cultural complexity as they learn to technologically harness more energy. The more energy is effectively utilized, the larger and presumably better the society can grow (White 1949). For example, large societies such as American, European, Japanese, and Chinese could probably not exist as large, complex entities (with all of the advantages provided by such size) without rapid transportation and quick communication. Increased technological control over the physical environment has made such societies possible.

In addition, Julian Steward (1955) and others have noted that there seems to be a series of stages of technological, economic, and sociocultural complexity that many societies have gone through. They have pointed to striking similarities in other aspects of cultures operated by people with similar "strategies of adaptation" (Y. Cohen 1968). They have thus been able to develop a number of valid insights concerning sociocultural change from an evolutionary perspective, and we should not too quickly reject such a perspective. We should not assume that because we disagree with theories of biological evolution we must reject the kinds of insights coming from cultural evolutionists, simply because the same name is used for both groups.

A simple illustration is afforded by peoples who, like the Hebrews, have moved from a nomadic way of life into a settled existence in a single territory. Nomadic peoples tend to have simpler technologies and fewer artifacts than more settled peoples. They also tend to consist of fairly small kinship groups that vest social, political, and religious leadership in the same person or persons who exercise overall leadership over the kinship group. Often in history, however, nomadic people have come to the point where they decided to settle down. At that point they have often tended to reduce their dependence on herding and develop agriculture. They then begin to have more and larger material goods. They also tend to increase in population and develop centralized governmental structures and armies to protect themselves and their territory from other people. Such developments tend to lead to greater specialization and greater complexity. Such a process has been observed within many societies and gives credence to much that current anthropologists who work out of an evolutionary paradigm are saying.

TECHNOLOGICAL DEVELOPMENT AND CULTURAL BALANCE

I am afraid the western technological focus, driven by a worldview bent on control and efficiency, has thrown western societies seriously off balance. We have become victims of our drive to control the universe and have made the vehicle of that mastery (science) our real religion. Though there is some erosion of our faith in science in recent years, traditionally we have exhibited an incredible faith in the power of scientific investigation to conquer everything, including food production, transport, physical health, weather, psychological problems, education, interpersonal relationships, government, even space. By putting our faith so totally in this one fairly tangible area of our culture, we have largely lost faith in the less-tangible areas, such as religion. "If we can control the world through our knowledge," we say, "who needs God?"

In addition, we have allowed our technology to entice us into settling for very superficial relationships with our families and other significant people in our lives. For the love of money and material, we have allowed ourselves to become job oriented rather than family oriented. We move far from our families and gather in cities to live among strangers for the sake of our jobs. People values then become secondary at best, and in many ways we become enslaved to our technology.

As badly as technology is affecting our cultural equilibrium, we have at least had the opportunity to work up to this over a considerable period of time. Much of the disruption in nonwestern societies is not so much the result of the introduction of technology itself but the introduction of so much technology so rapidly. It's the rapidity and the fact that they have not had time to adjust to each successive stage that is really disturbing. In some countries (e.g., Papua New Guinea) they have virtually skipped the horse and automobile stages of travel. They have moved straight from walking to flying. What kinds of meaning problems do they need to sort out? How are such people to interpret an airplane when they understand so little of manufacturing? Is it any wonder that movements spring up in these places that offer strange explanations for how and why such technological innovations have come?

Often such peoples point to such technological things as proof that westerners (whether Christian or non-Christian) have great power with God. Their assumption is that God has given us these things fully made because of our closeness to Him. So they go after such things (whether or not they are good for them) to see if, perchance, God will bless them also. In the process, they often lose more than they gain.

We need to be very sympathetic with peoples who are moving in one generation into even more serious unbalance than characterizes western societies. In such a short time they are moving from belief that they should largely submit to the universe to experiencing considerable control over it, from rural to urban, from agriculture to industrialization, from personal to impersonal, from supernaturalism to scientism, from family orientation to job orientation, from informal learning of subsistence skills to formal learning of technological skills.

Through such changes, many of these small-scale societies are becoming large-scale societies. The problem I see is that, though the technological value of efficiency has made such scale possible, it has done so at the expense of people values. I believe the well-being of people is not simply a control-the-environment-better thing. The crucial thing, as I see it, is meaningfulness of life. To the extent that technological development has increased that, I feel it is a good thing. But to the extent that such development has decreased such meaning in life, it appears to me to be a bad thing.

Not infrequently the quest for western goods has led people to make what seem to be very bad choices, such as to move to urban areas or put their energies into growing cash crops rather than their own food. This latter choice ties them into a world market that may be quite erratic, sometimes enabling them to become wealthy, but at other times (when the world price on their product drops) leaving them hungry and impoverished. There once was a time in many parts of the world when nearly every family grew its own food. If anybody went hungry, it was only the careless family. Now, in many of those same parts of the world, the energies of most people go into growing a cash crop (such as coffee, tea, or cocoa). When the world price of their crop goes down, they go hungry. For this reason and many others, primary blame for the widespread starvation going on in many parts of the nonwestern world today has to be laid at the feet of the westernization process.

The present world technological system is intricately balanced. It works reasonably well (at least technically—the people problems are still there) as long as it's working right. But when things go wrong, they go wrong in at least as large a measure as they go right. Indeed, it is likely that someday the whole great system will come tumbling down—not because a majority voted it out of existence but because somebody was clever enough to recognize how fragile the system is and decided to do it in. Technological efficiency has a lot to be said for it, but much to be feared as well.

Personally, I think our western societies (and now others) have grown much too large and that many of the more serious troubles we are experiencing are the result of the attempt to bring too many people into too great proximity. Technology has, of course, made this possible. We will, however, probably come to regret that technology has been allowed to carry things this far. As we are already discovering from the great amount of cultural breakdown taking place, mass societies are very hard on people and people values.

CROSS-CULTURAL WITNESSES AND TECHNOLOGY

The basic thing to say to cross-cultural witnesses concerning their use of technological and material things is, "Control them; don't let them control you." The Christian message that we seek to witness to is a people message. It is for people that Christ died. Any time people values are sacrificed for technological values, the message is compromised. An automobile may be a very helpful thing to have, but the way automobiles are used by Christian witnesses often denies the message we are supposed to be presenting. We are often so concerned with getting places quickly that we sacrifice spending time with people, which is necessary if the person orientation of our message is to get across. Eugene Nida illustrates this fact well by referring to a discussion he once had with an effective pioneer missionary to Guatemala

> who, then in his sixties, was getting ready to make one of his customary walking trips of several weeks out through the mountains in order to visit Indian congregations in the small villages. I asked him why he did not drive his car, in view of his increasingly poor health (he often took sick on such trips) and the new road which had just gone through that region, for he could have driven to many of the places he proposed to visit. His reply

was simply, "Oh, I never drive, for the people that I want to reach are not used to someone driving up in a car. What is more, I have never found a man I could not speak to about Jesus Christ, if only we were walking down the same road together" (1990:35–36).

This missionary had learned that the "people value" of walking with someone needed to be followed, rather than the technological values of efficiency and comfort, if the witness was to come out right. He exemplified what I'm recommending concerning using technology, rather than being captured by it. I knew missionaries who used their vehicles whenever possible and seldom carried Nigerians in them, even if the missionary was going the same way anyway.

The same is true of housing. Simple housing in which the people are welcome and feel at home promotes neighborliness better than the housing we often build for the sake of our comfort. Likewise with western communicational devices. We should (as I point out in chapter 17) try to use such devices according to indigenous patterns, if possible, rather than simply going for efficiency or up-to-dateness.

A good concept to get into our minds in this regard is *appropriateness*. Informed technical aid specialists seek to introduce "appropriate technology." By this they mean something that can be fixed by the people if it breaks, something that doesn't require an outside specialist to maintain it. We could well employ that concept with a bit of expansion. Let it mean both that the receptors are comfortable with it and can fix it and that it has the ability to convey to them the message of God without serious distortion. Let our use of technological ideas and objects be appropriate by being appropriate both to those to whom we have been called and to the messages God has called us to convey.

At the same time, we need to be appropriately sympathetic and helpful to those caught up in technological change. A lot of our job as cross-cultural witnesses is not so much initiating new things as working with what is already there, much of which may be counterproductive at best and perhaps even harmful to the cause we represent. We often find that the best we can do is sympathize with people who are already caught in the process of rapid westernization. We may, on occasion, be able to warn them, especially if the practice in question has already proven to be harmful in Euroamerica, but often our advice will be taken as a colonialist attempt to slow down their "progress."

Whatever we do in this regard, our primary aim should be to be loving and sympathetic, whether or not they seem to be doing what we consider the right thing, and whether or not they take our advice. We would probably not listen to them if the tables were turned. We should protect their right to make mistakes, but if given the chance either to warn them or to help them out of a difficult situation, we should lovingly do so. Most of all, though, we should model in our own lives the freedom of Christ to avoid the enslavement to technological and material things that so easily destroys both ministry and life itself.

CHAPTER 12

ECONOMIC CULTURE AND TECHNOLOGY

INTEGRATIONAL THOUGHT

There is much advice in the Scriptures concerning economics. Though Jesus didn't tell every rich person to give it all away, in Luke 18:22, 23, He highlights the fact that an attachment to one's riches can keep one from receiving eternal life. So He says to the rich man, "There is still one more thing you need to do. Sell all you have and give the money to the poor, and you will have riches in heaven; then come and follow me. But when the man heard this, he became very sad, because he was very rich."

The question the Master raises is a question of usage. Neither the form nor the function of money is evil in and of itself, but the usage and therefore the meaning can be evil, or at least provide a hindrance to one's attainment of things more valuable. So, if something that is potentially good and useful is found to block the attainment of something even more valuable, get rid of it and "Come, follow me."

It is sad that even many of us who have given up much for Jesus' sake may still be hindered by our materialism. We may not have much wealth in comparison to others, but what we have or what we think we deserve may still block our wholehearted following of Jesus. Furthermore, it may lead to our being perceived by others as trampling on one of their highest ideals—generosity. For many of the peoples of the world, greed is their worst sin and generosity their highest virtue. How Christlike!

We found this to be true in the area of Nigeria in which we lived. Their assumption was that everyone should be at approximately the same economic level. This meant that anyone with more of this world's goods had an obligation to share with those having less. Most of the more wealthy in the tribal societies around us in those days were helped in keeping this ideal by less-fortunate relatives who descended on anyone with means to take advantage of their surplus.

But what were they to do with a white family that seemed to have unlimited goods and money? Their perception was that we were incredibly wealthy, yet they could not treat me as they would one of their family members and "level off" our surplus. Some of them could, however, curry our favor and thereby gain whatever benefits we would grant them, plus the reputation among their people of being themselves wealthy—a reputation they often wished they did not have.

For our part, though our resources were severely limited, we could never convince the people of this fact. Though we were deep in debt personally, we had certain funds coming from the Mission that we were responsible to distribute for services rendered. But since we could not help everyone who appealed to us, we often came across to them as greedy.

The Gospel we proclaimed and the Scriptures we taught are against greed. To be Christlike is to give and serve. With their perception of us being what it was, how could we come across to them as Christlike? I don't know that we could have, if the economic barriers were the only things considered. But there may still be hope.

We were able to gather around us a small group of leaders, to whom we tried to explain ourselves in this area, as well as in many others. We spent time with them, learning what their life was like and explaining to them what ours was like, both in their country and in ours. Though we didn't reduce our economic standard to theirs (and probably couldn't have if we tried), we were able to develop a person-to-person closeness to some of them that enabled them to get beyond the blockage created by the economic distance between us. We were also able to share with them many of the technological benefits we brought into their area.

This enabled us to participate in the kind of relationship with them that Jesus was inviting the rich man to enjoy, for the key part of the above passage is when Jesus invites the rich man to come to be with Him. The passage is primarily about discipleship, not economics, and discipleship involves getting across whatever barriers there may be—ethnic, economic, status, educational—to get close. Jesus chose His disciples primarily "to be with Him" (Mk 3:14). The economic gaps we face as we go to other peoples may be formidable, but they must be traversed. Whether through selling all we have or in some other way, we must get beyond them to person-to-personness if we are to be truly Christlike.

INTRODUCTION

Economic strategies are an important aspect of technology. Among the strategies to be dealt with under this heading are the principles in terms of which societies organize such things as the production, distribution, and consumption of the goods and services they deem necessary for life. Such activities and the principles that underlie them are important to all peoples. They are also important to the Church, as we will see in the latter part of this chapter.

By way of *definition*, we will quote Hoebel:

> Economic institutions ... comprise the characteristic behaviors that center upon the production, the allocation and distribution, and the use and consumption of goods. Economic institutions include behavioral networks of food production and the manufacture of artifacts; gift exchange, trade, sale, preemption, and inheritance; utilization, hoarding, and consumption; and ownership, possession, and rights of use—everything which focuses upon production and utilization of goods and services (1972:343).

Robert Taylor shortens the definition to "the ways people, time, and materials are organized to produce, distribute, and consume goods and services" (1973:205). Note that in this chapter we are concerned with three entities—people, time, and materials—rather than simply with the materials employed and general techniques for their use (as in the previous chapter). In addition, we are concerned with the strategies people follow in the organizing, producing, distributing, and consuming of both goods and services.

As with each cultural subsystem, economics is all-encompassing, interlinked with all other aspects of culture. There is a sense in which everything in our cultural experience relates to the way in which materials are organized to produce, distribute, and consume goods and services, especially in western societies. As mentioned in our discussion of worldview, it is typical for one or another of the subsystems of a culture to have a predominant influence on the worldview. Within western societies, the influence of the economic subsystem on our worldview is very strong. Indeed, we tend to see even people and time as material things. Note that in this regard even our above definition of economics betrays a western bias.

One very troublesome area for westerners (especially Christians) is the influence of economic assumptions on the ways in which we view people. These lead us to divide people into three categories: scenery, machinery and persons (Iwanska 1957). As tourists, we go to all parts of the world to view the *scenery*. An important part of that scenery is the people. We don't get to know them, and we don't care about knowing them, except perhaps at a very superficial level. They are just there to look at, and we say, "How quaint! How nice their costumes are! How wonderful those people are!" They're not really persons to us, only part of the scenery.

Then (and here is where our techno-economic assumptions are most obvious) there are other people that we treat as *machinery*. These are the people who type our letters, bring our mail, or receive our money and ring it up on the cash register when we have been shopping. We're not interested in that person as a person, only as a thing (machine) that does a job for us. Suppose that person were to start sharing with us what his or her life is like. We'd think him or her completely out of line.

In a school situation, it is quite common for professors to view most students as scenery and for everyone to view secretaries and administrators as machinery. In addition, professors may well be viewed by students as teaching machines, and those students who work for a professor viewed by that professor as machines that help him or her to get things done. Administrators often see their employees more as machines than as fellow team members (persons). Unfortunately, even church and mission administrators often view their employees this way.

Then there are *persons*. These are the people we get close to and get to know beyond simply viewing them as scenery or using them as machinery. A student who gets close to a professor (or vice versa) soon takes a different attitude toward that person than that taken toward professors or students in general. For many professors there would seem to be a big difference between just any student and "my" student. Indeed, often when a genuine friendship comes about, both professor and student will find it uncomfortable to refer to each other in terms of the status label (the stereotype), since they have moved out of what Loewen and Loewen have called a "station-to-station" relationship, into a person to person relationship (1967). They have become friends, and friends are *persons* to each other.

Such basic assumptions as these are often a part of the equipment we take with us into cross-cultural witnessing situations. This fact can damage our effectiveness greatly, since our view is often quite divergent from the view of people our receptors are given by their worldviews. We unconsciously structure our relationships with them according to our assumptions and wonder why they don't respond to us or to our message as we would like them to.

ORGANIZING PRINCIPLES

The first economic strategies to be investigated are those that relate to the organization of the activities necessary to sustain the life of a people. We will focus on four of these and relate them to the three main types of society in the world today—*traditional (tribal), peasant, and industrial* (Shaw 1988). *Traditional* societies tend to be small, tribal, and largely self-sufficient. There are usually few specialists in traditional societies, most functions being cared for by kinship groups. *Peasant* societies tend to be agricultural and typically involve more specialization. Those who grow or make certain things depend on markets to enable them to exchange any surplus with those who have a surplus of goods they don't produce. In *industrial* societies, everyone is specialized and no one produces a very large percentage of what they need (and want) in life.

1. The first organizing principle is *kinship.* This is by far the most common organizing principle for any activity in traditional and peasant societies. Though we will deal with kinship more specifically in chapter 20, it needs to be noted here that in such societies, the kinship group typically is responsible for producing all or nearly all of the goods and food that they consume. The usual economic unit of these societies is the family, the clan, or whatever other kinship group is basic to the given social structure. This group is responsible for everything concerning goods and services, whether production, distribution, or consumption.

Traditional (usually tribal) societies often produce their foods by means of a system called "subsistence." This means that those (e.g., family or larger kinship group) who are going to consume the food are the ones responsible for producing that food. They must look after the organizing and carrying through of the activities necessary to agriculture, herding, or hunting if they are going to survive. Typically, such subsistence organization requires that all able-bodied persons be engaged in food production during most of their lives. In such societies, there tend to be few people who are specialized to the extent that they spend none of their time in food production.

While living in such a society, I noted (in the traditional segment of the society) only one significant group of people who did not grow their own food. These were a group of people who may be labeled tradesmen and formed a social caste at the bottom of the society's pecking order. They did things such as blacksmithing, leather working, pottery making, music, funerals, medicine, religious activities, and the like, which produced products and services that others gladly traded food to obtain.

As in every area of culture, each system has its strengths and weaknesses. Among the strengths of a kinship system is the fact that the responsibility for production lies with those who will be immediately affected if they do not tend to their responsibilities. The fact that they produce things from start to finish often gives them much more of a sense of accomplishment than western-type production does.

2. A second principle of economic organization is the fact of *specialization*. As we move from kinship societies into peasant societies, there is more specialization and a correspondingly lesser number of the people engaged in full-time food production. More of the people in these societies produce other goods and services that they trade for food produced by others. In *industrial* societies, specialization is such that the percentage of people producing the food may drop to something like 5 percent or less (as in the United States), while the rest of us work at other tasks and are paid in money that we use to buy food and other products.

Some sort of specialization on the basis of sex and age seems to be universal, even in traditional and peasant societies. Other types of specialization commonly found from society to society are based on family membership, social class, achievement, interest, and the like. With regard to *sex roles*, frequently they are so exclusive and clearly defined that men associate almost entirely with other men during most of their lives and women with other women, organizing the whole society into two groupings that might be referred to as the "men's community" and the "women's community."

With regard to *age*, in all societies, the very old people will have different kinds of occupations than the very young or those in the middle. There may be additional specialization on the basis of *family membership*. In many societies, those who belong to a family that has specialized in metal working (or any other trade) automatically follow that trade. The middle-class Anglo-American system is, however, just about the antithesis of this: if a father follows a certain trade, it is almost mandatory that his son find something else to do.

Specialization requires that people exchange the goods and services produced by one person or group for those produced by another person or group. See below, under Principles of Distribution, for more on this.

3. A third organizing principle is that of *task versus time orientation.* Until fairly recently, it was universal that people were rewarded for how well they did their task, not for how long they were at it. A few generations ago, though, a change was made within western societies that has resulted in quite a different practice. Now workers in these societies are paid for time spent at the task, rather than for the completion of the task itself. This often leads to workers not being as conscientious as they ought to be, since it is time rather than work that they are being paid for. I remember once seeing a coworker transferred because his fellow employees complained that he got too much work done each day!

In nonindustrial societies, the orientation toward work is not only task oriented, it is frequently much more casual than it is in western societies. The principle seems to be "if there's work to do, do it. If there's no work to do, don't work." They will often work very hard to achieve whatever their goal may be (e.g., clearing land, planting, harvesting, repairing a home), but once that goal is achieved, they see no need to continue working.

Another conflict we westerners have in relating to a system like that of most traditional and peasant societies is that we have both a very narrow definition of what work is and a strict dichotomy between what is work and what is leisure-time activity. For us, talking to others is leisure-time activity (unless it is a part of something like a formal, paid-for counseling process). Westerners frequently regard people who spend a high percentage of their time "merely" talking to each other as lazy.

When there isn't physical labor to do (and much of that time as well) traditional and peasant peoples tend to invest most of their time in interacting with people. This enables them to discuss and solve a high percentage of the problems that arise in their societies before the problems get to be large. We should see this as a very important kind of work, rather than (as our worldview dictates) as purely leisure-time activity.

4. A fourth organizing principle may be called *individual versus communal orientation*. In many societies, a large part of what westerners call work is performed communally. Such people will combine socializing with their work, for work is seen as a group thing. When there is a task to do, they will often spread the word and wait for people to gather before the work is started. They may get a lot less done in their task, but they are combining that with something enjoyable, which is socializing or even playing.

Our habit of dichotomizing between work and play proved quite embarrassing to me on at least one occasion in northern Nigeria. We had agreed to erect a church building, but, they said, nothing could get started until the drummer was free. "What has a drummer to do with building a church?" I wondered. When he became available, I learned that they don't do that kind of work without singing (and dancing). That mud-walled church got built to the beat of the drum! Work and play were combined in one big event—all to the beat of the drum. The work got done both enjoyably and communally, and I learned a lesson.

In the West, of course, we tend to be quite individualistic about our working situations. To us, work is an individual thing. We assume that individuals get jobs with organizations that hire people as individuals and consist of groups of individuals (rather than, say, a community that hired on together). It is rare that many of those working together in western establishments even knew each other before working together, but our system works reasonably well for us—as long as we only focus on getting work done. At least, this is the system that has made western societies great technologically. But a communal system has a lot to offer—especially if one is concerned with people values—though it will probably never enable them to excel technologically.

PRINCIPLES OF PRODUCTION

The organizing principles underlying the economy of a society are designed to assure that goods and services are produced or provided. This, of course, is necessary if they are to be distributed and consumed. But an economic system must also provide principles that govern the creation of the goods and services.

First there needs to be some sort of assessment of what is available in the physical and social environment, both the possibilities and the limitations. For most peoples, of course, these decisions have been made long ago, so the present generation needs to give little, if any, thought to the matter. They simply inherit an agricultural economy, a herding economy, or an industrial economy in which the resources available (both physical and social) are relatively well-known.

Assessing what a society has to work with would generate a listing of the resources and characteristics of the physical environment, a listing of the human potential, and a listing of other features, such as animals. In the physical setting, we might find, for example, plains, hills, rivers, trees, soil that is fertile in the plains but rocky on the hills, rivers that flood during part of the year but dry up at other times, a temperature that ranges from around 50 to 110 degrees (Fahrenheit), and so on. In the social group, we might find a preponderance of people who have developed agricultural skills, some who look after cattle, some who are able to make pottery from the clay in the area, some who make iron implements from materials that are traded for, and so on. These would be the elements available for the production of whatever is deemed necessary by this society for the living of life.

The worldview of the people provides the basic presuppositions concerning how the people should relate to such environmental givens. Following its guidelines, the people may use their territory for farming, hunting, herding, or industry. They may attempt to control their environment completely, partially, or not at all (i.e., to simply submit to it). They may determine what parts of that environment to focus on (e.g., the plains) and what to largely ignore (e.g., the hills) in the production of the necessities of life. Mixed in with and deriving from these worldview assumptions would be specifically economic assumptions, such as the assumption that production should be done communally rather than individually or that those who make pottery also need to farm, or that men tend the animals while women till the ground.

Differences between the principles governing production or procurement often result in societies looking quite different from each other on the surface, even when they inhabit similar geographical areas. On the other hand, similarities between such principles often result in societies looking quite similar to each other, even when they inhabit geographically different areas. Societies that produce their food through agriculture, for example, tend to look much more similar to each other than they do to societies that produce their food by herding animals. There are, apparently, only a limited number of ways to produce food agriculturally and perhaps an even more limited number of ways to herd animals. This restricts the creativity that might allow greater divergence.

What different societies choose to produce or procure may result in important differences between their cultures. Those groups that produce grains differ markedly in certain ways from those that produce root crops (e.g., yams, cassava). Those that herd cattle tend to show major differences from those that keep pigs. Those that hunt animals tend to differ in many ways from those that hunt roots.

All such strategies of production interact closely with the basic organizational principles discussed above and the principles of distribution, consumption, and ownership discussed below. They also become important factors in whatever changes are taking place in the society, and often in our day the change problem is a major one.

Take, for example, the case of a people who move from one habitat to another for some reason (war, famine, forced relocation). If the new habitat is significantly different from their old one, they will need to go through the process of assessing how to relate all over again. Contemporary examples are plentiful and include such diverse situations as that of the Ik of northern Uganda, moved from plains to mountains to make way for a game reserve (Turnbull 1972), Vietnamese refugees moving from tropical jungles to the northern United States because of war, and the large number of young people throughout the Two-Thirds World who yearly pour into the cities from rural areas, dislocated from most of traditional life through western schooling. All peoples are provided by their society with a strategy that works well as long as things go well but, because it is operated habitually, it is very difficult to change if conditions change.

PRINCIPLES OF DISTRIBUTION

Once the goods are produced, how do they get distributed to those who will make use of them?

1. The simplest principle is what might be labeled the *producer-user principle*, where those who produce the goods use them themselves. This principle is most widely utilized in subsistence economies and least evident (though never entirely absent) in industrial economies.

2. A second principle may be referred to as *reciprocal exchange*. This involves people providing others with something they have in exchange for a commodity of approximately equivalent value. Such exchange ranges from informal gift-giving situations, where a gift is given that elicits a return gift at a later date; to swapping, where goods are traded without benefit of any type of money; to customs such as "bride price," where the marriage arrangements involve the giving of gifts

by the groom's family to that of the bride, to help compensate for the loss of this very valuable family member. Sometimes, as in the case of Jacob in the Old Testament, what is given by one party is labor, rather than goods.

It is probable that some reciprocal exchange is found in every society. It is, however, much more prevalent in many nonwestern societies (e.g., Asian, African) than it is in America. In gift giving, though on the surface it may appear that nothing is expected in return, the rules may be such that a return gift of equal or greater value is quite obligatory. Christmas giving in America often involves the expectation that a gift will elicit another in response. In many situations, frequently including the giving of gifts by people of lower status to those of higher status, the commodity expected in return may be an intangible such as friendship or favor.

In many traditional societies, the major indigenous technique for reallocating resources has been the direct trading of products made by one person or group for those of another. If, for example, there were specialists in the society who made clothing all or part of their time, they might trade their product for surplus food grown by others. When a funeral was necessary, each group might trade what they produced for the services of an undertaker. And so on.

3. A third principle of distribution is that of *redistribution*. This method results in the goods and services getting to their destinations indirectly, as opposed to the directness of the first two methods. In most societies, there are at least some situations in which goods or services are pooled in a given place and redistributed. As examples, we may point to the stockpiling of grain, as Joseph did for the Pharaoh; gathering laborers into a labor pool; or even the giving of gifts to a king in a society where great generosity and hospitality is expected of the king. The form most familiar to westerners is the collecting of taxes, where all the funds are funneled into one central place, from which they are distributed to assist other people or provide goods and services (e.g., welfare, roads, army, and police) for the use of all or of people/groups other than the contributors. Unfortunately, there tends to be moderate to great slippage in this kind of system, resulting in the fact that what is distributed is often considerably less than what is funneled into the system.

4. The fourth principle of distribution involves another kind of indirectness— that of an intermediate medium. Though other valuables have been used in various places throughout history (e.g., salt, iron, shells, gold), what we know as coined and paper *money* is almost universally used today for this purpose. In using this principle, people need not arrange for the transfer of their own goods to the end user. Instead, they sell them to an intermediary for an intermediate currency that derives its value from the agreement of the people who use it to consider it as valuable. Such a system greatly increases the flexibility of the trading process (frequently at the expense of its personalness). For example, money enables at least one party in a transaction to travel a great distance without the necessity of carrying a heavy product to trade. The person need only carry money (or, increasingly, a credit card).

MARKETS

As we have seen, one of the characteristics of peasant and industrial societies is the presence of markets. These are centralized places into which goods and services are brought for the purpose of transferring them to new owners/users. In many societies to this day, a certain amount of the transfer is by means of direct swapping. The vast majority of exchanges that take place in today's markets, however, are negotiated through the use of money.

Markets, like every other social custom, are used differently by different peoples. Such differences exemplify certain important dissimilarities in worldview. Westerners, for example (especially in urban areas), tend to come to market expecting an impersonal experience, during which goods will be chosen and payment made with little or no personal interaction between buyer and seller, beyond what is absolutely necessary to complete the transaction. Though there may well be a more personal flavor to many such transactions in rural areas and a very personal tone in any situation where the participants are close friends, the pressure of our worldview is toward the depersonalization of the event and the participants. Furthermore, a market event is ordinarily understood by westerners primarily as an economic transaction rather than as a social event.

By contrast, the meaning of market to traditional and peasant peoples around the world is often more social than economic. What the worldviews of these peoples lead them to expect and enact is much more social interaction than economic transaction. Their markets may be weekly, semi-weekly, or daily, but they tend to be events people look forward to, whether or not they have anything economic to do. They go to market to see friends and relatives, hear the news, participate in recreation, make arrangements with others for such things as marriages, settle disputes, and occasionally buy or sell something.

The story is told of an anthropologist who stood by the side of a road leading into an African market and systematically offered the people much more than they could ever get for their goods by selling them in the market. He didn't get a single taker. When he tried to buy all their goods, they said, "If we sell to you, what will we do in market? What legitimacy will we have? How will we find a spot in market to sit and meet people?" So they wouldn't sell to him. Their market going was primarily about people and interpersonal interaction, even when the people felt they had to have something to sell to give them the excuse to be in the market.

The way traditional and peasant peoples buy and sell inside the market also requires more personal interaction, though westernization has already changed this in many places, especially in urban areas. Traditionally, people would expect to dicker or haggle, especially with prestigious outsiders who weren't expected to know the prices, so the price asked might be anywhere from slightly to quite a bit higher than the price expected. Many westerners find it difficult to get used to such a system, since we (in accordance with our worldview) expect buying and selling to be quite impersonal and efficient (i.e., completed in as short a time as possible). But in a traditional dickering system the seller prefers a person-to-person interaction, no matter how long it takes, to something approximating the western "quick and impersonal" style.

PRINCIPLES OF CONSUMPTION

Production and distribution of goods and services necessarily lead to consumption or use of the goods and services.

1. The first thing to note in this regard is that *consumption may be stretched out over longer periods of time or condensed into shorter periods*. With regard to food (and many other consumables, such as money), many people have what Nida

has called a "stuff and starve" mentality. Such people will grow their food and, if the harvest is abundant, consume enormous quantities of it. Then, when most of the food is gone, they can be very patient and very hungry until the next harvest. There is immediate consumption if there is plenty and going without if there is nothing.

Most people, of course, have to learn to spread things out, at least to some extent, if they are to survive, but not all people and not all circumstances easily lend themselves to storage or other forms of preservation. Often, for example, the worldview of a people provides them with a perspective that does not push them to plan ahead very much (*see* Mbiti 1971 for a discussion of this characteristic in African societies). For such peoples, what is in hand at the moment is to be used now, with the future taking care of itself. On the other hand, there are many peoples who might be called "future oriented." Such peoples often give so much attention to preparing for the future that they tend to sacrifice even legitimate present needs.

2. Another variable relates to *the totality of consumption*. Peoples who are living within close economic margins tend to be less wasteful than those who have enough of the necessities of life so that if they waste, they still live quite well. Yet even within these parameters, there are those who are more frugal and those who are less frugal. In societies where possessing one set of clothing is about all one can expect, it is quite normal for a person to use (consume) that outfit until it disintegrates. There are, however, a certain number of more wealthy persons who, contrary to what one would predict, show a similar tendency.

Change situations frequently result in severe problems in the area of consumption. Those whose environment has provided them an adequate food supply, for example, are often in serious difficulty if there is an environmental change (e.g., drought, plague of locusts or rodents, warfare that prevents normal planting or harvest, loss of manpower to the lure of cities). Their habits of life have been formed under the previous situation, and they are ill prepared to handle the changes. In western societies, the problems of air and water pollution, as well as the possibility of nuclear disaster, are confronting us with the necessity to change some of our patterns of consumption. Even greater pressure is put on many nonwestern societies by current changes.

3. A third variable relates to *possession and prestige*. In many societies, it is very prestigious to conspicuously display whatever one owns. When the worldview is supernaturalistic, it is common for people to regard material goods as signs of the blessing of God and to display them as indications of God's favor on them. Why do you wear that overcoat? Because I own (often understood as, "God gave me") an overcoat. Why do you show off your nice house? Because I am blessed with a nice house. People in western societies also often want to show off what they possess, but for a different reason. They tend to want to show off the results of what they perceive to be their "own hard work."

In certain societies, the custom may be to hide belongings, at least to the extent that one is not conspicuous about them. Many Americans are quite ashamed to have nice possessions, since their presence may indicate that we are more wealthy and probably less generous than we like to think.

Whatever the case in this regard, for most peoples (including most westerners), it is the keeping of possessions that gives prestige. Whether this "keeping" is an individual possession or that of a group, however, depends on the worldview of

the society. In many societies (as noted below), most property is actually or potentially communally owned and to be shared among the members of the community.
Generosity among the members of the in-group is required, and sharing within
that group is expected. No prestige attaches to doing what is expected, but great
shame attaches to not sharing one's property, especially necessities of life such as
food, clothing, and housing.

For at least some (e.g., the wealthy) in many societies, prestige is often
attained by distributing some portion of one's possessions to others. As mentioned
above, kings or chiefs are often required to be hospitable, and the more widely
they make their hospitality available to their subjects, the more prestige they
attain. There is a certain amount of such thinking among wealthy westerners as
well. This may result in the support of charitable causes, the throwing of parties,
and the setting up of foundations to give away wealth.

The use of possessions to gain or maintain power over others is another aspect
of the possessions and prestige topic. The ability to use one's wealth to hire services or buy products gives one great power. Such power is both a result of and a
contributor to prestige.

CONCEPTS OF PROPERTY

One of the factors interrelating with many of the topics we have been discussing is the way property is perceived by various peoples. As in all areas of culture,
there are quite a number of different ways of dealing with the ownership question.

1. The first consideration is *what can and cannot be owned*. For many peoples,
natural things (most of the physical universe) cannot be owned. Such things can
be used, but only things made by humans can be owned by humans. For other peoples, of course, nearly anything, natural or manufactured, can be owned.

When we think of property, we ordinarily think of material goods, yet in most
societies there are various nonmaterial things that can be owned. In western societies there are patents and copyrights. In many societies, it is possible to possess
exclusive rights to certain songs, stories, medicines, rituals, and other nonmaterial
items.

2. Another variable with regard to property is whether a given item is *owned
communally or individually*. A basic generalization would seem to be that communal societies tend to hold more property communally, while individualistic societies tend to allow more individual ownership. Another generalization would be that
property regularly used by many people tends to be owned communally, while
individual ownership tends to be more often allowed for those things that are used
exclusively by any given individual.

In traditional, kinship-oriented societies, it is typical for property such as live-
stock to be the possession of the kin group. Cooking utensils, on the other hand,
may belong individually to the wife to whom they were given on her wedding day,
or to the one who made them. Housing and clothing are also often communally
owned but "assigned" (perhaps quite informally) to the person who ordinarily uses
them. Indeed, if a person is not wearing a given set of clothing on a particular day,
that clothing is often considered available for someone else in the family to wear.

I had an interesting experience with this concept of ownership once when, as a
class demonstration of differences in people's definitions of stealing, I asked a
Nigerian the following question: "If your brother went into your home and took a

suit out of your closet without your permission, would you accuse him of stealing?" The answer was an emphatic "No!" followed by the reason, "Because he is my brother." When asked if the same rule applied to someone outside of his family, however, the reply was just as emphatic that that person would be guilty of stealing, since he was not a brother. In that society (and many others), such sharing of clothes approaches communal ownership.

In many such societies there is a kind of communal ownership of certain myths and other traditional explanations of life. Sometimes anthropologists have been blocked in their attempts to gain insight into cultures by the unwillingness of people to share what to them were secret things owned by their society. Sometimes the people have even misled the anthropologist into believing false stories concocted with the intent to mislead them, lest they learn the secret explanations that only insiders are permitted to know. Medical secrets are often owned and passed from generation to generation by given families. So are rituals used in healing or other religious observances.

3. One further concept of property to be mentioned concerns whether a given item is seen as *alienable or inalienable*. Something that can be sold or given away is called "alienable." Something that a people considers impossible to sell or give is called "inalienable." Land and other natural objects (e.g., rivers, trees) are often in the inalienable category. They may be seen as impossible for an individual to own (even westerners see air, rivers, and oceans in this way), or as owned by the society or its ancestors. If others need to use a given portion of land, the people might rent it to them or allow them to use it for a while, but they cannot sell it.

There is an interesting chapter in American history that revolves around the conflict between European and American Indian concepts of land ownership. On many occasions the American colonists offered money or goods to the Indians to purchase some of their land. From the colonists' point of view, they owned it. From the Indian point of view, however, no land could be bought or sold, and it never occurred to them that the settlers didn't understand that they were simply renting the land. After a period of time, the Indians came to the colonists to ask for their land back, but were denied. Furthermore, the colonists, since they had no understanding of the Indian point of view regarding land, concluded that the Indians were quite fickle and untrustworthy. From their point of view, they had bought the land fair and square. As a result of this kind of cross-cultural misunderstanding, a new (and prejudicial) phrase came into our language: a person who gives or sells you something and then later wants to take it back may be called "an Indian giver."

ECONOMIC STRUCTURE AND THE CHURCH

There are quite a number of areas where church structure interacts with economic structure. One helpful discussion of some of these areas is in Tippett (1967:180–85). Among the points he makes is that "the growth of a young church should be orientated to the economic pattern, not planned on a basis of western economy" (184). Such a principle leads us to ask a series of questions concerning how well any given church fits into the economic patterns of the surrounding society. Among these questions are the following:

1. *At what time should church services be conducted?* I've been told that the early Church met for worship very early on Sunday mornings. In that day, people had to work on Sunday, so the congregations met before their members had to go

to work. It is widely rumored that the eleven o'clock hour for church in Euroamerica was chosen to accommodate farmers, who would have had difficulty getting their chores and breakfast over with in time to make it to church at an earlier hour. In both cases, economic reality dictated the time of worship. Yet many of the leaders of young churches seem to have gotten the impression that it is God-ordained that church services must be at ten or eleven o'clock on Sunday morning, no matter how inconvenient this time might be for the participants.

I had quite a problem with this kind of mentality in my own ministry in Nigeria. There was a Sunday market five miles from us that got going well around nine or ten o'clock. There were several paths leading to that market. One of the major ones passed through our village. This meant that a fair number of people from villages near and far came along those paths on their way to market between seven and eight A.M. each Sunday. From my point of view, that would have been an excellent time to have our worship services, both for the people of our village who would then have gone to market and for those who were passing through and would have welcomed an event like church as an excuse for a rest from their long walk. But our leaders had learned (by example rather than verbal instruction) that God wants to be worshiped at mid-morning, not earlier.

This meant that the church services tended to attract mainly those who, for one reason or another, weren't going to market. Almost nobody came for worship who was not sick, aged, in the final stages of pregnancy, very young, or very sincere, especially if they had bicycles so they could get to market quickly after the service. Noting this, I tried to talk to our leaders and suggest that maybe the eleven o'clock hour wasn't sacred. This led to an experiment with meeting at seven-thirty. The building was always filled and overflowing at that hour. But eventually they went back to the sacred hour, probably because it was more convenient for the leaders, who, incidentally, often articulated a missionary point of view that if people were really spiritually minded, they would give up their Sunday marketing. Given the great importance of the weekly market in these people's lives, requiring such a sacrifice of Christians was truly unreasonable.

Do Christians have the right to set other Sunday hours for worship when there is this kind of interference from the people's way of life? Could Christians even change the day in a Muslim or a Hebrew area, where Friday or Saturday, rather than Sunday, is set aside? Some American churches are now scheduling their worship services on Saturday evening, Thursday evening (for those who regularly go out of town for the whole weekend), or Sunday afternoon to enable people to attend without unnecessary conflict with other legitimate aspects of their lives.

2. *Where should the church building or other place of worship be located?* Again, it behooves us to ask about the economic patterns. In the above-mentioned situation in my own ministry, not only was the time of worship a problem, we also had a place problem. The tendency of our church leaders was to want services conducted in buildings built by the Mission (in this case, school buildings), even though these were inconveniently located for most of the Christians (except the leaders) and were not close to the paths that were used by the people on their way to market. Though it seemed evident to the leaders that this usage communicated an unacceptable foreignness and inaccessibility of the new message, they had extreme difficulty countering the patterns they had learned.

In many societies, whether traditional, peasant, or industrial, it is important to consider questions relating to the placing (and timing) of Christian activities in proximity to the focal points of economic activity. In some situations (e.g., when people are entirely preoccupied with market or other activities so that any attempts at Christian witness or worship would be resented), it might be extremely unwise to try to make a Christian presence obvious. Many have, however, found quiet ways (e.g., a bookstall, a coffee/tea house, a small shop or "shrine" patterned after those of the dominant religion of the area) to create a witness even in busy places. The tendency for Christians to separate their meeting places from the world's market places needs to be constantly reevaluated to see if the gains (and there are many gains, especially for the already converted) are sufficient to compensate for the loss in the ability to witness to non-Christians.

3. *A third set of questions concerns support for the church and its staff.* In industrialized societies where everyone specializes, the western model of fulltime pastors may be quite appropriate, though often there is so little understanding of what pastors do to justify their salary that even committed Christians are sometimes suspicious. But what should the pattern be in societies that have few, if any, specialized workers or in which religious leaders are not paid? Even where neither of these problems occur, what if it is unreasonable to expect a small congregation to provide full support? Is it a good idea for the pastor in such a society to expect fulltime support?

Our western concepts of efficiency and specialization push us toward a "yes" answer to that question. But often problems such as the suspicion that is engendered, the decrease of the pastor's ability to identify with his or her parishioners (and they with him or her), the fact that fulltime pastors tend (in keeping with their training) to focus primarily on an intellectual, academic approach to the Scriptures (rather than on ministry) are so detrimental to their ministries that these western patterns should be carefully reanalyzed in relation to the specifics of each society into which they have been introduced. In many traditional and peasant societies, it is just not appropriate to have fully supported pastors (if the message of Christ is to come across intact).

One day Zrashukwi, one of our fulltime church planters, came to me saying, "I'm quitting my job." I asked why and was told, "This past Sunday I was out speaking in a nearby village. I preached my heart out, and afterwards a man came up to me and said, 'That's a very attractive message. But, of course, I would talk that way too if I were paid to.'" Zrashukwi then said to me emphatically, "Nobody is ever going to be able to say that to me again." I asked what his plans were. Was he going to stop speaking out for Christ? "No," he said. "I will never stop that. I am committed to continue witnessing for Christ. What I'll do is to go back to my family farm and grow all my own food. I'll have the best farm in the village, so that people will see that a church leader can be a full, respectable human being. Then I'll do church work on the side. Whatever the church leaders want me to do, I'm willing. If they don't assign me to a place, I'll go out and start another church on my own. Nothing will keep me from working for the Lord."

To this day, Zrashukwi is farming and leading a church. In working within the patterns of his culture, rather than in terms of the imported patterns, he has a much better witness than most of those who are pastoring fulltime. From the people's point of view, he has first proven that he is a full-fledged human being and then that he is totally committed to God. His is a powerful witness.

A further consideration, still very important in many areas of the world where people are not yet entirely comfortable with the use of money to support "people work" (as opposed to machinery work), is the matter of how such workers should be compensated. In such societies, the problem of specialization is not so great as the problem of how the specialists are to be compensated. Traditionally, such compensation would be in food, labor, or other necessary goods and services. The requirement that church workers be paid in money and that church offerings consist largely of money powerfully communicates foreignness. In a society similar to many in the world today, the Old Testament leaders taught that God expected at least a tenth of all produce to be used for the support of specialized persons and structures. Such teaching would be more appropriate today in many societies than the exclusive focus on monetary giving that many have fallen into.

A study of church history does not support the universality of the model of ministry that assumes a fulltime pastor paid in cash. Nor does it support the western practice of producing church leaders primarily by training young people as pseudo-academics and preachers. From earliest times, those who have been most successful in Christian ministry have related just as well to people as they did to God. These have often been laypeople who, like the disciples, have proven themselves in one career and then been set aside to devote fulltime to ministry because they have demonstrated the proper ministry and relational skills. The point is, even if the western pattern was working well in the West (which it is not), it should not simply be dumped on every society as if it were a universally valid pattern. *Church leadership patterns should be appropriate to the economic and social patterns of the receiving society, as they were in the Bible.*

4. A really sticky issue in many cross-cultural situations concerns *the use or nonuse of foreign funds.* Often the temptation for donors to try to control the receivers of donations (often unconsciously) and the tendency of the receivers to allow or even invite such control seems irresistible. In such cases, the issue of trust is added to the pressures exerted by each society toward conformity to the society's values. Unless, therefore, there is a very strong commitment on the part of the donors to trust the receivers (even when they err or when the donors do not understand the receivers' reasoning), the western compulsion to control through financial aid is likely to take over and distort the message.

Another factor in the area of outside financial support should be a strong concern for the *appropriateness* of whatever ministry a given Christian group gets involved in. Using the same definition of appropriateness highlighted in the previous chapter, we should aim at ministries that, if they "break," can be fixed by the people on the scene. Any ministry that requires outside funding or expertise should be seriously questioned. From my point of view, the first question to ask about such structures (as about all else in Christian ministry) is, "What is this approach communicating concerning the message for which God gave His all?" Often the heresy of the inherent foreignness of the Gospel is most strongly evident in those aspects of the church where foreign support is most necessary (e.g., institutions started by missions and turned over to the church).

5. Perhaps the most troublesome economic issue for many cross-cultural workers is *what to do about those practices that we label "bribery."* In Euroamerica, "tipping" applies in a fairly limited number of social situations. The most common of these occur in restaurants and hotels and relate mainly to the serving of food, the parking of cars, and the showing of a person to a hotel room. This custom involves the necessity of our paying employees of the establishment a small amount of money *after* they have provided some service for us. The fact that this is expected

often (not always) leads employers to offer lower salaries to such employees. It also leads such employees to habitually evaluate their clients in order to estimate how large their tip is likely to be and to provide whatever quality of service they believe the size of the tip will warrant.

The problem arises when Euroamericans find themselves in cross-cultural situations where the custom of providing tips for services is much more widespread (applies to almost any service rendered) and, in addition, the tips are expected *before*, rather than after the service is performed. Rather than seeing that custom as of the same nature as our tipping custom, we label it with a negative name, "bribe," and question its ethicality. The fact that this custom involves payment before the event does, indeed, provide much opportunity for exploitation on the part of the one who provides the service and for misinterpretation on the part of the one from whom the compensation is expected. However, like tipping, it is a normal custom and potentially neutral rather than inherently evil, in spite of the fact that the English label "bribe" prejudices us against the custom.

Having said this, we need to note that this custom, like many others, is often used in an unethical, exploitive way. Christian evaluation and critiquing of this custom should, therefore, be related to the misuse of it rather than to the custom in and of itself. Though outsiders (Euroamericans) may often err either in practicing or not practicing the custom, it seems clear that the misunderstanding stemming from our refusal to bribe/tip in cross-cultural situations that we only partially understand often is a poorer witness than going along with a judicious use of the custom.

CHAPTER 13

RELIGIOUS BELIEF AND TECHNOLOGY

INTEGRATIONAL THOUGHT

People are always making rules they expect God to obey. These rules then become an important part of the religious belief and technology employed by humans to express themselves in relation to supernatural beings and forces.

The early Church had a continual struggle with this aspect of human religiosity. In Acts 15, for example, the early Church leaders were faced with the fact that God had broken their rule concerning how Gentiles were to come into the Church. The rule was that Gentiles "cannot be saved unless [they] are circumcised as the Law of Moses requires" (Acts 15:1). That is, non-Jews were expected to convert culturally to Judaism if they were to be considered Christians. The early Jewish Christians fully believed that only Jewish culture was an adequate vehicle for Christian faith and expression.

This is understandable. What is more natural than to expect that the culture in which God has met us is to be the one He will use for everyone? Aren't these vehicles sanctified by His use of them? Isn't the way He has led us normative for all others as well?

But Paul and Barnabas reported an amazing thing. As they presented the Gospel to the Gentiles, God didn't wait for those who believed to change their culture. Instead, God gave them the Holy Spirit immediately, as soon they believed! What a dilemma! God had gone and broken a rule the early Church believed had come from Him. What should be done about a God like that? Imagine the discussions Paul and Barnabas and their ministry team members must have had on their way back to Jerusalem concerning how best to break this disturbing news to the leaders there.

When the report was made at headquarters, as with Church leaders in all ages, they argued over what to do (v. 7). Getting beneath the surface of the debate, it is clear that they had to decide whether or not to go along with what God had already begun to do, for it was He, not any humans, who had given the Holy Spirit to Gentile believers without requiring them to become Jews. After considerable argument, they narrowly agreed to go along with God (Acts 15:6–21).

But the history of the Church down through the ages shows a strong tendency to return to the earlier rule—the demand that converts to Christ also convert to the culture of the group in power. Luther broke with the Roman Catholic Church largely over its cultural requirements (including observance of Roman laws and rituals). Methodists broke with Anglicans largely over their cultural requirements. In fact, there is seldom a denominational split that does not focus in a primary way on the felt need of the splitting group to escape from what they consider undesirable cultural requirements.

But God's way is not the same as our ways. He is not a machine to be controlled by those who observe cultural rules—even if these are rules He once approved for a different set of people in a different set of circumstances. He is a person to be related to in ways appropriate to the present time and culture. He moves freely, according to His own desires and in keeping with principles highlighted in the Scriptures—whether or not those movements conform to the rules and traditions we think are important.

May we learn this lesson and be careful that we are not burdening people with cultural loads that are both too heavy and unnecessary.

INTRODUCTION

Turning from the technology used in the material world to that used in religion may seem (to westerners, at least) to involve a sizable jump in subject matter. Yet for probably most of the peoples of the world what we call religion is to them much of what science and technology are to us in the West—a means of relating to and dealing with an important part of the nonhuman universe.

In dealing with the concept of religion, even more than in dealing with most of the other subcategories of human culture, we become aware of the fact that the very categories we set up stem from a western view of things. As we will see from some of the definitions below, the antisupernaturalistic biases of westerners easily intrude into what is regarded as religious and what is not. By way of contrast, a high percentage of the societies of the world have no separate linguistic term or concept for the category of life that we westerners label religion. For them, the basic assumptions we call religious are at the heart of their worldview and the rituals are their normal techniques for dealing with the external world.

A survey of definitions by anthropologists shows a clustering around one pole of a dichotomy that is particularly characteristic of western perspectives, the natural-supernatural dichotomy. For most of the peoples of the world (at least prior to westernization), such a dichotomy does not exist. For them, most or all of what we call supernatural is as natural as anything we call natural. They expect spirits and God(s) to regularly make their presence known in human affairs. So, of course, does biblical Christianity, in marked contrast to the secularized Christianity practiced by most Euroamerican Christians (including most western/westernized missionaries).

A standard anthropological definition of religion is given by Robert Taylor: "beliefs and practices having to do with the concept of the supernatural" (1976:230). Similarly, Spradley and McCurdy (in keeping with their "culture is knowledge" theory) call religion "the cultural knowledge of the supernatural that people use to cope with the ultimate problems of human existence" (1975:424). Wallace elaborates a bit on the same theme by pointing to "a set of rituals, rationalized by myth, which mobilizes supernatural powers" (1966:107). Note that each of these definitions assumes the dichotomy between natural and supernatural beings.

The clearest statement of the problem I am addressing is given by Beals and Hoijer who, after providing a definition similar to the first ones given above, state that

> Although the definition sounds simple enough, its use depends upon the anthropologist's capacity to distinguish clearly between things that are natural or social and things that are supernatural. In many cases *the attempt to distinguish between natural and supernatural leads to a kind of ethnocentrism* in which the beliefs of scientists,

including anthropologists, are considered to define the realm of the natural, whereas all other beliefs are held to deal with the supernatural. As an example, the belief that garlic will prevent plague is likely to be placed in the area of the supernatural until such time as some scientist demonstrates that garlic really does prevent plague (1977:473, emphasis mine).

Beals and Hoijer see the dilemma created by such dichotomization when they point out, "In the end, a great many beliefs and practices are neither completely secular nor completely sacred and have to do with phenomena that are not clearly natural or supernatural" (1977:474).

Before we get further into our subject, I would like to mention two recent textbooks on religion written from a Christian perspective. I highly recommend Burnett (1988) and Steyne (1990) as more complete treatments than we are able to present here.

ANTHROPOLOGISTS AND "SUPERNATURALISTIC" SOCIETIES

An interesting spin-off from the western biases of anthropologists is important to the case we will make below concerning the distinctions between religion and worldview. The major portion of the history of anthropology to date has involved the almost exclusive study of nonwestern, largely small, tribal societies. Almost all such societies may be labeled "supernaturalistic." The westerners studying them were, however, "naturalistic," in the sense that they made the above-described dichotomy between those areas we think can be investigated scientifically and those we think cannot.

Since supernaturalistic concepts were so prominent among these peoples, anthropologists assumed that what they termed religion was more basic to those cultures than any other aspect. What they observed and labeled (according to western categories) religion included much of what I here term worldview, plus the surface-level rituals and behavior that provide religious expression for the supernaturalistic assumptions of the peoples they studied. That is, what the anthropologists called religion included all the supernaturalistic worldview assumptions that lay at the base of their whole cultures, simply because that's where they fit *according to the worldview of the investigators.*

The problem caused by such a confusion was not so important as long as anthropologists limited themselves largely to nonwestern societies. As long as they stuck to supernaturalistic societies, they could accurately contend that, in terms of western categories, "the core of this culture is their religion." But what happens when one looks at a western people who have substituted naturalistic science for supernaturalistic religion?

At this point we need to decide whether it would be best to redefine religion in such a way that western science is considered a religion or to approach the matter in a different way. If we call science a religion because it functions at the core of western societies much as supernaturalism functions at the core of most other societies, we end up with a naturalistic, atheistic religion. This is the course some have taken, however. Note the following definition from Paul Hiebert:

> In its broadest sense, religion encompasses *all specific beliefs about the ultimate nature of reality and the origins, meaning, and destiny of life*, as well as the myths and rituals that symbolically express them. In this sense, religions may or may not have gods, demons, and souls. For example, Christianity, Islam, some forms of Hinduism, and most

tribal religions have supernatural beings, but some forms of Buddhism and Hinduism and scientism do not.

Religion is also based on the person's ability to transcend the self, to step "outside" of and contemplate oneself, one's fellows, and the universe. It is based on the human need to "make sense" out of human experience and find some order and significance in the whole human situation (1983:372, emphasis mine).

Such a definition of religion, though possible (and not uncommon among anthropologists), raises sizable problems with an approach such as ours (and Hiebert's) when it comes to distinguishing between religion and worldview. If religion covers the items in the second paragraph and the italicized part of the first, there is a considerable overlap and confusion between what we call religion and what we have defined as worldview.

For this reason, as we have seen in chapters 3, 4, and 8, I choose to take a different approach—one that allows a rigorous distinction between religion and worldview. Worldview is defined as that which provides a society its basic perspectives on *all* of life—"all the specific beliefs [or assumptions] about the ultimate nature of reality and the origins, meaning, and destiny of life," that Hiebert (but not I) includes under the religion category. Religion, however, is but one of the surface-level subsystems, along with politics, economics, and the rest. There is no confusion in my analysis between worldview at the core of culture and religion that consists of surface-level belief and behavior.

From this point of view, religion is more than worldview, in the sense that it includes behavior (both ritual and creative) as well as belief. It is less in the sense that it does not, like worldview, include the assumptions that underlie the rest of culture. On the other hand, worldview is more than religion in that worldview, unlike religion, involves the culture-wide assumptions that apply to how humans behave in all contexts, whether these are labeled political, social, economic, religious, linguistic, or whatever. Worldview includes no behavior at all, only the underlying assumptions on which all of a society's behavior is based.

As we have seen in chapter 4, though, there tends to be an unequal influence of surface-level concerns on worldview. In each society, the surface-level concerns to which the people give the most attention have the greatest influence on the people's worldview. Thus in the majority of the traditional and peasant societies of the world, the religious subsystem is usually the most developed and the most influential on the worldview. In western societies, however, it is the technoeconomic subsystems (including science) that are much more highly developed and therefore more influential on the worldview.

The "religion as the heart of culture" view is, unfortunately, still alive and confusing, both in much of contemporary anthropology and among certain theologians (e.g., Tillich 1959; Conn 1984). Even though that is not the approach preferred here, we need to know it and to make sure we find out how any given author is using the terms. Tippett, for example, whose missiological writing is timeless, follows this older usage (*see* Tippett 1987:157–82).

ALLEGIANCES

One crucial dimension of the kind of distinction we are making between religion and worldview lies in the area of allegiance. We have said that the fundamental values and allegiances on the basis of which people live their lives lie in their worldview. People not only value things (including concepts), they commit themselves to them with varying intensities. That is, a group of people may value their own identity as a group so much that they even commit themselves to die to preserve that group as a separate entity. On the other hand, they may place such a low value on, say, whether they wear traditional or imported clothing, that they gladly accept the latter as their preferred attire. Few commit themselves to clothing, toothpaste, or other such items with the same intensity they reserve for their allegiance to family, tribe/nation, food staple, geographical locale, language, and certain aspects of their religion.

In dealing with religion, it is important to distinguish the allegiance aspect from the structure aspect. Though for some, especially those who serve as professionals in world religions, allegiance to the system may be an important thing, for most the system would seem to be more a vehicle for expressing allegiance than an object of allegiance. That is, the concern of most is to use the structures to express conscious or unconscious allegiance (including dependence on, loyalty, commitment) to the beings and powers that lie beyond the system. The attitude of most toward the system is utilitarian. They are therefore often open to change if presented in relevant ways with better answers to the questions for which they seek answers. People are not necessarily conservative when it comes to religion.

Allegiances and structures (including the belief structures) are two quite different things, both in their nature and in their importance. Among the allegiances expressed through the religious structures may be a person's ultimate or primary allegiance. If that primary allegiance is to the true God, the person is, of course, "saved," whether or not the structures through which that allegiance is expressed conform to those used in other parts of the world to express Christian commitment. If, however, the person's primary commitment is to another god, to family, culture, self, the religious system itself, or to any of thousands of other possible allegiances, the person is "lost," even if that person participates in structures that have been used by true Christians for ages.

If a person comes, through his or her religion, to a primary allegiance to the true God, it is more than simply a religious matter. It is a matter of the person's worldview, since that allegiance has displaced all other potential allegiances (e.g., family, job, nation, or tribe) offered by the other subsystems of the culture. That central allegiance to God will be played out through participation in all of the cultural subsystems, not simply via the religious structures. In fact, if that commitment is isolated to a person's religious behavior (as might be the case with many westerners), it may well be that the person is not truly God's child, since some other allegiance may be greater.

The cultural structuring of such aspects of religious practice as worship, prayer, myth, even belief, are of quite a different nature than this primary allegiance. We see in the Scriptures that God accepts quite a variety of such structures. For example, the Hebrews pledged their allegiance to God but used their own cultural structures (starting with those they had before Abraham met Yahweh) to worship God. In fact, one of them comes in for a lot of discussion in the New Testament.

The Jews circumcised their young boys in order to express their allegiance to God. Then, in New Testament times, Paul said that circumcision is not to be practiced by Gentile Christians. Paul regarded it as a hindrance to their faith. People of societies other than Jewish were not to be required to use this custom, no matter how meaningful it was to the Jews. But all peoples, Gentile or Jew, were/are to pledge the same allegiance to God. Without such commitment there is no salvation. The discussion in Acts 15 is about this very thing. Paul and Barnabas are saying that though Gentiles (like Jews) must respond to God in faith, they are free to use the religious structures of their own culture to express it. They do not have to convert to Jewish culture in order to be Christian.

At the end of this chapter, I will raise the possibility that people may be able to become Christian while retaining as secondary and tertiary allegiances their relationships to their cultures, including their traditional religious structures. If the allegiance is Christian, does it matter if the structures are more like Muslim or Hindu structures than like western "Christian" structures? The crucial dimension is primary commitment, not religious structures. If a people's primary allegiance is not to God through Christ, no set of structures will save them. If it is to God through Jesus, any structures that are meaningful will do. See Kraft (1979c) for a more detailed treatment of this topic.

RELIGIOUS BELIEFS

As indicated above, religion consists of belief (assumptions) and practice. We will first discuss the variety and nature of the religious assumptions made by the peoples of the world. Though at this point we will treat these all as religious assumptions, it should be noted that for many societies some of them are so basic that they function at the deeper level as worldview assumptions. For "supernaturalistic" societies, at least some of the beliefs described here would class as worldview assumptions, while for "naturalistic" societies they class as purely religious.

Assumptions concerning supernatural beings or powers constitute what is perhaps the most important area of religious belief. For what is probably the majority of the peoples of the world, the most important questions of life revolve around what to do about (or with) the supernatural powers that they believe surround them and constantly influence their lives. It is unfortunate that most of the westerners who have gone to other peoples as Christian witnesses have been from segments of Christianity that hold secularized western assumptions rather than biblical assumptions concerning such powers.

This has led to the presentation of a secularized, virtually nonsupernatural type of Christianity that, like western secular society, points to naturalistic, technological answers to what might be termed the "power questions" of life (e.g., health, agriculture, interpersonal relationships). The supernaturalistically oriented nonwestern recipients of the message, however, tend to be left without better answers to those power questions than they had before the Christian witnesses arrived. This fact gives rise to what is undoubtedly the biggest problem in worldwide Christianity, the problem of "dual allegiance." Dual allegiance is the condition of those who pledge allegiance to Christ but retain their previous allegiance to traditional power sources mediated by traditional religious practitioners such as shamans, medicine men/women, diviners, fortune-tellers, and priests. Since they find no power in the churches to displace the power they depended on previously, they continue to go the shaman to meet those needs (*see* Kraft and Kraft 1993).

The major human reason for the rapid spread of Pentecostal and charismatic Christianity in nonwestern societies is the fact that these groups are dealing with the power questions of life and are usually more on the wavelength both of those to whom they present the message and of the biblical societies in which the message was originally presented. Dual allegiance is much less of a problem in these approaches to Christianity, though there is often a kind of cultural insensitivity that raises other problems.

Ideas concerning supernatural beings and powers sort generally into two categories: those concerning personal beings and those concerning impersonal forces or powers. It is probable that most of the peoples of the world believe in both personal and impersonal beings/powers and often see little need to distinguish between them. As Christians, we see the source of all spiritual power in the Person of God. We also believe in personal angels and demons. Blessings, curses, dedications, oaths, and the like might be seen as examples of impersonal power, though that power originates in the persons who pronounce them. Impersonal power is not, therefore, nearly as prominent in Christianity as in some non-Christian belief systems.

Within anthropology, the term *animism* (originated by E. B. Tylor 1874) has been used in both a broad and a narrow sense. In the broad sense it is a label for any belief in personal supernatural beings such as gods, spirits, and ghosts. As Tylor wrote, "I propose here, under the name Animism, to investigate the deeply-lying doctrine of Spiritual Beings, which embodies the very essence of Spiritualistic as opposed to Materialistic philosophy" (1874:vol 1:425).

In this sense, Christianity, Judaism, and Islam are forms of animism. Christian missiologists, therefore, find it more helpful to follow the narrower usage that defines animism as "a belief in spirit beings which are thought to animate nature" and is

> typical of those who see themselves as being a part of nature rather than superior to it. . . . Among them, gods and goddesses are relatively unimportant, but the woods are full of all sorts of spirits. Gods and goddesses, if they exist at all, may be seen as having created the world, and perhaps making it fit to live in. But it is spirits to whom one turns for curing, who help or hinder the shaman, and whom the ordinary hunter may meet in the woods (Haviland 1982:541).

Many peoples believe in certain powers or forces that are not personal. Anthropologists usually use the Oceanic term *mana* to label this kind of belief.

> The Melanesians . . . think of *mana* as a force inherent in all objects. It is not in itself physical, but it can reveal itself physically. A warrior's success in fighting is not attributed to his own strength but to the *mana* contained in an amulet which hangs around his neck . . . *mana* is abstract in the extreme, a power lying always just beyond reach of the senses (Haviland 1982:541–2).

Such a force is not dissimilar to the western concept of luck, though it is often much more developed and taken quite a bit more seriously than in Euroamerica. It is often seen as "a supernatural attribute of persons and things [providing] the exceptional power to do things that are unusual" (Hoebel 1972:577).

Belief in other impersonal forces is also common. We have mentioned the western concept of luck. Concepts such as fate, kismet, destiny, one's lot, and the like are widespread. Such concepts generally hold that a person's or group's future is predestined and therefore unalterable. The Hindu concept of karma is a similar but more complicated concept.

Another universal belief is in various kinds of *supernatural beings*. The majority of the world's societies appear to believe in some kind of High God. Hoebel cites a statistical study of a selection of the world's peoples that shows a High God concept present in 97 percent of the societies of the Mediterranean area, 86 percent of those of Black Africa, though in somewhat less than half of those of East Eurasia and the Americas and fairly rare in the Pacific islands (1972:591). For many of the peoples who believe in a High God, however, He is distant and unapproachable.

For this reason, people often also believe in other supernatural beings (whether gods or spirits) who are subservient to God. Apparently few, if any, societies are genuinely polytheistic, believing in many gods that are equal to each other. More often they will, like the early Jews, hold to what is called "henotheism," which holds that there is one God above all the others but that there are other gods. When God said, "Worship no god but me" (Ex 20:3), He implicitly allowed the Hebrews to believe in the existence of other gods (for the time being) but not to give them their primary allegiance.

Most peoples believe in *spirits* of various kinds. Often these will be divided into good (angels) and evil spirits (Satan and demons), though it is not unusual for some or all of the spirits to be capable of either good or bad activity. Many societies will elevate some of their prominent ancestors to positions as "hero" spirits. Often, I'm afraid, Jesus is unconsciously reduced by Christians to this category. Some societies will believe in messenger or ministering spirits who function like angels do in Christianity. Though we in the West often do not understand angels (at least partly because nobody has bothered to translate the word angel), the biblical concept of a God who has various messengers that He sends out to do various tasks is often quite intelligible to nonwestern peoples.

The *ways in which supernaturals and humans relate* to each other is also conceived of differently from society to society. As mentioned above, a High God is often felt to be far off and out of reach for close contact with humans. The gap is often filled by evil spirits. As with most animists, the people I worked with in northeastern Nigeria reasoned that since God was far away and would be good to them, they could usually ignore Him. But they needed to do whatever they could to appease the evil spirits, who were close and troublesome. So when they sacrificed, they sacrificed to the evil spirits, not to God. When there were problems, they would try to do something that would call the evil spirits off. This was a very logical approach, given their assumptions.

In developing a strategy for winning these people to Christ, we found they were most receptive to an approach that enabled them to go directly to God, through Jesus, for protection from these spirits. We would ask them who they felt could control the spirits. They would say, "Only God." So we would present them the Good News about the way to get into close contact with God through Jesus Christ. We were thus able to affirm both their belief in God and the reality of their problems with the spirits (i.e., to start where they were) but also to show them the Christian answer to their most pressing felt need.

One further area of religious belief is that of *souls and ghosts*. A soul may be defined as "a nonmaterial entity existing within and fundamental to the life of the body" (R. Taylor 1976:233). Many peoples use a different term, such as the English ghost to designate a soul once its physical body has died. Some concept of soul seems to be present in nearly every society. Though within western societies we have argued over whether human beings ought to be seen as bipartite (body and soul) or tripartite (body, soul, and spirit), we don't get nearly as elaborate in this area as many societies do. One former student who worked among the Karen of

Myanmar (Burma) reports, for example, that they believe each person has thirty-three different souls, though he states frankly that he has only ever been able to get any kind of definition of nine of these varieties. But even nine could be confusing to outsiders, and many peoples approach that number.

Often a people explain death, illness, dreams, visions, and the like in terms of the presence or absence of the person's soul. For such peoples, "Illness may be due to partial or temporary loss of a soul, and death may occur when the soul is completely and permanently separated from the body. Dreams are accounted for as the travels and experiences of the soul while one is asleep" (R. Taylor 1976:233).

For such people, it is often considered a serious offense to wake a person too quickly, since this may mean that his or her soul will not be able to return from its wanderings in time, causing sickness or even death.

A person's shadow is often considered a soul, as are other perceived manifestations of one or another aspect of personhood. In some ways, certain multi-soul views of persons seem similar to certain polytheistic views of Deity in which one could postulate an original single Deity who had been split into a variety of separate functions, each of which had then become personified and regarded as separate deities. Were it not for the fact that a human person has a single body, we could well imagine the possibility of conceiving of a person as multiple beings labeled life soul, brain soul, spirit, death soul (ghost), dream soul, shadow soul, and so on.

A final area is *belief in an afterlife*. Concepts of some kind of immortality are nearly universal. Belief in *reincarnation* is also common. Heaven and Hell are familiar to us from Christianity. Concepts involving the desire for oblivion, such as the Buddhist belief in Nirvana, are somewhat rarer than those already listed.

It is frequently understood that at death certain people, if not all, continue to be a part of the living community, even though they no longer possess bodies. Usually such persons are thought to have greater power as ancestors than they had in biological life. They are often treated with great respect, lest they become angry and punish their people for not looking after them properly. Funeral arrangements and memorial ceremonies must be carried out "just so" if the biologically alive are to avoid misfortune at the hands of the invisible members of their community. The ancestors, however, often also have their duties and may be spoken to quite harshly by the biologically alive if they don't, for example, keep the rain coming or the land or women fertile.

A belief that *ancestors* are still alive after biological death has proved to be very problematic for westerners, especially for Christians. For example, with no more understanding of the spirit world than our western societies allow us, what name do we give to the supposed interaction between the biological living and the biological dead? Since what goes on looks to westerners like prayer and worship (i.e., the kind of things we do in relation to God), the usual designation has been ancestor worship. This term is frequently inaccurate, since people often make a fairly clear distinction between behavior due toward God and that appropriate for humans—including humans who no longer have bodies and therefore are considered dead by westerners. What westerners consider worship is usually, from the point of view of those who honor their biologically dead ancestors, simply the respect due to the most important members of their *living* community.

I conclude that a term such as "ancestor worship" as a general designation of such practices is prejudicial and should be abandoned. The term is the product of western worldview limitations, rather than an accurate designation of such customs. More appropriate would be a term such as "ancestor reverence" or "ancestor veneration" or even "ancestor cult." If we use a less biased general label, there is no problem in recognizing that with this custom, as with any human attribution of honor or respect, it is possible that many will actually put their respect of their ancestors ahead of their respect for God and will therefore fall into idolatry. But if they, like the Hebrews, are honoring God first and their ancestors second, they should not be accused of ancestor worship merely because we didn't take the time to develop a more charitable term.

RELIGIOUS PRACTICES

Magic is one of the most widespread religious practices. The basic concept underlying magic is the possibility for humans to control supernatural beings and powers through the use of certain language or ritual. It is, thus, a mechanical rather than a personal approach to supernatural beings and powers. It is believed that if the word or ritual formulas are said or done properly, the intended result is assured. People often distinguish between so-called black magic (sorcery), where the intent is to do evil, and so-called white or good magic, though from a Christian perspective, both appear to be empowered by the Evil One. Magical procedures are used to try to control the supernatural powers believed to be in charge of food supplies (e.g., crops, game), fertility, health, and the like.

Two types of magical procedures are usually distinguished: imitative (or sympathetic) and contagious. A commonly employed form of *imitative magic* involves magicians in producing a figure of the person or animal to be cursed (or, infrequently, blessed) and doing to that figure what they want to have happen to the person or animal. Pins may be used on the figure to induce sickness or death, or the image may be thrown into water to induce madness (Haviland 1982:552). A picture of an animal with an arrow through its heart may be used to bring about its capture. Ritual sexual intercourse may be engaged in at crop planting time (paralleling human seed planting with agricultural seed planting) (R. Taylor 1976:237).

Contagious magic involves the employment of something that was once in contact with the one to be cursed or blessed. Commonly such items as clothing, fingernails, spit, feces, hair, and teeth are used. These may be cursed or physically damaged by, for example, stamping on, submerging, or burning them in order to bring about a similar fate in the life of the victim.

Certain objects may be blessed and carried by people to attempt to control supernatural powers for blessing. Technically, objects called *charms* are those that attract supernatural aid, while *amulets* are those that ward off evil influences. Often both of these are lumped together and called by the nontechnical name *fetishes* (R. Taylor 1976:238).

Witchcraft, in the technical sense, is the use of human psychic powers to do evil. It is contrasted technically with *sorcery* (black magic), where supernatural power is invoked through magical incantation. Sorcery employs implements, objects, medicines, and other paraphernalia, while witchcraft does not and, in fact, may be done quite unconsciously by some. "Evidence of witchcraft can never be found," making accusations more difficult to prove or disprove (Ember and Ember 1973:275). The same people often practice (or are accused of practicing) both, and nonspecialists seldom make the technical distinction.

Various forms of *divination* are commonly used to evoke "knowledge of some secret or hidden thing by mechanical or manipulative techniques" (Hoebel 1972:509). Both magical (e.g., incantation and ritual) and nonmagical (e.g., appeals to personal spirits, spirit possession) techniques are used to discover such things as the causes of illness or other misfortune, the guilty party in a court case, the right day on which to hunt, build, and so on. Eskimo diviners tied a thong to some object and, after invoking spirit power, asked it yes-no questions. If the object was hard to lift, the answer was no, if easy, yes. Some American Indians would look for the reflection of the face of a guilty person in specially prepared standing water. The Trobrianders dug up corpses and analyzed their appearance to determine how they died. The Azande fed poison to a chicken and determined the guilt or innocence of an accused by what happened (Hoebel 1972:510). Diviners among the Kamwe of northeastern Nigeria use crabs walking in sand to indicate (by the patterning of their tracks) what people should do.

Tabus (*taboos*) may be seen as a kind of negative magic in which it is possible to control supernatural power, at least to the extent of avoiding negative consequences, by refraining from certain acts. A taboo is a negative rule, the breaking of which results in supernatural retribution. Hebrews and Muslims have taboos against eating pork. It is often taboo for warriors to engage in sexual relations before a battle. In Polynesia, where the concept is strong (and the word *tabu* originated), people of high rank are believed to possess such potent mana "that their very persons are surrounded with tabus, as is everything they touch. Sin, in Polynesia as elsewhere, is the violation of a tabu—an act punishable by supernatural sanction" (Hoebel 1972:582).

A helpful distinction is often made between the *attitudes that underlie magic and those that underlie religion*. This is especially valuable for Christians to recognize, since a magical attitude is by no means limited to those who practice magic. Whereas the "religious attitude" is submissive and reverent toward supernaturals, the "magical attitude" demands compliance from them.

> In the religious state of mind, man acknowledges the superiority of the supernatural powers upon whose action his well-being depends. . . . The magician, on the other hand, believes that he *controls* supernatural power under certain conditions. He has power over power. He feels confirmed in his belief that if he possesses a tested formula and if he executes the formula perfectly, barring outside interference, he will get the results which that formula is specified to give. The supernatural power has no volition or choice of its own. It must respond (Hoebel 1972:578).

Though thoroughgoing systems of magic are widespread, the magical attitude is apparent even in systems such as western Christianity, where only the religious attitude is approved. Prescribed prayers, other rituals, and certain types of behavior are often perceived by westerners to pressure God into doing our will. If this is true in the West, how much more apparent is it among recently converted peoples whose traditional religion involved great dependence on magic.

Wallace (1966:52–67) has attempted to summarize religious behavior by producing a more or less comprehensive list of twelve *types of activity found the world over*. Though any given people may not use every one of these behaviors, it would be unusual to find a system in which most of them did not occur. Much of such behavior occurs in *ritual* form. The activities are: 1) prayer, 2) music and dance, 3) physiological alteration or deprivation, 4) exhortation, 5) recitation of myths or codes of conduct, 6) simulation (as in magic, divination, dreams, drama or dramatic dancing and rituals), 7) tabu and mana, 8) feasts or other sacred meals, 9) sacrifices, 10) group activity, 11) inspiration of human beings and certain human activities by the supernatural(s), and 12) symbolism.

RELIGIOUS PRACTITIONERS

As with any of the cultural subsystems, it is important to discuss who does what. If the people are involved in the kinds of practices just described, who leads them? Though this differs to some extent from society to society, it is usually possible to label any given religious leader in terms of his or her approximation to one or the other of the extremes represented by the terms "priest" and "shaman" (or "prophet").

By way of definition, a *priest* is one whose authority comes from the system of which he or she is a part. "He or she is the socially initiated, ceremonially inducted member of a recognized religious organization with a rank and function that belongs to him or her as the tenant of an office held before by others" (Haviland 1982:543).

In a society such as ours, in which there are many specialists, such persons are fairly obvious. We call them pastors, ministers, priests, rabbis. In systems with less specialization, however, it is often true that the one(s) who serve the priestly function do so in addition to other duties. Abraham, for example, in a traditional society governed by kinship, served as general overall leader in all matters, whether political, economic, or religious.

A *shaman* or *prophet*, on the other hand, rises to prominence on the basis of his or her own claims and demonstration of a close relationship to supernatural powers. Shamans or prophets tend to be charismatic personalities who are able to convince people that they speak or behave on behalf of God or gods by performing miracles or by powerfully presenting messages from supernatural beings. Often shamans and prophets claim to be possessed by the god or spirits they serve. Such people often tend to be antiestablishment (whether we are talking about the religious or the political establishment). They are usually highly dedicated and often emotional, and attract followers with the same characteristics. Whether we think of the shamans of the American Indians or other tribal groups, or the prophets and apostles of the Scriptures, or the evangelists and faith healers of today, such people attract a lot of attention and are often disruptive to neatly ordered traditions. The role Jesus took was that of a prophet rather than that of a priest.

Though both types of leaders are often found in all types of societies, shamans tend to be more prominent in less complex societies, while priests tend to be more prominent in more complex societies. When they occur in the same society, they tend not to get along well with each other.

> Shamans and priests are frequently found in the same culture, but in societies with highly organized churches, there is often conflict between them. To priests, with their vested interests in the bureaucracy, the shaman, with his fierce individualism, is a threat to the whole religious structure. The shaman, on the other hand, may in time develop a following, organize a cult group, and thus become the founder of a new religious organization (Hiebert 1983:381).

That organization eventually becomes an institution and is structured in such a way that it is self-perpetuating. When this happens, its leadership is ordinarily chosen from those who have been faithful either to that or another similar organization (like priests) rather than simply emerging from the society at large (like prophets), as the founder did.

Shamans and prophets operate on the basis of revelation from spiritual beings. They have acquired their power and position (if any) individually, often through some sort of a vision quest or call. This may be sought after, as in the case of American Indian shamans (or Jesus or Paul) who went off into long periods of isolation for the purpose of fasting, praying, meditating, and seeking close relationship with God/gods/spirit(s). Often the call would come via a dream or vision and the person would be empowered to do marvelous things, frequently including healing.

Ideally for many religious systems, priests would manifest the same type of power. It is, however, often true that those in appointed positions come to rely more on human power, including the ability to maneuver politically within an organization, than on power from a supernatural source. Though evangelical Christianity theoretically requires of its leaders both the call of God and an organizational appointment, it is not always successful in assuring that they really have the prophetic gifting that its ideals assert is necessary. The same problem plagued groups such as the Pharisees (and nearly every other group within Christianity before or since). The history of Christianity is full of the rise of prophets (shamans) within our organizations who attempt to revive and revitalize (*see* below) the people of God.

RITUALS AND CEREMONIES

Though I have made the point that ritual (habitual) behavior characterizes every cultural subsystem, religious ritual often serves an important function in reinforcing worldview-level activity. It would seem, therefore, to deserve special treatment. Much of what is said above concerning religious practice is played out in religious ritual. As I have suggested, most of the activity pointed to in Wallace's list of twelve types of religious behavior occurs in ritual. There are, however, important functions of such ritual that we have not yet dealt with.

Two basic functions are indicated by the terms "rites of passage" and "rites of intensification/consolidation." The former relates to the subject of our next chapter, the life cycle. Cultures provide for their peoples "proper" things to do whenever there is a transition from one stage of life to another or whenever an actual or potential crisis comes along. If what is intended is a safe passage from one stage to another, the ceremony or other ritual activity supports that passage. If what is intended is support and strengthening within a situation that does not necessarily involve transition, a ritual designed to intensify relationships within the community and between the people and supernatural powers is provided. Many rituals serve both functions.

The classic work on *rites of passage* is that of Arnold Van Gennep (1960). The concept has been more recently popularized by Sheehy (1974). Van Gennep noted that at crucial times in the life of the individual and the society—birth, puberty, marriage, movement from one place to another, movement from one status to another, death, and the like—there are often quite elaborate rituals, such as naming ceremonies, circumcision rites, initiation rites, wedding ceremonies, and funerals. These designate and facilitate three important aspects of passage: separation, transition, and incorporation. During this process, an individual would typically "first be ritually removed from the society as a whole, then isolated for a period, and finally incorporated back into the tribe in his or her new status" (Haviland 1982:549). This process may occur in a single ritual or over an extended period of time via many rituals.

Such rites have great value both as social events and as techniques for defining and clarifying relationships. Before an initiation ceremony, for example, it is clear that the person is a child. After it, however, it is just as clear that he or she is a man or woman. Jesus knew He was a man, and related to His mother accordingly, after He had been through His Bar Mitzvah (Lk 2:49). Likewise with a wedding. Before the ceremony, the man and woman are single and expected by society to participate in life in terms of that status and the roles expected of it. After the ceremony, however, their status and the roles expected of the couple have changed dramatically—in a very short time in a western wedding ceremony.

Given the importance of rites of passage in healthy smaller societies, one wonders at the relatively low value put on them in at least certain sectors of Euroamerican societies. It seems that the lack of clarity on the part of many American young people of high school and college age as to whether they are, in fact, children or adults might be alleviated if there were a clear-cut initiation ceremony, after which all would agree they are adults.

Rites of intensification or consolidation are focused more on the needs of the group than of the individual. Indeed, many ceremonies that function as rites of passage for individuals serve as rites of intensification for the group (e.g., weddings, initiations). In addition to these, however, there are times of social crisis, in which other ceremonies are important.

> A severe lack of rain which threatens crops in the fields, the sudden appearance of an enemy war party, or some other force from outside which disturbs everyone [call for] mass ceremonies . . . to allay the danger to the group . . .
>
> What this does is to *unite people in a common effort in such a way that fear and confusion yield to collective action* and a degree of optimism. The balance in the relations of all concerned, which has been upset, is restored to normal.
>
> While the death of an individual might be regarded as the ultimate crisis in the life of an individual, it is as well a crisis for the entire group, particularly if the group is small. A member of the group has been removed, and so its equilibrium has been upset. The survivors, therefore, must *readjust and restore balance*. They must, at the same time, reconcile themselves to the loss of someone to whom they were emotionally tied. Funerary ceremonies, then, can be regarded as rites of intensification that permit the living to express in nondisruptive ways their upset over the death, and that provide for *social readjustment* (Haviland 1982:550, emphasis mine).

At what are usually less crucial times, rites of intensification or consolidation take place through worship services, reunions of families, friends or schoolmates, political rallies and the like.

Hiebert (1983:375–76) helpfully discusses seven *important functions played by religious rituals*. I have added the eighth. The quote in the following listing is from Hiebert.

1. Frequently *a great deal of information is stored and transmitted from generation to generation through religious rituals.*

2. Rituals enable the members of a society to effectively participate in the religious life of the community and to thus *discover their identity in the group.*

3. Rituals *provide people security and comfort* in times of crisis.

4. Rituals provide opportunity for people to *express and demonstrate their oneness and social cohesion*.

5. In such rituals is *often mirrored a people's worldview perception of "the total cosmic order* and the way people relate to supernatural beings, to one another, and to nature."

6. People also *relate to the natural world* through rituals. Rituals are often thought to maintain order or balance with nature.

7. Likewise, people *relate to supernatural beings or impersonal powers* through rituals.

8. *In rituals, religion can often be fun* and release from the uptightness of everyday cultural life.

MISSIOLOGICAL APPLICATIONS

Christian witnesses have often launched all-out attacks on what they considered to be the religion of the people they sought to win, condemning much of the people's worldview in the process.

How unlike the God of the Scriptures this attitude has been. In working with Abraham and his descendants, God worked *with*, not against their culture, including their religion. What He condemned was idolatry, the *meanings* in people's minds that elevated some god or some thing other than Yahweh to the place of primary allegiance. What He did not condemn was the use of the "pagan" cultural structures (the forms) of the Hebrews as a vehicle for expressing their commitment to the true God. This included the continued use of nearly every form and structure in their culture, including those we might label religious. They even continued, apparently with God's blessing, many customs that we find quite incompatible with such commitment to God (e.g., trial by ordeal, polygamy, casting lots).

I believe God wants to act in today's societies very much like He acted among the Hebrews and later in the Greek world, as portrayed in the Bible. I believe God is pro-culture, though anti-sin and anti- the satanic use of a people's customs. See Kraft (1979a:235–57) for a fuller presentation of this argument.

What, then, should be our attitude toward the religion of a people? In keeping with the definition of religion given above, I believe it should be virtually the same as our attitude toward the rest of the culture. In this area, however, we need to be especially concerned about allegiance and empowerment.

1. With respect to *allegiance*, we must maintain that people are saved or lost on the basis of whether or not their primary commitment is to the true God. Whatever the secondary allegiances, rituals, other beliefs and practices may be they are all of much less importance than the central issue of primary allegiance. Many of those customs will be changed in the process of Christian growth, as with the Hebrews, but God is still very patient with secondary things.

2. With regard to *empowerment*, the dedication of cultural practices and implements to gods and spirits has been a regular part of "pagan" religions and often of other aspects of pagan cultural life as well. Perceiving this, western Christians have routinely condemned at least the religion, if not the whole culture, of many of the peoples to whom we have gone. This led to our trying to replace their customs, especially their religious customs, with ours on the assumption that Satan had control of theirs but not of ours.

It has, however, become clear that *it is not culture or even "pagan" religion that is our enemy, but Satan working within the society.* We have been learning that culture (including religion) is simply culture. Culture is not the enemy; the enemy is the enemy. One of the ways we are to fight the enemy is by capturing the structures he has used for his purposes. This is done by disempowering them, breaking his power to use them, and then re-empowering them by blessing them for God's use.

With regard to customs, our task is to help people express (contextualize) Christianity within their own customs and thus capture those customs for Christ. With regard to satanic involvement in their sociocultural life, our task is to help people confront Satan within their own way of life and replace satanic empowerment with God's empowerment in the practice of their religious customs and all their other customs, since Christianity is to pervade all of life.

The mistake of trying to convert people to our forms of Christianity has, for many, radically changed the message of Christ into what is primarily a cultural rather than spiritual message. What they have heard is that *He*, not simply we, requires conversion from their cultural religion to our cultural religion (called Christianity, whether or not it is biblical).

The fact is that we now have at least *two "Christianities"* in the world—two very distinct things called by the same name. The one is biblical Christianity, that for which Jesus gave His life. I'll spell that with a capital "C." The other is the religion of western societies, also called Christianity. I'll use a small "c" for that one. Small "c" "christianity" is simply a cultural system or structuring that may or may not require saving faith (*see* Kraft 1963 and 1979a).

Allegiance to christianity (small "c") is not saving, as allegiance to God is. What is more, that system, with its beliefs, practices, rituals, and organization is not worth giving our lives for. Yet this is what we often export and transplant, complete with: western buildings; communication forms (e.g., monologue, intellectual preaching, overdependence on writing); schooled (and usually secularized) young leaders who know a lot about the world but often not much about life or God; foreign rituals such as western baptism and truncated communion services (that communicate lack of importance to peoples who are used to elaborate rituals on important occasions); intellectualized doctrine in place of spirit-power based behavior; western nonacceptance of people of other societies and their life in place of Divine acceptance, and so forth. In our western fear of heresy, we have often broken the greatest commandment and perpetrated a "failure in love" (*see* Barrett 1968).

I would maintain very strongly that we are not to simply propagate a religion. Christianity—essential biblical Christianity—is not and never was intended to be a religion. It is not our calling to take western christianity anywhere. It is our calling to take everywhere the message of the God who came in Christ to redeem those of every society on the basis of their faith relationship to Him alone. This relationship is then to be expressed and worked out within the only form of life really meaningful to a people, their culture, including the religious part of that culture. Unfortunately, we often perceive ourselves and are perceived by others as simply coming with a *competing religion*, and the battle is not for faith but for religious forms and structures. This obscures the fact that the real battle is with Satan, not cultural forms.

Once this principle is grasped, we begin to discover exciting possibilities for working within, say, Jewish or Islamic or Hindu or Buddhist or animistic cultures to reach people who will be culturally Jewish or Muslim or Hindu or animist to the end of their days but Christian in their faith allegiance.

Lest I be misunderstood, I am definitely not saying that people can be saved through other religious systems. For that matter, I would contend strongly that no one can be saved through the christian (small "c") system, either. If a Muslim is depending on the fact that he is a Muslim (i.e., on his system) to save him, he's lost. So is a Christian. Any primary commitment other than that to the true God is idolatry. But if Muslims replace their previous primary allegiance with a commitment to as much of Christ as they can grasp, that is saving, even if they remain in their previous cultural (including religious) structures. Those structures are their "place to feel at home," and the structures serve well as a secondary or tertiary allegiance. It is *within the structures, not extracted from them*, that God wants to meet people. I would say the same for a Hindu, though the problems raised by such Hindu worldview assumptions as monism, polytheism, reincarnation, karma, and the like are enormously greater than those raised by the worldviews of Muslims and Hebrews. I venture to suggest that millions of Muslims, Hindus, Buddhists, and animists have been lost because they never imagined they could follow Christ while still keeping the identity they prize so much as members of their traditional "religious" community.

In taking a position like this, we need to recognize that distinguishing between primary commitment and religious structuring is easier to make in our minds than in practice. But unless we make it in our minds, we are in great danger of not making it at all in practice. It is, in fact, likely that we will fall into the heresy of the Judaizers that was condemned in Acts 15. The early Christians, because they had experienced Christ within Hebrew culture and learned to express that faith in Hebrew religious forms, thought everybody had to be converted to the use of those Hebrew forms in order to be Christian. I'm simply saying that people do not have to be converted to Hebrew or Greek or American religious forms in order to be Christian. The change from non-Christian to Christian is based on faith allegiance, not on the customs that one uses to express that allegiance.

In working with people in their cultures, we never get far from the form-meaning dichotomy. From one point of view, what we are saying is that the meaning of faith-commitment to God is far more important than the forms through which it is expressed. After all, we are saved through faith, not through cultural or religious forms. It is precisely because the forms that people grew up with are so important to them that we need to take this kind of position. Those forms are loved by them. They belong to them. Other forms are not. They belong to foreigners and have (in people's minds) attached to them the reputation of the foreigners. If that reputation is prestigious, the foreign forms may have the "smell" of prestige about them and be accepted gladly (though often not for the right reasons). If, however, the people who introduced the forms are resented, the forms will have the "smell" of resentment about them and either be rejected or accepted with that meaning attached. Neither of these situations lets people know that Christianity is not owned by those who own the forms in which it came.

The forms of the people's religion that relate to a non-Christian allegiance have to be dealt with at two levels. First, the power issue must be confronted. Christians must not continue to practice their lives, or parts of them (as in the case of dual allegiance), under the power of Satan. They need to put their whole lives under the power of Christ, expressing through their cultural structures their allegiance to Him.

Living Christianity through cultural structures that once were used to serve Satan raises, however, a second important issue. This is the issue of *meaning*. Old meanings often die hard. Though learning to use the cultural forms of ordinary life for Christ usually doesn't cause too much difficulty in the meaning area, learning to use religious forms may. The leaders I worked with told me, for example, that certain drumbeats could not be used for Christ because they brought wrong meanings into people's minds. It was not difficult to find other drumbeats to use, however—drumbeats that didn't raise that problem. On the other hand, in areas where large numbers of Muslims are coming to Christ, they seem to have little difficulty in using their Muslim worship places, times, and rituals to exalt Jesus.

Can "pagan" songs, forms of prayer, times and places of worship be "captured" or transformed for Christian usage? What about shrines, dedication practices, divination, magical rites, and the like? In any of these areas, the power of Satan can be broken. With some of them (e.g., divination and magical practices), however, there will need to be replacement with scriptural ways of meeting the same needs with the power of God. Even though the power issues may be solvable in these ways, the meaning issues are sometimes more difficult. When old forms are used in new ways, the tendency is for people to interpret them as if they still carry the old meanings. This results in syncretism. The meaning problem must be constantly confronted with scriptural teaching concerning what the Christian meanings are intended to be.

Often the power issues and the meaning issues can be addressed together by focusing on the core concern, allegiance. With Israel, though they could keep their culture, including their religion, God was adamant against the idolatry that once was a part of it. Their former allegiance, both the power and meaning aspects of it, had to be confronted and converted at every point. Idolatry, whether in the form of images (Ex 20:4), arrogance (1 Sm 15:23), covetousness (Col 3:5), or the works of the flesh (Gal 5:20), is always to be replaced on the basis of the new allegiance. So are divination (1 Sm 15:23) and witchcraft (2 Kgs 9:22). God didn't seem bothered by the fact that most of the Hebrew sacrifices, most of their judicial code, most of their taboos, and most of the rest of their religious practices differed little from the religious practices of the surrounding related societies. These similarities paralleled those throughout the rest of Jewish culture at the start. What concerned God was that His people practice a different allegiance. This allegiance to Him, though it did eliminate a few customs (e.g., divination, witchcraft), was to transform rather than replace their traditional customs. The longer God worked within Hebrew culture and the longer this transformation process continued, the greater the differences that developed between Hebrew culture and those of the surrounding peoples. This is to be expected in contemporary societies as well.

What would be the right forms of prayer for Muslims who commit themselves to Christ? Their background would lead them to want to face in the direction of Mecca (and Jerusalem). They would probably be inclined to pray five times a day with particular postures at specified times. They would probably continue to recognize Muhammad as a prophet, worship (without singing) at a mosque, and so on. I doubt that any of these things would bother God (though the honor given to Muhammad would probably bother many Christians, since we have usually seen

Muhammad and Christ, contrary to the Koran's portrayal, as competitors). What might affect the Muslim Christian's commitment to Christ would be the continuance in a belief held by many (not all) Muslims that salvation is earned. A new understanding of the basis for God's mercy would have to be built, probably after their commitment to Christ. So will a new understanding of how God could remain all-powerful and still allow His prophet (Jesus) to die. But doctrinal issues such as these (and many others) come best after commitment, rather than before. That is, just like with the Hebrews, God can start with virtually anything culturally or religiously, as long as the allegiance issue is settled.

CHAPTER 14

LIFE CYCLE

INTEGRATIONAL THOUGHT

In Luke 2:41–52 we read of Jesus' response to a newly attained position in life. As we will see below, social life is segmented into "seasons" such as childhood, adolescence, adulthood, old age, and ancestorhood. These seasons are often entered into via "passages" involving rituals ("rites of passage") initiating a person into the next stage of life.

Jesus, as a normal Hebrew boy, would have passed from childhood into adulthood at the age of twelve. There was no adolescence in first-century Hebrew society. At twelve, Jesus became a man. This meant, among other things, that he became a full-fledged member of Israelite society, a "son of the law." He then took on the obligations of a Hebrew man, including attendance at the Passover. "So at twelve Jesus for the first time went to the Passover" (Barclay 1956:24).

It is likely that He went with a group of relatives, all of the adults from the extended family of which Jesus was a part. We should not, therefore, picture Jesus as a child being carefully tended by His parents or carelessly running off to play with other children. He was an adult and was expected to be quite serious about assuming His adult responsibilities.

While there, as we know, He went to the Temple to sit with and learn from the teachers of the Law (v. 46). This was to be expected of a serious son of Israel, for whom a life of sitting with the learned, discussing the things of God was held out as an ideal. None of this was out of the ordinary—and His parents should have expected it. Only His understandings and his "intelligent answers" (v. 47), plus perhaps the fact that He did not join the group from Nazareth when they left for home, should have surprised them, for He was a full son of Israel now.

The social relationships and expectations are reasonably clear (or would have been to first century Hebrews). So what is the point of the account? Is it that Mary and Joseph were unwittingly attempting to hold Jesus back from gaining the insight He would need later in His ministry? Perhaps they, like us, needed to be reminded that they shouldn't try to make rules for God or even be anxious concerning how He is going to work things out. They were clearly worried, and Mary said, "Son, why have you done this to us? Your father and I have been terribly worried trying to find you" (v. 48). That was an attitude of unfaith on their part.

Jesus clearly expected His parents to know where He was. He asked them, "Why did you have to look for me? Didn't you know that I had to be in my Father's house?" (v. 49). Why is it they didn't understand (v. 50)?

And what's this about "my Father's house?" This may have been the first time Jesus referred to God as His Father. Barclay considers this to be "one of the key passages in the life of Jesus" (1956:24). Indeed, Barclay calls this "the day when

Jesus discovered who He was" (p. 25). Though this may be carrying things a bit far, the following is helpful: "'Your father and I,' said Mary, 'have been searching for you.' 'Did you not realize,' said Jesus, 'that you would find me in *my Father's* house?' See how very gently but very definitely Jesus takes the name *father* from Joseph and gives it to God" (pp. 24, 25).

I wonder how long Jesus would have stayed if they had not returned to get Him. Would He, like Samuel, have taken up residence in the Temple and perhaps had quite a different start to His public ministry? One thing seems certain. Contrary to some sermonizing on this passage, Jesus was behaving appropriately in the Temple. He was merely participating in the regular Sanhedrin discussions of religious and theological issues. These were held in public at Passover time in the Temple court. But, says Barclay, "We must not think of it as a scene where a precocious boy was dominating a crowd of his seniors. *Hearing and asking questions* is the regular Jewish phrase for a student learning from his teachers. Jesus was listening to the discussions and eagerly searching for knowledge like an avid student" (p. 24).

Perhaps the point is, after all, that Jesus was being normal. But here, as elsewhere, when Jesus is normal and doing what should have been expected of Him, it puts others (even His parents) off. Perhaps when He does such "normal" things near us, we should learn to do what Jesus' mother did: treasure what He did in her heart (v. 51) even though she did not understand (v. 50).

INTRODUCTION

We now turn to a slightly different perspective on culture, though we do it here because it relates so well to many of the rites of passage rituals dealt with in the previous chapter. In most of the chapters of this book, we look at one or another of the cultural subsystems. This has been the case in the three chapters immediately preceding this one. It will also be the case in the chapters in the next section. But in this chapter we want to do an overview of the life cycle to see how any given individual understands and deals with those things that happen to everyone during the course of a lifetime.

As throughout all sociocultural life, a society's worldview defines how the life cycle is to be understood. Our Euroamerican worldview tends to focus on life as simply a biological thing, but it is the worldview perception of the biological data that people really work with, not biology in and of itself. We may assume that there is only one definition of life: "Life is life, isn't it?" But, as we shall see, even life and its components is defined differently from society to society.

Western societies have chosen to make their cultural definition of life correspond as closely as possible to our understanding of the biological facts in life. We believe that life begins with the biological start of life and ends with the biological end of life. In contrast, many of the world's peoples unconsciously go with a cultural definition of life, less tied to biological fact than ours. For many people live as long as they are perceived to be sociologically active in the community, whether or not they are still biologically alive.

In this chapter, I want to try to point out some of the alternative ways in which different peoples view the life cycle and certain of its component parts. We do this to expand our understanding of the variety of possible approaches to these topics. All of us will still hold to our own definitions in this area, as in every other. These are ours, and we follow them habitually. But when we go to another people, we need to be aware of the probability that they will define things differently than we have been taught to define them. If this is part of our awareness, we can be more appreciative of their point of view—whether or not we like it.

DIAGRAMS OF THE HUMAN LIFE CYCLE

Figure 14.1 below presents two diagrams to enable us to picture the process we are discussing. The first represents a linear understanding of life, where life is considered to start at one point, go through a process, and end at another point. The second portrays the same process conceived in a circular fashion, where people are seen as born, going through biological life, passing into ancestorhood, then passing out of ancestorhood through biological birth into biological life again.

1. A Linear Understanding **2. Circular Understanding**
of the Life Cycle

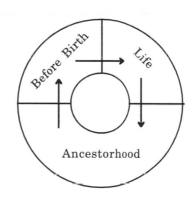

Before Birth

Biological Birth

Naming

Puberty

Marriage

Retirement

Biological Death

Ancestorhood

C H I L D — C H I L D H O O D

A D U L T — A D U L T H O O D

O L D — O L D A G E

Before Birth

Life

Ancestorhood

Figure 14.1 Linear and circular understandings of the human life cycle

In the linear view, life is seen as a kind of stream or river that begins at a certain point previous to biological birth, flows along through the various stages of life, and ends either at biological death or after a shorter or longer period of ancestorhood. Note that, though not indicated on the circular diagram, each of these stages is assumed during the period labeled "life" on that diagram.

In what follows, we will treat each of the stages of life in sequence. Our purpose is to survey the kinds of understandings of each of these areas of life that occur in the 6,000 or more ethnolinguistic groupings of the world. One of the important things we are trying to do is develop a perspective on the peoples of the world that considers their understanding of things as valid. We want this not for curiosity's sake but so that we're not shocked when we come across things that from our point of view seem quite strange. As we have repeatedly emphasized, each cultural way of life makes sense to the intelligent people who live by it, so we, if we are to relate lovingly to them, must recognize their intelligence and take their cultural patterns seriously.

Though we may find some of these beliefs and practices distasteful, immoral, or theologically unacceptable, our aim at this point is to *understand*, not pass judgment. We will, therefore, specifically ignore questions of rightness and wrongness for the sake of understanding the customs. This is necessary because judgments of rightness and wrongness are almost always made too soon and come across so colored by our ethnocentrism that they tend at the very least to be impolite and often selfish and unloving as well. Having said that, I don't want to suggest that there are never any wrong things in cultures. On the contrary, it is the repeated emphasis of this approach that all cultures include sin as well as enlightenment.

Each society is about as good or bad as each other society when it comes to right and wrong or doing things in sensible or misguided ways, but those judgments should be made by *insiders* under the leading of God. Our job is first to understand, then to accept (whether or not we like the custom), then to assist (not dominate) insiders in discovering what God wants them to do in relation to their customs. In this we must never forget how patient God has been with us and our ancestors. We must teach and, with our receptors, claim that patience for them and their people.

THE STAGES AND TRANSITIONS

In what follows, we will focus on two things: the stages that a person goes through during the life cycle and the transitions between these stages. The transitions often involve rites of passage to initiate the person into the next stage of life.

Before Birth

The first stage to deal with is what we will call the *prebirth* stage. Many of the peoples of the world believe that any child born has existed previously. Often such a belief is connected to a belief in reincarnation. If so, the understanding may be that the child existed either as an animal or as a human in a previous existence (e.g., Hinduism) or simply that the previous existence was human. In the latter case, if the baby looks like a deceased relative, this may be taken as proof that that person has been reincarnated in the child. Though such concepts are common, they are often not well-defined in the minds of the people who hold them.

Concerning *conception*, there are many different interpretations, varying from believing in a purely spiritual cause to believing, as westerners tend to, in a purely biological cause. There are, for the majority who accept the fact that humans play a part in initiating life, quite a variety of understandings concerning just what part humans play. Apparently the majority of the peoples of the world believe that the female is simply (like the earth) the "soil" or vessel in which the male plants the seed (R. Taylor 1976:281). Though that seed grows within her until birth, it is believed that she had nothing to do with its original formation. There have also been societies that believe the male has little or nothing to do with the process. The Arunta and other Australian aborigines are famous for believing "that a woman conceives as an ancestral soul enters her when she passes near places where the ancient totem ancestors entered the ground" (R. Taylor 1976:280).

Procreation is, however, "almost universally regarded . . . as being highly mysterious and full of religious significance" (Nida 1954:106). In a large number of societies, the belief is that no man and woman can produce a child by themselves. They need spiritual help, and if for some reason pregnancy does not happen, the reason is that God has denied His blessing. There are many examples of such an understanding in the Bible. Robert Taylor points out that among the things believed by various peoples to be necessary for pregnancy to occur are the proper phase of the moon, interaction with a fertility deity, and consumption of certain foods or juices (1976:281). Many societies therefore schedule religious rituals either to assure fertility at the start of a marriage or to correct an infertility situation. The corresponding rituals in western societies tend to be scientific (medical) rather than religious.

It is characteristic of a large number of societies to develop a mythological explanation of what happens, such as the following:

> The Hidatsa Indians of the American plains agree that intercourse is necessary for a baby to develop, but a certain spirit must also enter the mother. Spirits who are to become human beings live in special hills, each believed to be an earth lodge where the spirits are cared for by an old man. A woman who wants a child puts toys at the foot of these hills, and men who want children fast there. When a spirit baby wants to be born, it crawls across a ditch inside the lodge on an ash pole, and if it gets across without falling into the ditch, it will be born into the tribe before long. Some Hidatsa have memories of the time when they lived in the "baby hills" (R. Taylor 1976:280–81).

During *pregnancy*, it is common for some sort of restrictions to be imposed on the prospective mother. Food tabus are common, as are restrictions on intercourse. Sometimes these restrictions extend to the kind or amount of work a pregnant woman is allowed to do, though often she is expected to carry on as normally as possible.

Delivery is commonly surrounded with taboos, sometimes on the father as well as the prospective mother. The woman will usually be assisted by older women, often relatives, serving as midwives. Assisting in or even observing birth is commonly forbidden to men. Ford (1945:58) states that sitting is the most common position for childbirth, with kneeling fairly frequent and squatting and reclining less common. Birth is, of course, ordinarily difficult for the mother and sometimes for the father as well. "In a few societies he takes to his bed during and after his wife's parturition and even imitates her labor" in a custom known as "couvade." This custom is most frequent among certain South American Indians (R. Taylor 1976:283–84).

In many societies, once the child is born, the umbilical cord is either disposed of or saved in a religiously significant way. The afterbirth, too, is treated carefully. Bathing of the newborn immediately after birth appears universal. Mother and child are often kept secluded for a period of time, sometimes for several weeks. Usually sexual intercourse is prohibited for some period of time, often for most or all of the time of lactation (two years or more).

Initiation into Life

When children are born, they are not always automatically admitted into the status or stage that we may label "sociologically alive." Such admission will often involve some sort of *initiation into life*. Societies differ as to when they feel that sociological life begins. Though biological birth may be regarded as the automatic entrance into sociological life (as in the West), there is frequently a gap of from a few days to a year or more before the child is admitted into the status of full "human beingness." For many peoples, the initiation into such status is signaled by a naming ceremony. For the Hebrews, this was on the eighth day and also involved circumcision for boys, to signal that the boy had become "a son of the covenant" (i.e., a human being).

It is often possible to get clues concerning the point at which a child is considered a human being by finding out how things that go wrong are handled soon after birth. If the child dies, for example, the body may be treated quite differently if the death occurs before the naming ceremony than if it occurs after it. If infanticide occurs, it is likely that it is not defined as murder, since the child has not yet become a full human being.

Though *infanticide* is not all that common, it is practiced on occasion by peoples whose community life is threatened by too many births (e.g., traditional hunters, modern Chinese). Deformed or otherwise abnormal children may also be killed, especially if the belief is 1) that the child is not yet a human being and such a killing is not defined as murder or 2) "that the child's soul returns to the place it came from and can be reborn later in the same or another woman" (R. Taylor 1976:284). Certain of the ancient Greeks had a custom in which the officials of the city would come and examine a newborn child to see if the child should be allowed to become sociologically alive. If the child was judged by the officials to be weak or sickly or unfit to become a person, the child would be disposed of. Westerners would call such a custom murder, because we define life biologically. For them, though, it would fall into quite another category, perhaps similar to our contraception category, since it would be seen as preventing an undesirable life from coming into being, rather than terminating a life that had already started.

In some societies, biological children cannot be allowed to become persons unless they are part of a family. The concept of person or sociological life is intimately tied up with familiness, and a child without a family is felt to be a threat to the society. It may be even more specific than that. Often the child must have a mother. If, for example, a child's mother dies in childbirth or soon after childbirth, the child is not to be allowed to live (biologically), since without a mother and family the child can never be allowed to become a person. Orphans in such societies are by definition nonpersons. When they are rescued from biological death by Christian organizations, the message is seldom understood in the same way it was intended. Quite often it is understood as tampering with life as it should be, or with God's will. Life for those who are biologically alive but considered sociologically dead is often very difficult.

What Christians should do about orphans or any of these other customs is of great significance. We should not, of course, disobey what God leads us to do simply because our activity might raise cultural problems. Yet a recognition of how the people may be interpreting our actions will make it possible for us to formulate strategies that make more sense to the people than would those formulated in total ignorance of their point of view.

Among the Kamwe, the traditional understanding is that when the child is between one and two years old it will be decided, "This child has come to stay." The child has been biologically alive for about a year and a half, but sociologically that child is only a potential life until that point. Many children, of course, don't live to that point. In such cases, the Kamwe don't say the child has died. They say "he/she decided not to stay." They believe the child looked the world over and didn't like what he or she saw and left. The body would be disposed of, then, quite matter-of-factly, with no ceremony. Then they look for that child to be reborn at a later time. If a person dies after that "come-to-stay" period, there is a funeral.

Period of Childhood

Childhood, like every other part of the life cycle, is handled differently from society to society. Probably the most different customs (i.e., different from the norm of the cultures of the world) are found in western societies, particularly in the extension of childhood that we have created called adolescence. In all societies, childhood is a period of intensive learning, with a high degree of protection provided for these most vulnerable members of a society.

The mother is usually particularly important, especially in the early stages. However, especially in rural settings, her duties are often shared with other women who live with or close to her in extended family groupings. These women function along with the biological mother as sociological mothers or, if they are older, as grandmothers. This arrangement provides a very good form of social security. If the biological mother dies, the child still has other mothers. On the male side, a child in such societies will also have many sociological fathers and grandfathers.

With regard to motherhood, westerners dare not assume that every people sees motherhood (or women's roles in general) as we see them. We tend to highly value producing children but often regard raising them as drudgery, rather than as fulfillment. I've had American women argue with me that tending children is inherently unfulfilling. It is, therefore, often difficult for Americans to recognize that in many societies women feel total fulfillment from both bearing and raising children. They value very positively something that our society has decided to value negatively. Many Americans feel sorry for such women, as if they have been deluded. I suspect, though, that it is we who have been deluded rather than they.

At some point after weaning, the traditional practice in many societies was for boys to join the men's community in which they learn to be men. Girls in such societies learned to be women by being a part of the women's community and participating with the women. This was their primary educational system. It has now been seriously disrupted by schools in most societies.

Though the western stereotype of the tender, loving mother is frequently found, it is not uncommon in certain matrilineal societies (e.g., Trobriand) for the father to be the one the child goes to when he or she is upset, since it is the father who is the loving, nurturing parent. The father would never discipline what to us would be considered his child, since that child is not his, according to the rules of his society. In such a matrilineal society, the children he fathers belong to his wife's brother, who is the head of his sister's home. Any discipline is administered by the one who heads the home, not by the children's father. He can only discipline the children that belong to him—his sister's children.

The early years of childhood are primarily devoted to what is technically called socialization or enculturation. We will simply call it education (*see* chapter 17). It is common for children to learn adult roles through play. The toys traditionally used in many societies are scaled-down models of adult tools, rather than quite different things. Frequently, children are encouraged to use those "tools" to "work" alongside adults or older siblings, thus playacting themselves into learning adult roles.

For most societies, childhood has traditionally been a fairly short period of time, often terminated by an initiation ceremony (such as the Jewish Bar Mitzvah), after which the youngster is an adult. As mentioned in the previous chapter, such clarity of definition concerning one's status is largely absent from American society, leading to a good bit of insecurity on the part of American youth. Instead, we have created adolescence, a rather stormy several years when our youth (and their parents) can't quite decide whether they are children or adults. This period is seen "as a kind of social weaning from the family home setting with an expectation of religious maturity coming early (confirmation), political capacity much later (voting age), and legal responsibility (no longer being a minor) variously in between" (Keesing 1958:248). The period is often inadvertently extended by means of schooling. Indeed, if one can afford to pay the fees, it is now possible for one to extend childhood to close to age thirty or above! This is long past the age when young people in most societies have become important parts of the society.

Initiation into Adulthood

The end of childhood is often signaled by an initiation ceremony. Typically such a rite is performed soon after puberty and carries with it the expectation that from that time forth the person is to take on adult roles. In many societies (especially in Africa) it will involve a period of seclusion and instruction followed by circumcision for boys (and, in East Africa, sometimes for girls). In Brazil, the elaborate party thrown for a girl on her fifteenth birthday serves to signal her adulthood.

A girl's first menstruation is very often publicly noted. Whether or not girls go through extended initiation rites, there is often a ceremony marking the event. This may be seen as a celebration or "an occasion of danger and consequent seclusion" (R. Taylor 1976:289). Sometimes special costumes are worn for a period of time (e.g., Valley Tonga of East Africa). Many societies require isolation of menstruating women from this time on, sometimes in special menstrual huts (e.g., Ojibwa of North America).

Westerners may think the announcement of a girl's first period or a boy's attaining puberty is a rather crude custom. We must, however, understand that the purpose for such a custom is to announce a status change, not simply to focus on a physical event. The purpose is social, not biological, and the young people themselves are perhaps the ones most eager to have the event announced, since it puts them into a new and higher status within the society. They are as proud of that achievement as westerners might be of a graduation or some other major social achievement (e.g., getting one's driver's license).

The onset of sexual desire and response has to be dealt with by all societies, but concepts of what is erotic and the structuring of how and when sexual contact is permissible vary greatly. The popular notion that nonwestern peoples are highly permissive sexually is only partly true. Some are, but some are even more prudish than western stereotypes of the Puritans (e.g., Arab societies). In America, nudity is interpreted as erotic. Not so in many nonwestern societies where the body and bodily functions are accepted more matter-of-factly.

Some societies restrict premarital sexual activity largely by arranging for marriage to occur soon after puberty, especially for girls. Sometimes a couple is officially married or engaged even before puberty, with the understanding that there will be no sexual relations until after puberty. As we will see in chapter 19, it is common for nonwestern societies (in their traditional state, at least) to assign experienced people to arrange marriages and then surround the couple with a good deal of social support to help the young people.

The transition from youth to adulthood is a crucial time in everyone's life cycle. How it is handled is, therefore, very important and has a lot to do with how the rest of one's life turns out. We can point to at least four ways in which American society has not traditionally handled this transition very well:

1. First, American society *allows inexperienced young people to choose their own spouses* and often to go into married life with little or no support from their relatives.

2. Second, we prolong childhood by lengthening the period of adolescence, largely through schools.

3. Third, we create discontinuity between generations by producing disaffection and even enmity between children and their parents.

4. Fourth, we expect our youth to find their own way occupationally, rather than follow in the footsteps of their parents.

One result of all of this is that, to a disturbing degree, in mainstream American society young people cannot simply grow into adulthood as a normal, natural concomitant of the maturing process. Young people cannot feel secure in knowing that they are going to be important, productive members of adult society. Rather, *we are expected to achieve adultness*, to earn it. This results in our being insecure during our younger years for fear we will not succeed, and insecure in our adult years because we are not sure we have made it. Young men are expected to compete with peers to achieve a job and success in that job. Young women are expected to compete with all other women to achieve physical beauty, then marriage and home as well as a job. Few ever get to the place where they can claim satisfaction with what they have attained.

Period of Adulthood

Once young people have successfully negotiated whatever transitional expectations the society has for them, they are typically expected to center their lives around what are defined as adult activities. Adult status tends to be fully conferred only after marriage and sometimes, for a woman, only after she has borne one or more children. It is frequently symbolized by some form of distinctive dress, hairdo, jewelry (e.g., wedding ring), or other bodily decoration (e.g., scarification, red dot on the forehead). Though some societies prepare their youth better than others for adulthood, effectively accepting and participating in adult roles will still require a good bit of further learning.

In all societies

> the adult is faced with developmental tasks like selecting or learning to live with a mate; rearing children; organizing his or her nuclear family, perhaps within a larger extended family; executing occupational roles in satisfactory fashion; assuming some share of administrative responsibility in the village, nation, tribe, sib, or lineage; helping to enforce social pressure; and, finally, accepting emotionally the physiological changes that come with middle age (Honigmann 1959:582–3).

Adult life involves many stresses. Not that stress is absent in the earlier years, but as adults, people often have less social insulation from the problems of life than they did when, as minors, they received more protection from their elders. Pelto and Pelto (1976:411–13) list eleven such stresses, among which are the following:

1. *Inequality between people.* The authors cite class and caste distinctions plus role distinctions (e.g., those of males and females) that place one group in dominance over another.

2. *The stress of warfare and similar intergroup conflict*, or the threat of same.

3. *Competition for the limited resources* available to the society, whether these be food, money, housing, comfort, enjoyment, or other such tangible and intangible items. "Although a certain amount of such in-group competition is undoubtedly beneficial for the human organism and is in any case unavoidable, in-group competition can be psychologically painful for most individuals" (412).

4. *Restraints on various impulses and appetites*, such as those for pleasure, comfort, sex, freedom from restraint, etc. Such restraints can be severe.

5. *Pressure to conform socially* in areas such as clothing, language, religion, conformity to one's age, social level, or sex role, etc.

6. *Expectations and conflicting expectations concerning one's performance in the society*, especially as these relate to level of ability, tiredness, wealth, social class, and the like. "The society . . . may expect a person to work when he is tired, to give up some of his possessions for feasts . . . to perform rituals when he is not inclined to participate," etc. (413). Furthermore, such expectations may be conflicting as between one's family and one's workmates, one's spouse and one's relatives, or one's peers and one's friends and relatives of another generation.

7. *Monotony* seems to be a frequent adult experience.

8. *Dissatisfaction with social relationships.* Feelings of social isolation or alienation can be very painful. So can the stresses of too much or too frequent interaction, such as those that commonly occur with urbanization or other types of crowding. One of the most disturbing sources of dissatisfaction in urban living is "the high frequency of encounters with strangers, with whom we must transact business and successfully communicate without prior preparation" (413).

9. A further source of stress (not mentioned by the Peltos) that adults need to deal with frequently is the *preservation of good health*. For nonwestern peoples, disease tends to be more a theological than a technological (medical) problem, as it is in the West. In the nonwestern world (and increasingly in the West), the answers are more often sought through the use of religious techniques, either by themselves or in combination with medicine, than through medical technology alone. The need to deal with health problems is one of the major concerns of adult life.

Initiation into Old Age

Retirement of some kind, with or without ceremony, is the usual initiation into the period of old age. The age at which this occurs differs from society to society. Often one's physical condition is more significant than age in signaling the need for retirement (Honigmann 1959:583). "Retirement from an age class system, having grandchildren, loss of vitality, and passage of menopause are among the criteria of old age used in different [societies]" (R. Taylor 1976:293). For men, retirement is often associated with cessation of at least the most demanding physical work. In many societies, this will issue in a period when most of their time is spent thinking, talking, and advising younger men. For women, cessation of their childbearing capability often brings about a significant change in their status, either raising it or lowering it. This change may not, however, noticeably affect the amount of work they are expected to do, unless they are physically incapacitated in some way.

Initiation into old age may or may not be marked by a ceremony. In societies such as many in East Africa, in which age grades are important, the movement from adult to elder status for a man may be accompanied by elaborate ritual. In many western companies, retirement parties with or without the giving of a gold watch are common. Rituals signifying the initiation of women into old age are far less common. Usually for women, and not infrequently for men, the transition is a gradual, rather than a sharp one at this stage of life.

In Euroamerican and certain other societies (e.g., Eskimo), retirement often signals the beginning of sociological death. When the focus is on what one *does* to contribute to society, rather than on who one *is* within a social system, the cessation of one's primary adult activity has a powerful impact on one's status, both as perceived by the society and as understood by oneself. When at age sixty-five or seventy a man is told he can no longer do the job that has made his life meaningful for forty or more years, frequently something dies within him. He is sociologically "on the trash heap." Life may become quite meaningless, and feelings of rejection and despondency take over.

Period of Old Age

Older people may be greatly honored or consigned to "cheerless resignation or even despair" (R. Taylor 1976:293). The greater their prestige, of course, the more valuable and secure they feel. When prestige is low, insecurity and feelings of worthlessness and guilt over the burden they are to society tend to be prominent.

Typical of societies that grant high prestige to their aged are the Hidatsa of aboriginal America. They

> set great store on the wisdom of the aged. Their mythology validates the importance of taking good care of old people; stories tell of how aged persons with little visible evidence of supernatural power or wealth bring trouble on those who neglect them and bring great benefits to those who are good to them. Households with old people are thought fortunate to have them there to teach the grandchildren the sacred myths and lore, to explain how things used to be, and to give them the kinds of instruction they need to grow up to be of greatest help to people. The old men sit in the honored section of the lodge during ceremonial and social functions and are given many gifts by those performing the rituals (R. Taylor 1976:293).

In many of the world's societies, such as the Hidatsa or the Chinese, a person starts as a child at a fairly low prestige level that increases steadily with age to a very high level at biological death, sometimes issuing in a still higher level as an ancestor. In Euroamerican societies, however, prestige tends to peak during early adulthood and then descend during old age. Indeed, western peoples may even experience their greatest feelings of value while they are still quite young. This, plus the widespread propensity of western adults to seek to imitate youth, leads many to characterize western societies as "youth oriented."

"Old age may be a better time for one sex than the other" (R. Taylor 1976:294). It tends, for example, to be harder on men than on women in America. In many societies, as they age, women gain greater prestige, influence, and freedom from such things as work, tabus, and domination by their husbands. In Asia, the position of mother-in-law or grandmother is often very high.

Hunting and gathering societies often have been forced to live close to the margin and have tended to grant older people low prestige. The rigors of survival have often led such groups to develop customs that result in unproductive older or infirm persons relinquishing their lives (usually at least semi-voluntarily) for the sake of the living. Eskimo societies are famous for the fact that aged people who no longer can "carry their weight" in the society "walk off into the sunset" and deliberately expose themselves to the harsh weather of their environment without food or protection in order to bring about their own biological death soon after they perceive themselves to have died sociologically. They do this, usually voluntarily, to keep from being a burden on the productive members of the society. In American society, though we, like the Eskimos, consign older people to sociological death (*see* Henry 1963), our reverence for biological life would not allow such a custom.

The lengthening of the life span in western societies and others through the influence of western medical knowledge increases the number of older persons. This requires new attention to their place and condition in society. For western societies with wealth enough to provide institutions for the care of those whose families cannot or will not look after them, this is resulting in some creative new approaches to the problem. For societies living close to starvation, the results of the western drive to extend biological life are causing increasing problems for the people in the society who are required to provide both for themselves and for an increasing number of nonproductive aged with meager resources.

Initiation into the Hereafter—Biological Death

The attitude toward one who is dying reflects to some extent the prestige accorded the person during the latter part of his or her life. If the person was in the prime of life, there is typically much grief. In northeastern Nigeria, such grief may be combined with his wife's scolding, if the man who died was in the prime of life. He may be scolded for leaving his wife to fend for herself before he was supposed to. An aged person, "full of years," on the other hand, may not be treated very well in a society where aged people are not highly respected unless, as in western societies, the reverence for life for its own sake is very high. In such a case, the attempt to thwart the process of dying can take on ridiculous proportions through the use of medical techniques to keep heart, lungs, or other vital organs working long after they would have stopped if left alone. Dying persons may, however, be treated with extreme respect and caution in a society that believes they will soon become ancestors with greater and less-controllable power, lest they be interested in revenge after death.

Biological death is highly ceremonialized in most societies, especially for prestigious persons. Though funerals are often regarded as rites of initiation by groups who believe that ancestors continue to live sociologically, they also serve several important functions for the biologically alive. The major ones typically relate to the continuance and restoration of social and spiritual relationships. Funerals thus serve as rituals of intensification and consolidation for the living, as well as transition rituals for the departed. Though it is the custom of many to bury (or otherwise dispose of) the corpse immediately, many others wait for one or more days.

A wide variety of funerary customs occur:

> The corpse often is washed, attired, or wrapped in preparation for its final disposal. Where mortuary specialists are lacking these tasks are performed by persons of the same sex as the deceased, perhaps by particular kinsmen. Communities, therefore, expect that the rules of modesty will continue to be observed even toward a lifeless body. Other signs of respect also are customarily shown to a corpse although this generalization cannot be extended to cover enemy dead. A few communities insist on an autopsy of the corpse, perhaps to diagnose how death occurred (Honigmann 1959:584–5).

Not every people buries their dead. Other techniques include cremation or leaving the body in a cave, out in the open, on a platform, or in a tree. If buried, the body is commonly positioned in a special way. Sitting, squatting, and lying positions are used, and it is common for the head to be positioned toward a favored point of the compass. Sometimes the bodies of important people (e.g., wealthy persons, warriors), young people, or unimportant or disgraced persons are treated differently from others. There may also be differences in the treatment of males and females, if not in the burial itself, perhaps in the kind of decorations put on the grave. Sometimes one or more parts of the body will be retained to assist the living community to deal with the spirit world (R. Taylor 1976:295–6). In addition,

> People often take elaborate symbolic precautions to dissociate the soul (or ghost) of the deceased from living survivors. The funeral party, for example, may follow a circuitous route back from the grave, destroy articles of clothing that belonged to the deceased, and wreck the house in which death occurred. The local group, if normally mobile, moves from the scene of death . . . (Honigmann 1959:584–5).

A normal funeral among the Kamwe of northeastern Nigeria was a fairly elaborate three-day occasion, during which the people literally worked their grief out of themselves. The drums would beat and the mourners dance in a circle around the sitting corpse. The first day was primarily a grief day—lots of tears and weeping, lots of sadness. The second day provided a transition from grief to acceptance. The beer pots would be brought out to help the process. By the third day, the community had worked its grief out and decided that they can, in fact, go on without the biological presence of the deceased.

Without understanding the functional value of such a ceremony, the early Christian witnesses in that area condemned such funerals and required Christians to bury the body right away and conduct small "Christian" (= western) funerals. This, however, proved terribly unsatisfying to these people. They were accustomed to expressing their grief and working it out of their systems. They found that if they didn't have the opportunity to work out that grief, the grief (and often evil spirits) came back to haunt them. They never felt quite right. Indeed, there is evidence to suggest that some at least, perhaps many, have turned away from Christ because they knew they would not be given a proper funeral if they became Christians.

Period of Ancestorhood

Entrance into ancestorhood is almost universally regarded as of high spiritual significance. It is typical for a sense of mystery, danger, and fear to be felt. Often there is fear that the ghost of the deceased will not be satisfied with the ceremony. If he is not treated properly, he can come and get you afterwards. The idea is that the person has not ceased to exist but, rather, has entered into a new, more power-ful stage of life. He or she will continue to live and play an active part in commu-nity life in the powerful role of ancestor. Great care is frequently exercised, lest the ghost take revenge on the community.

For those who practice ancestor reverence, the deceased are considered to be still *alive sociologically*, even though they are not physically present with their group. They are talked to, honored, assigned responsibilities, sometimes even scolded (if they do not perform their assigned responsibilities). Ancestors are ordi-narily believed to participate in the life of the community with more power than when alive biologically. The more powerful they were when biologically alive, the more powerful they are as ancestors. The person is typically considered to be alive at least until the last biologically alive person who remembers that person passes into ancestorhood. At this point, as at all others, it is the sociological, not the bio-logical definition of life that people live by.

IMPLICATIONS FOR CROSS-CULTURAL WITNESS

From our consideration of this material, it is clear that 1) peoples perceive things differently and 2) the way they work out their lives differs according to such differences in perception. Life cycle concepts and practices are, like all of culture, deeply rooted in the worldviews of the people who believe and practice them. Our efforts to reach people for Christ are aimed at change in these worldviews. Let's deal, then, with some of the implications of these two considerations.

1. Definition of Life

In what I have written above, I have alluded several times to the important distinction between biological and sociological life. All societies define life in terms of their sociological (worldview) perceptions of what life is. The degree to which western societies attempt to conform their cultural interpretation of what consti-tutes life to biological facts is largely unknown among other peoples. In western societies this phenomenon is largely due, on the one hand, to our desire to be sci-entifically precise and, on the other, to the great ability we have attained to carry out that preciseness in biological matters. Perhaps such factors as our fear of death and the fact that we virtually worship biological life for its own sake also enter in. Such a view of life, however, not only makes us quite different from oth-ers, it makes it very difficult for us to understand other perspectives.

There are several important points for us to recognize, each of which will prob-ably become the subject of some controversy, given the strength of western beliefs in this area and the fact that we have often buttressed these western values by assuming that Christianity supports them.

a. One of the primary things that a society must look after is its own *self-pres-ervation*. The needs of the community must at certain points take precedence over the biological life of individuals. We often recognize the validity of a principle such as this when it comes to the termination of the life of a criminal. There is, though, the strong feeling in many societies that children without families are just as great a threat to social well-being as we believe murderers to be. Though this fact is often beyond a westerner's ability to comprehend, that is how they feel, and we need to learn to respect their conviction, whether or not we like it.

b. A second area of concern is *the conflict between the patience that it takes to wait for change to take place and our western concern to save lives*. In this regard, I often ponder the large number of people that Jesus allowed to go unhealed in His day in order that He would be able to stay on course with His training of the disciples and the other things He set Himself to do. There is no doubt He could have spent every waking moment healing the sick, raising the dead, and tending to the needs of the poor, but He took time for other things such as teaching, prayer, and even an occasional party. Did not the plight of these people mean anything to Him? Of course it did. But the overall ministry to which He had committed Himself was much more important than even the needs of the ill or poor that were always present (Mt 26:11).

The lesson I want to draw from this is to strongly suggest that an overall strategy that will hopefully result in the conversion of large numbers of people after a period of time is much more important than simply stemming the tide of sickness and death that has been going on before we got there and will continue after we leave. Doctors, especially, tend to get caught up in the fight to save as many lives as possible and often lose much of the potential for greater ministry that their specialization could give them. One doctor I know understood this and refused to become simply a "body mechanic." He told his mission before he went out that he would only do medicine half days, since he had more important things to do than to "be chained to an operating table." When asked what he would do with the time he wasn't practicing medicine, he replied that he would be out in the villages with the people, witnessing for Christ and studying their medical practices to discover how to make his own more relevant to the Christian witness he had committed himself to.

Many people died that he could have rescued, had he given full time to medical practice. But something much more significant was accomplished by way of Christian witness because he refused to allow his reverence for biological life to obscure the fact that the real object of his ministry lay beyond simple dedication to preserving the biological life of people destined for a Christless eternity.

c. I hope the foregoing discussion will raise to our awareness the great importance of *continually looking out for the quality of sociological life*. Things fall apart psychologically, physically, and spiritually when social structures fall apart. The fact that life is defined sociologically means that *social reality is reality as people experience it at the gut level*. Social reality is more real than biological reality. Anything that anthropological insight can do to enable and challenge Christian witnesses to be concerned in a primary way to keep from threatening social well-orderedness and build it up when it breaks down is extremely important.

d. In relation to all of this, I need to comment on *abortion*. In terms of "capital R" REALITY, I believe life starts at conception. In Ephesians 1.4 we learn that God chose (and therefore planned) each of us before the world was made. He put the life in each child at conception and formed him or her in the womb (Ps 139:13, 15). *The termination of a pregnancy is, therefore, the termination of a life*. Though a miscarriage is involuntary, an abortion is by choice and is murder in God's eyes, not simply the "disposal of fetal tissue." This is, I believe, "capital R" REALITY.

Having said this, we who enter other people's societies from outside need to behave as guests. We have been called first and foremost to win people to Christ, not to crusade against evil customs in someone else's society at the expense of our primary calling. Once people have turned to Christ, they are to listen to the voice of the Holy Spirit concerning which customs to change and when and how to change them. We who are American Christians need to oppose the murder of unborn children within our own society, because it is our task as insiders to recognize and confront such evil when perpetrated by our own people. In other societies, however, such responsibility falls on the shoulders of the insiders there, though we may need to tactfully raise such matters to their attention from time to time.

2. Orientation with Respect to Age of Leaders

It is important to be concerned about *the appropriate age for the leadership of Christian organizations and activities* in the societies in which we work. The conceptualization dealt with above of the relationship between prestige and age is a serious matter. If youthfulness is highly valued, youngish leaders may not be a bad idea. Though in western societies a group will usually not tolerate a very young and inexperienced leader, we consider capability to be more important than age and tend to encourage (if not always to accept) creativity and innovation. But what about societies in which the very idea of youthful leadership is despised, especially if accompanied by creativity and innovativeness?

As we have noted before, the Euroamerican practice is out of step with most of the world, especially when combined with belief that the primary instruction given to leaders should be intellectual rather than experiential. For most societies, age and experience are seen as necessary to wisdom and prestige. Furthermore, the ideal of such societies is ordinarily the preservation and continuance of tradition, rather than its change. If the society is age oriented rather than youth oriented and tradition oriented rather than innovation oriented, what characteristics should church leaders possess? Churches that appoint leaders without culturally appropriate characteristics have to recognize that such a procedure not only results in weak leadership and witness, it distorts the message they intend to convey, at least to the traditional segment of the populace.

How much more prestigious might the church be if it had the proper kinds of leaders—leaders who are regarded within the society as capable of leading? According to Jesus' example, the way to get leaders is to find those who are already looked up to in the society and bring them into leadership in the church. As my former colleague Ralph Winter was fond of saying, "Leadership within the church should always be a second career." The person appointed to lead should have demonstrated his ability to lead in some other sphere, some other context. Then he can convert that into ministry within the church. We would say this within western society as well as within other societies.

What, then, should be done with those younger people already in leadership positions? Many younger leaders have been wise enough to link up with older traditional leaders in a kind of co-leadership or sponsorship arrangement. It may be a mayor, chief, or other political leader who sponsors the church leader. That person becomes the sponsor, and the younger leader works with that person's permission and authority. Or an older, prestigious person may work with the younger person as a co-leader. The older person would then do certain things that fall within his capabilities, while the younger person does those things that correspond with his abilities, but always with the authority of the older leader.

The sponsorship model may even work in male-dominated societies as a way of enabling women to exercise leadership gifts. Often all that is needed is for an appropriately important male within the society to openly put his stamp of approval on the female so that everyone knows that what she does is done with his approval and authority. In some cases, such approval may need to be worded as the respected male leader "ordering" the female to perform the leadership task. Sometimes such sponsorship needs to involve the woman in living in or near the home of the respected leader, to make it clear to all that she represents the leader's household in all she does.

This discussion raises an issue that should be considered in other contexts as well: the relationship between "focus" and "power," or between the "power of authority" and the "power of influence." The point is, *some people have social permission to exercise power openly, while others are allowed only to exercise power in the background*. In many situations, including not a few marriages, one member of a partnership is in focus, wielding the power of authority, while the other wields even greater power in the background as the power of influence. In many tribal situations, though it is the chief who is in focus, he really has little power by himself. He is often more the spokesman for those who make the decisions than the maker of the decisions himself. In church situations as well, the person most visible is not necessarily the person with the power necessary to provide adequate leadership for the body. If those in pastoral positions can learn to work in tandem with one or more of those who have genuine social prestige, perhaps we can combine the best of the traditional customs with the best of western practices. Any young church leader can probably help himself considerably in this regard by spending more time with the older people than he would have ordinarily. He may come up with a sponsor.

One more issue needs to be addressed. By now, most societies are split into at least two groups—the traditional segment and the westernizing segment. What is appropriate for one segment is not always appropriate for the other. A youth- and schooling-oriented approach to church leadership is probably not as harmful for the westernizing segment as it is for the traditional segment (though it still needs to be questioned as a valid method for western societies). This is one reason why traditionalists tend to be more resistant to the Gospel than those who are westernizing. But such an approach is probably never the right thing for the tradition-oriented segment of the population. If we insist on only a single approach to leadership for the church, we may be alienating the traditionalists and unconsciously giving the impression that the only way into Christianity is through these westernized techniques.

3. Transitions between Stages

A third issue raised by the above life cycle considerations is the question of what kind of recognition should be given to a major transition such as becoming a Christian. In the West we do not tend to have elaborate ceremonies, even for important transitions. Though our weddings sometimes get to be big affairs and there's an occasional large funeral, we seldom do anything of the sort at the time of a person's most important transition—from death to life. We often settle for a mere five- to ten-minute baptismal ceremony. What does such a practice communicate to people who are used to elaborate rituals at the most important transitions of life? Might they conclude that Christian conversion is not a very important event?

As we have seen, many societies have a strong emphasis on marking the transition points in life. When a person is born or becomes an adult or gets married, there is some major event, a rite of passage, a rite of transition, a community ceremony that marks that particular transition, in a way nobody can forget, as something supremely important and meaningful. Furthermore, the whole community participates both in the event and in the changed treatment of the initiate.

If a given society is particularly careful to mark those transition points, what kinds of things does the church in that society do to mark the big events in its life? Traditionally, of course, we have advocated water baptism, a ritual of transition used in both Hebrew (e.g., John the Baptist) and Greek (e.g., Greek mystery religions) societies when the Church was born. But often the baptismal rite is done (as in Euroamerica) quite simply and with little fanfare. In a society where initiations are well-known and involve many people and the stopping of all work, such baptismal initiation into the church is likely to be quite unsatisfying, both because it is foreign and because it is too brief.

What I would suggest is that the expectations of the people with respect to transition rites need to be looked at to determine what ought to be done at baptism time. In societies used to elaborate ceremonies, in order to properly emphasize the importance of the meaning to be conveyed, the initiation ceremony into the church ought to be much more elaborate than it is. Let it be elaborate in a traditional way, including a lot of very traditional things, to which is added that foreign thing that we call baptism. Let the foreign thing be encapsulated into something that the people understand. If this is done, fewer people will see it (and Christianity as a whole) as simply a foreign thing and more will see it as "really ours," because people enter this new stage of life in a very meaningful, traditional way.

I would also suggest for such societies that other transition points with appropriate rites ought to be developed within the life of the church. People seem to grow better when they have a series of transitions to strive for. One of the problems within much western Christianity is that once one has gone through the initiation of baptism, there seems to be little more to strive for. Though we are taught that we are to do our best to grow more like Jesus, there are few, if any, stages in that growth that are formally recognized. Especially in societies used to elaborate transitions, it would seem important to provide more stages that can be ceremonialized toward which Christians may strive, stages signaling greater Christian maturity or the taking of greater responsibility in the church.

4. Continuity or Discontinuity between Stages

In the West we believe that youth and adulthood should be discontinuous. That is, we encourage our youth to launch out on their own, not simply follow in their parents' footsteps. There are other peoples that also believe in a sharp distinction at certain, if not all, of the transition points. But in many societies, even if they celebrate well-defined rites of passage, such transitions tend to be smooth ones, emphasizing continuity between the stages rather than discontinuity.

The question to be raised here is whether an approach to Christian conversion that emphasizes the discontinuities more than the continuities between Christian life and a convert's previous life is culturally appropriate. It may be that the wrong impression about Christianity has been given by emphasizing what seems important to us in the West—the discontinuity between people's lives as Christians and their previous lives as non-Christians. Becoming a Christian, then, is seen as intended to turn one totally against everything in one's culture.

Jesus' approach was different. His approach was not to destroy but to fulfill, "not to do away with [the God-given traditions] but to make their teachings come true" (Mt 5:17). The Christianity advocated by westerners is often understood as advocating a system that seeks to destroy, not to fulfill.

There is, of course, discontinuity. We cannot say that Jesus, even when He said that He came to fulfill, left all of the traditions intact. In fact, many of the seeds that Jesus sowed resulted in considerable disruption in the lives of people that He influenced. Jesus, however, planted seeds that germinated and transformed from within as they grew. He did not use a sledgehammer on the outer structure of peoples' lives, except on those He had given up on (e.g., the Pharisees). Social transformation came from people inside the society recognizing, under the guidance of the Holy Spirit, that they needed to make changes. It did not come from some outside body imposing foreign rules and regulations designed to conform their Christianity to that of another society.

One worthy attempt at discovering the continuities was worked out in a doctoral dissertation at the Fuller School of World Mission, in which a very perceptive missionary chose to investigate what was going on religiously before the missionaries arrived in the Papua New Guinean society in which he worked. He was able to interview several of the old men who had been around at the time, and found that God had raised up at least one prophet who had predicted the coming of the missionary and recommended that his people follow the new ideas. By focusing on such events and the large number of traditional values and customs that can easily be incorporated into Christianity, this missionary has tried to help these people recognize that there is a continuity between what was going on before Christianity came to them and what is going on now. In this way he wants, among other things, to help them have a Christianity rooted in their own history, rather than simply adopting a history from overseas. He has been able to demonstrate that what has happened recently in their acceptance of Christianity was prepared for within their own history (*see* Spruth 1981).

Richardson's *Eternity in Their Hearts* (1981) records quite a number of additional examples of God working among given peoples before the coming of missionaries. Cross-cultural witnesses need to look for such indications of God's prior working in whatever societies they go to and work in continuity with them.

5. Ancestors

As we have discussed, to many people the continued existence of the ancestors is real. What should be our attitude? We can deny their existence and cut off our opportunities for communicating effectively with those whose "reality" includes living ancestors. Or we can take their belief seriously (even though we may suspect satanic manipulation of their desire to honor their forebears) and seek to lead them from any form of idolatry they may be practicing into truly putting the God of the universe first. Several points may help.

a. It is important to recognize that honoring ancestors is not necessarily worshiping them. From a western point of view, such talking to spirits is considered prayer and, therefore, worship. Since we don't have a custom in which we talk to people who are not biologically present, *we attribute our motives to their actions*, no matter what they are actually feeling. We assume that they are worshiping whoever they think they are talking to.

But worship is putting somebody else in the place of God. For many of those who talk to ancestors, this practice is not rightly interpreted as a replacement of God by ancestors. In African societies, for example, what is usually happening is that those who are revering (venerating, honoring) their ancestors are fulfilling the fifth commandment, "Honor your father and your mother" (since they believe their loved ones are still alive), rather than breaking the first commandment, "No other gods before me."

b. This is not always the case, however. Ancestors, like material possessions, family, job, or any other facet of human life, can be made the object of primary allegiance and worshiped. This is called idolatry and is soundly condemned throughout Scripture. Many people whose allegiance to God is weak but whose allegiance to family is strong do put one or more revered ancestors in the place of God and fall into worshiping them. This is a form of idolatry and will require an allegiance encounter (*see* Kraft 1991b) that leads the people to turn from rendering primary allegiance to the ancestor to pledging that allegiance to the true God.

c. The Old Testament deals with this problem, since the Jewish people were constantly tempted to revere their ancestors to the point of worship. One phrase used over and over in the Old Testament to help the Jews with their struggle is "the God of Abraham, Isaac, and Jacob." The use of such a phrase enabled the people both to revere their ancestors and render primary allegiance to God. Often, though, western witnesses do not discover that such a phrase is usable in a given society, since we do not probe far enough to discover that the people know of a source of power greater than the ancestors.

I discovered something important in this regard while questioning some Papua New Guinean Christians concerning ancestors. I pressed them to trace the source of the power of their ancestors back to the beginning. They held that each ancestor received his power from a previous ancestor and, at first, seemed unable to press the source of power further back than that. Then one of them stated that she had once heard a story of their first ancestor running out of power and climbing a tall tree to request more power from someone who lived higher than the top of that tree. When this was stated, the rest agreed that they had also heard such a story and that that story must indicate that the ultimate source of the ancestors' power was in God.

d. For many peoples, the ancestors serve as intermediaries with God. In such cases, it may be valid to represent Jesus as the Supreme Ancestor, the Great Ancestor, the One who assuredly takes our requests to God. This can provide a start toward the truth that instead of talking to our ancestors, we can talk to Jesus. Jesus, being God Himself, has more power than the ancestors. As people learn to focus more on Jesus as the Mediator between themselves and God, they will come to focus less on the ancestors.

6. When Things Go Wrong in the Cycle

People have different understandings of disease and other misfortunes. The question to raise here is what the attitude of the cross-cultural witness should be. Traditionally, western missionaries have simply attempted (whether consciously or unconsciously) to convert nonwestern peoples to our naturalistic views of disease. Many people have become convinced of the efficacy of western medical technology, as well they should be. The record is impressive. But things may have been lost in that process.

One question to be raised concerns the totality of the theoretical underpinnings of western medicine. Is the well-nigh total faith that many westerners put in our kind of medicine really justified? Or are there some things that western medicine is good at and others that it is not good at? I believe there is ample evidence, even in western contexts, that this type of medicine is not as totally effective as we often assume. Nor are other approaches to medicine (e.g., chiropractic, osteopathy, acupuncture) totally without success.

Second, what about the faith element in healing, whether faith in people and procedures or faith in God. On the human level, there are studies pointing out that people who have faith in given doctors or in given medicine are more likely to be healed than those who don't have such faith. Could the same be true of nonwestern medical practitioners and procedures?

Third, what about the whole relationship between mind and body that western medical practitioners seem to know so little about? Could there be an even greater influence of mind on body than we have imagined? Even western doctors are suggesting that 80 percent or more of physical illnesses are psychosomatic. Could other peoples know more about this (and other) areas than we do?

Finally, what about the supernatural dimensions of the subject, those areas that western worldviews tend to completely ignore and even deny? Should we not be more concerned with Who does the healing and be more resistant to our society's exclusive concern for intermediaries in the process such as doctors and medicine? Should we not consult God first, even if we then turn for help to doctors and medicine that He allowed humans to develop? Experience has shown that when this is done, sometimes the doctors and medicine are not needed. At other times, however, the process involving doctors and medicine is speeded up. I believe God wants to be consulted first, not last. I'm afraid most of us, even in the name of God, have secularized Jesus' example, commands, and predictions concerning healing the sick and the way we are to be involved in it (e.g., Mt 10:1, 8; Mk 3:15; Lk 9:2, 10:9; Jn 14:12). See Kraft (1989) for more on this subject.

PART IV

RELATING TO THE HUMAN UNIVERSE

CHAPTER 15

COMMUNICATION: LANGUAGE

INTEGRATIONAL THOUGHT

When westerners think of language, we often focus on words, sentences, or the whole language in terms of *what these elements of life are*. We may not think so much of *the kinds of things that happen when they are used*. Thus language and its parts seem to westerners much more static than they really are. This is unfortunate, since language, of all the subsystems of culture, is the supreme stimulator of the "meaning construction" that goes on in people's minds as communication takes place. Language participates in what may be the most dynamic of the activities humans engage in—the process of communication. Therefore any tendency to see language as a static thing should be strongly resisted.

Christians often have another hang-up when they think of the word *word*. Our commitment to literacy on the one hand and to the Bible as the "Word of God" on the other often leads us to assume that when the Bible refers to the "word" of God, it is referring to the Bible. This is seldom the case, however. By far the majority of scriptural uses of the phrase "Word of God" refer to the speaking (not the writing) activity of God. Note, for example, the commonly used verses Isaiah 55:11 ("the word that I speak . . . will do everything I send it to do"), and Hebrews 4:12 ("the Word that God speaks is alive and active" *JBP*).

With these things in mind, note the impression of staticness that comes across in the traditional translation of John 1:1: "In the beginning was the Word, and the Word was with God, and the Word was God" (*KJV*).

Much of contemporary western Christianity seems static. At least some of the blame for this may lie in the way we express ourselves when we talk about Christian things. Take expressions such as "God is love," "God is my Father," "we are brothers and sisters in Christ," or even "the Lord is my Shepherd" and the like. Though these are true statements, the use of the word *is* reduces each to a matter-of-fact, static pronouncement concerning a state of being. Note the difference in tone when we rephrase each to the following: "God relates to me lovingly," "God treats me as a good father treats his child," "we behave toward each other as brothers and sisters in Christ," and "the Lord cares for me as a shepherd cares for his sheep." Though both sets of statements are true, only the latter set conveys the dynamism we are expected to experience in our relationship with God and His people.

John, like the other New Testament authors, was a Jew. Like most bilinguals, he probably thought largely in the concepts of his native language (Aramaic), even when speaking Greek. In comparison to either Greek or English, Aramaic and Hebrew expressed things more dynamically. Greek embodied much action in nouns which, when translated literally into English, result in an impression of staticness. We can assume, though, that when John used the Greek word *logos*, it was the meaning of the Hebrew word *dabar* that he had in mind, and *dabar* did not denote a static concept.

Indeed, some of the meanings of *dabar* are quite dynamic. Without going into a lot of detail, we can say that throughout the Old Testament, the word generally refers to the activity of speaking, with a bias toward the speaking activity of God. It occurs often, for example, in the formula, "the word (= the speaking activity) of the Lord" as used throughout the prophetic books.

I suspect that Phillips has better captured the original intent when he translates John 1:1, "At the beginning God expressed himself. That personal expression, that word, was with God and was God, and he existed with God from the beginning."

That God is still expressing Himself, still speaking, still acting. Both He and our relationships with Him are intended to be living and dynamic. Let's not let the language we use, or any other factor in our Christian experience, reduce either our relationship with Him or our expression of that relationship to staticness. Let's fight static Christianity!

INTRODUCTION

Language is the first of the several subsystems of culture devoted to relating people to people. See the diagram in chapter 8 for the overall picture of the various subsystems of culture that radiate out from the worldview core. The first two that we will discuss are communicational subsystems.

Before we get into our treatment of cultural subsystems, two preliminary points need to be made. The first is that we will make no attempt to be exhaustive in our treatment. We will not treat every subsystem of culture. There are too many of them, and we lack any precise definition of what is and what is not to be considered a full subsystem. Nor will we treat every aspect of those we deal with. This is an attempt to deal representatively, not exhaustively, with certain of the major components of culture. By dealing with this particular selection, however, we hope to alert you to enough of the complexity of culture to enable you to deal with these issues and discover aspects of culture not dealt with here (and deal with them as well).

The second preliminary point is to remind ourselves that any division of culture into parts has to be done fairly artificially and for analytical purposes. In real life, the cultural subsystems function like the parts of the human body—in tight integration and interrelation with each other and with the worldview. In spite of this, like medical people, we identify, label, and study individual parts of culture for the sake of gaining a greater understanding of the whole.

Such a tight relationship is certainly true between language and the other subsystems. In fact, there are many who would say that language is the most important subsystem of culture. Some have even gone to the extreme of contending that language exerts a formative influence on culture (e.g., Sapir and Whorf). Others have countered that it is culture that determines language. Such an argument is not very profitable. It seems to me to be similar to the discussion concerning whether the chicken or the egg came first.

What does seem worth saying is that *language mirrors culture at every point*. Language affects culture, and culture affects language. We learn our culture as children, along with our language. As we learn the names of things, we pick up the categories of our language, which largely correspond with the categories of our culture. Any change in language brings about some change in the culture (since language is a part of culture). When there are changes in other parts of a culture, they are usually reflected in some way in the language. Thus the relationship between language and culture is of the closest kind.

DEFINITION OF LANGUAGE

Language may be defined as *a system of arbitrary vocal symbols employed by the members of a society for a variety of inter- and intrapersonal purposes such as: formulating and communicating ideas, inducing others to action, attracting pity, instilling fear, and expressing oneself, as in letting off steam, showing off, and the like.*

1. Note, in the first place, that when we talk about language, we are talking about a *vocal* thing. Many people, especially in western societies, think primarily of something written when they think of language. From a cross-cultural perspective, however, we need to recognize that the basic thing called language (on which written language is dependent) is what goes on between people's mouths and their ears. Written language, though different from spoken language, is a derivative of vocal language and is only characteristic of perhaps a third or less of the world's societies. Though anthropologists recognize the importance of written language, when we use the term *language*, we are referring to the vocal communicational system that every society possesses, not to the written system that has been added by certain peoples.

Some varieties of sign language used among the hearing impaired are a partial exception to this statement, since they depend on hands and eyes rather than on mouth and ears. Systems such as American Sign Language are well developed and possess many of the major characteristics of vocal language. Some would, therefore, classify them as "full" languages. They are, however, structured more around picture symbols than around word symbols and are at base more like drama communication (*see* chapter 16) than like ordinary language. This fact and the limitations it imposes lead me to regard them as restricted or semilanguages. Alphabet-based sign languages are, of course, more like writing than like speaking.

A System of Arbitrary Vocal Symbols	Employed by the Members of a Society	For Interpersonal and Intrapersonal Purposes such as: 1. Formulating and Communicating Ideas 2. Inducing Others to Action 3. Attracting Pity 4. Instilling Fear 5. Expressing Oneself 6. Etc.

Figure 15.1 Definition of language

2. Second, a language is *systematic and structured*. Not infrequently, travelers have reported that "the language of these people has absolutely no system, no logic to it." Linguists and anthropologists have to date never found a single language that is not systematic and intricately structured. The problem that such travelers experienced was that no other language is structured exactly the same as theirs. Every language is organized according to its own system, its own logic, and may look quite unsystematic and illogical from the point of view of the patterning of another language.

Structurally, each language consists of a large number of grammatical patterns that are capable of allowing the users to create a well-nigh infinite variety of expressions. These expressions are used to enable the members of a social group to communicate with one another. This they can do because they have come via common indoctrination and shared interpretation of experience to attach the same, or nearly the same, meanings to the same forms and structures.

3. Third, we say that the vocal symbols of language are *arbitrary*. By this we mean that there is nothing in reality that requires that any given sequence of sound be associated with any given being or concept. Nothing in the universe requires that a canine animal be called a dog. In other languages, people choose to call that same animal a *chien* or a *perro* or a *hund* or a *kare*, or whatever. The linguistic labels used in the various languages of the world are assigned arbitrarily by the various societies that use those languages.

Once a community assigns a label, though, the arbitrariness is gone. That is, it is required that, in attempting to communicate with any given group, we use *their* term if we are to be understood. In relation to their language system and their culture, the form to be used is fixed. One cannot change the form and expect to be understood. We call language symbols arbitrary only because nothing in the universe—nothing outside the reality of the given language and culture—requires that any given sound be associated with any given concept.

4. Fourth, when we speak of the forms of language (i.e., the words, phrases, sentences, idioms, etc.), we are speaking of *symbols* that stand for something else.

Linguistic symbols, like other cultural forms, signify elements in the reality out-side our minds and function as the forms to which we attach meanings. Symbols are, however, specific to each language. That is, any given symbol cannot be counted on to represent the same reality in more than one culture.

No word (or other linguistic symbol) means something inherently. As we have said above, there is no necessary meaning attached to a word, no meaning that is necessitated by a relationship between the sound of that word and external real-ity. God doesn't attach inherent meanings to words, nor does nature. The mean-ings are attached by the community of people who agree to use the words to signify certain meanings and not other possible meanings. That's what we mean by symbols.

5. A language is the *property of a society or linguistic community*. It is agreed upon and structured in such a way that hearers within that community can pre-dict reasonably well what speakers intend when they use a given symbol. I can communicate with you who read this only if you agree with me on what the words and phrases I use are intended to signify. This is little or no problem if we are part of the same linguistic community, except perhaps when I use technical terms that come from my involvement with the anthropological community of which you may not be part, or if I use regional terms or terms specific to my generation but not to yours. If, however, you are not a native speaker of American English (of this dia-lect), you will understand only to the extent that your experience with American English speakers has enabled you to participate in the agreements that we of this American English-speaking community share.

6. Language is used by people both intra- and interpersonally. *Language is used intrapersonally* when people talk to themselves. This is, apparently, a univer-sal phenomenon. Many would say that the process of thinking is largely, if not entirely, a matter of people talking internally to themselves. *Reading*, too, is prob-ably a process in which we carry on a conversation with ourselves, one side of which is stimulated by printed materials. *Talking out loud to ourselves* is another type of intrapersonal use of language that many if not most people engage in from time to time.

Language may be *used expressively* whether or not anyone else is near. When we are hammering nails and by accident hit a finger, we will often use language to express ourselves very forcefully! Likewise, we often "let off steam" verbally when we are upset, even when we are alone.

But the most obvious uses of language are *interpersonal*—between one person and another. In language, we formulate and communicate ideas, we seek to get others to do things, express various emotions, *we* show off, and attempt to attract pity, love, or other types of concern.

LANGUAGE AND MEANING

There are those who contend that words and other forms of language *contain* their meanings. They see language forms as containers needing to be "unpacked" to discover what's inside. Many who specialize in interpreting Scripture have this theory of meaning. They tend to devote themselves to the study of the structure and origin (etymology) of words in order to discover their precise meanings. The origin of a word is, however, about as relevant to the meaning as a genealogy is to the meaning of a person. Occasionally the origin or genealogy is significant, but usually it contributes little, especially in comparison to the importance of contemporary usage.

The study of the meaning of a term needs to be a study of social agreements that come to light through gaining an understanding of how that term is used in actual life situations. It is on this basis that good dictionaries are made. Dictionary makers attempt to discover and describe all the ways the people of a society use any given word. They then attempt to categorize and label each of those ways to enable those consulting their product to select the meaning appropriate to the context in which they have found the word.

The fact that social agreement, rather than something inherent in a word or idiom, underlies meaning may be shown in several ways. One way is to point out that any given word may mean something different to different groups within the same society. Several years ago, for example, certain groups of American young people decided to use the words *cool* and *bad* in ways different from standard usage. I found that all of a sudden my children were referring to people of whom they approved as *cool* and things they considered good as *bad*. Though this was confusing to those of us on the other side of the generation gap, our youth understood each other because they had agreed among themselves to assign their, rather than our, meanings to these words. There was nothing inherent in these words that kept their users from changing their meanings. Now dictionary makers have to describe their usage as well as ours, since both are valid to different communities.

The fact that words are symbols pointing to a reality outside themselves, rather than containers to be unpacked, is well stated by Berlo (1960:175):

> *Meanings are in people*, [they are] covert responses, contained within the human organism. Meanings . . . are personal, our own property. We learn meanings, we add to them, we distort them, forget them, change them. We cannot *find* them. They are in *us* not in messages. Fortunately, we usually find other people who have meanings that are similar to ours. To the extent that people have similar meanings, they can communicate. If they have no similarities in meaning between them they cannot communicate.
>
> If meanings are found in words, it would follow that any person could understand any language, any code. If the meaning is in the word we should be able to analyze the word and find the meaning. Yet obviously we cannot. Some people have meanings for some codes others do not.

The elements and structure of a language do not themselves have meaning. They are only symbols, sets of symbols, cues that cause us to bring our own meanings into play to think about them, to rearrange them, and so forth. *Communication does not consist of the transmission of meaning*. Meanings are not transmittable, not transferable. Only messages are transmittable, and meanings are not in the message, they are in the message users.

As with all cultural forms (*see* chapter 9), meaning assignment is done on the basis of personal interpretation, and such assignment is done subjectively, individually, even though usually in terms of group conventions. It is also done habitually, on the basis of what I call "interpretational reflexes." When we learn another language, we are learning another set of habits of interpretation and meaning assignment. We learn another symbol system and the interpretational reflexes to go with it. For further elaboration of this perspective on language and meaning, see my *Communication Theory for Christian Witness* (1991a), especially chapter 7.

CHARACTERISTICS OF LANGUAGE

There are several additional things that can be said to characterize this marvelous thing we call language.

1. First of all, on the basis of the information we have from studies of thousands of the world's languages, we can safely say that *a language is always complex*. Linguists have not discovered a single primitive or simple language. Of course, most people think their own language is the easiest in the world—and any other language they may be trying to learn the hardest!

The problem is that any given language seems simple only to those who learned it from childhood, because they learned it before they could tell the difference between simple and complex. Outsiders, having already learned their own language (which also is not simple), find the deeply entrenched habits of hearing and speaking that language constantly interfering with their learning of the new language. Many cross-cultural witnesses end up with very poor command of the language of the people among whom they work, not because they're not intelligent, but because they just couldn't get out of the old patterns. Their native pronunciation habits interfered so greatly with their attempts to pronounce the new language that they could hardly make themselves understood. Their native grammatical habits likewise kept them from learning new word ordering and other new patterns that weren't in their first language. For many, fighting those patterns got to be so much work that they simply gave up.

Every language has tens of thousands of vocabulary items. Dictionaries have been produced for so-called primitive languages containing 40–60,000 different entries. Indeed, there probably is no language without a minimum of 20–30,000 vocabulary items and the potential for creating thousands more if and when they are needed, demonstrating again that they are not primitive or simple. In addition, every language has an intricately organized grammatical structuring.

2. Second, *every language is relatively adequate*. This means that any language enables its speakers to handle relatively well the concepts that the society focuses on. It is usually more difficult for people to discuss at any depth those things they consider of lesser importance. Vocabulary items are developed for things that are considered to be important and that people want to talk about. Things they are not interested in tend to get screened out by the worldview, so there are fewer vocabulary items or none at all to deal with those things.

The presence in Eskimo languages of about twenty-six different words for different types of snow and ice suggests that these people are very concerned about snow. When you look at their culture, you discover that snow is indeed very important. In fact, their ability to survive in their snowy environment requires that they carefully distinguish between various kinds of snow. They may distinguish between the kind of snow that you can drive a sled over and the kind of snow a sled will fall through. They have distinctions for the kind of snow that you can cut into blocks to make igloos and the kind of snow that won't pack well for such purposes. If they don't make such distinctions—if they treat all snow alike, as some of us do—they will be in big trouble.

Some languages do not even have a word for snow. The best we could do in Hausa was a word for ice. When we tried to tell these people about snow, the only thing we could do was open our refrigerators and point to the frost. I'm sure they didn't believe that that kind of thing could ever cover the ground, as we told them it did in our home country. But Hausa makes a four-way distinction between heat and cold—hot dry, hot damp, cold dry, and cold damp. Apparently this distinction was considered important enough by those who originated it for them to develop separate words for each category, and it is considered important enough today for the contemporary users of the language to continue to make this four-way distinction.

Likewise, it is said that Arabic has 1,000 words or more for knives or knife parts and a similar number of words for camels and their accoutrements. What should we conclude about the importance they attach to knives and camels? Or what should we conclude about the people who speak American English, with our thousands of terms for automobiles and their parts, household gadgets, electronic instruments and their parts, and any number of other material, technological, and scientific items? Our language also shows that we highly value abstract ideas in many areas of life, including philosophy, mathematics, and science.

Any given language cannot immediately handle every concept that its speakers think up or borrow. A part of language adequacy is, however, the fact that new terms and structures can be created or borrowed to meet the needs of the society. Languages are apparently almost infinitely adaptable, though sometimes the process of adaptation takes a bit of time and effort at first. Given this fact, we can say that anything that can be said in one language can be represented adequately (though never exactly) in another, if enough effort is put into it (*see* Kraft 1979a:272 and Nida and Taber 1969). See below on adaptability.

3. Third, *languages are unique*. No two are exactly alike. There are probably more than 6,000 distinct languages in the world. None is structured in exactly the same way as any other. There are always differences in sounds and grammar between even the most closely related languages. Human creativity has resulted in an amazing variety of grammatical and phonological patterning in the languages of the world.

Furthermore, no concept is dealt with in exactly the same way in any two languages (though the languages of peoples with closely related worldviews will sometimes come close). There is, therefore, no exact conceptual equivalence between languages. As was mentioned above, even a fairly simple concept like "dog" cannot be taken from one language to another and be expected to mean exactly the same thing, much less more abstract concepts. Furthermore, different languages are structured in ways that facilitate or hinder certain types of conceptualization. The Navaho language, for example, is structured to focus on movement, while English (and European languages in general) tend to focus more on states of being. We can speak of European languages being noun oriented and Navaho being verb oriented. As mentioned in the Integrational Thought Section, we say, "God *is* our Father," while they would probably be more comfortable with something like, "God *acts like* a father toward me." From the Navaho point of view (worldview) the world is full of movement, so linguistically they focus on movement. The first words their children learn to focus on are verbs (Goldschmidt 1954). From our Anglo point of view, things look more static. We teach our children the nouns of the language and basically use the verbs to connect the nouns.

It used to be thought that different languages were simply alternative codes for dealing with the same reality. In other words, the world was viewed as a single reality and each language seen as providing a different set of labels for each of the same elements in that one reality. With the insight we now have into the differences between REALITY (as God sees it) and perceived reality (*see* chapter 2), on the one hand, and cultural worldviews (*see* chapter 4), on the other, it looks as if it would be more accurate to speak, as Sapir did years ago (1929), of each language actually dealing with a different reality. Though such a point of view can be (and sometimes has been) taken too far, we must take very seriously the differences in the conceptual structuring of reality inherent in the world's different worldviews and the languages that represent them.

This causes great problems for Bible translators. If a translator ignores this lack of conceptual equivalence and produces a literal translation, it is automatically a poor translation because it has failed to take account of the differences between the way the source and receptor languages express thoughts. A noun-based translation in Navaho that focused on static relationships, as is appropriate in an English translation, would be perceived by Navahos as so far out of touch with reality that quite a different message than that intended by the authors would come across. *A good translation has to present the message as differently in the receptor language as is necessary to enable the receptors to understand as nearly as possible what the original hearers understood.*

Such a translation needs to include enough of what may be termed "legitimate paraphrase" to make explicit to the new receptors what was obvious, though not stated, to the original hearers. If the original intent is to come across, it must be clear to the receptors that when Jesus says, "Get behind me, Satan" (Mt 16:23), he is not asking for Satan's assistance (as would be the normal interpretation in some languages. *See* Nida 1954:216) or that the belief required for salvation is not simply the kind of intellectual assent that the English word ordinarily connotes. There is "illegitimate paraphrase," where the translator actually adds to the information intended by the original author. But legitimate paraphrase is simply intended to keep the author's intent from being misinterpreted due to the differences in the ways source and receptor languages handle information.

4. Fourth, *languages are adaptable*. People adapt their language to whatever changes take place in the culture. Many such changes take place from within as the normal processes of culture change take place. For most people today, the most obvious pressures for change are coming from outside. When a people freely borrows material items and concepts from another society, the tendency is to borrow linguistic terms also. We therefore find many English (and other European language) names for objects borrowed from western societies in the languages of many nonwestern peoples. It is not surprising, for example, to find the word "*mota*" (from "motor") or "*tica*" (from "teacher"), or even "*fidaburdi*" (from PWD—Public Works Department) in Hausa. Nor is it surprising to find in the same language a large number of Arabic borrowings brought into the language in an earlier day, when Arabic peoples were the most influential outsiders in Hausaland.

But borrowing is not the only way that languages adapt. Another way is by expanding the use of terms already within the language to cover certain items and concepts that are being introduced. When the Hausa people wanted a label for a railroad train, they didn't borrow the English name. Instead, they expanded the use of their word "canoe" by calling trains "land canoes." When airplanes were introduced, they labeled them "canoes in the sky." In this way, an interesting thing happened to the word for canoe. It has now come to mean something more like the

English word "vehicle" than like the English word "canoe." Another of my favorites within Hausa is the phrase they use for "guided missile." They put some words together and came up with "a bullet with a bridle!" To translate "United Nations," they came up with the concept of a "council for sewing the world together." Very creative! One of the most fascinating things about the way people use their language is this creativity.

A similar thing happened in Greek with the most common of the words usually translated "preach" or "proclaim." The word *kerusso* originally referred to what a herald did as he went from village to village shouting out the news. By New Testament times, the word had come to cover the communication, by almost any means, of a message originated by someone other than the messenger and given to that person to present in whatever way seemed appropriate (*see* Kittel 1967, vol 3). If translators took proper account of this fact, they would translate a verse such as Mk 16:15 "Go into all the world to *communicate* the gospel," rather than mislead people into thinking that it is God (rather than custom) that requires us to monologue from behind a pulpit to fulfill His command. Jesus, of course, felt no such restriction. He used a multiplicity of forms of communication—a lot of dialogue, a lot of life involvement, and occasionally some monologue (*see* Kraft 1991a).

There are also losses in the process of adaptation. We are aware of the loss of such terms as "thee" and "thou" in English. In America, a large number of terms that used to be commonly known relating to horses, saddles, and wagons are lost to all but those who work with horses, since the custom of using horses and horse-drawn conveyances as our principal means of transportation and load-carrying has dropped out of the culture.

In these and other ways, language shows great adaptability.

5. Fifth, *language mirrors culture at every point*. Among the many possible examples of this fact, we will deal with five areas: time, place, age, gender, and occasion. We will here draw from an audio presentation of anthropology done several years ago for radio (Goldschmidt 1954).

a. Language mirrors culture with respect to *time*. By this we mean that the way a culture has changed over time can be traced via the study of linguistic change. For example, in English we find a double set of terms for certain animals and their meat. This situation came about as a result of the French conquest of England in the eleventh century. The terms are presented in figure 15.2 below.

When the French conquered England, they established themselves as the upper social class. The English (called the Anglo-Saxons at that time) became the lower social class. The English (Anglo-Saxon) names were used for the animals when they were alive, because the lower class English were tending the animals. But when the animals had been butchered and the meat came to the tables of the French masters, they used French words for the meat. The French word *boeuf* (cow) was used for the cow as it appeared butchered on the table, the French word *mouton* (sheep) was used for the meat of the sheep, and the French word *porc* (pig) for the meat of the pig, even though back in the barns the native English people were still calling those creatures cows, sheep, and pigs. As time passed, both sets of terms were retained in the language, but each became specialized in the way we use them now. This kind of thing happens in many languages.

Another example of a language retaining such "historical overhang" is the English spelling system, which has not changed very much over hundreds of years. Our ancestors way back pronounced these words as they are spelled. The language (the spoken system) has changed quite a bit over the years (as all languages do), but the spelling system has remained relatively static, so now we have a spelling system that is far out of touch with the way the words are pronounced.

ENGLISH ANIMAL	ENGLISH MEAT	FRENCH ANIMAL
Cow	Beef	Boeuf
Pig	Pork	Porc
Sheep	Mutton	Mouton

Figure 15.2 Double sets of terms in English

b. Another area in which language mirrors culture is with respect to *place*. People who live in any given part of a cultural area tend to develop ways of speaking that differ to a lesser or greater extent from the speech of those living in other places. We call such linguistic varieties dialects. Linguists and anthropologists use this term for regional variations within the same language, such as differences of pronunciation or vocabulary that interfere a bit but do not keep people from understanding each other. A variety of speech not understood by a given group (even if it is not large or highly respected) is termed a separate language, not, as is the custom in some countries, a dialect.

In American English, we have several regional accents. Those from the southeastern states, for example, tend to pronounce their words quite differently from those from the northern parts of the country. There are, furthermore, African American and Hispanic dialects of American English, plus several urban dialects in which pronunciation differs markedly from that of so-called Standard Midwestern American English. Then, of course, there are British and Australian and Indian and African dialects of English, each with certain distinguishing features of pronunciation. In addition, each dialect has certain differences in vocabulary usage. For example, certain American dialects will refer to a kind of water container as a bucket, while others will call the same container a pail. Likewise, soft drinks will be called soda in many parts of the country but pop in other parts (and, at least formerly, tonic in some parts of the northeast).

Even wider vocabulary differences exist between American and British English. For example, Americans say napkin where British use serviette. Americans call certain parts of a car the hood, trunk, and windshield while British call them bonnet, boot and windscreen. Likewise for tack (American) and drawing pin (British), steal (American) and pinch (British).

It was because of their dialect that people easily identified Jesus and His disciples as being from Galilee when they went to Jerusalem. At Jesus' trial, Peter was identified as one of Jesus' disciples because of his Galilean accent (*see* Mt 26:73).

c. Language also mirrors *age*. Adults don't ordinarily talk baby talk except to babies, nor do children talk like adults. If, for example, a professor lectured by speaking as a child does or a child talked like a professor lectures, we would think it quite strange. When we go to another people to learn their language, we often (though not always) find that children talk more slowly and more precisely than adults. We can usually learn the language with less difficulty from children—as long as we realize that we can't keep talking like children. At the other end of the age spectrum, the very aged tend to speak differently from younger people. One important reason for this difference is the amount of change in the language that takes place as generation succeeds generation. The more rapid this change, the greater the differences between the speech of different generations.

d. Language also mirrors cultural *gender distinctions*. Apparently in all societies there are some differences between the way men and women speak. The greater the cultural differences between the behavior and associations of men and women, the more likely that the language differences will be great. Some peoples carry such differences so far that they have the men and women speak almost entirely different languages. Greater isolation between people, whether regionally or sexually, tends to produce greater linguistic difference. In American English, the gender-related distinctions are not nearly as great as in many other languages, yet a man who exclaimed, "Oh, that's darling!" or "Isn't that just precious?" would be regarded as strange, since he would be using women's language. Likewise, a woman who regularly uses vulgar and so-called swear words is considered out of place (at least in much of middle-class society) because she is using expressions traditionally reserved for men.

e. Language differs according to *occasion* in culturally prescribed ways. One of my favorite examples of this fact is the comment reportedly made by Queen Victoria of England (1819–1901) concerning the famous orator William Gladstone: "Mr. Gladstone always addresses me as if I were a public meeting." Such a comment indicates that the queen felt Gladstone did not properly "shift gears" when he moved from a public meeting into a private conference with the queen. He failed to adapt to these different occasions.

We are expected to behave differently on different occasions (e.g., work, play, at home, private, public, formal, informal, and so on). Our language, then, is expected to appropriately mirror whatever the social expectations for each occasion. A person who uses one style on all occasions is socially out of line.

LANGUAGE IS THE PRIMARY VEHICLE OF CULTURE

As indicated above, language mirrors the basic worldview structuring in terms of which a society organizes reality. The society's special way of looking at and interpreting reality (worldview) is built into the language. In serving the worldview, each language provides a framework for its people to understand what they are observing and perceiving. It gives them categories in which to organize and classify their everyday experiences.

From an anthropological point of view, there are as many different worlds upon the earth as there are languages. Each language is an instrument that guides people in observing, reacting, and expressing themselves in a special way, so the peoples on this earth can be seen as living in at least 6,000 different worlds. We may talk about one world geographically, or even refer to what some have called our global village. But geography is trivial, and to assume that we are all in the same "village" because rapid travel has made almost every part of the world readily accessible seems the height of naiveness. Each of us, in our own language and worldview, participates at the deep level in a separate reality, however similar we may look on the surface.

We have noted above that Navaho is verb based while English is noun based. Such differences relate to differences in the worldview that underlies the lan-

guage. As mentioned, Greek puts a lot of actions into nouns. "A baptism of repentance for the forgiveness of sins" (Mk 1:4 *RSV*), for example, is a literal translation
from Greek. Baptism, repentance, forgiveness and sinning are all actions, but
Greek puts all of these concepts into nouns. A translation that seeks to adequately
convey the author's thought in English will conform to English practice and render those actions with verbs. Such a translation would talk about baptizing people
who have repented so that they can be forgiven for committing sins. Literal translations such as the *RSV, KJV, ASV, NASV,* and *NIV,* however, use English nouns to
render the Greek nouns, giving English speakers the impression that Christianity
is intended to be much more static than a proper understanding of Greek modes of
expression would suggest.

Western languages tend to structure reality and interpret experience in terms
of a large number of either-or distinctions. Under the influence of our worldview,
expressed primarily through our languages, we divide reality up into the good and
the bad, the clean and the unclean, the tall and the short, the fat and the skinny,
the pretty and the ugly, the right and the wrong, the guilty and the not guilty, the
saved and the unsaved. We tend to polarize our total experience. In fact, as the
great Harvard anthropologist Clyde Kluckhohn has said,

> Traditional or Aristotelian logic has been mainly the analysis of consistencies in the
> structures of languages like Greek and Latin. The subject-predicate form of speech has
> implied a changeless world of fixed relations between "substances" and their "qualities"
> ... Aristotelian logic teaches us that something is or isn't. Such a statement is often
> false to reality, for both-and is more often true than either-or .... Actual experience
> does not present clear-cut entities like "good" and "bad," "mind" and "body;" the sharp
> split remains verbal (1949a:124–5).

Kluckhohn is saying that reality is more like a continuum than like the dis-
crete entities that English (and other western languages) requires us to focus on.
But because westerners have been taught to make such discriminations, we tend
to assume that reality is actually organized in such categories. On the contrary,
the organization we perceive is that of our worldview and language, not of REALITY
itself. The story is told of some Native Americans who were hired by Anglos to sort
oranges into "good oranges" and "bad oranges." After trying unsuccessfully to do
what they were hired for, they were dismissed by their employers because they
just could not divide oranges into those two categories. Their worldview led them
to see the oranges in a continuum from good to bad, rendering them unable to
decide which fell into their employers' "good" category and which into the "bad."

Most eastern languages (and many others) also do not think in terms of such
dichotomies. They too lead their speakers to plot things on a scale from better to
worse, from taller to shorter, from more true to less true. Such peoples don't just
have two options—one at either end of the scale—they have a number of options in
between. For example, "Chinese gives priority to 'how?' and non-exclusive categories; European languages to 'what?' and exclusive categories" (Kluckhohn
1949a:125). This is particularly bothersome to westerners in the area of religious
or political allegiance where, from a western point of view, there is no possibility of
a "both-and" allegiance. Easterners often see no problem with belonging to several
religions.

Each language embodies a whole set of unconscious worldview assumptions
about the world and life in it, so people see and hear largely what their language

makes them sensitive to and trains them to look for. *A people's language serves as both the indoctrination mechanism for and the constant reminder of the structuring of reality provided by their worldview.* Through it we learn to be sensitive to certain things and not to others, to be selective, to look for certain things while ignoring others.

A language provides its people with a certain number of *color terms*. In English we have about eleven major color terms. Many languages at least traditionally divide the color spectrum into three, five, or seven parts. Not that people don't see the other colors—they often note them as subcategories—they simply segment reality differently. The language of a people will also provide them with terms that bias them to identify certain things as good and others as bad. The language structure, verbs especially, designates a time system (past, present, or future) or an aspect system (indicating, e.g., continuing action, action that happens once and doesn't happen again, action that happens repeatedly, or action involving the viewing of something in the future). Probably most of the languages of the world are primarily aspect languages. Most European languages tend to be time or tense languages, however.

Many languages have two words for "we," one of which is inclusive, the other exclusive. The inclusive "we" means "Myself and all of you," the other word means "Myself and my people but not any of you." Notice what happens if a missionary says, "God loves us" and uses the wrong term for "us." He may use the term meaning "I and my people but not any of you." The people just sit there and say, "Okay, God loves him and his people, but He doesn't love any of us." What he meant to say was, "God loves us all," using the inclusive "we" that includes all of them.

As Kluckhohn has said, "the underlying conceptual images of each language tend to constitute a coherent though unconscious philosophy" (Kluckhohn 1949a:125). For example,

> In the Haida language of British Columbia there are more than twenty verbal prefixes that indicate whether an action was performed by carrying, shooting, hammering, pushing, pulling, floating, stamping, picking, chopping, or the like. Some languages have different verbs, adjectives, and pronouns for animate and inanimate things. In Melanesia there are as many as four variant forms for each possessive pronoun. One may be used for the speaker's body and mind, another for illegitimate relatives and his loincloth, a third his possessions and gifts (Kluckhohn 1949a:125).

Even distinctions between masculine and feminine, singular and plural, past, present, and future, and linguistic indications of preferences for identifying certain colors while ignoring others or for highlighting items rather than actions (as mentioned above) manifest this "coherent though unconscious philosophy." A fascinating example of different philosophical assumptions between English and Greek may be illustrated from the fact that the Greek word *opiso* may mean either "behind" or "in the future." Americans find such a combination illogical, since we (implicitly and unconsciously) picture time as a kind of substance that sits still while we move through it. The underlying assumption of Greek worldview in this regard was quite different. Greeks saw themselves standing still while future time moved up on them from behind, passed them, and then moved on into the past. The past was what they faced and the future lay behind them (Kluckhohn 1949a:127). Such a view is, of course, quite logical on the basis of their philosophical (worldview) assumptions, but quite illogical on the basis of ours.

In the American Indian language Wintu, the worldview assumption that it is important to know the nature of the credibility of a given report comes to the surface in an interesting way. A report such as "Harry is chopping wood" would have to be expressed in one of five ways, depending on whether the speaker knows this by hearsay, direct observation, or inference with high, medium, or low plausibility. The speaker has to indicate grammatically whether he directly observed the event, heard about it, or simply noticed that such an event seemed to have happened and that his inference seems highly possible, not very possible, or somewhere in-between.

Perhaps such illustrations are sufficient to indicate that

> Any language is more than an instrument of conveying ideas, more even than an instrument for working on the feelings of others for self expression. Every language is also a means of categorizing experience. The events of the "real" world are never felt or reported as a machine would do it. There is a selection process and an interpretation in the very act of response. Some features of the external situation are highlighted; others are ignored or not fully discriminated (Kluckhohn 1949a:129).

The structuring of a society's worldview is probably more obvious to the outsider through the analysis of such features of the language than in any other way. Though not all of the worldview will be identifiable in this way, a large number of the basic premises and categories in terms of which the people perceive and think, plus a general view of their world, will be evident from an analysis of the language.

The final thing we want to say about language as a vehicle for culture is that it is the primary means of enculturation or socialization—the process by means of which children learn to be and behave as adults. Children are pressed into the worldview of their culture primarily through their language. All the things we have said above concerning how the structuring of a people's language channels the basic perceptions and expressions of that people apply to the process by means of which children develop those habits.

Whether the worldview of a society focuses on items or activities, whether it advocates dichotomizing or seeing things in continuum, whether it discriminates eleven colors or three, whatever is valued at the heart of a culture is taught and reinforced to newcomers via the mirroring of these values in language.

LANGUAGE AND THE CROSS-CULTURAL WITNESS

What are the implications of these insights into language for the cross-cultural witness? First of all, we need to be clear that *our aim is to learn the people and their culture, not just to learn the language.* As we have pointed out above, the best way to learn the worldview of a culture is through learning the language. This is the most direct route into the heart of a culture.

Learning a language is one of the hardest things any of us ever have to do. Learning our first language was very difficult, though most of us don't realize how hard we had to work at it. Learning a second language is even more difficult, due primarily to the interference of our first language habits, but also due to the fact that as we get older, our ability diminishes to fight those habits in order to replace them with other habits. Any language is difficult to learn, but it is a necessary first step.

The thing that helps me most in facing such a difficult task is to recognize that on the other side of that language barrier are wonderful, exciting people. It helps me to talk about *learning people*, not simply about learning language. You have to learn language in order to learn people, but learning people is an exciting thing. That keeps one pushing through the drudgery and difficulty of learning the language.

As the Brewsters (1982) keep reminding us, language learning is a *social*, not merely an academic activity. A language cannot be learned primarily from books. *Language is a people thing and must be learned primarily from people*—people who are engaged as much as possible in normal life activities. This can only be done by participating in life situations. Not that nothing useful can be learned in a classroom, but if the classroom becomes the major situation, most of what a person needs to know to function effectively in the life of the people will have been missed. At the start of language learning, it may be advisable to spend time working privately with a language helper. But as soon as possible, and as often as possible, language learners need to get into a more natural environment—into the familiar territory of the host people. This is, of course, both frightening and embarrassing, but there is no other way if we want to learn well.

It helps to learn *how* to learn a language, and there are now courses to help us with this problem. The foremost teacher of language learning is Dr. Betty Sue Brewster, of the Fuller School of World Mission faculty (*see* Brewster and Brewster 1982). Her and her late husband's calling has been to help westerners to fight against nearly everything we have learned in schools (where we are taught to be taught rather than taught to learn under our own guidance), in order to teach people how to take charge of their own language learning experience and learn a language effectively. A major part of such a course is to learn what languages are like. Another part is to learn how to organize oneself. Still another part is to learn to handle the extreme embarrassment of a language learning experience.

Those who learn languages best are those who 1) have an intense drive to communicate with the people on the other side of that language barrier and 2) are able to swallow their pride and accept and even enjoy being laughed at. Children accept being laughed at, but we adults tend to shrivel and give up when we are laughed at. In a new language and culture we try something simple and botch it, so we get laughed at and we figure the people are telling stories behind our back (which, of course, they are—we do too when foreigners make mistakes with our language and culture). But we, like those who come to our country, are entering like little children into another society and must get over this fear of being laughed at. Indeed, we must learn to laugh at ourselves if we are ever to survive.

One of the other problems is that many people are so polite that they will never tell us when we make a mistake. The best language helper is someone who will laugh at us or in some other way tell us when we're making a mistake. I had a good language helper once who got lazy and stopped correcting me. I don't blame him for getting lazy. Helping someone learn your language is a desperately boring and frustrating job. But my future was at stake so, to test him, I deliberately made a mistake. He let the mistake stand, so I said to him, "I just made a mistake." This woke him up, and he asked me to say it again. I repeated it for him, and he agreed that I had made a mistake. "But you told me I was doing fine," I said. "If this continues, I'm going to speak this language badly, and people will ask, 'Who taught you?' I'll tell them and they'll simply conclude that you are not a good language teacher." This approach was very effective, since he was quite concerned about his reputation and I had attached my ability in the language to his prestige as a language teacher.

It is absolutely incumbent upon us who claim to be bringing a message of love from God to demonstrate that love by learning the language well. Learning the language well and accurately is an important way to demonstrate God's love. Since our actions speak much louder than our words, it is no good trying to convince a people that God loves them if our own inability in their language is perceived by them as a constant reminder of the falsity of what we claim.

This fact has never come across to me so forcefully as in an experience I had in Nigeria relating to a non-Christian linguist who was living in the area at the time. He had the reputation of being a homosexual (which was a custom quite abhorrent to the Nigerians). But he also lived with them, accepted them, learned their language and culture well, and in these and other ways, demonstrated what they perceived to be love for them. Some of my friends came to me one day asking, "How come this fellow loves us more than you missionaries do?" In reply, I asked "How do you know he loves you more than we do?" They replied, "First of all, he learns our language well. Secondly, he lives with us. He doesn't live in a castle like you people do!" What a horrible indictment! I'm not at all sure his actions were motivated by love (though they might have been). It was obvious, though, that he had learned their language better than the missionaries in that area (many of whom had been there much longer than he).

My feeling is that if we love people the way we say we do, the first priority is to learn their language and learn it well. If we spend forty years in cross-cultural ministry and do nothing but learn the language, we will probably be communicating Christianity more effectively than in any other way! I really believe that the most important thing we can ever do is to learn and use the language well. By doing that we show them politeness, love, concern, and we probably will not have to preach to them. They will know that God loves them. Why? Because we have learned their language well. And, as the Brewsters point out, *language learning is ministry* (1982).

I can make a statement such as the above because Christianity is so well demonstrated by those who take a learning posture. If we truly choose to assume a learning posture, we will automatically do a lot of things in a Christian way. For one thing, learners are seldom arrogant, they seldom assume that they know more than their teachers. If we respect and treat the people we go to as our teachers, we will be demonstrating the love of God to them. We will be very complimentary to them, very polite, very loving. We will ask them what they know and try to learn it. We will ask them their advice, whether it's language learning or culture learning or whatever. We will sit at their feet rather than being tempted to lord it over them. I think the example of Jesus is very important in this regard. He sat at the feet of the people of His society for thirty years before He started His public ministry. That may be a little longer than we have available to us, but it's a good example to follow. We, like Jesus, will be more effective if we first learn from the people and then seek to minister to them, rather than to lord it over them.

As learners, then, the proper sequence of events in language learning (contrary to what is often practiced in classrooms) is first to listen, then to speak, and only then to read and write. That's the way children learn their language. They listen for a couple of years, and then parents are amazed when they suddenly speak things that the parent has no idea the child picked up. Many times we can play a tape recording of a language while we're doing other things and just listen and listen, to get our minds full of it. Then we begin speaking (not too soon). And only then do we try reading and writing.

I simply don't believe we can emphasize the importance of language too much. From my point of view, it is absolutely crucial to perform well in the heart language of a people (not simply in a trade language) if we are to adequately communicate God's love to them. Heart concepts such as Christian conversion and growth seldom mean what they ought to mean in any language but the heart (usually the first) language of a people. There is no better way than to imitate God in this respect. He became a full human being, one who spoke the language of those He came to like a native. Jesus spoke Galilean Aramaic (even though it had little prestige outside of Galilee) to reach the common people of Galilee. That's the example we are to follow, no matter how difficult it may be.

CHAPTER 16

COMMUNICATION: BEYOND LANGUAGE

INTEGRATIONAL THOUGHT

The Christ life is intended to be a life of joy. Even as the shadows lengthened over Jesus' earthly ministry, He told His followers that the purpose of His teaching was "that my joy may be in you and that your joy may be complete" (Jn 15:11). Joy is one of the fruits of the Spirit (Gal 5:22). We are to "rejoice in our life in union with Christ" (Phil 3:3). We are even to be joyful in suffering (1 Pt 4:12, 13) and to persevere in suffering as Jesus did "because of the joy that was waiting for him" on the other side of the cross (Heb 12:2).

For most of the peoples of the world (including the Hebrews of the Old Testament), joy is expressed most visibly in song and dance. The Nigerians I lived among had no problem expressing even non-Christian joy with their bodies as well as their voices. How much greater was the desire of Christians to express themselves with their whole being! Their worldview not only allows bodily movement, it demands that singing be accompanied by dancing (to the chagrin of many western missionaries).

How, then, did the Christianity of much of the western world (including that in which I was brought up) get so somber? My generation of western evangelicals has been carefully taught that emotion is bad, especially if it is expressed in bodily movement.

To quote something on this subject that I've written elsewhere:

> My ancestors came from northern Europe. They had conformed Protestantism to their own stolid, unemotional image. They believed that emotion and overt expression of feelings are bad, especially for men. A cardinal rule of behavior is, don't let anyone know how you're feeling. If it feels good or bad, it probably is wrong unless, of course, the feeling is guilt. . . .
>
> Adultness and feelings don't mix. "Be a man," I was told as a boy, "don't show your emotions." The worldview assumption is that emotion, feeling, closeness, and bodily expression in general are improper adult behavior, especially for men.
>
> As members of the Anglo segment of American society, we are carefully taught to control our emotions (except at athletic events). And anti-emotionalism gets built into our Christianity as if it were a cardinal doctrine. Church life, then, becomes primarily a matter of "will" surrounded by intellect. We can sing, but don't dare to wiggle (Kraft 1992b:10, 53).

How different is the biblical picture! The Hebrews were very much into song and dance. They also were strong in other arts such as storytelling (e.g., parables), drama (e.g., the books of Jonah and perhaps Job are considered by some to be written in the form of dramas (*see* LaSor et al. 1982:353, 574), and poetry/song (e.g., Psalms). This provides the foundation for New Testament Christianity.

It is interesting to imagine what joyful, expressive Christianity would be like if we ever got beyond our cultural conditioning. Perhaps we can learn from the Pentecostals and Charismatics!

Though the New Testament doesn't mention dance except incidentally (Mt 14:6; Mk 6:22; Lk 15:25), it strongly recommends singing in passages such as Ephesians 5:18–20 and Colossians 3:16. In both passages, singing is connected with thanksgiving, while in the former it is also connected with the filling of the Spirit. "Do not get drunk with wine, which will only ruin you; instead, be filled with the Spirit. Speak to one another with the words of psalms, hymns, and sacred songs; sing hymns and psalms to the Lord with praise in your hearts. In the name of our Lord Jesus Christ, always give thanks for everything to God the Father" (Eph 5:18–20).

Our intellectual understandings need the balance of emotional expression if we are to experience all of the joy that is our heritage. "Christ's message in all its richness" (Col 3:16) can only live in our hearts if we give ourselves to both ends of the equation. We are called to joy. Let's not settle for less.

INTRODUCTION

Art is a western word for a body of cultural material, but that name betrays a bias concerning the material. The term "art," at least in American society, signifies something that we ordinarily consider to be in the recreation or play area of life and have pretty much pushed to the periphery of our culture. What we are referring to includes drawing pictures (graphic art), making statues or other kinds of sculptures (plastic art), music, dance, drama, storytelling, and the like. In many traditional societies, these are very central to the life of the people.

I know a Christian professor who specializes in cross-cultural art who found among an important tribal group of West Africa that the communication of the Christian message has been significantly blocked because their art is so important to them and is regarded as pagan by the missionaries. She was able to gain a high degree of rapport with the people because her interests were so similar to theirs. Her theory is that if the missionaries would learn to be positive rather than negative toward the art that is so central to their value system, these people would soon be receptive to the Gospel.

I wonder how many of the world's peoples are like this, and how often we who are westerners may reduce the attractiveness of the Gospel because of our biases in this area. Often by evaluating the artistic expressions of the people to whom we go as if their behavior has our meanings, we come up with improper understandings of them. Our assumptions concerning what their activities mean often keep us from really trying to find out what meanings they attach to them.

DEFINITION AND FUNCTIONS

Art may be briefly and broadly defined as any cultural behavior that involves an esthetic dimension. Artists typically attempt to create something that will please an audience at the sensory or emotional level. For the originating artists (and also for any intermediary artists such as musical or dramatic performers), the creation is expressive. For the audience, it is intended to be pleasurable. For all involved, communication takes place. Creative skill is important at the artist's end. Interpretive skill is important for the receptors if they are to derive pleasure or receive messages from the object or behavior.

Artists may seek to express themselves by producing either material or non-material objects (e.g., pictures or songs) or performances (e.g., dances or the singing of songs). Among the cultural behaviors in view here would be activities such as *singing, playing music, dancing, drama, oratory, drawing, sculpting, carving, or even, on occasion, playing a game*. Such behavior often results in cultural products such as pictures, songs, statues, speeches, and the like.

Human beings seem to be incurably artistic, some more so than others. Indeed, many people are apt at transforming certain rather ordinary activities into artistic productions of one sort or another. Many are artists with words, either orally or in print (and this is highly valued in many societies).

There are many functions of artistic behavior. The ten listed by Alan Merriam (1964) for music apply to any form of art: 1) Emotional expression, 2) Aesthetic enjoyment, 3) Communication, 4) Entertainment, 5) Symbolic representation, 6) Physical response, 7) Enforcing conformity to social norms, 8) Validation of social institutions and religious rituals, 9) Contribution to the continuity and stability of culture, and 10) Contribution to the integration of society. He might have added 11) Protest. Though we will focus primarily on the communicational function of artistic expression, most artistic events will also involve one or more of the other functions.

Much art can be performed. We may, therefore, speak of a *performance* function of art. This function is often the task of an intermediary, rather than of the original creator (e.g., when someone other than the creator of a song or drama performs it). Performance can be for the sake of communicating a message or for the sake of attracting attention to the performer. We will talk of the communicative use of performance below.

Many in the West regard artists (including musicians, dramatists, dancers, painters) primarily as performers whose main concern is to attract attention to themselves. We listen or watch and say, "Aren't they good?" "Don't they perform well?" Even in church we tend to have this kind of attitude toward artistic expression. Ordinary church members and many pastors so misunderstand the functions of music that they view choir and solo musical performances more as displays of ability than as valid and valuable communications of the messages intended by the words. The quality of a church's music program is often measured by the musical ability of the performers. As music communication specialist Roberta King has said,

> Although performance is involved whenever music is produced, we see [in 2 Chron 20:21–22] that the ultimate priority in the use of music is utilitarian. It serves a purpose to either signal or communicate particular thoughts. That does not mean that musical performance is not without aesthetic standards or a certain level of competence. In 1 Chron 25:7, 8 David selects the most skillful musicians to bring praise to the Lord. Note though that praising the Lord is the priority and performance skill is only a prerequisite for such service. Church musicians today often reverse this and attempt to make a display of technical skill the priority rather than seeking to lead in worship or minister through music (1983:28).

Though performance and expression are legitimate uses of art, our focus here will be on its use in *communication*. Even when artists are simply trying to express themselves, they are communicating something, though it may just be to show off their abilities. The communicative function of art goes much farther than this, however. In traditional societies, what we call art is usually among the most important vehicles for education and the sending of a wide variety of other messages between the members of a society. We will deal with some of these later in the chapter.

For now, let us illustrate from western society how singing may be used for educational purposes. The story is told of a conversation that took place between John and Charles Wesley in which the concern was over the relative merits of preaching and singing as teaching devices. Reportedly, Charles claimed that he would be able to teach more Christian truth via his hymns than John would through his sermons. History has, of course, proven Charles right. Both in his day and in this, many of Charles Wesley's 6,500 hymns have probably been much more influential as vehicles for teaching Christian messages than all of the best sermons of John and many other preachers.

The value of songs as teaching devices is probably proportionately even greater in many traditional societies and in non-Christian sectors of western societies than it is in western churches. Everything in human experience that can be interpreted communicates something. One anthropologist (oversimplifying a bit) says, "Culture *is* communication" (Hall 1959). But not everything in culture conveys messages with equal effectiveness. Because the artistic vehicle is perceived as pleasant, messages thus transmitted often have very powerful impact. Forms such as music may, in addition, lead people into a kind of altered state of consciousness in which they are more vulnerable to the messages transmitted. In this chapter we want to deal both with art forms as vehicles for communication and the increase in impact the greater use of such forms can have in the communication of Christian messages.

Many human activities effectively combine an artistic dimension with a communicative one, providing something to admire along with another, "more substantial" message. Good teaching or preaching often combines both. This is what is meant when we talk of the "art" of teaching or preaching. Those of us who attempt to communicate to large audiences have a need (or are required) to express ourselves. If we do it well, we do it with a certain flair that is artistic. We may, at times at least, submit to the temptation to simply show off. At such times what gets across is our own expertise, which obscures whatever we are trying to teach. But even when we are not stealing the show from our material, so to speak, it feels good to be up front expressing ourselves in ways that get beyond the merely pedantic. We are meeting some of our own needs to be creative and expressive, and at the same time we're communicating something more. To be a good teacher involves being an artist. We need skillfulness and creativity in the way we communicate to our students.

The same is true of singers, actors, dancers, musicians, storytellers, poets, and the like. To the extent that they are concerned with communicating a message artistically, they, too, combine the expressive with the communicative functions to whatever extent they are allowed by the medium they use. Not all media allow the same flexibility for communicating the same kinds of messages. Dance and instrumental music, for example, are ordinarily much more limited than drama and public speaking in dealing with cognitive messages. Public speaking, on the other hand, though suited to cognitive messages, is more limited in its appeal to the emotions. Whenever the message, whether cognitive or emotive in nature, is presented in a form not understood by the receptors, the latter are reduced to simply admiring the form in which the message comes.

ETHNOCENTRISM AND ART

There is a real tendency for westerners to be more ethnocentric about the artistic expressions of other societies than about almost any other aspect of culture. Perhaps this is because evaluations of the good and the bad are so subjective and unconscious. We have learned well to distinguish what we have been taught is "good art" from what we have been taught is "poor art" within our own society and socioeconomic class. Since we are in the habit of judging our own art forms by standards that we usually label good or bad, it's not uncommon for us to judge other people's forms accordingly. We judge art forms as good or bad depending on whether we like or dislike them, and simply carry this habit over into our evaluations of the customs of other peoples.

Many evangelicals seem to have fallen into the trap of evaluating as bad or evil or even satanic a whole series of forms of art they don't approve of. Whether it be rock music, slow dancing, drums in church, modern art, or some other type of expression, people tend to condemn the forms as evil rather than the meanings. Many of our churches have had conflicts over the introduction of new musical forms. The tendency is to unconsciously judge the new forms as good or bad merely on the basis of the preferences of our social group. Because we have become accustomed to making such judgments in our own society, we're already set up to begin with a critical mind cross-culturally. When we get into a cross-cultural situation and don't understand the meaning that the form is expressing, we feel very free to judge it negatively.

What people who condemn artistic forms as satanic mean is that Satan can and regularly does use these forms for his purposes. Furthermore, there are certain musical groups that make no secret of the fact that they are serving and working under the power of Satan. Our enemy is quick and persistent in his attempts to use whatever people allow him to use to carry out his schemes. Those who condemn artistic forms are right that Satan can and does use these forms, but the problem does not lie in the forms, as they suppose. It lies in the meanings associated with them in the minds of the people who use them. Particularly for new converts who have recently been immersed in those forms in worldly settings, these associations are often such that it is very easy for Satan to use those forms to drag people back into servitude to him.

But this same rule applies to every cultural form, even those often regarded as sacred. Satan frequently uses hymns, the Bible (see Lk 4:1–13), sermons, church buildings, church organizations, people who are committed to Christ (see Mt 16:23), and anything else he can. Working through his people, our enemy can use and empower any cultural form. But so can God. Satan is a counterfeiter; he depends on his ability to misuse cultural forms created by God or humans for better purposes.

In their home culture, missionaries feel relatively confident that they can make the necessary discriminations between whether it is God, Satan, or simply human beings behind any given artistic form. In cross-cultural settings, however, many missionaries found it impossible to discern who was behind what. Everything looked so strange, and it was easy to equate strangeness with evil. In fear of what was strange and, from their point of view, considered evil, such missionaries condemned virtually all artistic expression as satanic or at least immoral. After all, they reasoned, weren't such customs usually associated with religious rituals?

Again, however, *if there is evil in these media, it lies not in the media themselves but in any evil use made of them or in any empowerment of them by satanic power.* If they are used in pagan religious ceremonies, they have probably been dedicated to pagan gods or spirits. That power needs to be broken before they can even be considered for Christian usage. Even then, the strength of the pagan associations people have in their minds might be such that these forms should not be used, at least in the first generation.

By condemning a people's art, missionaries have often given the impression that God is against all, or nearly all, of the people's way of life. For the converts in tribal and peasant societies, this made suspect most of their traditional communicational, educational, and recreational systems. Even in industrial societies, such prohibitions negatively affect much of the richness and creativity of the Christian segment.

Nevertheless, in much of today's world, Christians do well to carefully evaluate the messages coming via television, videos, movies, and certain print media. One undesirable aspect of free societies is the fact that authors and producers with money and contacts are able to expose us all to their sometimes sick or evil fantasies via these media. They often use this opportunity to powerfully communicate to us and our children that acting like the purely fictional characters in their films and books is both normal and free of negative consequences.

The real problem lies not in any of the various forms of art but in the possibility of satanic empowerment and in the meanings people may attach to them. Though our ethnocentrism is applied largely to cultural forms, we need to learn another focus, a focus on meanings and empowerment. With this focus we will often come out questioning many of the same things that were questioned in previous generations. But we will be focused at a deeper, more important level and therefore able to avoid making the kind of unwise (and unchristian) blanket condemnations that plague both western and nonwestern churches to this day.

For example, in my generation, we were simply told that Christians should not dance, as if everything labeled "dance" was automatically evil. The problem was that we were taught to focus on forms, rather than on meanings. In this case the form was anything labeled "dance." This type of approach was carried to the mission fields of the world and activities labeled "dance" condemned, whether or not they were similar to the objectionable practices in the home country. This was done in our part of Nigeria without realizing that what was being condemned was much more like western games than like the western dancing the missionaries objected to. Indeed, the indigenous words used for Nigerian dancing would be more appropriately translated "playing." In the objectionable western dancing, a man and a woman hold each other close and move together. The Nigerians, however, danced in a circle, always men with men and women with women. They moved their bodies and kept time to the beat of the drum, but it was far from the same as western ballroom dancing.

The Nigerians also used this kind of game in ceremonies such as funerals and religious observances. In such cases, perhaps it could rightly be contended that the practice was inappropriate for Christians, since both empowerment and meaning issues might be prominent in such settings, but even this fact does not provide sufficient reason for condemning the practice whenever it occurred. The missionaries' principle seemed to be: always be suspicious of anything African (especially if it involves emotion or drums or bodily movement or "pagan" music). In our suspicion, we first condemned, then taught against, then, after a period of time, let the people make their own choice.

The reason lying behind such suspicion is fear of syncretism. Syncretism is the mixing of Christian meanings with pagan meanings in such a way that the result is not really Christian, though it may on the surface look like Christianity (*see* chapter 27 for more on this subject). There is good reason to fear syncretism. One of the last things we (and God) desire is to have people who look like Christians but really aren't. But the fear, like that of the man in the Parable of the Talents who buried what his master had given him, is *a fear of risk*, not a fear of the known (*see* Kraft 1979a:18–21 on risk). Often our definition of what Christians should look like is so conformed to what we see (or, usually, what we idealize) in our own society that we are suspicious of anything that doesn't look the same. We look at any given activity in another society (especially activities that seem to relate to their religion) and, often with little understanding of the significance of those activities and little advice from insiders who have not already been taught our biases, we constitute ourselves, as Reyburn once said, *judge and jury without really knowing the meaning of the trial*.

It seems to be characteristic of Euroamericans that our way of handling fear of the unknown is to prohibit it (if we have the power to do so). In this case, we seem to be afraid that if we don't immediately prohibit suspicious activities, we will find ourselves endorsing something that will later turn out to be syncretistic. We are afraid of that risk, probably due to the fear that neither the people nor God will be able to get out of a poor situation later on (*see* Smalley 1958a concerning our paternalism toward God), so we make what is often the worst choice of all—to condemn the practice.

At least two serious consequences then follow. First, without intending to, our condemnation of certain things (music, dance) leads many to the conclusion that large portions, if not all, of their culture are unworthy of God's using them. Second, we push them strongly toward a kind of syncretism that is at least as bad as the one we have tried to avoid. There are at least two kinds of syncretism. The one commonly spoken about occurs when the receiving peoples retain many of their own practices with their indigenous meanings and mix them with practices that look Christian. The other occurs when they adopt foreign (Christian) forms wholesale but retain their own meanings. When people feel pressured (whether or not we intended it) to do virtually everything in a western way, they inadvertently fall into this second type of syncretism.

ART, FORMS AND MEANINGS

All of this raises for us again the importance of the distinction between forms, meanings, uses, and functions (chapter 9). The mistake many early cross-cultural witnesses fell into was the automatic assumption that the forms of the receiving culture meant the same thing to those people that they would mean to Euroamericans if the latter practiced them. Without a good understanding of surface and deep culture, they tended to judge on the basis of their own interpretational reflexes (*see* Kraft 1979a:131–4). They assumed that any given cultural form always carries the same meaning—the meaning that they, the representatives of Christianity, attached to it. As we have frequently pointed out here, such is not the case.

In art, as in every other aspect of culture, the meanings of the forms are attached by those whose world the given culture defines, on the basis of shared agreements. Thus, whatever the art form, outsiders cannot be sure they understand the meaning until they understand what the insiders' agreements are. None of these forms has universal meanings.

I became more aware than usual of this fact during one discussion with some Nigerian church leaders. The topic was which parts of a traditional dance (game) would be acceptable and which unacceptable for use when Christians gathered for fellowship and recreation. The list they came up with (on the basis of what things would mean to those who participated) was fairly predictable to me, with two exceptions. First, they agreed that certain drumbeats should not be used, since they would not glorify Christ. This I would not have thought of, since I did not distinguish the connotations of the various beats as they did. When they had finished their list, however, they had not mentioned something that to me seemed an obvious practice to disallow, so I asked, "What about the bodily movements that many of the women make when they dance?" "Oh," they said, "there's nothing wrong with those. They're just ordinary sexual movements."

To me, of course, the fact that these were sexually oriented was just the point. I, coming from my background, felt such movements could have no place in an event that was to glorify Christ. But to them and their people, there was no problem. Certain forms that I would have included (the drumbeats) were a problem to them, while some of the forms that I would have excluded as not appropriate (the women's movements) turned out not to have a negative meaning for them. Here again we see that the meanings of cultural forms are in the people who do the interpreting, not in the forms themselves.

Even apart from the meaning differences, at the form level, the art subsystems of a culture are, like the language (or any other subsystem) likely to be structured quite differently from the corresponding subsystem in another culture. This being true, we cannot, from a cross-cultural point of view, speak of a single worldwide type of music or art, any more than we can speak of a single language. We must speak of "musics" or "arts." Each subsystem works according to the rules of the particular cultural system it is a part of, at least until the insiders change those rules.

Many (perhaps most) of the musics of the world, for example, are structured around a five-note scale (called pentatonic), rather than around a seven-note scale (called heptatonic), as are most western musics. Furthermore, in many musical systems it is the beat or rhythm that is central, rather than the melody (as with traditional western music). In fact, since probably half of the world's languages are tone languages, melody-based music often creates quite a bit of confusion. In tone languages, the pitch of each syllable or word is crucial to the interpretation of that utterance, so it is important that the pitch patterning of the music follow the words rather than, as in western musics, the words accommodating to the melody.

When you take a melody from the West and put words to it from a tone language, you frequently end up with rather serious distortion. Often two syllables will be an intelligible word if pronounced with a high-high tone pattern but will be nonsense if pronounced with a high-low pattern (e.g., Hausa *ruwa* with a high-high pattern means "water"; with any other pattern, it is nonsense). This is not, however, as serious as when such a combination of syllables is a completely different word when the pitch levels are different. I have heard Dr. Nida refer to a group in Liberia who were supposed to be singing the chorus, "Precious name, oh how sweet; Hope of earth and joy of heaven." But the tune so reassigned the pitch patterns that it came out, "Well done chicken, oh how sweet . . ." The people, not knowing they were supposed to be singing about anything other than the missionaries' favorite meal, thought things were fine!

Missionaries usually made such mistakes innocently. We have been accustomed to singing our faith and have simply introduced the only kind of music we know—western music. The fact that our Euroamerican music botches up the tone patterns of the language is something westerners discovered too late, often long after the national Christians had developed two important (and misleading) habits: that of singing our tunes to God and assuming that God wants it this way. Often their indigenous religion presents God (or gods) as unintelligible. How are they to know that the Christian God, unlike their own, seeks to be intelligible?

Take any western hymn, pick out any word in it that is repeated several times, and note the variety of pitch patterns assigned to that word by the melody in its various occurrences. Then imagine that hymn translated into any of the thousands of the world's tone languages (e.g., the Chinese languages, most African languages) with the translated word occurring in each of these places in the song with each of the various pitch patterns. Assume, then (as is often the case), that each time those syllables combine with a different pitch pattern, the result is a completely different word with a different meaning. Now imagine the confusion this must bring to the minds of people who understand even less of what is going on than we do and little or nothing of what is intended.

Such situations (and they occur frequently) make it necessary for the nationals to read the words silently to themselves, attaching the proper tones as best they can to discover what the words are intended to mean. Then, as they sing them, they have to turn off something in their minds in order to do so with understanding. This is standard procedure in Chinese churches and many others. It is an unnecessary burden, detracting and garbling the message, in contrast to the enhancement of the message usually experienced when it is presented in musical form.

In a discussion such as this, we need to be very careful that we do not go to the extent of denying the sincerity of those missionaries who took the kind of position we are questioning. Most of them did the best they could, far better than we might expect, given the limitations of their preparation. Had we been in their place, we probably would have done even worse. However, if God has helped us to understand things in a better way, today we are accountable for that better way. We have no excuse if we duplicate old mistakes. We will undoubtedly make plenty of mistakes of our own, but they should not be the same ones (we should be more creative than that!). With this recognition, I believe we should take responsibility for their mistakes and try, as politely as possible, to help those who are hindered in their relationship to God by them.

In recognizing that the issue is meaning rather than form, we should not go to the extreme of uncritically endorsing every practice in order to right the mistakes we believe earlier generations may have made. That would be as foolish as it is unfortunate. But we do want to contend that God can use most, if not all, of the cultural forms of any culture, even many of those that were once used exclusively by Satan, as long as the meanings are changed and the empowerment broken so that it is now Christ who is glorified.

In many societies, music and other artistic forms were more often condemned by first-generation Christians than by the missionaries. Often this was the right decision, at least for that generation, but the decision was right because the meanings were wrong for the people of that generation, not because the forms were evil forever and ever. For this reason, whatever was done in the first generation needs to be reevaluated in the second and third generations, to see whether it might now be possible to use some of these things, since over the passage of time the meanings change.

Let me illustrate from a western situation. For some of his Christian hymns, Martin Luther chose tunes regularly used as drinking songs. This both facilitated recognition and communicated the message that God is pleased to use familiar cultural forms rather than only those imported from other places and times. But what kind of impact might that music have had on somebody for whom it symbolized the drunken state in which he lived before turning to Christ? Probably such people struggled with those tunes all the time. Probably the tunes were not very worshipful for them since they dredged up memories of their past life that they would like to forget. In that first generation, it may not have been a good idea to use those songs for Christian purposes with those people.

This kind of thing happened in Mexico with the instrument we call a marimba. The first generation said it was used for the devil, and they wanted no part of it. A later generation did not have the same associations and reintroduced the instrument for Christian music. Without necessarily condemning the choices made in the first generation, it is often possible to reintroduce indigenous music and other art forms for Christian purposes at a later date.

USE OF ART IN ENCULTURATION

As mentioned at the start of this chapter, what we westerners call art and largely relegate to the periphery of our cultural awareness is often much more central in the life of nonwestern peoples. Even though this area of culture is often not in focus for westerners, there is much communication that takes place through these vehicles at a subconscious level. We could rightly contend that these cultural vehicles are at least as important in western contexts as in nonwestern, even though often less in focus.

In this section we will highlight the important function served by art in the *enculturation or education of children*. We will look at folklore, music, and drama/dance as means used for this purpose.

1. *Folklore* is a term commonly used to label a large group of practices including myths, legends, fables, proverbs, riddles, and the like. Technically, *myths* are stories that usually embody a good bit of truth, even though there is seldom the same concern for factuality that westerners feel necessary. The key function of myth is to explain how things got to be the way they are and how they stay that way. Unlike the way the word *myth* is used popularly, in this technical usage, the word has no connotations of untruthfulness. Many who have a high view of biblical inspiration are able to recognize that, in this technical sense, certain portions of the Bible (notably Gn 1–11) can be classified as myth. It is unfortunate that the ordinary usage of this term connotes untruthfulness. Evangelicals usually try to avoid using the term, even in the technical sense, to refer to scriptural materials,

lest they be misinterpreted as questioning the authority of the Scriptures. Here we will use the term in the technical sense (though we will not be applying it to the Bible).

The term *legend* is used for a story, usually of some past event, considered important by a people. Legends, like myths, often have some basis in fact that is no longer verifiable. *Fables and tales*, on the other hand, tend to be totally ficticious and are not expected to relate to either the origins or the history of a people. The telling and hearing of them is largely just for fun, but since they embody culturally characteristic ways of picturing and thinking about reality, their value as teaching tools is great. *Riddles* usually involve some sort of competition but, like fables, also embody culturally characteristic ways of picturing and thinking about reality. *Proverbs* are pithy ways of stating agreed-upon wisdom.

a. Through folklore, children are taught the society's explanation of how things got to be the way they are and why they remain that way. Myths and legends are the primary vehicles of such information. Almost every people has an explanation of where they came from, how they got to where they are, and why things continue the way they are. There is usually an origin myth that embodies a lot of truth, usually with a lot of additional elaboration. It is interesting to observe the similarities between biblical accounts and the origin myths of many peoples.

b. In addition to such explanations, folklore is also used to teach and support a society's worldview assumptions and values. This is done largely through such vehicles as proverbs, fables, and moralistic stories. Such vehicles are powerful methods for teaching and enabling people to remember their basic assumptions and values, since they enable people to picture reality as their society perceives it. The loss of such a system is a serious loss for any society.

c. A third way that folklore is used in the enculturation process is to train children in logic and thinking. This is done through all types of folklore, since each story, proverb, or riddle exhibits the logic of the society. The logic of one people is not necessarily the same as that of another, of course, so an uninformed outsider may not easily see the folklore's value in this respect. For those who recognize the value of folklore in enculturation, however, collecting, learning, and studying these vehicles can be a useful way to get into the heart of the culture more quickly (and more enjoyably) than would otherwise be possible. In addition, if you collect, study, and learn proverbs, riddles, and fables, you will be highly respected and loved by the people you serve. Such materials tend to be close to the hearts of people, and those outsiders who learn them get closer to the people's hearts than would be the case otherwise. Respect for and knowledge of a people's folklore is (like language ability) frequently interpreted as love for them.

In this type of educational system, repetition and memorization are extremely important. Often songs will be used at key points in a folktale to facilitate retention. Children hear, then tell and retell a folktale. In the process of retelling, they learn much of the information and values they need to function effectively as adults. They also often learn to like to hear the same stories repeated. Here in the West, we may start a joke or story with a statement such as, "If you've heard this one, stop me." With this as my habit, I've been surprised on a number of occasions to have Nigerians refuse to stop me because they wanted me to tell it again. In fact, often they would prefer an old, established story to a new one.

It is typical of tribal and peasant peoples to like such repetition. In addition, because they value the art of storytelling, they are usually eager to hear how each storyteller will interpret or embellish the story. They will then sit around and participate in the story and chime in with any details missed or altered by the storyteller. This is their familiar way of learning and demonstrating their oneness with each other. The introduction of Scripture stories into this kind of format is, in spite of the fact that the stories come from outside of their traditions, usually a much more effective way of communicating biblical truth than is western preaching. Repetition is especially important.

As mentioned above, we in the West tend not to take folklore very seriously. We tend to focus more on what we call history and science (without realizing how similar in validity many of our ideas in these areas are to what we call myth or legend in other people's cultures). For westerners, history and science have become our mythology (in the technical sense), but several generations ago, westerners also taught their children through myths, legends, and fables. Many of what we now call fairy tales have at the end of the story a sentence like, "The moral of the story is . . . ," followed by a proverb or other type of wise saying. It is interesting to see that our ancestors, like many in contemporary traditional societies, once made use of such vehicles to teach their children the important things in life.

When, however, we turned to schools (and away from homes) as the primary vehicle of education, we turned away from such a use of folklore and, more recently, pretty much away from teaching the moral content of those stories as well. Now, except for the occasional parents who continue to tell (usually read) stories to their children, we have allowed this powerful means of education to disappear.

The fact that westerners now regard the use of folklore as purely play and tend not to take it seriously often affects our attitude toward what we see (or often fail to see because we are not looking for it) in other societies. The early missionaries (and many quite recent ones as well), because they saw nothing that looked like a school, concluded that the people had no educational system. They introduced schools and (as had happened earlier in western societies) inadvertently moved the children away from a system that focused on the family-centered passing on of moral instruction and practical skills to the school-centered passing on of information, much of which has very little practical value. We will deal more with schools in chapter 17. Suffice it to say here that the change from a folklore, family-based educational approach to a western school approach is invariably detrimental, both to the arts-based communication system and to the ability of the society to pass on moral and practical learning to younger generations.

2. *Music* (often including *drama and dance*) is another important vehicle of enculturation. It is frequently used along with and as part of the telling of folktales, myths, legends, and the like. Thus nearly everything said above about these vehicles can apply to music as well. But music is often used by itself as well or, in many societies, invariably with dance. In such societies, they make little or no distinction between music without dance and music with dance. They are seen, often along with drama, as inseparable parts of the same concept for many people.

Both in nonwestern and western societies, the words of songs are powerful conveyers of the values of the society. Something sung to a catchy tune or beat is much more likely to be repeated than something merely spoken. In addition, something sung to a catchy tune or beat is more likely to be regarded positively than something merely spoken. Knowing this, those who want to influence young people regularly package their messages in songs.

It is fascinating to see how children learn group interaction skills while participating together in song, drama, and dance. In many societies where adults are divided into "men's community" and "women's community," such structuring is very evident in the ways in which the children sing and dance together. It is probably a cultural universal that such children's play is an important part of their education. In addition, in many societies, children are welcome to participate in adult singing and dancing. For adults, such events serve to reinforce values. For the children, however, this is learning time. Beyond this, of course, children are taught through such participation with adults to place the same value on singing and dancing that the adults do. They also learn to use singing and dancing in the same contexts as do the adults (e.g., recreation, mourning, communal work, religion, keeping people in line through ridicule, courtship, etc.).

3. *Drama* (often including music and dance) is a third important vehicle of enculturation. In some societies there are many rituals that involve the acting out of historical events or the imaginative acting out of a predicted event (e.g., a hunt). These are teaching tools for instruction of the young, as are the stylized dramas used in rituals such as initiation, planting and harvest, worship and celebration. Children's games often involve some acting out of adult roles. These, too, are instructive.

4. *Graphic and Plastic Art* may also be used to teach the young. In some societies, the people carve their history into walls, doors, and other material items. Masks are used by some in rituals and dramas in which the young are instructed, as are figurines, statues, paintings, carvings, and the like.

OTHER COMMUNICATIONAL USES OF ART

In addition to enculturation messages, older generations frequently send other types of messages to the youth. Among such are *messages of authority and expertise*, in which adults let youth know who is in charge or who has which abilities, and *those that keep people in line*, where the basic message is that the youth must behave or suffer the consequences. Folklore, singing, drama, masks, and other art forms are frequently used as vehicles for such messages.

Youth, when desiring to send messages to adults, often choose one or another form of art. In many societies, youth sing, dance, dramatize, or draw their acceptance of or challenge to authority. In societies that allow youth a large measure of freedom (e.g., western), challenges to authority or outright rebellion may be expressed quite openly. In less-open societies, such expressions have to be more subtle. In such, subtle stories or riddles are often used.

Artistic expression is also *used to communicate horizontally* within a society, between people of the same generation or social group. One of the most important ways that art forms are used in a society is to strengthen group solidarity. Groupness is strengthened through participation in work songs, dances, rituals, dramas, graphic and plastic art, and the like that belong to the group and therefore strengthen group awareness and cohesion. National anthems serve this purpose for many societies. Often a group will use characteristic art forms such as particular designs that may be carved on cooking utensils, painted on clothing, or carved (i.e., through scarification) or painted on their bodies. Societies also bolster their cohesion through typical musical styles, musical instruments, housing (and other) decorations, clothing styles, and the like. Particular patterns identify persons as members of a given society; it's their badge of membership. In such ways, art forms are used to increase group solidarity.

Still another way art forms are used in intracultural communication is as *vehicles of competition* between individuals and groups. Riddling, story telling, singing, dancing, and drama contests are widely used. Indeed, in certain Alaskan societies, singing contests are conducted between accuser and accused as a means of determining guilt.

Art forms are also used for *release of tension*. Much singing and dancing (and drinking) takes place during Latin American fiestas. These are times when an uptight society has an institutional form for letting off steam. During the several days of fiesta, people are allowed to express themselves with an abandon that would not be allowed during the rest of the year.

USE OF ARTS IN CHRISTIAN WITNESS

What are the implications of a discussion such as this for cross-cultural witness? By and large, we westerners have imported our own forms of communication in preference to using the kinds of vehicles we are discussing here. Is this proper? Would it be more effective to make better use of traditional media of communication?

Such considerations, looked at from a communicational perspective, certainly provide a lot of food for thought. On the one hand, there are a lot of possibilities here for assisting people to feel that God wants to be a part of their innermost beings. Communication via these vehicles gets to people on their deepest level. On the other hand, this is a high-risk area. As in all areas of culture, there are no forms to which people do not attach meanings. The more intensely the meanings are felt, the greater the difficulty in converting people from attaching an old meaning to attaching a new one to any given form.

The thing that should help us greatly in choosing our approach is, I believe, a consideration of our attitudes and the alternatives available to us.

Our Attitudes

1. As we have noted above, much cross-cultural witness has been conducted on the assumption that indigenous vehicles of communication (except language) have been so infested with pagan meanings that they are largely unusable. The close association between indigenous religious ritual and, for example, dance, music, and art, has given many Christians (both outsiders and insiders) pause when they think of the possibility of using these vehicles for Christ.

2. Mixed in with this attitude is the western assumption that anything artistic that escapes the above judgment is simply play or recreation and therefore not to be seriously considered when looking for communication vehicles.

3. A third basic attitude has derived from the intense attachment of westerners to literacy and preaching. We have not even been able to picture (much less advocate) a Christianity that is not thoroughly grounded in Bible reading and the study of other helpful written materials. We seem to assume (in keeping with western evolutionary views of history) that anything God was able to do before Gutenberg (prior to the invention of the printing press) is inferior to what He has

been able to do since. We simply assume that God intends a rewiring of the communicational system of every society so that they, like us, will depend rather totally on literacy. We tend to ignore the great differences between messages that come through writing and those that come orally and to denigrate those societies that consider oral communication superior and do not get as excited as we over literacy (*see* Klem 1982 for more on this subject).

It is exciting to see the United Bible Societies now recognizing that the Bible needs to be put out in oral form if it is to be used by most of the world. Nearly all of the Bible was transmitted orally for at least one generation before it was committed to writing, and quite a bit of it was only in oral form for much longer. As it is "re-oralized" today, it is exciting to hear how different it is from written versions and how excited oral peoples get when they hear the Word in their preferred communicational vehicle. See Søgaard (1991 and 1993) for more on this subject.

Our assumptions concerning preaching also get in our way. Our English Bible translations use the word *preach* to represent quite a number of Greek and Hebrew words, each of which covers a wider (or different) area than the monologue, pulpit, usually rather intellectual type of presentation that the word preach signifies in English. In addition, it is rare that a scriptural example of what is labeled preaching is anything like the kind of formal, academic monologue that we experience regularly in our churches. Scriptural presentations were usually dialogic and seldom, if ever, academic.

Our tradition comes from western history, not from the Scriptures. In the first place, the scriptural words refer to a much wider range of communicational vehicles than our word *preach* allows. The main focus of the most frequently used New Testament word (*kerusso*) was on the outside source of the message (God), not (as with our word) on the method employed to get the message across (Friedrich 1965). Meanwhile, we have inherited a custom developed during Reformation times to meet the need of ordinary church members of that time for greater understanding of the Scriptures. The academic lecture, customary in the universities, was at that time made central in the church service (replacing the Mass) and has been passed down to us as if it were the only God-ordained way of organizing church services.

Though one could validly criticize the effects of our tradition on the communication of the Gospel in western societies (*see* Kraft 1991a), that is not the purpose here. Our aim is to point to the way our tradition has hindered our openness to the usefulness of a wide range of indigenous communicational structures.

The Alternatives

1. One alternative is to simply import our communicational forms, as has been widely done. I believe there have been great benefits to this. Many people can now read the Word for themselves.

The problem, as I see it, lies in the failure to also put the Gospel into indigenous communicational structures. This has often communicated loud and clear that God is western, fairly impersonal, and intellectual, and that He is at best suspicious of—and at worst condemnatory of—traditional vehicles of communication and expression. Among the results of this approach are the westernness, the powerlessness, and the deadness of much of the Christianity resulting from western missionary efforts. Though there is much in the Two-Thirds World to be optimistic about, most of the real success stories have involved God and His people overcoming this problem and making use of indigenous communicational structures. The great problem areas are where the syncretism forced by the heavy hand of western patterns of communication and expression is most evident.

2. A second alternative would be to simply use and endorse whatever traditional communicational forms are available. The advocates of Christianity could uncritically accept everything from storytelling to religious ritual as valid ways of communicating and expressing themselves before God. Much good might come from this approach, but a major result would probably be the kind of syncretism that happens when only the labels are changed (*see* Hiebert 1984).

I believe it would be wrong for the advocates of Christianity to adopt the attitude that people are better off if nothing is changed. Christianity requires change, and Christian witnesses coming from another society ought, in love, to make available to their receptors anything that would benefit them.

3. A third alternative presents itself—that of attempting to use both western and indigenous vehicles. This alternative is complicated by the fact that so many mistakes have already been made, so many problematic attitudes and habits already developed by nonwestern peoples. But there is a bright side: for many peoples, customary vehicles that to earlier generations would have conveyed meanings incompatible with Christian faith and growth no longer bear such a stigma. Like the Mexican marimba or the German drinking tunes that Luther used, these vehicles are often much more easily recognized by Christians as usable.

In addition, media that originated in the West are widely used in most nonwestern societies today. Electronic and print media can often be used in such a way that messages are transmitted in very appealing, traditional ways.

COMBINING MEDIA

A wise communicator will look for ways to use whatever media will get the job done best. Euroamericans tend to think first of such media as print, lectures, radio, film, and other media widely used in western societies. Within those techniques, Christians have tended to make less use of drama than of lectures and print. The latter media have been highly overvalued as vehicles for bringing about change. On the other hand, I believe there has been a failure on the part of most to properly value the impact of vocal music (though music is widely used) and drama (which is not so widely used).

In breaking out of such habits, both western and nonwestern church leaders need to give strong preference to utilizing those media that are preferred by and carry the greatest impact with the receivers of the Christian message. Traditional media are usually high on this list, often in combination with western oral media such as radio or cassette tapes. We can learn a lesson from Scripture in this regard. The original presentations of most parts of Scripture were storytold or sung. The materials are highly person oriented (the doctrine flows from ministry to persons) and were originally presented largely in person. The recording of these materials in writing has preserved them for us, but (as is always true of writing) at the sacrifice of most of that personalness. It remains, then, for the contemporary communicator of the Scriptures to "repersonalize" their content. This is especially important among peoples who do not have a long literary tradition and therefore find it quite difficult to do the necessary repersonalizing on their own.

The peoples of such oral societies (*see* Klem 1982), like most of the people of highly literate societies, respond best to the kinds of media discussed in this chapter. They can usually be reached and taught best through such vehicles as songs that rise from within the society and contain Scripture or doctrine, dramatization of Bible stories or stories of their own history, storytelling of Bible stories as daily devotions, graphic and plastic art symbolizing Christian events, and the like. Though there are a growing number of exciting experiments going on in this area (e.g., drama in Thailand, puppetry in Indonesia, use of indigenous music in many places), much more needs to be done to help people understand that God does indeed want to be close to them. Much of this can be helpfully done by increasing the present efforts to combine western oral media (radio, cassettes) with indigenous techniques.

Radio and cassette tapes are very effective in utilizing the values of and encouraging the greater use of such things as indigenous music styles (with Christian messages in the words), storytelling (especially storytelling biblical events), and drama (including the dramatization of Scripture stories and of true-to-life and real-life experiences). Film, video, and TV, though often too expensive or not available to a large percentage of the population, can also be effectively used with drama, song, dance, and the like. One very valuable way these media can be utilized is in portraying ordinary Christian life-styles to those asking the question, "What will my life be like if I become a Christian?" One experiment in Thailand found this usage to be very helpful in village evangelism (*see* Conklin 1984).

Overall, studies show radio and cassettes to be more usable than TV and film. Though the cost is often an important factor, a more important reason is that oral presentations (such as those through radio and cassette) are often more impactful than visual presentations since they allow and require more participation of the receivers, particularly in the use of their imagination. Allowing and requiring more creativity on the part of the receiver of a communication usually results in more effective communication. Some of these issues, with special focus on the use of cassettes, are helpfully discussed in Søgaard (1975).

Something that should not be missed in this discussion is the fact that the medium of the communication becomes an important part of the message received (*see* Kraft 1991a). Media familiar to and appreciated by the receptors usually affect the message and the response to it in a positive way. Foreign or unappreciated media often have the opposite effect. If we want people to receive the message and the God of the message warmly and to accept it as genuinely theirs, we must give solid attention to discovering which media do the best job of conveying that warmness. A message that comes through "our" media is more likely to be regarded as "our" message than one that comes through "their" media.

It is very significant to me that Jesus was a storyteller. We westerners are sermonizers, and there is a big difference between the effectiveness of a storytold message and a sermonized message. One of the most disappointing experiences I ever had in church was in northern Nigeria, where I listened to a Nigerian preaching in Hausa deliver a whole sermon without a single illustration or proverb! In Hausa and many other languages, whether in ordinary conversation or public oratory, any major point will ordinarily be made with at least one proverb or illustration, but this man had learned to sermonize in a Bible school with a western curriculum. He had learned his lessons so well that he earned the inattention of his audience, most of whom were ignoring him, not because his message was poor, but because his method was foreign. There was no art to the way he spoke, no drama, no eventness, no recognition of the fact that to communicate to his own people, he needed to storytell and use proverbs.

Jesus came from heaven to communicate in the most effective way. He told stories to a story oriented society (and made little use of literacy, even in a literate society). I think we ought to imitate Jesus instead of western preachers. Missionaries serving under Gospel Recordings are helping us to realize that if we want to communicate via tape, we shouldn't simply read the Bible. It needs to be storytold and, if possible, dramatized. To do this, they look for a storyteller (sometimes they even have to settle for a non-Christian), explain the biblical story, and have that person tell it in his or her own way. I believe this is what Jesus would have done, had He come to any of the 70 percent or more of today's nonreading people.

	MESSAGE		MEDIUM		IMPACT
	Content	Formulation	Form	Use	
Foreign	X				
Indigenous					

Figure 16.1 Message, medium, and impact chart

In northeastern Nigeria, we started using a drummer instead of bells to call people to church. What a novel idea! All over Africa at that time, people were called to church with a bell. After we made this change, more people came, since the drum told them the event belonged to them, not to outsiders. Those who beat the drums discovered that if they gathered the people early, the congregation could have a wonderful time dancing together outside the building before the service began. We also started using drums to accompany congregational singing in the church services. We found, however, that in our small buildings, the drums were too loud, so we used indigenous stringed instruments inside the building, restricting the drums to outside use. The fact that they could create their own songs and use their own musical instruments to express themselves worked powerfully to develop the feeling that Christianity really belonged to them. This is *their* Christianity, and the Christian God is not a foreign God to them. He not only speaks their language, He sings (and dances) their songs.

If we are to do the kind of job we need to do in using either indigenous or foreign media, we need some way of evaluating the media and their use. A chart such as figure 16.1 above has been helpful to some in this regard.

Some such device as this provides a way to evaluate the impact of the final message (including the message conveyed by the medium or media used). On it you can indicate which parts of the combination of message and medium in a given communication event are foreign and which arise from the indigenous cultural structuring (are culturally appropriate in terms of today's cultural structures). Some assessment of what the communicational impact of such an event might be can then be gauged.

Note that I have placed an X in the box relating to the content of the Christian message. Since this content comes from outside the culture, it will always be foreign to some extent. Often, however, we take this foreign Christian message to another people and formulate it in a way that is foreign, as did the Hausa preacher in the above example. His message was formulated in such a foreign manner that this added another layer of foreignness to the message. In addition, that man was using a foreign medium (preaching) in a foreign way.

On the above chart, we would evaluate that man's message by placing X marks in each of the boxes corresponding to foreign. The impact would also be evaluated as foreign. What the value of foreign impact would be differs from society to society. Some people highly value foreign things if they respect the source, while others are generally against foreignness. With respect to the Christian message, though, I suspect that a high degree of foreignness (with or without a respected source) always distorts the message to some extent, especially if that foreignness lies primarily in the way the message is presented.

If we evaluate another event in which the foreign message has been formulated in an indigenous way (e.g., through the use of indigenous illustrative vehicles, proverbs, patterns of logic, and the like) and then use an indigenous medium such as storytelling, song, or drama in an indigenous way, the impact can be very high. In addition, it is often possible to compensate in certain ways for the introduction of foreign elements into the communication process by balancing, say, foreign form with indigenous usage. For example, if the medium in use is a sermon (foreign form) but the way the message is formulated is highly culturally appropriate and the speaker uses a storytelling style (assuming that this is culturally appropriate), the impact can be very high, even though the vehicle is foreign. The problem with the Hausa speaker mentioned above was not that he was using a foreign medium but that he was using it in a foreign way. Likewise with a medium like radio or cassette. As mentioned above, simply reading Scripture (a foreign thing to do) over such media is likely to have quite a different impact than employing them to convey storytold Scripture stories. This would constitute some sort of indigenous use of foreign media.

CHAPTER 17

EDUCATION

INTEGRATIONAL THOUGHT

Education, as we emphasize below, is much more than the mere accumulating of information. This is the consistent position of the Scriptures, where terms such as "teaching" and "doctrine" refer more to the behavior inculcated than to the information assimilated. Paul knew this, since he instructed Timothy to warn his people "not to fight over words. [This] does no good, but only ruins the people who listen" (2 Tm 2:14).

An information orientation, whether in life in general or in Christianity, leads to a focus on and disputes over the correctness of words and concepts. This diverts attention from the real purpose of education—to learn to live, behave, and use knowledge in effective, profitable, and (in the case of Christians), Christ-glorifying ways. Instead, Timothy, "Do your best to win full approval in God's sight, as a worker who is not ashamed of his work, one who correctly teaches the message of God's truth" (2 Tm 2:15).

Note that Timothy is to win God's approval by working, that is, by behaving properly, by turning "away from wrongdoing" (v. 19), by "Avoid[ing] the passions of youth, and striv[ing] for righteousness, faith, love, and peace . . . keep[ing] away from foolish and ignorant arguments . . . be[ing] kind toward all, a good and patient teacher, who is gentle as he corrects his opponents" (vv. 22–25).

Full approval comes from learning to do such things and by teaching them to others through one's example. Paul, like Jesus, taught by example, followed by analysis of that example. The aim was always to lead the followers to correct behavior. Here Paul instructs Timothy concerning issues that Paul has already modeled. The instruction is that Timothy, in turn, model these things for his followers.

Paul knew that the messenger is "the major component of the message he conveys" (Kraft 1991a:17). He knew that we teach what we model and therefore says several times, "follow my example" (1 Cor 4:16; cf. 11:1). Jesus taught the same way, by modeling. He called His disciples with the invitation to "Come with me, and I will teach you to catch men" (Mk 1:17). He didn't promise to merely inform the disciples *about* catching people. He promised *they would learn to actually do what He Himself had come to do,* and they spent twenty-four hours a day with their Teacher, learning to be like Him.

That's true education. It is extremely misleading to equate schooling with education. Schooling may provide opportunity to do the analysis part of education, provided the students have had enough experience to have something to analyze. Schooling, however, seldom provides education all by itself, unless one is learning to be the kind of teacher modeled by the teacher. *We learn what we do.*

So, as students, let's focus on learning how to live, not simply how to think. Imitate the behavior of your life models (whether they are teachers or not), as they imitate Jesus' behavior. Don't let your education devolve into mere analysis of and arguing over words and concepts for their own sake. Those of us who are teachers need to be greatly concerned that we live, and thus teach, as Jesus did. Let's model Him in attitude, deed, and word, that those who learn by imitating us may become like Jesus.

INTRODUCTION

We have defined "culture" as an integrated system of learned behavior patterns, ideas, and products characteristic of an individual human society. Elsewhere we have described what we mean by an integrated system, patterned behavior, ideas, and products. What we have not yet addressed is the matter of how culture is learned.

Every society must provide mechanisms for passing on to the young those patterns and habits considered necessary for meaningful life (including survival and whatever else a society considers appropriate). This teaching and learning process starts soon after conception and is carried on intensively throughout childhood. Throughout adulthood, we continue to learn (continue our education), sometimes fairly intensively, for the rest of our lives.

In attempting to understand this educational process, we will answer two questions:

1. What is the nature of this process called education? and

2. How do human societies provide for the transmission of particular cultural behavior, ideas, and products from one generation to the next?

As with all cultural phenomena, the process is complex, but basic to it is the teaching that is done by adults and the learning that is done by the youth of any given society. This process is called enculturation, socialization, or just plain education. In this chapter we will present an anthropological perspective on the important cultural subsystem called education.

WHAT IS THE NATURE OF EDUCATION?

The first question to address is, What do we mean when we use the term education from an anthropologically informed, cross-cultural perspective?

1. Education Is More Than Schooling

Actually, education is much more than schooling. It is unfortunate that the western world has so focused on the training of its youth in mass institutions called schools that for many the terms schooling and education are synonymous. But, as we attempt to demonstrate below, schooling may or may not be very helpful in the educational process. Indeed, schools often significantly hinder the process of preparing the young to effectively participate in adult life.

In all societies, whether or not there are schools, the most significant educational events occur without the benefit of formal school rooms, institutionalized programs, and paid professional teachers. Most education occurs without books and paper, lectures, and examinations. The basic ingredients are modeling and imitation. Largely through these informal techniques, a society transmits cultural behavior, ideas, and products from one generation to the next as the young imitate those with whom they frequently associate, especially those of greater authority or prestige than themselves.

Mead defines education as "The cultural process [by means of] which each newborn infant . . . is transformed into a full member of a specific human society" (1963:162). By such a process we are enculturated (trained into knowing and behaving according to the cultural patterns of our society) and socialized (trained into appropriate social behavior) and thus become functioning members of the society into which we are born. These technical terms, the first coming from anthropology, the second from sociology, may be used more or less synonymously (if one cares to use technical terms). We will simply use the term education to cover the whole territory.

2. Education Is More Than Simply Accumulating Information

Education from this point of view is much more a matter of learning how to behave than of learning how to think. True education is the process of total formation of the person being educated, and this formation is for the purpose of effective and approvable participation in the total life of the society of which the person is a member. Though the taking in of new information is an important part of this educational process, the central focus is on what the learners learn to do, and how they will behave as a result.

Education is a social, behavioral thing, not merely a knowledge thing. The result of education is proper behavior. So is the process by means of which education is obtained. We learn what we do largely by observing and imitating what's going on about us. Large amounts of information, of the sort we are likely to receive in a typical school room setting, are not necessarily helpful in the educational process. Such information is of value if it provides (as it often does) input that enables us to live more effectively. It is, however, a hindrance to the process if it diverts our energies to peripheral or unnecessary matters at the expense of more crucial things.

We learn in the process of what I've called "life involvement" (Kraft 1991a). Whatever we are involved in is what we learn, and the basic thing we learn through our involvement in going to school is how to go to school. Whether this learning is a help or a hindrance in the educational process needs to be discussed rather thoroughly from a cross-cultural point of view.

TYPES OF EDUCATIONAL PROCEDURES

Having defined what we mean by education and distinguished between education and schooling, we now turn to a consideration of the types of activities that are educative. There are several of these. Most of them will be found to some extent in every society.

Formal Education

We list formal education first not because it is most important but because this is the category of which we are usually most conscious. Schools are the most prominent type of formal educational procedures. Typically, formal procedures will demonstrate fairly impersonal characteristics. In western societies, they tend to be centered around the classroom, a fairly large group of students, and a professional teacher. They make use of specialized paraphernalia such as books, buildings, desks arranged neatly in a row, and other symbols of institutionalization.

Formal procedures make it possible to process sizable groups of learners simultaneously. Usually they are quite teacher oriented, in the sense that the initiative for learning by formal procedures typically rests with the teacher, while the student is more passive than in less formal types of learning. Though students are assigned to do such things as reading and writing, the initiative for these comes from the teacher rather than from the learners. The effort of the latter is in reaction rather than in initiation.

Formal education is now a part of nearly all of the world's societies. Usually the pattern for such schooling, even in nonwestern areas, is quite similar to one or another of the Euroamerican patterns. This means that in nonwestern contexts, what is taught often has very little relevance to traditional life. It thus serves to extract people from traditional life into the westernizing segment of society. This process has much to do with the emigration of people from rural to urban areas and from nonwestern to western countries.

Nonformal Education

The term "nonformal" has been developed to designate another very important type of educational activity. As Ted Ward has said,

> There are some educational activities that do not fall neatly into the informal nor the formal sectors. They are not a part of socialization, nor of schooling. They are a category apart, which we might label "other." Much of instruction in religion has historically been done in the "other" realm. For example, Sunday schools—though we call them schools, they are not really schools (1987:7).

Nonformal education, in contrast to informal education, is planned and usually directed toward adults. Seminars and workshops aimed at facilitating change in a semi- or non-directive way fall into this category. So does much of what happens in apprenticeship and discipleship (treated separately below). Many nonwestern societies practice nonformal educational procedures as a part of initiation ceremonies often held at the time a boy becomes a man or a girl becomes a woman.

Informal Education

Most education, whether in western or nonwestern societies, occurs informally. Informal procedures require much more life involvement between teacher and learner. They tend to be more learner centered, with the initiative taken more by the learners themselves. Techniques are usually less mechanical and more personal. Such elements as time, place, materials used, duration, and intensity of contact are more flexible.

Informal education is often person to person, involving modeling and observation, informal talking (as opposed to lecturing), storytelling, informal reading, and the like. It often happens in addition to formal or nonformal education or when the focus is on something else. Much informal education happens in the home, where parent-child relationships are central. Traditionally, western mothers have provided informal education for their daughters to teach them to handle domestic responsibilities. With so many mothers working nowadays, this system is breaking down for many daughters. Scouting organizations and athletic and musical programs in the schools are western examples of activities organized for purposes other than education in which a good bit of informal learning takes place. In many nonwestern societies, boys learn to be men by associating with adult men, while girls learn to be women by associating with adult women. In each case, the youngsters observe and participate as they are able in adult activities and thus informally learn their adult roles in society.

Apprenticeship/Discipleship

A very common approach to education employed in a great number of human societies is apprenticeship/discipleship. This may be seen as a formalized relationship between a teacher/expert and one or more students/learners within which most of the teaching/learning is done nonformally and informally. Some sort of contract may be involved, specifying what services or payment is to be provided to the master in return for the privilege of learning from him or her.

Apprenticeship/discipleship relationships frequently extend over long periods of time and involve learning a broad range of information and behavior. The focus is seldom on information for its own sake, however. Nor does learning ordinarily occur in contexts divorced from real life. Often teacher and learner experience life together twenty-four hours a day. Such a relationship is characterized by constant life involvement designed to profoundly affect the behavior of the apprentice.

This approach to education is, I believe, the one most likely to produce the kind of leaders needed by the Christian Church. Jesus, of course, employed it to produce the core of leaders who soon were blamed for turning the world upside down. In many societies it has been traditional to pass most occupations from father to son via apprenticeship. Even in western societies, many of the trades (e.g., carpentry, stone masonry, plumbing) are regularly (though not exclusively) taught in this way.

THE ORIENTATION OF EDUCATIONAL PROCEDURES

When observing or analyzing educational practices, it is helpful to ask certain questions concerning the intent or orientation of each procedure. What is a given approach best suited to accomplish? In what ways is it designed to reach its goal(s)? The answers to such questions will help the analyst understand what types of situations any given procedure is best suited for and make any recommendations for change on that basis. One may analyze the orientation of an educational procedure along parameters such as the following:

Mass vs. Individual: Is the procedure oriented toward dealing with masses of people or toward the formation of individuals?

Teacher Initiative vs. Learner Initiative: Does the procedure depend basically upon the initiative of the teacher or on that of the learner for its impetus, direction, and result?

Indoctrination vs. Discovery: Does the teacher simply attempt to transplant in a mechanistic fashion his or her own understanding, or is the learner stimulated and permitted to discover?

Information vs. Behavior: Does the procedure emphasize the transmission of desirable information or the formation of desirable behavior?

Thinking vs. Living: Correspondingly, does the procedure emphasize thinking only, or living as well?

Children vs. Adults: Is the focus on children or adults?

Discontinuity vs. Continuity: Does the procedure stimulate discontinuity or continuity between the learners and those in the surrounding society from other generations or other social or ethnic entities?

Integrative vs. Disintegrative: Does the procedure demonstrate an integrative conception of life and learning or a dichotomized, disintegrative conception? Does it treat life in compartmentalized units or as an integrated whole?

Change vs. Growth: Is the focus on change, as is so often true in western contexts, or on growth? Not all change is growth!

Protection vs. Participation: Does the procedure facilitate participation in real-life contexts or does it instead isolate, remove, and protect learners from participation?

PURPOSES OF EDUCATIONAL PROCEDURES

We have defined what we mean by education and considered several general types of educational procedures. But what *purposes* are served by educational processes?

Continuity with the Past

A principal purpose for educational procedures is enculturation, a term denoting training for effective participation in a specific society. Nearly every people is concerned about maintaining a strong continuity with the past. Especially at the informal and nonformal levels, this concern is played out in countless ways as people teach their children the customs that are precious to them. Though there is always change between generations, adults attempt to lead their youth into as close an approximation as possible to the way they do things.

When the concern for continuing the traditions of the past and protecting themselves from as much change as possible in the present gets carried to an extreme, it produces what might be called a closed society. Many nonwestern societies, and certain western subsocieties such as the Amish and the Hutterites, have traditionally attempted to close themselves as much as possible to the outside world. They have neither welcomed change nor trained their young to function outside their own cultural context. Children are trained to function only within the confines of their own homogeneous social enclosure. The name of the game is the preservation and continuance of their specific cultural system, with as little change as possible from generation to generation. The members of closed societies are not trained to function well in the world at large, nor are they well prepared to communicate effectively across cultural barriers.

Societies such as these value tradition and eschew change. The societies of the Old Testament are examples. A fictionalized though very accurate example may be found in the musical *Fiddler on the Roof*. Who can forget Tevye's love for tradition, expressed in the song by that name? When asked what tradition means to him, he states, "Tradition tells me who I am and what God expects."

Such societies are often very brittle. They tend to break apart when confronted by the kind of massive pressure for change that today's level of contact with other peoples and customs produces. Children trained to function within the strict parameters of a closed society usually are not well equipped to deal as adults with much diversity and pressure for change, especially when that pressure comes from sources such as Euroamerican societies that practice openness to a fault.

Press beyond Past: Discontinuity between Generations

In the western world, though the informal and nonformal educational processes show a concern for continuity, there is a different motif in the formal education sphere. Beyond the teaching of the basics, children are trained to be negative rather than positive toward most tradition and thus to value change over continuity from generation to generation. Change is considered progress, and progress beyond the past is considered to be one of the greatest goods. The enculturation of the children thus becomes training for discontinuity with the past rather than for continuity and preservation of tradition.

They are taught to press beyond the past, whether by going farther than their parents did in school or by achieving greater prestige or wealth than they did. Such a system teaches disdain for the past and for those who represent the past—the older generations. Each generation is molded into a peer group, largely through the schools, and this group becomes the primary reference group for, and the primary influence on, the youth who are a part of it. In this way we become youth oriented rather than age oriented.

This emphasis gets transported into societies with a tradition of closedness and age orientation via western schools. In this way, such societies are exposed to high levels of destructive pressure and often move into the kind of demoralization discussed in chapter 26.

Conversion to Another (Sub)culture: Discontinuity with the Past

Educational procedures sometimes serve another purpose: conversion from one set of assumptions and customs to those of another culture or subculture. Immigrants coming into North America became a part of the melting pot experiment. American leaders were faced with the problem of how to melt into one functional unit quite a diversity of immigrant peoples. The schools, buttressed by compulsory education laws, soon became the primary means of meeting this challenge. All immigrant children had to attend and, in the process, be converted into North Americans. The schools were used to melt peoples into as much of a homogeneous unit as possible.

This use of schools is now widespread in Two-Thirds World countries as well. Those who go to school go through a conversion process that effectively weans them from a large number of (but nowhere near all) traditional attitudes and behaviors and to the values and behaviors of the West. The disruption thus caused by the introduction of western schools is enormous, often putting the schooled sector of the society in a position where whatever value they have received from their training is only really applicable to a way of life not yet fully in existence in their cultural context (*see* Beals and Spindler 1973, ch. 9).

Escape or Involvement?

As noted above, certain educational procedures, especially formal procedures such as western schools (both in western and in Two-Thirds World societies), often tend to serve quite another purpose—to enable participants to escape, at least for certain periods of time, from the real world into a somewhat artificial world of thought and ideas. This happens rather unconsciously to both students and teachers, due to the sometimes large distance between what goes on in the artificial institutionalized setting and what goes on in real life. As pointed out by Robert Taylor, "Nowhere . . . is education divorced from everyday life to the degree that it is in Euroamerican communities" (1973:476).

This is not necessarily an intended function. Nor is it necessarily always bad, if indulged in sparingly. When, however, the condition becomes a way of life (as can easily happen), it can be quite damaging to individuals and to the society as a whole. People who are rather totally caught up in an artificial, academic world of thought and theory are of little use to themselves or to society.

SCHOOLING AGAINST EDUCATION: WESTERN WAYS

What we know as schooling in the West is a formal educational technique developed within western societies for the purpose of facilitating and making more efficient a major segment of the educational process. It involves the turning over of each family's children to experts (teachers) who have special training and presumably know more than the parents do concerning what needs to be taught and how best to get it across. To do this, large institutions have been set up, buildings built, and rather specialized processes developed, by means of which to transmit what it is assumed children need to know in order to live life effectively. The theory seems to make sense, but what is actually taught and learned?

Though nobody really intended it to turn out this way, I believe a sober analysis of the schooling process in western and westernizing societies shows the following lessons to be among the major things we learn in school. Though each has both positive and negative aspects to it, some would seem to include elements so detrimental to the intent of the educational process that I feel it important to highlight the dangers, lest we fail to take steps to compensate where possible in our own lives and in those of our children. Unfortunately, the schools are not the only part of western(izing) societies to convey many of these messages. But they are often the places where we and our children are most systematically exposed to them early in life.

1. *Since we learn what we do, it is clear that the primary thing we learn in school is how to go to school.* This is not necessarily a bad thing, since, if we are to learn through a technique, we must first learn the technique. It must also be recognized, on the positive side, that there are many other institutions in western society (e.g., clubs, government, church) that are patterned in many respects in a very similar way. One might contend, therefore, that learning to go to school teaches one how to participate in many other areas of the society.

But many seem to learn so well how to go to school that they never seem to function well in settings very different from school settings. Sadly, the result is often that students learn so well to avoid real life that they never recover from this habit. Many westerners spend fully one-third of their entire lives in school situations, pursuing one degree after another: high school, college, professional or graduate school. Some of these become "professional students," continually seeking higher levels of education as ends in themselves. Others try to escape from many life responsibilities by becoming more concerned with gaining and processing information than with really managing life in an effective manner. That is, they never quite get beyond the school-induced focus on collecting information to the necessity to use such information properly in the living of life.

Unfortunately, school life is often "make believe," a game we play, a baby-sitting system or summer camp seemingly developed by the society to keep young people from getting into adult life too soon. In conjunction with the schools, western societies have developed adolescence, a time when young people are largely protected from having to take responsibility. They are hindered in learning accountability, something that can only be learned by practice. Instead, many learn well what they practice—habits of irresponsibility. Many, of course, overcome such learning and do become responsible members of society. One wonders, however, if the delay and the large number of failures are necessary.

2. As schoolchildren, *we learn to place a higher value on what goes on in school than on what goes on at home*. We are, after all, graded on our performance in school, but not on our performance at home. On the positive side, young people need to learn how to function effectively outside their homes. Schools provide many social experiences quite similar to those the learner will have to face as an adult. In this respect, much important preparation is gained for adulthood.

But when one reflects on the fact that the family is in serious trouble throughout most of the western(izing) world and notes that the schools provide the primary challenge to the home, one wonders about the role played by what is taught at school. There are many factors contributing to family breakdown, of course, including rapid change, industrialization, individualism, mobility, and the like. But a look at the competition that has evolved between the learning that takes place at home and the influences coming from school-type education suggests that schools may be at least as significant as any of these other contributors to family breakdown.

Americans find that our children spend more waking hours at school than at home. They are engaged in more activities structured around the school than in activities structured around the family. Demands made at school usually capture our children's attention and imagination much more than the responsibilities of family at home. They learn to value school more than home, teachers more than parents, what they learn at school more than what they learn at home. In such a competition between the institution of family and the institution of school, the latter—being much better financed and often much better run—usually wins out.

3. *We learn in school to depend upon professionals* and professional paraphernalia such as teachers, experts, books, and institutionally approved patterning of the learning experience. Parents and others with age and life experience to offer tend to be relegated to a secondary place of influence.

On the positive side, this kind of specialization is consistent with the rest of western cultural patterning. Our youth will have to learn to look to specialists sooner or later. The fact that teachers, textbook writers, and curriculum designers are specialists provides a kind of expertise in the schooling system that most parents could not provide. In a fast-paced, forward-looking society such as ours, it is the specialists, the professionals, who stand the best chance of keeping up with the latest developments. We certainly want our children to gain the benefit of their expertise.

On the other hand, the question needs to be asked, What happens to our youth when they are given the impression that teachers know more than parents, thinkers are more important than doers, books are more important than people? This results in strange, destructive values. Parents are automatically "out of it," not because of anything they have or have not done, but simply because they bear the title "parent" rather than the title "teacher" or "expert." We learn to look outside the home, preferably to teachers and books, for nearly all expertise, even expertise that parents might legitimately claim. A professional though unmarried family counselor, for example, might sooner be turned to for advice than one who has successfully raised a family. We have learned to trust strangers, especially schooled strangers who charge us money for their advice, over relatives whom we know and who care for us, whether or not money is involved.

My older children, when they were in high school, once came to me with something their English teacher was teaching. I listened and told them their teacher was wrong about the matter. They objected rather strongly. Who was I, a mere parent, to question the word of a teacher? At first, I was taken aback, until I realized where the problem lay and how to get out of it. The problem was, of course, that the status "parent" is valued as quite inferior in our society to that of "teacher," especially in matters of knowledge. The way out was readily available to me (though not to every parent), since I am a teacher and have been trained at a higher academic level than their teacher in a partially overlapping area. Their teacher was dealing with English, and one of my specialties is linguistics, a field that deals more expertly with the issue in question than her more specialized field. This I explained to them and was able to correct the misunderstanding and gain stature in the eyes of my youngsters.

4. Additionally, *we learn to value formal, highly structured situations* (school) more than informal, less-structured experiences (personal conversations, family). *The clock* becomes our master. We learn to divide and compartmentalize our lives into concise, "efficient," and usually short time periods. We learn to *sit still* in neat rows, all facing the teacher, and to concentrate (more or less) on what is coming from that person, ignoring as much as possible what else may be going on around us. We learn to assume a dependent attitude vis-à-vis the teacher and a dependent attitude in general toward our own learning and development. *We learn to depend upon the pressure of externally structured conditions* such as well-formulated assignments, exams and grades to motivate us to do things. We learn that important things are accompanied by deadlines, measured by exams, and evaluated through grading.

Again, such structuring is not all bad. We live in complex, mass societies that would crumble if they were not highly structured. It is important that our youth learn how to conform their lives to such a reality.

But at what price? Has not the structuring often become a master rather than a servant? Focused on such structuring, guided by such experts, and dependent on such pressures, many fail to learn how to motivate and organize themselves in unstructured or self-structured situations. Homemakers and preachers, for example, often experience severe feelings of inadequacy centered around the feeling that they "are not accomplishing anything," since the structuring of time and activities they have been trained to depend on is not there. A pastor often values a structured Bible study over an unstructured conversation with a parishioner, even though he theorizes and will preach that personal relationships are to be top priority for Christians.

In addition, we learn to distrust our own life experience and the life experience of persons surrounding us (our community and family). Instead, we learn to trust most what is formally presented (lectures, books) or was received from an "expert." Some years ago, a student came to me, saying he could not write a thesis on his own people because virtually nothing had been written on them previously. Since he found no experts to quote and footnote, he believed, he could not do a study of these people. He failed to see the value of his own life experience and the possibility that he was the expert who could write that up. He had learned in school to distrust so "flimsy" an authority as his own personal experience.

It is interesting to note how pervasively this and other aspects of what we learn in school have invaded our church life. Lecture-centered ritual (very much like school in formality, timing, seating, and informational focus) has become defined as weekly worship for most of us (even though there may be little of real worship involved). In Sunday School, even the age grading of the public schools is employed. Our churches, like our schools, are also book and expert centered. A problem arises, however, with the fact that exams and grades are not given in church. This means that very little of the information presented is ordinarily retained, since our school-inculcated habit is to work at retaining informational things only under the pressure of exams and grades.

5. As already implied, *we learn in school to value information more highly than behavior.* On the positive side, an emphasis on information is very much needed in order to survive in what have been termed "information societies." If our youth are to cope with modern life, they will need to be up on the latest thinking at least in the area of their specialty. The problem lies, however, in the comparative value they learn to place on the information they accumulate versus the value they learn to place on their ability to live life effectively.

The commitment to teaching in classrooms itself predisposes the process in favor of the passing on of information and against the modeling of behavior. The problem at this point is not that the emphasis on information is bad, but that it produces a one-sidedness to the educational process if not balanced with an equal emphasis on the right use of that information. What can be "sold" by teachers and "bought" by students in classrooms, however, is information about things that happen outside the classroom context, most of which cannot be (or, at least, are not) demonstrated in the classroom. We are merely presented "facts" about this situation or that event, this problem or that solution, with little or no reference to whether these facts will be applicable in our present or future behavior (except, of course, in the passing of the examinations).

In spite of this, much of the information that is passed on to us would be relevant if we could only remember it long enough. But the fact that the information is presented in such large amounts and rather totally out of the context of our real lives puts us at a serious disadvantage in trying to retain it, even to pass the exam.

A lot depends on how old and experienced one is when one receives the instruction. Much of what goes on in elementary and high school classrooms is irrelevant, merely because it is given at the wrong time in the students' lives. The very same instruction might be quite different in value to those who have had a lot of life experience. This is because information divorced from experience is quite a different thing from information that relates to one's experience. Information that comes in the context of hunger for insight concerning the living of life or the conducting of vocation can be extremely valuable, even though it is presented in a classroom setting.

Even with experienced people, though, one must be careful of information overload, a situation in which too much information is presented. It has the effect of compromising the value of the useful information, since there is just too much to handle. Good education not only provides relevant information, it provides it in usable dosages.

Note again the undesirable effect a focus on information has on Christian practice. How easily the focus of sermonizing, from both the preacher's and the listener's perspectives, gravitates toward the amount and kind of information provided. Large numbers of sermons consist mainly of information *about* the history, geography, and language of biblical times. Western Christians often become walking sources of information about God and His works but impoverished in the crucial relational aspects of our faith. Even orthodoxy, contrary to Scripture, becomes defined as a matter of knowing correct information rather than practicing Christian behavior. In this regard, a prominent African leader (Gottfried Osei-Mensah) once said to me, "You westerners are concerned about intellectual heresy. In Africa we are concerned about interpersonal heresy."

6. Schooling, furthermore, *leads us into certain relational habits that, though socially approved, can be very troublesome.* For example, *we learn to compete with our peers* for such things as grades, the attention of our teachers, success, and popularity. We are constantly subject to comparison and contrast with others of our age, both in the areas emphasized in school and in such other areas as physical appearance, personality, and extracurricular activities (e.g., athletics, music, drama, etc.). We may be good in some other area, but that doesn't count. The academic part of such competition is often intensified through the custom of grading on a curve, so that the numbers of high and low grades in a class are determined by standardized percentages, with little reference to the pace of individual progress.

In our highly competitive societies, people would probably not cope very well if they did not learn how to compete, so it is not inappropriate for a certain amount of competitiveness to be taught in schools. Such learning does, however, often seem to carry people to extremes, especially when combined with another relational problem that arises—*the tendency to regard others as something less than persons.* This "thinging," or depersonalization of others, is an artifact of mass society. It is, nevertheless, disturbing to see and experience.

We also learn to conform to our peer group. Whether in dress, vocabulary, music preference, attitude toward adults, or general outlook on life, the members of an age group learn to value the attitudes and customs of their peers above those of the rest of society. The members of each generation thus get identified primarily in terms of their peer subculture and are cut off from much meaningful interaction with those of previous generations.

The positive side of peer group conformity lies in the fact that that's the way our society is arranged. If we don't learn to get along with those of our own age group, we are unlikely to find life as meaningful as we would like it.

In the competition-conformity process, unfortunately, *we seem to learn to envy success* as defined by our society at large and the dynamics of school society in particular. We envy, and yet we learn to seek flaws in the successful. We learn to want to be successful but, if that seems to evade us, to at least "cut down to size" anyone who has achieved what we desire. Teachers and others in power over us become special objects of our critiques.

Correspondingly, *we learn to fear failure* more, perhaps, than anything else. We hear the promises of our society that if we compete hard enough we can make it to the top, but the thought of either not attaining or of failing once we have attained is chilling.

wow!

All of this we are taught to handle individualistically. Whether as competitors, conformers, envyers, or those who fear failure, we are on our own. We are expected to do whatever we do as individuals, largely cut off from significant assistance from family or friends. We are to "take on the world," but our record is usually so spotty that most of us develop severe self-image problems along the way. Typically, we develop deep feelings of inadequacy over our failure to measure up in one area or another. There always seems to be someone doing better than we are. When that is observed, we have learned to blame ourselves, even if the standard by which we measured ourselves was unrealistic. Though it is clear that our society specializes in unrealistically high standards, we frequently allow ourselves to be deceived into measuring ourselves by them.

Again, a certain amount of individualism would seem to be necessary in our kind of society. But have we not carried it too far? Scripturally, a high degree of *interdependence* seems to be recommended. I believe such interdependence is more healthy than the kind and degree of independence advocated both in western societies at large and by those who are supposed to be helping heal persons who break down psychologically.

7. Lastly, let me point to the *pervasive secularism that western schools convey.* On the positive side, even most Christians would not want to return to the days before the development of contemporary science, when a somewhat obscurantist form of religious instruction was in vogue. We would say it is good to teach science and history and mathematics and reading. It is good to provide our youth with the tools to investigate life on their own. It is good to expand their horizons beyond the geographical boundaries of their own land and beyond the temporal borders of the present time.

But training that spends 90 percent or more of the time detailing what humans have accomplished gives the young a strong impression that what humans have done is far more important than anything God may have done— even if the subject matter is taught by Christian teachers in Christian schools. Even if the curriculum deals primarily with the Scriptures (as in seminaries and Bible schools), but treats them in an informational, knowledge-oriented way, there is something secularizing and spiritually deadening about the process.

From where I sit, it seems almost impossible to avoid secularizing and spiritual deadening over any extended period of time in a school-based approach to training, no matter how Christian the participants. I suspect that the seeds of secularization lie in the approach to education at least as much as in the curriculum and teachers. Perhaps there was no hope from the very beginning that Harvard, Yale, and the myriad other preacher-training institutions that have "gone bad" would succeed in their original mission. Is it the curriculum that causes this? Is it the artificiality of the setting, the out-of-context nature of the discussions? Is it the informationalizing of the subject matter? Is it the inexperience of the students? Is it the fact that in many school settings the teachers have little, if any, ministry experience (they were hired because of their academic abilities, not their effectiveness in ministry)? Doubtless each of these factors plays an important part.

These and many other things are learned in western school contexts, and many more items, both positive and negative, could easily be added to the list. It is hoped, however, that this much will suffice to show the many contrasts between schooling and the educational process cross-culturally understood. For further treatment of this subject, I recommend Beals and Spindler (1973) and Henry (1963).

EDUCATION IN CROSS-CULTURAL MINISTRY

Many churches and missions around the world invest thousands of dollars and hundreds of persons in operating western schools in other societies. What principles and practical assistance may be gained from a consideration of what I have presented above?

Purpose

We need to first ask at least two questions concerning the purpose of mission/church involvement:

1. What are the intended purposes or reasons for the mission or church involvement in this approach to education?

2. What purposes are actually being served by what is being done?
Having considered these questions a third question often needs to be asked.

3. If the intended purposes are not being served by these procedures, what should be done about it?

What purposes might we suggest for educational projects in cross-cultural contexts? Certainly churches should be concerned about the educational needs of children and the leaders of the churches. Providing for such needs represents the kind of works of love Christians are called to be involved in. As such, education is a legitimate part of the overall mission of the Church of Christ in the world. Service to a needy community of fellow human beings, whether medical, agricultural, or educational, represents a high and worthy purpose deserving of specific priority within the Church's agenda.

The question raised here, however, is just how genuinely educative are the techniques we are involved in? If what we are doing is starting and supporting western schools in nonwestern areas, have we not become captive to the naive assumption of westerners that schooling automatically promotes education? If we define our purpose as providing education, it is fundamentally important for us to ask if our techniques are, in fact, doing what we intend. If, as will often be the case with schools, we discover that most of what they are providing does not correspond with what we intend, we need either to conform our procedures to what will meet our goals or revise our goals to conform to what is actually happening.

Often the kind of institutionalized approach we associate with educational work frustrates the realization of our greater purposes. We have transplanted such institutions with all good intentions on the assumption that they are working well at home (an assumption that itself needs examining) and that, therefore, they will work well here. But they don't seem to live up to our expectations, and we often don't know why. Indeed, they prove disruptive to indigenous values and cultural traits that we would otherwise wish to maintain.

Our traditional missionary programs of *leadership training* provide an example. Up to the present, for most nonwestern churches it is standard procedure to pull potential church leaders out of their home contexts for three years for training in a traditional residential Bible school or seminary setting. This approach disrupts the students' relationships with their people, dislocates the family (if the student is married), trains them informationally rather than practically in an artificial context, often without opportunity for practice of the kind of ministry being trained for and, in many cases, is little short of disastrous personally and relationally. Seeing some of these problems, Ralph Winter and others began in the 1960s to develop "theological education by extension" to provide suitable training for leadership within the life context of the learners. Such programs represent a quantum leap in the area of methodology. Unfortunately, many such programs have tended to become merely a better way of presenting material that is still primarily informational and of little relevance to the daily life of those for whom it is intended. But Theological Education by Extension is a big step in the direction of providing training that is genuinely educational.

Another promising experiment is being conducted by the Assemblies of God (assisted by Australian missionaries) in Papua New Guinea. They conduct pastoral training only for persons already in pastoral positions and only for twenty weeks at a time. Leaders leave their positions for no more than one twenty-week period per year to be instructed at a central location. When the twenty weeks is up, they return to their churches. They cannot continue on for additional work at this time. Nor can they bring their families with them to the training site. They get a certificate for their work and, if over a period of several years they are able to accumulate enough credits, they receive a formal diploma. Thus they receive training, experience, and formal credentials during the same period of time.

Appropriate Model

Having carefully considered our purpose and the relationship between that and the procedures employed, we will often find the need to look for a more appropriate model in terms of which to increase the fit between what we intend and what actually occurs educationally. At this point we need always to remind ourselves that *an educational model having validity in one society may not easily be transferred to another.*

To assure an appropriate fit between the forms employed and the intended meanings and functions served in nonwestern contexts, we are well advised to investigate and evaluate educational models already indigenous to the society. Is storytelling an appropriate technique? (For most people it is). How usable are master-apprentice techniques? (This, too, is a very widely used structure). What about more formal techniques such as classrooms, central locations, and fixed daily hours? (These are indigenous to many non-western societies for certain purposes). In every case, we will want to build or modify the educational procedures used to make them as congenial as possible to the learning patterns most likely to be effective among the receiving group.

Educational procedures, including schools, do not have to be guilty of all the above problems. Especially if combinations of methods are employed, many difficulties can be overcome. Any method, including formal schooling, can be effective,

1. If proper attention is given to relating the nature and quantity of material presented to the real-life needs and the actual context in which the person lives,

2. If it is assured that students with enough experience to profit from whatever is presented are taught by teachers who themselves are or have been successful in the kind of ministry being advocated,

3. If instruction is done intensively for short periods of time, or

4. If discipleship/apprenticeship methods are employed over longer periods of time.

Education is like eating. People cannot simply gorge themselves during one month of the year or one period of life, on the assumption that they will then be able to live the rest of the year or life on what has been ingested during that short period of time. The body is made so that it will accept only what it can use at the time (more or less). It then eliminates the rest. So it is with the mind. In educating, as in eating, it is important to provide the right materials in quantities that can be used immediately. Otherwise even potentially useful materials get eliminated or the receptor gets intellectually "fat."

To prevent many of the potential dangers, educational procedures need to maximize such things as:

1. The relevance of the materials to the receptors' real needs and actual life contexts,

2. The "bite-sized" nature of the quantities of material presented,

3. The balancing of the input and the output of what is taught through providing in the educational model for timely use of the material presented, and

4. The behavior relatedness of the material presented and the way in which it is presented.

What to Do about Present Involvement in Schools

Is there a future for church-run schools in the Two-Thirds World? We have already affirmed the basic validity of "service" within the overall program of the Church, but are schools worth the bother? If we see the many problems, should we continue to be involved in schools?

There are indeed problems related to schools. One of the major problems is that in most situations we don't have the luxury either to do away with them or to start over. The question is not the presence or absence of schools but are they, we, and the people of the society in question adaptable? In many contexts, it is possible to adapt certain of the techniques used in schools to better serve the needs of the people. For example, such traditional educational techniques as storytelling, proverbs, riddles, and the like can often be introduced. The people's own traditions can be brought into focus, with older members of the society brought in as the experts. Even a certain amount of apprenticeship learning can often be combined with classroom learning. It is also usually possible to work within the system to do people-related things that enable us to transcend the impersonal, mass-production features of the system. Many Christian teachers, even in poorly operated schools, have found it possible to strongly influence large numbers of students for the Lord. They have discovered the principle we have been advocating throughout this book: it is usually possible to work with any cultural system to transcend it.

In many societies around the world, at least two rather distinct subsocieties have been created through the influences of westernization. There now exist within most language groups a westernizing segment and a traditional segment. It would be appropriate, if allowed by the government, to use different educational procedures for each of these segments. Both segments are valid, and it is a valid endeavor to tailor an educational procedure for each one. This means that some sort of school program (preferably with appropriate modifications) may indeed be right for the westernizing segment of the society. Yet to provide the same kind of schooling for the traditional segments would be quite harmful.

Unfortunately, what is often done is to devote most of our energies to the schooling of the westernizing segment and to forget completely those who, for one reason or another (often choice), will continue to be largely traditional in their orientation. This leads to tragic consequences for the cause of Christ. The traditional segment of society does need education, and their leaders need training, but they need to receive these benefits in ways appropriate to their own way of life, probably in informal and nonformal ways. If they are ignored, they will have no trained leaders. Furthermore, we are communicating to them that God has little concern for traditional people. I trust that one of the benefits of this discussion will be for us to pay more attention to that very important (often majority) segment of the societies of the world.

In sum, our chief concern ought certainly to be that the proper *functions* be carried out and the proper *meanings* conveyed, not that a given set of educational *forms* (whether originally foreign or originally traditional) be preserved. *The adapting of forms with primary consideration for function and meaning results in the kind of freedom at the cultural level that the Gospel promises at the personal level.* To this end we are to use whatever resources are available to us for the realization of genuinely Christian purposes. The mere transplanting of forms from one cultural context to another, without adaptation or solid attention to the results of such importation, brings about the kind of cultural enslavement and frustration that is antithetical to the aims of Christian witness and growth.

CHAPTER 18

FAMILY

INTEGRATIONAL THOUGHT

The English word "love" is perhaps the greatest problem in our language when it comes to understanding and practicing what God desires in family relationships. We use a phrase like "fall in love" to refer to what may be a very superficial and accidental emotional attachment to a member of the opposite sex, yet falling in love is considered a requirement for marriage. Furthermore, we use the phrase "make love" to refer to having sex (whether or not love in any meaningful sense is involved). Such usage can inhibit our understanding and practice of deeper kinds of commitment that we also label love.

Our society's virtual identification of love with sex leads many to feel that if a couple is not strongly sexually attracted to each other, they must no longer be in love and may justifiably break up or get divorced. Even those who do not so closely relate love and sex usually see love as primarily an emotion.

It is very difficult for Americans to deal with the fact that the Scriptures nowhere treat love as a matter of sexual feeling, nor even as an emotion. *Love in the Scriptures is something that is willed.* When God is represented as loving humans, it is because He wills it, not because He merely feels some emotional attachment to us. When we are commanded to love one another, we are expected to use our wills to love others, whether or not we feel like it and whether or not we even like them.

It is also difficult for us, when we go into other societies, to perceive love in the way many societies structure relationships between husbands and wives. When we see what looks to us to be little or no emotional attachment between spouses, we easily conclude there is no love. Love as faithful commitment, love as sacrifice, love as concern that the loved ones be well cared for may be there in abundance. But because it is not expressed in overtly visible emotional ways, we may assume it is not there. It may shock us to see a husband grieve uncontrollably at the death of his wife, whom we've never seen him touch, smile at, or even stay in the same room with, unless she was serving him. We may even accuse him of insincerely performing a ritual at such a time.

Such deep culturally inculcated difficulty with the concept of love affects our understandings of the Scriptures. How could God love (be emotionally attached to) us when we are so unlovable (not pleasant or attractive externally or internally)? Easy: He *wills* to *love us* (to do what is best for us at whatever expense to Himself). Or how can we be expected to love (be emotionally attached to) people we don't know well or who are unappealing to us? Easy: we are (like God) to *will* to love them (to want and do whatever is best for them at whatever cost to ourselves).

With this perspective on love, Paul commanded husbands to "love your wives just as Christ loved the church and gave his life for it" (Eph 5:25). We are to will that love, whether or not we feel like it. We are to will the serving, the giving of our lives, because that's what real love is all about. It is willed love that can keep a family together. Emotion may or may not be present. Unless the love is willed, however, there is no context in which healthy emotional attachment can thrive. Emotional love is not the proper basis for marriage. *It is the willed marriage commitment that is the proper basis for emotional love.*

I believe such willed love is the proper scriptural basis both for marriage and for ordinary Christian relationships in every society. Whether or not much overt emotion is expressed, commitment-centered, service-oriented, sacrificial love, modeled after that of our Lord toward us, His Church, is the standard we are to strive to live up to.

INTRODUCTION

Traditionally this chapter would be titled "Marriage and Family," since in the West we have the habit of making marriage the focus and the family an afterthought. However, it is the family that is the basic social unit of most societies, with marriage serving as the entrance into family responsibility. Marriage is an important event in that it serves as the doorway into the family. It may be helpful to think of the relationship of marriage to the family as similar to what baptism is to the Church. It is the Church that is the major focus, and it is the joyous event of baptism through which one gains entrance into the Church. In the same way, marriage is the door through which one enters into the major focus of the family.

So we will deal with the family first. With that context in mind, we will then turn to marriage later in the chapter.

FAMILY

"The family, in one form or another, is the primary unit of human culture and sociality" (Hoebel 1972:422). There are no known societies without some sort of family. In virtually all of these, it is the basic social, economic, and educational unit. At the core of the family is a nucleus consisting of a man and a woman and their offspring. This nuclear group usually, though not always, lives together and cooperates socially and economically. The husband and wife bring children into the world and usually are responsible for providing physical care, affectional support, and socialization for the offspring. In most societies, the family lives together in a home where the children grow up and receive most of their instruction as they learn to be adults.

There are several functions of the family in any given society. It is the basic unit in which economic, educational, and social functions are carried out and taught to new generations. Elaborating on certain of these functions, Hoebel says,

> The functions of the family may be stated as follows: (1) The institutionalization of mating and the channeling of sexual outlets, thus establishing a legal father for a woman's children and a legal mother for a man's children; each acquires a "monopoly" in the sexuality of the other. (2) The nurture and basic enculturation of the young in an atmosphere of intimacy, preparing them to accept the statuses that will come to them as the jural heirs of their established parents and kinsmen. (3) The organization of a complementary division of labor between spouses, allocating to each certain rights in the labor of the other and in such goods or property as they may acquire through their individual or joint efforts. (4) The linkage of each spouse and the offspring within the wider net-

work of kinsmen: the establishment of relationships of descent and affinity. These functions are universally performed by the family as a social unit (1972:422).

Having dealt with education and economics in previous chapters, we will deal primarily with Hoebel's functions 1 and 4 in this chapter. Families are the focal point for such social concerns as kinship (who is related to whom), marriage (how are couples legitimately brought together), residence (where does the newly married couple live), inheritance (how are goods passed from generation to generation) and child care and training.

Types of Families

There are different understandings of what the family is. Several years ago, I was told the following story by an African student. An American family had invited him to share dinner with them. During dinner, the hostess asked if he hoped to bring his family to America, to be with him. He was shocked at the question and replied, "No! I only hope to bring my wife and children." This answer, of course, surprised the hostess, since her definition of family included only those people the student had named. His definition, however, included many more people, far more than he could ever hope to bring to America to be with him while he studied.

In western societies, when we use the word "family," it is rarely more than the nuclear family—husband, wife, and children—that we have in mind. This is the norm for about half of the world's societies. For the other half, the norm is what we call the *extended family* (Hoebel 1972:424). An extended family in a patrilineal society will typically be headed by an older man and consist of his sons, their wives, and children. If a man has five sons, each of whom has one wife and five children, the family could consist of nearly forty people. If there are more wives and children, the number in the family could go considerably higher. In traditional rural Taiwan, it was expected that all the sons would bring their new wives back to farm, and new rooms would be added to the farmhouse to house the new family. In this way three, four, or five nuclear families would all be living and working together as one family unit.

There are many advantages to extended families. For one, they provide the basis for stable, secure marriages. Since a new marriage is very unstable and insecure, such societies have built into their cultural structures a support system to surround the newly married with assistance as they get started in their life together. Another advantage is that an extended family provides several "mothers" and "fathers" for the children. If the biological parent of any given child is not able or willing to provide good parenting, it is possible that another of the adults in the family will be able to fill the gap. There are, furthermore, economic advantages to an extended family in traditional and peasant societies. Typically, each family will be responsible for providing most of its own needs. The bigger the group, the more workers to provide for such needs. In addition, extended families usually are able to provide for the needs of those unable to work—children, the aged, and the disabled.

Though extended families also have weaknesses, each of these areas of strength points to weaknesses in cultural systems built on nuclear families. Such problems lead many anthropologists to suggest that the nuclear family is inherently unstable and ill-adapted to meet the problems of life. From an anthropological point of view, the high divorce rate in western society is predictable, because the nuclear family is not large enough to meet all the needs and help with all the problems a family has to deal with. In American society, we expect a newly married couple to physically and emotionally leave their natal family and most of the others they have depended on for support. We believe that young couples should be able to go it alone and criticize them if they have difficulties. Indeed, if they are not making it alone, newlyweds often are harder on themselves than are those around them, since they have been carefully taught the myth that they should be self-sufficient and not have to ask anyone for help.

Spouses, from the wedding on, are expected to meet all of each other's needs for love, friendship, emotional, economic, and physical support. The job is impossible. For this reason, Levi-Strauss calls the nuclear family the "restricted family," because it appears in societies where the family is given little functional value (1956:272).

Given the fragility of western nuclear families, it is disconcerting to hear that a number of western missionaries have taken it upon themselves to teach that nuclear families are God's ideal and more biblical than extended families. The Bible shows clearly, however, that God is willing to work in whatever cultural configuration there is, and the anthropological evidence suggests that people may function better in an extended family system. Not knowing such facts, a missionary to Taiwan who considered himself an expert on family constantly preached on the "betterness" and, from his point of view, the biblicalness of western family ideals. By so doing, he earned the disrespect of his hearers, who knew from their reading of the Bible that God is willing to use systems like theirs. This prompted the leaders of one Taiwanese congregation to say to a younger missionary whom they invited to preach, "You can preach on anything except the family. Your senior missionary has proved that you missionaries don't know anything about God's teaching on family life!"

Urbanization and mobility have greatly impacted family life around the world. So have various kinds of outside intervention, ranging from the advocacy of birth control to the Chinese government policy of one child per family, not to mention AIDS and homosexual activism. Each of these factors brings with it its own consequences. Urban families tend to be nuclear rather than extended, thus providing fewer relatives to care for the children. In addition, one or both parents are usually absent from the children much of the time, due to employment. Urban families also usually have to live in more crowded conditions, with less room for the children to play and a higher likelihood of short tempers and conflict within the family.

I am told that the one-child policy in China often results in the child becoming the "king" of the family, pampered, catered to, and protected. Whatever the specifics, such conditions as urbanization and family management create major challenges to thousands of families today.

Descent and Inheritance in the Family

Among the problems all societies have to deal with are those of descent and inheritance. Descent has to do with who is considered to be related to whom. Inheritance has to do with who inherits the goods left behind when the head of a family dies. We see in the Old Testament a system much like that in most of the world but quite unlike that in western societies. Old Testament Jews were *patrilineal*. This means that all children produced by a couple belong to the group of their father and his father, grandfather, and so on. Only sons are considered descendants, however, and inheritance goes from father to son(s), never to daughters. Daughters are "married out" into other families, their needs being supplied by their husbands and their husbands' families. The children they produce will be part of their husbands' families, often not even considered related to their family of birth.

An alternate system practiced by many (perhaps one-third) of the world's smaller societies is called *matrilineal*. Many American Indian groups (including Navaho and Hopi), tribal groups along the northern Thai border, and a fair number of African societies (including the Akan groups of southern Ghana) are matrilineal. One well-known matrilineal group is the Trobriand Islanders of Papua New Guinea, written about by the famous anthropologist Bronislaw Malinowski. In this system, the children belong to the group of their mother, grandmother, and so forth. Usually the sons "marry out" to become parts of their wives' families. Typically, the male authority in any given family will be exercised by the mother's brother, rather than by the children's father. Inheritance passes from mother to daughter(s). Spradley and McCurdy describe what look to outsiders like complications in such a system:

> Matrilineal descent provides some interesting problems for family organization. In every society about which we have information, males appear to have formal authority. Women may have strong influence, but it is men who take the lead in public. . . . in matrilineal extended families the women all belong to the same descent group, but the men, their spouses, do not. Since a woman does not head the family, who is to do so? The only males who can exert such authority are those belonging to the female line, the brothers of the women living in the household. So often it is they even though they usually live in other households, who assume formal responsibility for kin group decisions. To facilitate the exercise of such authority over her children it is common for a woman's son to move in with her brother (1975:173–74).

Both patrilineal and matrilineal systems are *unilineal/unilateral*, that is, descent and property are the privilege and responsibility of only one sex. Such a system contrasts with *bilineal/bilateral* systems practiced by about one-third of the world's societies (Hoebel 1972:445), including that of the United States. In a bilineal system, both sons and daughters are, for genealogical and inheritance purposes, considered related to their parents. This system seems more equitable, but is also more difficult to administer. Lest we be too critical of the inequities of unilineal systems, let's hear Hoebel, "By figuring descent through one parental line, kinship becomes more clear-cut, and societies needing to rely on kinship groups to perform most of their basic functions are able to develop more predictable and reliable social patterns" (1972:446).

Residence of Families

Usually, hand in hand with patriliny or matriliny goes the custom of living in the vicinity of the parent through whom descent is reckoned. *Patrilocal residence* is the label given to the custom of the family living in the vicinity of, or perhaps in the home of, the husband's parents. *Matrilocal residence* is the custom of the family living in the locality of the wife's parents. Some matrilineal groups practice *avunculocal residence*, in which the newly married couple goes to live with or near the wife's maternal uncle. Occasionally we find a practice called *matripatrilocal*, where a family moves back and forth, living for a period of time in the area of the husband's family and for a period of time in the area of the wife's family.

In western societies, the common practice is *neolocal residence,* where the newly married couple go to a new place where neither the husband's family nor the wife's family live. If newlyweds in Anglo American society live with either husband's or wife's family for any period of time, it is usually considered unfortunate and temporary. Minority groups in the United States may continue to practice as much as possible of their traditional custom in this regard.

Authority in the Family

In the formal sense, authority in the family is always in the hands of a male (*see* quote by Spradley and McCurdy above). This is often not the husband (in a patrilineal system) or the wife's brother (in a matrilineal system), but an older man in the grandparents' or even great-grandparents' generation. He will ordinarily be the most respected male member of the extended family. There is the possibility of matriarchal leadership, but apparently there are no societies where this happens in the formal sense. Female leadership can very definitely happen in the informal sense, such as in traditional Chinese families, where the grandmother is the real power in the family, or even in western society, where an older woman is very powerful and we call her the matriarch of the family.

Security Orientation versus Freedom Orientation

Underlying the family systems of the world's peoples are worldview values. Perhaps the most prominent value expressed through the family system of most societies is what I call a *security orientation*. With this value in view, the concern of the society is to provide the greatest degree of security for the most vulnerable people, with lessening degrees of security for those less vulnerable. The most vulnerable people in any society are the children. The concern is, then, to provide a maximum amount of security for this group. To do this, the family structure is arranged in layers like an onion, with the children in the middle and the women (of all ages) charged with providing them with security. In the next ring are the men, who provide the necessities of life, including protection (through such activities as settling disputes, engaging in politics, war, and business) in order to provide security for the women and children. Then comes the larger social group, the structuring of which is depended upon to provide security for all. God or other spiritual powers are appealed to for more ultimate types of security.

We can picture this very oversimplified but important dimension of traditional family and social systems as in figure 18.1 below.

In this orientation, security is the key concern, and those with the most "layers" of social protection are the ones most in need of that protection. We can say that in this kind of system, the family is for the sake of the children, aimed at providing maximum security for those who are the most vulnerable members of society. The children cannot take care of themselves, therefore they must be kept secure. This is the mother's primary job and her crown, her source of meaning in life. The father's job is to provide security for the mother and children. *The central relationship within the family is the mother-child bond,* and everything is to work to protect them. Marriage is for the sake of the children.

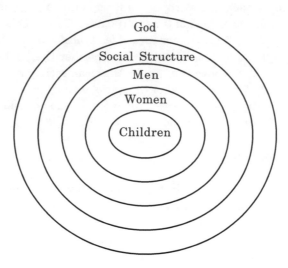

Figure 18.1 Security-oriented family structuring

There are important strengths in security-oriented systems. Though there are misuses of any system, in general, in a security-oriented system, parents feel satisfied with their assigned roles and children are made to feel that they belong and are wanted. Since the mother is expected to give nearly full attention to her small children, her husband can come to feel quite neglected. In addition, when a security focus gets carried too far, it tends to become oppressive. That is, too much security can restrict personal freedom to the extent that it feels stifling. This makes a freedom-oriented system look very attractive, and many people, when given the opportunity, opt for more freedom, even at the cost of giving up many of the good things offered by their traditional system.

Western societies tend to have what I call a *freedom orientation* in their approach to family, as in most of the rest of their social structuring. In a freedom-oriented society, the *central relationship is the husband-wife bond*. The most important job of the husband and wife is to work out, largely without help, a physical, social, and economic relationship between themselves that will survive the various challenges of life, including children. The children come into the family as semi-outsiders, too often consciously or unconsciously experienced as intruders. Parenting is often experienced as drudgery and the parents' job defined as surviving the kids long enough to get them into day-care or school as soon as possible. In school, the children learn to function in peer groups, developing greater or lesser antagonism toward their parents' generation and working largely within their peer group to find their own answers to life's questions.

Note that each set of parents (labeled husband-wife, since that is their primary relationship) is separated from their children by a peer group barrier. Meanwhile, the children of each set of parents are related more to each other within the peer group than they are to their own parents.

There are some very important strengths of a freedom-oriented system. Among them are the freedom of choice allowed in many areas of life and the fact that each husband-wife-children unit has at least the possibility of developing its own little subculture with its own appropriate, agreed-upon rules. When such a system gets off balance, however, people can experience an enormous amount of loneliness and internal and external conflict.

Our freedom-oriented system shows weaknesses in such areas as the lack of security many feel, discrepancies between promises made by the society and the ability of the society to provide for the fulfillment of those promises, and the large-scale conflicts that arise from competing loyalties. Individualism and the western catch-as-catch-can approach to courtship and marriage result in widespread insecurity and disappointment over the discrepancy between what society promises and what actually happens.

In addition, mothers frequently experience intense conflict between the need to satisfy their husbands and the obligation to meet the needs of their children. Though she may rightly judge that her children need her more than her husband does, the latter, having learned to unconsciously expect her to put him first, may not be as patient with her as he ought to be. Built into her through social conditioning is the feeling that she can adequately meet both these demands and that if she falls short, it is because there is some deficiency in her. Her husband, for his part, often comes to resent their children for depriving him of his wife's full attention, while the children may come to feel they are intruders and second-class citizens in their parents' home. The social expectations are impossible, and many live with a large amount of hurt and guilt because of this.

In spite of such major deficiencies, many western Christians, including some with worldwide reputations, go around the world teaching that an idealized form of western family is God's will for everyone. It is contended that God has ordained marriage primarily for the spouses, with the children regarded as guests. Scripture, however, seems to endorse a more child-centered ideal, one more like that practiced by security-oriented societies.

American Families: A Case Study

In cross-cultural perspective, we see American family practices in contrast with the traditional version of most of the family systems of other parts of the world at a number of points. They also contrast with many biblical ideals. Lest American practices be held up as more ideal than they ought to be, it might be helpful to list some of the these features (see R. Taylor 1973:265–66):

1. Mates are to be biologically unrelated.

2. Choice of mate is to be individualistic on the basis of personal romantic attraction (called love).

Physical appearance and appealing personality often are the main factors in selecting a spouse, and less attention is given to whether the person is industrious and dependable or what his family is like.

American parents usually have little to do with the spouse selection process, and sometimes a person marries without having met his spouse's parents (p. 266).

3. Neolocal residence is strongly preferred and almost always practiced, often at a great distance from other relatives.

The parental families may live too far away for significant interdependence to develop, and when they do live close, the diverse interests of the two units may prevent harmonious cooperation (p. 266).

4. Marriage is validated by a legal ceremony presided over by a pastor or other legally qualified person. Those who live together without going through this cul-

AMERICAN FAMILY	CHINESE FAMILY
Nuclear Family • individual above family • no relatives around to take responsibility	*Extended Family* • family surrounds, provides support
Youth Venerated	*Elders Venerated* • realistic attitude toward death
Isolation Between Generations • family restlessness	*Continuity Between Generations*
Old People Cast Off • not welcomed in children's home • in the way • young woman wants house to self • young—no interests in common with the old	*Respect for Old People* • grandmother status very high • considered wise • woman comes into her own as mother-in-law, grandmother • easier to grow old
Husband-Wife Relation Central • wishes of wife over father • wishes of children over husband • children don't listen to mother • mother free but alone	*Father-Son Relationship Central* • rigid tradition • authority comes with age • continuity
Problems • inexperienced people often lead • family often chaotic • insecurity, loneliness • too much change, too fast	*Good Points* • experienced people lead • family well-ordered • great security in the group

Good Points
 • youth free to make changes
 • people have "elbow room"
 • problems ease up if you survive long enough
 • women more respected
 • girl babies usually not resented
 • great individual freedom
	Problems
	 • conservatism hinders change
	 • woman's place very low
	   • girls looked down upon
	   • marry and move in with strangers
	   • husband sides with parents
	   • submission—"I am nothing"
	   • oppressive for individuals

Figure 18.2 Contrasts between American and Chinese families

tural form are considered unmarried, whether or not they successfully carry out the functions of the marriage relationship over an extended period of time.

5. Monogamy is the only legal form. Since there is a much larger number of marriageable females than of marriageable males in the society (100 marriageable women to 50–75 marriageable men, depending on the section of the country, according to one study), many females remain single or become the second or third wife of a divorced man, whose previous wife then becomes single.

6. Independent nuclear families are the ideal. These are, however,

relatively unstable. After marriage the couple's relationship, which depends so heavily on each finding the other's personality continually pleasing, often deteriorates. One circumstance that tends to pull the two apart is the husband's absence from the home most of the time for the purpose of earning a living. Frequently, a husband spends more time with co-workers than with his family. . . .

The independent nuclear unit is highly vulnerable, because it has so few ties to other supporting units, and the immediate small group must carry sometimes heavy

burdens. . . . the immediate family is made to carry most of the burden of intimate interaction, a function too oppressive for such a small group. This has been suggested as one
cause for the tensions and interaction breakdowns that plague many American families
(p. 266).

A helpful contrast between American and traditional Chinese family systems
as they were in the 1940s is presented by Goldschmidt (1954). Note that

> Each family system has its sources of strength and weakness. If we compare the Chi-
> nese peasant family with our own, we can see this. The Chinese family emphasizes
> unity and gives strength and support to its members, but the freedom of each person is
> lessened by the demands of family ties. The American family is discontinuous, it is
> small, and it offers less strength and support to each member. If a man dies, his widow
> may be put entirely on her own, and children do not regularly support their aging par-
> ents. But the system does give more freedom of action—particularly to the youth—and
> allows them more opportunity to find their own way and serve their own interests. We
> may well argue over which system is the better scheme for personal satisfaction; but it
> is hardly doubtful that our family pattern is better adjusted for life in America, with its
> rapid changes and need for free movement (Goldschmidt 1957:146).

MARRIAGE

We may define marriage as *the socially recognized partnership between a man
and a woman by means of which new families are established*. How this partnership is worked out varies from society to society. As we have seen, in the West the
new husband and wife normally set up a new, separate household and live as a
new family unit. But in some societies, all the men live together in one house and
all the women live in a separate house. Or all the men live in one community and
all the women live in a different community. These societies all have socially recognized partnerships between men and women, but these partnerships are worked
out in a very different way from the way things are done in the West.

In most societies, this partnership is not simply between a man and a woman
but between the family of the man and the family of the woman. As an old German
peasant proverb says, "It's not man that marries maid, but field marries field,
vineyard marries vineyard, cattle marry cattle."

There are various arrangements made to get young people together in marriage. There are social arrangements and ceremonies, economic transactions, frequently (though not always) religious events, and sometimes political activities.
These arrangements can be interfamily, interpersonal, intergroup, and contrac-
tual. These arrangements result in the privileges and responsibilities of marriage
and family, some of which are personal, many of which are social. There is usually
the expectation of permanence. Whether the marriage is actually permanent is
another story, but the expectation is there.

Spouse Selection

The ways spouses are selected are specified by the society, and there is a wide
variety in these customs. Hoebel states,

> Very few societies leave [spouse selection] to individuals who are to be married to decide
> for themselves. The American practice in this respect is most exceptional, although it
> represents a discernibly increasing trend in many parts of the world. . . . Most mar-
> riages either are still arranged by the families concerned or involve family consent and

participation. For this reason . . . it is necessary to grasp this basic principle: *marriage constitutes an alliance between two kinship groups in which the couple concerned is merely the most conspicuous link* (1972:409–10).

In some societies, who marries whom is totally arranged by others and the partners don't meet before the engagement or even the wedding ceremony. In such a case, as they say in Taiwan, the bridegroom won't know if his bride will be a bitter melon or a treasure until the day of the wedding. Usually, though, even in arranged marriages, the future spouses meet each other beforehand and may have some say in the selection process.

When marriages are arranged, finding a spouse for one's child can be relatively easy or quite a challenge, formal or very informal. Often any serious negotiations will involve quite an investigation of the background of the prospective marriage partner and his or her family. Such things as health, wealth, strength, any history of involvement with evil spirits, and the like will be checked into. In some societies, parents will seek to make pacts between themselves for the marriage of their children while the latter are quite young. In most, the arrangements are started much later. Many peoples have traditionally sought to have their daughters marry at about age fifteen. The coming of schools has disrupted this custom. Sometimes a matchmaker is involved (as in *Fiddler on the Roof*).

The assumption behind arranged marriages is that those with the most experience in society have the responsibility for putting together in marriage those with less experience. There is usually no thought given to whether the young people love each other. As Golda sings in *Fiddler on the Roof*, "My father and my mother said we'd learn to love each other." We see arranged marriage practiced in Genesis when Abraham sent his servant out with the command to "get a wife for my son Isaac" (Gn 24:4).

At the other extreme are western societies in which the young people seek out their own mates and may not seek guidance until after all has been decided. All the elders can do is go along with the decision already made. These couples believe that they are already in love and that, although they are the least experienced members of society, they know what is the best for the future. The high divorce rate in Euroamerican societies that practice this method of spouse selection shows that this is not necessarily the superior method.

What is considered appropriate premarital behavior varies from society to society. Some peoples have traditionally gone to great lengths to keep potential marriage partners separated, even if they allowed relationships with other young people to be quite free. Others have allowed fairly unrestricted interaction, even for those who may someday marry. A period of courtship between those who plan to marry is standard in some societies. This can be a formal time where the partners of an arranged marriage meet in a prescribed manner. Only in very extreme circumstances can the marriage be called off (e.g., Joseph and Mary in the Bible). Or the courtship period might be considered a time when it is the young people who set the rules and nearly any behavior, including sexual intercourse and living together, is allowed or winked at.

In some societies, it was traditional for young people to be relatively free to engage in premarital sexual relations. In others, such behavior would incur the severest of penalties. However, with the social disruption coming into most of the world's societies related to easy travel, urbanization, industrialization, western schools, and the like, there is widespread breakdown today of even the strictest standards.

In arranged marriages, whether or not the future spouses have much contact with each other, there is usually plenty of contact between the families of the couple.

Of the seven formalized modes of acquiring a wife, only two (marriage by capture and marriage by elopement) do not heavily involve the active participation of the kinship groups of the bride and groom. The seven modes are 1) by progeny price, or bride wealth; 2) by suitor service; 3) by gift exchange; 4) by capture; 5) by inheritance; 6) by elopement; and 7) by adoption (Hoebel 1972:410).

Frequently it is the custom for designated representatives of the two families to meet rather frequently to negotiate. Following such meetings between the family representatives, the latter meet with their families to work out details with them. They need to work out, both within and between families, such things as the economic arrangements and the myriad of other details involved in negotiating the new relationships between the spouses and between the families themselves. If this interfamily relationship is worked out before the wedding, when problems come up in the marriage, a system of support is already in place to help mediate.

The Wedding Ceremony

There is great variety in the customs employed to initiate a marriage. In many societies, there are elaborate wedding ceremonies, at least for those who can afford them. In others, once the arrangements are made, the couple simply starts living together without ceremony. Often the ceremony is quite elaborate and expensive, lasting for several days and involving many people and lots of food, drink, and gaiety. A typical church wedding in the United States, though often elaborate and expensive, may last only twenty to thirty minutes, with the following reception taking another hour or two. This is not much of a celebration, by cross-cultural standards.

Some societies take years to complete the wedding process. In northeastern Nigeria, some of the peoples traditionally extended the wedding process over as much as two years. Such arrangements would often have the couple living together for several months, after little or no ceremony. Then the "wife" would return to her parent's home for several months, hopefully to deliver their first child. This might be followed by another period when they lived together and still another time apart before the major ceremony, fully two years after the start. At that time the bride's goods get transported to her husband's home and several days of gaiety ensue. After that the couple, and hopefully a child or two, live together permanently. The question in westerners' minds is, Which of the ceremonies is the wedding? Robert Taylor reports a similar type of arrangement among Mexican Indians. The couple begin to live together without a ceremony. If they are still together and, hopefully, have at least one child after one and a half to two years, then there will be a formal wedding ceremony (1973:250–51).

This may be the traditional basis for the widespread practice of *common law marriage* in Latin America. Either because it is the tradition or because church weddings are too expensive (or both), many common people in Latin America and elsewhere simply start living together without the benefit of any ceremony. If they stay together for a period of time, they are recognized (even legally in many places) as formally married.

Missionaries and other Christians from middle- and upper-class backgrounds often have a hard time accepting as marriage something that doesn't involve (or hasn't yet involved) a church ceremony. In part, this is a social class issue. That is, the missionaries and other Christians who condemn such informal "weddings" have seldom faced either the economic or the "this is our tradition" issues. In part, though, the problem stems from a sincere moral concern over whether to define a given relationship as marriage or adultery. In Latin America, where for 500 years the Roman Catholic overlay has not succeeded in replacing many traditional customs, including this one, and where church weddings are far more expensive than peasants can afford, should informal partnering be looked at as a part of the people's tradition or as rebellion against Christianity? Much damage has been done to the cause of Christ by treating common law marriage and other forms of traditional informal partnering as rebellion (sin) rather than as tradition.

The approach of Euroamerican cross-cultural witnesses on this issue is often strongly affected by their attitude toward couples living together without a ceremony in the home country. We often assume that our own western youth are living together in defiance of Christian moral values. In many cases this is true, but in many cases it is not and, given Jesus' concern for evaluating people on the basis of their motivation rather than their outward behavior, we ought to be more charitable toward many of them. In any event, the issues underlying such practices in other societies need to be understood in terms of both the cultural context and the motivations of the people, not as related to our assessment of how to treat issues in western societies.

As in all other areas, so with weddings, we find from Scripture that God is willing to accept and bless whatever form a society deems appropriate. Western wedding customs are not necessarily scriptural or God-ordained, yet we may go to other peoples with some pretty firm ideas as to how weddings *should* be conducted. A wedding doesn't have to be conducted by a preacher or involve a sermon or a bride dressed in white to be blessed by God. It could be thoroughly traditional, with the blessing of God pronounced at appropriate times throughout and some form of dedication of the new relationship to God added to the traditional rituals or replacing any dedication to other spirits or gods that was a part of the traditional form.

As mentioned above, the degree of family and other group involvement in marriage varies greatly from society to society. This can range from a virtual marriage between two families to a lack of any involvement between the families of the bride and groom. Societies that have greater involvements of the families in marriage have the opportunity of providing more stability for the married couple. A problem between the husband and wife is not just a problem between themselves, but a problem between two families. There are greater pressures and resources to resolve conflict. This is quite a difference from western culture, where the parents may be the last to know when one of their children is going through a divorce.

For most of the world, a wedding is more for the sake of the relatives and the children than for the spouses. It is a social arrangement that legitimizes many transactions between the relatives and gives order to the production and rearing of children.

Economic Arrangements

Compensation by the groom's family to the bride's family (often termed *bride-price*) is very common. The purpose of this is to stabilize the marriage. It is usual for the goods and money to be almost immediately distributed among the members of the bride's family. Then if the bride decided to leave her husband, her family would have to collect all the goods and money (which would usually already be spent, often to acquire a bride for a brother) and return it to the groom's family. In the same way, if the bride should run off, the husband would not go looking for her. He would go to her father and say, "Please find my bride or return the money and goods." This is a strong motivation for the family to work hard for reconciliation.

On the other hand, if the husband did not like his new wife and sent her away, then his family would forfeit all the goods and money that had been raised for his wedding. The labor and savings of many years that had gone into raising the brideprice would then be lost. His family may not be willing to raise these goods a second time, so he would have no chance to find a second wife. The logical thing would be for him to accept his wife back and, with help, for them to work out their problems.

Often the bride will take goods and money with her into the marriage, her *dowry*. This is not to be confused with brideprice, which is money given by the groom's family to the bride's family. A young woman may work for several years in order to acquire a respectable dowry to take into the marriage. In societies in which both brideprice and dowry are practiced, it is common for the bride's family to use the brideprice, or part of it, to enlarge the dowry.

The economic exchanges that take place with dowry and brideprice work toward the stabilization of the marriage. There is a common Chinese proverb that says "Marriage makes kinsmen of bitter enemies." The idea being expressed in the proverb is that through such economic transactions, two families that may not have gotten along previously are welded together. In most nonwestern societies, marriage is not a matter of inclination but a negotiated alliance between two families that is cemented by the economic transactions.

Though the purpose of the brideprice and the dowry is the stabilization of marriage, many westerners tend to view such customs ethnocentrically and talk about people who buy or sell their brides. Some westerners have even suggested that this is a form of slavery. Though such practices can be abused, such evaluations are based on very serious misimpressions of customs that are intended to protect people and social institutions, not to degrade either.

Historians have recorded an example of the misuse of the dowry system in colonial America. Benjamin Franklin supposedly rejected his intended bride because her dowry wasn't enough to purchase the printing press he wanted to begin his printing business. In India, there have been a number of murders of young brides so the groom's family can collect a second dowry. However, these instances do not overrule the fact that brideprice and dowry provide stability to the marriages of many societies.

Who Marries Whom

Each society determines, often quite specifically, who may marry whom and who dares not marry whom. In all societies there are *rules of incest*. Incest may be defined as sexual relations between persons who are so closely related that their marriage is illegal or forbidden by custom. But a marriage that is illegal or forbidden in one society may be the required marriage in another.

There are no societies that as a general rule prescribe or prefer incestuous marriages, in which a son may marry his mother, a daughter may marry her father, or a brother may marry his sister. There are in the literature, however, a few examples of societies in which it was preferred or prescribed that, within a royal family, a brother would marry his sister. In western societies the custom is that we dare not allow cousins, especially first cousins, to marry. Westerners believe that this kind of "inbreeding" will result in mental or physical deformities, and sometimes it does.

However, many peoples specify that you *must* marry a cousin, or at least a certain kind of cousin. In kinship terms, cousins are often divided into two kinds (as we shall see in chapter 20), *cross-cousins* and *parallel-cousins*. The children produced by the mother and the mother's sisters will be parallel-cousins, as will children produced by the father and the father's brothers. That is, children of siblings of the same sex are parallel-cousins. Meanwhile, father and father's sister, or mother and mother's brother, will produce cross-cousins.

In many societies, it is prescribed that a person should marry a cross-cousin, somebody who is the son or daughter of either the father's sister or the mother's brother. In these societies, it is usually forbidden to marry somebody who is related to you by being the son or daughter of your father's brother or your mother's sister (a parallel-cousin). Probably one reason for this is that in many of these societies, father and father's brother are both called father; mother and mother's sister are both called mother. A parallel-cousin is thus considered a brother or sister, so marriage to a parallel-cousin would be unthinkable. A cross-cousin is not, however, viewed as a sibling and is regarded as acceptable for marriage.

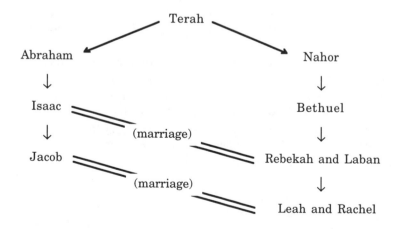

Figure 18.3 Abraham, Isaac, and Jacob's kinship chart

Only certain Semitic peoples (the ancient Hebrews and certain Arabs to this day) seem to recommend parallel-cousin marriage. We see in the Old Testament the requirement that people marry their parallel-cousins. This is what happened in the case of Isaac marrying his parallel-cousin Rebekah and Jacob marrying his parallel-cousins Leah and Rachel, though the parallelness goes back to Abraham and his brother Nahor. The relationship is shown on the above kinship chart.

Though the fact that Isaac, in marrying the daughter of his parallel-cousin, Bethuel, made Laban's daughters (Leah and Rachel) also cross-cousins of Jacob through Rebekah is incidental and irrelevant to the fulfilling of the parallel-cousin custom. The relevant fact is the relationship through the grandfathers. By custom, Jacob is marrying the daughters of his parallel-cousin, Laban, not cross-cousin daughters of Rebekah, his mother. Note that in Genesis 28:2 it is the house of Bethuel that is specified as the one from which Jacob is to take a wife.

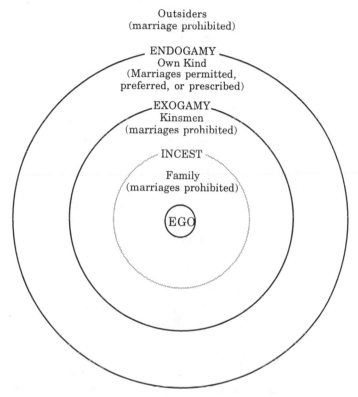

Figure 18.4 Marriage permitted in some relationships, forbidden in others

Marrying "In" or "Out"

Two concepts that anthropologists find helpful in discussing marriage arrangements are *endogamy* and *exogamy*. Endogamy means marrying within your group (clan, tribe, town), and exogamy means marrying outside that group. As pointed out above, all societies require that marriage partners come from outside the family (family exogamy), however the family is defined. Some groups have village endogamy. That is, they are to marry someone within their village. On the other hand, many groups practice village exogamy, requiring their people to marry outside their village. Tribal endogamy has been universal in traditional societies. This rule is, however, being broken more and more in modern times as people of one society become better acquainted with those of other societies.

The chart above is taken from Paul Hiebert's *Cultural Anthropology* (1983:199) and shows how marriage is permitted in some relationships and prohibited in others.

How Many Spouses?

In one sample of 450 societies around the world 80 percent of them either encouraged polygamy as the ideal or allowed it. (This is not saying that 80 percent of the world's *population* encourages or allows polygamy but that 80 percent of the world's *societies* do.) Or to put it another way, only 20 percent of the world's ethno-linguistic people groups hold monogamy as the only possibility (Hoebel 1972:425–30).

There are two kinds of *polygamy*, the marriage of one person to two or more spouses: *polygyny*, one man having two or more wives, and *polyandry*, one woman having two or more husbands. However, polyandry is very rare, known mainly for its occurrence in a small area in India. It is, therefore, common to use the term polygamy as synonymous with polygyny (one man, more than one wife).

Westerners tend to think that the main reason for polygamy is sexual, but this is seldom, if ever, the case. Indeed, in a discussion with a Nigerian polygamist with whom we were living at the time, I discovered that he considered the sexual obligations to his two wives a burden rather than a privilege. His statement was, "You Europeans are fortunate! You only have one wife. I have to sleep with each of mine in rotation, and it wears me out!"

Since, among western Christians, a man who has sex with more than one woman is seen as committing adultery, westerners tend to consider polygamy a form of adultery. This attitude accounts for the extremely negative view missionaries have taken toward the practice. In Jewish and many traditional societies to this day, however, polygamy is considered to be legitimate marriage, not adultery. In God's workings with the Jews, He never once condemned the practice. The statements in 1 Timothy 3:2, 12 and Titus 1:6 concerning the requirement that leaders have only one wife are not rightly applied to polygamy, since they are directed to Greeks, who never practiced plural marriage. The prohibitions most likely are intended, in accord with a Greek ideal, to prohibit *digamy* among church leaders. Digamy is a label for remarriage after the death or divorce of one's wife. The Greek ideal (even though not always practiced) was that marriage to one's wife is for eternity. A person, especially a leader, should only marry once and not remarry if his wife dies or leaves him. *In the Old Testament and in these passages we see that God takes seriously both the cultural definition of marriage and the socially defined requirements for leadership.*

In those large number of societies that allow plural marriages, the custom occurs as the result of arrangements agreed upon and approved by society. It is not outside the ideals of the society, as is adultery. Though God's ideal, as indicated by His provision at creation, is one wife for each man, He shows Himself throughout Scripture as respecting the cultural definition of marriage practiced by Abraham's ancestors and continued after Abraham and his descendants became "the people of God." The fact that the custom, though still allowed, was very seldom practiced among the Jews by New Testament times suggests that over the years God slowly changed His people in the direction of monogamy.

Though the custom of plural marriage is declining in many areas under the influence of westernization, it is still considered an ideal by many tribal peoples. It is also practiced by many urbanites who can afford to support more than one wife and her children. This sometimes involves all wives living with the husband in the city or, more frequently, the practice of a "city wife" and one or more "country wives" who live in the family's home area (usually rural).

There are several reasons considered valid by tribal and peasant peoples for practicing plural marriage:

1. One set of reasons is *economic*. In subsistence societies, each family has to provide for its own needs. The more workers in a family, the greater its ability to produce the food and other things it needs to survive. The primary ways to increase the work force in such societies are through marriage and childbirth. If an additional wife is added, there is both additional adult labor and the promise of additional children who will grow into laborers to increase the family's ability to cope and even, perhaps, to get wealthy.

2. Another reason for plural marriage is that *a man's first wife often wants another wife to help her with the work*. Raising children and working in the garden make a heavy load for a wife and mother, so it is often the first wife who asks for the second wife to lighten her work load. As one African told a missionary, the day the second wife came into the home was the first wife's happiest day (Smalley, 1978:233–235.) This fact, usually not understood by missionaries, has led to a curious situation with respect to the acceptance of members of polygamous households into the church. Many churches reject a believing polygamous man who may not have wanted more than one wife, while accepting a believing first wife who may have been the one responsible for her husband's additional marriages!

3. Another reason for plural marriage is *to provide the opportunity for every woman to marry and thus fulfill her proper role in life*. In most societies, it is the ideal for every woman to marry and to give birth to children. It is normal for traditional women to take great pride in their unique abilities in homemaking, producing, and caring for children.

But in most societies the number of women of marriageable age exceeds the number of men. There are two, sometimes three, reasons for this. First, though more boys are born than girls, more boy babies do not survive. This results in most societies in a slightly greater number of marriageable women than men (usually about 104 to 100) during the late teenage years. Second, before the impact of westernization and schooling began to raise the normal age of marriage for women, the tradition was for women to marry soon after puberty, usually at fourteen or fifteen years of age. The normal age for men, however, would be in the mid to late twenties. This made for about ten years worth more women in the "marriage market" than of men at any given time. Third, in some societies at certain points in their histories, many of the men had been killed in warfare, sometimes creating a very large disparity between the numbers of adult men and women.

A combination of this numerical disparity and the conviction that it is the responsibility of a society to provide marriage for every woman leads to polygyny. Women are considered so valuable that they are to be kept secure through marriage, and children so valuable that every effort should be made to bring the maximum number into the world. Thus, plural marriage.

4. A fourth reason for polygamy is *the desire for many children*. The expectation is that every woman will bear as many children as possible, thus increasing the work force.

5. A further reason is *to compensate for barrenness in a first wife*. As we see in both Abraham's and Jacob's families in the Old Testament, children were provided by another wife or concubine when the first or preferred wife was barren. Many men in polygamous societies will send a barren wife away. Many, however, will

love the first wife so much that they will keep her but, often at her insistence, take a second wife in order that the family will not go childless.

As in all other areas of sociocultural life, we see that this custom has been developed as a people's way of coping with real or imagined problems of life. Though the reasoning polygamous peoples use to justify their custom may differ from our reasoning, it needs to be taken seriously. Before we make any moral judgments concerning a custom or seek to change it, respect for the people who practice it demands that we make every effort to understand the custom from their point of view.

We in the West are quick to see the problems of arranged marriage and multiple wives, many of which are very real. There is, for example, often a great deal of conflict between wives and between wives and their husband in a polygamous home. Jealousy and favoritism, often spawning hate, are frequently there. In seeing such problems with plural marriages, however, we westerners and those imitating us need also to take seriously the flaws in western systems. Though to us women are so valuable they must be free, western women pay a high price in insecurity for that freedom. With regard to marriage, we cannot carry out what we promise. Furthermore, to get our youth married, we rely on a system where people randomly meet and marry on the primary basis of emotional attachment. This system also penalizes the woman, because while the men are allowed to be aggressive in seeking out wives, women are supposed to sit and wait for the men to do the choosing.

Those who advocate one system over the other tend to compare the ideal of one system with the actual or even the worst of the other. This is not fair. If we compare ideals with ideals, we find that an ideal polygamous system and an ideal monogamous system work about as well as each other, while an actual polygamous system and an actual monogamous system are about as bad as each other.

So the systems are relatively equal to each other, but what about God's standards? We assert that God's ideal is for each man to have one wife and each woman to have one husband for life. If this ideal does not happen, either because of human incompatibility (as in divorce), or because of cultural structuring (as with plural marriage), what should be done?

God is realistic. When divorce occurred, He regulated it, not because He approved but because He is realistic and patient. God says, "I hate divorce" (Mal 2:16), but He provides a rule that regulates it and assures the woman her rights when it occurs (Dt 24:1–3). With regard to polygamy, He never condemns it but works with the society invisibly toward monogamy. Cross-cultural witnesses need to be as respectful and patient as God is in dealing with subideal worldview assumptions and the surface-level customs that accompany them.

The widespread rapid and often destructive sociocultural changes taking place in the world today seldom allow us the luxury of working with systems, whether traditional or western, that are still intact. Mass media, urbanization, the mobility of individuals and groups, and a myriad of spin-off factors conspire to disrupt traditional courtship and marriage patterns. Polygamy is economically counterproductive and difficult to maintain in a city. Women who have obtained higher levels of schooling seldom agree to marriage arrangements made by their rural families. Not infrequently, they prefer to work in a city and, with or without marriage, give birth to a child from time to time. Or they may choose abortion when pregnancy occurs.

Incredibly high brideprices or dowries impose impossible economic burdens on many families. So do expensive western-style weddings. The refusal of youth who have been to school to farm, often accompanied by their choosing to live in the cities, deprives rural families of their work force. The lure of money gained through growing cash crops instead of food often reduces traditional people to poverty and starvation. Many family members no longer carry out their traditionally expected roles. Cultural disruption and social demoralization have replaced stability in most parts of the world. Will the family survive?

Divorce

All peoples have to deal with the fact that a certain number of marriages need to be dissolved. In most societies, the families play a major role in divorce proceedings, just as they do in marriage arrangements. In individualistic western societies, the major part of the responsibility in divorce, as in weddings, falls on the marriage partners themselves.

There are several reasons for divorce. In many societies, childlessness is a major reason. The marriage contract is seen as assuring that there will be children. If there are none after a few years, it would be typical for the husband in a patrilineal society to approach his own relatives about dissolving the marriage. They would then go to the wife's relatives to get them to return the brideprice or, in some cases, to supply a different wife for their son. In some societies, it is felt that the wife's obligation to the husband and his family has been fulfilled if she has borne them two or three children. If she is unhappy in the marriage, she may then leave without the repayment of any of the brideprice or upon repayment of a small portion of it.

In many societies, a marriage can be dissolved if the groom's family fails to pay the whole brideprice. Often the wife's family allows the couple to get married before the full brideprice has been paid. If after a period of time the remainder has not been paid, the marriage can be dissolved. Among some peoples, simple incompatibility is sufficient reason for dissolution. If one spouse is dissatisfied with the other, he or she may ask relatives to work out a divorce. If there is a brideprice involved, the relatives may exert considerable pressure against their daughter (since divorce would mean a return of the brideprice) or for their son (since divorce would mean receiving back the brideprice). Some traditions, where no brideprice is involved, allow a simple dismissal of a wife. For example, in certain Muslim societies, the simple statement, "I divorce you," said several times, is enough to dissolve a marriage.

In western societies, the dissolution of a marriage is much more formal than in most, involving lawyers and legal proceedings. Economic arrangements constitute a major part of the divorce proceedings, both in western and in nonwestern societies.

MISSIOLOGICAL APPLICATIONS

In addition to the applications for cross-cultural Christian witness pointed out above, we may add the following:

1. Most of the peoples of the world are very family oriented. At all points, therefore, family structuring, including interpersonal expectations, leadership,

and authority patterns, needs to be taken seriously in evangelism and the plant-ing and conduct of churches.

In family-oriented societies, the making of major decisions is family based. In an extended family, any major decision can involve quite a large number of people. The appeal for decisions for Christ in such societies should not, therefore, be made to individuals, unless they hold a prominent place in their families. Waiting to baptize family members—especially women and children—until the whole family has converted is highly advisable in most cases. Unfortunately, much western mis-sionary work has appealed to individuals with little, if any, reference to the place of such individuals in their families. This has often resulted in the conversion of only marginal people and a few others willing to stand against their traditions.

Appealing for conversion to heads of families, though usually resulting in a longer time before conversion, has proved to be a better strategy, unless they have completely rejected the message. Not infrequently, even when the family head rejects the message, he gives those under him permission to convert. When family heads are positive toward the message, typically they will consult those under their authority concerning conversion. When all or nearly all agree, the family makes a "multi-individual" decision, with all turning to Christ at the same time. Some of those involved in such a conversion may have already made individual decisions but wisely waited until those in authority agreed for all to move into Christianity at once. Wise cross-cultural witnesses advise such people to witness within the family, in hopes of seeing the whole family come to Christ, rather than stepping out of the family to be baptized soon after their individual decision. Often, at the time it is announced that a family group will move into Christianity, many in the group will not have made individual decisions. They make such deci-sions later, after the group as a whole has formally turned to Christ. Such deci-sion-making patterns then result in extended-family churches. These are more appropriate in such societies than churches made up of individuals or small seg-ments from different families. Much damage has been done to the cause of Christ by cross-cultural witnesses who have ignored traditional family-oriented decision-making processes in attempting to lead people to Christ.

Strategies should work *with* rather than against culturally appropriate lines of authority, leadership, and decision making. That is, every attempt should be made to win and incorporate into church life family leaders who have led in group decision making, rather than family "remnants" who have separated themselves from their families in order to become Christian.

2. After a family has moved into Christianity together, it is wise to disciple them together. Western patterns of separating family members into age groups (e.g., in Sunday school) may work reasonably well among westernizing segments of nonwestern societies. In the more traditional segments, however, the customary pattern of communication is likely to involve a primary focus on the older male leaders, with the women and younger men listening in. Such a pattern can be effectively utilized for Christian instruction, with the whole group hearing Chris-tian truth and making decisions as a group to follow the new principles.

3. The entrance of Christianity as a part of westernization has been hard on traditional family life. Whether we focus on the way western missionaries have opposed such customs as polygamy and brideprice or the destruction of family val-ues brought about by the schools, the results have usually been disastrous. In many societies, the exclusion of polygamists from the church has split families and

denied the church real leadership by keeping the traditional leaders outside of Christianity while women, children, and marginals have been allowed in. Those given leadership in the churches then are young men who have no status in society and have been alienated from their families through western schooling. Often, in addition, moral standards and traditional marriage patterns have also broken down and a wide rift developed between younger and older generations.

Such breakdown, whether in conversion and leadership patterns or in morals and marriage, present Christians with formidable challenges. Since the coming of the Gospel from western sources has had a lot to do with the breakdown, it appears to me that western Christians need to give attention to helping people seek solutions. The first steps toward solution need to involve Christians who are westerners, or westernized members of nonwestern societies, coming to better understandings of traditional patterns, values, and expectations and of how God worked among peoples with similar customs. From there, westerners and non-westerners can work together to come to realistic combinations of the best of traditional and western customs for the church to advocate.

4. In spite of contemporary disruptions in family solidarity, we should note that many families survive with a good bit of strength, often with both urban and rural components. When major decisions are contemplated by one segment of the family, the other segment will need to be consulted before the decision can be made. A missionary friend of mine discovered this fact when, after an evangelistic approach to a rural family, they informed him that, though positive toward Christ, they could not make a final decision until they consulted with their urban relatives. After consultation, they rejected the Christian way.

5. At least three kinds of sociocultural situations are resulting from the impact of westernization on traditional family systems. The first is a separation of given people groups into a more traditional segment and a more westernized segment. The second is the emerging of new patterns that are neither wholly one nor the other. The third is a high degree of demoralization. Often these three types of adaptation are well mixed in any given population.

When the society splits into traditional and westernized segments, each type of cultural organization needs to be taken seriously. It may be necessary to have separate churches for each group, in order to adequately convey the fact that God accepts and respects both kinds of cultural adaptation. In this case, the more traditional members of the family will likely prefer a church organized and worshiping according to traditional cultural patterns. Such churches are rarely developed, leading to the loss for Christ of large numbers of traditional peoples who choose to remain traditional. The more westernized segments of the same families will prefer organization and worship after more western patterns, perhaps conducted in the trade or European language. Such churches are more common, but they often give the heretical impression that God only accepts those who give up their traditional cultural patterns when they accept Christ.

When working with people who have effectively mixed traditional and western assumptions and practices, the resulting cultural structuring needs to be taken just as seriously as either of the source cultures. The new structures are the appropriate way of life for those who practice them. What needs to be carefully watched, both in this category and any others, is the blending of non-Christian assumptions with what *look like* Christian customs. It is common, for example, for people to attend church but to depend on traditional diviners and healers, rather than on God, in times of crisis. This "dual allegiance" (*see* Kraft and Kraft 1993) is the most serious problem in worldwide Christianity today.

A third possibility is that people simply get discouraged and virtually give up trying. Parents see their children "going to the dogs" and don't know what to do about it. They give up when they see that traditional forms of discipline no longer work and their children don't seem to care about the family and the maintenance of family traditions. Young people, for their part, often live in bewilderment, not knowing what is right and how to balance the conflicting expectations of parents and the youth society around them.

Unfortunately, in each of these cultural configurations we find members of the same families in different places. Frequently traditional parents have children who have largely westernized or worked out a combination culture. Either or both parents and children may suffer from discouragement or demoralization. The cultural imperialism that we so decry when it comes from western missionaries is often a factor in the relationships between nonwestern parents and children. Though it is often difficult to apply, the principle of dealing with each group in terms of its own culture still applies. Traditional parents need to be helped to understand the validity of their children's approach to life and to encourage structures, within or apart from their own churches, that work with their cultural and linguistic preferences. Young people need to be helped to understand and appreciate where their parents are coming from and to make decisions that are as considerate as possible of their understandings and practices. The command to honor our fathers and mothers, with its promise of long life if we obey, is still in the Bible (Ex 20:12), but so is the command to not discourage our children (Col 3:21).

CHAPTER 19

STATUS AND ROLE

INTEGRATIONAL THOUGHT

Jesus had an interesting perspective on status and role. In the Kingdom, things are different in many ways. For one, what is normal in the world is not to be normal in the Kingdom. He pointed this out to the disciples in the event recorded in Mark 10:35–45, in which James and John (and their mother) asked for special positions in the Kingdom. But the Kingdom works by other principles—what someone has called upside-down principles. What is to be normal in the Kingdom therefore involves quite a different approach to status and role from that of the world. Jesus summarizes His teaching on this subject by saying,

> You know that the men who are considered rulers of the heathen have power over them, and the leaders have complete authority. This, however, is not the way it is among you. If one of you wants to be great, he must be the servant of the rest; and if one of you wants to be first, he must be the slave of all. For even the Son of Man did not come to be served; he came to serve and to give his life to redeem many people (vv. 42–45).

High status is, of course, a cultural form, as is the role one adopts in carrying out that status. The question is, how is that status used and what does it mean to those affected by the use of the status? They all knew how leaders of the heathen and even the Pharisees used their status: they lorded it over those beneath them in status. That is, they used their authority, power, and prestige to display and enhance their authority, power, and prestige.

Jesus, more than anyone else, could have done this Himself. He had a perfect right to lord it over everyone. Except that this is not what God is like. Though we've often missed it, what God is really like is best said in Jesus' statement in v. 45 that He came to serve, not to be served, and in His demonstration of what this means when He washed the feet of His disciples, even those of Judas (Jn 13). Jesus/God serves His creatures out of self-giving love and concern, more for our needs than for His prestige. He is like the secure father who, far from feeling threatened by the need to lower himself to clean up after his children, gladly does the most menial tasks for their sakes, while asking no recognition for his part in their success.

The constant message of the Scriptures buttressed by the stunning example of Jesus is that *God's Kingdom people are to use their authority, power, and prestige to help and serve, never to hurt, those without authority, power, and prestige.*

The fact that the Pharisees misused their status perquisites is one of the major things Jesus had against them. Though He tells His followers to obey the Pharisees because of their position (status), He warns them not to "imitate their actions, because they don't practice what they preach" (Mt 23:3). The misuse of

313

status power is also the major thing God had against David in his affair with Bathsheba (2 Sm 11–12). As becomes clear from Nathan's message, David had misused his power to defraud and murder one who had less power than he.

Jesus, of course, was a living demonstration of how God expects Kingdom people to use the authority, power, and prestige He gives us. We are to use our status as members of His family to behave as He did. He has given us "power and authority to drive out all demons and to cure diseases" (Lk 9:1), but we are not to use these perquisites of our status to exalt ourselves. Instead, we are to use them lovingly to serve and free God's battered creatures, as Jesus did. He has given us the power and authority to bless or to curse others. We are to use this power as Jesus did, to "bless and curse not," to bless even those who persecute us (Rom 12:14; Lk 6:28). He has given us authority to grant or refuse forgiveness of sins (Jn 20:23). We are to use that authority (responsibly, of course) to help free those tormented by the Evil One from bondage to that which God has already forgiven.

We are to adopt the attitude of the Son of Man (Phil 2:5), laying aside all desire for prestige. Imitating our Lord, we are to use our status for the good of others, loving as He loved, serving as He served, using whatever position we attain or are given for the same purposes as He used His.

INTRODUCTION

Shakespeare has written, "All the world's a stage and all the men and women merely players. They all have their exits and their entrances and one man in his time plays many parts" (*As You Like It*). Such a quote serves well to introduce us to the subject of status and role, for this is an important feature of all societies. The terms *status/role* or, following Goodenough (1965), *social identity*, are used to designate the parts each human being plays in the game of life.

As we have seen over and over again on these pages, human behavior is patterned according to cultural rules. At the broadest level, culture is organized into subsystems and institutions. At the other end of the spectrum—the interpersonal relationship level—human life is just as structured. It is at this level that the social stereotype called status and the accompanying behavior called role are relevant.

WHAT ARE STATUS AND ROLE?

The term *status*, as usually used within anthropology, is a structural term referring to the position or rank a person occupies in a society. This is what Goodenough (1965) calls a social identity. Labels such as father, mother, teacher, pastor, president, professor, doctor, garbage collector, in addition to designating a function served by a person, also serve to indicate the position (status) occupied by that person. *A status is a social position or identity occupied by a member of a society to which are assigned rights and duties*. A status is typically labeled by a term that enables one who knows the social patterns of a society to describe the holder of that status in terms of the stereotypes and expectations of that society. A status is *a kind of social stereotype*, a part that we play in the drama of life.

For example, the label husband raises in a person's mind a stereotype that includes such things as a picture of how a husband ought to behave, what a husband looks like, what his relationship is to another person labeled wife, and what can be expected of him. The label garbage collector brings to mind a stereotype of one who fulfills quite another kind of function in society.

Role is how we play the part assigned by our status. Statuses are always coupled with roles. The status is the position, the role is the way one behaves in that position. The status is the part one plays in the game of life, the role is how one plays that part.

Though there is a range of behavior allowed within a given status, certain behavior is considered socially appropriate and other behavior is not. Behavior considered acceptable for a given status will range from ideal to marginal. When people act according to the rights and duties that society expects to go along with a status, their role performance is deemed to be appropriate. If somebody has the status of a rich man's son but acts like a poor man's son, he is likely to be told to act more appropriately. If a person has the status of college professor but acts like a child, he or she will meet with social disapproval. However, a professor who is a grandfather is allowed to act very childlike when playing with his grandchildren (I know, I do so regularly), though such behavior would be strongly disapproved of in other situations.

The role is the dynamic aspect of status. In a sense, status is rather static, a position that just sits there, a state of being. What one does in and with that position, however, is dynamic. That's the role. Status and role are always paired, but there may be a variety of creatively expressed roles played by people of the same status at different times. Roles are how actors play the parts society gives them in the play of life, but one actor does not always play a role like someone else does, or even like he or she did last time.

People adopt different roles when relating to people of other statuses. Students will ordinarily adopt one role vis-à-vis a professor, another in relation to other students, and still another when relating to the librarian. Men and women typically adopt different roles when relating to those of their own sex than when relating cross-sexually. Missionaries tend to behave differently in relation to nationals, other missionaries, home supporters, and mission board officials.

People frequently occupy many statuses and roles at a time. I, for example, am a son to my parents, a brother to my brothers and sister, an in-law to their spouses, a husband to my wife, a father to my children, a grandfather to my grandchildren, an uncle to my nephews and nieces, a cousin to my cousins, a teacher to my students, an employer to those I employ, a neighbor to my neighbors, a person of relatively high status, an American, a missionary, a Christian, a middle-aged male, on occasion a student, a visitor, a host, a messenger, a preacher, a dishwasher, a counselor, a softball player (retired), a stamp collector, a woodworker, a computer operator, and more. *Though I am only one person, there's a sense in which I am as many different people as the statuses I have and the roles I play.*

Given statuses tend to cluster together. A middle-aged male, for example, is likely to be son, brother, husband, father, grandfather, cousin, and uncle—plus, in American society, whatever statuses and roles his occupation brings with it. A middle-aged female is likely to be daughter, sister, wife, mother, grandmother, cousin, aunt—plus, in American society, whatever statuses and roles her occupation brings with it. This fact makes life easier by making it more predictable. When someone adopts an unpredictable status/role, relationships are made more difficult, as when a professor joins a softball team made up of his or her students.

Predictability/unpredictability is, however, different from acceptability. It may be totally acceptable, though unpredictable, for a foreigner to use the latest slang in a language not his or her own or for a professor to play softball. But when a prestigious person's role performance is such that others of the same status are ashamed of that person, the social consequences may be serious. Such behavior usually leads to the imposition of some social control mechanism, such as the person being ostracized.

Often there are conflicting expectations when we have more than one status in relation to the same people. This can lead to role conflict. What happens, for example, when I as a teacher have my wife or the wife of a faculty colleague as a student? I have experienced both. Fortunately, both my wife and the wives of my colleagues who have taken classes from me have been very good students.

If they weren't good students, I would have been faced with the agonizing decision as to which of my statuses to give priority to. If I give priority to my status as a professor—which, at least in American society, carries with it the expectation that I will not play favorites—I would have to give even the wife of a colleague a low grade, if that is all she earned. If, however, I give priority to my relationship as a colleague of my student's husband, I will give her a high grade, even if she did not earn it.

Such a dilemma is very difficult for a westerner to work out. For many non-westerners, however, it would be impossible to give a relative or friend a low grade, no matter how poor the quality of work. The personal relationship criterion for sorting out status/role conflicts would always outweigh any other criterion.

Other role conflicts arise when a mother has to choose between the needs or desires of her husband and those of her children. Or when a grandfather disciplines his grandchild in a way unacceptable to his son, the child's father, and that son has to choose between being dutiful toward his father and doing what he feels is best for his children. A conflict that is almost universal in American families (and by now in the rest of the world as well) is that between the expectations of one's employer and those of one's family.

KINDS OF STATUS/ROLE

As is obvious from the above discussion, statuses and roles come in pairs. The status parent presupposes that of child. That of husband requires that of wife. Other pairs are adult-youth, teacher-student, wealthy person-poor person, employer-employee, male-female, friend-friend, and so on.

Note that some of these relationships are *superordinate* or *subordinate* (arranged hierarchically) while others are *coordinate* (parallel to each other). In many societies (e.g., India, Korea), nearly every relationship is hierarchical, while in American society the trend is toward as many status pairs as possible relating coordinately. Even in America, however, super/subordinate relationships are usual between parents and children, adults and youth, teachers and students, employers and employees. Coordinate relationships are usual between friends and, in many societies, between siblings, age-mates, and others of "equal" status. In many societies, however, relationships such as male-female (including husband-wife), older-younger (including older brother/sister-younger brother/sister), one occupation-another occupation are almost entirely hierarchical.

There may be a relationship between the social structuring of status/role and psychological health. There has been some discussion within American medical and psychological communities concerning the possibility that the hierarchical doctor-patient model may be detrimental to health. It is said, for example, that in America, doctors and nurses who sit by a patient's bedside and are warm and caring aid healing more than those who stand or are more "professional." Though I know of no research to prove it, I suspect there may be something inherently damaging to the psyches of those continually involved in subordinate/superordinate relationships, even when such social hierarching is the norm.

Interactions between people may be *personal or impersonal*. Status and role distinctions are frequently influential at this point. Relationships between those of unequal status, for example, are often impersonal (teachers and students, doctors and patients, shopper and cashier). On occasion, though, an employer may become quite fond of (and personal with) an employee, a doctor may come to treat a patient as a person rather than as a patient, a student and a teacher may become close friends.

Since status is a matter of social stereotype, it is easy for people of unequal status to relate to each other in a manner that Loewens (1967), analogizing from experience with telephones, label "station-to-station" or "this-is-a-recording," in contrast with "person-to-person" interactions. Those concerned to be incarnational in their ministries should, of course, resist the social pressures to relate to people merely in terms of status expectations. They should, rather, seek to develop person to person interactions.

Status/role pairs involve relationship bonds between those so paired. Following Hiebert (1983:148–50), we may refer to those relationships joined by but a single bond as *simplex* relationships. People so joined would have only one relationship in common, e.g., parent-child, teacher-student, or neighbor-neighbor. Not infrequently, however, especially in smaller and more rural societies, any two people may be related by several status/role bonds. We may term such relationships *multiplex*. For example, a pastor and a parishioner who is a dentist and also a tennis partner, a good friend, and in addition a member of the same local service club may share at least five quite distinct status/role relationships. On Sunday, of course, the relationship is pastor-parishioner, but on Monday dentist-patient, while later in the week they take each other on in tennis, share committee duties, or simply discuss matters friend to friend. Such a complex of relationships is multiplex.

Note that in the two super/subordinate relationships (pastor-parishioner and dentist-patient) the status of the participants, at least with respect to who is in charge, is reversed. Such changes in status can often result in impoliteness and confusion. Suppose, for example, the pastor, since he is used to being in control in church settings, continues to act as if he has authority over the dentist's office or home. It is not unusual for those whose status in one situation gets them in the habit of being in control to unconsciously attempt to exert the same kind of control when they are expected to be guests in someone else's home or office.

Cross-cultural workers are frequently guilty of just such misjudgment. Whatever status we may have had in our home setting and however strong our desire to serve God to the ends of the earth, nothing gives us permission to act as if we own someone else's territory. We can learn from Jesus in this regard. He took quite a different status in the territory controlled by humans than He had in heaven. He then won his way in His relationships with humans, abiding by human rules all the while He was here, in order to relate in a winning way to humans.

ASCRIBED AND ACHIEVED

Statuses and roles are ordinarily spoken of as ascribed (assigned) and achieved. An *ascribed* status is assigned at birth or in relation to some other biological or social certainty such as age, initiation, parenthood, and the like. All societies ascribe some differences of status on the basis of sex and age. In many societies such positions as those of leader/follower, wealthy person/poor person, tradesman/scholar, plus class or caste membership, are likewise assigned at birth. Such assignments often do not seem fair. There seems, however, to be no way out of some such assignments. It is automatic that one born female is assigned the position(s) of a female in the society and will be expected to act (i.e., to carry out the roles) appropriately, whether she likes her status or not.

All societies have some differential in the assignment of sex roles. In some societies, the men are supposed to be strong and the women weak. The men are supposed to be leaders and the women followers. In others, women are supposed to be strong and men weak. In some societies, the men are supposed to be very emotional and the women unemotional. I think of the Bali people of Indonesia, where the men are trained to be artistic, sensitive, and emotional, and the women solid, staid, and dignified.

One can seldom do anything to change an ascribed status in any society. Those societies that are tightly organized and have discouraged diversity have traditionally tended to structure relationships by assigning their people to a fairly fixed position from one end of life to the other. Less tightly organized societies, on the other hand, tend to allow more room for individual variability and achievement. The same statuses that are ascribed in a tightly organized society may be open for virtually anyone to achieve in a less tightly organized one.

An *achieved* status is one that a person is allowed or encouraged by the society to work for. Such status is usually the result of a person doing things (e.g., working) or getting things (e.g., by inheritance). The necessary achievement takes place within whatever parameters the society has set up for a person in that category. A male will ordinarily be allowed to achieve only within those areas allowed to males, a member of a given caste only within whatever leeway is allowed to people of that caste, a young person only within whatever is allowed to a youth of his or her sex, an older person likewise.

Western societies seem to have carried the principle of achievement farther than most. This is one reason why westernization can be so disruptive to more tightly organized societies. In the West, for example, we often blur even the distinctions between male and female statuses/roles that for many societies are set in cement. In addition, status is often achieved on the basis of how far one has gone in school, rather than on the basis either of who one is (ascribed status) or even of what one has accomplished (a usual achievement criterion). Furthermore, the gain in prestige accorded by most societies (traditionally) as one ages is reversed by western societies so that fairly young and inexperienced persons often are granted higher status than the older and more experienced.

A major principle underlying the assigning (ascribing) of statuses seems to be that a society needs to decide how to get all the work done. There is more work to be done in life than any one type of person can do. Theoretically, a society could wait for everybody to grow up and find out what they are good at before assigning them. They could observe individuals, find out their skills, and plug each into whatever jobs (with accompanying status/roles) they are best suited for. That's what western society seems to want to do. People, however, don't wait to learn how they are to relate to others. They grow up relating to others and in that process create for themselves statuses and roles, if there are none assigned.

Most of the peoples of the world don't wait. They simply assign people, without reference to innate differences or abilities. If a male child is born, he is arbitrarily assigned certain tasks that fall to every male. A female is arbitrarily assigned certain other tasks without finding out whether or not she is good at them all.

With regard to sex roles, most societies try to bring about a high degree of complementarity between what men and women are assigned to do. This functions to reduce the amount of potential competition between men and women. In such societies, there is seldom any argument over such things as who looks after the children, does the cooking, and washes the dishes or who relates the family to the society at large, clears the land for farming, and repairs the house. Such tasks are clearly assigned to those of one sex or the other. American society, however, in trying to make nearly every possible position and job available to everyone, has greatly increased the amount of competition between men and women. This competition then becomes a destructive force in our society. In trying to be more fair to everyone, we have unwittingly let ourselves in for another set of serious problems.

Societies depend on assigned statuses (even though these may be unfair to those who weren't born with the abilities to do well at carrying out the necessary roles) to take care of the ordinary business of living. Assignment is usually on the basis of one of three reference points—sex, age, and family relationship. In many societies, the family a person is born into is assigned either to be leaders or to be followers. Such assignments are made at birth, just like the male-female assignment.

Certain assignments are, however, made some time after birth. Among these are occupation and the various assignments that depend on one's age. Though in America an occupation is seldom assigned, in many societies, one or more of the sons of a father are expected to adopt his occupation. If you are male and your father is a farmer, in most societies you will automatically become a farmer; it's assigned to you. What better person to be a farmer than one who has grown up in the home of a farmer?

Even in ascribed statuses there is room for some achievement. Though a person is assigned a context and his or her achievements are limited by the parameters of that context, there is still the question of how well the person is going to perform in that context. A person assigned by society to be a cook, a carpenter, or a musician, for example, may be a good one or a poor one. What kind of a cook, carpenter, or musician one is depends on how well one performs within the parameters of the assigned status/role. He or she may achieve the status of a *good* cook, carpenter, or musician or settle for mediocrity.

In some societies, an ascribed status such as being born into a wealthy home can make it possible for one to achieve other statuses. This commonly happens in American society when those born wealthy are able, because of their wealth, to go into politics. Those who are born into poorer families seldom have either the leisure or the financial backing to long survive this very expensive exercise, unless they have become wealthy through achievement or inheritance.

EVALUATION OF STATUS/ROLE

Societies not only assign statuses/roles, they attach particular values to them—often quite arbitrarily. Such statuses as ruler, wealthy person, physician, and scholar tend to be highly valued. Others such as laborer, garbage collector, poor person, and the like tend to be looked down on.

Often, however, some of the most necessary kinds of occupations are valued quite lowly and some of the least necessary are given a higher ranking in people's minds. Ask, for example, Which is more necessary to the proper functioning of a society, a professor or a garbage collector? In American society, the status of a professor is very high, and that of the garbage collector very low. I think, however, we could get along without professors more easily than we could get along without garbage collectors. If the professors go on strike, hardly anything changes. But if the garbage collectors go on strike, things become really snarled. Sometimes such a discrepancy in the evaluation of status is compensated for by those of lower status earning higher wages than those of "higher" status. But this is not always the case (doctors have high status and usually high salaries, while unskilled laborers have low status and usually low wages as well).

We experienced a kind of checks and balances situation in this regard among the Kamwe. That society is divided into two groups, the commoners and the blacksmiths (a label applied to all craftsmen). The primary characteristic shared by the craftsmen in this subsistence society is that they don't grow all their own food (though many grow some). Instead, they perform nonagricultural tasks such as working with metal and leather, making pottery, producing music, dealing with illness and medicine, divining, and burying. Though these people perform many important services, they are looked down upon by the commoners who grow all or nearly all of their own food and look on themselves as self-sufficient.

The separation between the groups is such that the craftsmen are not allowed to intermarry or develop other close social relationships with the commoners. What we have, then, is a caste barrier between the two groups. Among the functions served by the craftsmen, however, are several that require (from the Kamwe point of view) close contact between the craftsmen and the spirit world. Medical specialists, funeral directors, diviners, and those whose skills require spirit assistance, though looked down on, are also feared, sometimes greatly. I asked a commoner who he feared most, the chief of the village (who has great visibility and great power in the society) or the chief of the craftsmen. Without hesitation, he said, "The chief of the craftsmen." The reason he gave was the close connection that man had with the spirit world. Social prestige, high visibility, and political power was felt to be more than overbalanced by connections with the unseen powers. Though the commoners do not hesitate to criticize these people and refuse to associate with them, they grant them a fair amount of fear-engendered respect.

Women in Kamwe and many other societies are often treated in the same way—given relatively low status on the surface but respected and consulted when major decisions have to be made. In Kamwe society, a chief will rarely even consider announcing a major decision unless he knows the women and the craftsmen are in favor of it. As can be seen, higher status is closely related to the visible exercise of power. There is, however, a considerable amount of power wielded in less visible ways by those of lower status.

Often visible power can be termed *the power of authority*, while the less obvious exercise of power (e.g., that of women) can be labeled *the power of influence*. In many situations, it can be argued that the power of influence is greater than the power of authority.

Age is highly valued in many societies and great respect accorded those who have had long experience. In traditional and peasant societies, people usually gain respect as they age and achieve those things expected of them as they pass through the various stages of the life cycle (*see* chapter 14). The great prestige given to youth in western societies and the desire people have to remain youthful makes our way of life quite distinct in this regard.

APPLICATIONS TO CROSS-CULTURAL MINISTRY

The applications of this material to cross-cultural ministry are many. In what follows, several important questions are raised and approaches to answers presented in terms of the above considerations.

1. Who should lead the church?

It has been the usual practice for westerners involved in cross-cultural ministry to simply introduce their own cultural structures (i.e., some sort of school based on literacy) as if these were the God-ordained means for producing leaders. This has ordinarily been done sincerely and without the slightest intention of disrupting the receiving society. One problem is that the receiving societies invariably have their own structures for obtaining leaders, usually based on principles quite different from those of western societies.

Another problem is the fact that the Scriptures endorse no school-based method of obtaining leaders. We see, rather, a focus on gifting (1 Cor 12; 1 Tm 4:14), behavior (1 Tm 3), and apprenticeship (the practice of both Jesus and Paul) as the bases for the appointment of leaders. These criteria were employed within the guidelines of the society, with one notable possible exception—when Timothy is advised to practice and teach that gifting supersedes youthfulness (1 Tm 4:11–16).

A leader is one who is followed, and those who follow ordinarily abide by cultural rules concerning who is worthy of being followed. Often, for example, a person's family or social class, age, and perhaps achievements will be more important to any potential followers than his or her attainment of a particular set of academic credentials.

What, then, is the reputation and the ability to attract adherents of a church led by someone not qualified (from the point of view of the society) to lead? What happens in an age- or gender-oriented society if the pastor is young or female? Or what if the pastor comes from a family or social class not allowed to lead?

Among the Kamwe, the tradesmen were not allowed to lead commoners. This meant that, in spite of his schooling, one of our pastors, a tradesman, could never pastor a church in the normal way. Another tradesman, however, was able to solve the problem and grow a church quite successfully. What he did was to function somewhat in the background, except that he led the singing. This was a role appropriate to a person of his social class. When it came to the preaching, though, he regularly turned things over to a man of the "proper" social class.

Another man had continual success, however. Every place we assigned him, things went well, for he was the son of a chief. Though he was young, he was born to lead. He knew it, and all the people knew it. Even when he was assigned to a congregation at a distance from his own village, people responded well to him.

In another situation, Dr. Alan Tippett, a founding faculty member of the Fuller School of World Mission, was asked by an Episcopal Church mission to study their work among the Navaho Indians. Many of their churches were not growing, and the missionaries did not know why. At one point Tippett asked if the missionaries had noticed that each of the more "alive" churches had a strong woman song leader. They had not. Nor did they know the significance of this fact. The Navaho are matrilineal. If they are to be true to the people's understanding of how things ought to be, their churches need to have women in prominent positions. Tippett's advice to them was that if they wanted improvement in their churches, they would need to learn to work in terms of the indigenous ideas concerning status and role.

I give these illustrations to show both the possibility of working with the cultural structures and the consequences of not working in terms of the only understanding of life of any given people. Though the examples are from rural settings, while some of my readers may be working within an urban setting, the principle of working within the expected structures still applies. Indeed, though urban settings look very different from rural settings, a large percentage of the people living in the urban situation may still be thinking rural thoughts. That is, though their setting is urban, their expectations may be more like those of rural areas than it would seem to an outside observer.

2. What about sex roles?

There is currently much discussion concerning sex roles. Three aspects of this discussion would seem to be of great importance to cross-cultural witnesses. They are: 1) The determining of God's attitude, 2) an evaluation of American understandings in cross-cultural perspective, and 3) the development of helpful guidelines in terms of which cross-cultural workers can function in a loving, Christian way in other societies.

Under the influence of American and more broadly western understandings of equality, many western Christians feel compelled to include a message concerning status and role equality in their presentations of the Gospel. They will frequently buttress such a concept with scriptural interpretations that focus on the supposed "very low" status of women in Hebrew society and the supposedly very different attitude demonstrated by Jesus in His dealings with women. Though there is some truth in the contention that women were not as well treated as they might have been in Jesus' day, it is also true that the judgments Americans make are dependent upon a set of worldview assumptions that themselves need to be examined critically.

For example, our concept of equality is firmly rooted in a perspective that consistently rates positively most of what have traditionally been regarded as male statuses and roles (overt leadership, intellectual training, jobs and relationships outside the home, freedom of movement and thought) while downgrading traditionally "female" statuses and roles (homemaking, child rearing, covert leadership, intuitive thinking, person [as opposed to job] orientation). As a result, Americans have developed a single standard of evaluation for males and females in terms of one set of criteria—that traditionally considered appropriate for males. By teaching this value and training both males and females (largely in schools) to strive to achieve and evaluate themselves in terms of their accomplishments in these areas, our society has brought about wholesale competition between the sexes.

We have also come to define equality as sameness and given ourselves to attempting to produce as much similarity as possible between men and women. If men and women are to be equal, we believe, they have to achieve in the same areas of life. If women do not achieve in these (traditionally men's) areas at as high a level as men, they are regarded as second-class in terms of their achievement on the traditionally male ladder. In these terms, women who do not "make it" are second-class persons. Many women, of course, do better than men in traditionally male areas, constituting a grave threat to many men.

A major reason for any lack of achievement in these terms by women is the fact that most American women are also expected to perform what have been traditionally considered female roles (homemaking, childbearing and rearing, hospitality, covert leadership). Since these roles are systematically devalued by our society, females often feel they are oppressed in two ways. What they are expected to do in traditionally female roles is not highly valued (except in the abstract) and, in addition, these involvements keep them from doing those things that will earn them high status in the society. Women are expected to carry a double load. This starts in childhood when, if they are to learn to be "women" (in the traditional sense), they have to learn it from their mothers and other women via a separate outside-of-school educational process (cooking, homemaking, child care) that competes for time and energy with the schooling process. In addition, if they are to have a career, they are still expected (and usually expect themselves) to get married and produce children, even though marriage and family responsibilities will interfere with that career.

One result of combining traditionally male goals with traditionally female goals is the fact that women are now expected to add a career to the already heavy set of demands placed on women by our society. Basically, four things are required for a woman to feel successful. She must 1) achieve sexiness, 2) get married, 3) produce children (though raising children is defined by our society as drudgery), and 4) have a career. These expectations are backbreaking, but they have the advantage of being fairly clear and well-defined. On the male side of things, nearly all the equivalent of this fulfillment is to be achieved in one's career. One important source of insecurity and tension in husband-wife relationships is the fact that a woman often has achieved three or all four of the things expected of her a full ten to fifteen years before her husband has achieved a similar degree of fulfillment in his career.

Without pursuing this track any further, let me simply suggest how things might have been different. Suppose, for example, our society had chosen either of two other alternatives: 1) to value traditionally female roles more highly than traditionally male roles, or 2) to define equality in such a way that people could be thoroughly different yet regarded as equal. If the first course had been followed, we would have a situation similar to the present situation, but with the standards slanted in the other direction.

If the second option were pursued, we could end up with complementarity in place of the present competitiveness between the sexes. Men could then feel completely fulfilled in doing male things without fear that some female might come along and do them better. Women would find their activities valued just as highly as men's activities, even though their activities were completely different from and noncompetitive with those of men. There would be little opportunity for argument over who does what. Women could again feel proud of their accomplishments at home, their ability to raise their children properly, and their role in helping their husbands become important. Instead of the present arrangement of first-class (mostly male) persons and second-class (mostly female) persons, men and women could each be first-class, even though they are assigned to and feel fulfilled by completely different tasks.

If this analysis is accurate, the contemporary feminist movement within western societies may be seen as a perfectly legitimate (given western assumptions) attempt on the part of "second-class" persons (females) to become "first-class" persons. There is, however, a major problem when westerners carry "gender-equality" ideals to societies with traditional sex-role differentiations that effectively eliminate competition between genders by eliminating overlapping social roles in work, community, and family order. These societies are ideally working on the basis of assumption two above—that men and women can be thoroughly different yet completely equal. Ideally, then, women in these societies can feel totally fulfilled as homemakers, childbearers, and child rearers. A great many did until western ideals were imported without recognizing the losses as well as the gains resulting from changes in these societies' own ideals and practices.

There is, however, a major problem in this analysis. It is idealized. Though, ideally, societies with such no-competitive male and female roles allow for first-class men and women, actually men are often given more opportunity than women to use their power to make the life of women less fulfilling than it would ideally be. The security orientation of such societies spoken of in chapter 18, which puts men in charge of keeping the women and children secure, also gives men opportunity to make life hard for women, if they so choose. And, sinfulness and selfishness being what they are, men frequently avail themselves of this opportunity.

Western judgments concerning the reasons for the difficulties of female life in nonwestern societies and western tactics for correcting the situation are, however, usually quite wide of the mark. They tend to start from the assumption that it is evil in and of itself for a society to operate with fairly watertight distinctions between male and female roles. That view, however, needs to be argued and demonstrated, not assumed on the basis of modern western worldviews. Debates on gender relations should be conducted, in other words, on the terms of a given culture. It should not be simply assumed that traditional patterns based on distinct gender roles are bad while western patterns that blur gender distinctions and inadvertently increase role competitiveness between men and women are good.

It is here recommended, then, that westerners seek first to understand both the positive aspects of sex role distinctions and the negative aspects of western anti-role-distinction attitudes before we attempt to advise other peoples. With such understandings we should be better able to help other peoples to strive to reach their own ideals, rather than disrupt their societies by aiming at ideals that are very destructive in western societies. Women (and the societies that depend so much on them) are, for example, often more hurt than helped by programs that send girls to schools (to become more like boys) rather than assisting them to learn better homemaking and child rearing skills. These latter skills are ultimately much more important than school skills to any society, and ignoring them is at least as destructive to other societies as it is to our own. *Cross-cultural workers need to consider the possibility that women may feel more fulfilled by and proud of the ability to carry out tradition-assigned female roles than they would by being trained to compete with males.* Local persons should, as they grow in their understanding of the gospel, be empowered to soberly evaluate and even resist the disruption of goals, motivations and behavior of certain vocal western groups. Though these have certain valid complaints, they spring from experience within quite a different cultural world with their basis in quite a different set of assumptions. At the very least, sound anthropoligical and theological criteria need to guide us in an area of extreme delicacy like gender relations.

3. What is God's attitude toward sex role distinctions?

Though it would be presumptuous to claim to know God's attitude beyond a shadow of a doubt, it will be useful to attempt to guess on the basis of the indications we can derive from Scripture. One major problem arises, however: the cultures of the Scriptures all show a similar status/role structuring, with men in authority over women in all matters outside the home and with ultimate authority within the home as well. The assumption at all times seems to be that women will be married. The Scriptures thus leave us to infer either 1) that God wants all societies to be arranged as are those in Scripture, or 2) that He would have adapted just as thoroughly to other structurings of status and role as He did to those of the Hebrews and the Greeks.

What might God have done in a matrilineal society (or matriarchal, if there be any)? Or what patterns would we see Him using in a society such as that of contemporary America, where there are less than 75 marriageable men for every 100 marriageable women and polygamy is not allowed? Would He work with or against a society, such as American, that has chosen to be negative toward rigid role distinctions?

My basic position in this issue, as in each of the other issues raised in these pages, is to suggest that God is willing to work with and in terms of any cultural structuring, but will not endorse any cultural usage in which those with less power are mistreated by those with more. Even in the patriarchal societies in which the events of Scripture took place, we see God allowing many customs that one suspects fall somewhat below his ideals (e.g., enslaving of Gentiles [Lv 25], trial by ordeal [Nm 5], divorce [Dt 24], polygamy [2 Sm 12]).

I believe, therefore, that God will accept whatever status/role patterns He finds in a society as the place to start. His basic message will then be that people relate in love to Him and to all fellow human beings with all their heart, soul, mind, and strength from within the social structure in which they live. Whenever status/role relationships are used to oppress others, however, God comes down against the oppressor, especially if the oppressor claims to be on God's side.

From anthropological evidence, it looks as though a healthy society will be structured in such a way that the positions of people within the society are fairly well-defined, to minimize competition between potentially competitive segments of society. Such structuring is done through status and role assignments in terms of which males and females, younger and older, those of one occupation and those of another, those who lead and those who follow are expected to carry out certain relatively nonoverlapping responsibilities. I believe God is in favor of such structuring, whether or not He prefers that males be in authority over females. I suspect He would at least be willing to start with any reasonable arrangement in which each person knows his or her place and carries out his or her responsibilities.

What I assume He would be against (though I think He would be willing to start with even such a sub-ideal arrangement) is any setup in which one segment uses its power to oppress another segment. I also think He would be against any arrangement that allows unhealthy (destructive) amounts of competition between segments. I believe He wants to provide His people with insight, desire, and power to change the way such cultural patterns are used, whether or not the structures themselves are changed. As Christian witnesses, then, I believe we should be careful not to oppose a pattern simply because it is being used wrongly (i.e., oppressively). We should stand, rather, for a usage of their patterns that is more Christian and against usages that are less Christian (as I believe God would), without simply submitting to our ethnocentric tendencies to advocate our own cultural pattern as if our pattern in and of itself were better than theirs. Note how God did this in David's case by condemning his misuse of power while supporting his practice of polygamy (2 Sm 12:7–9).

4. What kind of status or position should we as outsiders take when we go into another society?

In order to relate properly to the human beings of another society we need to be in an understandable relationship to them. That is, the label (standing for status/role) assigned to us, whether by ourselves or by them, must make sense within their frame of reference. We need to ask ourselves, If our position in our home society is labeled missionary or pastor or even Christian, what will our status be in the receiving society if that label is simply carried over? What is their stereotype of someone who carries that label? Will it gain us understanding and acceptance, or will it hinder the work we are called to do? If the latter, is there a possibility of doing things in such a way that we are reassigned to a different status?

In many societies, such terms as the above elicit a positive reaction. Where, however, the understanding is negative, we need to consider what, if anything, can be done about it. Is this a society that allows an outsider like me to choose a different role? If so, under what conditions and with what consequences? Can I legitimately present myself as a scholar (as Wycliffe Bible Translators do), or as a relief worker (as World Vision representatives do), or as a student or business person (as many Christians working in "closed" countries do)? Or can I establish myself (hopefully noncompetitively) in a way understandable within the society as a teacher, agriculturalist, medical specialist, or the like?

Sometimes a person's ministry so demonstrates the presence and power of God (according to their expectations) that the people assign him or her to the position of religious specialist. I know of a case where a missionary couple is used so often to heal that the people consider them the most powerful shamans they have ever seen. In parts of India, where a holy man is expected to be ascetic, certain Christian witnesses have been able to win their way into the holy man category in people's minds by becoming ascetic. In both of these cases, the Christian witness has been enormously enhanced, even though there have been certain aspects of these statuses and their roles that the Christian witnesses have chosen not to adopt. Unfortunately, most western missionaries have not done whatever was necessary to be perceived by the people as genuinely from God and have usually been more effective at secularizing than Christianizing (*see* Newbigin 1966:18).

Though there are limitations, it is often possible to work toward reassignment if one discovers that the assigned status/role is a hindrance to what one is attempting to do. Much of what has been said above provides clues to enable one to overcome a disagreeable stereotype. If one is labeled missionary, for example, and would like to escape that stereotype, he or she may, by developing intimate personal relationships with insiders, get into the position where people remark, "You may be a missionary, but you're different."

The basic problem, as I see it, is that of getting out of whatever social stereotype (status/role) one is assigned to and into the receiving people's "human being" category. "Missionary (or teacher or doctor, etc.) but different" usually means "human (and, therefore, understandable) like us." So the trick is to learn and do what it takes within their frame of reference to win their reassignment. Usually this involves either playing the role assigned to a status differently than expected or playing a different role altogether. Either can be done only by the permission of the insiders, so careful attention needs to be given to developing close personal relationships with opinion leaders who can both give one permission to act differently and sponsor one in the new position. On this basis we can work for the kind of position within the society that we believe is more conducive to the effective communication of the Gospel than that previously assigned (e.g., foreigner, outsider, dominator, competitor, etc.). See Kraft 1979a:156–59 for further discussion of this issue.

5. What functional roles can be adopted by cross-cultural witnesses?

Apart from the status/role associated with whatever label we may wear, there are a variety of functional roles that may be adopted by the cross-cultural witness.

One may choose to relate to the members of another society as an insider or as an outsider. Though I argue that we should ordinarily follow Jesus' example and become insiders (Kraft 1979b, 1991a), Loewen and Loewen (1967) raises some important counter arguments that may apply, at least in certain situations. Insiders, it is pointed out, though occupying an understandable position in the society, may by virtue of that fact find themselves involved in reciprocal obligations that seriously interfere with the tasks they came to fulfill. An experience is related in Paraguay, where someone felt that he should become an insider and found a family willing to adopt him. He found out later, however, that they had a reason he hadn't suspected for wanting a North American in their family—a reason that hampered his intended ministry. Though his aim was to communicate the Gospel, their strategy was to invite an outsider to join their family who had enough money and prestige to bail out one of their sons who kept getting drunk and locked up by the police!

Though those admitted to insider status run the risk of being pressed into serving the desires of their receptors, those who function as outsiders usually fare even worse. They may be regarded as spies, used simply as status symbols or those who supply status goods and services (schools, hospitals), or used as go-betweens with government or economic agencies. Even so, Loewen wonders if he did the right thing in trying to become so totally an insider. He theorizes that perhaps a cross-cultural witness should seek to become a partial insider/partial outsider. Though such a position would sacrifice some of the incarnational nature of one's ministry, it would avoid the potential crippling of that ministry by the kind of problem Loewen experienced. There are several very valuable functions that can be performed from such a position. Among them are the ability to 1) serve as a mirror to help people take a fresh look at themselves, 2) get people to share them-selves and thereby discover their own needs, 3) provide a source of alternatives from which they can select when searching for answers to pressing questions, and 4) be a catalyst who provides a bit of push but disappears from the process once it gets underway.

Another choice we may have with regard to the functional role we adopt is that between *cooperator* and *competitor*. With the strong support of western world-views, much of the approach to Christian witness engaged in by westerners has been competitive in nature. We have tended to interpret God's mandate to us as involv-ing an "our side against their side" mentality, which to some extent it is. But in taking this approach we have (in keeping with our worldview) often taken things too far and ignored the many senses (supported by Scripture) in which Christian-ity is to work in continuity, rather than in discontinuity with the culture of the receiving society. Instead, we have set up competing religious structures (western church policies and practices), competing medical structures (clinics and hospi-tals), competing educational structures (schools for children and church leaders), and even competing communicational structures (writing and monologue preaching).

Though each of these (and other) innovations has brought substantial cultural benefits to nonwestern societies, they have also conveyed in a none-too-subtle way the message that the Christian God sets Himself in opposition to much or all of the way of life of the receiving people. How much more like the character of God as shown in Scripture would it have been for His cross-cultural witnesses to cooper-ate with the social structures already in place than to compete against them as if they were of no value to God? Contemporary cross-cultural witnesses should look for ways to work cooperatively with the receiving people and their patterns of life, rather than simply following the western way and competing with them and their ways.

But what about the evil in the societies we take the Gospel to? Yes, there is much evil, but in these societies, as in our home society, the evil is the work of Satan and those who do his bidding within the society. It is not the society or the culture that is in and of itself evil. To repeat a clever saying some have found help-ful to keep us alert to this fact, "Culture is culture. Culture is not the enemy. The enemy is the enemy." Let's oppose the right enemy, not the wrong one.

One way of working toward such an approach is to first enter the receiving society in a subordinate position as a *learner*. Jesus spent the first thirty years of His life learning to use the structures of Palestinian society and building up the credibility He would need for His later ministry. We need to spend a substantial proportion of the time and energy available to us in a learner role. We need to be learners in language, of course, and to see even this as ministry (*see* Brewster and Brewster 1984). But we also need to be learners in religious matters, medical mat-ters, educational matters, social matters, communicational matters—recognizing that, as with language, God wants to use these local structures (not simply their western counterparts) for His purposes. In the process of learning, accompanied by the building up of good relationships, the cooperator role is easily earned. One earns the right to be regarded by insiders as nonthreatening—one who opens up rather than keeping to oneself, engages in easy give-and-take rather than lording it over and dominating people, and contributes what one has to offer for their betterment.

6. Summary of possible roles of cross-cultural workers

Hiebert (1985:255–83) has discussed several roles that cross-cultural witnesses have or can play in relation to various other persons or groups with whom they regularly interact. Often these roles were detrimental to the effective communication of the Gospel but were assumed without realizing this. Frequently the witnesses were quite unconscious of the nature and type of social relationships inherent in and expected of those assigned these roles. With this recognition and the understanding that if one knows what one is doing, then it is frequently possible to behave in such a way that one attains a different status/role, we summarize Hiebert's list in figure 19.1.

Roles in Relation to Nationals	
Negative roles:	"missionary," colonialist, landlord, policeman, reformer, empire builder, spiritual father, administrator, technician, saint, paid preacher
Positive roles:	some insider role, learner, brother, servant, mirror, catalyst, fellow sinner, signpost
Roles in Relation to Other Cross-cultural Witnesses	
Negative roles:	professional missionary
Positive roles:	fellow team member, colleague, co-student
Roles in Relation to the Sending Agency	
Negative roles:	antagonist, "visiting fireman"
Positive roles:	fellow team member
Roles in Relation to the Constituency	
Negative roles:	"missionary on furlough," defender of the missionary image, builder of an empire
Positive roles:	friend, fellow Christian using one's gifts cross-culturally
Roles in Relation to One's Family	
Negative roles:	"missionary" in relation to spouse and/or children, "spiritual giant," dictator
Positive roles:	human being, nurturer, guide, comforter

Figure 19.1 Several roles played by cross-cultural witnesses

As the Apostle Paul exhorts us to "set [our] hearts . . . on the more important gifts" (1 Cor 12:31), so I believe God wants us to set our hearts on filling those statuses and roles in the receiving society that will be most usable in the work of His Kingdom.

CHAPTER 20

GROUPING

INTEGRATIONAL THOUGHT

There's a sense in which the thing called "church" (Greek *ekklesia*) was something that God brought newly into existence after the ascension of Jesus. Certainly a spiritual newness came at that time into God's community. Many preachers and commentators focus on that newness. The community experiencing that newness may be thought of as God's people grouping together for worship of God and working together in service for God. That group has been baptized and empowered by the Spirit of God to be the People of God, doing the Works of God in territory presently ruled by Satan (1 Jn 5:19) but claimed, bought, and paid for by Christ. This all is true and wonderful. We glory in our position and authority as the People of God, the Church.

But there's another sense in which "people of Godness" is not new. In fact, the word *ekklesia*, usually translated "church" in the New Testament is the same Greek word often used (translating Hebrew *qahal*) in the Septuagint (the Greek translation of the Old Testament) to designate the community of God that existed long before what we call the Church came into existence.

The fact is, God has always worked with people in groups. People are made for relationships and can't exist very well (if at all) without them. When He dealt with Abraham, it was with Abraham as the head of a group (Gn 12:5). He worked with Israel as a people and with individual Israelites in their relationships to that people.

People were converted in groups both in the Old Testament and New Testament. These were what Tippett, following Barnett (1953:15), came to call "multi-individual, mutually interdependent" conversions. When Abraham decided to follow Yahweh, his group decided with him. When Cornelius decided for Christ, he did so with his "relatives and close friends that he had invited" (Acts 10:24). When the Philippian jailer believed, he did so with all of his household (including slaves, Acts 16:31–34).

Christians are called the "body of Christ" (1 Cor 12:27), each with his or her own job to do, each interrelating with the others and working together for the good of the whole.

Groupness is as crucial to the people of God as it is to humanity in general. We cannot live our ordinary lives without other humans. We cannot live our Christian lives without other Christians. We are made for relationships both on the natural plane and on the spiritual plane. We should by no means try to go it alone.

Many of the peoples of the world know and experience more closeness between persons than do individualistic westerners. Their customary groupness provides a much better model of what the Church should look like than do western organizations, made up as they typically are of collections of individuals. For the peoples of such societies, the group is often more real than are individuals.

So it should be for Christians in relation to the Church—being in interrelationships with God's people in church groupings should be the ultimate for us. As it is, I'm afraid many of our western churches are quite like parking lots—we drive in and we drive out, one or two persons per car, and about the only time we make contact is when we open our doors too wide and scratch each other's paint!

So let's focus on groupness in our Christian experience. Just as we need each other just to stay healthy in the ordinary human realm, so we need each other to attain and maintain any kind of spiritual health. Let's give solid attention to avoiding "relational heresy" by turning against western individualism, learning to genuinely love, share with, and closely relate to our brothers and sisters in Christ.

Tightly related groupings committed to Christ are necessary on both the human and the Kingdom levels. Let's make sure we are part of them. Let's also make sure we learn as much as we can from our nonwestern brethren concerning how to conduct truly interdependent groupness effectively.

INTRODUCTION

All societies arrange people into groups. Wherever there are people and whatever people are doing, it happens in groups. Even when acting as individuals, the individual actions are conditioned by the fact that each individual is a member of a group or groups. At any one time, an individual is a member of several groups and is relating to several other groups. For many in nonwestern societies, the group is often more real to its members than they themselves are as individuals. To westerners, the individual is the reality, and it is harder thinking about the reality of groupness.

BASES FOR GROUPING

Societies are organized into various groupings on the basis of a variety of different principles. We present these in summary form first, after which the three main types of groupings will be treated in more detailed fashion:

1. *Biological*. This is common to all societies. Each person is born into a group. It may be a small group like the nuclear family or a large group like an extended family or clan. This is an involuntary group; it is not chosen by the person.

2. *Marriage*. Young people get together in marriage and begin a new group. For most societies, this is an involuntary group, since the young people don't choose who they will marry. *Biological groups and marriage groups are lumped together and termed kinship groups.*

3. *Common Interests*. People interested in the same thing get together and form a group. The interest might be hiking, stamp collecting, knitting, nuclear physics, or whatever. This is a voluntary grouping, chosen by the participants.

4. *Ranking*. Ranked groups may be involuntary or voluntary. Groups such as those based on social classes, castes, or slavery are usually involuntary, with membership based on birth. In many societies, however, there are ranked groups that may be entered by achievement. Achieving wealth, education, political position, expertise, or some other respectable position may enable a person to move into a socially higher rank than he or she was born into. Politicians, research scientists, and astronauts are regarded as elite, based on their achievements.

5. *Territory*. People are born into a family in a particular area and become a part of whatever grouping exists in that territory. I am writing this book in Pasa-

dena, California, and people living in Pasadena are part of a group that shares things such as a moderate climate, smog, freeways, and the Rose Parade. For some this grouping is temporary, but for others more permanent. This grouping can be voluntary or involuntary.

Now we will discuss three bases for grouping.

1. The Kinship Basis

Kinship is a term used to refer to groupings based on birth or marriage. At least in the case of birth, and for many societies with regard to marriage also, kinship groupings are entered into involuntarily.

Children are born into a group of relatives. Mothers, fathers, brothers, sisters, grandparents, aunts, and uncles are determined by factors others than choice. The individual may be happy or unhappy with the kin he or she inherits, but can do nothing about it. Kinship is the first grouping system for all societies and remains the basic one for most.

Marriage often results from the arrangements made for young people by representatives of the previous generation. In such systems, it is not voluntary. In other systems, however, the choice of partners is quite voluntary. This has been discussed in chapter 18.

Societies organize kinship relationship into a very wide variety of complex kinship systems. In fact, as we look at kinship organization, we often marvel at the variety, complexity, and human ingenuity that has gone into developing these systems.

Western systems tend to be quite simple ("primitive") in comparison to many nonwestern systems. Westerners basically have a mother, father, brother, and sister whom they consider family. Father and mother have parents whom their children call grandparents. In addition, father and mother have brothers and sisters, all of whom are called aunts and uncles, and they have children who are called cousins. These are the people who are the "kin." Beyond that, westerners make few kinship distinctions.

People from other societies wonder how westerners can be so casual about all this. The Comanche kinship system has thirty-six different kinship categories, each labeled with a different kinship term. None of these categories are identical with any of the traditional western kinship relationships. To westerners, these kinship relations seem to defy logic. For example, the mother's sister's husband may have the same name as the father's brother. But to the insider, it is all logical, and any Comanche child can understand the system.

As complicated as some kinship systems are, no system provides a separate and distinct term for every possible position in the kinship chart. Each society specifies certain relationships and lumps together others. When a system lumps together people related differently to each other under one kinship term, that term is called *classificatory* (cousin, aunt). When a term is specific to but one relationship, that term is called *descriptive* or *particularizing* (father, oldest brother). This lumping and specifying is in accord with a people's worldview values.

The Anglo-American system specifies within the nuclear family: father, mother, son, and daughter. But it classifies with respect to cousin, uncle, aunt, niece, nephew, grandparents, and grandchildren. Even within the nuclear family, though, we Americans lump where other societies specify, since we make no distinction between younger and older brothers and sisters or first son and second son. Since the focus is on the nuclear family, the system is most particular within the nuclear family and general outside of it.

The Comanche kinship system, while much more complex and specific than the Anglo-American system, also classifies at points. For example, a single kinship term is used for father, father's brother, and mother's sister's husband, a lumping that makes no sense to us at all. The Comanche feels that these three people are in some sense in the same relationship to the child. The children grow up assuming that these people are to be classified by that term, and the system thus perpetuated develops its own rationale.

Figure 20.1 shows one kind of very simple kinship chart that enables us to picture a typical set of relationships over three generations.

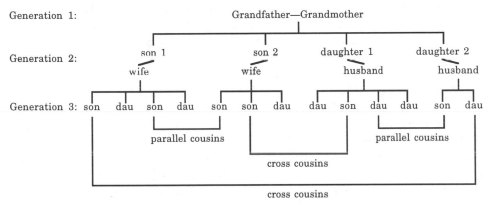

Figure 20.1 Kinship chart

All persons in a given social category (mother, father, sister, brother, uncle, aunt) are likely to be treated in the same way. With regard to cousins, note that the above chart labels two distinct types of cousins. The term *parallel cousin* refers to the children of siblings of the same sex (father's brothers, mother's sisters); *cross cousins* are the children of siblings of opposite sex (mother's brothers, father's sisters). This distinction is very important in societies in which marriage is preferred between one type of cousin and discouraged or forbidden between the other type. Most often when this occurs, the preferred or required marriage is between cross cousins, these being considered unrelated, never between parallel cousins, these being considered brothers and sisters and any marriage between them incest.

Kinship terms are labels for social statuses. What one calls another person carries with it prescriptions for how one behaves toward that person. If the biological father is called father and the biological father's brothers are also called father (as is often the case), the chances are that the person addressing them in this way will relate to each of these persons in a similar manner. Likewise, all persons called mother are likely to be treated in the same way, as will cousins, aunts, and uncles.

In the same way, if the biological sister is called sister and both sets of parallel cousins—the mother's sister's daughters and the father's brother's daughters—are also called sister (a fairly common occurrence), the likelihood is that no marriage will be allowed between these girls and any of their parallel cousin "brothers," just as a western man would not be allowed to marry his sister. Within that society, the incest taboo that says a brother can't marry his biological sister will also forbid marrying all others in the same sociological category, since this would be considered just as much incest as marrying the biological sister. As throughout cultural reality, social categorization overrides biological relationships.

Criteria Employed in Kinship Classification

We may point to at least nine criteria employed by the societies of the world to distinguish kinship relationships (Hiebert 1983:235–8). Though not all of the criteria are used by any one society, a study of them can help us understand the bases both for our own system and for that of others. The Anglo-American system uses only the first five principles. Other more complicated systems may use more (the Comanche system uses the first seven).

1. *The generation level* of those related to each other is indicated in the kinship terminology of most societies. Separate terms will be used for at least certain members of the grandparent's generation, the parent's generation, and the children's generation. There are, however, societies that call grandparents and grandchildren by the same term. In dealing with cousins, the American kinship system allows a general classificatory word, cousin, to lump them all together. Or the generation of the cousin can be specified by such terms as first cousin, second cousin, or first/second cousin once removed (the child of your first cousin is your first cousin one generation removed).

2. *Lineal and collateral relatives* are usually distinguished in the kinship terminology. That is, a distinction is made between relatives in a direct-line relationship (grandfather, father, son) and those in a parallel/collateral relationship (uncle, aunt, who are parallel to father, mother and brother, sister who are parallel to you). In many societies, collateral aunts are referred to as mother (as if they were in a lineal relationship to the person) and collateral uncles as father. In American society, the collateral distinction between biological mother and aunt is carefully maintained.

3. *Sex* is a distinction represented in some ways in all kinship systems. Terms such as brother/sister, father/mother, son/daughter, aunt/uncle are all sex specific. When Americans want to speak of children of the same parents, we ordinarily use terms that specify which sex they are (son/daughter, brother/sister), unless we use the technical term siblings. When it comes to cousins, however, our normal term (cousin) does not specify.

4. *Affinity distinctions* refer to those made between blood relatives and relatives by marriage. The distinctions between mother and mother-in-law, between brother and brother-in-law, are affinity distinctions.

5. *A polarity distinction* is made when two kinsmen refer to each other by distinct names that specify a polar relationship between them. Father-son, grandmother-grandson, uncle-niece are examples of this. In the American system, the terms cousin, sister, and brother are nonpolar, since each calls the other by the same name.

6. *A relative age distinction* is commonly made between those of different ages within the same generation. Though this distinction is not made in English, in Chinese and many other societies, a brother is always known as younger brother or older brother, an uncle as younger or older brother of the father. Often there will be separate terms for each of these distinctions. Respect is granted according to relative age.

7. *Bifurcation distinctions* are those made according to the sex of the person through whom the relationship is established. When distinct terms are used for cross cousins and parallel cousins, they are made on this basis. So are differences in the terms used for a father's brother and a mother's brother, since they are related through parents of different sexes. Since Americans don't make such a distinction, we call both of these kinsmen by the same term, uncle.

8. More rarely, a distinction is made according to the *sex of the speaker*. In such a system (Haida, an American Indian society), a brother and sister would use different terms to refer to their father.

9. Also more rare are systems in which a distinction is made according to the *status or life condition of the person through whom the relationship exists*. If this person is living, one term is used, if dead, another. Likewise, if the person is married, one term would be used, if unmarried, another.

Fictive Kinship

Many societies have techniques for at least occasionally accepting as kinsmen those who are not related by blood or marriage. *Adoption* is one kind of fictive kinship, since adopted children take their adoptive parents as their real parents.

Another process that results in a real family relationship is *blood brotherhood*. In 1 Samuel 20, David and Jonathan made a covenant with each other, becoming blood brothers. They thereby became fictive blood relatives—that is, actual brothers. This, of course, made King Saul very angry when he found out about it, since it made his enemy David a legitimate heir to his throne.

The *godparent-godchildren* relationship may, when it is taken seriously, also be a kind of fictive kinship. When the child is very young, often at baptism, another set of adults will be adopted as the godparents of the child. These godparents will then have some responsibility toward the child as he or she grows older. A typical responsibility would be that if anything were to happen to the biological parents, the godparents would take over full responsibility for raising the child.

Things to Remember Concerning Kinship

For many, especially westerners, dealing with kinship seems like an intolerable burden. The subject seems so technical and complicated. Many want to simply ignore the whole matter and focus on the more interesting and less technical areas of culture and social life. Unfortunately, this is not a helpful attitude. People live in worlds bounded by kinship categories, and to enter and work in those worlds, we must become familiar with and work in terms of their (not our) categories. Nevertheless, we have presented only the very basics of this subject in an attempt to keep the reader from getting too tangled up in the details. What follows are some things to keep in mind as we approach this area of the life of the people we seek to assist.

Westerners especially need to be aware that *most kinship systems are unilineal*. This means that ancestry and inheritance are traced through only one line of descent: either the male line (in patrilineal systems) or the female line (in matrilineal systems). Our Anglo-American system (like a minority of other systems in the world) is *bilineal*, tracing ancestry and granting inheritance through both the male and female line. A familiar example of a unilineal (patrilineal) system is that of the Old Testament Hebrews, where inheritance was passed from father to eldest son and ancestry was traced (e.g., in the genealogies) *only* through the male line.

Many of the peoples of the world are so structured by the kinship system of their society that they have great *difficulty relating to anyone they cannot give a kinship label to*. In order to be considered truly human in such a society, outsiders may have to be adopted into a family, so the receiving people can understand and relate to them. Though this requirement may seem strange to us, it is more understandable if we recognize that their system is the only one that enables them to make sense out of the world. There are often great advantages to becoming adopted in this way, since the adoptee thus becomes a part of the kinship system and from that point on has a legitimate position within the group. But there are also difficulties involved, since the outsider not only inherits all the family friends and relatives but also inherits enemies and problems (*see* Loewen and Loewen 1967). Yet becoming adopted into the society may provide the only realistic way for an outsider to be understood within that group and thus the best way to become an incarnational witness to those people.

Whether or not we are adopted into a system, it is extremely important that we *respect the people enough to memorize and learn to use their kinship terms in their way*. Though it is usual for their system to be more complicated than our native system, we must learn it, just as we must learn their language if we are to communicate effectively. For our purposes here, it is not important that we learn all the different types of kinship systems so far discovered by anthropologists. We have tried to spare you that. For illustrations of such systems, see Hiebert 1983:226–34; Hoebel 1972:457–66 or the chapter on kinship in another good introductory anthropology text. But *it is important to learn and use the terms employed by the people you work among*.

We must be aware of the categories our hosts feel to be important and learn to see this part of reality in terms of those divisions, for those divisions and labels are important and probably the only ones that make sense to the people who use them. If we are to work incarnationally, we must be willing to learn how that group categorizes people in kinship relationships. When seeking to learn the language and culture of a people, work hard to learn who calls who by what name, in order that you may function appropriately within that system.

When we go to another society to work and live, we need to do some elementary anthropological fieldwork in a number of areas, not the least of which is kinship terminology. Anthropologists have developed a way of charting kinship relations that can be a great aid to learning these relationships. We can follow one of these systems or develop our own (as I have above). In either case, it is often helpful to attempt to picture on paper, in as simple a way as possible, who is related to whom and what each calls the other.

We can also chart prescribed marriage patterns to help make sense of these relationships. Some cross-cultural workers use cameras (especially useful are Polaroid cameras that immediately develop the photograph) to take pictures of people in their family units. They then ask the family specific questions about each person in the picture. In this way, the kinship relations can be learned from the people involved and recorded for constant reference in such a way that we don't have to rely totally on our memories.

2. The Association Basis

The second basis for grouping to be treated here is what are called associations. Associations are based on having things other than relatives in common. All societies have associations, technically called *sodalities*. These associations may be voluntary or involuntary.

Western society is very association oriented. "In no country of the world has the principle of association been more successfully used or applied to a greater number of objects than in America" (Hoebel 1972:481, quoting de Tocqueville 1945:I:198). Westerners even have networks of associations. We belong to a local church and automatically are associated with all the churches that church is related to in a denominational network. Nonwestern societies tend to be less associationally oriented and more kinship oriented.

One very common type of association is *sex-based groups*. These are involuntary in the sense that any choice we are given is limited to those of our sex, but there may be a choice as to which associations one decides to belong to. Many societies elaborate them into socially very important communities, one of men and the other of women. In such societies, a man's closest friends, even after marriage, will always be men, and a woman's closest friends will be women. It is not expected, as in western societies, that people will give up their friends of the same sex when they get married. Nor are marriage partners expected to develop the intimate friendship relationship expected in western marriages. In such societies, it is common to see men going to market in exclusively male groups and women going in exclusively female groups. In communal gatherings such as church, the men and boys sit together (often on one side of the aisle) and the women and small children sit apart. Traditionally, men and women, especially spouses, would seldom be seen associating with each other in public, either as groups or as individuals.

In western university societies, fraternities and sororities provide examples of other sex-based groups. Some people groups have secret societies that are also sex based. In the United States (until recently), youth groups such as Boy Scouts and Little League (baseball) were sex-based groups for boys only. Today both boys and girls are allowed to participate, and these groups are no longer exclusively one-sex groups.

The functions of sex-based groups are varied: fellowship, education, aid, task performance, or merely common interest. In a society with men's and women's communities, traditional education was and is carried out within each community. As soon as a boy was old enough to leave his mother, he joined the men's community and learned how to be a man by participating in that community. A girl learned how to be a woman by associating with the women.

There are also *age-based associations*. Some societies have age sets that are formalized. Certain tribal groups in eastern and southern Africa (e.g., Maasai) are famous for their systems of age grades or sets. Around puberty all the boys in the society go through an initiation ceremony that moves them into a young manhood age set. Those same men will together go through an initiation rite of passage every ten years or so, to move them into the next category. Categories may be labeled as young warriors, family men, junior elders, senior elders, and retired.

In the United States we can see age-based associations in the Boy Scout organization. Cub Scouts are ages seven to nine, Boy Scouts are ages ten to thirteen, and Explorer Scouts ages fourteen to eighteen. Above age eighteen, the Scouts can be junior leaders, and then adult leaders. As noted in chapter 17, there is a sense in which the peer groups produced by the schools result in a kind of age grading as well.

There are also *associations based on interests*. These are usually voluntary, whereas the sex-based groups and age-based associations may be involuntary. Many different societies have sports clubs. In the United States, there are hundreds of different kinds of clubs attended by those with common interests such as social service (Lions, Rotary), stamp collecting, sailing, motorcycle riding, computers, and so on.

Associations based on *occupation* are common in some societies. Guilds, labor unions, and professional societies are all examples of this. I belong to the American Anthropological Association, the American Society of Missiology, and the American Scientific Affiliation. Each of these groups is related to my occupation.

Another kind of association is that based on *ranking* or the evaluation of a status by the society. The most prominent kind of ranking is social class. Though involuntary, in that one is born to a family in one class or another, this is an associational rather than a kinship grouping. In many societies there is a voluntary dimension to social classes in that a person can achieve a position in a higher social class through voluntary activity.

Far from being universal, as Marxists contend, social classes are rare among smaller societies. In a survey of 547 representative societies, 68 percent were virtually classless (*see* Hoebel 1972:485–88). Many recognized some difference between the wealthy and the nonwealthy, but most were classless. Only 8 percent of this sampling of 547 cultures had a multiple-class system, and these were almost exclusively from the Mediterranean and Asia. Eighty-seven percent of the New World societies (American Indian, etc.) and two-thirds of the societies in Africa and the Pacific were classless. These are largely small societies, and the tendency is that as the number of people in a cultural group increases, divisions arise. But the fact remains that a significant percentage of the world's societies are classless. Those of us going to other peoples from America and Europe cannot assume that our new host society is divided into classes.

The bases on which social classes are determined ordinarily include ranking by birth, wealth, or occupation. The most frequent ranking is the division between nobility and commoner. In the United States, we divide classes by wealth, but other criteria such as education or occupation might be more important in certain cases. For example, a university professor will likely be considered in a higher class than a garbage collector, even if he makes less money that the latter. In the same way, a doctor in the United States is considered to be in a higher class than a plumber, whether or not he or she earns more money. In some societies, wealth does not determine social class. In traditional China, the farming class was always poorer than the business class, but the farming class was ranked higher because farming was viewed as a more honorable profession than doing business.

A kind of social class that is much more rigid is *caste*. Castes are often defined as *frozen classes*, with no mobility or intermarriage. In a class system, the mobility may be restricted to a great extent, but usually there is some possibility of moving from one class to another. In a caste system, the structure is such that ordinarily there is virtually no possibility of moving from one caste to another.

Caste is often based on occupation or ethnic identification. Supposedly the caste system in India resulted from various tribal groups finding themselves in a multi-tribal situation, becoming specialized to a specific occupation, and then becoming frozen socially with respect to their interrelations with each of the other tribal/occupational groups. The present castes are now basically occupational groupings that are interdependent occupationally but sociologically isolated and insulated from each other in terms of intermarriage and other social interaction, such as eating together. Hiebert provides helpful insight into the Indian system:

> Castes . . . are integrated into a common social system on the basis of hierarchy. Each caste has a rank based on its ritual purity. At the top are the priestly castes, referred to in general as Brahmins. Beneath these are Kshatriya castes, once comprised of rulers and warriors; the Vaishya castes, which handle banking and trade; and a great many Shudra castes, comprising the farmers, craftsmen (Weavers, Winetappers, Potters, Tailors), and servicemen (Barbers and Washermen). At the bottom of the social scale are castes comprising workers such as the Sweepers and Leather workers, sometimes referred to as "untouchables." The number of castes in a village may range from a half dozen to more than forty, and in the country, as a whole, in the thousands (1983:282–83).

Though the Indian caste system is probably the most well developed, it is not the only one in existence. In Japan there is a butcher caste. We experienced among the Kamwe a caste division between the common people and the tradesmen. Furthermore, American social structure can be analyzed to show a caste division existing in most parts of the country between whites and blacks.

There are also combination systems in which castes and classes both exist. The white-black relationship in the United States has been so analyzed. Within both white and black society there exist high, middle, and lower classes. But there is a caste border between the two societies that is very strong in many parts of the country, though it has broken down to some extent in other places. What this means is that though a black may be in the upper class in black society, he or she may be virtually ignored or even treated as low class within white society. This, of course, ought not to be. It is encouraging to see it breaking down in many parts of the country.

Another association based on ranking is *slavery*. This has occurred often where one group enslaves another and those enslaved become a part of the social system, usually at the lowest level. In the seventeenth and eighteenth centuries, slavery occurred in over 50 percent of the world's societies (Hoebel 1972:495). Slavery occurred most often among the peoples of Africa (78 percent of them), Circum-Mediterranean (61 percent), and Eurasia (56 percent).

Slavery has often been less evil than it may seem to us in western societies. Some societies have groups that are technically slaves, but they are treated as people, not property. In New Testament times, we see that in the Greek system a slave could be put in charge of all the financial dealings of his master. If the master either didn't have a son, or his son died, he would often adopt his slave, who would then become a free person and heir. There are a variety of slavery systems, many of which are not nearly so bad as what we've known in the West.

3. The Territorial Basis

Another basis for associations is territorial. Territorial groupings into which one is born are, of course, involuntary. People are born into a particular community, so their associations are with the people in that community. The territorial community can be a neighborhood, village, town, city, state, nation, or the like. As a community gets larger, there is often more opportunity for people to voluntarily move to a different location, putting them in association with groups within the larger community other than those they grew up with. When a village grows into a town or city, different neighborhoods develop as territorial groupings. Such urbanization often implies greater ease of moving to a different neighborhood than was possible in more rural settings.

In many societies a geographical community will also be largely united on the basis of kinship. The larger the community grows, however, the greater the likelihood that it will extend beyond the bounds of kinship or that various segments of the kinship group will stop relating to each other in a primary way, creating social divisions even though the group still lives in the same geographical proximity.

Common terms for territorial groupings are tribe, nation, state, city, or country. It should by now be evident, however, that the territorial or geographical reality of such groupings is ordinarily not nearly so important for human relationships as are the cultural and social realities. Indeed, the larger territories may well include several cultural groupings that, in turn, may include more than one social grouping. In a geographical entity such as the United States, for example, we have many cultural groupings, within which are distinct social and subcultural groups (e.g., varieties of Asian, Latin American, Afro-American, and other populations that have come from various countries). The problems raised by cross-cultural relationships and the need for cross-cultural insight are not, therefore, important only for those who go overseas.

Cities around the world tend to be made up of people from numerous sociocultural groupings. Whether in Africa, Asia, Latin America, or Euroamerica, there are certain similar characteristics of urban territorial groupings. Cities tend, for example, to be made up partially of long-term urbanites and partially of recent immigrants. They also tend to be more cosmopolitan, more influenced by contemporary influences such as mass media, easy mobility, and western schooling. Therefore, they allow less isolation from world trends and influences than rural life. For this reason, the effects of modernization tend to be more prominent in cities.

Nevertheless, rural attitudes and values tend to be very important, especially among the more recent immigrants. If in any given city there are enough members of an ethnolinguistic group, they will ordinarily band together to form a distinct community in the new geographical area. If there are not enough, they will tend to band together with others from their own region of the country—even with those who at home would have been their enemies. Cities, therefore, tend to be made up of a large number of distinct communities, some of which, in spite of living in close proximity with other ethnic groups, are able to maintain a good bit of social isolation. Village people living in cities have to make major modifications in their ways of life, to be sure, but the deep-level worldview values and attitudes are usually much less affected than the changes in surface-level behavior might lead the outsider to assume.

The cosmopolitan culture of the cities, though made up of many parts and greatly influenced by world cultural trends, is to be taken as just as valid as any other culture. It is inappropriate for outsiders, especially those who come in the name of Christ, to regard only traditional cultures as valid. People have the right to reconstruct their cultural life in any way they choose. This means that city people (as well as others) have the right to adopt customs and ways of thinking that have come from outside sources, either as additions to or replacements of their previous customs. The resulting cultural structuring, even though made up of western as well as traditional parts, is to be respected and taken every bit as seriously by cross-cultural witnesses as the more traditional cultural structuring of rural peoples.

With city dwellers, as with traditional peoples, we are to start with them where they are culturally. With city dwellers, as with traditional peoples, however, there are dissatisfactions with their present way of life. We often find those most dissatisfied with their cultural life in cities, since they tend to be those most affected by the tragic aspects of rapid sociocultural change. Though urban lifeways are to be taken as valid, they are often felt by the people to be quite unsatisfactory. The felt needs springing from such attitudes, if discovered, often point the way to opportunities to present the Christian message.

CULTURALLY DEFINED GROUPNESS AND THE CHURCH

1. *How should the people of God group themselves?* With the Bible as our guide, we note that there is no single pattern for grouping presented there. In the Old Testament, we find tribal, kinship grouping predominant. In the New Testament, it appears that we have more an association of families as the basis for "churchness." The Jewish synagogues were organized in this way. In Acts 16:31, Paul tells the Philippian jailer, "Believe on the Lord Jesus Christ, and you will be saved, *and your household.*" It seems clear that the grouping of God's people was according to appropriate cultural guidelines.

In contemporary kinship societies, we should expect to have kinship churches, and in associational societies, it is appropriate to have associational churches. People living in the same geographical region can be expected to group with others in that region according to the cultural guidelines employed in the rest of their lives.

When large extended families are a major part of the local society, as in many parts of Latin America and elsewhere, any given church may appropriately be made up largely of a single family. In rural United States, we often have churches comprised of associations of families. In urban areas, where our associations tend to be more of individuals or nuclear families, our churches reflect this. This is right and good, for there is not a single pattern for churches in all parts of the world. God uses whatever the culturally appropriate practices of groupness may be to provide the social basis for His local churches. This is the point of the so-called *homogeneous unit principle* that has been a part of church growth theory from the start (*see* McGavran and Wagner, 1990).

2. We also need to think about *the maximum appropriate size for a church in any given society*. Several years ago, one of my students came to me, contending that church growth is impossible in Kinshasa, Zaire. When I asked why he said, "Because there is no more land left on which to build church buildings." When I asked what size church buildings he had in mind, he referred to a large 2,000 member church in the middle of the city.

I asked him where most of the people in Kinshasa come from. He answered that they are moving in from the villages. I then asked him what were the largest groupings people would experience in the villages, which provided the models in their minds regarding the appropriate size of groups. He thought that it was thirty to forty people. I then asked him what size church did he think would be most in line with the sociocultural expectations of the people of Kinshasa. On reconsidering, he said thirty to forty sounded about right.

When churches ignore the ideas of appropriateness concerning the size of groupings that people carry in their minds due to sociocultural conditioning, they will run into problems. Some churches with exceptional leaders or circumstances may be able to become larger than what is normally culturally appropriate. In the long run, however, ignoring this principle will cause problems.

3. The *appropriate style of church government* also needs to be thought out. How differentiated can a group be and be handled by a given organizational style? In a society where the oldest male member of a group is automatically the leader, a Baptistic, democratic style of church government usually will not work well. In such a society, leaders are not elected; they attain their position through experience with life. If a church insists on electing leaders, the real leaders may be forced out of the church. In many societies, even Baptist churches that claim to have a democratic church government have in reality (often unconsciously) adapted to the society's expectations and have a hierarchical church government, with the oldest men running the church.

We have already discussed the tragedy of young church leaders in age-oriented societies. It might be possible in such societies to work with a kind of dual leadership. Reportedly this is what was done in Middle Ages Europe. To do this, an older traditional leader is paired with a younger, better trained leader (perhaps chosen by election), each providing what he has to offer to the furtherance of God's work. The function of the older leader may often be no more than sponsorship, but such sponsorship can be crucial to the acceptance and progress of the work of God.

In more urban settings, both age and training can be very important. If we were to follow the example of Jesus, we would find those who are older and established in their careers and enroll them in a discipleship training program. I think it has been well demonstrated, both within and outside the western world, that choosing young people and training them in classrooms results in relatively poor church leadership.

4. *Geographical considerations* also need to be taken into account. We in the West are used to great mobility and think of a church as covering a wide geographical area. In many societies, travel patterns are different, however, and even people who could travel fair distances strongly resist such travel due to cultural conditioning. They may be especially resistant if going to church means going into or through the territory of another sociocultural group. In such cases the idea of small "parishes" may be the best idea.

In discussing church planting with a pastor in Japan, I found he was successful in starting churches very near subway stations. Travel patterns in this urban area were such that people found it easy to get on a train to get to church but difficult to get there if the church was far from the station.

One way or another, patterns of grouping need to be carefully considered in the work of Christ. These are but a few of the issues that need to be considered in this regard.

CHAPTER 21

SOCIAL CONTROL

INTEGRATIONAL THOUGHT

Our God is a relating God. From the beginning of time, He has shown Himself to be primarily concerned about the relationships between Himself and His creatures. He apparently likes to be in close relationship with humans. But many have misinterpreted Him to be a God of rules and regulations, One who delights to judge people once they have broken the rules.

In Galatians 3, Paul deals with this issue. He points out that Abraham responded to God by putting his trust in Him and "because of his faith[fulness] God accepted him as righteous" (v. 6). He then makes statements concerning that relationship, such as, "the real descendants of Abraham are the people who have faith[fulness]" (v. 7), "God would put the Gentiles right with himself through faith[fulness]" (v. 8), "Abraham believed [was faithful] and was blessed" (v. 9), "only the person who is put right with God through faith[fulness] shall live" (v. 11), "God made a covenant with Abraham and promised to keep it" (v. 16), "it was because of his promise that God gave that gift [the Covenant] to Abraham" (v. 18), and "if you belong to Christ, then you are the descendants of Abraham and will receive what God has promised" (v. 29).

He says, concerning the rules and regulations, however, "did you receive God's Spirit by doing what the Law requires?" (v. 2; cf. v. 5), "those who depend upon the Law live under a curse" (v. 10), "it is clear that no one is put right with God by means of the Law" (v. 11), "the Law has nothing to do with faith[fulness]" (v. 12), "the Law, which was given four hundred and thirty years [after the Covenant], cannot break that covenant and cancel God's promise" (v. 17), "What, then, was the purpose of the Law? It was added in order to show what wrongdoing is" (v. 19), and "Does this mean that the Law is against God's promises? No, not at all!" (v. 21).

Among other things, these statements are about social control. The question lying behind them is, Are we in line with God's plan because of rules or because of relationship? Clearly, according to Paul, it is a matter of relationship. But even as exciting a thing as a relationship needs guidelines, the rules. Adults as well as children have to have clear standards to enable them to know what is expected of them. And, as Tevye says in *Fiddler on the Roof*, it is tradition (the Law) that "tells me who I am and what God expects of me."

So we have rules and relationship to focus on in any social interaction. The problem with many of the Jews of Jesus' and Paul's time was that they had made rules the basis for their interactions with God and humans, rather than relationship. Rules are good as guidelines, but they are deadening if they become the central focus in social interaction. Yet there seems to be a tendency for humans to gravitate toward a focus on external rules.

We must constantly push ourselves to look more deeply to the relationships underlying behavior. Our questions concerning our own and others' behavior should always be, How true or faithful is that one being to the relationship? How carefully is he or she obeying the rules? Obedience to the rules automatically springs from faithfulness to the relationship and automatically suffers when a person is unfaithful to the relationship.

Whether we are dealing with interaction between humans or interaction between humans and God, the most effective basis for social control is the relationship basis. This is one reason why societies where kinship relationships are all-encompassing tend to produce greater conformity than those (like American) based more on rules and law.

God works on a relationship basis, requiring faithfulness above all. The joy, peace, hope, love, and pure excitement that comes in that relationship with Him provide the most powerful motivating factors available for us to obey the rules. Are you into relationship or rules in your social interactions with God and those whom you supervise?

INTRODUCTION

As should be clear by now, people normally behave according to cultural guidelines. We have pictured these guidelines as roads on which people travel by habit or as a script that actors memorize and follow closely. The places of learning and habit in keeping people on the road or following the script are clear. These influences come from inside a person. But not everyone keeps on the road or follows the script all the time. People make mistakes and even deliberately wander away from these guidelines. What happens then?

We have seen that culture is based on community agreements, so following cultural guidelines is a matter of loyalty to the community. But factors such as self-interest, willfulness, rebellion, and sin disturb that loyalty from time to time. What techniques does a society use to keep people from overstepping the guidelines, or punish them when they do?

How do people traveling along the road of culture recognize when they are getting close to the edge of the road, or when they have gone off the road? We learn as we grow up that there are rules for acceptable behavior. If a rule is broken, there is a consequence. Loyalty to the community and to its rules is enforced. Some kinds of transgression are punished harshly, some more leniently. Some of the roads we travel are wide, allowing considerable leeway for diverse behavior, but some are narrow, allowing little, if any, optional behavior, and we learn the difference.

These are the concerns of the sociocultural area we call social control. What enables a society to function is the behavior of its people enacting group agreements according to cultural guidelines. Some of that behavior makes the society "go." Some, however, is designed to steer the behavior or even to apply the brakes. In order to function well, a society needs to have cultural guidelines for steering and stopping as well as for going. This is the cultural area of social control.

Note that this area is specifically labeled social control, not cultural control. The steering and stopping of cultural behavior is a people thing, not a structural thing. The road or script of culture controls nothing; only those who follow the road or the script can control the way these vehicles are used.

AN ILLUSTRATION: HOW TO DRESS

If someone (other than a street person or other social misfit) should appear in church some Sunday morning dressed in very old raggedy clothes, we might look at him askance, communicating, in effect, that very old clothes are inappropriate in church. But unless we are very bold or very offended, we would not likely confront him to his face. We would depend on our disapproving look to communicate our message, and we would with our look be attempting to exercise a measure of social control. If the offender heeded the message, he would dress acceptably the following Sunday. The cultural guideline is that one dresses up for church.

But if someone, especially a woman, were to appear in Sunday worship dressed in a bathing suit, we might not feel that a look of disapproval would be enough to get our message across. We might well confront the person, letting him or her know verbally that a bathing suit is not appropriate attire for Sunday morning worship. We would probably feel that this is such a flagrant violation of cultural guidelines that we need to take a more direct approach. Yet we would not likely go so far as to call the police or attempt to throw the person in jail. We would expect our verbal confrontation to suffice as the social control mechanism appropriate to that situation.

However, if someone should appear in Sunday morning worship naked, we would probably feel justified in calling the police. We might attempt to wrap something around the person first and get him or her to go home to get dressed. But if the person refused, we would likely seek to have him or her arrested for indecent exposure. The level of this transgression of cultural guidelines is such that neither an askance look nor a direct, verbal confrontation would be considered adequate, for in North America, public nakedness is not allowed, especially in church. Clothes, often a particular kind of clothes, are required for church.

Yet here, as with most other customs, there is variation from society to society. Though it has changed now, during our first Nigerian stay, we worshiped regularly with women who wore nothing above the waist and little below but felt no shame about it. I visited a group of tribes to the north of us in which (at that time) nakedness was required of both men and women. Since then I have visited Papua New Guinea and Irian Jaya, where appropriate male dress consists of little more than a penis sheath (a longish gourd enclosing the penis and sticking out in front). There are no askance looks when people dress in these ways in these societies. Indeed, traditionally in a society where people wore no clothes, it was considered immodest to wear clothes, since people interpreted such behavior as indicating that the person had something to hide. The social pressure exerted by that group at that time would have been directed toward keeping people from putting on clothing.

As this discussion indicates, there are several mechanisms employed by the peoples of the world to keep everyone within the cultural guidelines. These mechanisms are designed to prevent unacceptable behavior and, directly or indirectly, to define, identify, and reward what the society sees as acceptable. Following are a number of the many specific mechanisms by which human societies accomplish social control.

MECHANISMS OF SOCIAL CONTROL

Positive Reinforcement

Though most of the mechanisms of social control have a fairly negative bias, we will start with two that are more positive. All societies have ways of encouraging appropriate and especially valued behavior. Whether it be overt symbols such as medals, titles, or degrees, or less tangible reinforcers such as social status, an appeal to pride, or, more directly, words of congratulation from respected persons, each society provides many techniques to designate and reinforce the behavior selected for emulation.

Whatever is done in a society that results in a person feeling good about herself or himself fits under this category. Among the things used by various societies are pats on the back, hugs, smiles, lack of criticism, thanks, and praise—whether verbal, written, sung, or communicated through silence.

The prominence of encouragement and praise for achievement in western societies points to the fact that competition is a highly valued behavior among these peoples. In many traditional societies, however, it is cooperation that is highly valued, and competitiveness is clearly eschewed or even punished. The kind of competitive behavior that is rewarded in the West by high social rank and financial profit engenders shame in many nonwestern contexts, while the compliant and cooperative mood dominating there is distasteful to westerners.

Logic

Another more or less positive form of social control found in most if not all societies is logic. Though the ways of reasoning differ from people to people, some appeal to a person or group's common sense can often turn people away from seriously overstepping the guidelines. People learn deep-level worldview assumptions and values, but they often forget or ignore them in the living of life. When such assumptions are called to consciousness before or after a decision is made, embarrassing situations can often be avoided.

Priests, prophets, counselors, lawyers or other designated persons are often those charged with using logic to call to the attention of others the fact that they are not living up to what they profess. The aim is to motivate people to change their behavior so that they live up to their own ideals.

Gossip

Perhaps the most important mechanism of social control in most societies is gossip. When gossip is employed, a person is usually shamed. Gossip is powerful because people fear the possibility of negative opinions toward them by others in their group. These negative opinions are communicated throughout the community through gossip. People are gossiped about when they are perceived by the community to have let the group down by behaving in a way that is disloyal to the group and its guidelines. The gossip is intended to shame such persons so they get back into line. This technique is usually very effective.

The mere possibility of embarrassment, before any transgression even occurs, is usually sufficient to keep people in line. People do not ordinarily like to be talked about in negative ways. The fear of this happening makes the gossip mechanism very powerful. When a person has stepped over the line and gossip occurs, the embarrassment and shame provide powerful motivation to conform to established norms the next time around.

Shame

Shame is ordinarily seen as the distress caused by strong negative public opinion when a person has stepped out of line. In its weaker forms, it may or may not be a powerful motivator, depending on the person's need for group approval. Even in its weaker forms, however, shame can be a powerful means of social control in societies with a strong group consciousness. In its strongest form, it involves raising questions about the legitimacy of a person's very existence. Whereas guilt involves distress over *what a person has done*, shame may involve the questioning of *who a person is and whether it is legitimate for that person to even exist*. In its stronger forms, it functions at a level much deeper than guilt and may motivate suicide.

Unlike some of the more formal means of social control discussed below, shaming through gossip usually occurs informally, but shame also comes to people as an accompaniment of the more formal procedures. When, for example, a person is taken away by a policeman or judged against by a court, both that person and his or her family normally feel ashamed. That shame, though a by-product of the more formal social control mechanisms, is a powerful mechanism in and of itself to bring conformity to social guidelines next time.

In some societies, there are more formal mechanisms specifically devised to shame people into acceptable behavior. In colonial America, displaying people publicly with hands and feet locked in stocks was a formal shaming device. Certain Eskimo societies have traditionally employed ridicule songs, a semiformal procedure to bring shame on persons who have transgressed social norms. Offending individuals were made the subject of spontaneous singing, the function of which was to shame the offender so that he or she abandoned unacceptable behavior in favor of acceptable patterns. Less formally, both Kamwe and American youth use ridicule expressed in song to shame their peers.

Shame, like any of the other social control mechanisms, may be misused by individuals with power and prestige, or even by whole communities, to pressure people into conformity to their values. Since shame is always related to social standards, all the powerful have to do is manipulate the standards. If the standard is atheism, for example, as in Communist societies, a belief in God is considered disloyalty by those in power and something to be ashamed of. The elite of a community who value literacy, schooling, certain clothing styles, a particular dialect of their language, or any number of other concepts and practices, are often found to be using shame to press other members of their community into conformity. Even Christians who highly value certain practices and doctrines may be found to be unlovingly shaming people into feeling inferior and even unacceptable to God. I suggest that church leaders misuse their power to shame when they proclaim acceptance by God on the basis of faith alone but then relegate to second-class citizenship people who practice traditional customs unacceptable to these leaders (e.g., traditional marriage customs) or other cultural behavior not condemned by Scripture.

Guilt

Guilt is distress over what one has done or not done. It, too, is a powerful mechanism of social control. Guilt operates internally and receives its power from the internalization of the social norms that have been taught to us, norms that assume within us the status of absolute moral standards underlying the operation of our consciences. Shame relates primarily to external social pressure and is activated by pressure or fear of pressure in the here and now by the people around us. Shame may not operate, or at least not be very powerful, if we transgress but are not discovered. Guilt, however, functions internally. It may or may not include shame. We have been imprinted deep within with certain standards and have a conscience that travels with us wherever we go to let us know when we have overstepped, whether or not there are others around to notice.

The shame factor leads us to ask, "If I behave in such and such a manner, what will my friends or society at large or perhaps God think of me?" The guilt factor is more likely to raise the question of the rightness or wrongness of the act in relation to the standards we have internalized as we learned our culture.

Theologians have often contended that all people, no matter what their culture, know intuitively (in their consciences) that certain things are right and other things are wrong. Anthropologists contend, however, that conscience is a product of sociocultural conditioning. Though I don't know how to prove it, I believe both are partially right. That is, I think there is evidence that people of all societies naturally feel some guilt over the taking of another life, even if they are shamed into doing it by their peers. Likewise, I believe that all people carry within them certain moral principles, such as that it is right for mothers to protect their babies (including the unborn) and for children to respect their parents, and that it is wrong to exploit others sexually or to take their property. I believe these and whatever other universal moral principles there may be are manipulated, defined, and structured in the process of culture learning, but not obliterated. The conscience God has built into us to keep us operating by those principles can, however, be ignored to the extent that it no longer functions to advocate the right and prevent the wrong. When this happens, even God gives up on us, allowing all kinds of evil behavior (Rom 1:18–32). Whether or not there are whole societies that God has completely given up on is a point for discussion.

The available research from the field of anthropology suggests that all societies employ both shame and guilt as mechanisms of social control. What appears to differ from people to people is the relative proportion of each. Group-oriented societies are often referred to as "shame cultures," since they seem to use shaming a lot, with guilt apparently playing a minor role. More individualistic societies may be labeled "guilt cultures," because the internalized guilt control seems to be more important in them than shaming. Whether these designations are helpful or not, what certainly remains the same throughout the entire spectrum of human societies is that shame and guilt provide powerful (perhaps the most powerful), and effective mechanisms for the control of human behavior.

Reciprocity

Reciprocity is another powerful mechanism of social control in many societies. Its operation is based on a simple premise: If I behave (or do not behave) in a certain way toward someone else, that person will behave (or not behave) toward me in the same way. If I want another person to treat me well, I need to treat that person well. The popular saying, "I scratch your back, you scratch mine" captures the essence of reciprocity. This is not simply the Golden Rule, where we are to treat others as we would like to be treated, though that is a good place to start when we are taking the initiative.

Positively, reciprocity is bargaining for good treatment. Negatively, it is revenge for bad treatment. The glue that maintains friendships and even entire social units is reciprocity, but so are the dynamic underlying feuds and the need to pay people back for what they have done to us. Many parents find reciprocity a helpful mechanism for social control in the home. They tell their children, If you do as I want you to (clean your room, wash the dishes, etc.), I'll do something nice for you (take you to the movies). It is a simple but effective logic: conformity is exercised in hopeful expectation of reciprocity. But reciprocity is withheld when one does not acceptably conform.

Reciprocity is also a major factor in economics (*see* chapter 12), where buying an item requires that the seller be recompensed what the latter considers to be the worth of the item. Gift giving is also often a function of reciprocity. At Christmastime, many Americans would be embarrassed if they received a gift from someone they forgot to buy a gift for. Reciprocity also lies behind the giving and receiving of intangibles such as love to receive love, respect or obedience to receive favor, conformity to social rules in exchange for social security. Such relational reciprocity both keeps people under control and binds them together.

Mediation

Mediators function in many societies, either informally or formally, as instruments of social control. Informally, ordinary people often function to settle disputes. Counselors and lawyers handle more serious disputes on a formal basis. Formal mediation occurs internationally through ambassadors and envoys. In many societies, marriage arrangements are worked out, whether formally or informally, through intermediaries who may hold the official position of matchmaker. In each case, the goal and purpose of mediation is to direct social behavior according to acceptable patterns.

Law and Legal Norms

"Law is more than custom and less than social control" (Hoebel 1972:503). When we speak of social control, we may think first of formal law, but this is far from the only mechanism for keeping people in line. In this sense, law is less than the whole story. Being more formalized, law is more than simply informal, customary tradition.

Western societies may be said to be law oriented. In the United States, when something in society is not working right, our first response will often be to call for a new law or regulation. It seems to be our belief that any social or behavioral problem can be solved by legislating another rule! We have so many regulations we can't keep track of them all, and people still break them. As many western missionaries have discovered, informal social control mechanisms are usually more effective than laws in nonwestern contexts. The fact is that informal techniques are also more effective in the West. It is the breakdown of these informal mechanisms, not the inability to enforce our laws, that is the primary source of current social disruption.

Yet all societies have rules and legal norms, some formal and some informal. Formal laws are often written down. In nonliterate societies, they are transmitted from generation to generation by word of mouth. Informal laws, however, form the far larger category across the spectrum of human societies.

How do formal and informal laws relate? Let me illustrate. Not long ago I was stopped for speeding. The officer confronted me with the radar-analyzed facts: I was going 42 miles per hour in a 25 mph zone! I was guilty; no doubt about it. The facts are the facts. What surprised me was the way the officer used the facts. He told me that, in spite of the fact that the posted maximum speed was 25 mph, his department judged that a speed up to 33 mph would be safe. So he fined me only for the difference between that speed and my speed of 42 mph, rather than that between the posted 25 mph and my speed! The formal law written in the books and on the traffic signs was 25 mph. But the informal limit was 33! On the highways, we know we can travel according to the informal speed limit, at least 5 to 10 mph above the posted speed limit.

In many societies, there are both formal and informal rules for many services performed by government and other officials. The informal rules prescribe that a bribe be given, and even the appropriate amount of the bribe. Likewise, there are often formal and informal rules for marriage. Formal and informal laws exist together, often treating the very same area or category of behavior. The formal law is official, in literate societies written down, and made the point of reference for the behavior in question. Yet often the informal law overrides the formal.

In addition to laws with both formal and informal components, there are purely informal rules and regulations. These are customary principles in terms of which groups operate. They are usually unwritten and seldom even verbalized, but often quite binding. Families often have slightly unique ways of doing things, indicating that there are informal rules known to those within the family but sometimes puzzling to outsiders. Whether, in contrast to Hoebel's statement above, to consider all of the rules of a society as laws or not is a matter of definition. In a certain sense, however, rules for speech and social behavior may legitimately be understood as informal laws.

A basic principle of law, as of other social control mechanism, is that if we conform, all goes well and nothing bad happens. If we obey the laws, we are not bothered by those charged with enforcing them. Our behavior is judged to conform to the legally defined norm. It is only when a law is transgressed that negative sanctions apply.

Government

The term government refers to the governing of a people. There are many forms, from traditional kinship society governance, in which the head of each extended family is its governor, to the complicated set of parliaments, congresses, supreme courts, presidents, and prime ministers that characterize large western nations. Between these lie structures governing groups of extended families, structures that govern fairly sizable but relatively homogeneous peasant societies, and structures by means of which large multicultural nations are governed. At either end of the scale, the structures may be operated despotically or more or less democratically. Tribal societies, for example, may be governed rather ruthlessly by a powerful chief or on the basis of consensus democracy, in which every decision requires agreement by every one of the significant leaders in the society.

Government exerts social control in a myriad of ways. As the highest authority, a government typically empowers each level of authority under it to maintain order and provide protection both internally and externally. In larger societies, this entails the maintenance of formalized structures such as police and military, as well as smaller entities, such as cities and states. In smaller societies, the largest percentage of what it takes to maintain order and protect is tended to through informal processes.

Within formal governmental structures, as within the other formal structures we have discussed, exist informal processes. Within the context of western-style democracies, for example, such activities as lobbying and important discussions conducted in smoke-filled rooms, cloakrooms, restaurants, and cocktail parties represent informal political procedures. Informal promises are made, and deals are struck (reciprocity), often quite apart from and frequently antithetical to the interests of the formal relationship of constituency to representative that is supposed to control the system.

The governing of institutions other than the government also contributes markedly to the maintenance of social control. Business, educational, religious, law enforcement, military, and all other institutions within a society are operated in terms of similar formal and informal procedures to enable them to effectively function, both internally and in relation to the rest of society.

Governing involves power, and power is easily misused. In many societies, checks and balances are built into the system of governance to protect society from the misuse of power. In democracies, for example, voting for those who represent us in government is intended to protect us. So is the court system. In many systems, however—either because there are not enough checks and balances or because they are not effective—the power that ought to protect a society is used against it by its leaders. Examples of despotic leaders abound, whether in tribal or national settings. So do examples of misuse of power within so-called democratic systems. It is, unfortunately, not uncommon for people in power to put themselves above law and custom, making use of their power and position to hurt rather than to help those who are under them. Nevertheless, Paul admonishes Christians to honor and obey those in authority over them, because their authority comes from God Himself (Rom 13:1–7).

Spiritual Mechanisms /(Taboos)

People with supernaturalistic worldviews often employ a variety of techniques that depend on spiritual power. Sorcery, witchcraft, curses, and threats of natural or supernatural retribution are commonly used to discover who committed a crime (as defined by the society) or to take revenge on someone deemed guilty. The existence of these techniques and their practitioners engenders great fear in those who might consider performing antisocial acts, and fear, as we have seen, is a powerful motivator for social control.

Curses can be leveled either formally by specialists in spiritual power or informally by nonspecialists. Unfortunately, in many societies it is believed that certain people can perform witchcraft unknowingly. To control this, witchcraft eradication societies have sprung up in many societies, with the aim of discovering witches and prosecuting them. This is usually an extralegal mechanism of social control. Both within and outside of Christianity, there are people who cast out demons, using spiritual power to limit the social consequences of demonization. Unfortunately, like the witchcraft eradication societies, many such efforts often do more harm than good. The fear engendered by the use of spiritual mechanisms often becomes a powerful tool in the enemy's hands, keeping people in his grip.

Taboos are an important mechanism of social control, probably in all societies. The concept is that if people do certain things, they offend spirits, gods, or God and will have to pay for it. Prohibited behavior includes such things as incest, appearing in public during menstruation, avoidance of certain places (e.g., sacred groves), avoidance of certain people or their names (e.g., mother-in-law), eating certain foods, and the like.

As American Christians, many of us grew up under the influence of rather strong taboos against such things as drinking alcoholic beverages, smoking, dancing, masturbation, going to movies, using vulgar language, neglecting daily devotions, missing church services, necking, and thinking lustful thoughts. Our leaders were often not very subtle in their suggestions that God is a fearsome divine Punisher who is ready at any moment to lean over His heavenly balcony and bring justice to any who stray into the taboo areas. This approach to Christian morality amounts to the use of taboo for the control of behavior. Our leaders did well to be concerned that we not fall into most of these things, but the manner in which the warnings were given amounted to control by fear and guilt, the power behind taboos. Many of us have ever since had difficulty relating to a God who seeks to motivate through love rather than fear.

Punishment

The threat of punishment exists whenever a guideline is transgressed, whether the vehicle of punishment is embarrassment because of gossip or being put in prison for breaking a formal law. Ridicule is a higher form of punishment than gossip. So are such things as fines, isolation, and deprivation. Physical force is often used, as in disciplining children, beating, and capital punishment.

Fines are widely used as punishment, whether the fining of a man in a tribal society for committing adultery with another man's wife or the fining of an American for speeding. Isolation and deprivation of social contact are the primary techniques involved in imprisonment. Social isolation is the intended result of criticism and ridicule, at least if the person doesn't change his or her behavior.

Determining Guilt

There are various techniques for deciding whether or not a person is guilty. In many smaller societies, the primary techniques are spiritual. When trouble or death comes to a family, the head of the family may consult a diviner or shaman to learn who caused the trouble or death. The diviner or shaman then may be asked to perform sorcery on the person deemed to be guilty.

In many of these and other societies, a procedure called trial by ordeal may be resorted to, usually with an appeal to spiritual power to assure the accuracy of the process. Though ordeals are of many kinds, a biblical example of an ordeal to discern adultery is found in Numbers 5:11–31. This ordeal involved drinking cursed water that would make a woman's stomach swell if she were guilty. Other types of ordeal include requiring the accused to drink poison or immerse his or her hand in a pot of boiling oil. If the person survives without harm, she or he is presumed innocent. An ordeal that employs spirit power very overtly is one where a length of rope on the ground is commanded to rise, form a noose around the accused's neck, and choke him or her if guilty.

Probably the most common way of determining guilt is for someone to hear the case and make a decision. Whether in a highly structured way, as in western societies, or in a less structured manner, as in small-scale societies, accusations are carried to designated adjudicators. In many societies, including ours, the ultimate decision may be made either by one person (a judge) or by a group of people (a group of elders or a jury) who come up with a joint decision.

What we have presented above is a partial list only. Several other mechanisms and varieties of those discussed are employed to maintain social control in various societies of the world.

THE INTEGRATIVE NATURE OF SOCIAL CONTROL

Besides keeping people in line, social control mechanisms function to relate one aspect of social life to another. Social control is based on worldview assumptions concerning correct behavior. Thus, like language, it is not a subsystem parallel to the others but pervasive of the others. That is, social control is not maintained separately from religious, economic, and political subsystems. Nor is it maintained separately within each of the subsystems, though there are some specific behaviors with sanctions for and against within each subsystem. Rather, the controls ordinarily apply to all types of behavior throughout the society.

For example, the guidelines for relating to a leader ordinarily apply whether that leader's sphere of influence is political, religious, or economic. Though, as with all the subsystems, there will be some specific subsystem assumptions that will apply to how one relates to each type of leader, the assumptions concerning how to show honor and respect and who to show it to spring from worldview. In a hierarchical society such as Korean or Japanese, you bow to an important man, no matter how he gained importance, or to an older man just because of his age. An egalitarian society will have other guidelines to follow, but they will apply to everyone in a given class.

In supernaturalistic societies (and subsocieties such as American Christians), the taboos relate to all of life, not just religious behavior. Likewise with guidelines enforced through gossip, logic, reciprocity, law, or any of the other mechanisms discussed here.

The fact that social control is based upon worldview assumptions concerning how people should behave suggests that it is an especially important area for cross-cultural workers to study. When you find out what is allowed and prohibited and why, you are close to the heart of what makes a people tick.

First of all, we need to study social control to learn how to behave appropriately in the receiving society. Secondly, it is important to discover the reasons and motivations for behavior in order to appreciate it. Only on the basis of such understanding and appreciation should we dare to suggest changes, starting with changes in assumptions, then moving to changes in behavior. In learning the significant mechanisms of social control pertinent to the receiving society, the cross-cultural worker gains important insights into the worldview and fundamental values operating in that society.

Obviously, the individual items valued and promoted will differ significantly from society to society. Cross-cultural communicators must recognize that every element of social control, whether prescriptive or proscriptive, positive reinforcement or negative prohibition, is culturally conditioned and defined. It will, therefore, differ in relative importance and meaning from society to society, as fundamentally as do all other worldview assumptions and values. For example, all societies have some regulations against incest, murder, adultery, and stealing.

These things are universally proscribed. But different societies may define each prohibition differently.

In the story told in chapter 12 concerning stealing, for example, we see the Nigerian defining stealing quite differently from the way I, as an American, define it. The Nigerian and I agreed that taking something from nonrelatives should be defined as stealing. We differed, however, in that I would probably (perhaps not always) consider it stealing if my brother took something of mine without permission, whereas he would not accuse any brother of his (probably including parallel cousins), even if he disagreed with what he did. Definitions of incest, murder, and adultery likewise vary from society to society. If my Nigerian brother's society is one of the many that regard parallel cousins as brothers and sisters, his people would consider sex with one of them incest. My society would not, though we would consider it adultery. In many societies there are sexual relationships outside of marriage that are not considered adulterous. Nor do they consider polygamy adultery, whereas westerners would. Even in American society there are different definitions of murder, some of which include the unborn some of the time (e.g., when a pregnant woman is shot and her fetus dies) but not at others (when a doctor kills the baby).

It is important to recognize that a society employs social control to support its own, not our, guidelines. We may differ at many points as to what principles should be upheld, but their moral consciousness has been formed within the sociocultural structures through which reality was mediated to them, not within ours. And *they* must be convinced that any changes we recommend are the right thing, before we can expect them to agree to change.

MISSIOLOGICAL APPLICATIONS

1. *When people change from one system of social control to another, great disruption takes place.* As cross-cultural workers, we work in many societies that have been severely disrupted through colonization, western business, western schools, and myriad other powerful outside influences, including Christianity. In many societies, societal cohesion and stability have been damaged, perhaps beyond repair. Parents are often puzzled because they can no longer discipline or even maintain the respect of their children, who spend most of their time in school, learning things their parents know nothing about. Governments often function poorly because the nationals running them base their activities on assumptions quite different from those of Europe and America, from whence these governmental structures came. Individuals experience high levels of stress and emotional breakdown because they don't know who they are personally or where they are socially. As one Nigerian put it, "We are like bats, neither birds nor animals. We are betwixt and between, neither European (though trained in schools to be European) nor African (though destined to live out our lives in Africa)."

In the churches we have leaders attempting to work according to partially learned western principles in nonwestern contexts. In a society where neither traditional nor western social control mechanisms are working, they are expected to hold their members to higher (biblical) standards than those ever advocated in their society. With little going for them, they are called on to face certain discipline problems we in the West never imagined, much less helped them to solve, plus many that we ourselves have never been able to handle. Is it any wonder that church leaders are often at least as demoralized as others in their societies?

What kind of roots does this massive disruption have?

To attempt to understand the kind of challenge brought by a western system of social control, we can look at several examples. The first comes from colonial Sudan. Prior to British colonization, adultery was punished in some Sudanese tribes by chopping off one of the offending party's knuckles. The punishment was personal and effective, communicating without ambiguity societal norms proscribing adultery. When the British arrived, however, they condemned the practice as barbaric and forbade it. Instead, they put offenders, when they caught them, in prison. But the new punishment did not have the same impact as the old. In fact, for some offending parties it was an attraction rather than a deterrent: in prison the offending party was well fed and taken care of. He lived in luxury by their standards. Many Sudanese reached the only logical conclusion—that the British condoned, even promoted, adultery.

In India, a Christian man's home is robbed. He knows who the thief is but also knows that the local police will be ineffective in getting him justice. So he goes to the diviner and starts a process through which the thief will be punished in a traditional way.

In Nigeria, teenage girls who traditionally would have been protected from pregnancy by their mothers at home go away from their home villages to board at a mission secondary school. The traditional structures governing boy-girl relationships are not in force at the school, and the western structures are ineffective, so boys there take advantage of the girls, and a certain number of them become pregnant. Since pregnancy is embarrassing and likely to keep the girls from finishing school, they seek abortions from traditional medicine men. This often results in physical damage, future infertility, and even death.

A Korean leader is in charge of collecting and banking the weekly offerings. A family member gets in trouble and badly needs funds. The church leader knows better but is shamed by his family into borrowing from church funds to help his family member, fully planning to pay back the loan. He never obtains enough of a surplus to repay it. The traditional value that says "Any family member who has access to funds is obligated to use those funds to help a brother, even though they are not his" wins again!

Whether it is morality that has suffered, or the inability to learn a new way to deal with money, or the inability to effectively keep children or wife in line, when the traditional social control rules no longer work and the new ones are not yet fully accepted, people have big trouble.

2. *To analyze the situation, look at the changes in sanctions.* It is the change from one type of sanction to another that gives people the most difficulty. When the sanctions (the basis of the control mechanism) change from personal to impersonal, from informal to formal, from horizontal sanctions (interpersonal) to vertical sanctions (supernatural), or from vertical to horizontal, widespread confusion and disorganization is likely to result.

Consider, for example, when sanctions are changed *from personal to impersonal* with regard to the offense of stealing. In many nonwestern societies, stealing is an offense sanctioned by personal retribution. Offenders may be beaten or publicly shamed by the offended party or his or her representative. The sanction represents a powerful mechanism of social control. But where such personal sanctions are replaced by impersonal sanctions (e.g., civil suits that may or may not land one in jail), people become confused. People then may "logically" conclude that stealing is acceptable, for now it offends no one personally, only the impersonal state. The original sanction was personal; the new sanction is impersonal. The original sanction applied between persons, the offender and those offended. The new sanction applies between the offender and some impersonal force, the government, that has not been wronged directly and probably is considered an enemy anyway.

Problems also ensue when societies change *from informal to formal sanctions.* In many nonwestern societies, offenses are sanctioned informally, often as a matter to be resolved between the family of the offender and the family of the offended. But if such an informal sanction is converted rapidly to a formal system (a legal court system), confusion is sure to result. The original sanction was often direct and immediate; the new sanction is frequently far removed from the actual moment and circumstance of the offense incurred. The original sanction was personally meaningful to the individuals between whom it was negotiated. The new sanction may be less meaningful personally, having derived its meaning from abstract and formal legislation. The original sanction was negotiated face-to-face between the offending and offended parties. The new sanction is negotiated by professional third parties—lawyers—and may depend for its satisfactory result upon the relative cleverness of one lawyer or another.

Or consider the problems raised by a change *from horizontal to vertical sanctions.* In many nonwestern societies, stealing is purely a horizontal matter. It occurs, it is defined, recognized, and sanctioned *between persons.* Now a westerner arrives on the scene and ignores the horizontal sanctions already operative in a particular society. He insists that vertical sanctions are now to be observed. If the offender has stolen, he should ask forgiveness of God. If he has committed adultery, he should ask forgiveness of God. The missionary goes on to teach that God is ready, even eager to forgive the offender. What sort of message is communicated here? This missionary's strategy is likely to promote exactly what it was supposed to prohibit: further stealing and adultery. The functioning horizontal sanctions were by-passed, but the vertical sanctions were not yet functional.

Or, as often happens, consider the problem of a change *from vertical to horizontal* sanctions. In many traditional and some not-so-traditional societies, many of the most serious sins—including adultery, stealing, incest, witchcraft, and the like—are normally dealt with through vertical sanctions. That is, whether automatically or after an appeal, God, the gods, or the spirits are expected to punish the offender. Those offenses that westerners consider serious, however, are punished horizontally if at all, and usually after a lengthy process quite foreign and unsatisfying to the people involved. Even within the church, instead of helping people to appeal to God rather than to their traditional gods, we have usually secularized the process. By turning people to secular processes rather than to God, we have unwittingly demonstrated our belief that God is either not concerned about or powerless to handle such matters.

The point in all of this is not that sanctions ought never to change. The point is rather that changing sanctions is risky business. Cross-cultural witnesses need to recognize this dynamic and devise plans to deal with it. Sanctions must communicate effectively within the parameters of the specific sociocultural context if they are to be of any value at all as mechanisms of social control.

3. *Some practical suggestions.* We have in this chapter discussed and illustrated the fundamental mechanisms of social control. We have explained that social control performs an integrative function in society and that changes of social control forms and mechanisms are therefore disruptive of societal stability. This is especially true when changes are abrupt or artificially transplanted from one society to another. We have illustrated some of the problems that arise when changes are made in sanctions from personal to impersonal, informal to formal, horizontal to vertical, and vertical to horizontal.

What practical help might our analysis represent for the cross-cultural worker confronting situations of social disorientation related to breakdown in systems of social control? We offer two general guidelines:

a. Where abrupt change or breakdown in systems of social control has contributed to societal disintegration, *work toward a new integration.* But first, study and seek to understand the actual function or dysfunction of existing mechanisms. What are the prominent mechanisms of social control existing in the society? What behavioral norms do they serve? Are they affecting behavior congruent with established societal norms? Have they changed recently or received significant impact from foreign systems of social control? What sanctions apply in the system? Are they impersonal or personal? Formal or informal? Horizontally oriented or vertically oriented? In short, find out to what extent the present configuration of social control mechanisms is and is not doing its job. Such an analysis will help the cross-cultural worker to begin where the people actually are.

Now the cross-cultural worker must ask if individual mechanisms, or even the entire configuration of the existing social control system, will need to change. He or she may then attempt to assist in the process, mindful that changes should contribute toward a new integration and should make sense to the people involved. As we have already intimated above, the worker will want to be especially wary of changes toward the formal and impersonal parameters of social control sanctions.

b. If we were to suggest an *ideal direction* for the development of systems of social control, it would be this: *From the personal/horizontal toward the personal/ vertical.* Nonwestern peoples tend to be both personal and supernaturalistic. Personal sanctions are therefore both better understood and more effective than impersonal sanctions. Supernaturalistic sanctions are also more appropriate, but a change usually has to be made in the power source. A sober charismatic approach to this issue provides a better resolution than that traditionally offered by evangelicals. The ideal combination for most people would be a largely personal system with total dependence on God working through it. Probably it will be impossible to avoid certain impersonal and naturalistic importations (police, judges, and prisons). A Christian community that takes both vertical and horizontal relationships seriously, however, and practices what it preaches, can probably avoid most contact with these impersonal mechanisms.

PART V

CULTURAL AND WORLDVIEW CHANGE

CHAPTER 22

Stability and Change

INTEGRATIONAL THOUGHT

In Romans 12:2 the Apostle Paul says, "Do not conform yourselves to the standards of this world" or, as Phillips translates it, "Don't let the world around you squeeze you into its own mold." We have learned to distinguish between the cultural structures and the people (the society) that by habit lives according to those structures. Some have made the mistake of identifying the biblical term "world" (Greek, *kosmos*) with the human structures we call culture. If this were true, we would have to reject as evil those structures we have been taught. And, if this were true, we would be puzzled by the fact that throughout the Scriptures God made use of cultural structures to work with the people who lived according to them.

It is not the structures we are being told not to conform to; it is the way people use the structures. The warning is against allowing ourselves to be enslaved to a human and satanic empowerment of any cultural system. That is why Phillips translates, Don't let the "world" (i.e., society) squeeze you into its mold. The concern is with the pressure put on us by the people who run the system, not by the system itself. We are not to allow ourselves to simply follow the guidelines and standards of our society, guidelines and standards enforced by social control. Rather we are to recognize that God enables and empowers us to live above such standards, beyond the reach of the satanic influences on society, to live in a way that transcends the way the people around us behave.

We are to be transformed through adopting a new perspective (a renewed mind) on the basis of which, under God's direction and empowerment, we make changes in our habitual behavior. For, as we will discuss below, all sociocultural change starts with changes in the minds of individuals. The starting point for change is a new perspective. We can thus change our habitual use of cultural structures to enable us to serve God, rather than the ends ordinarily recommended by the society of which we are a part.

Jesus is our model here, as in all other matters. He lived within the cultural structuring around Him and according to most of the worldview assumptions underlying that culture. There were, to be sure, differences in some of the things He assumed, differences that came from His Kingdom perspective (*see* Kraft 1989, chapt. 9 for more on this). *But the main thing that differed about Jesus was His commitment to live within those structures in total faithfulness to God. He did not introduce new structures; He used the old structures differently than did the society (the world) around Him.*

Jesus seldom opposed any of the cultural structures, but He loved when society allowed Him to hate, He forgave when He was allowed by the society to curse, He refused to judge when society allowed Him to condemn, He served when society allowed Him to be served. His attitude toward the structures was different because His allegiance was to the true God (not any of the gods of this world) and His commitment to His Kingdom. He refused to be captive either to Satan or to society.

INTRODUCTION

At this point we turn in an ordered way to the very important subject of change. We have been aware throughout the preceding chapters that change is going on, but now we'll take a closer look at the principles and processes by means of which it takes place in the culture, especially in the worldview.

This is an important topic for cross-cultural workers, for we are agents of change. We are interested in seeing people make changes that enable them to serve Christ better. We are anxious that those changes cause as little disruption as possible in the cultural lives of a people, so we need to learn as much as possible about culture change—what causes change, what things happen when people change their cultures, and so on.

Anthropologists view sociocultural change as a constant. That is, there is no such thing as a society that is not constantly in the process of changing its culture. Thus we dispute the claim of those who say they have discovered a group of people that "hasn't changed for thousands of years." Anthropologists are often accused of not wanting a society to change its customs. Though there are some (called "salvage anthropologists") who would seem to hold such a view, most anthropologists are not against culture change as such. We have observed, however, that the kind of change that results from the coming of outsiders (including missionaries) is often very destructive to the people. It tends to affect them psychologically and often results in demoralization and death to people, as well as to their ways of life.

We are thus not against change but concerned about what kinds of change are brought about, who brings them about, and how they are introduced.

Christian anthropologists especially cannot be against change. The Gospel always results in changes—changes in people who initially change the way they use their culture and may then go on to alter the structures themselves to become more adequate vehicles for God's working. But questions have to be raised concerning what changes are to be made, how they are to come about, and who does the changing, for even Christian influence, done in the wrong way, has often resulted in cultural, psychological, and even spiritual destruction. Though we want with all our hearts to defend our right and obligation in obedience to God to engage in cross-cultural Christian witness, we must be honest about the results and attempt with God's help to correct any approaches that in His name hurt the people He wants to win.

Whether or not there will be change is not the issue. Our concern is for such things as the nature, rate, direction and advocates of change. The principles underlying such concerns are the subject of the next several chapters. In this chapter we will deal with general principles related to change, in the following, we will develop several more specific topics.

In this chapter and those to follow we will lean heavily on the excellent presentations in Luzbetak (1963:195–316) and Foster 1973:76–259). Indeed, most of the outline followed and many of the illustrations used are closely related to Luzbetak's treatment of this topic. I am grateful to him for permission to gear my presentation so closely to his.

CULTURES BOTH PERSIST AND ARE CHANGED

Many of us are so aware of the changes going on around us that sometimes we don't ask, Just how similar is our culture as we operate it today to the way our parents and grandparents lived before us? If we compare, we find certain changes, but the vast majority of what we do is more similar than we thought it was. Many young people in rapidly changing societies grow up with the impression that everything is different today from what it was when their parents were growing up. They are fond of saying to their parents, "It's all different now than when you were growing up. You just don't understand. You were brought up in the dark ages." As they grow older, though, they usually come to feel that things aren't as different as they thought they were.

There have, of course, been changes. There always are changes. But often a sober estimate of what has actually occurred yields less substance than our feelings led us to expect. It is as if we have been fighting to swim in a river with a strong current. We get out and say, "Boy, that current is strong. I'll bet it's flowing at thirty miles per hour." Then someone comes along who has measured the current scientifically and tells us it's only flowing at five miles per hour—plenty fast, but not as fast as it felt to us when we were in the water.

1. *General persistence.* In spite of continual change, an anthropologist would expect two varieties of any given culture that are, say, one or two hundred years apart, to show such a strong resemblance that there is no doubt concerning their close relationship. Customs and cultural structuring show great persistence and a tendency to remain surprisingly the same over long periods of time.

The inventory of a culture is, of course, very large. Even though many things may be changed from generation to generation, many things remain pretty much the same. In addition, most of the changes are quite small, so even a fair number of alterations to a custom often leave a contemporary custom's relationship to an older form of that custom quite readily discernible.

There seems, furthermore, to be a kind of ethos or personality to a culture, to which new or altered customs tend to be fitted and conformed. This integration of the new into the old enables a people to maintain the same distinctiveness in its cultural structuring over the generations. This factor seems similar to the personality structuring of an individual who, though he or she grows, develops, and changes much, is still easily identifiable, even after many years, by those who knew him or her as a youngster.

2. *Yet continual change.* Parallel to the persistence is continual change. As people use their cultural structures, they adapt them to new situations. They develop new approaches, new strategies, new structures as they go along. With many people in a society adapting and creating, much newness is produced. One important result of this process is that we never pass on to the next generation exactly what we received from the last.

There are at least four reasons for such changes: 1) First of all, *children never learn perfectly* what the adults of the society try to teach them, so a certain number of changes are the result of imperfect learning between generations. 2) Then there are *mistakes* that people think are clever and imitate. The mistake itself does not constitute cultural change; it is the fact that people imitated it and made what started out as a mistake an accepted custom. 3) *Creativity* accounts for the introduction of many changes into a culture. People are simply too creative to continue to do things in the same ways forever. 4) Lastly, changes are introduced into a culture through *borrowing.* Something that another group has or does is observed or heard of by the members of this group, and they like it and adopt it.

3. *Changes result largely from people choosing a different allowed alternative.* Most of the changes in a culture are not caused by the adoption of some previously unknown practice. Changes tend to result from decisions made by people to follow a different *known* custom in preference to the one usually followed.

In chapter 10 we talked about culture as providing guidelines for behavior. Within guidelines, more than one possible behavior is ordinarily allowed, with 1) one kind of behavior specifically endorsed, 2) other behaviors allowed but, if followed, resulting in the person feeling socially uncomfortable, 3) other behaviors allowed but, if followed, resulting in the person feeling guilty, and 4) still other behaviors definitely forbidden.

To take clothing customs as an illustration, in the preceding chapter, we discussed the social control mechanisms that would be put into effect if a person came to church in America dressed inappropriately. It is obvious that Americans are required to wear clothing in public. If we don't, the police are called in to enforce our cultural rule. Within the requirement that we wear clothes, however, are subrules specifying patterns we are to follow concerning what is proper in various settings and on which occasions. These rules specify, for example, that we are to wear formal clothing on occasions defined by our society as formal occasions, informal clothing on occasions defined as informal, and casual clothing on still other occasions. Social pressure such as that discussed in the previous chapter is exerted to keep people in line.

Over several generations, however, some interesting changes have occurred within these patterns. There has been, for example, a noticeable change in the United States in the number of people who wear informal clothing to church and seminary classes. Church and seminary were once defined as fairly formal occasions and, in at least some traditions, a person could be refused admittance if not dressed "properly."

What has happened is that the definition of proper clothing on such occasions has changed over the years. When the formality of the situation was strongly in focus, social control mechanisms such as disallowing a person not dressed properly would be regularly used. Other dress customs were, however, known and used at other times and places. Some more daring persons began to test the custom of dressing formally by dressing in one of the other known ways. They found that though they became the subjects of gossip, disapproving looks, and the like, they were not often ushered out. Others imitated the more daring, and the custom of dressing less formally in such settings became the preferred custom for many. A previously known but disapproved alternative pattern has now come to be the preferred custom.

We may analyze this change by dividing the process into "time periods." In the *first time period,* a given practice was prescribed and enforced. Other practices, though known, fell into categories that elicited reactions ranging from mild disapproval to strong punishment. In *time period two*, however, some of the more venturesome begin to practice a custom that falls into the "mild disapproval" category. This formerly disapproved custom moved from being practiced by a small minority (say 10 percent of the population) to being practiced by the majority (say 60 to 70 percent). By *time period three*, the new practice completely or partially replaced the former practice as the option most frequently chosen by most of the people, with the former custom still practiced by the more conservative.

By way of illustration, we may cite the change that has taken place in the use of pants by American women. Not long ago, women wore dresses in public. Pants were worn in private, in the house. Over time, skirts began to shorten so much that many women became uncomfortable wearing them and made the change to wearing pants. This appeared to have happened quite suddenly, but there was a long period of preparation leading up to it. American society is so conformist that when such change begins, it moves quickly throughout certain segments, especially the young.

In time periods two and three, since that radical change occurred, the use of pants has become very widespread, extending even to more formal situations such as church. This change has, of course, been encouraged by the manufacturers of women's clothing, who have provided styles in pants to suit every taste, every size and shape, and every occasion. The change has not, however, been total. In some parts of this country (south and mid-west), there may still be social pressure against women wearing pants to church.

Note that the movement is usually from the present practice to a known but mildly disapproved practice. Seldom will a practice that receives a stronger negative reaction be attempted at this point unless it is considered highly prestigious (as are many customs coming from the West in the eyes of nonwestern peoples). With such customs, those who adopt them usually find that they sacrifice much of their rapport with the traditional community. In the case of women's clothing, note that American women did not go from short skirts to wearing bathing suits or short shorts in public (though some in warmer parts of the country seem to be moving in this direction now). At the time of the initial movement, these forms of dress were in a more strongly disapproved category.

It might be helpful to provide a diagrammatic summary of what we've been saying about the change in what American society feels is proper public attire for women. Note in figure 22.1, on the one hand, the scale from preferred to forbidden and, on the other, the changes in the ordering of the lists for each time period.

PROPER "NEAT" PUBLIC ATTIRE FOR AMERICAN WOMEN		
	Time Period 1	*Time Periods 2 to 3*
Preferred Alternative	1. Dress	1. Dress, Skirt, Fitted Pants
Allowed Alternative	2. Skirt	2. Designer Jeans 3. Jogging Suit, Nice Pajamas 4. Non-Fitted Pants, Culottes 5. Short Shorts 6. Miniskirts
Unacceptable Alternative	3. Slacks (Pants) 4. Culottes 5. Jeans	7. Bathing Suit
Forbidden Alternative	6. Short Shorts 7. Pajamas 8. Bathing Suit 9. Underwear 10. Naked	8. Underwear 9. Naked

Figure 22.1 Proper public attire for women

4. *Some changes are the result of choosing a more radical alternative.* Though most changes are the result of a group choosing a known but only slightly less approved alternative, some result from a more radical choice. Usually if some within a society choose a much disapproved alternative, they will have to pay a high social price. An example within American society would be the "hippies" of the 1960s who chose several greatly disapproved practices to symbolize their rebellion and, at least at first, paid a high social cost in terms of rejection by society at large.

Among the disapproved practices they chose were long hair, beads and earrings for men, sexual promiscuity, sloppy clothing, and going without bathing. That countercultural rebellion was a very interesting phenomenon from many points of view, and since similar things are happening among the youth of other societies, it may be helpful to analyze it a bit.

Americans expect their young people to rebel to some extent against the previous generation. American youth are expected to outdo their parents, from whom, largely through schooling, they have been at least partially alienated. Through schooling and other processes, a youth peer group mentality is created, by means of which peer (rather than parental) pressure becomes the most important social control mechanism for probably the majority of American youth. When a movement begins among the youth, large numbers of other youth readily respond to their peers and join it.

In a society where rebellion on the part of the youth is expected and parents largely ignore their children, the youth ask, How are we to get the attention of the society as a whole? Small-scale choosing of alternative behavior won't do the job—that is expected. The kinds of alternative behavior that will attract attention must involve practices that will really upset the "proper" people. Important social rules must be broken, rules pertaining to clearly unacceptable things, or the movement will go unnoticed. So they chose sex, hair length for men, and cleanliness, three strongly valued areas, as symbols of their rebellion. I'm not sure anything positive was accomplished, but these choices brilliantly served the aim of attracting the attention of the older generations, since the alternative behavior chosen came from the unacceptable and forbidden categories.

In a society in which the social control mechanisms are more effective, if a person or group should choose to begin practicing a disallowed alternative, extreme social pressure would likely be exerted to bring that individual or group back into conformity. As pointed out in chapter 21, such techniques as gossip, ostracism, or even physical force may be used. The object of such mechanisms is, of course, to assure the persistence of the people's way of life—or at least of those portions of it felt by the people to be most important—in the face of certain change.

Kinds of Persistence

We talk about persistence rather than lack of change, because it's a matter of customs continuing, customs persisting, in spite of the certainty of change. There are, however, several types of persistence. People do not always attempt to preserve the whole of the cultural structuring. Often they seem to protect certain portions of their culture while gladly changing others.

1. *General persistence of the culture* is the condition when the members of a society are more or less successful in their attempts to resist change in all areas of their culture. Though contemporary pressures for change have now changed things for many peoples, the prevalent attitude of small-scale traditional societies around the world has usually been conservative. For many, though, conservatism probably stemmed more from the lack of opportunity than the lack of openness to new things. Such societies were often isolated from neighboring societies because of geography or because of antagonism between themselves and their neighbors, thus cutting them off from the most likely sources of new ideas.

Within the United States, there is a group with German roots called the Amish. In spite of the positive value put on change by the society around them, the Amish in general, and especially one of their groups called the Old Order Amish, consider it very important to maintain as much as possible of their old ways.

They believe that God's chosen people are not of this world and therefore must not conform to it, whether it be in matters pertaining to travel, clothing, haircuts, or modern conveniences. Even the lapels and buttons seen on "worldly" coats must not be found on the apparel of the Amish. Cars, bicycles, television sets, radios, phonographs, and pianos are all for "worldlings," not for the Amish. Positive effort is made to inculcate in the young a dislike of radical change. Particularly "dangerous" is a "worldly" secondary education through high school and college, for it threatens the very foundation of the Amish way (Luzbetak 1963:198).

The Old Order Amish and a group called Hutterites that is in many ways similar (*see* Hostetler and Huntington 1967) are attempting a general persistence approach to culture change. Both groups perceive (I think, correctly) that in order to maintain themselves, they will have to carefully control the schooling their children receive. To maintain this control, both groups have had to fight against local school authorities.

Change does go on within such encapsulated societies, of course, but at a very much slower rate than in the surrounding society. Evidence of such change lies in the fact that by as early as 1942, the Old Order Amish had accepted such new crops as tobacco and tomatoes, adopted the use of tractors, and increased their involvement in dairying. The Hutterites, though practicing general persistence overall, have chosen to learn and incorporate modern agricultural techniques and machinery into their way of life. If such an approach to change were more common, we might need to develop a new category labeled "sectionally open to change," to cover those groups who choose one area of life to open up for change while attempting to maintain the status quo in all other areas.

2. *Sectional persistence*, the acceptance of change in certain areas but not in others is more characteristic of contemporary societies than is general persistence. It seems to result from a desire on the part of a people to preserve certain of the more meaningful things in their way of life, while allowing most other things to change. The Hutterites could be considered sectionally persistent, since they encourage change in the agricultural area, except that the "section" of their way of life that they try to protect from change covers nearly all of their culture, while there is basically only one section of life in which they advocate change. Since agriculture is their means of livelihood, changes in that area involve changes throughout the rest of their culture. Nevertheless, they fit best in the general persistence (or sectionally open) category.

Japanese society, unlike the Hutterites, seems to have opened up much of its way of life to western influences (material technology, economics). Yet it may be labeled sectionally persistent in that it has, to date, done a good job of maintaining most of its tightly structured social system (though currently there are signs of some breakdown) and a good bit of traditionalism in religion. Both Hutterite and Japanese societies tend to be closed societies, in that they tend to be oriented to protect their members from as much outside influence as possible. American society, by contrast, is much more open, encouraging the incorporating of outside influences.

Most western societies exhibit a much more restricted form of sectional persistence than the Hutterites and the Japanese. In the United States, in spite of our commitment to technological change and our tolerance for the concomitant disruptions of social life, we find strong persistence in such areas as spelling, political organization, sports rules, and religious organization and attitudes.

3. *Token persistence* is a kind of sectional persistence that is considerably more restricted. This is where things that once were important in the culture are retained, but only in a token way. In American society, horses were once the primary means of long-distance travel and transport. They were also depended on for farming and warfare. But engine-powered vehicles such as automobiles, trucks, tractors, and tanks were invented and came into wide usage, pushing the horse and all of the materials and skills employed in horsemanship to the periphery of our culture. Now, instead of being one of the most obvious and useful features of American society, horses only appear in such activities as horse racing, military funerals, parades, and recreational horseback riding.

4. *Survivals* are even more peripheral parts of culture. These are parts of a culture that once served reasonably important functions but now serve only as decorations or formalities. Buttons on the sleeves of men's suit coats are the survival of the buttons that once tightened the sleeve, as do the buttons on a shirt. Neckties are a survival of scarves, academic robes of a past form of dress. Coloring Easter eggs and putting up mistletoe at Christmastime survive from ancient religious practices. Typically, as in each of these cases, the cultural form survives, but there is a change in its meaning.

In such ways cultural items and practices persist in spite of the fact that changes are constantly occurring.

CHANGE: GENERAL CONSIDERATIONS

As has been pointed out, the processes of change are working at the same time as the processes of persistence. On the one hand, the participants in a society are attempting to keep it as similar as possible to its past structuring and configuration while, on the other, constantly altering old approaches and creating new ones. There are several general things to say about the change process before we turn to the more specific aspects.

1. Locus of change. All change in culture is initiated in the minds of the people who live by that culture. So we say, with Barnett (1953) and Luzbetak (1963), that *the "locus" of change or the place where change originates is in the mind.* As pointed out previously, culture is not something that acts on its own. Culture in and of itself is not like a person with the power to act and do things. Culture has no power to "do" anything. Its structures are activated and altered by people. *Culture, therefore, does not change; it is changed*, and when it is changed, it is changed by people who change their behavior, sometimes following, sometimes preceding a change of mind.

All culture change is rooted in mind change. People, of course, frequently change their minds, and most of these mind changes never result in significant change in the culture. But certain people have followings and are therefore likely to be imitated by others when they change their minds. These are called opinion leaders. An opinion leader is not necessarily one who is highly visible in a society, but simply one whose opinions are followed. Each society has many opinion leaders. They function at all levels and in every segment of the society.

When any change made in the behavior of such influential people is imitated by others, a change occurs in the structuring of the behavior (the culture) of that particular group. If other groupings of people imitate that behavior, it can result in a change that affects the whole cultural structuring of a society. This may then be passed on to the next generation in its changed form. Changes thus pass from individuals into the cultural structuring.

2. Rate of change. The rate of change is the speed at which changes are made. Cultures are always being changed, but not all are changing at the same rate. Traditionally, many cultures underwent fairly slow change. In our present world, however, the rate of change for most peoples, especially under the influence of ideas and items coming from the west, seems to be quite rapid and accelerating. This often leads to a good bit of unbalance, particularly on the part of people whose orientation is more toward slow than rapid change.

There are several rates of change, with several terms we can use to designate them. Among them are revolutionary change, cultural drift, long-term trends, styles, and historic accidents.

a. *Revolutionary change* is the most rapid rate. This type of change is typically sudden and disruptive. It usually affects (disrupts) a considerable portion of the culture, even beyond those areas of the culture that the advocates of the change had in mind. Though revolutionary change may be brought about through political change, many other kinds of change may also be revolutionary. Certainly much of the technological change in which nonwestern peoples are presently involved is, for them, revolutionary.

b. One type of slower change is called *cultural drift*. Such drift comes about as minor alterations occur over a long period of time, moving the culture in a given direction. We have had this kind of movement within western culture as, over a long period of time, we have moved from God-centeredness to science-centeredness, from a place where nearly all explanations of what happens were in terms of God's involvement to the place where today most westerners (including most Christians) attempt to explain almost everything that happens as cause and effect. We seldom explain things as God's activity except, regrettably, when an insurance company describes a tragedy such as an earthquake or tornado as an act of God. Unfortunately, one of our worldview values is that if we can explain something, God is not in it.

c. A *long-term trend* is less extensive than a cultural drift, since it affects but one or several items in the cultural inventory. Some recent trends in western societies are toward smaller cars, wives who work outside the home, children spending more years in formal schooling, and overeating. In nonwestern societies, the trend toward accepting technological products and ideas from the West has, for many peoples, developed into a cultural drift, characterized often by a disturbing uncriticalness concerning what is borrowed and what the implications of that borrowing might be for the receiving society.

d. A short-term change may be called a *style or fad*. Some things that start out looking like styles or fads are eventually adopted and become long-term trends. It looks as though the change from skirts to pants for women may fall into this category. There are, however, many changes in western clothing that stay for a short while but then are replaced. Among such are the continual changes in skirt length and necktie width. Car manufacturers also seem to specialize in minor changes in style.

e. One type of change that affects the rate at which changes are made is the *historic accident*. Historic accidents happen abruptly and unpredictably. They often result in unguided change, sometimes of a rather widespread nature. The occurrence of a war that radically changes the face of a society or results in a people that once were independent becoming subservient to another people may be seen as historic accidents. The colonialist takeovers of nonwestern societies during the nineteenth century are another tragic example, as are devastating volcano eruptions, earthquakes, floods, and fires.

Many key scientific inventions were also historic accidents. See below under "discoveries."

3. Stages in rapid acculturation. "Acculturation" is the term used by anthropologists to label the process a people goes through as they adapt to and adopt parts of the cultural system of another people. When such adaptation and adoption takes place rapidly, a people tends to go through certain stages, such as the following (*see* Foster 1973:65ff).

a. First, there is usually a *fairly negative attitude* toward the new practices and the possibility of adopting them. Older people, especially, may be quite antagonistic. Even during this period, though, the people may be open to accepting at least certain material items that appear to provide better solutions to problems they face than do traditional techniques.

b. Next comes *increasing acceptance by the more daring*. The daring tend to be in two social categories: the secure and the desperate. Often the latter are quite marginal, socially, so whatever they become associated with may, like them, be looked down on by people of the social mainstream. Christianity is often readily accepted by such people and thus becomes suspect in the eyes of the majority. Youth also are often more daring and open to experimenting with new items, ideas, and practices. This openness, however, may only be temporary. In Japan, for example, youth are allowed to experiment but expected to conform when they marry and assume family responsibility.

c. If the process continues, a third stage involves such wholehearted acceptance of the new that *a good bit of the traditional culture is rejected*. The social controls (e.g., gossip, ostracism, etc.) designed to keep people in the traditional paths begin to break down, so those who choose the new ways disregard the advice of traditional leaders and even scorn traditional ways. Not only the daring, but all but the most conservative members of the populace (e.g., the aged and those with positions of importance in traditional society) seem to rush headlong to accept and practice whatever comes from the prestigious outside source (in our day, western societies). Outsiders are imitated and traditionalists labeled "backward." Those who function best in the new ways become a new elite and get to govern and impose their will on the rest.

d. After some time in stage three, however, *disillusionment* tends to set in. Those most disillusioned are often those who have given themselves most wholeheartedly to adopting the new ways and who, in the process, have become the new elite. They often discover that no matter how hard they try, they are not able (often not allowed) to fully participate in the society they have tried to enter. They will never be regarded as fully European. Furthermore, they perceive that in the process of adapting to western ways they may have lost more sociocultural security in what they have given up than they gained in what they have adopted. They have gone to school and learned how to participate in a society that exists overseas but does not yet fully exist in their own land. In the process, they missed their chance to learn the traditional underpinnings that, at least for the foreseeable future, their own society will have to be based upon, even with all the changes it has recently undergone.

The elite, who a few years earlier eagerly sought to identify themselves with the ways of the West in dress, education, food, and politics, and who often deprecated their own culture and its achievements, now lead their people in a search to discover the essence of their traditional cultural forms. The values inherent in ancient ways are recognized, and attempts are made to restore and perpetuate them (Foster 1973:66).

e. At this point, many attempt to achieve *new cultural rootage* by creating a movement incorporating as much as possible of the old blended with as much as possible of the new. Such a movement may be political (nationalism), religious (Cargo Cults or new religious movements), or "cultural" (with an emphasis on the preservation of such things as indigenous arts, crafts, and rituals). People who feel they have been deprived of their traditional roots but have not been able to fully root themselves in the European (or other) worldview commit themselves to a cause that they feel gives them something to live for.

We will take this topic up again in chapter 26. There we will raise the question of whether Christianity can provide the kind of matrix for reformulation that could lead to both spiritual and cultural health.

4. *Manner of change.* Our final general consideration concerns the way a change takes place. We will deal here with substitution, loss, addition and fusion.

a. Changes often happen by *substitution*. Once Americans traveled on horseback and lit their houses with gas lamps and candles. In those days, men used straight razors to shave. Over a period of time, the horse was replaced by the automobile in general usage, electricity was substituted for gas and candles in lighting, and safety or blade razors replaced the old straight edges.

These substitutions have been well-nigh *complete*, in the sense that very few people still use horses, gas lamps, or straight razors in the same way that once was the rule in our society. Often, though, a substitution is *partial*. That is, both the new custom and the old continue side by side. This is the case with store-bought cakes and pies and also with electric razors, each of which have to share the territory with their predecessors—homemade cakes and pies and blade-type razors.

b. Another manner of change is by *loss*. Over a period of time, some customs die out. Scarification and tattooing have been dying out of certain nonwestern societies, as has long convalescence after childbirth or certain operations in American culture.

c. Change in the culture by *addition* has taken place in many societies with the introduction of such products as radio, television, tape recorders, bicycles, new forms of packaging, and the like. Each of these items adds a whole complex of related items and concepts to the culture, such as the wider dissemination of information and music through radio, antennas, stores, and repair facilities to go with TV, similar kinds of things relating to tape recorders, tires, and other accessories for bicycles. Such products and processes, though they do affect other parts of the cultural structuring, function more as additions to the cultural inventory than as replacements or substitutions for items or customs already in it.

d. There are, furthermore, changes that result in *fusion*. This is a process in which something new is combined with the corresponding item or custom already in the culture. Old-style houses made with new-style materials would be one illustration. In language, a kind of fusion takes place when the meaning of a word is extended to cover new territory without relinquishing the old meanings (e.g., the Hausa word *jirgi*, "canoe/vehicle" discussed in chapter 15). The various pidgin languages of the world (e.g., West African Pidgin, Melanesian Pidgin, Haitian Creole) provide another clear example of linguistic fusion by combining vocabulary from European languages with indigenous semantic and grammatical structures. In contemporary America, a kind of fusion has come about through the decision of movie makers to allow their products to be aired over television. The various accommodations of major athletic events to the desires of television producers and sponsors, even including certain changes in rules, also class as fusions.

CHANGE PROCESSES

Turning from such general things as the locus, rate, and manner of change, let's now look at certain of the processes involved in culture change. These can be divided into primary and secondary processes. Among the former we can discern changes that result from origination (from inside a society) and those that result from diffusion ("borrowed" from outside a society). As secondary processes, we will treat the reinterpretation of an item or concept that occurs when it is borrowed and the ramifications that result within the culture when new things are introduced.

1. The *primary processes* are origination and diffusion. These are labeled primary because they are the means by which new things are introduced into a culture.

a. *Origination* occurs when cultural insiders come up with new things without outside influence. These new things may be arrived at either intentionally or unintentionally. The term *discovery* may be used if the process is unintentional, and the term *invention* if the process is intentional. Either term is, however, often used for both.

In western societies, vulcanization (the process of treating crude rubber so that it will last), penicillin, brainwashing, shock treatment for psychological illness, and countless other innovations have been discovered unintentionally. On the other hand, the development of a multitude of new varieties of plants, animals, and manufactured products has been quite deliberate. One can imagine large numbers of both unintentional and intentional discoveries extending back through history in every society. Such techniques as fire, the alphabet, the various approaches to kinship, types of marriage arrangements, housing patterns, economic, political, and religious rituals and beliefs all were originated somewhere by someone.

What can be originated at any given time is restricted or enhanced by what is already in the culture. People who have no understanding of the principles of leverage, for example, are not likely to develop implements based on those principles. Nor are people who believe the world to be flat likely to try to go around it. Contemporary airplanes and space vehicles could not have been developed 200 years ago, not because the people of that day were not intelligent and creative, but simply because a whole series of insights (originations) had to be developed before the modern techniques could come into existence.

Origination is also helped or hindered by the relative freedom or lack of freedom to express creativity felt by the members of the society. Such freedom, plus the tradition of sharing information with others (enhanced by literacy and the wealth and leisure to engage in research and publish the results), have greatly aided western societies in this regard.

b. *Diffusion*, the movement of cultural "materials" from one society to another, is the other important primary process. Perhaps most cultural change is, in one way or another, dependent upon the movement of ideas from one group to another, whether these groups are parts of separate societies or subgroups within the same society.

Most people seem to borrow at least some things quite readily, if they have the opportunity. Opportunity is, of course, restricted for people who are not in close contact with other peoples. Those with the greatest number of outside contacts are usually those most given to borrowing.

There are several types of diffusion. What may be called *pure diffusion* involves the simple borrowing of an element from a foreign society. When the Yir Yoront borrowed steel axes to replace their stone ones, they participated in pure diffusion. Likewise with a society that borrows an alphabet, particularly the alphabet of another group, such as that of a colonial power that has ruled them.

Often, however, what happens may be called *stimulus diffusion*. In this process, the idea alone is borrowed. It is then elaborated on within the receiving society in their own way. Often certain members of a society travel to another area, where they hear of something but may or may not get to see it. They then go back to their homes and produce something equivalent, but in their own way. The classic example is of the Cherokee chief who, in the early contact period, heard that Whites wrote their language. He then produced a writing system for Cherokee that provided a symbol for each syllable in the language (called a syllabary).

The diffusion process, like any culture change, can be *gradual or rapid*. The difference may tie in with the relative fit or complexity of what is borrowed. Or it may center in the attitudes of the people toward borrowing in general, toward borrowing from that source, or toward borrowing the particular item in question. Diffusion can center on the *borrowing of an object or simply a technique*. In fact, though people often borrow cultural forms (material or non-material), they also often borrow new usages, functions, or meanings for old forms. Almost any combination is possible.

2. Once borrowing has taken place, there are a number of other processes that occur. We will call these *secondary processes* because they represent a second (not a less important) step in the overall movement of change. Among these are reinterpretation and ramification.

a. *Reinterpretation or adaptation* of some kind always happens when a cultural form is taken from one society to another. There will, for example, always be some differences in what that form means to those receiving it. There are usually differences in usage and function as well. Terms such as contextualization, localization, indigenization, reformulation, reworking, and the like, point to other aspects of the reinterpretation process.

The *cultural forms themselves* may or may not be changed when they are borrowed. Material forms such as an axe, a saw, a piece of clothing, or a machine are typically borrowed with little or no change. Nonmaterial forms, however, such as a ceremony or a language, will usually undergo considerable change, as when non-westerners sing western hymns or when a westerner learns (borrows) a nonwestern language. In the latter case, the pronunciation is typically changed considerably from that of a native speaker, under the influence of the language patterns of the learner's native tongue.

More obvious changes often occur in the *usage* of the forms. Even material forms are often used differently than in the source society, as when an African wears a heavy western overcoat in the hot sunshine as an item of decoration (rather than to keep warm); or when an Iranian uses the bumper of a car offensively, to bump another vehicle out of the way, rather than defensively, as the western manufacturer intended it to be used, or when a New Guinean Christian carries a Bible (which he cannot read) to increase his spiritual power. The way nonnative speakers perform linguistically, of course, provides many examples of reinterpretation of usage. Europeans in northern Nigeria have long (unknowingly) misled Nigerians concerning their real intentions by misusing the Hausa word *watakila* to mean "maybe" rather than "almost certainly," and English-speaking Nigerians regularly mislead native English speakers by using "used to" to mean "usually."

Reinterpretation also regularly occurs in the *function* of a borrowed item. The so-called Kachina dolls and sand-painting designs bought by many tourists from the Navaho and Hopi Indians, though used decoratively by the purchasers, function indigenously as sources or vehicles of spiritual power in the religious life of their originators. The New Guinean arrows I have hanging in my living room serve a decorative function for me, though at least some of them were intended by their maker to function in food getting or protection.

Reinterpretation of *meaning* is always a concomitant of borrowing. Meaning is personal, existing in the minds of the persons who practice the processes of culture, rather than inherent in the cultural forms themselves (*see* Kraft 1991a). Whenever an item or practice passes from one group to another, we can be certain that it will be reinterpreted from the point of view of the receiving group. When the overcoat, Bible, automobile, words of a language, Kachina dolls, or the arrows are used with a different function, they are automatically interpreted differently by their new users.

b. In addition to and intertwined with the process of reinterpretation is the process of *ramification*. Since the various aspects of a cultural system relate closely with one another, a change in one part will affect other parts. The introduction of new items and practices will have an influence on other parts of the system.

There are many illustrations of undesirable ramifications resulting from the introduction of new practices by missionaries. In an attempt to enable cross-cultural Christians to avoid such mistakes, this text is full of them! For instance, there have been destructive ramifications of the introduction into nonwestern societies of western schools. Youth who spend their days in school cannot, of course, help their parents during that time. Nor will they learn as well what their parents would like to teach them. Thus a generation gap develops. They are, furthermore, secularized, and their people skills diminished. See chapter 17 for more of these ramifications. There are, however, more positive ramifications. Such youth learn reading, writing, science, math, and other skills that put them in good stead in relation to the world outside their home villages.

Often the ramifications resulting from the borrowing of one item or practice result in a people feeling the need to borrow additional items or practices. At one time, the Winnebago Indians allowed their children to go naked. Then somebody introduced housing with wooden floors. Naked children on wooden floors, however, frequently result in very slippery floors! This ramification led to the borrowing of two additional customs—diapers and earlier toilet training (Luzbetak 1963:218; Honigmann 1959:14).

Things invented or developed within a society also produce ramifications. Within western societies, for example, the ramifications of the internal combustion engine, the automobile, the airplane, radio, television, industrialization, and urbanization have been enormous.

The process of ramification does not take place evenly. Typically, some people in a society adopt a new practice while others reject or take longer to incorporate the change into their way of life. As mentioned, the very secure and the desperate in a society are more likely to accept new ways. When the change turns out to be a good one, those who adopt it tend to gain an advantage over those who refuse it. In India, it was the outcastes who turned to Christianity and westernization. This has given many of them an advantage over those socially in the middle of the society, with respect to employment in western occupations.

If a change turns out to be a poor one, however, those who have adopted it may find themselves at a serious disadvantage in relation to those who have rejected the practice. A leader in a polygamous society who becomes a Christian, and is therefore allowed only one wife, finds himself (and his wife) at a serious disadvantage in attempting to carry out the hospitality required of a person of his standing. He may, in fact, lose his position and his wife (who may well leave him because she is overworked) if he insists on remaining monogamous. Another kind of disadvantage faces many subsistence farmers who turned exclusively to cash crops such as cocoa, groundnuts, or coffee or who left their farms to take employment as miners. They often discover that the ups and downs of world demand for the products they have turned to often leave them without the necessities of life.

Even if the majority of the people of a society adopt a practice, they may use it only in certain parts of their cultural life, without fully incorporating it into other areas. Languages are often used like this—one language at home, another in the office, perhaps a third at market. Christianity, unfortunately, often becomes specialized in this way, used on Sunday but forgotten for the rest of the week.

Another type of uneven change occurs when only part of a given custom is adopted. Frequently those who give up subsistence farming to work for money do not learn how to store (save) money for lean times, the way they knew how to store food. When they get money, they tend to spend it all quickly, often by being overgenerous to unemployed relatives. Then when they find themselves out of work, they also find themselves without resources to take care of their needs, because they have not saved.

Perhaps the greatest problem of Christianity in the Two-Thirds World is the fact that large numbers of those who call themselves Christians still go to traditional shamans, diviners, and healers when they feel the need for supernatural power. Probably because of deficiencies in the way the Christian message was presented to them, they only learned part of it and therefore retained those practices on which they had learned to depend for spiritual power, not knowing that the Christian God has provided for that part of life as well.

RESULTS OF CHANGE

Once a change has taken place, there are certain definable results within the cultural system. Among these are development/decline, elaboration/simplification, specialization/generalization, and equilibrium/disequilibrium.

1. New items or practices in a culture may result in *development*, a greater ability of a society to control the material, social, or spiritual forces that affect it. The borrowing of material technology from the West has increased the ability of many societies to control their physical environment. With this has often come, however, *decline* in their ability to control social factors such as crime, delinquency, intergenerational alienation, and the like.

2. *Elaboration*, the increase of complexity in the culture, is the usual result of the frequent introduction of new customs. Each new item or practice adds to the cultural inventory. Such additions then require additional relationships between the new and the old, increasing the complexity of the system as a whole. At the same time, other parts of the cultural system may be moving toward *simplification*. In American society, we are surrounded by scientific, technological, and institutional elaboration. At the same time, however, customs of address involving titles for people of different age or status seem to be undergoing reduction in the direction of addressing everyone by his or her first name. It would seem to be a

general principle that as the complex dynamics of mass populations invade a society in, for example, urbanization, there will be simplification in the terminology used to address and refer to other people.

3. As the cultural inventory increases and the system gets more complex, the twin tendencies toward *specialization and generalization* develop. People find they can no longer keep track of everything, so they specialize. Specialization by age and sex are already a part of most small-scale societies. Added complexity, however, gives rise to additional specialization based on such things as occupation, social class, and talent. Meanwhile, to cope with the increasing complexity, more generalized concepts are introduced into the thinking of the people. A very small-scale society, where everyone knows everyone else's family relationships, can get along without general terms for such relatives as brother/sister, uncle/aunt, and cousin. A larger scale society, however, finds frequent need for such broader categorization.

4. In all of this, careful attention has to be given to the *equilibrium or disequilibrium* occasioned by the various changes coming into a society. Changes that increase a people's control over such things as food production and health may create a greater sense of balance and security, if they are not accompanied by too many disruptive changes. When change is rapid or forced, however, people often lose the sense of security they once felt. They may even change their attitude toward their culture, from respect to disrespect. This can lead to demoralization, and psychological and social breakdown.

War and conquest are among the most prominent destroyers of equilibrium. They often result in demoralization and disequilibrium. Urbanization, industrialization, and migration (especially if forced) are also enemies of balance and security. People who come out of a rural situation where they feel important, into an urban situation where they don't feel important, often feel keenly the depersonalization of the city. They often then lose their balance and become self-centered and irresponsible. We will discuss this area further in chapter 27.

MISSIOLOGICAL APPLICATIONS

As we have frequently pointed out, Christian cross-cultural witnesses are agents of cultural as well as spiritual change. The insights and applications emanating from the considerations raised in this chapter (and the section it introduces) will almost surely be very helpful. It is our hope that the following suggestions for application will make the chapter even more valuable.

1. *Opinion leaders.* A point of considerable significance for cross-cultural witnesses is the recognition that sociocultural change is basically a matter of changes in people's minds. It is easy to get bogged down when we ponder the complexity and power of sociocultural change; the whole business seems so complex, so strong, so unmanageable. What can we as individuals ever expect to do to affect such forces?

When we scale the process down to what is going on with individuals, however, some hope emerges. Opinion leaders are more influential than others. When they change their minds, others follow. Those who develop close friendship with opinion leaders often find that their suggestions for change are taken seriously and sometimes adopted. There are, however, at least three important things to consider:

a. *Identifying opinion leaders is not always easy.* Each group within a society will include one or more opinion leaders. Some influence small groups, others have a larger influence. Political position does not always assure opinion leadership. Indeed, often those in official positions are hampered in making changes by the fact that their main job is to *support*, not change the system. Often the persons who advise the leader in focus are the ones most likely to influence the opinion of the leader. The cross-cultural witness needs to develop the ability to discover those within the society whom others listen to. Whether these people are in focus or out of focus doesn't matter; they are the ones to appeal to, if one's suggestions are to have the broad influence desired by us and by God.

b. *Can such a strategy be in the will of God?* Aren't we recommending insincerity, manipulation, and even deceit? These are indeed possible, and we must carefully guard against them, but they are not inevitable. What is inevitable is that we will need to approach people. This being true, which persons should we select to form relationships with? When Jesus had this decision to make, He chose Galilean opinion leaders as His disciples. Having decided to make Galilee His area of concentration, He chose to relate to those in respectable positions within that target area—successful fishermen, a tax collector, a politician. They all had achieved positions of prominence, and all would be listened to by Galileans. Had Jesus targeted Jerusalem, He would have chosen a different group.

Was Jesus insincere or manipulative to have chosen opinion leaders? Of course not. He was simply sensible. He was loving in His approach to them. He invited them, He did not coerce them. They could have refused His invitation or left Him at any time later, as many others did (Jn 6:66–7). He loved them and worked with them for their own sakes as well as for the sake of His strategy. Nor did His choice of those disciples involve rejection of others. It is clear from the Gospels that there were many others who, with the disciples, had witnessed the whole of Jesus' ministry (Acts 1:21). He simply chose to develop a special relationship with certain persons as a matter of good strategy. Such an approach need not be insincere or manipulative. Let's then choose this strategy in preference to a poorer one.

c. Having identified opinion leaders and chosen to work with them, *what kind of relationship should we work toward?* First of all, it should be a friendship relationship, not simply a working association. Jesus did not "lord it over" His disciples. He related to them as friends (Jn 15:15). He taught them, but He also trusted them (in spite of frequent indications that they should not be trusted). In a helpful passage concerning what is involved in this kind of approach, Luzbetak (1963:229–38) lists the following as important to the kind of rapport we need with opinion leaders: mutual understanding, common tastes, common interests, mutual assistance, mutual admiration, and mutual accessibility. That kind of basis provides the best possible soil for the kind of witness we seek to bring. The task is to plant and cultivate the right kind of seed in that soil.

The discussion in chapter 24 builds on this approach.

2. *Syncretism and contextualization (= appropriate Christianity).* During sociocultural change, the adoption of the new usually takes place gradually and unevenly. This means that it is the usual state of affairs for those who enter Christianity to change certain things in their lives right away, others more gradually, and still others after a long period of time, if at all. Intermediate states may look quite unlike what is desirable. This is normal in the process by means of which a

people make Christianity genuinely theirs. This is contextualization, the process of learning to express genuine Christianity in socioculturally appropriate ways.

The question faced by Christian witnesses is, however, whether any given undesirable state is but a step in a continuing process or whether the changes have virtually come to an end and the people are settled in their present beliefs and behavior. If the latter is the case, some sort of renewal is called for. If, however, the people are simply in the middle of a continuing process, patience and continued assistance in the right direction are what are needed.

If the undesirable condition is a settled state it is frequently labeled syncretism or Christopaganism. What these terms are intended to label is a blend or mixture of Christianity with pre-Christian beliefs and practices relating to supernatural beings and powers. One common form of such a blend occurs when people adopt surface-level forms from those who bring Christianity while attaching to them deep-level meanings coming from their pre-Christian religious allegiances. What may on the surface look like Christianity may be anything but.

There are at least two roads that lead to syncretism. The "undirected selection" of elements from the new way that allows people to draw their own conclusions and attach their own meanings to the new practices is the road ordinarily focused on by those who talk of syncretism. But overdirection or domination can also lead to syncretism.

The change processes leading to the planting and growth of the Church have produced at least four kinds of form-meaning combinations. Each of these is a frequent response to the entrance of Christianity. Though the first type does not result in anything really Christian, combinations b, c, and d each result in a different kind of church.

a. Forms Local, Meanings Local ⟶ Local Religion. Local forms combined with local meanings result simply in a local form of religion. There is nothing necessarily Christian about this alternative, though certain Christian elements may well be incorporated. People may listen to the Christian message and choose to remain in their traditional state with traditional forms and meanings. Or they may develop a new or partly new approach to the expression of their supernaturalism, such as the Japanese "new religions" that have sprung from Buddhism or a nativistic movement such as a Melanesian cargo cult. Such systems are often the result of frustration over the rate of change, whether too fast or too slow.

In response, people create some reformulation of their traditional beliefs and rituals that is not exactly the same as what existed previously but usually makes no pretense of identifying with Christianity. Some of these are "anti-acculturative" in that they seek to react against the changes by creating something the people can control that is closer to their previous religion. Some, however, are "pro-acculturative" in that, though they constitute a reaction against the domination of foreigners, the leaders are desirous of westernizing even more rapidly than they were able to under foreign tutelage.

b. Forms Foreign, Meanings Local ⟶ Christopagan Syncretism. If a people have adopted the foreign forms but interpreted them largely in local ways, we have what we may call christopagan syncretism. In such systems, the meanings intended by those who brought them are not learned by the receivers. Instead, they connect the new forms with old ideas and practices and, as throughout Latin America, end up with traditional deities called by names coming from Roman

Catholic Christianity. Thus often their sun god is renamed God the Father, another god is named the Virgin Mary, and others are given the names of saints. Furthermore, "Christian" rituals are interpreted as magical and local healers conduct their businesses, using satanic power, right in the Catholic cathedrals.

Lest Protestants get too smug, there is much syncretism in Protestant churches as well. Many people who regularly attend church take communion as a magical procedure and prefer to appeal to the local healers using satanic power rather than to God for healing. The Bible, likewise, is often considered magical.

c. Forms Foreign, Meanings Foreign ⟶ Domination Syncretism. Domination by the advocates of Christianity to the point where the receptors have largely adopted both foreign forms and foreign meanings (whether those of the change agents or new meanings they have created themselves) results in what I call domination syncretism. This is a worldwide phenomenon that has resulted unconsciously and consistently from the interaction between foreign missionaries and peoples of traditional societies. It is characterized by western forms of organization, worship, music, preaching, training, doctrine, buildings, and all the rest, plus the western meanings that go along with them. These latter have been carefully taught more or less effectively, and though the people are usually conscious of the fact that they are practicing a foreign religion, they think that's the way Christianity was intended to be.

d. Forms Local, Meanings Christian ⟶ Appropriate Church. The ideal, a church that is thoroughly biblical and thoroughly appropriate to the sociocultural setting, consists largely of local forms to which are attached Christian meanings. In this case, the meanings come neither from the sending nor the receiving societies, but from the Scriptures. Though the meanings are always subject to interpretation, they should be understood and followed from the point of view of the receiving society. When the Christians

> think of the Lord as their own, not a foreign Christ; when they do things as unto the Lord meeting the cultural needs around them, worshipping in patterns they understand; when their congregations function in participation in a body, which is structurally indigenous; then you have an *indigenous* Church (Tippett 1987:381, original 1969).

Note that it is extremely important what forms are used and where they come from, since they have to convey the proper meanings if the result is to be properly Christian. Any society can, of course, borrow cultural forms from another society. If, however, the proportion of borrowed forms is very high and the proportion of indigenous forms very low, the character of their Christianity is strongly affected. Paul Hiebert has written an important article dealing with the evaluations that have to be made to enable people to work toward what he refers to as "Critical Contextualization" (1984).

The four types of response are summarized in figure 22.2.

a. Forms Local, Meanings Local ⟶ Local Religion
b. Forms Foreign, Meanings Local ⟶ Christopagan Syncretism
c. Forms Foreign, Meanings Foreign ⟶ Domination Syncretism
d. Forms Local, Meanings Christian ⟶ Appropriate Church

Figure 22.2 Summary of types of churches

3. *The cross-cultural Christian worker and sociocultural breakdown*. In many areas of the world today, it is sociocultural disorganization and breakdown rather than mere change that is the issue. None of us have to be told that serious social and personal problems arise as a result of such breakdown. What can cross-cultural Christian workers do in relation to such phenomena? Sometimes it seems the only thing we can do is to "be there," to sympathize with those caught in sociocultural breakdown, to figuratively hold their hands and let them know somebody cares. Though the problems are enormous, the answers few and, it seems, expertise all but nonexistent, perhaps a few suggestions can be advanced.

a. First of all, it is important to recognize both the complexity of the processes we are dealing with and the fact that it is at the individual, personal level that the problems manifest themselves. Sociocultural breakdown shows up in psychological and social problems. This being true, the possibility emerges of working for change at the personal level, employing the same principles we have been discussing. It is still individuals who make changes in their own behavior and opinion leaders whose ideas are followed by others. Ministry on the basis of Christian principles to individuals and small groups can at least help those persons and potentially be of benefit to larger groups as well.

b. Secondly, we need to be realistic rather than idealistic concerning the kinds of sociocultural patterns we recommend and work toward. We as outsiders are not in a position to dictate or control the change process (*see* chapter 24 for more on this topic), but we are often in a position to counsel, recommend, and work with the Christians toward improvement in their sociocultural and spiritual life. We should by now have come to recognize the great importance of solid cultural foundations to the well-being of any people. I wonder if people who are culturally ill can ever become spiritually healthy.

c. As those who function as counselors and recommenders, we need to recognize that there is no special value in preserving or returning to the patterns of the past. This is true in spite of the fact that even recently introduced present practices provide more satisfaction if they can be understood as extensions of and developments from traditional ways. The need is for coping with the present, not retreating to the past. This is why we choose to use the terms appropriate and local, rather than indigenous, as the labels for what we aim at, since the latter term seems to many to recommend a retreat to a past form of a people's way of life.

d. The questions are, What cultural structures will be appropriate for this people (especially the Christians) at this time? What of the past should be retained or recovered to provide a familiar and solid basis for whatever lies ahead? What of the new practices need to be grafted onto that basis, in order for these people to survive and thrive in the modern world? Considerations such as those raised in this and the following chapters should make us cautious about recommending too complete a break from the past, for the least disruptive changes (both socially and psychologically) are those most easily perceived as extensions and elaborations of existing patterns and habits.

These considerations should also help us recognize both the possibility and the potential effectiveness of working with a small, manageable group in constructive ways to assist them in overcoming the ravages of cultural breakdown. A realistic approach asks what is "do-able" and sets about doing it, rather than sitting around deploring the unmanageability of the situation. The people we work with need help to face and adapt to the present, not our counsel that they retreat from it.

CONCLUSION

In conclusion, we have surveyed certain general principles relative to cultural stability and change. We turn now to some more specific aspects of change. First we will look at the matter of what hinders and what facilitates change.

CHAPTER 23

CHANGE BARRIERS AND FACILITATORS

INTEGRATIONAL THOUGHT

Tradition is a powerful deterrent to change. It seems easier to continue with a tradition, even if it is widely acknowledged to be deficient, than to go to the effort of changing it. As someone has pointed out, the seven most deadly words are the phrase, "We've never done it that way before."

Thus it was with both Jesus and Paul (not to mention the other followers of Jesus). Their worst enemies were those who should have most readily supported them (the Pharisees and the Jewish Christians), but the changes Jesus and Paul were advocating and the success they enjoyed led the religious leaders to fear for their own influence. They took Jesus and Paul's popularity as a threat and sought to get rid of the cause, rather than make the recommended changes. They chose allegiance to their traditions and the support of their positions afforded by those traditions over the newness of life and experience they could have entered into, had they followed the recommendations of these men of God.

Again, the words of Tevye in *Fiddler on the Roof* are to the point. "Why do we do this?" he asks. "We don't know," he answers his own question, "but it's a tradition!" Thus it ever seems to be.

This problem was the subject of Jesus' interaction with the Jewish leaders recorded in Mark 7. The Jewish leaders had noticed that the disciples were eating food without ritually washing their hands first. That is, they broke one of the religious traditions that the Pharisees saw as their duty to enforce. So they asked Jesus, "Why is it that your disciples do not follow the teaching handed down by our ancestors, but instead eat with ritually unclean hands?" (v. 5).

Jesus called their bluff and made a statement about the wrongness of their heart attitude: "You are hypocrites, just as [Isaiah] wrote: 'These people, says God, honor me with their words, but their heart is really far away from me. It is no use for them to worship me, because they teach man-made rules as though they were my laws!' You put aside God's command and obey the teachings of men" (vv. 6–8). Tradition, of course, flows from worldview and, in turn, constricts it. Religious leaders seem even more prone than others to assume that their traditions are close to infallible. They tend to claim divine sanction for both their convictions and the cultural outworkings of these convictions. It is easy for us to drift in the direction of the Pharisees and, in the name of God, to hinder the working of God.

INTRODUCTION

We have surveyed the subject of change in a general way. Now let's look at some of the things that encourage or discourage the process of change. Though there are many angles from which to tackle this subject, we will approach it in terms of the universal categories of worldview discussed in chapter 4. We will also frequently draw on the excellent presentations concerning barriers to change in Foster 1973 (chapters 4, 5, and 6) and that on facilitators of change in Luzbetak 1963 (chapter 10).

BARRIERS TO CHANGE

The first question we want to face is, What are the things that tend to minimize or hinder change? If, as we have contended, we are to be change agents, what are the factors that are likely to keep the changes we are advocating from happening?

Worldview assumptions underlie all sociocultural behavior. These are the basic principles, the foundation for the rules and regulations from which social control techniques flow. Since people tend to be quite protective of their worldview assumptions, these provide the primary barriers to change. These *worldview* barriers are in the patterning, the script that people follow.

At the personal level, however, lies another formidable set of barriers, *the social barriers*. These flow from the fact that we ordinarily behave habitually and unthinkingly, according to the patterns we have been taught.

Worldview Barriers

First the worldview barriers to change. As we have mentioned, these lie in the structuring of a people's assumptions. Basic assumptions in each of the areas listed as worldview universals (chapter 4) provide blockage.

1. *Categorization, Classification, Logic, and Picturing* are terms I have used to point to that aspect of worldview that provides a people with their basic conceptions concerning how the various components of their universe are to be compartmentalized and related to each other.

In some cases, the way people classify and define items and events appears to provide little hindrance to change. Indeed, often when change occurs in the basic assumption, though the technical classification may change, the popular classification remains the same. Such is the case in American worldview with animals such as the whale and the bat. Scientists tell us that the whale is not a fish and the bat is not a bird, but at the popular level, we are tempted to say, "So what?" Most of us still consider swimming in water and flying in air as the primary criteria for classifying these animals and so think of whales with fish and bats with birds. We also know that technically the sun and moon do not rise and set, but popularly we continue to talk as if they do. Our real classification system has remained the same, in spite of scientific change.

The logical incompatibility between something introduced into a society and what is already there can be a barrier to acceptance. People are more likely to stay with the familiar, even if they recognize its problems, rather than adopt the new and risk a lot of other problems. The attempt to introduce monotheism to a polytheistic people would run into such a logical incompatibility problem. To the person who believes in many gods, it often seems arrogant and irreligious to claim there is but one God. In the first century Christians were called atheists.

A serious problem for cross-cultural communicators of the Gospel lies in an area where, for many of the peoples of the world, their logic puts such things as

material prosperity and physical health in the same category with spiritual blessing. Though there is also a causal dimension to this (*see below*), it is the classification that interests us here. From the point of view of their logic, the category
wealthy automatically implies spiritual. These peoples therefore tend to see
wealthy westerners as close to God (or other good spiritual powers) and assume
that if they themselves get close to God, westerners, or other blessed beings, they
will become wealthy also. Even after people in these societies have observed the
excesses of wealthy non-Christians and become Christian themselves, such a
worldview classification is hard to overcome.

2. Barriers in the *person/group* area of worldview may be very great. Especially difficult changes for Christians often lie in their worldview-based assumptions concerning in-group and out-group, the characteristics of an ideal person,
and the relationship between group and individual.

a. The fact that God accepts people where they are leads Christian strategists
to endorse the practice of *appealing to people in terms of the interests of their own
people group*. This is the approach sometimes called the homogeneous unit principle (*see* McGavran and Wagner 1990). It takes advantage of the groupness and in-
group cohesiveness felt by a people whose way of life derives from the same worldview. Taking advantage of such a factor can be an effective and, I believe, a scriptural strategy for reaching the lost (*see* Kraft 1978a). Christians are, however,
commanded to love outsiders, even enemies. In the process of Christian growth,
such natural in-group/out-group barriers are to be weakened and abandoned in
favor of the Christian principle of oneness in Christ. But this seems to happen
infrequently. The presence of such a person/group assumption and the strong allegiance people pledge to it provide a formidable barrier to change in this area. And
such blatant resistance to replacing the traditional worldview assumption with a
Christian perspective, as in the case of South African apartheid, is an embarrassment to us all.

b. Concepts of *what is ideal in personal characteristics and behavior* also often
constitute barriers to change. Richardson (1974) documents some of the difficulties
experienced by Sawi Christians with respect to the high value they have traditionally placed on treachery toward outsiders. When an idealized personal characteristic turns out to be diametrically opposed to what Christianity recommends, a high
barrier is produced. Even western Christian men often find that assumptions
inculcated by our society concerning what "manliness" is all about get in their way
in their attempts to become more Christlike. Western ideals such as strong individualism, aggressiveness, competitiveness, fear of weakness and self-revelation
can be strong barriers to change in the direction of scriptural assumptions and
attitudes.

c. Understandings of *status and role* that do not coincide between the agents of
change and the potential adopters of change can provide significant blockage to
acceptance. Typical western roles for women, for example, often provide models
that the men of the receptor society are afraid will be imitated by their women.
Likewise with children. Traditional men may therefore be quite resistant to Christianity, lest their women and children become like those of the advocates.

d. Either *strong groupness or strong individualism* can generate major barriers to Christian change. In many group oriented societies, unless the whole group
decides to make a change (such as conversion to Christ or adoption of some new

agricultural technique) at the same time, no individual is allowed to. In some societies, though, if permission is obtained from the leaders, some will be allowed to make such changes, even if the whole group does not go along with it. In individualistic societies, on the other hand, serious barriers to group cooperation frequently occur. These often lead to such things as unchristian competition between those supposed to be brothers, inability of fellow Christians to function as parts of the same body, severe weaknesses in relationships and behavior among members of the same church, and the like.

e. Perception concerning the *role of government* can also provide a barrier. Either traditional ideas concerning what is expected or reactions to disagreeable experiences with the current government can block openness to new ideas, especially if these are associated in people's minds with disagreeable governmental practices. Often people are suspicious of their government, so if the government supports something, they will automatically be negative toward it.

f. The worldview valuing of the *means of communication* employed is another person/group factor that often provides a barrier to change. Much depends on what language is used, especially when one deals with heart things like Christianity. In many parts of the world people need to function in three or more languages, but each is valued differently. For example, in the part of northeastern Nigeria where we worked, people spoke an indigenous language at home, a regional (trade) language (either Hausa or Fulani) in the market, and, if they knew it, a national/world language (English) in school and in their broader contacts with the outside world. For most, the use of English was quite restricted. Hausa or Fulani, however, would be used anytime one was interacting with a member of another tribe, ordinarily to discuss subjects such as buying and selling, politics, government, travel, schooling, and the like. But they very seldom used Hausa to talk about deep things inside their hearts and minds, since they used Hausa or Fulani primarily with outsiders. When insiders conversed, only the home language would be used and, for most people, only this language is adequate for discussing deep things such as a person's relationship with God.

When people talk about change at the worldview level, the kind of change that Christianity seeks to bring about, what is the appropriate language? Is it the language they use to speak to outsiders about outside things, or is it the language they use to speak to insiders about important personal things? There are deeply held worldview values attached to the vehicle through which any suggestion of change comes. If Christianity comes through an outsider language, what's to prevent people from thinking it's nothing but a foreign, outsider's way? Bible translators often speak of the excitement in the voices of people when they first hear God speaking in their heart language. "Now I know God really cares for me, really loves me," they often say. Changes advocated are associated with the values placed upon the vehicle through which they are presented.

The same is true of the art and music used in association with the Christian message. As pointed out in chapter 16, the message is received much more positively when represented in familiar art forms than in foreign clothing.

3. Many of the major barriers to the communication of the Gospel lie in the area of *causality and power*. The question of who is in charge of the universe (God, spirits, humans) and what should be our relationship to Him/them is, of course, a major item. But the existence of and attitude toward the power of humans over

other humans (e.g., in relation to family, position, politics) is also a crucial issue, both in communicating Christianity and in the personal growth of Christians. In addition, there is the matter of what kind of power Christians have been given by God in material, human, and spiritual spheres.

Those who believe in no god or many gods find their assumptions hindering any desire to accept the Christian God. Should they accept Him, they find constant interference from their old belief as they seek to understand and relate to the true God. The barriers raised by assumptions and attitudes such as the following can be very high: fatalism; a concept of God as distant and uncaring or as judgmental and harsh; taboos generated by such concepts of God; the belief that humans are (through science and education) potentially all-powerful; or the nearly opposite belief that capricious spirits control the universe and human destiny.

To give an example of the blockage caused by *fatalism*, I once got into a discussion with a Nigerian whose relative was dying. His attitude was that God wills such things and that, therefore, we cannot interfere. He told me his relative was dying because "God wants him to die." "How do you know?" I asked. "Because he's sick." "Why don't you take him to the hospital?" "Because God wants him to die." "If you took him to the hospital, perhaps he would live. Then what?" "Then I would know that God doesn't want him to die." "Well, why don't you take him to the hospital and try to find out?" "Because God wants him to die." "How do you know God wants him to die?" "Because he's sick?" On and on it goes. It was hard for me, as a westerner, to deal with such fatalism, since my worldview sees humans as virtually all-powerful and human life as something close to the most valuable thing on earth. I saw no conflict between believing that God is in charge and believing that we are allowed and encouraged by God Himself to make every attempt to save a human life.

Another aspect of causality is raised when we consider the *power of human habit* (as discussed in the previous chapter) in the perpetuation of traditions and attitudes. *Ethnocentrism* often breeds the attitude that a people's approach in any given area is already the best approach. Why do they need to change? *Pride and dignity* in their present way of life can result in the same resistance. A *fear of losing face* is often associated with such pride at the individual level. *Insecurity*, both individually and on a group level usually shows up in a fear of risk. *Norms of modesty* can be particularly troublesome when changes in such things as clothing, housing, and toilet customs are suggested.

4. A people's concept of *time/event* can hinder change as well. Efficiency in the use of time needed (or at least felt by westerners to be needed) for the smooth operation of industrial and other organizations (including church) is often neither appreciated nor practiced by those with nonwestern concepts of time. An "event orientation," in which people more or less go with the flow of whatever is going on until it peters out, with little regard to the length of time it takes, is not conducive to organizational efficiency. On the other hand, the tendency of westerners to structure even interpersonal interactions by the clock is not conducive to healthy relationships between people. Any attempt to introduce greater community and intimacy into western church structures has to overcome the barrier erected by western values with respect to time.

5. Concepts of *space* can also interfere in the processes of culture change. One major area of difficulty has been the fact that the worldview of many peoples does not allow them to buy or sell land. To them land is not owned, only used. When

practices are introduced from the West that require individual ownership of land (e.g., to build buildings on), there can be considerable misunderstanding. In the early days of the United States, the European settlers often bought (from their point of view) land from Indians who, from their point of view, were loaning it to them. Later there was trouble when the Indians felt they needed to regain control of the land.

I am told that for at least some of the aborigine peoples of Australia, important meetings take place outdoors in the evening. Church meetings that are scheduled for midday and indoors are therefore considered by the unacculturated to be unimportant and are poorly attended. Such values provide barriers to either group adopting the custom of the other.

The size of something is also a matter of space. A fascinating story of blockage based on size perception comes from the South Pacific, where a group of health specialists from the West were trying to instruct people concerning the dangers of houseflies. They made a poster with a foot-long picture of a house fly on it. Under it was a caption such as, "Kill the housefly because it causes disease." The people, though they were fascinated by the fly in the picture, came to a conclusion quite different from that intended by the outsiders. They agreed that such flies looked like an enormous threat to life and health. They also agreed to kill them if they saw them. But their interpretation, based on worldview assumptions concerning how to interpret such pictures, was that there was no real problem in their area of the world. "If we had flies that large around here," they concluded, "we'd see that they were dangerous and kill them also. But our flies are just tiny things. We don't kill them because they're not big enough to hurt anybody."

Social Barriers

As pointed out in chapter 4, though the worldview provides the basic assumptions, it is *people* who actually follow through on those assumptions. The worldview does not block change; it is people following the guidelines of the worldview who throw up the barriers. It is people who will, emote, think, interpret, evaluate, make commitments, explain, relate, and adapt on the basis either of the traditional assumptions or changed assumptions, and people tend to do this habitually, without thinking. We now want to look at certain social habits that provide barriers to change.

1. The first of these habits may be labeled *group solidarity*. People behave in groups, even when they highly value individualism. Public opinion seems to be extremely important to all peoples. A powerful hindrance to change is the fact that people always ask themselves the question, What would anybody in my group say if I broke from the accepted patterns and changed in the way you're suggesting? Among group-oriented peoples, there is usually an intense all for one, one for all mentality that becomes especially evident when they feel threatened or insecure. This mentality can be a strong barrier to change, even if logic would seem to indicate that the change would be helpful.

The *attitude of the group toward those introducing the change* is important in this regard. If the group respects the advocates in the area in question, it is much more likely to accept the innovation.

Internal factors that crosscut the overall solidarity also play a part. Often there is *conflict between subgroups*, producing various factions. If one faction accepts something, the other will automatically reject it. In many parts of Latin

America, for example, if one extended family accepts evangelical Christianity, then automatically other families that don't like them will reject it.

2. Another important social factor is the nature and relational characteristics of the *authority structures*. In all societies there are several levels of authority. When *personal authority is high*, as in individualistic societies, barriers to change may often be dealt with at that level. Conversion to Christ, for example, can usually be expected on the basis of an individual decision. Though the individual considers the opinions of others in the decision-making process, any blockage occasioned by such influence is ultimately evaluated and processed at the individual level.

When, however, the *family is strong* and the person approached is under the authority of others, the decision-making process in major areas of life may be totally out of the individual's hands. We often found in Nigeria that a recommendation that an ill person go to the hospital was met with the statement, "I have to ask my family." Quite often the authority in the family would not let the sick person go get the medical attention we thought he or she needed. The authority to make such a decision was in the family, and the person did not have the right to make that decision on an individual basis. Where is the authority? is a crucial question when change is introduced.

3. *Traditional leadership and organizational patterns* can also influence change in major ways. Foster (1973:128–9), citing Gordon Brown (1957), points to the differential acceptance by Samoans of three Christian denominations as a case in point. The Congregational Church was accepted better in Samoa than were the Methodist or Catholic Churches, "in spite of the fact that the elaborate ceremonial of the latter church undeniably appeals strongly to tribal peoples." The reason suggested for this difference is "the similarity in sociopolitical structure between native Samoa and the Congregational Church." Samoans were strong on village autonomy. Thus

> The Congregational Church fitted into this organization because the individual church is autonomous. It lends itself to village separatism and enables the Samoans to identify church and village as one. . . . The more rigid central control of the Methodists has less appeal. As for the Catholic [Church] . . . its hierarchical organization is a serious handicap (G. Brown 1957:14).

4. Social structures such as *caste and class* often also present barriers to acceptance of change. In India, if the members of one caste accept Christianity, very often they will have no ability to communicate it to members of other castes. The fact that it is the outcastes, the *harijans*, who have flocked to Christianity in India automatically means that high-caste people are not interested unless they can be approached separately and have their own churches. Indeed, the harijans usually do not want upper-caste people to become Christians because 1) if they convert and join the harijan churches, they may well take them over, and 2) if they have their own upper-caste churches, those will have more prestige than the harijan churches. The planting of an innovation such as Christianity must therefore be done separately within each caste if it is to be effectively introduced to all of the peoples of India. We can't ordinarily expect the message to flow from one caste to another. Such caste barriers tend to block movement of ideas from upper to lower as well as from lower to upper.

Class barriers, though not as difficult to permeate as caste barriers, also provide significant blockage to change. Ideas tend to flow from person to person within classes, rather than from members of one class to those of another. There is, however, some flow of ideas from upper to lower classes and a much lower flow from lower to upper, usually between contiguous classes. We must, however, be aware that God sometimes breaks the normal social and communicational rules. He did this in Acts 2, when He brought about a revival in Jerusalem through despised Galileans.

As we conclude this section on barriers to change, I would like to raise one caution: *that we attempt to look deeper than either the worldview or the social barriers to discover if there may be areas of dissatisfaction with existing patterns.* Often there are latent tensions caused by the lack of fit between the present social and worldview structuring and the needs of the present generation. The structuring of a culture always comes from the past and is often ill suited to the present or the future. We must learn to *look for the felt needs that are not now being met by the present structuring.* Felt needs are a personal, not a structural thing. Things that seem to be incompatible with the society as it is are often appealing to a people in relation to a felt need to get out from under the tight control of some aspect of the society.

For example, people are often tired of the tyranny of the spirit world as represented to them by the traditional religious leaders. They may also be weary of social pressure to marry only in certain ways (sometimes fathers of potential brides can get very greedy and set the brideprice unreasonably high) or of political structures controlled by a small handful of people whose power comes from birth rather than achievement. Such dissatisfactions can often be discovered and tapped as facilitators of change.

FACILITATORS OF CHANGE

On the opposite side of the coin from barriers to change are those things that facilitate change. Many of these can be deduced simply in contrast to most of the barriers. In addition, there are four major areas to be covered: 1) characteristics of receiving groups that facilitate change, 2) characteristics of individuals within these groups that facilitate change, 3) characteristics of donor groups that facilitate change, and 4) characteristics of the potential innovations themselves that make them likely to be accepted. These facilitators are in overview chart form in figure 23.1 below.

It should be clear, both from what has already been presented on this topic and from what follows, that we are dealing with great complexity. We are also looking at a large number of factors of high relevance to cross-cultural witnesses as we seek to communicate Christian messages to peoples around the world.

Characteristics of Receiving Groups That Facilitate Change

1. A *Favorable Social Climate for Change.* In the West, change is regarded as a positive thing in most areas of life. This attitude favors the continuance and acceleration of change. It is, however, no longer characteristic only of the West. The attitude itself seems to have been borrowed widely throughout the Two-Thirds World, for better or worse. Often, however, such openness is selective. As with the Japanese, people are often quite open in technological areas but remain relatively closed in social and religious areas.

Characteristics of Receiving Groups That Facilitate Change

1. A Favorable Social Climate for Change
2. The Evaluation of the Fit of a Change in Relation to Perceived Needs
3. Suitable Innovators and Advocates
4. The Complexity and Size of the Cultural Inventory
5. Heterogeneity of the Society
6. Being Away From the Home Area

Characteristics of Individuals That Facilitate Change

1. A Feeling of Need
2. Openness to Change
3. Freedom to Pursue Change
4. Belief in the Possibility and Advisability of Change
5. Desire for Gain in Personal Standing
6. Literacy

Characteristics of Donor Groups That Facilitate Change

1. Prestige of the Donor Group
2. Aggressiveness and Enthusiasm
3. Ability to Influence Opinion Leaders
4. Duration and Intensity of Contact
5. Friendliness of Contact

Characteristics of the Potential Innovations Themselves

1. The Innovation Fills a Gap
2. Compatibility
3. Not Complex, Easily Observable
4. Forms Easier to Borrow Than Meanings
5. The Timing Right

Figure 23.1 Characteristics that facilitate change

Change itself becomes a factor in encouraging and facilitating change. People who are used to changing are more likely to change than those used to not changing. In addition, each new idea or thing introduced will usually require additional changes. The introduction of literacy, for instance, may demand a whole chain of adjustments in the culture, including such correlates as a school system, teachers, teacher-training centers and programs, textbooks, libraries, newspapers, printers, publishers, higher standards of living, higher employment requirements, higher wages, and so forth. (Luzbetak 1963:273; Barnett 1953:92).

Freedom of inquiry and action is another characteristic of a society that favors change. Though no society allows total freedom to change, some societies are more free than others in encouraging their people to question, inquire, and act. Even when quite open, however, they exert some control over the process. When people are in a period of social disorganization or confusion, they are usually more open to change than when things are going well for them. Many contemporary societies are therefore very open to at least certain changes.

People have to be interested both in the need and in the solution if they are to accept change. Interest in something new is often only stimulated when the practical value of the suggestion is demonstrated. In our ministries, as in that of Jesus, it is the *demonstration*, not simply the theoretical explanation, of the betterness of the Christian way that will lead people to be interested in it.

A high motivation to change is likely to produce change. One example of a motivation producer from western society is the tremendous drive we seem to have to overcome anything we consider disagreeable or uncomfortable. Our tolerance for accepting the status quo in the circumstances that surround us seems low. We consider work, especially menial tasks, to be disagreeable, so we seek to develop new ways of doing things that will save us from it. We consider sitting or lying on hard surfaces uncomfortable, so we create soft sitting and sleeping materials. We consider walking long distances to be drudgery and a waste of time, so we have developed means of transportation that get us places quickly and without much effort.

The effectiveness of social control is an important factor of a different kind. As noted above, when social control mechanisms are strongest, the possibility of change is lessened. When there is a lessening of the effectiveness of social controls, there is more openness to change. Even when social controls are tight in certain areas of the culture, they may be looser in other areas, allowing for more change in those areas.

Factionalism can also be a factor. When a group perceives that they can gain an advantage over another group by adopting something new, they are usually open to it. Christianity has sometimes been adopted with this motivation. Many young people see in Christianity the opportunity to escape from such things as the control of the traditional leaders, having to work on the farm, and having to live in a rural area, by going to school and gaining prestige based on western criteria.

Notice that the New Testament shows Paul using the factionalism of his opponents on at least three occasions: Acts 13:46, 18:6, 23:6, 7. In the first two, Paul rebuked the Jews and turned to the Gentiles. In the third, he fomented a dispute between the Pharisees and the Sadducees over the doctrine of resurrection. Sometimes factionalism can be used for constructive purposes. In Christian witness, we may find a given group open to the Gospel just because their enemies are resistant. I think we would do well to follow Paul's example, however, and to make use of factionalism only as a last resort.

2. *The Evaluation of the Fit of a Change in Relation to Perceived Needs.* People are much more likely to accept something new if it is perceived to meet a need and, in addition, fits in well with what is already there, especially at the deep level. Practices that require the breaking of a taboo, for example, are seldom accepted.

The sociocultural context into which an innovation is to fit is crucial to its acceptance. It is safe to say that all human structures are imperfect. Cultural structures always have gaps in them, especially in contemporary situations of rapid sociocultural change. These are areas in which the "promise" of trouble-free life is not carried out, because the structures are not capable of handling all the situations the people face. Youth, for example, tend to expect they will be provided with physical, social, and spiritual security. They usually expect health, marriage, family, meaningfulness in life, and the like. These expectations are often frustrated, raising felt needs at points where the system doesn't work as "promised." These gaps provide places into which new ideas and practices can be fit.

Suggested answers need, however, to fit in with what is already there in the system and the minds of the people. The change agent must be especially concerned with deep-level values. For example, the introduction of white chickens into a part of China where the people had a taboo against raising and eating white birds met with rejection. If red chickens had been introduced, the project might have been successful (Foster 1973:165). In many areas, however, attempts to introduce large European chickens of any kind are frustrated by the fact that the people cannot conceive of the need to feed and protect such animals. The chickens are allowed to run free and forced to find their own food, with consequent high mortality and small size.

A further matter of fit relates to the differences in receptivity of the various segments of the group within which the change is introduced. In general, those who feel most secure and those who feel most desperate are likely to be more receptive than others. Those who feel their position or wealth gives them security are often (not always) more likely than others to experiment with new ideas, items, and practices. At the other end of the spectrum are the desperate ones, those for whom the answers provided by their society don't seem to be working at all. These often (not always) have high motivation for change. Those just above the desperation level may, however, be the most conservative people in the society. They fear that any experimentation may result in their dropping to a worse position than they already occupy, so they tend to resist new ideas and practices. Others in the middle, who are not desperate enough to grab anything but not secure enough to play around with whatever comes along, will also tend to be more resistant to change. But for the genuinely desperate, the idea that God and His people will love a person may have great appeal. Likewise with anything that promises economic gain or social advancement.

Fit with regard to the present social position of the person or group considering a change can also be an important factor. Social position is accompanied by authority and power that one who possesses them is loath to risk. "Will the change support or detract from my present social position or my authority?" is an important question to those who feel neither totally secure nor desperate.

3. *Suitable Innovators and Advocates*. It seems that in every society there are some people who have the privilege to innovate. Often these are older men who have earned the right to make changes. Or it may be there are persons who possess personality characteristics that seem to propel them into the position of being among the first to identify and adopt new things. Though they may have this right, however, those with the privilege or the compulsion to innovate are not always opinion leaders. It is not a sure thing that others will follow them. If they are followed, though, substantial change may occur.

As mentioned above, one problem often faced by cross-cultural Christian witnesses is that our appeal, either by design or default, is often to people who are not allowed to be innovators. When they make a change, nobody follows them. In fact, since they make the change, many people turn against them. See the following chapter for more on advocates and innovators.

4. *The Complexity and Size of the Cultural Inventory*. Larger societies, because there are more people active in producing more cultural activities and products, end up with more cultural "material" and greater cultural complexity. This leads to greater opportunity for discovery and invention than is present in smaller societies with smaller inventories. The more people there are and the more cultural material they have to work with, the more stimulus to creativity.

5. *Heterogeneity of the Society*. Diversity within the community often seems to make it more open to change, whether through invention or borrowing. The internal exposure to different opinions often (not always) seems to make a people more aware of the existence of other ideas. Thus, when through contact with an outside group they are attracted to something practiced by that group, they often are more willing to accept it.

When there is heterogeneity within a society, there is inevitably *competition*. Competition is one of the greatest encouragers of the seeking of new ideas. The competitiveness may center around personal goals (prestige), economic goals, political goals, religious goals (for more power), and the like. Though competition is often thought of as primarily interpersonal and intergroup, there is a sense in which the development of technology designed to conquer the material environment is due to competition between humans and that environment.

6. *Being Away from the Home Area.* When people move from a rural area to an urban area or from one part of the world to another, whether voluntarily or under pressure, they are usually more open to change. Perhaps they feel they have left their traditions behind, so they might as well open up to other changes. Or perhaps they see a new habitat requiring new strategies or allowing new freedoms. In any event, we find people more open to Christianity when not living in their own home territory. For example, there is great resistance to Christianity among the Japanese who live in Japan. Those living in Brazil, however, are much more receptive.

Characteristics of Individuals That Facilitate Change

1. *A Feeling of Need.* People have needs, both as individuals and as groups. Messages presented as answers to felt needs are often (not always) quite acceptable, if presented by the right people in the right way. Feelings of deprivation may be present, especially where media and other sources promise so much. Dissatisfaction or disaffection with the way things are can provide a powerful impetus toward change and a desire to improve one's situation in life, whether economically, socially, or spiritually. Whatever the motivation, a felt need for change opens people up for new suggestions. It may propel at least the more venturesome to seek new answers, even if such behavior is contrary to their tradition. Though it has often been overemphasized, the necessity that is supposed to be the mother of invention can be a powerful motivator.

Among the more important felt needs evidenced by the peoples of the world are desires for greater power and control over material, relational, and spiritual aspects of their lives; for greater meaningfulness to life; and for prestige. Those who would suggest changes would do well to attach them to such felt needs. It is tragic that many who deeply feel the need for a new approach to spiritual matters reject the very answer they seek when it comes in the wrong way or from the wrong person.

2. *Openness to Change.* It is obvious that people will be more likely to change if they are open to changing. Usually such openness is conditioned on such questions as when, how, and by whom the change is suggested. Underlying these factors are such factors as interest, curiosity, an inclination to experiment, and whether or not there is friendship with one who can suggest change.

Openness often depends on interest. Many will admit they have a need for something—say greater spiritual power—but will not pursue it for lack of interest. They may be devoting so much of their time and energy to other things that this area of life simply doesn't interest them at this time. Curiosity, too, can be a powerful motivator in the direction of change. Often information concerning some aspect of life not completely understood can stimulate such curiosity, and curiosity in one area may well lead to openness in others. Those inclined to experiment or even to play with new ideas are more likely to innovate than those not so inclined.

The power of personal relationships is demonstrated in the fact that often people are opened up to change through the development of friendship with and respect for the change agent. Whether it is a material object or a spiritual relationship that is being advocated, people respond to friendship. The importance and effectiveness of friendship in incarnational Christian ministry cannot be overemphasized.

3. *Freedom to Pursue Change.* For change to take place, there has to be enough freedom for people to receive and implement new suggestions. In addition, if people are to invent and discover, they need a certain amount of leisure. When all of one's time and energy is expended in merely surviving, creativity tends to be squelched. If, however, there is the pressure of problems that need solving, along with freedom and leisure, much innovation can come about. Leisure without pressure does not necessarily have the same result; it may simply lead to laziness.

Collaboration and cooperation stimulate innovation. When people and groups work together, challenging, stimulating, perhaps even goading each other on, more happens. This has been a primary factor in scientific developments. But willingness to share what one knows with others is crucial. Many people in traditional societies possess good and original ideas that are not shared with those outside their immediate family or kin group. Often, for example, effective medical treatments are owned by particular individuals or families and not shared with those who would have the potential of combining such ideas with other good ideas to come up with something better. In addition, learning from outside sources is usually productive. People in a society who, often through reading, become aware of the ideas of others in areas relatable to their own often become very creative.

4. *Belief in the Possibility and Advisability of Change.* If people are to get involved in changing something, they must believe the change is possible for them. They must also see it as advisable. As we have seen in our discussion of worldview, something believed to be impossible, either in general or for the individual, is likely to be dismissed, even if seen. The human ability to interpret in terms of what is believed is incredible. Often people will reject a solution to their problem because they don't believe there could be any solution to it.

Seeing something as possible and also believing it to be advisable produces a bias toward that change. If, however, it seems to people that the disadvantages of the change outweigh the advantages, it is likely to be rejected. Such seems to be the problem with English spelling reform. Many believe reform to be possible but see the problems posed by the need for relearning, reprinting, and the like to be greater than the problem we now face of not being able to spell well.

5. *Desire for Gain in Personal Standing.* Among the very powerful desires that motivate people are those for meaningfulness, economic gain, prestige, and power, whether spiritual or social. Meaningfulness in life is a general desire that can be defined as a major or minor part of each of the quests discussed here. Sometimes people seek meaning through economic gain. Many people, observing the wealth of western Christians, have become Christians out of a desire to improve themselves economically.

The quest for meaning through attaining social prestige has been around for a long time. Though definitions differ as to what prestige is, the desire to attain it often leads people to adopt new strategies. Again, the prestige of the advocates of Christianity has often resulted in acceptance of the Gospel for the purpose of attaining greater prestige.

The desire for greater spiritual power is certainly one of the most potent motivators to change. Perhaps the majority of the peoples of the world feel themselves oppressed by evil spiritual powers or forces. Their question is, How can I cope with or even gain an advantage over these powers or forces? Contrary to the religious conservatism of most westerners, many peoples are quite ready to change religious ideas and practices if there is some demonstration of greater power.

Seeking meaning through gaining greater power in human relationships can also be a strong motivator. Though most societies attempt to strictly limit potential competitiveness between their various segments, the desire of one person or group to attain an advantage over another is powerful. This desire strongly motivates some to seek new ideas and items. Again, though, the marginal people of a society, those who have most to gain by obtaining an advantage and the least to lose if their attempt doesn't work, are usually the most ready to respond positively to new things on the basis of this motivation.

6. *Literacy.* People who read tend to be more open to change than those who don't. Though not all of the changes that come through literacy are to be recommended, reading is still a potent force for change. Part of this is due to the fact that literacy itself is an innovation and those who accept one innovation are more open to others. In addition, reading puts people in touch with a world outside their own, frequently introducing them to new ideas that stimulate them to change.

Characteristics of Donor Groups That Facilitate Change

1. *Prestige of the Donor Group.* The prestige of the group from which the change comes is of great importance. Though people regularly borrow sparingly from groups they don't respect (e.g., Americans have borrowed corn, tomatoes, moccasins, and several other things from the Indians), they tend to borrow heavily from those groups they consider more prestigious. There is usually a great difference between people's openness to new ideas from societies and subgroups they respect and their openness to ideas from other sources. If there is a determined closedness or a special animosity toward the source of a potential change, the chances that the ideas will be accepted are slim.

The response is emotional rather than rational, both to the potential borrowing and to the source from which it comes. People who are prejudiced against a given people are likely to be reluctant to accept change coming from that source. On the other hand, a positive bias toward the donor group can result in the acceptance of harmful things as well as helpful ones.

2. *Aggressiveness and Enthusiasm.* The activeness and aggressiveness of the introducing group is frequently a factor in stimulating change. Those so sold on their ideas that they would die for them (e.g., Communists, sometimes Christians) are often much more likely to get their ideas accepted. The size of the introducing group is often quite secondary to its enthusiasm.

The enthusiasm of the group within the society that accepts the new ideas is also important. If the adopted idea is to spread, the advocating group must also be aggressive.

3. *Ability to Influence Opinion Leaders.* The ability of either (or both) the introducing group and those within the society who initially adopt the change to influence opinion leaders is crucial. As pointed out above, a dispossessed group often accepts innovations more readily than any other group in a society. If such a group accepts the innovation, it usually has little ability to influence the opinion leaders of the society at large. A prestigious group, however, can become a valuable springboard from which the innovation spreads throughout the whole society.

4. *Duration and Intensity of Contact*. The nature and intensity of the contact between those advocating change and the potential receptors is critical. Less intense, unfriendly, and short contacts are less likely to produce the spread of new ideas than those that are more intense, friendly, and extend over a longer period of time. These factors work closely together. Thus even a very intense relationship, if it is of short duration, may not produce much change, and sometimes reasonably unfriendly contacts, if intense and long-lasting, will result in a great amount of change.

For example, the greatest amount of westernization has occurred in those countries dominated by the West in colonial situations, even though there was much unfriendliness. Christian witnesses living among the people they seek to reach are likely to have a greater influence than those who simply visit from time to time, especially if the contact is friendly.

5. *Friendliness of Contact*. As noted, the friendliness of the contact is also crucial. If the relationship between two groups is unfriendly, you find less interest, and less likelihood of change than if the contact is friendly. Neither unfriendliness, lack of intensity, or short duration, however, keep borrowing from happening. People will frequently borrow from a prestigious source even if they are at a distance and unfriendly toward that source.

Characteristics of the Potential Innovations Themselves

1. *The Innovation Fills a Gap*. If something introduced is believed to relate better than a previous custom to a basic need, such as for survival or safety, it is likely to be accepted. With the increase in crime in American urban settings, many (who can afford them) consider it necessary for safety's sake to install an alarm system to protect the home from being broken into. Ecological innovations related to basic survival are not, however, being well received by Americans, because they conflict with the deep-seated worldview assumption that such things as air, water, forests, and land are inexhaustible.

Something perceived as useful is more easily borrowed than something people have to be convinced of. From the point of view of the communicator, the key concept is "demonstration." If the usefulness of something can be demonstrated, it is very likely to be accepted. Tools often fit into this category, as do healing techniques that work and foreign words and phrases that seem to express a thought better than expressions already in the language (e.g., *déjà vu, vis-à-vis, status quo*). Jesus' primary method of communicating God was by demonstrating Him.

Something that is complementary to what is already in the culture is more likely to be accepted than something that contradicts something already there. The principle of felt need is based on this fact. If something felt to be missing in the cultural system is provided by what is introduced, the new thing is likely to be accepted—provided it does not contradict some other value in the culture. A more efficient cutting implement such as a steel knife or ax may be readily accepted as meeting an important need by many in a society such as the Yir Yoront (Sharp 1952). Those in that society whose status partly depended on their control of access to the implements being replaced, however, though recognizing the superiority of the steel implements, found another important value being contradicted by the way the new implements were introduced and accepted (see chapter 26). The form was all right for all, but the meaning wrong for the group in authority.

2. *Compatibility*. It is important that the new idea or item relate well to what is already there. What are the characteristics of these items? As Luzbetak points

out (1963:292ff), something that people see to be useful is more likely to be accepted than something they don't see to be useful. Something that is compatible with what is already there is more likely to be accepted than something that contradicts it. Something related to a basic need such as survival is more likely to be accepted than something that relates to some other area of life. Something related to their cultural focus, that fits in with their primary values, is more likely to be accepted than something that contradicts those values.

People are often quite ready to adopt something that clearly assists them in an area of cultural focus. If, as it appears, most of the peoples of the world are greatly concerned to gain more spiritual power to fend off the evil powers that plague them, they are likely to be open to Gospel presentations that emphasize and demonstrate this feature. The greater effectiveness of those churches with this focus testifies to the fact that this is true. Two important cautions need to be registered, however: 1) many people will gladly avail themselves of the greater power of God without making any commitment to be faithful to Him, and 2) Christian experience based on power without knowledge and wisdom (*see* 1 Cor 1:22, 24) is unbalanced and easily moves into syncretism.

Especially important is whether the new fits with the basic assumptions (worldview), attitudes, and goals of a people. Practices that fit in with or can be built upon unconsciously held attitudes or deeply ingrained habits stand a better chance of acceptance than those that go against such attitudes and habits. Things that don't fit are generally either rejected or adapted. This is why democratic government was all right for the Samoans but would ordinarily be rejected by peoples whose governance is strongly in terms of family loyalties. Attitudes and habits developed in early youth are especially difficult to break (areas such as nutrition, sanitation, toilet). However, when ways can be found to work with such early conditioning to promote betterment, these attitudes and habits become solid foundations for constructive change.

3. *Not Complex, Easily Observable.* Less complex cultural items are more easily borrowed than more complex ones. Many material items fit into this category, leading to the easy acceptance of such things as pots, pans, and other carrying and cooking implements; clothing, beads, and other implements usable for bodily decoration; machetes, knives, and other utensils usable for protection, clearing land, and the like; even new fetishes to increase spiritual power. The complicated technology required to produce such items is, however, seldom borrowed. Nor are complicated ideas and symbols easily borrowed.

Customs that allow flexibility and alternate uses in the way they are practiced, applied, and interpreted are more likely to be accepted than those that are more limited in their use and interpretation. Machetes, spoons, and all-purpose fertilizers, for example, are more widely usable than forks and single-purpose fertilizers and are more likely to be adopted.

Observability can be an important factor. Curative medicine that almost immediately cures a headache, a fever, or some other obvious malady is readily accepted as soon as people see what it can do. Preventive medicine, however, is much more difficult to put across, because it takes time to prove its effectiveness.

4. *Forms Easier to Borrow Than Meanings.* As we have already noted, meanings always change in the process of borrowing. This is because the receiving people reinterpret the borrowed item, idea, or practice from their own point of view. To get Christian meanings across is much more difficult than to get people to adopt the external trappings through which those who carry the message express their

faith. Meanings that appeal to deeply felt needs such as the quest for greater supernatural power, however, may more easily be accepted if they are presented in ways that are easily understood by the potential receptors.

5. *The Timing Right.* The timing of the introduction of a change can be crucial. Helpful things introduced at the wrong time are usually rejected. The question is, Does this change fit at this point in a sequence of new things coming into the society? Innovations frequently require what might be called supporting circumstances (Foster 1973:167). In American car manufacturing, for example, compact cars did not fit well into the American mind-set until the supporting circumstance of higher prices and smaller quantities of gasoline came about.

In many previously nonliterate societies, literacy is not readily accepted or maintained until the supporting circumstance of Christian allegiance, accompanied by a desire to read the Bible, comes about. Reading is hard work for most people and is often felt to bring little reward as a mechanism of communication between humans. But when the motivation is to be enabled to hear from God at any time, the felt need increases considerably.

One aspect of timing that is important to Christian witnesses is to recognize that the Holy Spirit seems to bring people to greater openness to the Gospel at times that seem unpredictable to us. We need to be observant, looking for such times and employing the scarce resources of the Church in such a way as to maximize their effectiveness during times of openness, times when the fit between felt needs and the Gospel message will be greatest.

STRATEGY FOR CROSS-CULTURAL WORKERS

In addition to the frequent comments along the way designed to assist cross-cultural Christian workers in the application of these insights, the following considerations may be helpful.

1. It is important to specifically *study the barriers to and facilitators of change in the sociocultural context in which we operate.* Observe. Ask questions. Attempt to discover what is changing and what is not, and why. Look for felt needs and areas of dissatisfaction. Look for opinion leaders and discuss with them what they think can be done. Are the people open to change or closed? If they're open, are they open in all areas or just in certain areas? Have they been swept off their feet by changes they feel powerless to control? If so, has this made them less open to change in spiritual areas for fear they will lose out there as they feel they have in other areas?

Another set of important questions relates to what part we can play in the situation. Often we can help most by helping people evaluate the changes they are making and sometimes reject certain things or slow down the process. Often the changes being made are not so bad, but the process is going too fast. The people are off balance, not because the changes are necessarily bad ones, but because they are happening too rapidly. Our primary task is often helping them to recognize what's going on.

To do this, we need to develop informed policies designed to enable us to help rather than hurt the people God has called us to minister to. Love must undergird all we do, but love without understanding them, their situation, and the possibilities and limitations of our position, is deeply flawed. We need to recognize and work with suitable innovators (opinion leaders), to win their confidence and support, deal with felt needs, and apply all the insight and principles we have been learning to the tasks God leads us into.

2. In line with such insight, we need to *assign ministry personnel strategically*, with the aim of applying a maximum amount of helpful influence in spite of the limitations of our resources. Strategy considerations relating to such things as how change takes place, who is receptive to what, what hindrances and helps exist in the present personnel and strategy, who are the opinion leaders and how can they be reached, and the like, all bathed in compassion and love, need to figure prominently in our thinking. A realistic appraisal in these terms of the actual situation needs to replace any tendency to simply assume that God will bless whatever we do if we are sincere enough. This needs to be followed by what McGavran calls "hard, bold plans" to correct and improve the ministry.

3. *Study and use of the social mechanisms by means of which information and influence flow* should also be a part of our strategy. Reading and courses in the area of communication can be very helpful for this purpose (e.g., Kraft 1991a). What kinds of mechanisms are there, and how can they be used? In some situations, the Gospel has been propagated effectively because Christians have used gossip as the main mechanism. They are "gossiping the Gospel."

One communication study sought to discover who in a housing project talked to whom, and when. It was found that people talked to others in their same building and to those in the next building, but seldom, if ever, to anyone across the street. The main vehicle for the flow of information was the talk that took place between the women as they hung their clothes out on lines hung between the buildings. Getting the Christian message into this channel could be very important to its spread. The planting of the message would, however, have to be done separately on either side of the street.

We'll end this discussion of the barriers to and facilitators of change at this point. We turn now to the place of advocates and innovators in the processes of change.

CHAPTER 24

ADVOCATES OF CHANGE

INTEGRATIONAL THOUGHT

In Acts 1:8 Jesus prophesied to the small band of those still faithful to Him that they would become witnesses as soon as they were empowered by the Holy Spirit. Their witnessing was to take place both in their home territory of Jerusalem and Judea and in foreign territory, Samaria and the rest of the world.

In terms of the anthropological concepts presented in this chapter, Jesus was predicting that His followers would become both in-culture and out-culture advocates/witnesses of the Gospel. That is, they would be those who, once they had themselves accepted an innovation, would now seek to bring others into accepting it, both within their own society and in other societies.

Before they could advocate that others accept, however, they had had to become *acceptors* themselves. This they had done, starting in Galilee where Jesus had attracted a small group of Galilean opinion leaders as His first followers. When they agreed to follow Jesus, they began to *implement or innovate* new ideas and behavior into their lives. They first became acceptors and implementors, then advocates of Christianity.

The process, in keeping with the flow of innovation as presented in this chapter, went: *From original* Advocate/Witness *to* Acceptors/Converts *who became* Implementors *of the new faith in their lives and, in turn, became* Advocates/Witnesses *presenting the message to others.*

Down through the ages, God has depended on insiders within the human context to first become acceptors and implementors, then to become advocates for His cause. Abraham, Moses, the Prophets, the disciples, and Paul all played both these roles. God, however, since He is always outside the stream of human life, could only be an outside Advocate until Jesus came. As a human being, Jesus could be both an implementor and an inside advocate for God's way.

Implementors, since they are insiders, can *demonstrate* the message they bring; advocates can only *recommend*. Both witness to what they have seen and heard (1 Jn 1:1–3), but the insider is the "person on the spot," the person who actually makes whatever changes are made and pays whatever social price must be paid for deviating from the expected sociocultural patterns. If the going gets tough, the advocate who came from outside can leave, but not the implementor.

God needs both types of people. How shall the insiders hear unless an advocate—a witness—is sent to let them know what God has done (Rom 10:14, 15)? The expected fruit of that witness is that insiders accept, implement, and themselves become witnesses/advocates for the cause.

God's plan is to empower a change strategy that involves witnesses going to other people, advocating acceptance of the Christian way. Those who accept will implement it in their own lives, demonstrate a new quality of life (2 Cor 5:17) and, in turn, become empowered advocates of the same innovation to others.

God has demonstrated this plan in Jesus and now entrusts it to all of His own, whom He has empowered. As Jesus said, just before He empowered His disciples, "As the Father sent me, so I send you" (Jn 20:21; cf. Jn 17:18). He sent them out as ambassadors (= empowered advocates) (2 Cor 5:20) to do His works (Jn 14:12), and He *trusted* them to do the job.

Do we trust those we send out?

God's method is good anthropology, plus empowerment. His work is not done well without either the empowerment or the anthropologically sound approach.

INTRODUCTION

We have dealt with some of the general issues in sociocultural change. In the process we have pointed several times to the important place occupied by individuals in bringing about culture change. Now we turn more specifically to the place of the individual, as defined by Homer Barnett (1953). We will then turn to the broader matter of advocating change and introduce some important insights from Foster (1973) concerning attitudes and approaches of organizations that advocate change.

ADVOCATES AND IMPLEMENTORS

Barnett uses three terms in his discussion of advocacy: advocate, acceptor, and innovator. I prefer the term implementor to the term innovator (with the same meaning), since it speaks more obviously to the function of the one who makes a change.

Advocates, as indicated in the devotional above, are those who seek to convince others to make a change. They are recommenders, witnesses who seek to convince others of the advantages to be gained by doing something in a new way. Advocates may be outsiders who come from one society to another and advocate or recommend a change. Whether in the area of agriculture, medicine, or Christianity, advocates seek to win people over to their point of view. Like the term witness, this term implies politeness and a rejection of the desire to dominate.

The older, ethnocentric concept that many of us have worked with in missions was quite different from this point of view. It was expressed by a missionary colleague of mine who objected to my contention that, even in our pioneering situation, our people should be encouraged to make their own choices and work out their own style of Christianity. He simply stated, "We have a right to tell these people what they are to do in Christianity. We've had 2,000 years of experience." My reply was, "On the contrary, we haven't had even one year of experience with Christianity *in this society.*"

Our job as he saw it is simply to deliver Christianity to Nigeria as a postman delivers a package. He felt that 2,000 years after the Christ events, scholars have pretty much worked out all of the intricacies of biblical interpretation. Those who organize have, furthermore, pretty well worked out things in that area, so now all we have to do is deliver the package. This missionary thought it incredible that these brand-new Christians should be encouraged to develop their own brand of Christianity.

My desire was not to simply get them to conform to our image. We should, rather, try to present our messages in such a way that they learn to respond directly to God, instead of primarily to us and our ways. We are privileged to plant seed and then watch and advise, but always with the understanding that we are outsiders. The culture is not ours but theirs. They are the ones to do what needs to be done and to develop what needs to be developed in their context. We know many good and helpful things, and we are to contribute these whenever they are acceptable to the receptors, but we really don't dare assume that the things we think we know from our own experience will apply in this cultural world. The worlds are not the same, as this missionary was assuming. We don't know what form the Church ought to take in this society so it will be attractive and win other people for whom this is the only valid way of life.

An advocate can be an insider or an outsider to the society. *Outside advocates* come to one society from another. They introduce new ideas that may or may not be picked up by insiders (acceptors/implementors). A missionary or cross-cultural witness can be an advocate even though he or she is an outsider.

This concept parallels some of the insights of communication theory and contextualization theory (*see* Kraft 1979a, 1991a). It recognizes that though outsiders can do important things, it is up to the insiders in the society to accept, reject, modify, or otherwise do whatever they want with what is recommended. Just as, in psychological counseling, any changes must be made by the receiver of the counseling, in sociocultural matters, changing is the right, privilege, and responsibility of those who "own" the culture.

What, then, can outsiders do? The outside advocate/witness is a planter of seed, a raiser of awareness, an introducer of ideas that were not previously present in the receiving society. This is an extremely important function, since it involves stimulus, without which people wither and die. Our job is stimulus—witness. We cannot and should not try to coerce people into responding to God in our way.

The patterns of church, conversion, and sanctification need to be patterns *appropriate* to the insiders of the society. Though the stimulus may come from the outside, the nature of the response is always up to the insider, even in situations that seem to be effectively dominated from the outside. There will always be contextualization, whether guided by those more mature in the faith or not. Theological understandings will automatically differ from society to society, since they are the products of the insiders' attempts to interpret from their point of view. As we have learned, no forms (e.g., theological understandings) can be simply carried from one society to another without reinterpretation.

Implementors (spelled -ors) are persons who make the change. They are always social insiders. Though outsiders can, consciously or unconsciously, exert influence, they never have the right to make changes in somebody else's way of life. It is only insiders who can implement whatever they accept of the advocate's recommendations. An innovation or new custom doesn't take place until insiders accept and implement it.

The first step, however, is acceptance. Insiders listen to and observe the advocate and either accept or reject what is recommended. If they accept, they become what Barnett calls acceptors. Having accepted, they implement the change(s) in their own lives, thus becoming what Barnett calls innovators and I prefer to call implementors. Implementors, having made the change in their own lives, often go on to recommend the change to others. At that point they become in-culture advocates. The process is pictured below.

Person I:	Person II:	Person III:
Out-culture advocate →	1. Acceptor 2. Implementor 3. In-culture advocate →	1. Acceptor 2. Implementor 3. In-culture advocate

Figure 24.1 The process of advocate to implementor

Note that there are two processes going on: 1) the process of communication from out-culture advocates to acceptors and 2) the process that goes on within the acceptors as they move from acceptors to implementors to in-culture advocates.

In-culture advocates fulfill the same function as the out-culture advocates, but within their own society. Such persons can typically speak their own language, work from their own worldview assumptions, and be assured that when they model the change within the culture it is more likely to be properly interpreted and imitated than if they were working in a different society. These are distinct advantages in most respects though, as Jesus pointed out, prophets (recommenders of new ideas) are likely to not be respected in their own society (Mt 13:57). This problem tends to be lessened, however, if the in-culture advocate is an opinion leader.

We cannot assume that whenever people advocate something in their own language within their own society they will be regarded by the receptors as a part of their group. Most societies are divided into a number of subgroups. Often an inside advocate, though a part of the larger society, is attempting to influence those of another subgroup. If the advocate comes from a less-prestigious group than the one he or she is attempting to reach, there may be even greater lack of acceptance than a total outsider would experience.

Some of the Old Testament prophets had this problem (e.g., Amos, who was sent from Judah to the Northern Kingdom). Likewise, Jesus and His disciples had a problem when they ventured outside of Galilee where, at least originally, they were well respected. But in Jerusalem it was another story. Galileans were not respected there, especially those who had not studied under prestigious teachers (Acts 4:13). They were not, therefore, regarded as insiders there, especially by the religious and political elite. They were treated as out-culture advocates (or worse) from a known and negatively valued social group. Thus their appeal was mainly to the socially disadvantaged.

The main principles behind what we are discussing are summarized here.

- Persons from outside a society cannot implement change within that society.
- Outsiders can only recommend. They may, however, recommend persuasively. We call such recommenders advocates.
- Those who respond positively to the recommendations of outsiders are called acceptors.
- Acceptors, as soon as they put the change into practice, become implementors or innovators (Barnett).
- Implementors who get excited about a change and recommend it to others (either via word or deed) become advocates within their societies.

FOCUS ON ADVOCACY

George Foster, in his discussion of the nature of the sponsoring organization in the process of guided change (1973:175–80), raises some extremely important considerations for Christian cross-cultural workers. He points out that almost all of the analyses of directed social change "have focused on the recipient group, on its social structure, its economy, its customs, and its values" (p. 175). Well and good, but often we have neglected the fact that any blockage to acceptance may be the fault of the sponsoring organization rather than the recipient group.

He suggests that we regard the sponsoring organization as a culture and analyze it in these terms. As cultures, organizations behave on the basis of their worldviews. These basic worldview perspectives, Foster contends, are the main source of problems in the advocacy process. They need to be studied.

We who go as church leaders or missionaries go not only as individuals but also as representatives of our organizations. Many of us feel an extreme tension between the demands of our denomination or mission organization and the demands of the people to whom we go. I've talked to many who felt forced to choose between the people and their desires and their organization and its desires. Some side with the people and often get sent home and have to look for other employment. Others seem to side with their organizations and get to stay there longer— but often at the cost of their effectiveness with the people.

This kind of tug-of-war springs from contrasts between the desires of the organization and the needs of the people. Our organization usually expects us to achieve within its own culture, we are expected to learn the rules and procedures of the organization, to recognize and submit to those with experience as our leaders, and to be loyal to the system and its decision makers, whether or not such loyalty enhances our work. Not infrequently, newcomers who have better training than the veterans are looked on as threats. Such newcomers may learn the language faster and better than the veterans or challenge time-honored rules or gain a larger following than their seniors. Such people often don't last long—not because they serve the people poorly, but because they are regarded as threats by the leadership of the organization culture.

Foster describes three organizational approaches (models) that have been used in cross-cultural work, each with its strengths and weaknesses. We find each of them employed by Christian organizations.

1. The first is what he calls *the primitive technical assistance model*. This is an ethnocentric model in which those who run an organization, like the missionary quoted above, simply assume that their ways are best, whether we are talking about the activities of church, missionary, or other private organizations, or of government and internationally sponsored programs.

The striking thing about all of the early technical assistance work was its ethnocentric premise: *techniques, programs, and solutions that have worked well in the most developed countries will work equally well in developing countries.* The first program planners and technicians assumed that technologies are absolutes, divorced from culture, equally suitable and efficacious in all sociocultural and economic settings (Foster 1973:176).

Though church work involves much that is not, strictly speaking, technological, the same assumptions were almost universally made by the advocates of Christianity. *Techniques that were familiar in the West, including church organiza-*

tion, schools, hospitals, agricultural strategies, and the like, were felt, often with slight modification, to be culture-free and even endorsed by God. Furthermore, "the superiority of Western ways [was thought to be] obvious to anyone who observes them" (Foster 1973:176). We thought, therefore, that the peoples of the Two-Thirds World would be anxious to adopt them.

Anthropologists and others came along, however, and observed that people who accepted the things we in the West offered were not necessarily better off. They noted that imported machines often broke down with no one in the society able to repair them. People who became Christians often lived more sinfully than the non-Christians around them. People who went to school were often unable to find employment. Orphans and people with disabilities who were saved from physical death were often consigned to sociological "living death." Helping people to grow products for world markets often simply put them at the mercy of world economic forces they could not influence, so many who never went hungry before found themselves starving every time the world market price went down on the commodity they learned to produce.

2. So a new set of assumptions came into vogue that Foster labels *the anthropological technical assistance model*. This approach tries to take into account the needs of the receptor peoples. It still assumes we have many techniques and ideas to give them that, if they would accept, would make them much better off. But it sees *the major barriers to the communication of these innovations in the receptor societies*.

Under this approach, we still assume we know what's best for people and set up our strategies so they will find it possible to accept our ideas. We seek all the anthropological insight we can get to enable us to accommodate our programs to their frame of reference and thus get them to accept our ideas. This model assumes that people are generally less than totally happy with their way of life. They will, therefore,

> modify their behavior *if* innovation is presented to them in such a fashion that they perceive advantages and *if* the social cost in disruption of traditional and valued ways is not too great. Consequently, says the model, the recipient peoples must be studied in their social, cultural, and psychological dimensions so that (1) innovations will in fact represent functional improvements, and (2) they can be tailored and modified to conform to local cultural expectations (Foster 1973:176–77).

There's much to learn from this model. We do need to try to understand the receptor people and ask the right kinds of questions before we make judgments. We do need to focus on the receptors, their felt needs, and the relationship between what we offer and their needs. But *the model still assumes that we outsiders are in charge*.

We should ask ourselves, *who put us in charge, especially in their homeland?* Who gave us the power to allow or forbid anything? Does our mandate to witness to the Gospel to the ends of the earth give us permission to take charge of their sociocultural destiny? Do we really know what is best for them? These are embarrassing questions not asked by this model. Perhaps answering them is even more difficult than stating them. But their existence indicates that we need a better model, a better set of assumptions to work from.

3. Foster begins to work toward this by developing what he calls *the donor-culture model*. This approach is not the new comprehensive model we should be aiming toward. It is, rather, the highlighting of a component neglected in the other

approaches, and it significantly advances our understandings by pointing us to the donor organization as a probable source of blockage and alerting us to the fact that we should treat that organization as a separate culture.

The organization that works out and administers the change program and hires and supervises the personnel involved needs to be seen as a distinct culture, mostly but not totally governed by the worldview of the society out of which its members came. Though much of the behavior of cross-cultural change agents is similar to that of their compatriots in the home country, some is not.

We in the West are so familiar with bureaucracies in our daily life that we take them for granted. In reality, we need to treat them as in need of study and "to carry out institutional research comparable to that carried out on target cultures" (Foster 1973:177).

If we look at overseas Americans (whether church workers or representatives of governmental or other agencies) as a culture, we find a group of people who neither grew up together nor would have chosen each other to associate with. They are not a "natural" grouping. Yet they are bound together socially as well as occupationally due to the fact that the community of those who think and speak alike is so small. They often unconsciously embody a "siege mentality," feeling they are a small island of sensible people surrounded by a sea of others who don't think or reason as they do and are liable to overwhelm them at any moment, if they don't watch out.

The outsiders probably have fairly concrete ideas of what they would like to see happen in the receiving society—though seldom are they as agreed on how it is to happen. But they are accountable to an organization or a constituency back home that look for and evaluate results in terms of their own cultural criteria, whether or not those are appropriate to the receiving society. All these factors set in motion complex and often disturbing dynamics within the community and between the community and those other groups to which it is related.

Just as we are learning to study the specific characteristics of receiving societies, so we need to study the characteristics of the sending organization, for we need to take careful account of both at all times.

THE ORGANIZATION AS A CULTURE

In working toward a better approach, we need to take Foster seriously. What follows is a synopsis of his presentation. Following this, we apply his insights specifically to mission and church organizations. A bureaucracy, Foster contends (1973:178), possesses at least six important characteristics that identify it as of the same nature as a culture:

1. An organization possesses "most of the same structural and dynamic features found in such 'natural' communities as a tribe, a peasant village, or a city. Like these, it is composed of members of both sexes, with a wide age spread, organized according to functional tasks, in a hierarchy of authority, responsibility, and obligation."

2. Second, a bureaucracy has a social structure that defines roles, relationships, and statuses of all members of the group. New members continually are introduced into the system (through recruitment rather than birth); they are socialized and enculturated to accept the fundamental premises, values, and goals of the organization; they perform their professional assignments as long as they remain with the group; and through retirement, resignation, or separation (rather

than death) they leave the organization, thereby making room for newer and younger members who are essential to organizational viability.

3. A bureaucracy has "structural integration."

4. A bureaucracy has "institutional and individual behavior based on explicit and implicit premises."

5. A bureaucracy has "personality and psychological variation among employees."

6. Sixth, as with all structurally integrated systems, no change comes about in isolation: new goals, new programs, new modes of operation imply rearrangement of role relations within the organization, bringing increased authority and status for some and lessened power and prestige for others. Bureaucrats, like all other human beings, jealously guard their traditional perquisites and positions, willingly surrendering vested interests only in exchange for something as good or better. Consequently, rearrangements in role relations, which favor some and threaten others, always meet with resistance. In bureaucracies this leads to organizational inflexibility, which makes it difficult to meet changing conditions and new needs. Structural integration may be just as much a barrier to change in bureaucracies as in peasant villages.

Foster next (1973:179–80) points to a number of worldview assumptions that underlie the behavior of those who serve under western organizations seeking to promote social change cross-culturally. There are at least three levels of these: 1) general cultural assumptions (from the culture of the participants), 2) bureaucratic assumptions, and 3) professional assumptions.

Among the *general cultural premises*, Americans tend to assume such things as that rural is better than urban, that people should seek "progress," that change is improvement, and that there is unlimited potential in the universe for people to attain goods, position, etc., including room for nearly everyone who works hard to get to the top.

Bureaucratically, we tend to assume such things as that an administrative organization must continually grow if it is to remain healthy; that the importance of a position is determined by the number of people the person supervises; that if it looks like there will be a surplus in your budget, you should spend it (even needlessly), lest the home office decides you don't need as much next year and cuts your budget; and that it's preferable to fill an opening with a mediocre or totally unsuitable employee than to risk the loss of that position.

There are *professional assumptions* that influence the way we go about our tasks. For example, we believe that biological life is sacred, so medical (and other) personnel feel that no effort is too great to save a life. Agriculturalists (and others) assume that the best crops are those that yield the most while requiring the least possible effort. Educators and missionaries believe that literacy is crucial to nearly anything we hope to see happen.

Whether these premises and many others are correct or incorrect is beside the point. Their existence will strongly influence how technical specialists (including Christian workers) view their assignments, shape their work plans, and measure their success and that of their peers (Foster 1973:179–80).

CHURCH AND MISSION ORGANIZATIONS AS CULTURES

It is very interesting to analyze Christian organizations working cross-culturally, to discover just how culture bound they often are. For example,

1. Like cultures, *the church/mission has certain membership requirements.* Among these are loyalty to the organization or denomination and its leaders and agreement to strive for position and status in terms of the values of the group. In a natural society, people learn society's expectations as children and rarely challenge them.

In a church or mission society, however, the members have not grown up in the group and often have different expectations concerning how they should relate to the organization. The leaders of the organization expect the members (especially new ones) to "pay their dues" by pledging allegiance and submitting to the leadership until such time as they achieve positions on committees and are thus able to advocate change in a manner considered appropriate within the church/mission society. Challenging traditions before such position has been achieved is usually perceived by the leaders as inappropriate. If, therefore, the threat to the authority system is considered to be too great to take care of internally, the person(s) who mount the threat are eliminated from the organization.

2. Second, often because of greater access to finances and greater cultural prestige, the donor society is very powerful. In addition, western organizations tend to be paternalistic toward those we help. This issues in *unequal power relationships* between outside helping organizations and the local church organization. Sometimes the church leaders aren't even consulted.

Even organizations who seek to cooperate with the churches often fall into difficulty by working on western assumptions concerning how to go about such cooperation. Often the solution is seen in arranging that there be 50 percent representation from the donor organization and 50 percent from the national church. The way that worked in our area was that even though the numbers were equal, the missionaries did almost all the important talking, and the nationals did the majority of the listening and almost none of the decision making. The latter knew who controlled the money and had great respect for them as the founders and real owners and operators of the foreign structures they had started. So, in spite of good intentions on the part of the missionaries, such a scheme often did not work, because of the power differential and the foreignness of the system. This foreignness often carries with it the fact that only great amounts of money (more than can be raised by the nationals) can keep it going.

Another set of problems often arises over rules that were instituted by the missionaries when they were in charge that spring from their cultural background and manifest a questionable use of power. We have often set up churches with rules that nobody in the home country practices. On our field, we had certain rules pertaining to what to do with (national) Christians if they fell into sin. These were not rules practiced in the home churches. They were, I believe, rules instituted in good faith as an attempt to help the emerging church to be more pure than the home churches (over which many of us have felt guilty). Notice, however, the focus on rules rather than on relationship. This is the western way.

The rule in our area (as across Africa) was that if people fell into sin and were caught, they were "put on discipline." This was a kind of excommunication procedure designed to lead them to repentance. If they understood the procedure (many did not) and desired to repent, they would come before the church committee, confess, and repent. The practice was for the church committee to decide how large the offense was and set a period of time when they would be "on discipline." This would usually be up to three months for a minor offense and considerably longer for a more major one. During this time, the people would not be allowed to take communion. The idea seemed to be that Africans were considered unable to accept full pardon when they repent of their sins, so the church needed to give them some additional penalty.

The issues of power and paternalism are large ones, often rooted in lack of trust of the people we work with and, unconsciously, a lack of trust in God. In addressing himself to the frequent lack of trust in the people we work with, Smalley concludes his article, "Cultural Implications of an Indigenous Church," with the following telling comment, "I fear that our paternalism is not only a paternalism toward the people to whom we go but a paternalism toward God. We regard the indigenous church as a complicated toy too difficult for God to handle" (Smalley 1958a:65).

Smalley, writing about the concept of indigenous church, points out that it is entirely possible to have a church, self-governed by people who have been thoroughly indoctrinated by outsiders, that is not by any stretch of the imagination indigenous. Such leaders, whether trained in Bible schools and seminaries in their home countries or overseas, have been carefully taught to operate the church according to western patterns. Such a church is not an indigenous church. Nor is one that is self-supported after western patterns, rather than after indigenous patterns, or one self-governed according to *Robert's Rules of Order.*

3. A quite different issue related to this topic is the question of *whether donor and receiving group members should ever meet separately.* Should missionaries ever hold meetings just for missionaries? To answer such a question, we need to distinguish between the need for doing business and the very human need for fellowship with "our own kind."

With regard to fellowship, all people are cultural beings who feel most at home when interacting in their own language and understanding all the jokes. People need such gatherings for psychological reasons, for purposes of rest and relaxation. Without them, the chances are increased of psychological breakdown due to culture stress. Fellowship get-togethers of subgroupings of cross-cultural workers from different societies working within the same organization should especially be encouraged, since the smaller numbers of such people from each society raises the risk of breakdown due to culture stress. Seeing the separate groups as separate sociocultural entities, each with its own needs and each with responsibility for the psychological care of its members, is an important start toward dealing with the problems raised in cross-cultural ministry.

Meetings for the conducting of business, however, are another matter. The group in power needs to be especially careful not to conduct business that affects the other group(s) without their participation.

4. The *worldview assumptions underlying our church/mission organizations* need to be probed.

a. In terms of Foster's three types of assumptions detailed above, just what are the *general cultural* assumptions we carry into cross-cultural church work? Do we assume what he calls the *pastoral ideal*? Sometimes this leads us to assume that churches and other mission structures run according to indigenous principles are automatically better than those run by western or semi-western techniques. We need to be realistic rather than idealistic in this regard. Indigenous principles are not necessarily better or worse.

What about our assumptions concerning *progress*? Are we far enough along by now to recognize that not all change results in improvement? Nor, of course, is change always bad. Change is change; sometimes it is helpful, sometimes it is disruptive. Sometimes it seems to be neither.

What about resources—time, money, personnel, opportunity, room at the top? *Are resources unlimited or limited* in this situation? The middle-class western assumption that enough effort expended will result in the expected result because there are always enough resources needs to be questioned.

b. With regard to *bureaucratic* assumptions, then, *must a church continually grow to remain healthy*? Is it best in every society for churches to grow in an unlimited way? I think we need to examine such an assumption. I wonder whether a church ought to grow to a much greater size than is appropriate for other groups in that society. I even wonder if the "megachurches" in our society wouldn't be more effective in ministry if they were divided up into four or five smaller churches. Whatever the case, we need to carefully examine our assumptions and be able to defend them on both social and spiritual grounds.

What about the positions created in the institutions we deal with? Should the *importance of the position* be judged by the number of people supervised or influenced? Are those who work with large groups automatically more blessed and used by God than those who ordinarily relate to smaller groups? If so, what about Jesus' decision to work primarily with twelve?

c. *Professionally*, then, within church institutions, such assumptions as Foster mentions also come up. For example, is God's attitude toward the *value of biological life* the same as ours? Could the western value put on biological life for its own sake take us beyond where God wants us in our emphasis on medicine or, for that matter, on faith healing? It seems that in God's eyes, a short life (e.g., Jesus') well lived is preferable to long life for its own sake.

The principle of *efficiency of effort*, whether in agriculture (e.g., attempts to produce the highest yields with the least effort) or in organizational structuring (e.g., consolidate as many functions as possible under as few leaders as possible), also needs to be questioned. I wonder if God doesn't prefer a maximum number of people working with less skill in ministry to a minimum number of the more skillful operating such ministries with greater efficiency. Likewise with schools, medical work, agriculture, and other activities often engaged in by churches: a larger number of people performing meaningful activity is probably much more socially and psychologically healthy (and desired by God) than a lesser number doing the work while others have little that is meaningful to do.

Our assumptions concerning *literacy* also need to be constantly examined. See chapters 15 and 16 for discussions of this factor.

In cross-cultural church work, as in secular activities, it is important to hear Foster when he says,

> It is essential to realize that barriers to change are at least as prevalent within the innovating organization as within the target group. We need consciously to face up to the fact that bureaucracy places absolute limits on what we can do, that it burdens us with heavy costs, human and monetary, and that it must be studied just as thoroughly as a target group if results are to be optimized (1973:180).

FOCUS ON THE ADVOCATE

At the center of this whole discussion is the advocate. Still following Foster, let's look at the preparation of those who work cross-culturally and then at some of the common pitfalls into which cross-cultural workers frequently fall.

1. *Training*. We usually assume, in keeping with American values, that the right kind of training will take care of any problem. Like the Greeks, we assume that our basic problem is ignorance, therefore our need is for more knowledge. Yet we find that over and over again, people we thought had learned the right knowledge don't do the right job. Why? Perhaps they just did not have the right combination of personal characteristics to function effectively in another society. There are certain kinds of personal characteristics that suit anyone to work effectively in another society—flexibility, adaptability, tolerance for ambiguity. Can these be developed through training? Sometimes.

The fact is, however, that the training available for those who would be cross-cultural workers is seldom adequate. Whether university, professional school, seminary, or Bible school, at best the training is designed to equip the student to live and work in his own society. Much of what is learned isn't even useful for that. In the home country, there is no need to teach the average student to identify major problems and then work out solutions to them. The major problems are quite obvious; the need is to ameliorate, not identify them. The professional knows the kinds of questions his society will ask of him and the job demands it will make upon him. These are the tests he must pass successfully (Foster 1973:181).

With respect to ministerial training, the potential leader has ordinarily been taught to handle theological understanding in an academic way, and only from the point of view of western society. Due to the inadequacies of such training, this usually means the trainees are very poorly equipped to deal with real people and issues, even in their own society.

Medical training is usually more practical, at least with regard to physical problems faced in the home society, as long as the practitioner has access to an antiseptic hospital with electricity and the latest drugs. Unfortunately, researchers are discovering that most supposedly medical problems have deeper psychological (and spiritual?) roots that medical training does not equip for. When those with such training go overseas, they tend to be very poorly prepared to deal with either the physical limitations or the cultural and psychological differences.

The situation is similar for those trained to be teachers. Trainees come out able to work the mechanics of the western system but often with little or no understanding of what education really is. They, like the others, have been trained merely to maintain a system already in existence.

Concerning this problem, Foster says,

> most professional training is designed in terms of programs rather than underlying problems, and the technician comes to judge himself by what he has to offer to the programs in which he participates. Professional training produces program-oriented specialists. Only rarely does it produce problem-oriented specialists. . . . Man is so much a product of his culture—he is so ethnocentric—that he assumes that the advanced programs and techniques that work in his society are equally fitted to less developed countries (1973:181).

The combination of training for the programs in operation in the home country and the assumption that these programs are superior and needed in the receiving society leads to "false and dangerous definitions," both of what a good program is and of what a good specialist in that area should look like (p. 182). For example, contrary to the trained expert's usual assumption, it is highly unlikely that a genuinely effective church, medical, or educational program would look very much like the western-style program the expert will most likely attempt to duplicate. For

In developing areas the answers to the major problems have not been worked out. The task of the technical specialist is not to reproduce a standard American product, but to know how to adapt the scientific knowledge and operating techniques of his country to the economic, social, educational, and political reality of the country in which he works. The successful technical expert is the one who has learned to be problem oriented and not program oriented (Foster 1973:182).

2. *Common Pitfalls of Cross-cultural Workers.* The first pitfall is one already alluded to.

a. The tendency for westerners (and those trained in western ways) is to be *program oriented rather than problem and people oriented.* Perhaps it is the mechanistic view we seem to have of the universe and all that it contains (including people), or our tendency to think in terms of masses of people, that leads westerners to focus largely on how to launch and maintain programs, even at the expense of the good of the people involved in them. Even when we note problems in a present program, our tendency is to launch another program! We see this constantly in western industries, political life, and even in churches.

The need for approaches that seek to discover and solve problems and put primary focus on the needs of persons has been the constant focus of this book. Dr. Ronald Seaton had a radical conversion to such an approach shortly before he came to Fuller. He had been a typical medical doctor in a mission hospital, spending most of his time repairing bodies. One day, however, he thought he recognized a man on the operating table. As he operated on him for tuberculosis, he remembered that this was the man he had passed by every day on his way to the hospital, sitting beside the road rolling and selling cigarettes.

The question that then formed in Dr. Seaton's mind was, How many of the others that I operate on for tuberculosis have contracted the disease because they have bought and used the cigarettes made—and licked—by this man? This experience convinced Seaton that he should give his life to the problem of preventing disease. He began to realize that he, like nearly all other western doctors, had been taught only to *do* medicine, not to use their knowledge to problem solve and *communicate* what they discover. Seaton became committed to communicating medical insight for prevention. For years he has specialized in medical education by extension. He has written his insights in a book entitled *Here's How: Health Education by Extension* (Seaton and Seaton 1976).

Another doctor recognized the futility of being "chained to an operating table" before he went out and laid down certain conditions to his sending agency (a Lutheran mission). He said something like, "I will go to Nigeria as a doctor only if you will let me restrict my involvement in the hospital to half days. If I must serve in the hospital full days, I will not go." The board secretary asked, "What will you do with the other half of your days?" He said, "I'm going to be out in the villages with the people. I will still do medical work, but I will do it in the villages, not in the hospital." He refused to be simply a "body mechanic," fixing up people's bodies without real opportunity to minister to them as whole persons. Doctors with a passion to minister to people (as opposed to simply fixing their bodies) frequently become disappointed and demoralized if they are not able to arrange their lives in some such way as these two doctors have.

The frustration may be just as great for teachers, translators, agriculturalists, and even pastors who allow themselves to get caught up in running, maintaining, and promoting programs. God is people oriented; so should we be. No program is worth damaging people to maintain it, even if the program is done in God's name (e.g., the programs of the Pharisees and other Jewish leaders).

b. A second pitfall cross-cultural workers often fall into is the *desire to produce perfection*, often in a mechanistic manner. The illustration given above concerning the matter of church discipline is an unfortunate illustration of this pitfall. The missionaries, perhaps laboring under a guilt complex concerning the general lack of discipline in their home churches, set up rules designed to make the Nigerian churches more "pure" and perfect than those at home. Their way of going about this seems quite mechanistic, based on rules, not relationships. The result was that these rules were usually considered to be totally the concern of the outsiders, the missionaries. The local Christians seldom felt the rules were really of the essence of the new life they had found in Christ. Thus few were brought to discipline who were not caught by the missionary or someone who "had it in" for the person. The "perfection" was simply an external thing, never really penetrating to the level of the people's motivations (or their understandings of Scripture).

To the extent that the disciplinary procedures did work, they frequently resulted in the prosecution of people who transgressed missionary rules. Those sins (pride, greed, selfishness, arrogance, cultural bias) that the missionaries were soft on usually went unnoticed. "Sins" such as polygamy and others that, from the missionary point of view, were of a sexual nature, were frequently prosecuted. The church committee therefore became a kind of marriage court charged with dealing with whatever matters offended the missionary conscience. Though many of the issues were genuinely sinful, such a system does little to train consciences in scriptural ways.

c. A third pitfall lies in the area of *professional pride* in the rightness of what one is doing and the important contribution it is making to the cause. This pitfall is easily divisible into two rather distinct problem areas.

The first can be easily highlighted by noting the rhetorical question in many church workers' minds: How could I be wrong when I am so sincere? Armed with the conviction that God wants us to commit ourselves to cross-cultural work, plus the dedication to spiritual life and growth that keeps us in close touch with God, we easily assume that whatever way we go about carrying out God's program is the right way. It often comes as a great shock when we realize that God did not prevent us from making some very serious mistakes.

One manifestation of this pitfall occurs regularly when someone from the "younger" church asks advice from those who represent the "sending" church. The latter are frequently asked some such question as, "Is this cultural practice a good one?" It's very easy for us to answer with a simple yes or no. Giving such a response is seldom the right thing to do, since we are outsiders. It increases dependence on us, rather than helping the insiders to depend on God for guidance. A better approach would be to do as Jesus might have done—ask another question or tell a story to bring the matter into greater clarity.

Loewen (1975) suggests that when people ask us something like this, we should always present two or three alternatives. Instead of saying yes or no, we should probably say, "In a certain society they faced this problem and solved it this way. In another part of the world, they faced this problem and solved it this way. In still another place, they faced it and solved it this way." The national is likely to say, "Which do you prefer?" Again we can fall into the trap of becoming directors and stating our preference. We probably should say, "Which do you prefer? Which alternative would result in other people saying, This is our God, this is our Christ, and we want to follow Him?" The chances are that the person(s) receiving such advice will creatively develop an alternative even better suited to their context than any of those we might have suggested. This is the proper kind of activity for an outsider, but it may grate with our ideas of our own expertise.

A second manifestation of this professional pride in the contribution we can make surfaces in the fact that specialists usually feel that their own area should have the major focus in the overall ministry. The medical facilities, the schools, the agricultural programs, the church work all compete for a larger share of the budget, each with the conviction that the rest of the operations should provide support for them. Often such competition leads to animosity between members of the same team. This should not happen in the Lord's work.

Nor should the pride that easily develops from having studied missiology be allowed to intrude into our work. I'm afraid I myself allowed this pride to become a factor in our missionary experience. It is easy to seek ego gratification by claiming (or seeming to claim) knowledge superior to that of our colleagues. We may, indeed, have greater knowledge. If so, we must lean over backwards to affirm the value and the contributions of our colleagues in every way, so the effort can be cooperative rather than competitive, so we and they can love and encourage rather than criticize and work against.

d. Still another pitfall is the often subtle *need for ego gratification*. We are conditioned by our society to seek recognition from peers, clients, and supervisors. We have learned to feel good when those above us affirm us and to feel bad when they don't. We have learned to value highly structured situations (*see* chapter 17) and to not feel good when we find ourselves spending most of our time being interrupted by people in need. We have learned to strive to achieve titles (even if these are only committee memberships) and to be disappointed if we aren't elected or appointed to ever more prestigious positions. We usually aren't able to turn this kind of conditioning off when we move into another society. We then feel (often quite unconsciously) pushed to measure our achievements in terms of what the system calls for, even at the expense of the good of the people we are supposedly ministering to.

In church and mission organizations, we have often seen people who once campaigned for changes elected to positions of responsibility and changing from advocates of change to supporters of the status quo. Once the pressure for ego gratification begins to be satisfied, such persons begin to behave in such a way that the continuance of their position will be assured. They are often governed by the fear that if they make a misstep, they might lose their position, so they stop advocating any causes that are unpopular with the leadership, at whose behest they have "moved up in the world."

All of these pitfalls, then, are made worse by the constant presence of culture stress (often called "culture shock"). This stress "is precipitated by the anxiety that results from losing all our familiar signs and symbols of social intercourse" (Oberg 1954:1). See Oberg 1954, Luzbetak 1963:84–103 and Foster 1973:191–96 for good discussions of the phenomenon.

A major contributor both to culture stress and to the tendency to dominate stems from the fact that those who go to other societies to advocate change are often those who have stood forcefully for certain things in their own societies. They have been "movers and shakers" at home, both accepting, advocating and implementing change. Under the pressure that comes from culture stress, therefore, they tend to revert to familiar patterns and often take a more active role in the receiving society than their position as outside advocate/witness warrants.

Working in another sociocultural matrix can almost always be counted on to produce stress, anxiety and off-balancedness to one degree or another. Some people are able to minimize the effects of such stress because of personal characteristics and/or through effective adjustment to the host society. But it is usually safe to assume that whenever people working cross-culturally manifest problems, those problems are complicated to some degree by the influence of culture stress.

WHAT CAN BE DONE TO IMPROVE ADVOCACY SITUATIONS?

It is the purpose of this whole text to help us answer this question. We do this by seeking 1) to help develop a point of view, a perspective that will enable us to see beneath the surface of cross-cultural situations. We also seek 2) to provide some factual knowledge, including analyses of specific cases that will enable us to gain new insight into how things are in other societies. Such knowledge provides us with illustrative solutions and helps keep us from being crippled through surprise at the unexpected. It expands our horizons, allowing us to prepare emotionally, to some extent, for the unexpected.

In addition, we 3) gain some research techniques that will enable us to know how to seek and solve basic problems. By first understanding how little we are likely to know from our own background but then recognizing that we can use insights such as those provided here to go to an area and search out the answers, we are virtually assured of greater success than otherwise. Not that we can (or should) all become primarily engaged in research, but all of us need to use whatever insight we have gained to search more effectively for better ways to minister.

Such insight is neither a panacea nor a substitute for the Holy Spirit. It should, however, enable us to work with and under God in a different and more effective way, simply by providing us with tools to understand and avoid some of the more detrimental sociocultural conditioning we carry with us. Hopefully we then can be more free than we might have been to minister in a more loving way, a way more concerned for people.

We will say more on the subject of research and study in chapter 28.

CHAPTER 25

ETHICS OF CHANGE

INTEGRATIONAL THOUGHT

"'We are allowed to do anything,' so they say. 'We are allowed to do anything'—but not everything is helpful. No one should be looking to his own interests, but to the interests of others" (1 Cor 10:23–24).

So Paul approaches the topic of whether or not Christians ought to eat food that has been offered to idols. The basic question is, Just how far can we carry the freedom we have in Jesus Christ? Are we accountable only to God, so that we may do anything we want to do, as long as it is moral? Or are we also accountable to other people, such as "those who are weak in faith" (1 Cor 8:9)?

That is the basic question of this whole chapter. Is the term "ethical" to be defined only in the abstract, or does the definition get quite specific—relating not only to the motives of the one who does something but also to the perception of the observer? Paul, of course, comes down in favor of the latter interpretation, concluding his treatment with these words, "Well, whatever you do, whether you eat or drink, do it all for God's glory. Live in such a way as to cause no trouble either to Jews or Gentiles or to the church of God. Just do as I do; I try to please everyone in all that I do, not thinking of my own good, but of the good of all, so that they might be saved. Imitate me, then, just as I imitate Christ" (1 Cor 10:31–11:1).

We are to glorify God in everything, just as Jesus did. He and Paul both taught, though, that glorifying God means, among other things, always being concerned for the good of the receptors. It is the receptors of the world that "God so loved that He gave" (Jn 3:16). It is the receptors of the world that Jesus said He came to serve and to give His life for (Mt 20:28). Glorifying God means putting others first, ministering to them in ways that are meaningful to them and that communicate effectively the caring, loving, accepting, forgiving nature of God to the weak, the damaged, and the needy.

There is another group that neither Jesus nor Paul accommodated to. These are the hypocrites—those who take advantage of their position as religious leaders to dominate and oppress those over whom they have power. The Pharisees and other rulers of the Jews fell into this category in Jesus' ministry. The Judaizers, Jewish Christians who insisted that Gentiles convert to Jewish culture in order to follow Jesus, were the ones who caused problems for Paul. Such people who use their power to oppress in the name of God are not to be accommodated to; they are to be opposed.

But the "weaker ones," those who are not willfully blind and opposing God, are the ones before whom we are to "Live in such a way as to cause no trouble . . . so that they might be saved" (1 Cor 10:32–33). These may be Christians as well as non-Christians, since the term "saved" has a much broader reference than simply spiritual salvation. It can apply to anyone who needs to be rescued from any problem—spiritual, physical, psychological, or material.

We must, however, get our message across to these receptors in an ethical way, and our approach must be perceived as ethical by those who are reached through it, or it simply is not ethical. Our end, our aim, is to help, to rescue, to save (in a spiritual sense). How, though, are they to relate to that aim? *They will know our aims only through observing and experiencing the means we use!* With people, unlike with machines, how we get there is even more important than what we're aiming at. The Golden Rule is still in effect: we are to treat those we work with as we would like them to treat us if we were looking at and experiencing things from their perspective.

Our means must be perceived as ethical if our aims are to be considered ethical. The nature of the process is crucial, since most people never see our ends, only our means. It is even more important that our means be perceived as ethical than that our ends be so perceived! It is more important that our means be understood as ethical than that our ends be understood at all.

I believe this is what Jesus was getting at when He said, "All who take the sword will die by the sword" (Mt 26:52). I think He was saying, We are captured by whatever means we employ. Therefore, only proper means, those perceived by the receptors to be in line with what God wants to get across, are allowable. Any means that communicates a perception of God and His intentions different from those shown in Jesus Christ are unethical.

Let's practice "receptor-oriented" ethics, as Jesus did.

INTRODUCTION

The question as to whether what we do is ethical or not is a difficult and scary one. Often people say that it's simply meddling and unspiritual to raise questions about God's work and those who do it. If we are prayerful enough, spiritual enough, and committed enough, surely God is going to see to it that things work out well. I believe those who say this are sincere, and I wish they were correct. I wish it was just a matter of prayer and commitment. Our experience, however, seems to tell us that even dedicated, sincere, committed, Spirit-filled people doing the Lord's work can come up with very different results, some of which are pretty questionable. Why God allows this, I don't know, but He seems to frequently allow even His most dedicated servants to make some big mistakes. On the other hand, when God's servants better understand what they are doing, they seem to make fewer big mistakes.

Many internationals are looking at the work of sincere, dedicated, prayerful missionaries and nationals and asking how things could have come out so badly. The missionaries seem to have done everything they could to make sure they were getting the right directions from God, but something went wrong. Many of us as missionaries look at our own work and say, "I prayed about this, I thought about it, I read the Scriptures, I did everything I could before I made a given decision or a certain approach. I just don't understand why it seems to have worked out poorly."

That's the kind of circumstance that I want to raise to our attention as we ask questions about ethics. *Ethics* is a technical term with a long history of study and discussion in theological circles. Without going into all that discussion, we will simply say that something is ethical if it is right in God's sight, and in line with

God's intent. If it is wrong in God's sight or out of line with God's intent, we'll call it unethical.

The understanding of the human processes involved in getting a message across ethically is, of course, no substitute for the spiritual dimensions. We do not, however, see them as mutually exclusive. We cannot say we need either deep spirituality *or* an understanding of the dynamics of ethical communication. We must advocate prayer, sincerity, and commitment, *plus* an understanding of the processes of effective communication. Our intent is that both the power of God, which is available to those who are truly spiritual, and the effective use of human communicational insights be operative in a way that enables the whole message of God to come out properly at the other end.

It's very interesting to attend meetings of professional anthropologists and find that within the past several years even they have been raising questions concerning the ethicality of what they are doing. For example, what are the relationships of anthropologists to nationals? Are anthropologists justified in exploiting nationals to get information from them that the anthropologist will publish in a book and get a degree and reputation for? Can an anthropologist do this without feeling an obligation to at least share the results with those who helped? If a researcher publishes material on a given people, what is done with that material? Is it simply for the purpose of study, or are the insights to be used for the benefit of the people studied?

We as Christian cross-cultural witnesses dare not ignore some of these questions. I'm very happy for a chapter on ethics in Foster (1973) that raises questions concerning the validity, the ethicality, of what we are doing. It's so easy for us to simply assume that whatever we do—especially since we do it in God's name—must be okay. Experience is a hard master in this respect, because we're frequently pulled up short and begin to recognize that many of the things we do as individuals—even though we do them in God's name—probably are not done in a way that God approves. We want to raise this kind of issue not so much so we can come to definitive answers but so we will ask these questions concerning the ministries we are engaged in. Perhaps thereby we will learn more about how to do Christian things in a Christian way. I think it is very important that we not be found doing Christian things in ways that can be called unethical or sub-Christian.

A SECULAR PERSPECTIVE

Foster notes that the belief that we should help those less fortunate than we is deeply embedded in the consciences of Americans and other westerners. But we seldom ask questions such as "Why are we doing this?" or "What right have we to assume that our efforts to help others will be really helpful?" We simply go out and help them as best we can. "Yet very genuine moral and ethical problems arise in every instance in which attempts are made to change the way of living of others" (Foster 1973:246).

We have, for example, been able to extend the life expectancy of peoples around the world through improvement of medical services. We have assumed that the aim of bettering health and lengthening biological life is sufficient to entitle us to export western techniques to other societies. "Yet failure until very recently to integrate birth control with death control has produced a population problem far more threatening to man's future than unchecked disease . . . [raising the question] 'Will four billion undernourished people be more desirable than two billion undernourished people?'" (Foster 1973:247).

Both within and outside Christian circles, the western reverence for biological life has ordinarily been unquestioned as a basis for intercultural intervention.

Other basic assumptions stemming from western worldviews have also been prevalent (again, both within and outside Christian circles). Among them is the assumption that western societies have learned how to make "progress" happen and that such insight is suitable for export. Large numbers of those who work cross-culturally share, perhaps with the majority of Americans, the belief that in their heart of hearts all peoples really want to live and be like us. The experience or remembrance of millions of immigrants or children and grandchildren of immigrants who came to America seeking greater opportunity to achieve "the good life" may well have contributed to this belief.

> Poverty, coupled with poor health, primitive agriculture producing insufficient food, and limited education—these, it was argued, were the conditions that inhibited peoples in most of the rest of the world from making the progress they desired toward the American way of life. . . . [It was believed] that developing nations had neither the technical skills nor the financial means to lick poverty, disease, malnutrition, and ignorance (Foster 1973:248–49).

The answer seemed simple, whether from the point of view of Christians or (especially after World War II) of western governments: send people with technological skills to provide education, medicine, agricultural insight, and the like. The justification was on humanitarian grounds for both groups—as defined in terms of western worldview assumptions. We assumed, furthermore, that all peoples would see the value of our efforts and praise and be loyal to us (and, for Christians, to our God) because of them.

But, Foster points out, "professional aid looks very different to the recipient than to the donor" (1973:252). He asks, "What does an offer of technical aid imply to potential recipients? It implies many things. . . . Above all it says, in essence, 'if you people will learn to do more things the way we do them, you will be better off.' This is not a very flattering approach" (Foster 1973:253).

The same might be said of spiritual aid. Whether in technical or spiritual areas, traditional peoples may be wrong. This is often the case. But, and this is often overlooked, they may also be very right in many areas. Furthermore, we may be right or dead wrong in recommending a change, especially when their custom fits their life situation (whether technical or spiritual) better than our custom does.

As Foster notes with regard to technological matters, "It is wrong to assume that a method, because it is modern, scientific, and Western, is better than a traditional one" (1973:254). If, for example, it is not appropriate to the receiving context, can it be better? We may assert the same thing with regard to spiritual matters and contend, with Foster, that "until we are sure they are wrong on a particular point, it is unwise and *morally wrong* to try to 'improve' them" (1973:254 emphasis mine). What about appropriateness in spiritual matters as well? What's wrong or inappropriate, and according to whose definition?

One perspective comes from an old woman in a central African village. "You Europeans think you have everything to teach us. You tell us we eat the wrong food, treat our babies the wrong way, give our sick people the wrong medicine; you are always telling us we are wrong. Yet, if we had always done the wrong things, we should all be dead. And you see we are not" (Read 1955:7, quoted by Foster 1973:254).

Questions of right and wrong are ethical questions. The answers to such questions are deeply influenced by the cultural matrices in which people live.

THREE SETS OF ETHICAL STANDARDS

We assume, of course, 1) the existence and concern of God for His creatures, 2) the distinction between "big R" and "small r" reality, and 3) the validity or adequacy of any cultural structuring that enables those who use it to survive. Since, however, no cultural life way is without its problems, and since God is always in favor of human betterment (according to His "big R" standards), we also believe in change. We stand, therefore, in favor both of cultural continuity and of certain kinds of intervention by certain outsiders with certain aims and motivations for the purpose of improving a people's way of life. What is done, how it is done, and who it is done by are, however, crucial questions, even when we are in general agreement with the aims and purposes of those who intervene.

A position such as this, which espouses a caring God and takes an informed view of human culture, yields two levels of ethical standards.

1. *Transcultural ethical standards*, or "big E" ETHICS. These are the moral ideals built into the universe that, if lived up to, enable the peoples of the world to experience whatever God intends for them (tentatively postulated to be a more meaningful and fulfilling life). *Transcultural morals*, are the guidelines for correct behavior established by God. Discerning what these ethical and moral ideals are, however, is quite another matter from merely postulating them.

2. *Culture-specific ethical standards*. These are the "small e" ethical ideals (principles, standards, values) of a society that the members of that society are taught and presumably expected to live up to. *Culture-specific morals* are the guidelines for correct behavior generally accepted, approved, and sanctioned by a social group.

There are many groups attempting to assist peoples of societies other than their own. For purposes of this discussion, I will assume that it is the intention of most of these groups to conduct their interventions in an ethical manner. They will, however, inevitably define ethical according to their own cultural values. Will what they define as ethical be perceived as ethical by the receptors, given the fact that those receptors will define ethicality from their own cultural perspective?

The critical realist epistemology contends that there is a REAL (ETHICAL) above and beyond the cultural (perceptual) real (ethical). The problem is, of course, that if such a REAL exists, humans can only see it through their cultural (perceptual) lenses. We are, therefore, guessing at what that REAL might be. The fact of cultural limitations and distortions makes the question of how to discover that REAL a very large one.

As an anthropologist, I would claim that examination and comparison of cross-cultural data yields insight into cultural universals (or near universals) in the area of ethics that may be regarded as candidates for a transculturally valid ethic. As a Christian, I would contend that God has revealed at least some of His ideals in the Christian Scriptures. The problem of interpretation is, however, just as large with respect to such a revelation as with the cultural data—we still see and understand in terms of our own cultural grid.

Nevertheless, pending further discussion of this problem (*see below*), I will here postulate three sets of ideals (ethics) to consider in any cross-cultural encounter: 1) that of the communicators (source) and their culture, 2) that of the receptors and their culture, and 3) the transcultural. A triangle diagram can be used to illustrate the relationships between these.

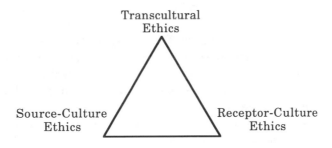

Figure 25.1 Three kinds of ethics

WORLDVIEW ASSUMPTIONS THE BASIS FOR ETHICAL JUDGMENTS

It is assumed that the underlying reason for differing understandings of ethicality lies in differences in the deep-level worldviews of the peoples of the world. As we have come to understand throughout these chapters, these assumptions are basic to cultural behavior, having been carefully taught, though seldom proven. They provide the perspective through which a society views reality. Many of these assumptions concern what exists, how it got here, and what the nature of it is. These are what Hoebel calls *existential postulates* (1972:26). But, he continues, "There are also deep-lying assumptions about whether things or acts are good and to be sought after, or bad and to be rejected. These are called *normative postulates or values*" (1972:26).

Such assumptions are the ones in terms of which we make evaluations. These are learned in the process of enculturation, along with the rest of our worldview assumptions, and become the basis in terms of which we make ethical judgments.

Worldview assumptions give rise to what I have called interpretational reflexes (Kraft 1979a:131–34). That is, we ordinarily interpret what is or happens automatically, habitually, and without thinking. Accompanying each interpretation is a judgment, an evaluation of the rightness or wrongness, goodness or badness of whatever is or happens.

Ethical judgments are thus a form of interpretation. They are based on worldview assumptions and made automatically as a part of our interpretational reflexes.

RECEPTORS, MEANINGS AND MOTIVES

As noted above, we are alerted by communication specialists to the fact that though messages pass between humans, meanings do not. "Meanings are in people," not in the messages themselves (Berlo 1960:175). Meanings are *attached* to message symbols by the users of those symbols; they are not inherent in the symbols themselves.

One implication of this fact is that the meanings understood by the receptors of a given message are likely to be at least slightly different from the meanings

intended by the communicator of the message, especially if the receptors are interpreting from the perspective of a worldview different from that of the communicators. Yet it is the receptors, as the "end point" of the communicational process, who
play the crucial part in determining whatever the outcome (the meaning) of the
interaction will be.

Meaning attachment is a form of interpretation, and interpretation is always
accompanied by evaluation of the goodness or badness, the rightness or wrongness
(the ethicality) of an interaction.

Behind the meanings in the minds of those who try to help others are *motives*.
The intent of such people is almost always worthy, but, worthy or unworthy, the
motives of the originators of helping activities are also evaluated and judged by
the receptors. Our intent, our motives, like all other meanings, will only be understood through the means we employ.

Understanding, evaluation, and the resulting meaning attachment—whether
concerning motives, ends, or means—is determined from the perspective of the
receptors within their frame of reference. When communicator and receptor come
from different cultural frames of reference, it is virtually certain that the meanings of speech and behavior will be interpreted and evaluated differently by each
participant. *What may seem quite good or right (ethical) from the communicator's
point of view may be interpreted as unethical from the receptor's perspective.* When
such an evaluation takes place, all the benefits of good motivation, sincerity, careful planning, and all the rest go down the drain.

WHAT RECEPTORS HAVE A RIGHT TO EXPECT

A key to this approach is to attempt to look at things from the point of view of
the receptors. This I call a "receptor-orientation" and define as an orientation on
the part of sources of messages (behavioral as well as verbal) characterized by a
primary concern that those sources do whatever possible to enable the receivers of
the messages to understand their intentions as clearly as possible within the
receivers' frame(s) of reference (*see* Kraft 1991a).

The doctrine of sociocultural adequacy has helped us appreciate the essential
validity of other people's ways of life, including their basic assumptions (worldview). *Sociocultural adequacy is an anthropological statement of the Golden Rule.*
It advocates granting the same kind of respect and appreciation to another people's way of life as we would like them to grant to us, were we in their place.

Some have, however, carried the doctrine to the point where no outside evaluation is allowed. These seem to assume that all cultural structures are neutral (the
term "functional" is often used) and all those who use them well motivated.

Though it might be contended that most structures are indeed neutral, there is
a great deal of evidence that even apparently neutral structures are regularly misused, especially by those in power. It is therefore difficult for most anthropologists
to take such "absolute relativism" seriously, at least with respect to the way cultural life is actually lived out. Most anthropologists would recognize the possibility
that in certain (perhaps many) ways, any given way of life can be improved.

Believing this and knowing just what needs to be changed and how and how
fast the change is best brought about are quite different things, however. We have
learned enough about the depths of our own enthnocentrism to be suspicious of
our own judgments in this regard.

Nevertheless, we can, with Elvin Hatch, assert that human well-being is a value that transcends every culture (1983:134), relating to a level of human being-ness that is deeper than culture. Though defining just what this means as a trans-cultural value poses numerous problems, Hatch advances two principles in this direction, and I will add a third. Hatch suggests

> 1. It is good to treat people well. . . . We can judge that human sacrifice, torture, and political repression are wrong, whether they occur in our society or some other. Simi-larly, it is wrong for a person, whatever society he or she may belong to, to be indifferent toward the suffering of others. . . . [Furthermore,] we may judge it to be wrong when some members of a society deliberately and forcefully interfere in the affairs of other people.
>
> 2. People ought to enjoy a reasonable level of material existence: we may judge that poverty, malnutrition, material discomfort, human suffering, and the like are bad (1983:135).

I agree with these, but would add a third principle:

> 3. People ought to be free from spiritual oppression. Spiritual oppression is real because evil spiritual beings are real and actively oppress people in physical, psycholog-ical, material, and relational ways.

Thus we are aiming beyond the validity of specific cultural matrices, toward what we might assume those cultural structures ought to be providing for their peoples: *genuine quality of life in interpersonal and personal areas, in material areas, and in spiritual areas.*

PROBLEMS TO CONTEND WITH

1. *The Problem of Interpretation by Insiders.* Interpretation is based on world-view assumptions. Worldviews, however, are culture-specific and therefore yield differing interpretations. Like all meaning assignment, interpretation is usually more felt than reasoned (Kraft 1991a). Meaning assignment is, furthermore, done reflexively, on the basis of habit.

The activities of a foreigner will therefore be regularly interpreted by insiders on the basis of what those activities would signify if they were performed by insid-ers. On this basis, both the meaning of the activity and the motivation of the actor are judged.

Outsiders must be prepared to have their motivations and intentions evalu-ated purely on the basis of the insider's perception of their overt behavior. Their means, seen from the perspective of the insider's worldview, therefore become the basis on which their ends are understood.

2. *The Problem of Cultural Goals/Ideals.* People are conditioned to have certain expectations. Many of these seem to have at least some rootage in basic human needs. Others seem to be constructed. All of them, no matter how basic, seem to be culturally elaborated.

In physiological, psychological, and spiritual spheres, humans are conditioned to expect their society to provide for them satisfaction of what are defined cultur-ally as their needs. The nature and extent of such satisfaction is culturally defined, as are the ways in which the satisfaction is to be delivered. Freedom from want or lack (as defined by the society) in such areas is a very important ideal of any people.

In the physiological sphere, people are conditioned to expect satisfaction of their biological needs for food, housing, safety, health, and the like. In the psychological sphere, there seem to be needs for meaning, communication, "love and belongingness" relationships with other humans (Maslow 1970), esteem, security, structure, and the like. In the spiritual sphere, the quest of most peoples could perhaps be defined as a search for a positive and beneficial relationship with (often power over) benign supernatural beings and powers, and protection from evil supernatural beings and powers.

3. *The Problem of Interference of Donor Society Goals/Ideals.* As with those who are receiving, so with those giving, the tendency will be for all activities to be interpreted and evaluated on the basis of what those activities would signify if they were happening in the sociocultural context of those doing the interpreting. Donor society participants will, from the best of motives, regularly attempt to provide such things as they believe to be necessary or advisable from the standpoint of their own values.

Westerners, for example, regularly assume that peoples of other societies want the same things we want: material prosperity, individualism, comfortable housing, schooling, clothing, rapid and effortless transportation, physical health, long life, "equality" (by our definition) of women, even our religion. Furthermore, we assume others are willing to pay the same price in terms of other values that we pay. Thus, we assume others will (should) value individual rights and freedoms over group concerns; material prosperity and creature comforts over family and group solidarity; easy mobility over isolation; mass, information-oriented education in schools over individualized, person-oriented training at home; impersonal, naturalistic medical procedures over personal, supernaturalistic procedures; women who are "free" (by western definitions) like males over women who are secure; even our religion over their "superstition," and the like.

Most of the things we seek to provide fall into the category we define as good in terms of *our* values and aims. Whether the receptors also consider them good, and how many other good things they are willing to sacrifice, are serious questions that need to be faced realistically by those who would help people of other cultures.

TOWARD A SOLUTION

1. *Prior Considerations.* A belief in the validity of every culture predisposes us to take seriously the goals and aspirations of each people. If so, the place to start in determining which of the potential interventions might be appropriate would be with a serious attempt to ascertain just what those social ideals might be. But here we are faced with several problems. Among them are the following.

a. *The conservativeness of people with regard to their cultural structures.* As is always the case, the people of this generation have been taught the cultural structures that the members of the previous generation employed to handle the life problems they faced. To the extent that today's problems differ from those, the available perspectives (worldview) and structures may be unsatisfactory and disappointing. There would seem to be plenty of evidence that many cultural structures that served people's needs fairly well in previous generations are not working in this generation. Yet those are the structures that have been taught to today's peoples with the promise that they would be adequate.

Especially in rapidly changing situations, cultural structures never seem to be up-to-date. Thus there is no assurance that an outside observer will be able to accurately discern the most important felt needs of a people through a study of the culture as it is at the present time. Nor, often, are the people caught in such a situation able to effectively articulate either their real needs or adequate answers to them.

b. Even without the complications of rapid social change, there may often be *latent dissatisfactions* among the people with certain ways in which their lives are structured by their societies. It is no longer possible to believe (with the older functionalists) that the relationship between a people and their cultural structures is always an agreeable one. Often people who appear to be quite satisfied with a given approach to life readily give that up when they become aware of the possibility of an alternative approach. Discovering such latent dissatisfactions is, however, a considerable problem for the researcher. Determining what can be done about it and how to carry out the change is an even greater challenge.

c. Even if outsiders carefully research the desires of a people, what do they do when *different segments of a society come up with conflicting ideals*? Given the pervasiveness of self-interest on the part of those consulted—a characteristic that can be expected to skew all information obtained through interviews—how does one arrive at a proper basis for intervention, even after one has carefully researched the situation? It is one thing to be able to look back at mostly bad examples of outside intervention and analyze what went wrong; it is quite another to plan beforehand and carry out an intervention that will not result in similar mistakes.

d. Another set of problems relates to the fact that a large number (perhaps most) of past interventions, no matter how sincere the agents, seem to have caused enough *social disruption* that one might question whether the benefits are sufficient to offset it. This raises the question of just how good anyone is at cultural manipulation in a positive direction. To put it more pointedly, would anthropologists have done a significantly better job than the missionaries of introducing change among the Yir Yoront? Perhaps. But perhaps the concomitants of a fairly small change in technology might not have been much (if any) clearer to anthropologists before the event.

2. *Principles for Intervention*. To the extent that the goals of a people can be ascertained, let me suggest a few candidates for transculturally ethical principles of intervention in another society. I will present these along with a discussion of some of the difficulties in their application.

a. *Golden Rule*. I propose that, whether on a religious or nonreligious basis, the Golden Rule be regarded as a transculturally valid ethical principle of intervention. We are to treat others as we ourselves would like to be treated, were we in their position. This means we are to seek to understand, respect, and relate to a people and their way of life in the same way that we would like them to understand, respect, and relate to us and our way of life, if the tables were turned. It also means that we need to find out from them how they would like to be treated, what *their* (not our) definition of understanding, respect, love, is and so on and to treat them that way.

The problem of discovering, defining, and (through participant observation) coming to actually feel what this means is an enormous one. Outsiders can seldom, if ever, learn to really feel what it's like to be in the skin of another people. Another problem is defining what to do in relation to the perceived "good" of the individual versus that of the society as a whole. Westerners, whose primary orientation would predictably be individualistic, would likely have to resist those tendencies without overreacting in the opposite direction.

In a sense, the following principles are but amplifications of the Golden Rule principle. Perhaps the Golden Rule, defined in receptor-oriented terms, is all we need. Nevertheless, we will attempt to articulate four more principles.

b. *Person/Group Orientation.* This principle recommends a primary concern for persons (as organized in groups, of course) and speaks at least as much to the methods as to the goals of intervention. I suggest that any approach to intervention be grounded in what I will call "person factors" that lie at a level deeper than culture. At this deepest level, "people are more alike than cultures" (Goldschmidt 1966:134). Person factors would be such things as *the quest for well-being in relational, material, and spiritual areas* mentioned above. Such a quest and the expectations surrounding it are, to be sure, all culturally defined, raising again the need for working in terms of a receptor-oriented definition of what intervention should bring about. But the universality of the quest for these things (and perhaps others) would seem to indicate that it is rooted in basic human beingness, rather than simply in culture.

This emphasis I see as in contrast with a primarily structural emphasis, such as preserving a culture simply because cultures are believed to be good in and of themselves. The question to ask is not, What can be done to preserve the culture? but, What will provide the greatest good for the person/group? The problem of making judgments concerning what that greatest good would be is an enormous one, and those who make such judgments will need considerable anthropological insight from both emic (insider) and informed etic (outsider) perspectives. I believe, however, that it is unethical in the transcultural sense for change agents to put any goals ahead of those that will seek the greatest benefit for persons/groups.

This principle relates, I believe, to an important insight coming from communication theory, where a distinction can be made between information or "word messages" and "person messages" (Kraft 1991a). News broadcasts, solutions to mathematics problems, science and history teaching, plus most of the rest of what is taught in school, can be passed from person to person rather impersonally through words designed to convey information. However, messages designed to lead people to make changes in their way of life need to be demonstrated in life and passed on in life-related ways through the impingement of the behavior of one person on the behavior of another person. It is not enough for such messages to be reduced simply to information passed from mouth to ear. In this way, the person-oriented message is both conveyed by and is part and parcel of the method used to convey it.

One of the major problems with this principle is the tendency for change agents to spend far too little time with the people they seek to assist. Participant observation is the proper approach to study and planned change, but true participant observation requires more investment of time (and especially life) than even change agents (other than some missionaries) are usually willing or able to give.

c. *Ethnic Cohesion.* Any intervention in another society should give careful attention to helping the people to maintain what Tippett (1987) calls their ethnic cohesion. This is an elusive factor, perhaps made up of some combination of pride in one's cultural heritage and a determination to survive, no matter what. Its presence keeps a people struggling to maintain their sociocultural existence, even in the presence of great pressure to change. The breaking of such cohesion results in the loss of the will of a people to continue living as a viable social entity.

Even though, according to the last principle, we are to focus on person/group over cultural structures as such, it is clear that persons/groups require effective sociocultural structuring to function properly. They also need a measure of pride in their way of life. My theory is that one of the functions of culture is to serve as a kind of protective coating/clothing and psychological support system for human psyches. If damage is done to that protective coating/clothing, people become psychologically naked, lose self-respect, and become vulnerable to harm from outside influences. If this process goes far enough, people begin to break down psychologically and, as individuals and groups, lose the will to live. Such breakdown signals the loss of ethnic cohesion and, unless followed by revitalization (à la Wallace 1956), moves into personal and social disintegration. I believe it is unethical in the transcultural sense for an advocate of change to seek change that will result in a loss of ethnic cohesion.

One problem is, of course, the difficulty of knowing when and how what one advocates damages such cohesion. Another is the fact that for many of the peoples of the world, much damage has already been done. Widespread personal demoralization is an indication that ethnic cohesion is in danger. Sympathetic understanding and genuine personal caring may be the best we can do to help stem the tide, at least in some of the people.

d. *Involve Receptors*. A receptor orientation requires that any decisions relating to the future of the receiving people 1) be made with their permission and 2) involve their participation, both in the decisions themselves and their implementation. People are to be treated as people, not as things. They are to be respected and consulted, not simply dominated. Potential innovations are to be politely advocated (Barnett 1953), not rudely mandated, even when the power of the change agents is considerable. I believe it is unethical in the transcultural sense to attempt to change people without involving them in the decision-making process.

Problems arise with respect to this principle not only when the power differential is great but also when there is a significant differential in expertise. For example, public health specialists may not be able to convince people to boil their water or dig latrines, even when it is clear that failure to take these steps results in a lack of the quality of life the people ardently desire. A person orientation involving patience, personal friendships, and a willingness to work at winning over persons and groups through carefully planned demonstration can turn the trick, if continued long enough. Working within their categories will usually require close attention to establishing and maintaining the right kinds of relationships with the right persons. It will probably also require a willingness to take seriously and work in terms of their understandings of the influence of spirit beings and powers on their lives.

e. *Use Power to Serve and Show Love*. In many situations those who intervene in another society are perceived—both by the receptors and by themselves—as more powerful than those they seek to change. Whether it is the power of political relationships, of wealth, of cultural prestige, or of that which comes from God, they are easily tempted to use such power to achieve what they define as worthy ends, whether or not this is done in a loving way. I believe whenever power is used without love, it is unethical in the transcultural sense, even if the ends seem justified.

Problems arise with this principle when westerners with an egalitarian per-spective fail to perceive themselves as more powerful than those they work among. It is very easy for them to miss or misunderstand the significance of, for example, rapid agreement from the receptor group to what was intended as merely a sug-gestion. Westerners must learn to perceive such situations as characterized by unequal power relationships and to lean over backwards to attempt to compen-sate. I point again to Loewen's suggestion that in such situations, the change agent never offer only one alternative but, at the very least, two alternatives, thereby making it necessary for the receivers to choose between alternatives or come up with their own solution (Loewen 1975).

A CASE STUDY: THE ETHICALITY OF MISSIONARY ACTIVITIES

We have discussed the problem of ethicality in Christian cross-cultural wit-ness. We may now look at certain western-style approaches to the communication of Christian messages, to see what we can learn about how things actually turn out. To do this, we will attempt to evaluate *how such activities rate when measured by the ethical principles listed above*. That is, do they carry forward God's work 1) in accordance with the Golden Rule of cultural respect, 2) with a primary concern for person factors, 3) with serious attention paid to maintaining ethnic cohesion, 4) involving the receptors in decisions that affect them, 5) being careful to use all power in helpful, loving ways so that 6) God's intent is perceived by the receptors and 7) our activities contribute to what receptors have a right to expect in the area of well-being?

We will ask these questions concerning some of the typical activities initiated by missionaries. This is done, not as a definitive statement of rightness or wrong-ness of the activities, but to suggest how we may attempt to evaluate the activities we are involved in.

It has been pointed out that the tendency of westerners is to be program and institution oriented rather than person oriented. The vast majority of the peoples of the world are, however, person oriented. So is God. To the extent that our pro-grams and institutions are impersonal, they are out of sync with both receptors and God. But those who work within such programs and institutions can fre-quently be person oriented, so even these activities can be brought more into line with God's intent.

This points up an interesting facet of our discussion. Though we may decry the western propensity for programs and institutions, we cannot evaluate the ethical-ity of the structures themselves, only the ways in which they are used. This points to another important observation: it is unlikely that all of those who participate in these activities will use them in the same way. It is likely, therefore, that any pro-gram or institution will turn out to be partly ethical and partly unethical, depend-ing on who it is used by and how.

1. First, let's look at an institution such as the hospital and clinic program in which our mission was engaged. Our mission leaders had set up this program to help people with one of their most deeply felt needs, the need for better health. They and we saw this as an available way of using western expertise to demon-strate the love of God to the people among whom we worked.

This is, I believe, a worthy goal. Unfortunately, such a goal easily gets sub-merged under the western value that assumes that the primary purpose of a hospital is simply to bring better health and longer life. The doctors were trained to support these western secular goals in America and assumed that enhancing health and prolonging life would automatically be understood by the people as communicating love. They made little or no adjustment in the way they used the hospitals and clinics, beyond the many physical adjustments they had to make because of lack of equipment, irregular electricity, and the like.

In terms of criteria such as obeying the cultural Golden Rule, being personal, consulting the receptors in deciding on how things should be done, and using power in loving ways, these programs often fell short. Though there have been many exceptions in each of these areas, times when people were treated as persons and their way of life respected, it was usually clear that these were foreign institutions operating almost exclusively on western assumptions. In keeping with western assumptions, the relationship between healers and patients tended to be impersonal and the healing process dependent on a mechanical relationship between medicine and body. How could the patients discover the personalness and lovingness of God? How could they receive what they had a right to expect from life except in the narrow range of concern for physical problems? Sociocultural and spiritual problems, if addressed at all, were treated in western ways that did not connect with their ways.

In addition, these programs exacted a high social cost, threatening the societies' ethnic cohesion (though that cohesion was also being threatened in even greater ways by other factors coming from the outside). These programs and institutions were set up in direct competition with parallel institutions already present in the society. Though the native medical practitioners were often no match for western medical techniques, they were holistically focused, rather than narrowly dealing only with the physical. In contrast with western medicine, they took seriously the social and spiritual dimensions of people and the healing process. Though western medics often talked about the place of God in healing and sometimes prayed with the patients, there was little in these programs to connect with the spirituality of the receptors or extricate them from their bondage to evil spirits, and the western approach to healing did nothing to help them with the social and relational problems of life that likely underlay most of their physical problems.

In one area of western expertise—the ability to repair the body as if it were a machine—our mission programs were usually seen by thinking people to be superior. Some, especially those in the process of becoming westernized, did perceive the love of God coming through. The partially westernized church leaders I worked with told me that for purely physical problems, they would much rather have the western dispensaries and hospitals than the native medical practitioners. They contended, however, that not all diseases were better handled by western medicine than by traditional medicine. It was clear to them that social and spiritual problems were largely ignored in the western programs and the society had to pay a high social and spiritual cost for their presence.

A disturbing part of the spiritual cost derives from the fact that though these programs teach people to put their faith in medicine and western medical technique rather than in spirit power, they also unconsciously teach against faith in God for healing. Even when secular medicine is done by Christian doctors, there is usually a deeply secularizing aspect to it. Traditional doctors know how to work with both spiritual and medical technique. Western doctors, though they may pray before they treat a person, seldom show the deep spiritual sensitivity and expertise to satisfy what these people have rightly come to expect from healers. Instead, people learn to be treated secularly for physical problems, many of which are not healed anyway, since they are emotionally or spiritually based. For problems related to social and spiritual relationships, major sources of emotional, physical, and spiritual problems, they are left to turn to usually less effective western churches (*see below*) or native practitioners.

Some missions and churches have been able to lessen parts of this problem by consistently highlighting the place of God and faith in Him in any healing process. They teach that God alone heals, even when He uses medicine and western technique to bring it about. And, because they pray authoritatively with patients for healing before any medicine or other technique is used, many are healed directly. Thus people are confirmed in what they already know (but we seem not to)—that medical healing is closely related to the spiritual dimension of humans. In accord with what we say we intend to communicate, they are directed to a new spiritual Source and taught that it is He (not some other spirit) who works through these medical techniques. The social relationship part, however, is still neglected.

In our medical program, as in many others, the western assumption that the main issue is physical healing rather than communicating God's messages into the receptors' world has done extreme damage to the work of God through medical programs. The down-deep secular nature of this and other underlying assumptions led to virtual enslavement to the press of sick people and the press of other technical duties, to the neglect of meaningful spiritual (and social) realities. Typically, the doctors and nurses give the medicine without praying, and often the people get well. This leads them to put their faith in the medicine, because apparently the medicine did it without spiritual assistance.

The situation on our field was not all as deficient as the above analysis suggests, however. Up until about the mid-fifties, we had a leprosarium that included a colony made up of those receiving treatment, plus their families. Though the hundreds (at one time thousands) of people in the colony came from various places, they were able to create a community that worked at supplying its members' social, spiritual, and physical needs. This fact went a long way toward making up for at least some of the deficiencies in the western approach to medicine.

This leper colony had a direct relationship to the growth of the church in the area in which my wife and I served. Though it was nearly 100 miles from our area, in the 1940s, one of the young men from our area made his way there, stayed for about fifteen years, and returned to our area with his leprosy arrested and his soul on fire for the Lord. His evangelistic work before missionaries came provided the foundations for what is still a thriving church among the Kamwe.

2. Though I'll not go into it in as much detail, this kind of an evaluation of western schools in such a traditional context would be even more harsh. Much of what I've said in chapter 17 concerning schools leads me to the conclusion that our use of them in missionary work smacks of unethicality at every turn. Both what they stand for and the way they are operated in every context that I know of find them breaking all seven of the principles we are using for evaluation.

However, schools will not go away, so the practical question is, Is it possible to use any parts of them in ways that would satisfy any of our criteria for ethicality? The answer is yes. For example, it is possible for teachers to establish personal relationships with some of their students and, beyond that, with some of their families, if they will go out and visit them. From this basis, they may be able to demonstrate respect for the society and its culture to both students and their families. If, in addition, teachers are able to connect with the people they spend time with in ways that speak to them spiritually, they may be able to reduce at least a little the disastrous effects of the schools on some of their students and their families.

3. I believe the ethicality of much of what is done in and through churches planted by western organizations can also be questioned. Though their aim is to communicate God's intent in ways intelligible to the receptors, their westernness gets in the way. In many parts of the world, there is little in the churches that even connects with the people's spirituality. In India, for example, one who claims to be close to the spirit world is expected to be an ascetic and to be able to tell, not ask, a person what is wrong with him or her and then heal it. Western-style pastors usually don't even come close on either count. Nearly worldwide, the expectation of traditional peoples is that one who is close to God will also heal. In this expectation they have both the Bible and their traditional culture.

Church leaders often show precious little respect for the traditional culture or concern over the threat they represent to its ethnic cohesion. Church leaders trained in western subjects often are puzzled by the myriad of social, spiritual, and psychological problems their people face. Some are deeply person-oriented and good models of how to use God's power in loving ways. Unfortunately, many lord it over their people and badly misuse their power. One major reason for the latter problem is the insecurity that young leaders especially feel when they are required to operate a foreign system with little relevance to the society around them, either in organization or in the way its message is presented. Though I feel sorry for them, I must contend that much of what they do is unethical.

4. What about a Bible translation program that is based on the western principle of specialization of technical tasks but works among people whose tradition is to relate to each other holistically, rather than in terms of specializations? The receptors are deeply person oriented, but the translators are expected by their organization to be specialists, not to do church work, because the organization considers that someone else's task.

The way this sorts out is often that those who follow their organization's guidelines most closely are those who would by these criteria be least ethical. There are others, however, who go beyond those guidelines to become personal—respecting and supporting the cultural cohesiveness of their people, involving the receptors in decision making, and all the rest. Through these, God's intent is often communicated very clearly (*see* Dye 1980).

5. In many parts of the world, especially in more urban settings, there are Christian home fellowship groups functioning either as parts of churches or as the primary form the church takes in those places. I believe the New Testament speaks of such churches meeting in places such as Lydia's house (Acts 16:15, 40) and that of Aquila and Priscilla (1 Cor 16:19). When such groups meet in culturally appropriate ways, they can measure up in each of the ways we have specified as ethical.

SUMMARY

Both the theoretical part and the case study in this chapter have attempted to draw our attention to ethical issues in intercultural intervention, with a focus on how the receptors of such intervention perceive it. We have not solved all the problems, by any means. Indeed, I would contend that it is only in concrete situations, rather than in abstract presentations such as this, that such problems can effectively be dealt with. Nevertheless, I believe it is very important to raise these issues so that the cross-cultural worker for Christ will be constantly concerned to do His work in His way. It is hoped the seven principles we have formulated will be of value in guiding us in this direction.

One lesson to learn, however, is that things *often* do not turn out as they were intended to. I think of the businessman I once heard say, "This is a nonprofit business. We never planned for it to be nonprofit. It just turned out that way!" Though he intended that his business make a profit, it turned out differently. I'm afraid the same can be said of our business, the cross-cultural communication of the Gospel.

For example, our western propensity for starting institutions has been mentioned. Our intention is to go to the ends of the earth to demonstrate the love of God. To do this, we often set up an institution and then get captured by it to the extent that the real (as opposed to the stated) purpose of the institution changes imperceptibly from serving to demonstrate God's love to the need to perpetuate itself. Institutions are not intrinsically bad. The question is, however, Just what does the institution now stand for? What is it really communicating? And what now is its real purpose?

The history of institutionalization is that almost inevitably the institution becomes primarily a means for perpetuating itself, no matter how worthy the goals that brought it into being. The history of American universities, seminaries, and not a few churches bears this out. Seminaries, for example, promise to prepare students for church ministry. In most seminaries, however, most of what is taught and modeled by the teachers equips students not for churches but to teach the same things their professors taught them. The ideal being taught is to teach in a seminary. I call this unethical in that what is promised is not delivered and what is delivered is quite different from what the students are led to believe they will receive.

In just such a way, whether in the home country or in another society, the person message of God, who came all the way down to reach us where we are, gets changed into an institution message. Though people may be promised the true message, the one that Jesus gave His life for, what they get is a chance to learn how to perpetuate the institution that made the promise. This institution may be the church, a school, a hospital, or a club. It may be a large institution or a fairly small program.

Our problem is, how can we keep God's person message from becoming merely a word message, an institution message, or an academic discipline message? How can we deal with spiritual issues, poverty issues, health issues, training issues so we deliver what we promise in a way that is appropriate to the receptors? If we do something that changes God's messages into something else, I'd say we are doing something unethical.

The purpose of the above analysis is to help us ask, What is our intent, and what are the receptors at the other end really getting? Is there anything we can do along the way, any mid-course corrections when we see our programs misleading people, to make sure that what they understand is closer to what God intends? We ask these questions seriously. If the work we are called to is as important as we believe it to be, we must regularly examine our motives and assumptions. We can't always assume that our motives line up with God's, are understood properly, or are even the same as those we started with.

If we intend to be ethical, we will need to do what we do with a primary concern that it be done so that *God's intent is perceived by the receptors*. The meanings intended by God must be communicated in ways appropriate to the receiving people and understood by them, at least approximately, as He intended them to be understood. If this is to happen, the communications will not be limited to verbal messages. There will be certain concomitants of the words spoken and the deeds done, such as love, personalness, and respect for both receptors and their sociocultural context.

Furthermore, our activities will genuinely *contribute to the receptors' wellbeing* in terms of the things they have a right to expect from life. Among these things are reasonable treatment by other people (insiders and outsiders), a reasonable level of material existence, and a reasonable degree of freedom from spiritual oppression.

Where does this leave us? I am reduced to a single principle of operation: John 1:14. The communication of God became a real, credible human being. Why do *I* go as a cross-cultural witness? What have I to offer? My conclusion is that in communicating, the only thing I have to contribute is my *God's message wrapped up in myself as a person*. Whatever my talents, abilities, or skills, these are secondary to myself as a single, dedicated human being committed to God, willing to live in *this* place for the sake of *this* people. I see myself as a person. The line I have to cross is to become a person or human being according to *the receptors'* definition.

Definitions of human beingness differ. One thing they have in common, though, is that they require *participation in the receptors' life*. At a basic material level, one of our missionary students found he could not be considered a person in his part of Papua New Guinea unless he owned some land and a pig. I was able to work toward becoming a person to the Kamwe by doing such things as dancing (though not very well) with them, sleeping on a grass mat when I visited their villages, eating with them, living for a period of time with a family in a village, and spending lots of time talking, ministering with, and discipling a small group of leaders. The Apostle Paul, in more urban settings, participated with them in the trade of tent making.

We have been entrusted with a *person message* (see Kraft 1991a). We go out as persons to become persons by their definition, so that the person message brought by our Lord can come across to the receptors as it was intended by Him. Such a message involves first a relationship with us. Paul said, "Imitate me as I imitate Christ." Jesus said, "If you relate to Me, you're related to the Father." That relationship to us results in a relationship with God as person. Whether we speak of the initial relationship, that first response that leads to salvation, or growth in spiritual maturity, it is still a relational thing, a personal message. Christian institutions should be giving degrees to people who show maturity in relating to God, not just to those who gain more knowledge about God.

Remember the question. Is what we are doing perceived as ethical? I'm afraid the answer may often be No from the receptors' point of view. Though we perceive it as ethical by our standards, we need to remember that the only standards our receptors really can judge by are theirs. The only place they can start is with their standards. If what we intend as ethical comes across to them as unethical, what does that do to the communication? It comes out at the receptor's end as unethical.

We are accountable for their perception of what we do. We have to get within their frame of reference as credible human beings who live as well as speak God's messages, recognizing that we are accountable for whatever they understand from within that frame of reference.

Those interested in pursuing this matter further will find Mayers 1974 to be of great help. Pages 279–363 of that book provide several useful cases to be considered.

CHAPTER 26

DYNAMICS OF WORLDVIEW CHANGE

INTEGRATIONAL THOUGHT

The New Testament gives many examples of those who refused to change their worldview. Before we start our treatment of worldview change, let us take a look at the major barrier to worldview change—the human will. Our text will be John 9, the story of the healing of a man born blind.

It has been said, "Our vision is more obstructed by what we think we know than by our lack of knowledge" (Stendahl 1976:7). The story in John 9 gives us a glimpse of this principle in action. As we look at the text, let us ask ourselves what the participants thought they knew about the situation and how this supposed knowledge blocked their ability to understand what God was doing.

First, let us consider the disciples. In v. 2 they ask Jesus, "Whose sin caused him to be born blind? Was it his own or his parents' sin?" The disciples *knew* that blindness is a consequence of sin and undoubtedly expected a straight answer from the Master. How startled they were when Jesus answered, "His blindness has nothing to do with his sins or his parents' sins. He is blind so that God's power might be seen in him" (v. 3). I assume that Jesus would have made such a statement even had He not planned to heal the man, for I suppose that any condition is intended to be used to demonstrate God's power. Nevertheless, the Master healed the man. The disciples, however, suffered from a worldview blockage that lay in their supposed knowledge, rather than in what they would have considered ignorance.

Next we see the "knowledge blockage" of the Pharisees. Jesus rubs mud on the man's eyes and sends him to wash in the pool of Siloam. When the man returns, his sight has been restored. In verse 16 some of the Pharisees say, "The man who did this cannot be from God, for he does not obey the Sabbath law." They *knew* Jesus could not be from God, because He didn't obey their rules. Others, however, were at least flexible enough to ask how a sinner could perform such a miracle (v. 16). The Pharisees were divided at this point between those who *knew* and those who questioned what they knew.

The man's parents were then approached. They knew the former blind man was their son. They also knew, however, that if they defended his relationship with Jesus, they would be thrown out of the synagogue (vv. 20–23), so they refrained from answering any further questions.

The Pharisees then turned back to the former blind man, asserting what they *knew*: "this man who cured you is a sinner" (v. 24). After questioning the man further, they continued, "We know that God spoke to Moses; as for that fellow, however, we do not even know where he comes from!" (v. 29). Amazing! Back and forth they went, between the former blind man and his parents, trying to get one or both of them to change their story—simply because they refused to believe the obvious.

The one who had no knowledge blockage was the man himself. Undeterred by whatever he thought he knew, he simply stated, "One thing I do know: I was blind, and now I see" (v. 25). Then, in spite of the fact that he would surely be expelled from the synagogue (see v. 34),

> The man answered, "What a strange thing that is! You do not know where he comes from, but he cured me of my blindness! We know that God does not listen to sinners; he does listen to people who respect him and do what he wants them to do. Since the beginning of the world nobody has ever heard of anyone giving sight to a blind person. Unless this man came from God, he would not be able to do a thing" (vv. 30–33).

Finally, when this man found out who Jesus was, he put his faith in Him (vv. 35–38).

What an incredible story of obstinacy based on what a group of committed religious leaders thought they knew! These were Pharisees, the group in first-century Palestine that should have been most receptive to Jesus, but because the Messiah did not conform to their preconceived ideas and obey their rules, many (not all) of them refused to open their minds and hearts to Him.

To summarize, the participants in this story respond to Jesus' challenge of their worldview in four distinctly different ways. 1) Some of the Pharisees, like many people today, chose to protect their worldview rather than change it. 2) Other Pharisees came at least to the brink of change (v. 16). 3) The blind man both changed his worldview and came out into the open with his decision. 4) The man's parents seemed to change but, for fear of the consequences, refused to openly admit it.

All four of these responses are common today, as well. In fact, now as then, *one of the greatest hindrances to worldview change is religious certainty*. It seems that a belief that God has had something to do with our present knowledge can act as a powerful force to keep us from learning anything new. We must watch this tendency in ourselves and not be surprised to see it in others with strong religious convictions.

INTRODUCTION

In the preceding chapters, we have discussed the basic ingredients of human societies. We have examined, piece by piece, the fundamental cultural building blocks so necessary to the life and survival of every human society. We have, however, also examined the cultural core of human societies—the worldview—the underlying assumptions, valuations, and allegiances that enable a society to function.

Now we arrive at the practical heart of the matter for cross-cultural agents of change: the questions of, How are worldviews transformed? and What are the patterns of worldview change? As Christian witnesses, we do not seek merely the alteration of superficial customs. We do not seek change on the surface of the cultures in which we work, change simply of external traits and institutions. Rather, we want to understand how cultures are transformed at their very heart. To these matters we now turn.

A BASIC MODEL OF WORLDVIEW CHANGE

As we discussed in chapters 3 and 4, worldview is at the heart of a culture and consists of the paradigmatic assumptions, valuations, and allegiances that underlie the culture. On the basis of these assumptions, a society interprets and understands the world that surrounds it and learns to operate effectively within that world. On the basis of these interpretations and evaluations, people explain, pledge allegiance, relate, and adapt. As we have seen, their worldview also provides people with patterns for willing, emoting, reasoning, and structuring motivation and predispositions.

These activities are the functions of worldview. The ideal for a society would be to operate in a healthy manner, with these functions carried out well and the entire society pervaded with a sense of equilibrium and cohesiveness. People would have a sense of security and perceive their sociocultural life to be uniquely "real" and destined to endure. Unfortunately, such an ideal state never happens. But it is a worthy goal to strive for.

Whether close to or far from such an ideal, however, societies change, as we have seen in the preceding chapters. In our day, such changes are often taking place too rapidly and on too large a scale. The result is that people's sense of security and satisfaction in their way of life is disrupted. This disruption frequently leads to sociocultural crisis followed by breakdown, plus or minus a regrouping and return to relative equilibrium. This chapter focuses on this process, with special reference to what happens at the worldview level.

We may borrow a basic model of the process of worldview transformation from Anthony Wallace (1956). It consists, simply, of three idealized conditions:

Old Steady State ⟶ Crisis Situation ⟶ New Steady State

The first stage represents the idealized equilibrium we have been describing above. All systems are "go," stable, and enduring.

The second stage represents the introduction of some radical challenge to a people's steady state. A crisis has come: war, perhaps, or natural calamity, or the imposition of the customs and worldview values of some foreign society. In this stage, an increasing number of traditional valuations and allegiances are called into question by the new circumstances. Many of the familiar rules and guidelines, especially in the area of social control, no longer work, and many traditional assumptions no longer satisfy.

The third stage represents the ideal resolution of the crisis: the survival of the society living within the formulation of a new steady state. Though such a steady state is usually a long time in coming, if at all, we present it as the goal toward which a society strives. As we will see below, there are several possible directions in which a society can move in dealing with the crises that occur in the second stage.

Worldviews are changed because of pressure—pressure that comes from inside the society but is frequently stimulated by something from outside. That is, though it is the inside implementors who feel the pressure and make changes, it is often the case that they were influenced primarily by their contact with outside factors and advocates. Such influences, especially those coming from contemporary western sources, tend to breed dissatisfaction with traditional assumptions and approaches to life. This, in turn, pressures people to develop new ways of understanding and coping with the new circumstances. New assumptions about the world, what is possible and appropriate and what is not, and new strategies to deal with it, are generated. New valuations and allegiances are formulated. People press toward what they hope will soon issue in a new steady state.

The generation of new suppositions, valuations, and allegiances implies the concomitant rejection of old suppositions, valuations, and allegiances. Yet, the new assumptions and strategies, whether those of the transitional period or of the new steady state, are not entirely continuous with the old assumptions and strategies. Even radical paradigm shifts, such as accompany, for example, the introduction of Christianity into previously unevangelized societies, permit a large measure of continuity with antecedent worldview assumptions and the strategies built on them. New experiences will have impinged upon traditional understandings. New conceptions and perceptual models will have influenced the old strategies and precipitated change at important junctures. Especially significant, new allegiances will have emerged. Yet many features of the old will continue on, often in modified form, into the new.

A model of culture will elucidate the matter further.

CHANGE AT MANY LEVELS: A BASIC MODEL OF CULTURE

In chapter 8 we presented a pie-shaped model or picture that portrayed culture with worldview at the center and the subsystems of the culture surrounding it. Here, however, we will picture culture in a slightly different way, following Alan Tippett (1987:157–82), though substituting worldview for what he labels religion at the core and adding some subsystems:

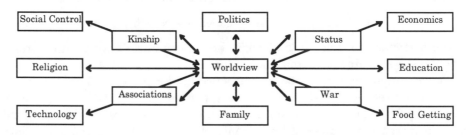

Figure 26.1 A model of culture (Tippett 1987:162, modified)

What this picturing of culture enables us to show are the many and varied interrelations between subsystems and between each subsystem and the core assumptions of worldview. Arranged about the core, each box represents an integral cultural subsystem: economics, social control, religion, war, kinship, and so forth. Subsystems interrelate with more than just the core, however. Each one interfaces with every other. The model attempts to portray culture as a living organism with muscle and ligament, tendon and sinew connecting an entire array of parts and members into a living, functioning whole.

As with the human body, what affects one part affects the whole. Even if the change is in a peripheral subsystem, the "lines" of connection between that subsystem and the worldview will see to it that change also happens at the core. We have spoken of the fact that pressure for change at the worldview level is what precipitates the crisis situation discussed above. We have also made it clear that it is at the level of worldview that the cross-cultural Christian witness seeks to bring change as a result of the entrance of the Gospel of Jesus Christ.

Often threats to a worldview come via one of the lines from a subsystem. Frequently such threats have resulted from the people's response to Christian witnesses who have pressured for changes in peripheral matters. Pressure for change of customs, even whole cultural subsystems, without corresponding transformation of worldview assumptions, is one of the surest roads to syncretism, for it frequently results in the adoption of foreign cultural *forms* to which are attached meanings that derive from the traditional background.

PATTERNS OF WORLDVIEW CHANGE

The following model presents various possibilities for the process of worldview change and its results.

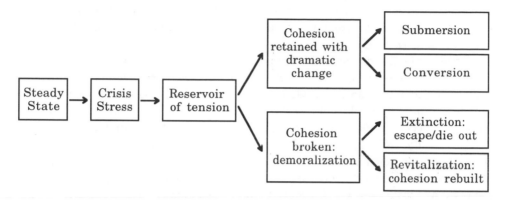

Figure 26.2 The process of worldview change and its results

As in figure 26.1, we begin with the ideal of a steady state. Then comes something from inside or, usually, from outside, that produces significant cultural stress. This stress builds and produces what Tippett calls "a reservoir of tension." Tippett explains, "It may be an intellectual, emotional, or spiritual build-up, or a complex of them all. This reservoir of tension may be a feeling of expectancy or an intense passion for emancipation" (Tippett 1987:287–88). The society, though experiencing this buildup of tension with its explosive potential for dramatic cultural change, yet preserves what Tippett describes as "ethnic cohesion"—the fundamental cultural glue that makes and keeps a people a people. At some point, however, something may happen to "ignite" the reservoir, precipitating dramatic change and innovation, issuing in conversion or submersion, yet without disrupting the fundamental configurational patterns that hold a people together, providing it with security and an identity.

Once this reservoir of tension has built up in a society, people may respond in one of a variety of ways, depending on whether the former cohesion is retained or broken. If the cohesion is retained, a people will usually move into what Tippett labeled submersion or conversion. If the cohesion is broken or severely damaged, people tend to move into some state of demoralization, issuing in either extinction or revitalization.

In *submersion*, the ethnic cohesion is preserved and traditional worldview configurations survive, though submerged under a veneer of the new. Submersion is a defense and coping mechanism on a cultural scale. When traditional worldviews are threatened with sweeping external changes, their only hope for survival may be to submerge, to hide "behind" the changes, to adopt the external form of the change while maintaining essentially the same worldview within. Such a response is "survivalist." It often leads to a syncretistic melding of worldview characteristics and has frequently occurred in reaction to colonialism. Within Christianity, submersion has often occurred in response to the requirement that converts Europeanize in order to be acceptable to those in power.

Conversion also retains the basic patterns of the sociocultural structuring of a people, but in different ways. Conversion (we're talking of culture conversion, not necessarily Christian conversion) is the approach of those who convert to a new worldview allegiance, keeping the rest of the social structure pretty much intact. Culture conversion may happen in response to any pressure on a people's worldview (e.g., coming from secularism, Islam, Hinduism, or Christianity). It is, however, typical of "people movements" into Christianity (or any other faith), when entire sociocultural groups choose to come into Christianity together. When such a movement happens, far from westernizing to become Christian, people bring their social structures with them.

Once again, the pressure for change usually comes from without—typically in the form of a message that represents a radically new perception of the universe, at once challenging traditional perceptions and precipitating the formation of new perceptual paradigms. It is a message that touches the very core of a culture, at the level of its fundamental presuppositions, evaluations, and allegiances. It issues in radical change internally (at worldview level), with only those changes required by the new allegiances and values at the surface level. When we speak of the conversion of a worldview, therefore, we are not referring to a complete conversion. We are looking at partial conversions in terms of the extent of the assumptions that are changed. But we are speaking of significant conversions in terms of the importance of the changes and the significance of the people's new commitment.

Both submersion and conversion are responses to pressure for worldview change, in which the basic cultural structuring and large portions of the worldview remain intact. But when ethnic cohesion is broken, when the worldview of a culture is so damaged that no one can mount a movement to rescue it, the society experiences *demoralization*. Neither traditional nor novel adaptations to life and answers to problems and challenges are perceived as effective. Even though a society may survive its encounter with a crisis such as westernization, an epidemic, or war, it may allow itself to enter into demoralized reasoning that undermines the last vestiges of security. The people's attitude may be, "We are lost. Everything we do is wrong. Whatever is good anymore comes from somewhere else. Our god no longer protects us; he must have died. We are weaklings and fools. What is there now to live for?" Psychological attitudes such as these quickly ramify through an entire society, calling into question its will to persevere. The result can be either extinction or revitalization.

Extinction eventually occurs if a demoralized society does not regain its cohesion. There are a number of paths that can lead from demoralization to total extinction of a culture. People may try to *escape* their society to align themselves with another society altogether. Such a response may occur suddenly and dramatically or gradually over generations. The more gradual course may happen through intermarriage, for example, or by the natural processes of assimilation that accompany invasion and colonization or large-scale emigration. In the United States, we have seen an entire spectrum of ethnically distinct immigrants "escape" their cultural distinctiveness—their language, customs, and traditions—in favor of "Americanizing." A society may also become extinct because people are no longer willing to reproduce. When a group has abandoned the search for security and cohesion altogether and is overtaken by hopelessness, procreation may be halted entirely.

However, not every demoralized society moves into extinction. When there is a conscious effort to rebuild a workable sense of cohesion, *revitalization* can occur.

The processes that lead to revitalization are a kind of rebound from the pulls of demoralization. Revitalization, like the other responses, results from the attitude of the people, not merely from the external pressures. If a society responds to demoralization with an attitude that says, "This can't happen to us. We will not allow ourselves and our way of life to disintegrate," then it takes steps to restructure and reorganize.

Such determination drives people to search for something new around which to reformulate their way of life in the face of unsatisfying anomie. They recognize that their cultural system has become inoperable and deliberately seek to rebuild a more satisfying cultural system. If the members of the society recognize the inadequacy of their system to deal with the crisis at hand, and if they possess a will to survive, the stage is set for revitalization. They are then able to discover a new paradigm, a new worldview allegiance, around which to reorganize themselves and their culture. Very often the new paradigm, the impetus and pattern for reorganization, will be supernaturalistic in nature.

FOUR MISSIOLOGICAL CONCERNS

In light of what we have just observed about the processes of worldview change, it is important for us to care for people who are in the midst of such change. Whether we focus on people within their social matrices or at the individual level, we need to concern ourselves with the following.

1. *The place of stress.* Our model of worldview transformation is built upon the progression from steady state, to crisis situation to new steady state. Basic to the model is the notion that sufficient stress impinging upon a society at the level of its worldview will result in a crisis situation. In our day, many societies are under great stress, and many have moved far down the demoralization road toward extinction. As Sharp has pointed out, "In such a situation the missionary with understanding of the processes going on about him would find his opportunity to introduce his forms of religion and to help create a new cultural universe" (1952:22). A Gospel "seed," properly planted at the right time, might be most effective in providing the spark around which a demoralized society might revitalize.

2. *The interrelatedness of the parts of a culture.* We must never forget that changes in core worldview presuppositions will ramify throughout an entire culture and all parts of its subsystems. Even apparently superficial changes produce a ripple effect throughout a culture, affecting both surface and deep-level structures. Extreme damage has been done by cross-cultural agents of change who, whether through ignorance or neglect, have not considered the interrelatedness of the many parts and aspects of a cultural configuration.

3. *Cohesion of the total configuration.* If a society is to survive in spite of stress, it will be because it is able to maintain or regain its ethnic cohesion, the cultural glue that keeps a way of life together. Where cohesiveness has been damaged, we should seek to introduce things that will repair and rebuild it. Where it is still intact, we should do our best to refrain from threatening it. God wants every people to be a people of God, secure both in their relationship to Him and in their relationships with each other.

4. *The maintenance of equilibrium.* Some degree of equilibrium, some sense of stability, is essential for the normal operation of human societies. It is easy for a people to become unbalanced under stressful conditions. When change (even "good" change) comes too rapidly, people have no opportunity to properly absorb

and integrate it with what they retain of the old ways; the result is an unsatisfying, even unintelligible, way of life. As we work with people in the throes of such destabilizing factors, we should be concerned that our efforts contribute to balance rather than to greater imbalance. In many cases, we are in a position to help people rebuild a balance they have lost.

TRANSFORMATIONAL CULTURE CHANGE

As we have seen, human cultures may be changed in response to a wide variety of circumstances, some of which are explosive catalysts, such as war or serious epidemics, and some of which are more subtle catalysts, such as the gradual erosion of values as new generations challenge and modify the conceptions of their mothers and fathers. Indeed, we have discovered that cultures are being changed constantly, through a wide variety of means.

Whatever the specific catalyst, we will describe change that touches a culture at its essential center, at the level of its worldview, as *transformational culture change*. By transformational culture change we refer to *the change that takes place within a society and its culture due to a change in worldview*. It is change that begins at the worldview heart of culture and courses, as it were, throughout the many veins and arteries of the surface-level subsystems, until it has touched everything and altered, to whatever extent necessary, whatever needs changing to accommodate the new assumption(s).

The reader will recall our basic model of culture (figure 26.1). We have depicted an organic unity, with the foundational assumptions, allegiances, and values of worldview at the core, fleshed out all around by the surface-level behavior arranged in subsystems that surround the core. Transformational culture change must be understood in relation to this same model. It assumes that change introduced at the deepest level of culture, at the level of worldview, will ramify through every surrounding subsystem, effecting integral change throughout.

Having examined this model of change, we must ask ourselves, How does all of this, all of our study, apply in the context of our own cross-cultural ministry? How can we go about the tasks of Christian mission in an informed way, touching and changing people and cultures in accord with principles endorsed by God?

Jesus described the "touch" of the Kingdom of God to be like the touch of yeast in a lump of dough (Lk 13:21). This is an image of how transformational change works. It affects the most fundamental level of things, the internal "chemistry," and eventually pervades the entire "lump." Transformational change is not superficial change painted over the surface of a culture like frosting on a cake. It is change that works from within. This change is not rapid or violent. It changes the loaf by leavening rather than by blowing it up. It works from the inside out, from worldview to surface-level behavior. Eventually, the entire "lump" of both social behavior and cultural structuring is transformed.

To use another analogy, Jesus described the radical changes attending the Kingdom of God to be like the planting and growth of a seed (Mk 4:26–32). As with yeast, the change comes from within. But notice this further point of analogy: just as a mustard seed, "the smallest seed in the world," can eventually produce "the biggest of all plants" (Mk 4:31–32), so small changes introduced at the level of worldview can eventuate in sweeping transformation throughout an entire culture. The analogy also suggests that for the growth of great shrubs and the trans-

formational change of cultures, everything depends upon the selection and place-
ment of the appropriate seed.

The Apostle Paul commanded the church at Rome to let God transform them
(Rom 12:2). He also showed us some of the steps we need to take and to recommend to others, as well as one of the results of those steps, when He said,

> So, then, my brothers, because of God's great mercy to us I appeal to you: Offer your-
> selves as a living sacrifice to God, dedicated to his service and pleasing to him. This is
> the true worship that you should offer. Do not conform yourselves to the standards of
> this world, but let God transform you inwardly by a complete change of your mind. Then
> you will be able to know the will of God—what is good and is pleasing to him and is per-
> fect (Rom 12:1–2).

The aim for the Christian is nothing short of transformation at the deepest
levels. For this to happen, though, we need to offer ourselves completely to the
only One who has the power to do the job—God. This offer of ourselves is to be like
that of a lamb about to be sacrificed, holding nothing back. As that lamb was committed without the ability to turn back, so we are to totally dedicate ourselves to
Him and His plan for us. Such dedication, however, involves the choice to refuse to
conform to the standards of the world. As Phillips translates it, we should not let
the society around us ("the world") press us into its mold. Building from this commitment and refusal, then, we submit to God for transformation through a complete change of mind (= perspective) that leads to a knowing (= experiencing) of
His will in continuous operation in our lives. (The Greek words for mind and
knowing are better translated "perspective" and "experiencing," respectively.)

This submission and dedication to the transformation process is, of course, a
tall order for mere human beings. When we apply it to a whole society, we can
imagine an incredible number of complications. Yet this is God's way and must
therefore be our practice and our teaching. Perhaps the real reason why transformation, either on the individual level or with groups, is so uncommon is because so
few do it God's way and with His empowerment.

The above analogies illustrate change. They do not suggest the wholesale
transplantation of entire shrubs, but the introduction of seeds. The New Testament is full of such seeds—new conceptions, new paradigms and definitions of
reality, new understandings of what is possible and what is not, of what is vitally
important and what in the end is of little importance at all—"seeds" that when
fully grown produce radical transformations. Here is illustrated the fundamental
principle of transformational worldview change: the process of cultural transformation is best pursued through the planting of new worldview assumptions in
people's minds. The Christian agent of change should concentrate on planting a
few crucial seeds, worldview seeds, rather than attempting vainly to replace or
transform surface-level behaviors. Both people and cultures are transformed from
within!

AN APPROACH TO TRANSFORMATIONAL CULTURE CHANGE

Now let us move on to outline a practical approach for the cross-cultural agent
of change. First we need to recognize that there do not seem to be any surefire
techniques that will work for every change agent in every cross-cultural situation
to initiate transformational culture change. Indeed, since transformational change

issues from within, we must be very careful about anything we as outsiders attempt to do to bring it about.

To reiterate a principle often stated in earlier chapters, constructive change cannot be imposed from without. External manipulation may bring success in altering surface-level cultural behavior. There is, however, often a reaction against such changes at a later time. Such reactions tend to undo or destroy whatever temporary benefits may have been gained.

In spite of the lack of surefire methods and the warning about outsiders attempting to effect worldview change, there are principles that can be helpful if followed. Cross-cultural witnesses can learn an attitude, or better, an approach, if not a technique. Such an approach can inform and enlighten our ministries and, hopefully, protect those we work with from most of the kinds of mistakes that have characterized cross-cultural witness in the past.

1. An important part of a constructive approach to transformational change springs from recognition of the *advocate-implementor or advocate-innovator* (Barnett 1953) *distinction*. We have already discussed the distinction in chapter 24. Here, however, we recall this important relationship to emphasize that outsiders can only advocate, never implement. An outsider can only recommend, never actually introduce and put into effect a change in someone else's culture. Something in the very nature of cross-cultural dynamics makes it true that only cultural insiders are able to genuinely implement change. Those working from outside to bring about transformational culture change need to be constantly aware of this fact.

Though we as outside advocates can and often do play important parts in the introduction of ideas, we must not overstep our boundaries by trying to do something we are not in a position to do. This means that outsiders (and cross-cultural agents of change will always be outsiders) can only *advocate* change, *witness* to alternative assumptions, values, and allegiances, and commend their acceptance. It is very destructive when outsiders, no matter how wise they are, attempt to impose even desirable changes on a society not their own.

Equally important, the cross-cultural advocate should not expect to control the natural processes of the spread and implementation of a change in another society. Again, we can advocate such spread and innovation, but most aspects of the process are for us to watch, not to control. In a very real sense, gospel-prompted changes within a society and its culture are a matter to be decided between the people themselves and God. The outside advocate possesses no inherent veto power over the process.

2. Another important facet of our approach to transformational culture change is the fact that culture change of any sort consists fundamentally in *a change of ideas* (Luzbetak 1963 after Barnett 1953).

> When cultures change it is not so much the houses, farming, techniques, wedding customs, dances, funerals, and religious rites that change as the *ideas* (the patterns) of houses, farms, weddings, dances, and religion. When cultures change, socially acquired sets of ideas change.
>
> The shared ideas of a society, which we call "culture," as such exist only in the mind, not on streets, farms, or in places of worship. To change cultures, therefore, means to propagate new *ideas* (Luzbetak 1963:196).

This, of course, is exactly what we have been saying. *Truly transformational change issues from transformed* ideas *at the level of worldview*. It is the transformation of worldview assumptions, values, and allegiances, either before or after the changes in behavior, that provide an adequate and lasting foundation for culture change.

3. The *principles of effective cross-cultural communication* make a third facet of our basic approach. What has come to be called the S-M-R model will help us here. If communication is to be effective, it is important that the communicator (or source, S) present the message (M) to receptors (R) in such a way that the latter will understand and do something about what they receive. In this process, however, sources have choices as to whether they will focus on themselves (as for example, in dealing with issues only important to S), on the message (as in focusing on truth in irrelevant ways), or on the receptors (as in relevantly dealing with the message in terms of their concerns and needs). Our choice is the latter.

If we are to communicate effectively for deep-level change, it is not enough that our messages are true and important to us. They should be both, but they also need to be relevant to those who watch and hear us. It is crucially important that the receptors be able to make sense of the message from within their own way of life and be able to apply it there. We do not endorse relevance simply for the sake of relevance. There are many messages that would be relevant but not Christian, even though some of them might be life transforming. Our aim, however, is to present the truths of the Gospel in such a way that our receptors perceive their relevance and applicability to their real life. If we are to do this, it is obvious that we will need to investigate thoroughly and experience for ourselves the sociocultural milieu in which we are to labor. What are these people's felt needs? What are their unfulfilled desires? As these questions are answered, we discover strategic bridges, points of engagement for the communication of the Gospel.

Once we have at least begun to discover such bridges, Jesus Himself provides us with our best model for ministering cross-culturally. Just as He moved from above culture to within culture, so we are to move from one cultural context into another. The way He operated on this side of the gap He crossed is instructive for us. Following are ten of the points concerning Jesus' communication that I treat in more detail in my book *Communication Theory for Christian Witness* (1991a).

a. Jesus *identified* with His receptors. In His case, He was incarnated in the receiving society. We cannot become incarnate, but should do our best to enter sympathetically into our receptors' way of life with understanding and empathy, even learning to participate with them to some extent and to share ourselves with them in person-to-person self-disclosure. As a former student of mine who felt that the goal of incarnation was too unrealistic put it, we can at least aim at *friendship* with those we seek to win (Hill 1990, 1993).

b. Jesus, as a participant in the society around Him, was *receptor-oriented*. That is, His primary concern was that those who heard and watched Him have a decent chance to understand and do something about His messages. To that end He spoke a language they could understand and used cultural forms (e.g., parables, healings) that would be familiar and attractive to His audiences.

c. An important part of the impact of Jesus' messages lay in the fact that *He gave Himself to His hearers in two-way communication*. He was out with the people constantly, seldom putting Himself in formalized monologue situations. His hearers could ask Him questions, challenge Him, interact with Him over every issue. He especially gave Himself to the twelve, training a group who would carry on the ministry after Jesus was gone.

d. He didn't settle for simply communicating verbally, however. Jesus *demonstrated the Father*. As He said to Phillip, "If you have seen me, you have seen the Father" (Jn 14:9). He employed the power of God to demonstrate the love of God. He showed the forgiveness and acceptance of God, demonstrating what God is really like to people who had a wrong understanding of Him.

e. As Jesus communicated, *He earned, rather than demanded, the respect He received*. He did not depend on His position or reputation to establish His standing with the people around Him. He spoke and did things that led people to accept or reject Him on the basis of their real-life experiences with Him.

f. Jesus did not simply approach people in general, *He dealt with specific people*. Though His messages were for all mankind, He treated each individual, even outcasts, as important, loved by, and acceptable to God.

g. Likewise with His messages. *He spoke to specific situations*, contextualizing His messages in appropriate and specific ways to meet concrete situations. He spoke in pictures but not in abstractions, focusing more on applications than on generalities.

h. *Jesus refrained from information overload*. Unlike our ordinary approaches to teaching, Jesus regularly gave people enough to chew on but not so much that they were inundated with information, much of which they would forget before they could make use of it.

i. Jesus' teaching method involved *inviting people to discovery*. Much of what He said and did was difficult to interpret until a person pondered it a while and discovered what Jesus was driving at. Our tendency is to predigest our messages and present them in terms of generalizations and implications, leaving the hearers little to discover, yet meanings discovered have much greater impact than meanings prepackaged and simply delivered.

j. *Jesus put great trust in His receptors*. In spite of the continual ups and downs of His followers, Jesus trusted them, first to understand and then to go out into the whole world to continue the job He had started. He simply said, "As the Father sent me, so I send you" (Jn 20:21). This trust made men of them.

In presenting these points, I am suggesting that Jesus has shown us not only what to communicate but *how* to communicate it. If we are to see Jesus' work done properly, we need to do it in His way. He wants to be understood and to draw all people to Himself through us. If we can do our part according to these principles, the sociocultural transformation we seek can become a reality.

SOME PRACTICAL STEPS TO TAKE

With this background, the question is, What do I do now? The steps are three, each implicit in what we have already said in the above pages, but each worthy of being repeated.

1. *Study*. As will be emphasized in chapter 28, the quest for understanding starts with the recognition that we don't know. Hopefully, these chapters will help us to go about this quest more effectively than might have been the case. To gain that understanding, we need to study the people we work among and their way of life. Though we need to be concerned with such study as early as possible in our preparation, we need to continue it throughout our career.

We should study the people we are attempting to influence as thoroughly as possible. Find out what is important to them and what is not. What occupies their attention and captures their interest, what are their basic assumptions, allegiances, and values (their worldview), what are their patterns of behavior, what is their societal organization, what are their methods of social control, what are their structures of religious belief and behavior? The list of important questions could go on and on.

We do not mean academic study only, though as cross-cultural agents of change we ought certainly to familiarize ourselves with the pertinent literature. The most important study, however, is *experiential study*. We need to experience the society into which we desire to introduce change. One aim of these chapters is to enable us to get beyond the literature to study the people. No culture exists in the abstract. Cultures exist only insofar as genuine human beings live them, think them, incarnate them. This means that cultures cannot be transformed from within the study cubicles of an academic library, but only as an agent of transformation significantly understands and touches a particular people.

2. *Analyze*. This is an additional step beyond study, though we often do it automatically as we study. We need to especially analyze and investigate the basic assumptions, values, and allegiances that comprise the worldview of a culture, plus the themes in which they function. We need to ask questions concerning a people's assumptions in each of the universal categories discussed in chapter 4, then analyze the information we receive and employ the insights in our interactions with the people.

As we analyze, it becomes apparent that the structuring of the people's assumptions and values can be arranged into a series of themes. This can be done in at least a tentative way by following the examples of worldview analyses presented below. Once this is done, there are still a number of questions to ask relating to the specific concerns of ministry. Among them are, What are the worldview assumptions on which we need to focus as we attempt to conduct Christian ministry among these people? Which assumptions should be focused on first and which can be left until later? How do these assumptions interrelate with other assumptions in the worldview? What are the likely ramifications if certain assumptions and values are changed? The answers to such questions inform the third important step. A particularly helpful analysis that can serve as a model for us is my wife's (Marguerite G. Kraft), *Worldview and the Communication of the Gospel* (1978) which is, unfortunately, now out of print, though available in many libraries.

3. *Strategize*. On the basis of such study and analysis, we are in a good position to produce a tentative strategy for introducing or redirecting transformational change. To this point we have been fact-finding and processing. As we worked through those areas, we started to ask questions related to our specific goals. At this point we turn more pointedly to the matter of what to do to maximize the influence of biblical input in the receiving society, so we begin in earnest to evaluate assumptions and themes in the light of the Gospel.

We also need to focus on needs felt by the people, especially those they feel are not being met by their present way of life. Often there is an amazing and strategically God-ordained correspondence between what people feel to be missing in their lives and what the Gospel offers. Thus it was that Paul was able to brilliantly connect God's grace with the Greek emphasis on grace (Gr. *charis*) while with Jews, Paul and the other New Testament authors focused more on meeting their desire for peace (Heb. *shalom*). In many contemporary societies, a primary quest is for power to deal with the spirit world. Jesus met Jews in terms of their felt need for this dimension. For many, the quest for relational harmony provides a good place to focus. For others, peace or forgiveness may be an appropriate focal point for strategy.

A clear word of caution is in order here. It is altogether too easy for Christian agents of change, even after studying anthropology, to allow ethnocentric assumptions to creep in concerning what they need and what the Gospel offers. As we have seen to some extent already and will emphasize in the next chapter, even our theological perspectives need to be affected by this cross-cultural approach. We may, for example, find ourselves unconsciously evaluating a target culture's values and practices by the standards and values of our own cultural understanding of the Bible, rather than from a cross-cultural perspective. It is not only westerners who fall into this trap. *It is easy for Christian witnesses (even those who have studied anthropology) to forget that the Gospel means allegiance to Christ, lived out in relationship of "grace through faith" in a culturally appropriate way.* We are not called to win people to or to train people in whatever our own cultural approach to Christianity may be. The specific outworking of expression and behavior, the particular integration of emphases, values, and thematic configurations, must be discovered and worked out (perhaps with our assistance) by each and every society as it responds to the Gospel of Christ in its own unique fashion.

To strategize for transformational change means to select specific cultural themes for engagement. It means, further, to develop a "game plan" for initiating this gospel contact and a notion of evaluative criteria by which successful progress in the direction intended will be demonstrated. In initial evangelism, this means uncovering such key areas as a people's *ultimate allegiance* and what they look to for authority and security and developing a systematic plan to introduce Christ at those points. In introducing change at later stages, we also seek to discover basic allegiances, values, and assumptions that stand in the way of the advocated change.

The seeds are then planted at the points of engagement. The basic seed leading to Christward transformation is, of course, allegiance to Christ as Savior and Lord. As this all-important seed takes root and grows, any human society will undergo radical changes that begin at worldview level and reverberate throughout the culture. Later seeds of transformation increase and enhance this "leavening" in the direction of enabling human cultural structures to be more usable by God. Though our primary goal is to see people transformed, the transformation of their cultural structures so that their cultural institutions and customs will be more easily used for God's purposes is a worthy secondary goal.

CHAPTER 27

THEOLOGICAL IMPLICATIONS
OF THIS APPROACH

INTEGRATIONAL THOUGHT

We have just been discussing the importance of worldview assumptions to cultural behavior. One area of cultural behavior strongly influenced by worldview is the doing of theology. As pointed out in chapter 7, worldview assumptions underlie the way people approach and interpret the Bible. A study of the worldview underlying the biblical writings is basic to theological hermeneutics, the science of biblical interpretation.

For example, asking worldview questions enables us to understand why Matthew used the expression "kingdom of heaven" instead of "kingdom of God" and called the Lake of Galilee a sea. Since he was writing to Jews, he needed to be careful about their sensibilities concerning the speaking of the name of God, so he used the euphemism "heaven" to keep from breaking the taboo. Since the Jews, unlike the Greeks, were more focused on inland bodies of water than on the Mediterranean, Matthew labeled "sea" a body of water that Greeks called a lake.

Likewise, an understanding of worldview enables us to understand what the problem was when Jesus said to the Samaritan woman, "You are right when you say you haven't got a husband. You have been married to five men, and the man you live with now is not really your husband" (Jn 4:17–18). Most American preachers, not understanding the underlying assumptions that would motivate such behavior in a society such as that of first-century Samaria, regard the Samaritan woman as an adulteress. A knowledge of the worldview assumptions underlying her behavior, however, enables one to recognize that her problem was more likely to be barrenness than adultery.

Again, insight into the underlying assumptions of the people Jesus worked with allows us to understand why they were so confused over His insistence on identifying with the poor and the outcast. It was their belief that wealth meant a person was righteous and therefore blessed by God. Poverty meant that one was unrighteous and cursed by God. On the basis of these assumptions, the fact that Jesus associated with the poor could only mean that He was not from God. And Jesus' statement that for rich people to get into heaven was like a camel going through the eye of a needle led the disciples to gasp, "Who, then, can be saved?" (Mk 10:26). From their point of view, if the rich (by cultural definition accepted and blessed by God) could not enter heaven, who could?

Another Jewish assumption enables us to understand why Peter and the other disciples were insistent that Jesus leave them after they had pulled in two boatloads of fish (Lk 5:4–10). It was their belief that if God got close, they died! (*see* Is

6:5). Since it was obvious to them—from what He had done by bringing in the fish—that Jesus had come from God, they felt His presence was bad news for them. Jesus, however, spent His ministry demonstrating to those open to God that when God gets near, things go well.

Looking beneath the surface permits us to see that the argument over whether or not Gentiles were to be circumcised (e.g., Acts 15) is an argument over cultural conversion rather than merely over a physical operation. Similarly, the discussion in Galatians of whether or not a Christian is to follow the Law is seen to be a broader issue, since Law as used there is virtually synonymous with what we call culture.

To interpret Scripture faithfully requires that we learn as much as possible about the assumptions underlying the statements and allusions made by the various authors. Just as we have learned to look for worldview assumptions to interpret the attitudes and behavior of our receptors, so we must look behind the surface-level statements of Scripture to understand the authors' intended meanings. Whether in theologizing or simply in communicating the Gospel cross-culturally, there are three points at which we must give attention to worldview issues: in dealing with the biblical authors within their cultural context, in attempting to understand ourselves in relation to our own cultural context, and in seeking to gain understandings of those to whom we seek to communicate. The diagram below may help us to picture this.

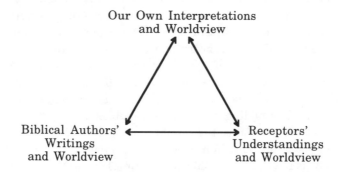

Figure 27.1 Three understandings conditioned by worldview

As we return to the implications of anthropological understandings for theologizing, the importance of worldview cannot be overstated, either at the interpreting end or at the communicating end of our activity.

INTRODUCTION

As has been clear throughout this volume, it is impossible, and even inadvisable, to avoid theological reflection as we attempt to approach anthropology from a Christian perspective. Those committed to Christ and His cause must seek answers to a series of dilemmas raised by the necessity of communicating messages from a supracultural God concerning ultimate things within a relative, sociocultural context. At the beginning of this volume we attempted to develop a perspective from which to view such issues, and we have raised and attempted to tackle quite a number of them throughout this text. What remains is to summarize and tie things together as we conclude.

In chapter 7, we weighed the relationships between western theological thinking and the attempts of western anthropologists to produce a broader understanding of life by developing a cross-cultural approach. Though many anthropologists have so embraced a relativistic approach that they reject the existence and claims of a supracultural God, and many Christians have not learned how to handle differences of cultural perspective, we have adopted a *critical realist* position that allows for both absolute supracultural REALITY and relative cultural realities. This approach to theological thinking we have labeled *Christian ethnotheology* (*see* Kraft 1979a). This chapter further outlines that approach.

GOD AND CULTURE

Throughout this text, we have implicitly and explicitly committed ourselves to the Protestant Bible as the revelation of God and therefore normative with regard to the understandings we advocate concerning God and His relationships with and desires for humans. We see the Bible as "capital R" REALITY, even though our interpretations of it fall into the "small r" reality category. On the basis of our best understandings of Scripture we affirm the presence and crucial importance of a Creator and Sustainer of the universe who is Himself uncreated. He originated, oversees, and keeps working all that exists. We see God as existing above and outside of culture yet working through culture in His interactions with human beings. Among His creations are humans whom He endowed with the capacity to create and alter the cultural "water" in which we must swim.

Humans and the sociocultural matrices in which we live are relative to and dependent upon God, yet the various perspectives extant in human communities are taken seriously by God and are to be taken seriously by us.

We pointed to 1 Corinthians 9:19–22 as the verses that most clearly articulate God's perspective on culture:

> I am a free man, nobody's slave; but I make myself everybody's slave in order to win as many people as possible. While working with the Jews, I live like a Jew in order to win them; and even though I myself am not subject to the Law of Moses, I live as though I were when working with those who are, in order to win them. In the same way, when working with Gentiles, I live like a Gentile, outside the Jewish Law, in order to win Gentiles. This does not mean that I don't obey God's law; I am really under Christ's law. Among the weak in faith I become like one of them, in order to win them. So I become all things to all men, that I may save some of them by whatever means are possible.

Just as the Apostle Paul sees each cultural matrix as usable for Christian witness, so we see God working in terms of Jewish culture to reach Jews yet refusing to impose Jewish customs on Gentiles (Acts 15; Galatians). Instead, non-Jews are to come to God and relate to Him in terms of their own cultural vehicles. We see the Bible endorsing a doctrine we call *biblical sociocultural adequacy*, in which each culture is taken seriously but none advocated exclusively as the only one acceptable to God.

Though this position accepts the relativity of culture, *it rejects ethical or moral relativism*, the doctrine that allows those within a society to adopt practices specifically forbidden by their society and by God simply because they have heard that such practices are allowed in other societies.

JESUS AND CULTURE

Jesus came into a single human culture, learning His way—as all humans do—into full participation in His society. But He was not simply a child of His society, since He had a higher allegiance. He became fully human (Jn 1:14), laying aside the use of His divinity (Phil 2:5–8) to demonstrate to us how Adam was and we are intended to live—fully cultural but obeying God and living in total dependence on Him.

As a human being, Jesus had a worldview (Kraft 1989:101–15). This consisted mostly of those assumptions He shared with other Galileans. It included, though, what may be called "Kingdom Principles" that resulted from the infusion into His worldview of things He learned from the Scriptures and directly from the Father. Among the characteristics of Jesus' worldview were the following, many of which challenged that of His countrymen, and most of which challenge ours:

1. Jesus assumed the existence of God. Like His contemporaries, He saw God with absolute authority over His creatures. Unlike His contemporaries, He saw God as a loving Father, favorably disposed toward humans, especially those who are hurting. Jesus saw God as actively involved with His creatures (Jn 5:17) and good to have close, One who stands against oppressors (Mt 23:13–22) and is willing to demonstrate His love to all who turn to Him (Jn 3:16–17). In addition, God is seen as understanding and relating to people on the basis of their motives rather than their behavior (Mt 23:25–28).

2. Jesus assumed the existence of a spirit world divided into two kingdoms, God's and Satan's (Mt 12:22–29). Human life is lived in the context of the war between these kingdoms, being both affected by it and involved in it.

3. Humans, including Jesus, are to receive the power to live properly in this context from the Holy Spirit (Lk 3:21–22; 24:49; Acts 1:8; 10:38). Under the influence and guidance of the Holy Spirit, we are to exercise both gifts (1 Cor 12:1–11) and fruits (Gal 5:22–23).

4. Jesus lived dependent on the Father, doing only what He saw the Father doing (Jn 5:19) and saying only what the Father instructed Him to say (Jn 8:28).

5. To Jesus, believing God leads to seeing (Lk 8:9–10) and obeying God to knowing (Jn 7:17).

6. Jesus considered love toward God, others, self, and even enemies as mandatory for God's people (Mt 22:37–40; Lk 6:27–36).

7. Jesus taught (Mt 6:12, 14–15) and demonstrated (Lk 23:34) that we are to forgive rather than to judge or condemn if we expect God to forgive us. We must also acknowledge our own sins (1 Jn 1:9).

8. Again, Jesus taught (Lk 6:29) and demonstrated that people are not to fight back when attacked.

9. Concern for the Kingdom of God and faithfulness to God are to be the primary goals for God's people to aim at (Mt 6:33).

10. God's people are to be stewards, risking with God rather than preserving for God (Mt 25:14–30).

11. Jesus modeled how to become great by serving (Mt 20:25–28). If we are to be great in the Kingdom, we are also to serve, even becoming like children (Mt 18:1–5).

These and other kingdom principles were a part of Jesus' worldview, though they did not arise from His cultural conditioning. They came directly from God the Father. Our commitment to follow Jesus implies that we are to adopt such assumptions and principles into our worldview as He did, even when they conflict with what we are taught within our society. As with Him, these assumptions and principles are to underlie our behavior in our own cultural contexts.

THE WAR IS *WITHIN*, NOT BETWEEN CULTURES

Since God exists and He and His Kingdom are to be our supreme value, we are to participate in the war between Him and Satan. This battle is not to be conceived of, as it was by early western missionary theorists, as a battle between our "Christian" culture and the cultures of pagans that have been so thoroughly affected by Satan that they need to be replaced. Such missiologists assumed that God had somehow purified our western cultures so that we have a right to impose them in His name on people whose societies are dominated by Satan as the approved way of bringing pagans to Christ. In keeping with this assumption, the missiology of a century ago rallied around the cry, "Civilize in order to evangelize." Attempts to school people and govern them into westernization were widely applauded as means to bring them truly into the Kingdom.

Nor should we go to the extreme that many have gone to in reaction against this negative view toward nonwestern societies and their cultures. In the middle of the twentieth century many of us who had been trained anthropologically turned to a distorted positive view of the cultures of mankind. With these assumptions, we often completely ignored the kinds of influence the enemy wields through people and their cultures. (I say "we" because I have been a part of this reaction.) We rightly saw that cultural structures in and of themselves are not evil. However, we often neglected the fact that structures created by humans under satanic influence are unlikely to be either totally neutral or easily usable for God's purposes.

Though we cited Jesus' and the early Church's easy use of most of the cultural structures of first-century Palestine, we failed to see that the considerable amount of previous use of those structures by God's people made a big difference in their usability by the early Church. More appropriate to our point was the ability of the early Christians to make use of Greco-Roman cultural structures as Christianity moved out into the world beyond Palestine. This fact still encourages us to advocate the contextualization of the Gospel in any culture. In such advocacy, however, we must give adequate attention to the difficulties of adaptation as well as the possibilities.

These difficulties in the early days of Christianity usually centered around the spiritual conflict between the followers of Satan and those of God in the use made of the cultural structures *within* whatever sociocultural setting was involved. The point is not the essential badness or goodness of the structures themselves, but the ways in which people (societies) influenced by Satan or God used these structures on behalf of their god. The Jewish Christians, even though their cultural structures had long been used by some people for God's purposes, could neither advocate the rightness of their structures nor deny the fact that Satan had also been making use of them. In our day, we who have inherited long experience of God's working within our western societies need to be as aware of the enemy's influence on our society and its culture as we are of his influence on other societies and their cultural structures. The battle between God and Satan takes place *within* every sociocultural context, not between sanctified structures and pagan ones.

Christian witness involves recommending, both to our own people and to those of other societies, that they live as Jesus did in what might be called "Kingdom normalcy." We are to use whatever is usable of our heritage (as Jesus did) but freely supplement by reinterpreting, altering, or replacing what we started out with in order to grow in our relationship with Christ and to capture as much as possible of our cultural heritage for Christ. The assumptions and principles we advocate accept as much of the cultural heritage (whether theirs or ours) as is compatible with Christian faith but assume that wresting cultural structures from satanic use may be difficult and will always involve reinterpretation, altering, and replacing.

This will involve us as witnesses, both in the incorporating of such assumptions and principles into our cultural worldview and behavior and in the teaching of those who call themselves Christians to incorporate these same kingdom principles into their worldview and behavior. The result would be that all Christians would live out the Gospel in ways appropriate both to their cultural heritage and to the Scriptures. This will mean that Christians in every society should, in ways appropriate to their sociocultural contexts, practice both the fruits and the gifts of the Spirit to do the works of Jesus in their societies. Among these would be the winning of people to Christ and the freeing of them from illnesses, demons, enslavement to poverty and sin and other symptoms of Satan's activity in the world.

CONTEXTUALIZATION AND ENCOUNTER

In dealing with the warfare between God and Satan within each society, it has become accepted to speak of *power encounters*. This term was coined by Alan Tippett (1971) to label the kinds of events he found were usually crucial in the South Pacific in the turning of large social groups to Christ. Since these people served gods invested with spiritual power (from Satan), it was crucial for them in considering Christianity to discover which god had the greatest power. When, either by design or accident, it became clear that the God of Jesus Christ was able to wield more power than their gods, they abandoned their allegiance to their gods and turned to Christ. The events in which God's power was shown to be greater are what Tippett called power encounters.

In Scripture, we have a series of power encounters between Moses and Pharaoh (Ex 5–12). Later, Elijah took on the prophets of Baal in another dramatic power encounter (1 Kgs 18). Jesus' ministry was full of power encounters in which, through healing or deliverance, He challenged and defeated the power of the Evil One to hold a person captive. Scripture records a large number of other events in which enemy power was challenged and defeated by those wielding the power of God.

For people like the Hebrews and most of today's peoples, for whom spiritual power is a primary concern, power encounters are often the clearest way to demonstrate the superiority of God over their spirits and gods. To reach them within the assumptions and principles that govern their lives, the exercise of the power of God in this way is crucial. Much of the world's Christianity is anemic because it was not presented with such exercise of divine power as a part of it. Pentecostal Christianity, on the other hand, is usually more acceptable and meaningful to most of the world's peoples because it includes this dimension of the Christian message.

But power encounters are not the only encounters portrayed in Scripture. There are two others: *allegiance (or commitment) encounters* and *truth encounters*. Jesus spent most of His time teaching truth, inviting people into truth encounters. As He taught, though, He constantly invited people into greater and greater allegiance to Him and His Father. In conjunction with the teaching of truth and the appeals for allegiance, He regularly freed people from the enemy's captivity through His use of God's power.

In Jesus' ministry and throughout the Scriptures, God calls people to commit themselves to Him as their primary allegiance. The Christian message involves an invitation to this initial commitment, followed by a continuing series of invitations to greater and greater commitment to God. These are what I am calling *allegiance encounters.*

Allegiance encounters have to do with *relationship.* The initial commitment to Christ brings us into a primary relationship with Him in replacement of the primacy of relationships with other gods, spirits, people, material objects, organizations, or whatever. Subsequent commitments confirm and deepen that relationship.

Truth encounters are about *understanding.* Prior to making a commitment to Christ, we need a certain level of understanding of the truth. Whenever truth is taught, it confronts or encounters ignorance and error. As we grow in our commitment to Christ, we need a continuing deepening of our understandings of God's truth to fight any ignorance and error to which we are exposed.

Power encounters are about *freedom.* To come to allegiance to Christ, people need freedom from the blindness (2 Cor 4:4), deceit, and other kinds of hindrances that the enemy throws at them. As we learn more truth, we need freedom from the enemy's power to divert us into error. We also need freedom from illness, accident, and demonization.

A summary of the purpose and results of these encounters as Jesus Christ and His followers confront Satan follows:

- Concerning *Power* resulting in *Power Encounters* to release people from satanic captivity and to bring them into *Freedom in Jesus Christ*
- Concerning *Allegiance* resulting in *Allegiance Encounters* to rescue people from wrong allegiances and to bring them into *Relationship to Jesus Christ*
- Concerning *Truth* resulting in *Truth Encounters* to counter error and/or ignorance and to bring people to *Correct Understandings*

There is, at all points in Christian experience, the need for all three of these kinds of encounters, and all of them need to take place within the sociocultural context appropriate to the given receptors. That is, these encounters will need to be contextualized.

Unfortunately, the majority of Christian witness coming from the West has neglected the advocacy of power encounters in the presentation of the Gospel. Though Pentecostal and charismatic witnesses have done better, evangelicals have stressed allegiance and truth but been deficient in the power dimensions of the biblical message. This has resulted in what is undoubtedly the biggest problem in worldwide Christianity: *dual allegiance.*

As mentioned, most of the peoples of the world, like the peoples of the Bible, may be referred to as "power oriented." They see the universe as filled with spiritual beings, many of which can hurt them. Their primary concern is to be able to command enough spiritual power to avoid or correct problems in their lives caused by the evil spiritual powers. When they hear biblical stories demonstrating the power of God, they are often very receptive. When, however, they find that western Christianity provides little or none of that power, they continue to make use of their traditional approaches to power. In spite of their pledge of allegiance to Christ, they continue to go to traditional priests, shamans, diviners, medicine men, and the like for healing, direction, and blessing. Their allegiance to God is thus compromised, and their Christianity syncretistic.

It is important, therefore, for evangelicals to add the power encounter dimension to their presentation of Christianity, if their churches are to avoid this problem, but not at the expense of their continuing emphasis on the other two types of encounters. Pentecostal and charismatic approaches need to be careful not to go to extremes in their emphasis on power. Power-oriented peoples will usually be content to accept any power available to them. They usually have difficulty understanding the exclusivity of God's claims. For example, Christian healing campaigns often attract many in nonwestern societies, and see many healed. Usually, however, such campaigns result in few who totally commit themselves to Christ. Most will just as gladly go to non-Christian sources for healing the next time they feel the need—in spite of the fact that they may continue to believe that Jesus' power is greater than the others'.

	START	NEED	PROCESS	RESULT
STAGE 1	Satanic Captivity	Freedom to Understand	Power Encounters	Commitment to Jesus
	Ignorance/Error	Enough Understanding	Truth Encounters	
	Non-Christian Allegiance	Challenge to Commit to Jesus	Allegiance Encounters	
STAGE 2	Commitment to Jesus	Spiritual Warfare to Provide Protection, Healing, Blessing, Deliverance	Power Encounters	Growing Relationship to God and His People
		Teaching	Truth Encounters	
		Challenges to Greater Commitment and Obedience	Allegiance Encounters	
STAGE 3	Growing Relationship to God and His People	Authoritative Prayer	Power Encounters	Witness to Those at the Beginning of Stage 1
		Teaching	Truth Encounters	
		Challenges to Commitment	Allegiance Encounters	

Figure 27.2 Summary of the encounters in three stages

It is crucial, therefore, that we emphasize power in such societies (as Jesus did). But it is also crucial that we emphasize allegiance and truth encounters as well (as Jesus did). Power demonstrations are extremely valuable but do not in and of themselves get the whole message across. They are means, not ends. The teaching of truth and the constant challenge to greater allegiance need to go hand in hand with power encounters.

The figure 27.2 above summarizes the above discussion, focusing on the use of the encounters in three successive stages of Christian experience.

For more detailed treatments of the three encounters and the problem of dual allegiance, see Kraft 1991b and 1992b and Kraft and Kraft 1993.

MEANING EQUIVALENCE CHRISTIANITY

Just as Jesus is our model for personal belief and behavior, the ideal we advocate for Christian belief and practice in the broader sense is an equivalence of meaning to that recorded in Scripture. The biblical documents record for us both Jesus' example and what was done with it by His earliest followers as they lived and proclaimed the Gospel within and outside of its original context. We suggest that, since God adapts to people within their cultures, *this equivalence should be in meaning, function, or dynamic, not merely in form*. Thus we speak of meaning (formerly "dynamic") equivalence Christianity. This would contrast with what might be termed *formal correspondence Christianity*, an approach in which the cultural forms of Christian expression are simply exported from one society to another, always looking like foreign imports in the receiving society.

In my book *Christianity in Culture* (1979a), I discuss the fact that much Christianity in nonwestern societies looks like literal Bible translations such as the King James Version, American Standard Version, Revised Standard Version, and, unfortunately, the more recent New International Version. The language of these literal translations is formal at best and "Greekized" and "Hebrewized" at worst. It does not flow as if the writing had been done by someone who really knows English and could write expertly so ordinary people could understand it. The impression is given that God only comes partway down to meet us in language and that He has not worked very hard to be understood. This is quite unlike the original documents, which were largely in the highly communicative common people's vernaculars of their day.

Those who translate literally from one language to another make the mistake of assuming that languages are more similar than they are in the way they express given meanings. As we learned in chapter 15, languages are unique and often express essentially the same meanings in quite different ways. A good translation will express the message as differently from the original as necessary to get the message across effectively to those who can be expected to know no other reality than their own language. Literal translations create the impression that God requires us to learn a strange variety of our language in order to understand Him. Such translations do not live up to what J. B. Phillips contends ought to be two of the basic rules for a translation. First, a translation

> must not sound like a translation at all. If it is skillfully done, and we are not previously informed, we should be quite unaware that it is a translation, even though the work we are reading is far distant from us in both time and place . . . and [the] final test which a good translator should be able to pass is that of being able to produce in the hearts and minds of his readers an effective equivalent to that produced by the author upon his original readers (Phillips 1958:ix).

Though there are no perfect translations, the Phillips, the Good News Bible, and the Living Bible come closer to this ideal than the literal translations mentioned above. These come closer to being what we call *meaning equivalence translations* than do the others. That is, there is a greater likelihood that people will respond to such versions as if they were not translations and that that response will be more like that of the original hearers than would the response to the literal translations.

Using the contrast between meaning equivalence translations and the literal, formal correspondence translations as a springboard, I suggest several areas within Christianity that often look foreign in nonwestern societies but ought to be more meaning equivalent to biblical models. Among them are transculturation of the Christian message, theologizing, church, conversion and cultural transformation.

1. By *meaning equivalence transculturation* of the message, I mean that we are to go beyond the adaptations allowed in translation as we present the messages of Christianity. "The term 'transculturate' is intended to signify with respect to cul-

ture what the term 'translate' signifies with respect to language. . . . A translation is tied to historical facts. In transculturation, however, the aim is to represent the meanings of those historical events as if they were clothed in contemporary events" (Kraft 1979a:280).

As we found in chapter 16, there are many more ways to communicate than simply through words, and even with the use of words, there are more effective ways than simply to monologue. Transculturation makes use of whatever techniques are appropriate to the receptors. It also attempts to make messages that were first communicated in other places and other times come across as if they had first been crafted in the receiving society. Translation, for example, presents Jesus as walking the dusty paths of first-century Palestine. This is historically accurate. Transculturation recognizes that Jesus could have come into any other society at any other time in history and therefore presents Jesus as if He were a member of a contemporary society. Both approaches represent truth—the one historical truth, the other the broader truth of what could have been.

A verbal form of transculturation appears in several presentations of parts of the Bible for special groups. For example, several years ago, a version of Paul's letters was produced for "street people" entitled *Letters to Street Christians* (Two Brothers from Berkeley, 1971). James 2:15–17 is rendered: "Like if a brother or sister doesn't have any clothes or enough to eat and you say 'see ya around, keep warm and eat right.' If you don't give them any food or clothes, what good is all your rhetoric? A plastic trust in Jesus that doesn't cause you to act like Him is DEAD."

Even though this rendering goes beyond what is allowed a translator, for a particular audience, such a presentation could have an impact very like that experienced by the citizens of the Roman Empire who first heard it in Koine Greek. Good, down-to-earth sermonizing can also be effective transculturation, as can drama and the life-specific daily living of the Gospel of committed Christians.

2. *Meaning equivalence theologizing* is a second application that can be made of this model. I have spoken in chapter 6 of the contextualization of theology. The theologizing process involves people reflecting upon God and His workings as presented in Scripture and experienced in contemporary life from their own perspectives. Theologizing, then, involves data (e.g., Scripture and experience) reflected upon from a cultural perspective. We contend that, just as God is pleased to work in terms of human cultures to interact with human beings, so He respects the culturally conditioned perceptions of the people He works with. So we speak of a number of different *theologies*, each conditioned by the perspective of the person(s) who developed them.

In certain parts of Scripture, we have recorded the results of theological reflection. Paul is especially given to such theologizing. It is my contention that Christians from every society are allowed and should be encouraged to reflect from their perspectives and organize those reflections in whatever ways are appropriate to their society for use within that context. Not all theologizing needs to be done by academics, or even by literates. Much Old Testament reflection is in ritual form or in the names of God. Song was and is a favorite way. The point is that people today should be doing theology in ways that are as appropriate to their contexts as was the theologizing of biblical peoples.

3. We should encourage *meaning equivalence churches*. Many churches look in their contexts like literal translations look in their languages—imported. One can travel all over Japan or nearly any other nonwestern country and easily identify

the churches because of their foreignness. But the foreignness does not stop at the buildings. The organizational, leadership, educational, and worship structures are usually foreign as well. Sunday mornings too often find nonwestern Christians meeting at a foreign time in a foreign building, seated in a foreign way, singing translated songs to western tunes guided by western instruments, followed by a western-type monologue presentation called a sermon.

Such church custom did not come from the first century, though it would have been equally inappropriate if it had. It came from foreigners who simply imported their cultural practices and imposed them on people, whether or not they conveyed the intended meanings. In most parts of the world, Christianity is distinctly foreign.

Meaning equivalence churches, on the other hand, would look and sound like they belong in the receiving society. People might then get the impression that God accepts them within their own cultures, rather than only on condition that they practice their Christianity with a foreign accent within their own land.

4. There can also be *meaning equivalence conversion*. Again, with respect to conversion, the patterns are often very foreign. As we have learned, most of the peoples of the world are group-oriented rather than individualistic. In the West, though, we convert largely as individuals and theologize that this is the scriptural way for conversion to happen. This is appropriate for an individualistic society.

For much of the world, however, major decisions are always made within the group and announced at the appropriate time by the leaders. Once announced, the whole group accepts and follows the decision. Biblically, such a pattern was employed by Abraham and probably all other Old Testament characters. In the New Testament, the Philippian jailer of Acts 16 was told by Paul that his decision would result in the salvation of his whole household (v. 31). The point is, conversion patterns should be as appropriate to the cultural context as all other aspects of Christianity. God requires a response, but He desires that it be understood by those responding from within the only way of life they have known. They do not have to respond in a foreign way.

5. *Culturally appropriate transformation of a people's way of life* is a desired outcome of the introduction of Christianity. Though God is willing to start where people are, within their cultural context, the planting of Gospel seeds will always result in changes. God accepted Abraham's culture as His starting point with Abraham, but as soon as Abraham responded, the changes started. As he lived his customs for God, he and God shaped them to be more adequate vehicles for their interaction. As we have seen, God works in and through people to change cultures. To do this, He uses people to change cultural structures for His purposes.

CONCLUSION

These are some of the ways in which this approach to Christian witness impacts our theological positions. Many of us have gone to the field as missionaries armed only with western theological understandings. And many, though working within their own nonwestern societies, have been taught such understandings as if they were the only possible correct interpretations of Scripture. Both groups have found such theological understandings often inadequate and sometimes quite misleading in nonwestern contexts. This is not necessarily because the theology taught in western institutions is wrong. Indeed, it is usually quite right for those who developed it, but these have usually been western scholars speaking in a western scholarly context.

The problem is that a change of sociocultural context requires that scriptural data be looked at in terms of perspectives and questions appropriate to *that* context. Though the Scriptures are from God, the interpretive perspective in terms of which God's messages can connect with the receptors must be that of the receivers of the messages, if those messages are to be understood and acted upon as God intends that they be understood and acted upon. This is why we consider it so important to take a new look at our theologies from a cross-cultural point of view: that the world may hear clearly. See Kraft 1979a for more on this topic.

PART VI

RESEARCH AND STUDY

CHAPTER 28

RESEARCH AND STUDY

INTEGRATIONAL THOUGHT

Proverbs 3:5, 6 are among the most familiar verses in the Bible. The Good News translation, however, brings a refreshing clarity to these verses (as to many others)—clarity in an area that we need to pay close attention to, if we have taken the approach of this book seriously. The verses read: "Trust in the Lord with all your heart. *Never rely on what you think you know.* Remember the Lord in everything you do, and he will show you the right way" (emphasis added).

Verse 7 adds, "Never let yourself think that you are wiser than you are."

Knowledge is a dangerous thing, but only if we trust it! In this book, we have been seeking knowledge and insight. As we have noted continually, it is not enough for the cross-cultural Christian worker to be dedicated and committed to Christ. Too many with only spiritual commitment have made what look like disastrous mistakes in cultural areas.

We have cited the research concerning the cultural disruption brought about through the unwise introduction of steel axes by missionaries among the Yir Yoront (Sharp 1952). I don't think we have any right to criticize the spiritual qualifications of those missionaries. They probably were beyond reproach in their relationship with God. Nevertheless, He allowed them to make what looks in retrospect like an enormous blunder.

I don't know why God allowed such a blunder, yet it appears that He frequently leaves uncorrected even major errors made by His most committed servants. Other evidence suggests, however, that those of God's servants who understand more of the things presented in this book make fewer mistakes than others—at least in cultural and communicational areas.

We should seek knowledge and understanding in these areas with all our hearts. God has given us this insight to use in His service. By absorbing it, we can avoid some of the mistakes of the past and do His work more effectively. Right?

Well, maybe, but only if we are careful to recognize that 1) God's work cannot be accomplished through purely human means and 2) human knowledge can never be trusted.

Apparently we are called to some kind of balance between spiritual dedication and human insight. Even in the most "secular" of the things we do for God "we are not fighting against human beings but against the wicked spiritual forces in the heavenly world, the rulers, authorities, and cosmic powers of this dark age" (Eph 6:12).

We are, therefore, to "put on all the armor God gives [us]" and to "do this in prayer, asking for God's help" (Eph 6:11, 18). But Jesus frequently compliments those who make good use of human wisdom as, for example, in Luke 16:8, where He says, "the people of this world are much more shrewd in handling their affairs than the people who belong to the light."

Seek that balance. Never relax in your quest for spiritual vitality or human understanding. But take heed of the advice of the writer of Proverbs 3:5—*never trust your knowledge*. God alone is to be the object of our trust. We are to trust in Him "with all our heart"—and in Hebrew "heart" includes the mind. *Knowledge is to be sought, but never trusted.* What God really wants is not knowledge but that we "do what is just . . . show constant love, and . . . live in humble fellowship with our God" (Mi 6:8). We must never forget, no matter how knowledgeable we become, that all human insight is "small r" reality and never to be relied upon in the way we can rely on God.

This is a good word on which to launch our chapter on research and study, for the only valid starting point for research is the assumption, "We don't know." Especially in cross-cultural research, we must always maintain a fairly humble attitude toward our ability to penetrate with much assurance a world built on assumptions often radically different from our own.

INTRODUCTION

It would be a sad thing if we completed this book and had too high an opinion of what we have learned. This has been barely an introduction to what human cultures are like, and only from a single point of view. My hope is that your horizons have been widened, your imaginations stimulated, and your minds alerted to some of the kinds of help available to you in this area.

There is, however, still a lot to gain, a lot farther to probe, so we want to conclude this book by talking about research and study. We want to challenge you to continue the quest you have started and to point you to some of the possibilities for learning more.

What you have received is a gift or possession that you are not to bury. Remember the Parable of the Talents (Mt 25:14–30). The man who had the one talent thought, "My master is a shrewd master, so I will bury this." The master said,

"No. Unless you have risked, you have not fulfilled my will. Unless you use what you have and risk losing it by using it, you are to be condemned." The talent was taken from that person not because the master was unfair but because that person refused to use what he had. *The whole purpose of what has been said here is that it be used.* Using these insights will lead to new insights; neglecting or burying them will lead to loss of whatever you have gained.

THE NEED TO STUDY AS WELL AS TO DO

No two situations are ever the same. We cannot, therefore, assume too much, even if we think we recognize what is going on, for we come into every situation as outsiders. Even when working in our own society, each situation has a newness to it, since it has never happened in exactly that way before. We have to recognize the newness as well as the familiar aspects and face both as wisely as possible.

Furthermore, we often come into situations more or less uninvited, or invited for reasons different from what we assumed. This raises problems for us as we attempt to build bridges into the situation. If we don't study it thoroughly, we're likely to make many more mistakes than we ought to.

Speaking mostly to Americans at this point, we Americans are able to enter any situation with an open mouth. We usually begin talking before we have listened. We are likely to assume we know what's going on and, therefore, to begin teaching before we have really learned anything about the people and their needs. Often, though, most of what we know is from books. We usually have not learned how to study people by associating with them, yet it is people we seek to reach, people in their own cultural contexts, people who are very different from us, people we need to learn about and from in *social, not academic contexts.*

Perhaps the most important part of this chapter is that *the starting point for all solid investigation and ministry is the statement,* "We don't know, *but we're going to try our best to find out.*" If we'll start with that assumption, we'll enter every situation with a proper *learner attitude.* Even if it looks familiar, we'll protect ourselves from overconfidence by asking questions rather than attempting too soon to give answers. We need to see ourselves as learners rather than teachers.

Our task is to communicate Christ, usually to those who have a worldview at least partly different from our own. This is undoubtedly the most demanding task in the world. Whether our job is to communicate to those who have never heard or to disciple those who have responded, the task is not easy, and there are many pitfalls.

Such a task demands, in the first place, the best we can give. In the second place, it demands that we participate fully with the Holy Spirit. Third, it demands that we follow God's plan and become human beings within the receptors' frame of reference in order to win and disciple them.

It looks as if *when we do our job better, the Holy Spirit does His job better.* That may seem a bit presumptuous. But we must wrestle with questions such as, How come when we mess things up, the Holy Spirit doesn't straighten them out? And how come when we do things well, the Holy Spirit blesses? The constant in the situation is the Holy Spirit; the variable is us. We are trying to improve our part so there will be greater freedom for the Holy Spirit to work *through* our wisdom, rather than to have to counter our ignorance. With that desire, we try to use the materials that anthropologists have provided for us to serve the Lord.

Serving God in His way requires that we imitate God's approach and work incarnationally. We are, therefore, to become human beings to people within a foreign cultural world. This is even more difficult than it would appear, since every people, every group, has its own definition of what a human being is. We come "from Mars," as it were, and don't know what human beingness is to insiders. We are presenting a person message, not a word message, a message that God Himself felt had to be communicated person to person. The God of the universe, who could have done anything in any mechanical way He wanted—through microphones, satellites, etc.—came as a human being.

Throughout this book, the goal in view is to communicate the person message of Christianity in a person-to-person way, as human beings to other human beings. We go to them not so much with our talents as with our person. This is the way the message is to get across. Whenever God wanted something done in the Scriptures, He worked through persons, not through mechanical things. The mechanical things can be used as long as they are proper extensions of the person, as long as they do not depersonalize that message.

I think some of the greatest heresies abroad today relate not so much to theological beliefs as to the mechanization and the depersonalization of the Christian message. When the method is impersonal and Christianity becomes merely a matter of doctrine rather than behavior, of intellectual knowledge rather than a matter of response and actual living, we have, I believe, a greater heresy than most of the kinds of heresy theologians talk about.

Yet we're likely to do just that—to go as bundles of knowledge and ability, specialists who see ourselves as purveyors of knowledge, as teaching machines. We are likely to evaluate ourselves in terms of the amount of information we get across, rather than in terms of our personalness and our ability to influence human beings to be all that God intends them to be.

PREPARATION FOR THE TASK

In considering the preparation we need, I would like to focus on three areas. 1) The one we have spent most of our time on in this volume is learning about the receptors in their cultural contexts. It is at this point that an anthropological approach makes its greatest contribution. 2) Always implicit and sometimes explicit in our study here is the use of this approach to enable us to see more clearly the biblical meanings God wants us to communicate. 3) Not to be ignored is the need to focus these tools and whatever others may be available to learn about ourselves. We need to study ourselves and, if necessary, free ourselves up from cultural, spiritual, emotional and any other hindrances to doing the job God has called us to do.

1. As Foster (1973) points out, western schooling at best prepares people for living and working within western settings. It tends to confirm and increase the ethnocentrism of westerners and do little, if anything, to enable us to function in relation to the sociocultural diversity of the rest of the world. For nonwesterners, western schooling, even when it is received in one's (nonwestern) home country, tends to glorify western customs and values and denigrate those of one's home society.

The upshot is that westerners ordinarily learn virtually nothing that will be helpful in cross-cultural work. Nonwesterners often find themselves strongly driven to go to or to stay in the West, since it is western society (not their own) that they have been trained to function in. The so-called educational process to which they have been subjected has been a process of weaning them from the life they are supposedly preparing for, rather than of preparing them for that life.

Within western societies, even those who recognize the need for training for cross-cultural workers are often not very aware of what is needed. Indeed, the very idea of training for cross-cultural ministry is often squelched by an attitude such as, "If you're going to work in a western society, you need a high level of preparation. But if you're just going to work in some nonwestern area, you don't need to be that well prepared."

By this point in this volume, readers are well aware that only by means of a rather thorough retraining program can we achieve the skills we need to function effectively in cross-cultural settings. We need training that will prepare us to meet, learn, and function in a world in which all the rules are different.

2. The Bible, the medium for us of the messages God wishes to communicate, is a cross-cultural book. We need, therefore, to study and teach it from a cross-cultural perspective in order to understand its riches for ourselves and communicate them to others with a minimum of distortion from our cultural background.

3. In addition, we need to attain as high a level of spiritual maturity and intimacy with Christ as possible. This is seldom developed simply by attending seminary or Bible school. We should give solid attention to searching books and attending retreats designed to assist us in developing and maintaining our spiritual life in difficult places. Learning how to teach ourselves in this area is at least as important as in any of the other areas mentioned.

Closely related to the need to develop intimacy with Christ is the need to get rid of whatever spiritual and emotional garbage has collected within us. With so much family dysfunction and so much breakdown in traditional values, I find a disturbing number of cross-cultural witnesses needing a lot of healing and often deliverance from demons. As we research the receiving society and the biblical meanings, we must not forget to research ourselves and, if necessary, to seek healing. Unfortunately, I have found many cross-cultural workers crippled by the enemy because they were carrying unresolved spiritual and emotional issues that gave the enemy a legal right to harass them. They were not like Jesus who, when the ruler of this world came along, he "could find nothing in Him" (Jn 14:30). Kraft 1989, 1992a, and 1993 have been written to deal with these needs.

With regard to all of these issues, I suggest a lifetime program of research and study. I suggest, furthermore, that it be a program that you, the learner, take charge of. Whether it involves advanced degrees or not doesn't matter much, though, to be realistic, we often find that our previous conditioning is such that we will learn more in a program in which the pressures of exams, grades, and theses are prominent. What does matter is that we first learn how to learn and then go about the process of instructing ourselves quite intentionally. The habit of studying and analyzing may be one of the best habits you ever developed.

RESOURCES AVAILABLE

Many Christians and their organizations don't seem to know what the world knows about how to research, strategize, and organize work such as ours. Perhaps we feel that God will overrule any deficiencies in our strategies if we only pray enough. Perhaps we feel that the strategies themselves are ordained of God. Perhaps we are simply too conservative and unwilling to learn the lesson of the Parable of the Talents; we must risk if we are to get anywhere in the Kingdom. In this regard, I'd like to raise several questions concerning what we do with the resources available to us.

1. First, let's ask if and how Christian organizations attempt to discover how to do God's work better. How much time, money, and skill do we put into evaluating, testing, and experimenting with our approaches? In a day when many secular industries put 5 to 15 percent or more of their financial resources into research so they can learn how to sell their products better, how much do Christian organizations spend in this important area? Manufacturers of such things as soap, toothpaste, drinks, automobiles, electronic equipment, cameras, and even those who sell "better" ideas for weight reduction, health, beauty, financial investment, and the like, all know they cannot survive if they do not do the research necessary to enable them to keep ahead of the competition.

Shouldn't those who are in competition with Satan for the souls of the creatures God cares most about be at least as wise as those who seek to sell soda and cars?

How much is put into research by your mission or your church to try to learn how to do the most important job better? Usually the percentage is zero or slightly above. We think that as long as we are sincere, we can't do things very badly, and God will make up for our lack of understanding. A percentage ought to be put into research. Mission boards and churches ought to support some of their members as they study and research both on the field and in overseas institutions (e.g., in graduate programs that focus on such study and research). Then, of course, the results of the research will need to be listened to, discussed, and implemented.

Unfortunately, the idea of researching God's work seems to be considered threatening by many Christian organizations. They are often afraid to allow their work to be subjected to the scrutiny of research. Or perhaps they have heard of research that has been done and has not turned out well. Yet there seems to be so much of God's talent and money wasted because there is no research, or because the approach to research was not wise. Often it does not take much research and study to figure out what is wrong with the present approach and what to do about it. However, research can go bad. There have been times when someone claimed to have done some research and succeeded in getting his or her colleagues to change their approach, only to discover later that nothing better has resulted. This often happens either because the research was done wrongly or the idea was not tested before the group decided to adopt it and pour its resources into it. People may assume that the person who did the study and suggested the change was godly and therefore couldn't go that far wrong.

But research is, like everything else we do, a human endeavor, so things can and do go wrong from time to time. But things go more wrong when we do not do the evaluation, testing, critiquing, and changing that God expects us to do, so we recommend research and study.

2. Research may be done by those inside or outside of the organization, or by a team made up of both kinds of people. Often there are those within an organization who are gifted in the area of research. Such people should be trained and set aside to carry out this very important task for the benefit of all. The most important contribution certain people could make to the organization of which they are a part might be to study the whole operation and suggest changes. This might be their gifting. In any event, someone within each Christian organization of any size

ought to be so occupied for at least part of the time, if the rest of the members are to do their jobs properly. Wycliffe Bible Translators has been a pleasant exception among missionary organizations in that it has built research into its ordinary operating procedures at several points.

At The Fuller School of World Mission (as well as in equivalent programs at such institutions as Asbury Seminary, Biola University, Columbia International University, Trinity Evangelical Divinity School, and others), people are trained to do such research. Several years ago, an executive of a mission board called me regarding one of their missionaries who had studied here. His basic question was, "How can we best utilize this person now that he has gained the insight you have taught him?" My suggestion was that they appoint him as their "designated researcher." In that position, he could do research on any problem identified by his colleagues as significant and report his findings to the body as a whole. I suggested that the missionaries and church leaders get together at least twice a year for the purpose of hearing and discussing his report and recommendations and then choosing the problem(s) he would be assigned to during the next six months. Such an assignment would be appropriate to that missionary's gifts, training, and interests and, in addition, would be a very good step in the right direction for a mission that has been experiencing quite a number of problems lately. They didn't take my advice.

A growing number of church organizations working cross-culturally are beginning to take at least first steps in the direction we are suggesting by sponsoring some of their members for study in missiology. Sometimes they are foresighted enough to send both a missionary and a national to study together. Many master's and doctoral theses are solid contributions to bettering our understandings of how to work more effectively with God in cross-cultural ministry. I know of at least one missionary team (about five couples) who trained as a team, required that each couple do research while on the field (which they reported to each other annually), and encouraged each participant to continue study and research while on furlough.

I know of another mission that set up its pioneer workers in teams consisting of church planter, anthropologist, linguist and literacy worker. Each trained and did research in his or her own area of expertise for the benefit of all. Though they worked together in the broad spectrum of Christian ministries that were the central focus of their commitment, they worked complementarily in their special areas.

In addition to such research by members of the organization, much help can be gained from outside consultants. From the early fifties—when people such as Eugene Nida, William and Marie Reyburn, and William Smalley were doing anthropological consulting under the auspices of the American Bible Society—some of this has been going on. A decade or so later, Donald McGavran and Alan Tippett began to be similarly involved with missionary organizations from time to time. There are many others by now who, either as individuals or as representatives of research-oriented organizations, are able to serve as consultants. Though the amount of insight and expertise is increasing, not nearly enough is being done to really grapple creatively with many of the pressing cultural problems encountered by missions and churches across the world.

One of the most exciting things to see is the cooperation that often develops between perceptive cultural insiders and the westerners who seek to serve God among them. Sometimes the cultural insiders seem to come by their perceptiveness naturally. In other cases, certain of them are getting training that enables them to take advantage of the kind of insights being taught here. Then they can discuss problems that need to be dealt with both as cultural insiders and as those with technical missiological expertise. To bring about such a possibility, some mission organizations have sent a national and a missionary together for advanced missiological study. Such a combination of informed cultural outsider and informed cultural insider working together to research and strategize a given church situation has great potential.

3. Getting research done is, however, only part of the problem. Sometimes a church or mission is farsighted enough to arrange for the research, but then does not follow the recommendations. I remember reading one research report produced several years ago that perceptively, helpfully, and comprehensively analyzed the total mission situation. The mission, however, in spite of the fact that they were in deep trouble, totally ignored the report, perhaps because the changes recommended were so radical. As the researchers predicted, the consequences were dire, and the work did not end happily.

In another case, Dr. and Mrs. William Reyburn were asked to study the situation of a Mennonite mission working in Argentina and to make recommendations. They spent some time studying the situation and concluded that much of the problem stemmed from the opposition of the missionaries to the Pentecostal type of Christianity the people were already practicing when they came. Since this was not their tradition, the Mennonites had felt called to convert both those who were already believers and the new converts to Mennonite ways. It was not working. The recommendation of the researchers was that the missionaries recognize the validity of the brand of Christianity already being practiced, refrain from opposing it, and offer their services to the people to help them in areas where their own resources were inadequate. The mission took this advice, changed its policies, and became quite successful in aiding a Christian movement very different from its tradition but fitting the receptors well. They chose to work with God in what He was already doing, rather than push for their own approach to Christianity.

Often what comes up in the research process is a facet of the culture of the people that has been overlooked by the Christian workers. Once Alan Tippett was invited by a mission working among the Navaho to do a study of their mission. During his research he noted that the growing churches each had a strong woman song leader. He asked some of the missionaries if they had noticed this. They hadn't. So he asked, "What leadership positions do women have in the church?" They replied, "None." Then he asked, "Don't you know that these are matrilineal people?" Apparently they had been working there for years and didn't recognize that among a matrilineal people, women have to be in important positions if anything is to work properly. Most of their churches were not growing due to some extent to the strongly male-oriented leadership patterns being required by the mission. But some of the congregations had successfully circumvented the problem, and people were responding to female leadership in the song-leading position. Often an outside researcher can see things that the insider cannot see.

4. As aids to research and study, whether on an institutional or an individual level, it is encouraging to see more and more informed writing being done. The number of missiological books incorporating solid anthropological insight is increasing, as is the number of theses and dissertations at the schools mentioned above and elsewhere. In addition, we have several good journals, such as *Interna-*

tional Bulletin of Missionary Research, Missiology, and *Evangelical Missions Quarterly,* that are putting out helpful missiological articles. Subscribe to these journals and encourage the libraries of your institutions to have them as well.

TIMES OF RESEARCH AND STUDY

Though we believe research and study should be a constant focus of cross-cultural ministries, the kind of activity appropriate for any given individual at any given time may differ according to the stage in which one finds oneself. It is important for one to do a good bit of *pre-field learning* prior to leaving for the field. I believe it is not usually a good idea to spend more than one year of specialized schooling before going to the field. A solid year of missiological study at this time can, however, enable cross-cultural workers to better understand what they are experiencing and thus avoid many of the pitfalls awaiting the uninformed. The movement toward spiritual and emotional freedom, plus the development of a strong and intimate relationship with Jesus, should be important focuses of pre-field learning as well.

At this stage, a person needs to learn how to learn—both spiritually and in the transformation of worldview—to accommodate new insights in areas crucial to cross-cultural ministry. Given the fact that western schooling does not ordinarily teach us how to learn (only how to be taught), this may mean the acquiring of a completely new skill. An important part of learning how to learn is learning how to organize one's learning without the guidance of a teacher or the pressure of examinations and grades.

In both biblical and cultural areas, we need to acquire the proper attitudes and learn such things as the kinds of question to ask. We also need to learn how to go about learning the language and the cultural perspective of the receiving people. Though much of the training given in these areas won't really make sense until we are on the field and putting what we have learned into practice, it is better for us to have been instructed than to not have been instructed. It is enormously helpful for one to go into a cross-cultural situation with one's mind and imagination already expanded to the point where "strange" things are expected and accepted, rather than coming as shocks and automatically rejected and condemned.

Previous to going to the field, it is possible for us to expand our understandings of what is possible and to learn to appreciate diversity. Pre-field training in both spiritual and cultural areas can be the catalyst for such learning and can go a long way toward warding off the worst effects of culture stress. The value of such training has been proven if one develops a "learner" attitude, enabling one to say, "I don't know but am willing to learn." In many ways, our education is just beginning when we get to the field. If, therefore, we go out with the attitude that our education is complete and doesn't need to be added to, tragedy awaits.

With the proper attitude toward the need for further learning, it is important for research and study to continue all the time we are on the field. We should never stop studying ourselves, the people to whom we go, our relationship with them, the impact of our presence and activity on them, and the influence of all of this on our relationship to God and our understanding and application of His messages in that context. A good plan is that adopted by the group mentioned above that trained together and went as a team. Each member of the team did a study each year in preparation for a yearly get-together at which they presented and discussed the various studies. They then each took another assignment for the next year. This gave a formalized way of studying while they were serving. Though that group focused almost exclusively on studying and discussing cultural and language factors, I would add the need for us to study and discuss spiritual factors as well. Living in a cultural context not our own raises many spiritual issues we may not have faced at home. Among these is the fact that in cross-cultural contexts we face forms and intensity of spiritual warfare we may not have experienced at home. Books such as my *Christianity with Power* (1989), *Deep Wounds, Deep Healing* (1993), *Defeating Dark Angels* (1992a), and *Behind Enemy Lines* (1994), plus numerous other books cited in the bibliographies of these books, are designed to assist cross-cultural witnesses with this area.

Missionaries who have regular furloughs can spend at least parts of their furlough time in analysis and reflection. As they get away from the immediate problems of the situation, they can see things in a broader perspective, especially if guided by the faculty and students in a good missiological training program.

The following chart is an attempt to suggest how much time and energy might profitably be put into study and research, versus how much might be put into ministry during the first three terms of the career of a cross-cultural worker. The exact percentages are not as important as that both research and ministry be planned for.

Stage of Career	Learning	Ministry
Pre-field	100%	
1st Term	85%	15%
1st Furlough	70%	30%
2nd Term	50%	50%
2nd Furlough	50%	50%
3rd Term	30%	70%

Figure 28.1 Suggested percentages of time put into learning and ministry

I suggest that 100 percent of pre-field preparation time be spent in learning, including research, study, and spiritual preparation. During the first term, a large percentage of one's time and energy should be given to learning, and a smaller percentage to ministry. Likewise on the first furlough. As time goes on, the amount of time devoted to ministry rises, but learning never completely stops. We always need to study what we do, as well as to do it.

METHODS OF RESEARCH AND STUDY

We've mentioned the "participant-observation" method of anthropological field investigation. This is simply a method for studying people in their regular life pursuits. It depends on the investigator first becoming thoroughly familiar with whatever can be learned concerning people in culture in general and concerning the people to be studied (or related peoples) in particular. On this basis, we are prepared to observe the people with greater insight and accuracy than otherwise. We observe them as we live among them, participating (as a learner) in as much of their life as possible. In this way we seek to develop both knowledge about the people's way of life and an appreciation for how it feels to be an insider (a participant) in the society. There are several valuable published guides to this and other anthropological research methods, among them Pelto and Pelto 1978, Spradley 1979, 1980, and Bernard 1988.

We should, likewise, be observing and analyzing our own behavior and attitudes and making mid-course corrections as necessary. In analyzing ourselves, we should not fail to focus on the spiritual dimensions, including our own spiritual life in general and our perspectives on the Scriptures. These latter may change dramatically as we attempt to see Scripture through the eyes of another people.

Though we can never fully become cultural insiders, participant-observation enables us to understand as much as we can, given the limitations springing from the fact that we were not enculturated by one of their mothers. If secular anthropologists are willing to go this far to understand and identify with the peoples of other societies, how much more should those whose aim is to communicate Christ?

In addition to participant-observation, a method that has served anthropologists well over the years, many anthropologists are now employing an approach to research in which a cultural insider becomes a co-researcher. The aim of such an approach is to produce research that more effectively blends the insights of an informed outsider with those of a genuine insider.

Previously anthropologists tended to use insiders simply as informants, often in a more or less exploitive way. Anthropologists saw themselves as the analysts, with the insiders simply as sources of information (never of interpretation) collected and interpreted by the researchers. The latter would then write up their findings either in doctoral dissertations or for publication and get famous for their presentations of materials provided by cultural insiders. The ethicality of such a procedure is being questioned and, for some at least, is being replaced by more of a partnership model for doing research. Such a model regards both outsiders and insiders as researchers and requires that the name(s) of the insider(s) appear on any publications along with that of the anthropologist(s). As Christians we can only applaud, and imitate, such a model.

Some governments are even beginning to require that the results of anthropological research be made available to them. They will allow anthropological work in their area only if researchers will agree to provide all their findings in a written report for their use. Sometimes governments will be even stronger than that and allow outsiders to study their people only on condition that they do something helpful for the people they are studying. Perhaps that kind of pressure is a good idea.

As Christians who claim to live ethically, we too should be careful about what we do with the information we get, lest we also be found guilty of exploiting the people for our purposes rather than learning about them in order to help them.

DIFFICULTIES IN CROSS-CULTURAL RESEARCH AND STUDY

1. The first difficulty to consider is that of *bias*. Though it is impossible for humans (even those who are anthropologically trained) to be unbiased, we should always strive to protect our research as much as possible, from either negative or positive bias. We should attempt as researchers to get as much inside their world as possible in order to understand things from their point of view. We should be careful to evaluate their customs as a part of their context without (at least at this point) passing judgment on them. Any judgments concerning the usability of their customs within Christianity should be made at a later stage, and always by insiders under the guidance of the Holy Spirit (with or without assistance from outsid-

ers). The research and study stage should, however, be kept quite distinct from the later evaluation stage, no matter how objectionable the outsider might find the custom.

In considering the potentially negative effects of bias, it is important to recognize that the kind of personal involvement we have been recommending is not necessarily the kind of hindrance that has often been felt in scientific circles. I remember listening to an anthropologist who made no pretensions of being a Christian, as far as I know. She was talking about her study of the religion of a people in Africa and expressed her frustration. She said, "I have come to the conclusion that no anthropologist should study somebody else's religion who is not deeply committed to some religion herself." She was recognizing that in the study of human beings, one's ability to understand is increased rather than decreased by participation in the equivalent activity within one's own society. She also seemed to be bemoaning the fact that her own lack of religious commitment seemed to block her in her attempt to study the religion of an African people.

Sometimes anthropologists will give missionaries the impression that we are so biased, because of our religious convictions, that we cannot do an adequate job anthropologically. On the contrary, I think we can say to these anthropologists that the very doctrine of participant-observation and the recognition of our own subjectivity mean that we have a tool to understand supernaturalistically oriented people that goes beyond the tools that irreligious anthropologists have. We don't need to apologize for this, even though we, like they, must still be aware of and take steps to counter our own ethnocentrism.

2. A second problem we may face is a *lack of cooperation by the people we seek to study*. They don't know why we ask all these questions. Often they can't conceive of anybody not knowing what we are asking about. They likely assume that we have been taught the same things they have been taught. If, therefore, we had listened to our mothers as we were growing up, we would have gotten it. What they don't realize is that we had different mothers. We may therefore meet some resistance. Yet if we are observant and careful in the way we ask questions, we can get much good information.

In some cases, the people we seek to study will not be truthful with us. They may seek to hide from us the information we want, or they may simply be playing a game entitled, Let's see how frustrated we can make this foreigner. Or they may not know the answer to our question and, being too ashamed to admit their lack of knowledge, decide to make up an answer to keep us happy.

E. E. Evans-Pritchard ran into another serious hindrance to research in his fieldwork among the Nuer of East Africa. After a period of initial hostility to his presence among them, they insisted

> that he live as one of them—as a full-fledged member of the community. He had no choice but to live intimately with them, and this put such demands upon him that it was impossible to escape their everyday life enough to hold confidential interviews with trained informants. . . . the compelled participation (even the most intimate aspects of life had to be performed before an audience) meant that information came to him in small fragments and, in spite of the intimacy—or because of it—he learned relatively little about them (R. Taylor 1973:109 based on Evans-Pritchard 1940).

3. A further set of difficulties we may experience arises from *improper attitudes on our part*. We may, for example, *not respect the people* we seek to study and work among. As Smalley (1958b) points out, many cross-cultural witnesses (both

westerners and nonwesterners) carry with them to other societies an unconscious unwillingness to respect the people they seek to serve. This kind of attitude cripples both research and ministry.

Cross-cultural workers may have a *poor self-image*. Their own insecurities may lead them to dominate those they work among, even though they know better. Insecure persons, feeling unconsciously threatened by others, often become harsh, dominating, and judgmental. They may believe that each group has the right to produce its own brand of Christianity but, because of their insecurities, may dominate in spite of themselves. Kraft 1993 is a publication aimed at helping with this problem.

Persons in *culture shock* may behave in a similar manner. Culture stress throws people off balance. This often results in their making desperate attempts to regain their psychological equilibrium at the expense of both sound thinking concerning what they are doing and healthy relationships with those with whom they are involved.

A *know-it-all attitude* cripples ministry. The researcher's, "I don't know, but I'm going to learn," attitude enhances ministry. Such an attitude often leads the receptors to ask their own questions about the aims and motives of the Christian witness. Those questions are asked in their time, when they are ready for them, and give the best kind of opportunity for witness.

4. A final area of difficulty that impedes both research and ministry is *the temptation to hold the people we work with accountable to live up to too high a standard too soon*. God is very patient with people who, though striving to live up to His standards, are still far short of them. He has been patient with us for years, yet it seems to be the tendency for cross-cultural witnesses to expect too much too fast from their converts and disciples.

We have often worked out theologically what the ideals of Christianity are. We have diligently studied the Scriptures to discern the biblical ideal in any given area. We know that God's ideal for marriage is loving monogamy; that His ideal with respect to His own existence is that people will believe in and follow Him as the only God there is: that He is against idolatry, oppression, murder, adultery, stealing, lying; that ancestors are not permitted by God to continue to participate in the life of their former community. Sometimes we research these practices in order to get our people to drop their traditional beliefs and practices in such areas and to immediately live up to God's ideals.

One of my missionary colleagues exemplified such an approach. He did research to discover what the customs of the people really were. He would, often by means of participant-observation, check out what the people believed and how they behaved. But his understanding of what he was to do with the insight he gained seemed to be guided by 1) an over-simplistic understanding of how easy it is for people to change their customs, 2) the view that we in the West, having studied the Scriptures for so long, have a pretty good understanding of what customs God really desires, and 3) a very western competitive approach to changing such customs. Once he got the information he felt he needed, he would (so my Nigerian friends told me) produce sermons that described in detail both their custom and what he regarded as the Christian custom (which usually turned out to be some idealized form of a western custom). He then would compare and contrast the customs, carefully pointing out how superior the "Christian" custom was to their custom and how important it was to God that they adopt it.

The same mistake is made in print in a book by Geoffrey Parrinder entitled *The Bible and Polygamy* (1950). This is a carefully researched book—on both the biblical and the cultural sides. But since he finds (correctly, I believe) that the biblical ideal is monogamy, and since the African custom is polygamy, the strong implication is that if Africans want to be true Christians, they are going to have to change their custom as soon as possible. Where the book fails is lack of attention to the fact that the polygamy custom is in the Bible, and the Bible shows both the custom and how God dealt with that custom. God, unlike western missionaries, first accepted people on the basis of their response to Him, then patiently, without condemning them for merely practicing a custom that had been passed down to them, He worked over a long period of time (hundreds of years) to move the society toward His ideal. By New Testament times, the custom was virtually dead.

Our tendency (like Parrinder's) has been to study the Scriptures to discover such ideals but to ignore the fact that in those same Scriptures we see displayed the patient, slow process by means of which God led His people toward those ideals. We are often hardest on others in those areas where, usually for cultural reasons, we have the least problem. For example, for those of us who are members of western societies, customs such as polytheism, ancestor reverence, and polygamy do not occur close enough for us to be concerned about them in our society. We tend to be very impatient with those of other societies who don't seem to be able to give up such practices within one generation. We westerners, of course, are happy to accept God's patience with us as we struggle with our own besetting sins such as gluttony, naturalism, materialism, individualism, pride, misuse of power, and the like. Granting such patience to others, however, is difficult for us, especially when we are in power.

We need, in love, to grant to others the same patience that we receive from God with regard to the process of change that is to spring from our commitment to Christ—especially in areas where the ordinary cultural practice differs from the scriptural ideal. We need, therefore, to balance our concern for and research into the ideals of the Scriptures with a search for understandings of what God is willing to settle for at the start of the transformation process and how slowly He presses for change in most areas of cultural life. God's focus always seems to be on the most important area—the person/group's relationship to Him. Changes in custom can come more slowly.

OUR PRIMARY CONCERN

No matter how important research and study are, and no matter how fascinating they become, these cannot be our primary concerns. Research and study must always be servants, not masters. Some, however, have become so involved in the excitement of studying people that they have forgotten that their main purpose is to minister to them. We must not let that happen to us. We have not been called by God to do research simply for the sake of doing research, but to minister His love to the people He has called us to.

It is infinitely more important that we do ministry than that we do research. It should be clear by now, however, that our ministry can be much more effective if we recognize that there are lots of questions we don't know, lots of answers we need to work out. We need, therefore, to do research along with ministry. Furthermore, very often we come across best in ministry when we take the attitude that a researcher needs to take—that of a learner, that of the person who says, "I don't understand, but I am going to study the practice until I do."

To do things right, both biblically and culturally, I believe we have to discover from the Bible the answers to three questions: 1) What are the biblical ideals? 2) Where is God willing to start? and 3) What can we learn from the Scriptures concerning the process God uses in moving people toward His ideal?

1. Though there is still plenty of room for discussion, I believe we have a good bit *of insight into answering the first of these questions*. We can, for example, usually explain reasonably well what the ideals are (i.e., their meanings) and the forms in which they should be expressed in our culture. The problem is that most of us, as cross-cultural witnesses, have not thought through how such meanings might be appropriately expressed through the forms of other cultures. In cross-cultural situations, we tend to recommend a high percentage of cultural forms that strongly resemble those of our home culture.

In addition, our tendency is to focus almost exclusively on customs that we, because of our own cultural experience, have learned to condemn, and to ignore areas where their practice may be closer to scriptural ideals than our own. For example, we focus on the "speck" of polygamy in their cultural "eye" but miss the "beam" of greed in our own cultural "eye." That is, the ideal would be for them to practice loving monogamy and generosity. We already practice monogamy (though we may not always live up to the loving part), but fail regularly in the generosity area, without even noticing it. Yet since we have more power and cultural prestige than they, we make them feel guilty (or, worse, keep them out of the church) for their "failure" while neither judging ourselves for our failure nor allowing them equal opportunity to comment on it. Likewise, we may be hard on them for their practice of honoring ancestors but ignore equal or worse idolatrous attachments on our part to material goods.

When we compare their practices with ours in such areas, we tend to contrast our ideal practice with the worst examples we can find in their life. For example, we usually compare an ideal monogamous relationship (though they are rare) in our society with examples of poor polygamous relationships in theirs. To be fair, we ought to compare ideal with ideal or poor with poor. We will find that in most societies, an ideal polygamous relationship is of about the same quality as an ideal monogamous relationship and a poor relationship of either kind just about the same as well. With respect to generosity, westerners would probably excel at both ideal and actual levels when it comes to giving impersonally to people and causes outside the kin group, while many of the peoples of the world would put us to shame when it comes to being generous on a personal level to members of their ingroup.

However, as pointed out in the chapter on ethics, ends can only be as ethical as the means employed to reach them, so there is a sense in which the next two questions are more crucial than the first, at least in actual ministry situations.

2. In the area of cultural practice, *where is God willing to start*? Only if we can support from Scripture the contention that God is not willing to start with a given custom do we have the right to require change in that custom (along with a faith commitment to Jesus Christ) as a precondition to joining the Christian community. I know of only one custom that God is not willing to start with—primary allegiance to another god. God is not willing to be patient with such an allegiance and the idolatry that accompanies it. Supreme allegiance to another god or to some-

thing other than God means that you have no part in the Kingdom. If a group pledges allegiance to the true God, however, the Scriptures show God as patient with all other customs, though He then begins a process that leads to change in many of them.

Our initial concern should be, Does this custom fall within scripturally allowable limits as a starting point for God's working? We'll find that nearly all customs except another primary allegiance (idolatry) do.

3. Our concern needs to be *that new converts seek the mind of God (not the traditions of humans) to discover what His program is for change* of the many customs that He desires to see moved from less ideal to more ideal. As God raises things to their attention, we can be of further assistance by helping them discover what the ideals are and researching constructive ways for changes in the right direction.

In any event, the understandings that come from our commitment to research and study should 1) reduce our fear of the continuance of indigenous customs within their practice of Christianity, 2) lead us to be more open and patient with both the people and their customs, and 3) enable us to be more helpful to them in the changes God requires of them as they grow. Our commitment to God and His ability to lead people to change their own customs should enable us to refrain from attempting to dominate the change process. We will be able, rather, to simply let them know that God expects them to constantly evaluate every aspect of their cultural life in relation to their new allegiance and that He will show them the priorities if they ask Him to. We can then step back and be content to pray and give advice only when they seek it.

CONCLUSION

It is my hope that this book will have provided the ability to gain insight into at least three areas:

1. Where the receivers of your cross-cultural ministry are within their culture,

2. How we, the advocates of Christianity, are affected by our culture, and

3. How to better understand and interpret the biblical meanings we are to present, since they also are presented in and through cultural vehicles.

This book is intended, therefore, to enable us to function more freely and intelligently, under the direction of the Holy Spirit, as effective Christian witnesses working to win and disciple the people God loves. Since we, they, and the biblical record are immersed in "cultural water," my prayer is that an understanding of what that means and how to keep from being crippled by it will be blessed by God to that end.

BIBLIOGRAPHY

American Scientific Affiliation

1978   *Origins and Change.* Special issue of *Journal of the American Scientific Affiliation.*

1986   *Teaching Science in a Climate of Controversy.* Ipswich, MA: American Scientific Affiliation.

Archer, Margaret S.

1988   *Culture and Agency: The Place of Culture in Social Theory.* Cambridge: Cambridge University Press.

Barbour, Ian G.

1974   *Myths, Models and Paradigms.* New York: Harper and Row.

Barclay, William

1956   *The Gospel of Luke.* Philadelphia: Westminster.

Barnett, Homer G.

1953   *Innovation: Basis of Culture Change.* New York: McGraw-Hill.

Barney, G. Linwood

1957   "The Meo—An Incipient Church," *Practical Anthropology* 4:31–50.

Barrett, David B.

1968   *Schism and Renewal.* London: Oxford.

Beals, Alan R., and George and Louise Spindler

1973   *Culture in Process,* 2nd ed. New York: Holt, Rinehart and Winston.

Beals, Ralph L., Harry Hoijer, and Alan R. Beals

1977   *An Introduction to Anthropology,* 5th ed. New York: Macmillan.

Beekman, John

1959   "Minimizing Religious Syncretism among the Chols," *Practical Anthropology* 6. Reprinted in Smalley (ed.) 1978, pp. 602–11.

Bellah, Robert N., and R. Madsen, W. Sullivan, A. Swidler, and S. Tipton

1986   *Habits of the Heart: Individualism and Commitment in American Life.* New York: Harper & Row.

Benedict, Ruth

1934   *Patterns of Culture.* Boston: Houghton Mifflin.

Berlo, David K.

1960   *The Process of Communication.* New York: Holt, Rinehart and Winston.

Bernard, H. Russell

1988   *Research Methods in Cultural Anthropology.* Newbury Park, CA: Sage.

Bohannan, Paul, and John Middleton

1968   *Marriage, Family and Residence.* Garden City, NY: Natural History Press.

Brewster, E. Thomas, and Elizabeth S. Brewster

1976   *Language Acquisition Made Practical* (LAMP). Pasadena, CA: Lingua House.

1982   *Bonding and the Missionary Task.* Pasadena, CA: Lingua House.

1984   *Language Learning Is Communication—Is Ministry.* Pasadena, CA: Lingua House.

Brown, Donald E.

1991   *Human Universals.* Philadelphia: Temple University Press.

Brown, G. Gordon

1957   "Some Problems of Culture Contact with Illustrations from East Africa and Samoa," *Human Organization* 16:11–14.

Buell, Jon, and Virginia Hearn, eds.

1994   *Darwinism: Science or Philosophy?* Richardson, TX: Foundation for Thought and Ethics.

Burnett, David

1988   *Unearthly Powers.* Nashville: Oliver-Nelson.

1990   *Clash of Worlds.* Nashville: Oliver-Nelson.

Campbell, Bernard G.
  1974 *Human Evolution*, 2nd ed. Chicago: Aldine.
Cohen, R., and J. Middleton
  1967 *Comparative Political Systems*. Garden City, NY: Natural History Press.
Cohen, Yehudi A.
  1968 *Man in Adaptation: The Biosocial Background*. Chicago: Aldine.
Cole, Michael, and John Gay, Joseph Glick, and Donald Sharp
  1971 *The Cultural Context of Learning and Thinking*. New York: Basic Books.
Conklin, Harold
  1955 "Hanunoo Color Categories," *Southwestern Journal of Anthropology* 11:339–44.
Conklin, James
  1984 *Worldview Evangelism*. Doctor of Missiology dissertation. Pasadena, CA: School of
        World Mission, Fuller Seminary.
Conn, Harvie M.
  1984 *Eternal Word, Changing Worlds*. Grand Rapids, MI: Zondervan.
Delson, Eric
  1984 *American Anthropological Association Statement on Evolution*. Washington, DC: Ameri-
        can Anthropological Association.
Dooley, Thomas A.
  1956 *Deliver Us from Evil*. New York: Berkley Publishing.
  1960 *The Night They Burned the Mountain*. New York: New American Library.
Douglas, Mary
  1973 *Natural Symbols*. New York: Vintage.
DuBois, Cora
  1955 "The Dominant Value Profile of American Culture," in M. Lantis (ed.), *American Anthro-
        pologist* 57:1232–39.
Dye, T. Wayne
  1976 "Toward a Cross-Cultural Definition of Sin," *Missiology* 4:27-41.
  1980 *The Bible Translation Strategy*. Dallas, TX: Wycliffe Bible Translators.
  n.d.   *Three Types of Cultural Systems*. Unpublished ms. Pasadena, CA: School of World Mis-
         sion, Fuller Seminary.
Ember, C. R., and M. Ember
  1973 *Anthropology*. New York: Appleton-Century-Crofts.
Evans-Pritchard, E. E.
  1940 *The Nuer*. London: Oxford.
Ford, Clellan S.
  1945 *A Comparative Study of Human Reproduction*. New Haven, CT: Yale University Press.
Foster, George M.
  1973 *Traditional Societies and Technological Change*. New York: Harper and Row.
Friedrich, Gerhard
  1965 "Kerusso," in *Theological Wordbook of the NT*, vol. 3. Translated by G. W. Bromiley.
        Grand Rapids, MI: Eerdmans.
Geertz, Clifford
  1973 *The Interpretation of Culture*. New York: Basic Books.
Giddens, Anthony
  1979 *Central Problems and Social Theory*. London: Macmillan.
Gilliland, Dean S.
  1989 *The Word Among Us*. Dallas, TX: Word.
Goldschmidt, Walter
  1954 *Ways of Mankind*. Audio record series. Boston: Beacon
  1957 (ed.) *Readings in the Ways of Mankind* (2 vols.). Boston: Beacon.
  1966 *Comparative Functionalism*. Berkeley: University of California Press.

Goodenough, Ward

1963 *Cooperation in Change*. New York: Russell Sage Foundation.

1965 "Rethinking Status and Role," in M. Banton (ed.), *The Relevance of Models for Social Anthropology*, A.S.A. Monographs no. 1. London: Tavistock, pp. 1–24.

1970 *Description and Comparison in Cultural Anthropology*. Chicago: Aldine.

Goodman, Mary E.

1967 *The Individual and Culture*. Homewood, IL: Dorsey.

Grunlan, Stephen, and Marvin Mayers

1979 *Cultural Anthropology: A Christian Perspective*. Grand Rapids, MI: Zondervan.

Hall, Edward T.

1959 *The Silent Language*. New York: Doubleday.

1966 *The Hidden Dimension*. New York: Doubleday.

1977 *Beyond Culture*. New York: Doubleday.

Harris, Marvin

1968 *The Rise of Anthropological Theory*. New York: Crowell.

Hatch, Elvin

1983 *Culture and Morality: The Relativity of Values in Anthropology*. NY: Columbia University Press.

Haviland, William A.

1978 *Cultural Anthropology*, 2nd ed. New York: Holt, Rinehart and Winston.

1979 *Human Evolution and Prehistory*. New York: Holt, Rinehart and Winston.

1982 *Anthropology*, 3rd ed. New York: Holt, Rinehart and Winston.

Henry, Jules

1963 *Culture Against Man*. New York: Random House.

Hesselgrave, David J.

1978 *Communicating Christ Cross-Culturally*. Grand Rapids, MI: Zondervan.

Hiebert, Paul G.

1982 "The Flaw of the Excluded Middle," *Missiology* 10:35-47.

1983 *Cultural Anthropology*, 2nd ed. Grand Rapids, MI: Baker.

1984 "Critical Contextualization," *Missiology* 12:287–96.

1985 *Anthropological Insights for Missionaries*. Grand Rapids, MI: Baker.

1989 "Form and Meaning in the Contextualization of the Gospel," in Gilliland, D.S. (ed.), *The Word Among Us*, pp. 101–20.

Hiebert, Paul G., and R. Daniel Shaw

1993 *The Power and the Glory*. Unpublished ms. Pasadena, CA: School of World Mission, Fuller Seminary.

Hill, Harriet

1990 "Incarnational Ministry: A Critical Examination," *Evangelical Missions Quarterly* 26(3): 196–201.

1993 "Lifting the Fog on Incarnational Ministry," *Evangelical Missions Quarterly* 29(3): 262–69.

Hillman, Eugene

1975 *Polygamy Reconsidered*. Maryknoll, NY: Orbis.

Hoebel, E. Adamson

1954 *The Law of Primitive Man*. Cambridge, MA: Harvard.

1972 *Anthropology: The Study of Man*, 4th ed. New York: McGraw-Hill.

Honigmann, John J.

1959 *The World of Man*. New York: Harper.

Hostetler, John A., and Gertrude E. Huntington

1967 *The Hutterites in North America*. NY: Holt, Rinehart and Winston.

Hsu, Francis L. K.

1961 "American Core Values and National Character," in *Psychological Anthropology: Approaches to Culture and Personality*. Homewood, IL: Dorsey.

Iwanska, Alicja

1957   "Some American Values." Paper read to the American Anthropological Association Annual Meeting, Chicago (discussed in Smalley 1958c).

Jensen, Arthur R.

1981   *Straight Talk about Mental Tests*. NY: Free Press.

Johnson, Phillip E.

1993   *Darwin on Trial*, 2nd ed. Downers Grove, IL: InterVarsity.

Jolley, Clifford, and Fred Plog

1976   *Resource Manual for Physical Anthropology and Archeology*. New York: Knopf.

Kearney, Michael

1984   *World View*. Noveto, CA: Chandler and Sharp.

Keesing, Felix M.

1958   *Cultural Anthropology*. New York: Holt, Rinehart and Winston.

King, Roberta

1983   "Crucial Dimensions in Intercultural Music Communication." Unpublished Ph.D. Tutorial Paper. Pasadena, CA: School of World Mission, Fuller Seminary.

1989   *Pathways in Christian Music Communication*. Ph.D. dissertation. Pasadena, CA: School of World Mission, Fuller Seminary.

Kittel, Gerhard, and Gerhard Friedrich

1965–76 *Theological Dictionary of the New Testament* (trans. and ed. by G. Bromiley). Grand Rapids, MI: Eerdmans.

Klem, Herbert V.

1982   *Oral Communication of the Scriptures*. Pasadena, CA: William Carey.

Kluckhohn, Clyde

1949a *Mirror for Man*. New York: McGraw-Hill (Fawcett Edition 1957).

1949b "The Philosophy of the Navaho Indians," in F. Northrop (ed.), *Ideological Differences and World Order*. New Haven, CT: Yale, pp. 356–84.

1953   "Universal Categories of Culture," in *Anthropology Today*, A. Kroeber (ed.). Chicago: University of Chicago, pp. 245–84.

Kluckhohn, C., and O. H. Mowrer

1944   "Culture and Personality: A Conceptual Scheme," in *American Anthropologist* 46:1–27.

Kraft, Charles H.

1963   "Christian Conversion or Cultural Conversion," *Practical Anthropology* 10:179–87.

1973   "Dynamic Equivalence Churches," *Missiology* 1:39–57.

1978a "An Anthropological Apologetic for the Homogeneous Unit Principle in Missiology," in *Occasional Bulletin of Missionary Research* 10:121–26.

1978b "The Contextualization of Theology," *Evangelical Missions Quarterly* 14:31–36.

1979a *Christianity in Culture*. Maryknoll, NY: Orbis.

1979b *Communicating the Gospel God's Way*. Pasadena, CA: William Carey.

1979c "Dynamic Equivalence Churches in Muslim Society," in McCurry, Don M., *The Gospel and Islam*. Monrovia, CA: MARC (World Vision), pp. 114–28.

1989   *Christianity with Power*. Ann Arbor, MI: Servant.

1991a *Communication Theory for Christian Witness* (revised edition). Maryknoll, NY: Orbis.

1991b "What Kind of Encounters Do We Need in Christian Witness?" *Evangelical Missions Quarterly* 27:258–65.

1992a *Defeating Dark Angels*. Ann Arbor, MI: Servant.

1992b "How Our Worldview Affects the Way We Worship." *Worship Leader* 1,3:10 and 53.

1993   *Deep Wounds, Deep Healing*. Ann Arbor, MI: Servant.

1994   *Behind Enemy Lines*. Ann Arbor, MI: Servant.

Kraft, Charles H., and Marguerite G. Kraft

1993   "The Power of God for Christians Who Ride Two Horses," in Grieg, Gary S. and Kevin N. Springer, *The Kingdom and the Power*. Ventura, CA: Regal Books, pp. 345–56.

Kraft, Charles H., and Tom N. Wisley, eds.

1979   *Readings in Dynamic Indigeneity.* Pasadena, CA: William Carey.

Kraft, Marguerite G.

1978   *Worldview and the Communication of the Gospel.* Pasadena, CA: William Carey.

1995   *Understanding Spiritual Power.* Maryknoll, NY: Orbis.

Kroeber, Alfred

1948   *Anthropology.* New York: Harcourt, Brace and World.

1950   "Anthropology," in *Scientific American* 183:87–94.

Kuhn, Thomas S.

1970   *The Structure of Scientific Revolutions.* Chicago: University of Chicago Press.

Langness, L. L.

1987   *The Study of Culture.* (Revised ed.) Novato, CA: Chandler and Sharp.

LaSor, William S., David A. Hubbard, and Frederic W. Bush

1982   *Old Testament Survey.* Grand Rapids, MI: Eerdmans.

Levi-Strauss, Claude

1956   "The Family," in H. L. Shapiro (ed.), *Man, Culture and Society.* NY: Oxford.

1969   *The Elementary Structures of Kinship.* Boston: Beacon (orig. 1949).

Levy-Bruhl, Lucien

1923   *Primitive Mentality.* (Translated from French by L. A. Clare). New York: Macmillan.

Lewis, Oscar

1959   *Five Families.* New York: Basic Books.

Lingenfelter, Sherwood

1992   *Transforming Culture.* Grand Rapids, MI: Baker.

Lingenfelter, Sherwood, and Marvin K. Mayers

1986   *Ministering Cross-Culturally.* Grand Rapids, MI: Baker.

Linton, Ralph

1936   *The Study of Man.* New York: Appleton, Century, Croft.

1945   *The Science of Man in the World Crisis.* New York: Columbia University Press.

Loewen, Jacob

1975   *Culture and Human Values.* Pasadena, CA: William Carey.

1986   "Which God Do Missionaries Preach?" *Missiology* 14:3-19.

Loewen, Jacob, and Anne Loewen

1967   "Role, Self-Image and Missionary Communication," *Practical Anthropology* 14:145–60. Reprinted in J. Loewen 1975, pp. 412–27.

Luzbetak, Louis

1963   *The Church and Cultures.* Techny, IL: Divine Word. Reprinted, South Pasadena, CA: William Carey, 1975.

1988   *The Church and Cultures* (revised and enlarged). Maryknoll, NY: Orbis.

Mair, Lucy

1965   *An Introduction to Social Anthropology.* London: Oxford.

Malina, Bruce J.

1981   *The New Testament World: Insights from Cultural Anthropology.* Atlanta: John Knox.

Malinowski, Bronislaw

1922   *Argonauts of the Western Pacific.* New York: Dutton.

1925   "Magic, Science and Religion," in *Science, Religion and Reality,* J. Needham (ed.). London (Reissued 1948 as *Magic, Science and Religion.* Boston: Beacon Press).

1929   *The Sexual Life of Savages in North-Western Melanesia.* NY: Harcourt.

Maslow, Abraham

1970   *Motivation and Personality,* 2nd ed. NY: Harper.

Mayers, Marvin K.

1974   (revised ed. 1987) *Christianity Confronts Culture.* Grand Rapids, MI: Zondervan.

Mbiti, John S.
  1971　*New Testament Eschatology in an African Background*. London: Oxford University Press.
McGavran, Donald A., and C. Peter Wagner
  1990　*Understanding Church Growth*, 3rd ed. Grand Rapids, MI: Eerdmans.
McLuhan, Marshall
  1964　*Understanding Media*, 2nd ed. NY: McGraw-Hill.
Mead, Margaret
  1930　*Growing Up in New Guinea*. New York: New American Library.
  1940　*The Mountain Arapesh*, vol. 2. New York: American Museum of Natural History.
  1956　*New Lives for Old*. NY: William Morrow.
  1963　"Our Educational Emphases in Primitive Perspective," *American Journal of Sociology* 48:633–39 (reprinted in Mead, *Anthropology—A Human Science*. Princeton, NJ: Van Nostrand, 1964, pp. 162–74.)
  1970　*Culture and Commitment*. New York: Doubleday.
Menninger, Karl
  1973　*Whatever Became of Sin?* New York: Hawthorn Books.
Merriam, Alan P.
  1964　*The Anthropology of Music*. Chicago: Northwestern University.
Messenger, John
  1959　"The Christian Concept of Forgiveness and Anang Morality," *Practical Anthropology* 6:97–103.
Morgan, Louis Henry
  1877　*Ancient Society*. New York: Holt.
Murdock, George P.
  1945　"The Common Denominator of Cultures," in Linton 1945: 123–42.
  1949　*Social Structure*. New York: Macmillan.
Newbigin, Lesslie
  1966　*Honest Religion for Secular Man*. Philadelphia: Westminster.
Nida, Eugene A.
  1952　*God's Word in Man's Language*. NY: Harper.
  1954　*Customs and Cultures*. Reprinted 1975. Pasadena, CA: William Carey.
  1959　"The Role of Cultural Anthropology in Christian Missions," *Practical Anthropology* 6. (Reprinted in Smalley 1978, pp. 837–43).
  1990　*Message and Mission* (revised edition). Pasadena, CA: William Carey.
Nida, Eugene A., and William D. Reyburn
  1981　*Meaning Across Cultures*. Maryknoll, NY: Orbis.
Nida, Eugene A., and Charles R. Taber
  1969　*The Theory and Practice of Translation*. Leiden: Brill.
Niebuhr, H. Richard
  1951　*Christ and Culture*. New York: Harper and Row.
Oberg, Kalevro
  1954　"Cultural Shock: Adjustment to New Cultural Environments," *Technical Assistance Quarterly Bulletin* (reprinted in *Practical Anthropology*, 1960, 7:177–82).
Opler, Morris E.
  1945　"Themes as Dynamic Forces in Culture," *American Journal of Sociology* 51:198–206.
Parrinder, E. Geoffrey
  1950　*The Bible and Polygamy*. London: SPCK.
Pelto, Gretel H., and Pertti J. Pelto
  1976　*The Human Adventure: An Introduction to Anthropology*. New York: Macmillan.
  1978　*Anthropological Research*, 2nd ed. NY: Cambridge.
Phillips, J. B.
  1958　*The New Testament in Modern English*, rev. ed. New York: Macmillan.
Pike, Eunice V., and Florence Cowan
  1959　"Mushroom Ritual Versus Christianity," *Practical Anthropology* 6:145–50.

Pike, Kenneth L.
  1967   *Language in Relation to a Unified Theory of the Structure of Human Behavior*, 2nd ed. The Hague: Mouton.
Pozas, Ricardo
  1962   *Juan the Chamula*. Trans. by L. Kemp. Berkeley, CA: University of California Press.
Radcliffe-Brown, A. R.
  1933/1965 *Structure and Function in Primitive Society*. New York: Free Press.
Read, Margaret
  1955   *Education and Social Change in Tropical Areas*. Camden, NJ: Nelson.
Redfield, Robert
  1953   *The Primitive World and Its Transformations*. Ithaca, NY: Cornell University Press.
Reyburn, William
  1957a "Missions Male and Female," *Practical Anthropology* 4:140–46.
  1957b "The Transformation of God and the Conversion of Man," *Practical Anthropology* 4:185–94.
  1958   "Motivations for Christianity: An African Conversation," *Practical Anthropology* 5:27–32 (Reprinted in Smalley 1978, pp. 73–76).
Richardson, Don
  1974   *Peace Child*. Ventura, CA: Regal.
  1981   *Eternity in Their Hearts*. Ventura, CA: Regal.
Rogers, Everett M.
  1983   *Diffusion of Innovations*, 3rd ed. New York: Free Press.
Rogerson, John W.
  1979   *Anthropology and the Old Testament*. Atlanta: John Knox.
Rynkiewich, Michael A. and James P. Spradley
  1976   *Ethics and Anthropology*. NY: John Wiley.
Sahlins, Marshall and Elman Service, eds.
  1960   *Evolution and Culture*. Ann Arbor, MI: University of Michigan.
Sapir, Edward
  1929   "The Status of Linguistics as a Science," *Language* 5:207–14.
  1931   "Conceptual Categories in Primitive Languages," *Science* 74:578.
Schaeffer, Francis
  1976   *How Shall We Then Live?* Old Tappan, NJ: Revell.
Schusky, Ernest L.
  1972   *Manual for Kinship Analysis*, 2nd ed. New York: Holt, Rinehart and Winston.
Seaton, Ronald S., and Edith B. Seaton
  1976   *Here's How: Health Education by Extension*. Pasadena, CA: William Carey.
Service, Elman R.
  1962   *Primitive Social Organization*. New York: Random House.
  1968   *Peasants*. Englewood Cliffs, NJ: Prentice-Hall.
Shapiro, H. L.
  1952   "Revised Version of UNESCO Statement on Race," *American Journal of Physical Anthropology* 10:363–68.
Sharp, J. Lauriston
  1952   "Steel Axes for Stone Age Australians," *Human Organization* 11 (reprinted in *Practical Anthropology* 7:62–73).
Shaw, R. Daniel
  1988   *Transculturation*. Pasadena, CA: William Carey.
Sheehy, Gail
  1974   *Passages*. New York: E. P. Dutton.
Sire, James
  1976   *The Universe Next Door*. Downers Grove, IL: InterVarsity.
Skinner, B. F.
  1971   *Beyond Freedom and Dignity*. New York: Knopf.

Smalley, William

  1958a   "Cultural Implications of an Indigenous Church," *Practical Anthropology* 5:61–65 (reprinted in Smalley 1978, pp. 363–72).

  1958b   "Respect and Ethnocentrism," *Practical Anthropology* 5:191–94 (reprinted in Smalley 1978, pp. 711–13).

  1958c   "The World Is Too Much with Us," *Practical Anthropology* 5:234–36 (reprinted in Smalley 1978, pp. 701–3).

  1978   *Readings in Missionary Anthropology* II. Pasadena, CA: William Carey.

Søgaard, Viggo

  1975   *Everything You Need to Know for a Cassette Ministry.* Minneapolis: Bethany Fellowship.

  1991   *Audio Scriptures.* United Bible Societies.

  1993   *Media in Church and Mission.* Pasadena, CA: William Carey.

Spradley, James P.

  1972   (ed.) *Culture and Cognition.* New York: Chandler.

  1979   *The Ethnographic Interview.* New York: Holt, Rinehart and Winston.

  1980   *Participant Observation.* New York: Holt, Rinehart and Winston.

Spradley, James P., and David W. McCurdy

  1975   *Anthropology: The Cultural Perspective.* New York: John Wiley.

Spruth, Erwin

  1981   *And the Word of God Spread.* Doctor of Missiology dissertation. Pasadena, CA: School of World Mission, Fuller Seminary.

Stendahl, Krister

  1976   *Paul among the Jews and Gentiles and Other Essays.* Philadelphia: Fortress Press.

Steward, Julian

  1955   *Theory of Culture Change.* Urbana, IL: University of Illinois Press.

Steyne, Philip M.

  1990   *Gods of Power.* Houston: Touch Publications.

Taylor, John

  1988   "Goods and Gods," in Tony Swan, and D. B. Rose, *Aboriginal Australians and Christian Missions.* Bedford Park, South Australia: Australian Association for the Study of Religions, South Australia College of Advanced Education.

Taylor, Robert B.

  1973   *Introduction to Cultural Anthropology.* Boston: Allyn and Bacon.

  1976   *Cultural Ways.* Boston: Allyn and Bacon.

Thaxton, Charles B., and Walter I. Bradley, and Roger L. Olsen

  1984   *The Mystery of Life's Origin.* NY: Philosophical Library.

Tillich, Paul

  1959   *Theology of Culture.* New York: Oxford.

Tippett, Alan R.

  1967   *Solomon Islands Christianity.* London: Lutterworth.

  1969   *Verdict Theology in Missionary Theory.* Lincoln, IL: Lincoln Christian College Press.

  1971   *People Movements in Southern Polynesia.* Chicago: Moody.

  1987   *Introduction to Missiology.* Pasadena, CA: William Carey.

de Tocqueville, Alexis

  1945   *Democracy in America.* New York: Doubleday. Originally published in French in 1835.

Toffler, Alvin

  1970   *Future Shock.* New York: Random House.

Turnbull, Colin

  1972   *The Mountain People.* New York: Simon and Shuster.

  1984   *The Human Cycle.* London: Jonathan Cape.

Two Brothers from Berkeley

  1971   *Letters to Street Christians.* Grand Rapids, MI: Zondervan.

Tylor, Edward B.

  1874   *Primitive Culture*. 2 volumes. New York: Holt.

Van Gennep, Arnold

  1960   *Rites of Passage*. Chicago: University of Chicago Press. First published in French in 1909.

Wallace, Anthony F. C.

  1956   "Revitalization Movements," *American Anthropologist* 58:264–81.

  1966   *Religion: An Anthropological View*. New York: Random House.

  1970   *Culture and Personality*, 2nd ed. New York: Random House.

Ward, Ted

  1987   "Putting Nonformal Education to Work," *Together* (World Vision), July–September.

Washburn, Sherwood L.

  1951   "The New Physical Anthropology," *Transactions of the New York Academy of Sciences*, series II, 13:298–304.

  1963   (ed.) *Classification and Human Evolution*. Viking Fund Publications in Anthropology, no. 37.

  n.d.   AAA Statement on Physical Anthropology. Washington, DC: American Anthropological Association.

Welbourn, F. B.

  1961   *East African Rebels*. London: SCM Press.

White, Leslie

  1949   *The Science of Culture*. New York: Grove Press.

Whorf, Benjamin Lee

  1956   *Language, Thought and Reality* (ed. John Carroll). New York: Wiley.

Williams, Thomas Rhys

  1972   *Introduction to Socialization*. St. Louis, MO: C.V. Mosby.

Wolff, Hans W.

  1981   *Anthropology of the Old Testament*. Philadelphia: Fortress.

GENERAL INDEX

Abortion, 229

Absolute relativism, 18

Absolutism, 70

Acculturation, 367–68

Achieved status, 318

Adoption, 335

Adulthood, 222–24

Advocates, 399–400, 402–4, 408–13; in-culture, 401

Afterlife, 204

Age-based associations, 337

Alienable, 191

Allegiance, 11, 210; encounters, 452–54

Alternatives, 155

American culture, 81–84

American family, 297–98, 299

American Indians: Comanche cultural patterning, 128–29; dissecting culture of, 128–29; diviners among, 206; prehistoric, 108; race and, 109–10; shamans, 207, 208

Amulets, 205

Anang Ibibio, 26–27

Ancestors, 204, 227–28, 233–34

Ancient Society (Morgan), 171

Angels, 203

Animism, 202

Anthropology: as a behavioral science, 4–5; communication and, 10; as a cross-cultural perspective, 8–9; cultural forms and, 10–11; culture change and, 12–13; development of culture concept by, 6–7; holistic view of people through, 7–8; importance of, 2–4; nonwestern peoples addressed through, 5–6; research methods developed by, 12; worldview concept developed by, 11–12

Apprenticeship/discipleship, 277

Archer, Margaret: on culture, 35

Art: combining media and, 269–72; definition of, 255–56; ethnocentrism and, 258–60; forms of, 260–62; functions of, 256–58; meaning and, 262–63; messages of authority and expertise sent through, 266; tension released through, 267; used by Christian witnesses, 267–69; used in enculturation, 263–66; as a vehicle of com-

petition, 267; youths' communication to adults through, 266

Ascribed status, 318–19

Association basis groupings, 337–39

Assumptions, 11

Authority structures, 386

Avunculocal residence, 294

Baptism, 140

Behavioral sciences, theology and, 87–96

Berlo, David K.: on language, 241

Beyond Freedom and Dignity (Skinner), 151

Bible, oral form of, 268, 271

Biological groups, 331

Black magic, 205

Blood brothers, 335

Boundaries, 153–56

Brown, G. Gordon: on nature versus nurture, 117

Cain and Abel, 104

Cassette tapes, 270

Castes, 338–39, 386, 387

Ceremonies, 10–11, 208–10

Change, 12–13, 125–27, 359–60, 374–79, 396–97; acculturation and, 367–68; advocates of, 399–401, 402–4, 408–13; barriers to, 381–87; continual, 361; encounters and, 452–54; ethics of, 415–18; facilitators of, 387–94; general persistence and, 360–61, 364–65; implementors of, 400–401; the individual and, 160–62; locus of, 366; manner of, 369; meaning equivalence Christianity and, 454–57; potential innovations, 394–96; primary process of, 370–71; in proper clothing, 361–64; rate of, 366–67; results of, 373–74; secondary process of, 371–73; sectional persistence and, 365; survivals and, 365–66; technology and, 172–73; token persistence and, 365; transformational, 440–44

Charms, 205

Childhood, 221–22

Christian ethnotheology, 95

Christopaganism, 376

Church: analysis of cultural structure applied to, 130; bribery and, 194–95; economic structure and, 191–95; foreign funds and,

SCRIPTURE INDEX

OLD TESTAMENT

NEW TESTAMENT